"Christians routinely dismiss objections advance͏͏ ... ground that they are outsiders who are not in a position to understand the doctrines they presume to criticize. Nobody can say that about John W. Loftus. As an ex-pastor and Christian apologist, he understands these doctrines from the inside and is able to expose the logical flaws of the arguments offered in support of them—textual, scientific, theological, and philosophical—with luminous clarity and devastating force. His scholarship is impressive, but he also knows how to write in a way that engages the nonscholarly reader. The result is a startlingly honest book that ought to be required reading for every Christian."

Dr. John Beversluis
Author of *C. S. Lewis and the Search for Rational Religion*

"Of the spate of books coming from the so-called New Atheists that have appeared in the past few years—Hitchens, Dawkins, Harris, and so on—John W. Loftus's critique of Christian theism is by far the most sophisticated. Where, say, Dawkins might be found attacking a man of straw, Loftus understands and assesses the arguments of today's premier Christian apologists and philosophers. Evangelicals cannot afford to ignore *Why I Became an Atheist*."

Dr. Mark D. Linville
Christian philosopher and contributor to
The Blackwell Companion to Natural Theology

"Scholarly unbelief is far more sophisticated, far more defensible than any of us would like to believe. John W. Loftus is a scholar and a former Christian who was overwhelmed by that sophistication. His story is a wake-up call to the church: it's time for us to start living in, and speaking to, the real world."

Dr. James F. Sennett
Christian philosopher and author of
Modality, Probability, and Rationality:
A Critical Examination of Alvin Plantinga's Philosophy

"Loftus writes with great honesty and candor about his experiences from both sides of the theistic/nontheistic landscape. His chapters on the problem of evil offer a fine overview of the complex historical debate over the obstacle that evil presents to rational theistic belief. His writing is admirable for maintaining conceptual accuracy while engendering accessibility for the nontechnical reader. Highly recommended— both as a valuable sourcebook for all involved in religious debate and as a good read."

Dr. A. M. Weisberger
Nontheistic philosopher and author of
Suffering Belief: Evil and the Anglo-American Defense of Theism

(Of "The Outsider Test for Faith . . ." chapter) "That's an excellent chapter. The logic of it is insurmountable, in my opinion, even by a so-called reformed or 'holy spirit' epistemologist."

Dr. Richard Carrier
Author of *Sense and Goodness without God*

"Loftus wrote his book primarily to explain why he ceased to be a believer, but its main value is that it spells out the falsifying evidence that finally cured him and will cure anyone who reads it. Loftus has brought together sufficient evidence of religion's Achilles' heel to cause all but the most intransigent believers to ask themselves: Could he be right?"

Dr. William Harwood
Author of *Mythology's Last Gods: Yahweh and Jesus*

"What is unusual about Loftus is his breadth and depth of research in defense of the Christian faith before finally rejecting his faith. Loftus applies himself in this book with the same intellectual rigor he had applied to defending the faith, and effectively dissects those very same arguments. I found myself marveling at the impressively contorted reasoning used by apologists through the ages in defense of their received traditions. They are worth reading from the standpoint of cognitive psychology alone."

Dr. Valerie Tarico
Author of *The Dark Side: How Evangelical Teachings Corrupt Love and Truth*

"The book's central strength lies in its information-rich content. John speaks the language of competent and well-known Christian scholars and apologists of both liberal and conservative affiliation, employing their own words against them, demonstrating that they themselves recognize the grave position they are in when facing the critical eye of a skeptical, modern world. 'The Outsider Test for Faith . . .' is one of those chapters that says what every doubter of religion has always thought but perhaps never said so well. The chapter is an absolute jewel. This work covers some ground that is seldom touched on in other comparable free thought works."

Joe E. Holman
Founder of www.ministerturnsatheist.org
and author of *Project Bible Truth: A Minister Turns Atheist and Tells All*

"This book is an absolute 'must have' for anyone who has left the Christian faith or is having serious intellectual doubts about the Christian religion. While the book starts out explaining some of his experiential reasons for leaving Christianity, the volume goes far beyond a mere personal testimony and dives deeply into the elemental contradictions of Christianity. Loftus deals evenly with the issues, carefully explaining the strengths and weaknesses of each argument. Loftus's coverage of the problems inherent in the claims of Christianity is comprehensive. Much of what he wrote sounds like an echo of many of my own introspections except expressed through the well-oiled mind of an academician."

David Van Allen
Webmaster of www.ex-christian.net

"I have read hundreds of Christian apologetics books. I have read all of C. S Lewis, all of Francis Schaeffer, all of Peter Kreeft, all of Dr. Geisler's works, along with the writings of Josh McDowell, William Lane Craig, Ravi Zacharias, J. P. Moreland, Richard Swinburne, N. T. Wright, Paul Copan, and so on. I was until recently enrolled at Dr. Geisler's school to study apologetics and philosophy. This year I decided, in order to be fair and honest, to read all the top skeptical books on religion. John's book was one of the first I read. It was the first skeptic book I read that made me seriously realize that I could be dead wrong! I think John has written by far the best overall refutation of Christianity in print. John's book is much more accessible, it covers a lot more arguments, it has the best chapters on the problem of evil you can find, it is more interesting to read, it refutes more apologetic arguments than any other book, and it addresses more central issues."

Andrew Atkinson

"If you have questions about your faith, read this book. Those nagging questions are addressed and exposed. Every skeptic should have this concise reference book on the desk, dog-eared, tagged, and highlighted. I've read Sam Harris's book *The End of Faith* and Richard Dawkins's book *The God Delusion*. The other books hit the target but John's book hits the bulls-eye. I doubt anyone with faith could walk away from this book with that faith intact. Awesome book!!!! It is honestly everything I've been looking for so far in my 'quest' for knowledge. Thank you!"

Chris Knight-Griffin

"This book is one of the best introductory texts on the philosophical problems with Christianity."

Matthew J. Green

"I have read numerous publications on this topic, but I don't believe I've ever seen as many great reasons to reject religion in one place. John's arguments are numerous and rock-solid. The level of research and brutal logic applied to the Bible is absolutely stunning, as is the sheer number of examples given. There is 'no stone unturned,' as Loftus takes on nearly every apologist angle ever conceived. This book will give more insight into scholarly unbelief than you ever thought possible."

Greg Meeuwsen

"If you read Christian apologetics, you owe it to yourself to have this anthology of the best arguments against Christian apologetics in your library."

Paul Harrison

why i became an
ATHEIST

why i became an
ATHEIST

A Former Preacher Rejects
CHRISTIANITY

john w.
LOFTUS

Prometheus Books

59 John Glenn Drive
Amherst, New York 14228–2119

Published 2008 by Prometheus Books

Inquiries should be addressed to
Prometheus Books
59 John Glenn Drive
Amherst, New York 14228–2119
VOICE: 716–691–0133, ext. 210
FAX: 716–691–0137
WWW.PROMETHEUSBOOKS.COM

12 11 10 09   5 4 3

Library of Congress Cataloging-in-Publication Data

Loftus, John W.
    Why I became an atheist : a former preacher rejects Christianity / by John W. Loftus.
        p. cm.
    ISBN 978–1–59102–592–4
    1. Christianity—Controversial literature. 2. Christianity and atheism. 3. Atheism.
4. Loftus, John W. I. Title.

BL2775.3.L64 2008
211'.8—dc22

                                                                          2007051795

Printed in the United States of America on acid-free paper

CONTENTS

Foreword by Edward T. Babinski   7

Introduction   11

PART 1: THE BASIS FOR MY CONTROL BELIEFS

1. My Christian Conversion and Deconversion   19

2. The Christian Illusion of Rational and Moral Superiority   35

3. Faith, Reason, and the Cumulative Case Method   46

4. The Outsider Test for Faith . . .   66

5. Does God Exist?   78

6. The Lessons of Galileo, Science, and Religion   106

7. The Strange and Superstitious World of the Bible   124

    7:1 Pseudonymity in the Bible   167

    7:2 Archaeology, Exodus, and the Canaanite Conquest   177

8. The Poor Evidence of Historical Evidence   181

9. Do Miracles Take Place?   199

10. The Self-Authenticating Witness of the Holy Spirit   213

11. The Problem of Unanswered Prayer   220

12. The Problem of Evil—Part 1: My Specific Case   228

13. The Problem of Evil—Part 2: Objections Answered   243

PART 2: THE BIBLICAL EVIDENCE EXAMINED

14. Science and the Genesis Creation Accounts   265

15. Science and Genesis 1–11   281

16. Prophecy and Biblical Authority   289

17. Was Jesus Born of a Virgin in Bethlehem?   317

18. Was Jesus God Incarnate?   329

19. "The Passion of the Christ": Why Did Jesus Suffer?   344

20. Did Jesus Bodily Rise from the Dead?   351

21. The Devil Made Me Do It!   383

22. Hell? No!   387

PART 3: WHAT I BELIEVE TODAY

23. Why I Became an Atheist   399

24. What Is Life without God?   406

Bibliography of Selected Works   417

FOREWORD
Edward T. Babinski

J ohn W. Loftus is a former conservative Christian apologist who at some point admitted that he could no longer honestly use the term "Christian" to describe his present beliefs or state of mind since he now doubts many Christian doctrines, beliefs, and biblical interpretations he once formerly accepted as rock-solid truths. His book is a clear, honest, and concise summary of some of the questions he encountered along his spiritual, theological, and philosophical journey. Neither is it as isolated and fearful a journey as some conservative evangelicals may think, because many of today's top biblical archeologists and biblical scholars from William Dever to Bart Ehrman and to Hector Avalos (including many professors in the Jesus Seminar) all began their own journeys as conservative Christians with few doubts, only to discover more questions and uncertainties.

Hence a diversity of opinion exists in modern-day scholarship. In fact, the majority of the world's educational institutions, though founded originally as conservative Christian seminaries, have also taken similar journeys to John's when engaging the learned opinions among scholars. Within two hundred years of Calvin's death, the very College of Geneva that John Calvin founded became open to all sorts of Enlightenment ideas and doubts concerning how literally to take the Bible and Christian doctrines. So John's experience not only parallels that of other individuals, like Dever, Ehrman, and Avalos, but also seminaries once founded to promote conservative Christian views. Yale, it must be remembered, was originally founded in reaction to the "theological excesses" of Harvard, yet today look at Yale!

Meanwhile, the types of institutions that continue to defend the "inerrancy of the Bible" are all relatively young institutions. In time, however, if they grow and attract the brightest and the best, they will have to interact with the scholarly world and read not simply evangelical or inerrantist publications, but engage with ongoing

worldwide interdisciplinary biblical research and questions. If a conservative evangelical Christian pokes his nose in theology books, journals, Bible dictionaries, and
Bible commentaries published by Oxford, Yale, and/or Cambridge University—to
name just a few (not to forget the Anchor Bible series of commentaries)—he is
bound to begin running into the diversity of opinion among scholars concerning the
meaning and relative importance of passages from Genesis to Revelation. Even
evangelical scholars at Wheaton like Professor Walton are beginning to catch up
with scholarly questions concerning how literally the ancient Hebrews probably
understood their own "primeval history" in Genesis and conclude we need not take
them so literally today.[1]

Another service John's book provides is demonstrating to many who are having
doubts that there are others out there like them. His book helps support others
making the sometimes difficult transition, which usually involves some isolation and
loneliness, since your former best friends in church have little idea why you need
time away from church to read and reconsider your beliefs, or why you might not
feel right about repeating the creedal affirmations aloud or singing the old choruses.

Again, speaking as someone who has himself spent years of his former Bible-
believing life trying to hold on to every word of the Bible "without error," I wonder
today just what conservative Christians *do* believe, or even if they themselves really
know. There are probably a lot more unspoken doubts going on in the Christian
world than anyone cares to personally relate. For instance, do conservative Christians imagine a literal talking serpent was "the shrewdest beast of the field God created," but then God cursed it to "go on its belly"? (Not much of a "curse" to put on
a serpent, come to think of it.) Do they all believe in the story of forbidden edible
fruit, and that all the natural causes of suffering on earth and throughout the
cosmos—including volcanoes, hurricanes, earthquakes, as well as diseases, poisonous microbes, and insects—were all simply the result of one human couple's disobedient hungering for a piece of fruit? Do they believe a woman named Eve was
cloned directly from Adam's rib? Do Christian apologists really doubt none of those
old mythological tales out of Israel's primeval history in Genesis? Do they plead that
Lot's wife must have indeed turned into a literal pillar of salt? Or do some of them
simply make embarrassed excuses for the tale of Noah, admitting, "it was only a
local flood." Do they accept the true scientific age of the earth, regardless of what
the "ages of the Patriarchs" adds up to, and regardless of the fact that Genesis states
that the first light of the entire cosmos was created simply to accommodate
"days/nights, evenings/mornings" as measured on one tiny planet, the earth? (How
geocentric, that is, the whole cosmos created to suit earth's "days," the time of revolution of only one planet in the whole cosmos.)

If Christian apologists *do not* imagine such things, or have even the barest of
doubts concerning them, then what exactly *do* they believe, and how can they tell
others they are so sure? It's the old crossroads that even Christian conservatives
eventually come to: either try to compress all of geology and cosmic astronomical
time into the thimble-full of years of the "primeval history" portions of Genesis,
whose names of patriarchs and events of their lives even Jesus alluded to, or admit

that Jesus was merely repeating back the prejudices of his day just so others would understand him? But by doing so, did Jesus know that he'd be legitimating today's "young-earth creationists" two thousand years hence? Can the Old Testament language in the primeval history easily be interpreted to make room for a cosmos billions of years old, with the earth created later in cosmic history, with humanity appearing very late on earth geologically?

All Christians also have to face the evidence of changes in teachings over time, or explain them away as progressive revelation or "different dispensations," because the Bible's views of God, Satan, the afterlife, and what you needed to do to please God changed over time, from the oldest Old Testament works to later ones, and from the Old Testament to intertestamental works, and from those works to the earliest New Testament writings. There are changes internal to the Gospels themselves that can be seen when you compare and contrast stories of, say, the resurrection from Paul to Mark, Matthew, Luke, and John (not to forget the later Jesus tales in the apocryphal Gospels concerning the resurrection and heaven and hell, because Christians did not cease writing stories of Jesus after the four Gospels were finished, but continued composing tales).

Two thousand years and forty-five thousand separate Christian denominations and missionary organizations later, we have modern-day "Christianity," including everything from Trappist monks and Quakers who worship in silence, and meditating Christians dialoging with Eastern faiths, to hell raisers and snake-handling Christians. We have damnationists and universalist Christians, and many more groups besides. Even after the Roman Empire adopted and enforced Christian faith, Arian and Athanasian Christians rioted, killed, and persecuted each other, as did Donatists and Catholics. And none of the older ideas ever fully die out, because some of the Bible verses and arguments used by Arians were much later revived and used by deists and Unitarians, while the Donatists never gave up their fight to appoint their own priests rather than Rome, kind of like today's ultraconservative Catholics who think the papacy is wrong but the rest of Catholicism is good. And there are many differences of opinion on everything in Christianity today from social issues to religious issues like tongue speaking; baptism; miracles; when and how to best honor the Sabbath; what Old Testament laws ought to be enforced today for the good of society; what signs to look for in the "saved," including "short hair in men"; or using the King James Bible above all other translations. Meanwhile some things that the early church emphasized are little emphasized today, except among the Catholics, by which I mean clergy celibacy, as seen in the words of Jesus and Paul and the author of Revelation. Christianity continues to evolve and branch into further new rival denominations and suborganizations as time goes on. How Darwinian of the churches!

Those like John who finally do climb off the Christian merry-go-round are indeed dizzy after leaving and wonder why others choose to stay. There is, after all, something to be said for self-reliance and allowing one's inquisitive mind to ponder questions for a season, even if doubting can make one feel less secure and less ecstatic than riding the merry-go-round. At least you begin to feel more like yourself, less at the mercy of your brain, which mindlessly pops out proof-texts, or fearing hell for even spending time away from church. You begin to feel more, well, "human," and hence begin to view others as having similar doubts and fears and also similar hopes and joys.

Edward T. Babinski
author of *Leaving the Fold:*
Testimonies of Former Fundamentalists
http://www.edwardtbabinski.us

NOTE

1. See the *NIV Application Commentary on Genesis* (Grand Rapids, MI: Zondervan Books, 2002).

INTRODUCTION

This book may be unlike any other book you've ever read. It is specifically written to devout Christians by a former Christian minister and apologist for their faith who is now an atheist. It's also written for Christians who are questioning their faith, as well as for skeptics who want to learn how to effectively argue against Christianity. Sadly to say, those two latter groups of people will be more likely to read it and gain the most benefit from it. There are many books that "preach to the choir" in the marketplace, on both sides of this great debate. Mine is not intended to be one of them. Because of this, some skeptics may not appreciate why I argue the way I do, but someone has to bridge the gap between us by speaking to Christians in ways they will understand.

Atheist professor Dr. Daniel C. Dennett is recommending this book to those who inquire, as is Christopher Hitchens, but my hope is that Christians will consider the recommendation of Dr. Norman L. Geisler, who is a Christian apologist and author of more than sixty apologetics books, including *The Baker Encyclopedia of Christian Apologetics.*[1] He is recommending this book of mine to his students. He said, first, it "is an honest and open account of how a Christian became an atheist. Seldom are unbelievers so candid and open. Second, every Christian—let alone Christian apologists—can learn some valuable lessons from it on how to treat wayward believers. Third, it is a thoughtful and intellectually challenging work, presenting arguments that every honest theist and Christian should face."[2]

Let me put it to you this way. Most Christians want to read books that are uplifting and produce within them a greater faith and trust in their God. But how often does the thought occur to them that they could be wrong? How often do they seriously consider whether they believe based upon their upbringing in a Christian family or a Christian culture? There are billions of people who have been brought up with a different religious faith because they were born into a different family and a different culture. The truth is that we are all probably wrong on many topics, especially when there are opposing sides that make good cases and when there isn't a mutually agreed-upon reliable scientific test to determine between rival theories.

Anyway, Christian, for once in your life, you need to seriously examine your faith. By virtue of the fact that your faith is something you prefer to be true, you should subject it to a critical analysis at least once in your life. If you laid aside the fact that you think Christianity is true and merely asked yourself if you prefer that it's true, you'll see quite plainly that you do. How do you know you don't believe what you prefer to be true? Socrates is reported by Plato to have said, "The unexamined life isn't worth living." Maybe you have never seriously questioned the truth of what you believe. Maybe you think you've examined your faith, but instead of reading a book by a skeptic like me, you've read a book by a Christian apologist who defends your faith. There is no comparison between these two types of books. You owe it to yourself to read firsthand what someone like me has to say. You can also read what Christian apologists like Dr. Geisler and others will say in response to what I write, of course. But nothing is quite like a firsthand reading through a book like mine.

This book is my effort to critically examine biblical, conservative, evangelical, or fundamentalist Christianity. As a former evangelical myself, I had already rejected Catholic, liberal, and "cultic"[3] versions of Christianity, and in my journey to becoming an atheist I reconsidered and then subsequently rejected liberal theology all over again. I believe evangelical Christianity has a good chance to be correct about Christianity as a whole. By rejecting it, I also reject Christianity in general.

I'm writing to explain why I rejected Christianity. It's sincere, and it's honest. I'm doing so on the level of a college student, not the professional philosopher, and I have usually tried to quote from accessible books whenever I could. In it I present a cumulative case argument against Christianity. It includes my own personal experiences with the Christian faith, along with the arguments that I find persuasive enough for me to reject that faith. *I consider this book to be one single argument against Christianity, and as such it should be evaluated as a whole.* As an introduction to what follows, I'll begin in the first chapter by telling my personal story of how I converted and then deconverted away from the Christian faith. Chapter 1 forms the backdrop for understanding me and why I wrote this book. My method is explained in detail toward the end of chapter 3. Suffice it to say that I consider part 1, "The Basis for My Control Beliefs," to be the most significant part of my whole case. In this part of my book I articulate and defend my skeptical control beliefs, some chapters of which are philosophical in nature while others are biblical in nature. If you find some of the philosophical arguments difficult to comprehend, you can probably skip over them without too much of a loss. However, you should read the rest of chapter 3, starting with page 56. But since my skeptical control beliefs don't tell me what to think about the specific evidence itself, I'll also examine the biblical evidence in part 2, and then conclude with what I believe today in part 3. My claim is that the Christian faith should be rejected by modern, civilized, scientifically literate people, even if I know many of them will still disagree. I'm just sharing the reasons that convinced me, and I think they should convince others. If someone is persuaded by the same reasons I argue for in this book, then I'm pleased.

Whether you realize it or not, there are probably many Christian professors who have had some serious doubts like me. Dr. Ruth A. Tucker, in her book *Walking Away from Faith: Unraveling the Mystery of Belief and Unbelief*,[4] shares her own doubt and how she overcame it, hoping to challenge unbelievers to reconsider what they are missing. But in one place in her book, as she was contemplating her own doubt, she candidly confesses what sometimes crosses her mind. As a seminary professor she wrote, "There are moments when I doubt all. It is then that I sometimes ask myself as I'm looking out my office window, *What on earth am I doing here? They'd fire me if they only knew.*"[5] While she remains a Christian, her specific challenge to the Christian believer "is that you seek a better understanding of those who do not believe—particularly those who have walked away from the faith—and that you listen carefully to their stories and respond with honesty and sensitivity."[6] According to Tucker, for those who walk away from their faith, "the process is full of sorrow and a sense of loss."[7]

Christian philosopher James F. Sennett is another one who has seriously struggled with his faith, as seen in his as yet unpublished book *This Much I Know: A Postmodern Apologetic*.[8] He confesses to having had a faith crisis in it, and wrote his book as a "first-person apologetic" to answer his own faith crisis. In chapter 1, called "The Reluctant Disciple: Anatomy of a Faith Crisis," he wrote, "I am the one who struggles with God. I am the Reluctant Disciple. . . . Once I had no doubt that God was there, but I resented him for it; now I desperately want him to be there, and am terrified that he might not be." Prompted by a study of the mind/brain problem, he added, "Sometimes I believed. Sometimes I didn't. And it seemed to me that the latter condition was definitely on the ascendancy."

Drs. Tucker and Sennett are not the only Christian believers out there who have seriously struggled with their Christian faith. Many others do too, like philosopher Terence Penelhum, who has expressed similar doubts.[9] I had my doubts, just like they have. At some point my faith just came crashing down on me.

I was a Christian apologist with the equivalent of a PhD degree in the philosophy of religion, set for the express purpose of defending Christianity from intellectual attacks. I was not afraid of any idea because I was convinced that Christianity was true and could withstand all attacks.

I graduated from Great Lakes Christian College, in Lansing, Michigan, in 1977. Then I attended Lincoln Christian Seminary (LCS), in Lincoln, Illinois, and graduated in 1982 with MA and MDiv degrees, under the mentoring of Dr. James D. Strauss. While at LCS I was the founding editor for the now-defunct apologetical quarterly *A Journal for Christian Studies*. After LCS I attended Trinity Evangelical Divinity School (TEDS), and graduated in 1985 with a ThM degree, under the mentoring of Dr. William Lane Craig, considered by many to be the foremost defender of the Kalam cosmological argument for the existence of God, the empty tomb of Jesus, and his bodily resurrection from the grave. I also spent a year and a half in a PhD program at Marquette University with a double major in theology and ethics, but I didn't finish. I have also taught classes for several Christian colleges and secular ones.

Above is a picture of Dr. William Lane Craig and Dr. James D. Strauss together with me at my 1985 Trinity Evangelical Divinity School graduation. Dr. Craig is on the left and Dr. Strauss (in a light suit) is on the right.

Here's what Dr. Craig said a few years after I graduated from TEDS: "In my former capacity as a professor at Trinity Evangelical Divinity School, I enjoyed the privilege of having graduates of Lincoln Christian College in my classes. I was amazed as one after another distinguished himself as among my brightest and most capable students. What was it about this little Christian school in midstate Illinois, I thought, that it should be such an academic powerhouse generating good philosophers? The answer was always the same: Dr. Strauss!"[10]

The fact that I was a former student of theirs should mean nothing to either side of this great debate, even though skeptics may revel in it and Christians may scoff at me for it. I mention it only because it helps people know something about my educational background, and I am very happy to have studied with both of them. People come to their own conclusions; that's all. I would still like to consider these two professors as my friends. My rejection of Christianity isn't anything personal with them. I think very highly of them both. They are both good men. The arguments just weren't there, period.

I was also ordained into the ministry of the centrist Restoration Movement Churches of Christ by Jerry M. Paul, when he was at Christ's Church at Georgetown, in Ft. Wayne, Indiana. I served as an associate minister, a minister, a senior minister, and an interim minister for several churches. I had ministries in Michigan, Wisconsin, and Illinois. I was in the ministry for about fourteen years. My last ministry was for the Angola Christian Church, in Angola, Indiana, where I served as the senior minister. While there I served in the Steuben County Ministerial Association, and for a year I was its president.

I am now an atheist. The major reason why I have become an atheist is because

I could not answer the questions I was encountering. I became an atheist precisely because that's where the unanswerable questions led me. The arguments just weren't there, period. Now as an atheist, I turn that same intellectual muscle into arguing against the things I formerly defended.

From the outset, you should know that I am not an angry atheist. I am certainly not angry with God, since I can no more be angry with a God that doesn't exist than a Christian can be angry with Allah or Zeus. Life for me has been good for the most part. So let me state for the record that although I reject Christianity, I do not reject Christian people, most of whom I respect as good people, nor do I wish to offend them. I will even capitalize the term "God," and refer to God as "him," so as not to offend Christians any further than they may already be with this book. I just consider Christians to be deluded about their faith, like I was. I think they are wrong, that's all.

I know with further research this book could be bettered in some areas. No one today can master all of the relevant issues, certainly not me. If I fail to deal with an important Christian argument, someone else has. I quote from and refer to many different resources that support and further argue for my position, and I don't think with additional information I'll change my mind. Many of the authors I quote from are liberal Christian scholars. I quote from them because I think they offer the best arguments against evangelical Christianity. I don't always state whether the authors I quote from are professing Christians or not because the arguments themselves are what I consider to be the important thing. It should go without saying that the Christian scholars I quote from don't conclude what I do, but I say it anyway.[11]

Finally, I dedicate this book to my wife, Gwen. She is an absolutely wonderful person, without whom I wouldn't have had the time needed to write this book. I never want to be without her. A big thanks goes out to several other people, including Hector Avalos, Graham Oppy, Andrea Weisberger, John Beversluis, Richard Carrier, Joshua Sharp, Felipe Leon, and Matthew J. Green, who all offered insightful comments in one way or another on various sections of this book for which I am very grateful, along with the various Bloggers and commenters on my blog who helped by discussing these issues. All errors are mine and mine alone.

To read updates and discuss the issues in this book with me, visit my Blog on the Web: http://debunkingchristianity.blogspot.com/. Look for my companion book as well, titled *Why I Became an Atheist: Personal Reflections and Additional Arguments*, which can be found online.

NOTES

1. Norman Geisler, *The Baker Encyclopedia of Christian Apologetics* (Grand Rapids, MI: Baker Academic Press, 1998).

2. Norman Geisler, "From Apologist to Atheist: A Critical Review," *Christian Apologetics Journal* 6, no. 1 (Spring 2007): 93–94. Dennett, Hitchens, and Geisler are recommending a previously self-published edition of this book. I'm sure that with this extensively revised Prometheus Books edition they will do likewise.

3. By this I mean those versions of Christianity that evangelical Christians deem as intellectual deviations from "true" Christianity. See Walter Martin's *The Kingdom of the Cults* (Minneapolis: Bethany House, 1985), which addresses some of these "cults." I myself am no longer in the habit of defining who is a Christian and who is not.

4. *Walking Away from Faith: Unraveling the Mystery of Belief and Unbelief* (Downers Grove, IL: Intervarsity Press, 2002).

5. Ibid., p. 133.

6. Ibid., p. 12.

7. Ibid., p. 13.

8. As a good personal friend of mine from seminary days, Sennett told me he's planning on revising this book significantly in light of some personal events that have taken place in his life. He's provided me with a copy of this manuscript.

9. Terence Penelhum, "A Belated Return," in *Philosophers Who Believe*, ed. Kelly James Clark (Downers Grove, IL: Intervarsity Press, 1993), pp. 223–36.

10. This quote can be found on the back cover of *Taking Every Thought Captive: Essays in Honor of James D. Strauss*, ed. Richard A. Knopp and John D. Castelein (Joplin, MO: College Press, 1997).

11. To read my critique of liberal Christian theology, go to my blog and do a search for "Part 1, The Problem with Liberal Theology." When it comes to the Catholic Church, I maintain that if the church has been wrong in the past with the inquisition and witch hunts, then I have no reason to think she is correct today. And with regard to liberal "communities of faith," I think it's very probable that whole communities of faith can be wrong about religious truth claims, given their proliferation.

THE BASIS FOR MY CONTROL BELIEFS

MY CHRISTIAN CONVERSION
AND DECONVERSION

If there is one thing that can be said for me, it's that I am a very passionate man. When I focus on something and/or commit myself to it, I give it my all. My conversion experience was dramatic—so dramatic that it stunned everyone around me. There is no one who knew me during my early years as a Christian who would say that I was not on fire for God. I burned with passion for the Lord. And for good reason; I believed God turned my life around.

I was born in 1954 and grew up in Fort Wayne, Indiana, in a Catholic home. I went to parochial school up until the fourth grade. It was in my youth when I heard of God's love for me, and of several Bible stories. Our family went to church, but we were a nominal churchgoing family, for the most part. I never experienced true faith growing up, but I did learn that whenever I was in need I should call out to God.

I was not always a good boy, being the middle child in a home with three boys separated by two and a half years on both sides of me. I seemed to be in almost every fight in the household, first with my older brother, Tom, and then with my younger brother, Jim. Tom was just too big for Jim to get into many fights with him. But not me! I fought with both of them.

My mother earned a college degree and started teaching elementary school just when I was about to enter the eighth grade. But since neither my mother nor my father would be home when we boys got home from school, they knew I would get into trouble from time to time with my brothers once school was out. So to eliminate the problem, they thought it would be good for everyone if I considered attending Howe Military School, in Howe, Indiana, for eighth grade. My mother's extra income would help pay for the costs, it would help discipline me, and my two brothers would be okay at home unsupervised.

Howe was a good school, and I learned for the first time that I could do well in school. I just hadn't applied myself before, for whatever reason. Howe required an hour of silence every night for doing homework, and because of this I received higher grades than ever before, B+s and above. I also had a yearlong math class taught by Mr. Utz, who actually taught us symbolic logic. Yes, that's right, symbolic logic! He said it was the new math. Since we didn't know any better, we thought it *was* math. I didn't realize what he had taught us until sometime after graduating from college, primarily because I never thought much about it. Later on in life, I actually found myself teaching logic classes for college students.

I have never claimed to have a higher IQ than others, nor that I was better than others at remembering things—sometimes I lack common sense—but what Mr. Utz gave this young passionate boy was something in addition to his passion. He gave me the intellectual tools to think through arguments. When something is taught at an early age, it can make you different than others simply because others were never exposed to it. If I seem to be smart, it's mainly because of Mr. Utz, who gave me the tools for thinking at an early age.

I didn't want to go back to Howe the next year, nor did I have to. But on the first day of school in ninth grade, I found myself walking to school next to a fellow ninth-grader who lit up a cigarette on the way. So in order to be cool, I had one too. It wasn't long before I was in the wrong crowd. I also began to do terrible in algebra class. I just barely passed with D–s. Somehow it didn't dawn on me that the reason why was because I hadn't had eighth-grade math, which would have prepared me for algebra. I just thought it was a higher, more advanced form of math, and I just wasn't getting it. Plus, when I started hanging around the wrong crowd, I wasn't interested in school and all of my grades plummeted.

I was a problem teenager. I had several problems my ninth-grade year at Lane Jr. High School. I got kicked out of Snider High School the next year several times for several different offenses. Then came my problems with the law. I spent many weeks in the Wood Youth Center, in Ft. Wayne. I dropped out of school. Most of my law breaking occurred during the time my mother and father were separated and divorced, and they found it hard to corral me in. They eventually remarried. But in the meantime, I was arrested six different times as a juvenile offender for various offenses. I think I just wanted to fit in. But I fit in with the wrong crowd, and I had no goals at that time.

While I never encountered any skeptics that I could tell, I did find people who told me that God loves me and that Jesus is the one person who could help me through troubled waters. That's all I ever heard. So it seemed natural that when I was a troubled juvenile, I would reach out to the God of the Bible and find the meaning of these Bible stories for my life. But at that age I had no way to know whether or not the Bible was true. I had never investigated it with a critical mind. I just assumed it was true. And so I began reading the Bible uncritically. I thought these were God's words and that he was speaking directly to me every time I read them. It all just seemed so real.

My life was radically changed. After I accepted Jesus, I attended a youth group called the Adam's Apple in Fort Wayne, Indiana, during the height of the Jesus

Movement. It was affiliated with the Calvary Temple Church, and it was Pentecostal in nature. I got heavily involved with several Christian friends, who went street witnessing every Friday and Saturday night on Main Street, where there were a couple of strip joints and one gay bar. We witnessed during a city July 4 celebration, and even after hockey games outside the War Memorial Coliseum. I would even go hitchhiking with the express purpose of witnessing to whoever picked me up. I witnessed to everyone almost all of the time.

In Fort Wayne in 1973 it became cooler to be a "Jesus Freak" than a druggie. Being Jesus Freaks for us was rebelling against the establishment and the old comforting values of our parents just as much as those who followed Timothy Leary's escape through drugs. We could look the same, have long hair, wear bell-bottom studded jeans, and we could use the same slang when describing Jesus as "hip" and a "cool dude." We evangelized with sound bites like "get high on Jesus" and "turn on with Jesus."

My parents had started to attend Christ's Church at Georgetown where Jerry M. Paul was the minister. He eventually baptized me, preached at my ordination, and married me to my former wife, Kathy. That summer he had Brant Doty Jr. as a youth minister—my youth minister. He was attending Great Lakes Christian College (GLCC) and his dad, Dr. Doty, was one of the professors. He told me that with such a passion for Christ I should consider attending there too, so I did. My parents helped me with tuition. After all, I was no longer getting arrested, and I was no longer doing drugs. While at GLCC my freshman year, I took the GED test and got my high school equivalency degree so I could eventually graduate in 1977.

At that point I began investigating my faith. I saw a book at the bookstore by Josh McDowell, called *Evidence That Demands a Verdict*, and I read it completely through. He offered what some critics said about the Bible, and then he countered those critics with quotes from Christian apologists who argued against them. After reading that book, I thought that Christianity also passed intellectual muster. It could handle the attacks of all of the critics. I thought, "It's true! Christianity is true!"

I also read a book by Hal Lindsey, called *The Late Great Planet Earth*. It was a popular treatment of end-time Bible predictions along with the events around the world that seemed to confirm that Jesus was going to return to the earth within our generation. So I once again thought to myself at the time, "It's true! Christianity is true! Jesus might return any day now."

A friend told me about Francis Schaeffer's books, and so I began reading them. I began with *True Spirituality*, then *The God Who Is There*, *Genesis in Space and Time*, *Escape from Reason*, and also *He Is There and He Is Not Silent*. With each of his books that I read, my faith was confirmed even more than before. I also read several of C. S. Lewis's books, especially *Mere Christianity*, *Miracles*, and *The Problem of Pain*. I had every reason to believe, especially since Lewis's and Schaeffer's books were philosophical in nature. There was no reason not to believe. So I thought, "It was true! It was really true!"

At this stage in my life, I probably had no doubts about my faith at all, and with good reason. I had never encountered anything at all to the contrary. It just all made sense. Later I found out that none of these initial reasons for believing had any real merit to them. Christian philosopher Thomas V. Morris effectively dealt with Francis Schaeffer's apologetics in his book *Francis Schaeffer's Apologetics: A Critique*.[1] I learned that the critics of the Bible are right, not Josh McDowell.[2] I am also no longer convinced by C. S. Lewis's arguments.[3] Furthermore, Hal Lindsey's timetable for Jesus' return has been shown to be wrong. Jesus has not yet returned to earth. Failed predictions of Jesus' return have become such an embarrassment for Christians that there is now a movement to embrace *Preterism*, which is the belief that Jesus returned to earth to reign from Jerusalem in a spiritual sense around 70 CE. I've concluded that I believed in the Christian faith for initial reasons that were just inadequate—reasons that I have subsequently come to reject. I just did not have the ability to think through the intellectual foundations for my faith at such a time in my life. I believed what was presented to me because that's all I knew to believe.

So here are a couple of key initial questions: First, what bias or presumption is the correct one when approaching the Christian faith? None of us sets out to study Christianity without some bias one way or another. But as is usually the case, the presumption we start out with will usually be the presumption we end up with— usually. And the presumption we start out with is usually adopted by us before we are properly informed. This is a catch-22. Second, at what point can someone say she can make an informed decision about the Christian faith? When could it be said that I had personally made an informed choice for my faith? In my early years I simply didn't know enough, did I? Who does? Did you? But in my later years, I con- tinued to approach my Christian faith with the presumption I had from my early years—that my faith was correct.

Later when I was in the ministry, I visited Israel, the "Holy Land," in 1989. I was one of nine ministers from Indiana who went to Israel, paid for by the Knights Templar organization in Angola. In a devotional written for the local *Herald Repub- lican* newspaper (March 8, 1989), I shared what I had learned:

> The stories of the beginnings of Christianity have a historical connectedness to them when contrasted with the eastern religion stories. In Christianity God reveals to man through actual historical events real answers that can be satisfying like nothing else can. For instance, Christ's claim to be "the Way, the Truth and the Life" (John 14:6) has a real historical basis in actual time, and actual places of which I visited. I visited Bethlehem where Jesus was born. I visited Nazareth where Jesus grew up. I touched the Jordan River where he was baptized. I visited an ancient Jewish synagogue in Capernaum where Jesus had surely preached. I walked in and around Jerusalem where he ministered. I stood in the Garden of Gethsemane where Jesus prayed, "Not my will but thine be done." I stood on the very stones Jesus walked on the night he was betrayed. I stood in the very area where Jesus was cru- cified, and I visited the empty tomb from which he arose from the dead. I also stood on the Mount of Olives where he ascended into heaven.
>
> There is such a close historical connectedness to the Christian faith that one is extremely hard pressed to deny Jesus' claim to be our only Savior without also denying early first-century Jewish history. Its faith claims are also claims about a

history that was checked by first-century people of that day. Since it is impossible to deny such a historical setting for my faith, it becomes extremely difficult to deny the claims of the Christian faith. Christ is the Way, the Truth and Life—truly!

Five years after I wrote the words above, I would find myself in the throes of doubt. Some of the seeds for my doubt had already been unwittingly sown at Lincoln Christian Seminary (LCS). While there I studied with Dr. James D. Strauss, a professor with a great deal of understanding and a passion for learning. This man lit me up like a firecracker. He was what I was looking for. Following his example, I became passionate for Christian studies and in defending my faith from all intellectual attacks. However, he also set me on the intellectual path that would eventually lead me away from the faith. As I'll explain later, he drummed into his students the perfectly reasonable Christian idea that "all truth is God's truth"—that all truth comes from God whether considered sacred or secular. Later I'll share why this idea eventually was damaging to my Christian faith.

After graduating from LCS, I wrote an article called "A Christian Defense of the Gospel in a Twentieth Century Land,"[4] and later I wrote a devotional for the local *Herald Republican* newspaper (August 10, 1989), summing up and elaborating on it. I'll quote from it extensively here:

Can you prove that God exists? When asked that question what do you say? In answer to the question, you couldn't say that you believe God exists because the Bible says so. Belief in the Bible as truth only comes after one believes in God. Nor could you say that you believe because God answers your prayers. To the unbeliever this is circumstantial evidence. Nor could you say that you believe because your parents have taught you to believe. What if they're wrong? Nor could you offer the fact that God changed your life as proof that God exists. Perhaps you're deluded as to the source of the change?

You might want to argue that biblical miracles prove God exists. Here the burden of proof is yours to show that such events really occurred. Yet, for someone who doesn't already believe in God, miraculous events cannot occur. Of course, the miracle of the resurrection of Christ is a powerful testimony for the existence of a God who raises the dead, but is it proof?

What about fulfilled prophecy in the Bible? We would first need to show that the prophecy was written before the prophesied event actually occurred. Even if it was, then we'd have to show that it wasn't just a lucky guess. The many prophecies concerning Jesus as the Messiah in the Old Testament, taken together, serve as a powerful testimony to a God who sees the future, but is it proof?

I think I can prove that God exists. Does that surprise you? But before I can attempt that feat, I have to know what standard of proof you are looking for. Scientists cannot prove with certainty that the sun will rise tomorrow, only that it has risen in the past. Neither can they prove with certainty that we have existed for more than one day, because every argument used to show this could be a pre-programmed memory in you. There is no proof that other minds than our own exist with whom we can converse, because it could all be in our heads. Nor could you prove that you exist as you appear to exist, rather than being brains in some future mad-scientist's vat who is causing you to experience the life you once lived all over again. Isn't that a scary thought? Now it is reasonable to believe the sun will rise tomorrow, that other minds exist, and that we have existed as we appear to have existed, even if these things are not subject to proof talk.

In the last few centuries philosophers asked theologians to prove that God exists with a certainty that is simply not possible to attain in any field of learning, as witnessed above. Yet, because God's existence couldn't be proved by this impossible standard, people grew to believe that God's existence couldn't be supported by reason. Of course, this does not follow. For if it's reasonable to believe we are who we experience ourselves to be without proof, then it can be reasonable to believe God exists without the same kinds of proof demands.

I can prove God exists then, only if we mean proved according to the same standards that allow us to believe we are who we experience ourselves to be. Unfortunately, to offer a proof of something doesn't mean that it's going to convince others. Most of us could offer proof that the earth is round, but there will always be people who remain unconvinced, as seen by those in the Flat Earth Society.

God's existence can be shown to be reasonable by examining consistent sets of answers to questions concerning the basic makeup of the world and man, called "world-views"—there are seven of them. If reasonableness is the standard, the Christian set of answers wins hands down. Christianity makes possible the standard of reasonableness without which modern science would never have arisen. Christian theism is more reasonable than any other total world-view system.

Pretty confident wasn't I? That was all to change in a few years.

WHY I CHANGED MY MIND: MY DECONVERSION

As I share my experiences in what follows, keep in mind that I don't speak for all skeptics. This is my life, not theirs. The experiences I've had are not typical of why people leave the Christian faith. Some former believers have rejected their faith based upon the evidence itself. My initial arguments for rejecting the Christian faith are not the same ones that others have had. Former Christians leave the faith for a wide variety of reasons since there are so many problems with the Christian faith.

For me there were three major circumstances that happened in my life that changed my thinking. They all happened in the space of about five years, from 1991 to 1996. These things are associated with three people: a woman I'll call Linda, Larry, and Jeff. It was Linda who brought a major crisis into my life. Larry brought new information into my life. Jeff took away my sense of a loving Christian community. *These are the three things that changed my thinking: a major crisis, plus new information that caused me to see things differently, minus a sense of a loving, caring, Christian community.* In the midst of these things, I felt rejected by the Church of Christ in my local area. For me it was an assault of major proportions that if I still believed in the devil, I would say it was orchestrated by the legions of hell.

LINDA

I was the founding president of a shelter for the homeless in Angola, Indiana, where I ministered. It was devoted to giving temporary shelter to people in need. I worked day by day with Linda, the executive director. She practically idolized me. She did everything I said to do, and would call me daily to ask for help in dealing with various situations that came up from the running of the shelter, along with her own personal issues. I was also having problems with my marriage at the time, and Linda made herself available to me. I succumbed and had an affair with her.

There's so much more I'd like to say about this, but few people would believe me. As a former stripper in her younger days, she had it in for preachers, and she took out her wrath on me. Perhaps because I was a moral crusader in town and stood against abortion and X-rated video rentals, she chose to humiliate me. Suffice it to say there are some women out there who, akin to Potipher's wife in the Bible, find it challenging to see if they can sack a minister, and she did.

How many sermons have you heard about Potipher's seductress wife in which preachers wonder aloud if many men could've overcome the temptation to sleep with her as she continually made herself available to Joseph (Gen. 39:6–20)? In order to bolster our confidence in Joseph's faith, they conclude not many men would've overcome this temptation. But when someone like me actually does succumb to such a temptation, even if it wasn't exactly the same, these preachers are quick to condemn me. There are mitigating factors here, even if I did do wrong. And I did do wrong. But until you experience something like this, you will never understand. This lack of understanding doubles my pain.

As far as the affair itself goes, ethicist Richard Taylor wrote a book on *Having Love Affairs* in which he discusses whose fault it is when there is an affair. Sometimes a married couple mostly ends up sharing the same house and children with each other. I am not excusing myself here, since it takes two, but as he explains, there may be more to it: "Though a wife may be ever so dutiful, faultless, and virtuous in every skill required for the making of a home, if she lacks passion, then in a very real sense she already is without a husband, or he, at least, is without a wife. Similarly, a husband who is preoccupied with himself and his work, who is oblivious to the needs of his wife and insensitive to her vanities, who takes for granted her unique talents and who goes about his business more or less as though she did not exist, has already withdrawn as a husband, except in name." Taylor continues, "What must be remembered by those persons who wish to condemn adultery is that the primary vow of marriage is to love, and that vow is not fulfilled by the kind of endless busyness exemplified in the industrious and ever generous husband or the dedicated homemaking wife. . . . What has to be stressed is that the first infidelity may or may not have been committed by the one who is having an affair. The first and ultimate infidelity is to withhold the love that was promised, and which was originally represented as the reason for marriage to begin with."[5]

But there is more. After only a few months I finally decided I could no longer reconcile the affair with my faith or my family life. So I told Linda that it was over. Well, William Congreve is right, "hell has no fury like a woman scorned." She went off in a rampage and told the board of directors at the shelter that I had raped her. She went to the prosecutor with my former associate minister and tried to press charges against me, too. They were all lies. No charges were brought against me, thankfully.

I thought everyone had heard of her accusations and that most people believed her. I received a phone call from someone who threatened my life, and it sounded like he would kill me, too. One man for whom I had a great amount of respect had heard her accusations. I said to him, "You don't believe her, do you?" He replied, "John, I don't know what to believe." This really hurt.

I was supposed to be smarter and better than that, or so I thought. How could I have done this? How could I have an affair with her and sin like that against my God and against my family? How could I allow my reputation to be sullied by claims that I had raped her? The biggest question of all was why God tested me by allowing her to come into my life when she did if he knew in advance I would fail the test? All of this devastated me: my sin, the strange mitigating factors, the Christian people who wouldn't forgive me even though I repented of this sin, the false accusation of rape, and God not seeming to care about his wayward soldier. I do thank my ex-wife, Kathy, for forgiving me and for standing by me during this period in my life. She is a wonderful woman. She understood.

LARRY

While I was still feeling the devastation from Linda, I carried on a correspondence debate with my cousin Larry Strawser, who was a lieutenant (now a colonel) in the air force and a professor of biochemistry at a base in Colorado. I handed him a book arguing for creation over evolution and asked him to look at it and let me know what he thought of it. After several months, he wrote me a thirty-one-page letter and included it with a box full of articles and books on the subject. Some of them were much too technical for me to understand, but I tried to read them. While he didn't convince me of much at the time, he did convince me of one solid truth: the universe is as old as scientists say it is, and the consensus was that it is between thirteen and fifteen billion years old.

This was the first time I really considered the theological implications of the age of the universe. Two corollaries of that idea started me down the road to being the atheist I am today. The first is that in Genesis chapter 1 we see that the earth existed before the sun, moon, and stars, which were all created on the fourth day. This doesn't square with astronomy. So I began looking at the first few chapters in Genesis, and as my thinking developed over time, I came to the conclusion that those chapters are folk literature—myth. The second corollary for me at that time was this: If God took so long to create the universe, then why would he all of a sudden snap his fingers, so to speak, and create human beings? If God took his time to create the universe, then why wouldn't he also create living creatures with greater complexity during the same length of time? Why did it take God so long to create the stuff of the universe, which is less valuable and presumably less complex to create, than it did to create the most valuable and highly complex creatures to inhabit the earth? Astronomy describes the long process of galaxy, star, and planet formation. It then becomes uncharacteristic of God to create life on planet earth by divine fiat instantaneously. I concluded that God created human beings by the same long process as he created the universe as a whole, if he created us at all.

Nearly two years later, I came to deny the Christian faith. **It required too much intellectual gerrymandering to believe.** *There were just too many individual problems that I had to balance, like spinning several plates up on several sticks, in order to keep my faith. At some point they just all came crashing down.* This book presents the fullest explanation of my reasons for rejecting that faith.

THE CHURCH OF CHRIST

At this point, I want to describe why I left the Church of Christ in my area. The Angola Christian Church asked for my resignation in December 1990. It had nothing much at all to do with my affair with Linda, although some thought I was getting too close to her, and they wondered. I had offended John and Sybil Love, camp managers with Lake James Christian Assembly, in Angola, Indiana. They are decent, hardworking Christian people. But they were opposed to my ministry for various petty reasons, in my opinion, so they left our church and started attending the Pleasant View Christian Church, also located in the small town of Angola. This was a church that had split off from ours a few decades back. Since the Loves had relatives and friends in our church, the pressure was on to get them back, and the church elders felt that one way to get them back was to ask for my resignation. So they did. It's not uncommon for ministers to be asked to leave a church when their effectiveness is gone. At the time, I argued that doing so would not bring the Loves back, and they didn't go back, as I predicted.

We didn't feel comfortable in attending a church from which I resigned, so our family attended the Pleasant View Christian Church a couple of times. We sensed from the church leadership that they didn't want us attending there, either, probably because that's where the Loves attended now. (The Christian Church has its *bishops*, after all, despite their doctrinal position on church polity.) At this point, neither one of the closest Christian Churches in our area wanted me.

What bothered me was that Jerry Paul, my home minister in Fort Wayne at the time, didn't call me. Somehow I couldn't call him either. I was just too embarrassed. But I needed to hear from him, and I've concluded he just didn't want to get involved. Jerry baptized me, was my ordaining minister, and married me to my wife at the time, Kathy. A minister friend named George Faull told me that the Linda I mentioned earlier had called Jerry Paul and told him I had raped her, and so on. She was hell-bent on destroying me, is all I can figure. But Jerry never called me to talk, or pray with me, or comfort me. When George told me that Jerry had heard from her, my heart just sank. Why? Is this what successful ministers do? They don't get involved with people who have become "hot potatoes"? Did he care? Was I just a black mark on his list of accomplishments such that he wanted to avoid me? That's how I felt. I really don't know his reasons. Maybe he thought that if I wanted help, then all I had to do was call, and he'd be right there with me all of the way. That's a nice way to do ministry, isn't it? Maybe that's just how he is, and maybe I could've gotten the encouragement I needed. But at the time, I felt rejected by someone I had respected the most.

After a while, I found myself teaching classes at Great Lakes Christian College (GLCC). My brother-in-law at the time, Tom Spoors, became the head of the Leadership Institute. It was a degree-completion program that GLCC set up and ran for a few years from about 1992 to 1996. I taught philosophy and apologetic classes there. Shortly after beginning to teach at GLCC, Jerry Paul became the president of the college, but we never spoke about anything except those things related to my classes. Neither of us brought other things up.

Partly because I felt the Church of Christ leadership in my local area had rejected me, but also because I tend to stretch people's minds anyway, I wrote a controversial essay on Christian baptism for *Integrity* magazine.[6] The editorial board of *Integrity* included the late Dr. Brant Lee Doty and Curtis Lloyd. Both men had been acting presidents for GLCC in the past, and both were well-respected Church of Christ people. The board said it was "thoughtful and worthy of being printed in the interests of a dialogue about the subject." But the reaction was intense. Sherman Nichols preached at a men's meeting in the heart of Michigan and denounced that article, and me. This put the pressure on President Jerry Paul and Tom Spoors to let me go from my teaching responsibilities at the college. And they did. Jerry said that many people previously had reservations about my teaching for the college and that this was the last straw, although Jerry also said he couldn't exactly pinpoint whether or not those reservations were legitimate ones. So I did the only thing I knew to do. I fired back in print with a second article on Christian baptism for *Integrity*.[7] One minister friend said that this second article was "superb," and another writer said that he didn't think my baptism articles could be refuted. At that point, I was done with the Church of Christ.

Several other people did encourage me at that time, including a few Bible College professors. I'm the sort of person who has a very hard time asking for help, and I was hurting badly. Even so, Curtis Lloyd, Virgil Warren, John Castelein, and George Faull all encouraged me in various ways, and I was grateful for that.

You'll notice that although I taught at GLCC, and was still involved in various churches, my doubts were growing in intensity. I continued in the church because I didn't yet know where my doubts would lead me. But when GLCC cut me off from its oversight and approval, I no longer had anything to lose by expressing my doubts, especially when my livelihood no longer depended on what I believed. And my doubts took over at that point, especially after I experienced problems with my cousin Jeff at his church, a month or two later.

JEFF

The previously mentioned correspondence with my cousin Larry over evolution took place while I was trying to maintain my faith in the Pleasant Lake Baptist Church. As I just said, I felt rejected by the Church of Christ in my local area. After my experience with Linda, I didn't even go to church for several months. But my other cousin, Jeff Stackhouse, became the pastor there, and I said to myself, "Here is a safe place to worship where I won't get hurt." So I gradually got involved. I helped wherever I could, and our family liked it very much. I taught Sunday school, preached on occasion, and eventually became an elder in that church with people who loved me and whom I loved, and I still do.

As best as I can tell, Jeff was suspicious of my motives—my own cousin! Without going into great detail, he and his wife, Lurleen (now Loren), suspected that I was secretly trying to oust him to become the pastor there. I'm sure they felt threatened, but I didn't mean to threaten them. The farthest thing from my mind was to oust him so that I could become the new pastor. I just wanted to help. But he left the church and blamed me. An elder even asked me in an elder's meeting after Jeff left if I would consider being the new pastor, and I turned it down. I really didn't want to do it at all.

I have no ill feelings toward Jeff and his wife and I wish them well. After all, we are just people, and people sometimes feel this way. I still consider them my friends. But the thing about this experience was that I had to wrestle with the question of why someone who is as close as a cousin to me could misread my intentions so badly. How could he get it so wrong? And he was wrong. From this I began to reflect on the many different interpretations people have of the Bible, and I began to ask whether it's possible to have a correct understanding of the Bible if people as close to each other as he and I had such a misunderstanding. I began to doubt that people with our passions and living in our day and age, so removed from the Bible, could properly understand that book when people living in the same age and as close to one another as he and I couldn't understand each other.

This last thought hit home extremely hard after Jeff left the church. In his wake, he left a rift in that church between a few important people who liked me and a few who didn't. Soon after Jeff left the church, a problem developed between Mark, an elder, and the director of the children's program, whose name was Conny (neither of them attend there anymore). Mark didn't like Conny, or her husband, or me, and he blamed us for Jeff's having left the church. I thought a lot of Conny, but she had a problem with her temper and got into a confrontation with Mark. She made a child sit out from an activity because he was unruly, but Mark told the child to participate anyway, and he did so in front of her! Well, she blew up at him on the spot.

Afterward, a debate ensued among the elders of our church. In the first place, I disagreed totally with how they wanted to handle the problem. I argued from the Bible that the two people who had the problem should sit down and talk about it first, but few agreed with me on that point. Beyond that, there were a few elders on one side who wanted to discipline (or punish) her by removing her from her position, and there were a few elders on the other side, including me, who wanted to forgive her. The interesting thing is that both sides claimed that they were motivated by love. We all had our Bible verses to back it up, too! Once again, the thought occurred to me how people living in the same day and age in the same church could have different understandings of what the Bible wanted us to do. I left that church over it, and so did most of the people involved. The people of that church are just like people of any church, caring for the most part, but we can all get riled too.

It sometimes still surprises me what people who are of the Christian faith will do with what they consider a clear conscience. I wonder to myself how these consciences can differ so widely, especially when Christianity is the only faith that claims God the Holy Spirit actually takes up residence in their being. I often ask myself why Christians don't seem to act any better than others when they alone claim to have the power, wisdom, and guidance of God right there within them. Apparently, the Holy Spirit didn't properly do his job here. *This was the last blow to my faith and one of the reasons why I am an atheist today.*

By then the damage was done both psychologically in my experiences and intellectually as I continued to study the issues. Massive doubt crept upon me until I didn't want to be a part of any church much at all.

MY DIVORCE AND REMARRIAGE

Finally, I decided I wasn't going to live out the rest of my life not being happily married. So I left Kathy and decided I was going to find love again. I did feel guilty for this, but neither of us was happy in our marriage. Pollster George Barna's research has shown that "a surprising number of Christians experienced divorces both before and after their conversion."[8] Why should it be different for skeptics when they leave their religion?

I found Gwen, a woman who is as passionate about me as I am about her. Gwen has gone with me to church whenever I have wanted to go, and I do go when visiting my mother or when someone asks me to go on a special occasion, but she, too, is an unbeliever—an atheist. She's got the kind of character that most church people do not have. To a large extent, because of my divorce from Kathy and my remarriage to Gwen, I've stayed away from churches. The longer I was away, the less I believed, and the less I believed, the less I wanted to attend church.

In the era of tell-all books, I think honesty is what's required so that readers can see and judge for themselves about the totality of the reasons why I rejected Christianity. I don't believe conversion or deconversion experiences take place strictly because of epistemic reasons in either direction, in most all cases. There are most always social and psychological factors too. Anyone who ever hears most Christian conversion stories knows exactly what I mean. All of the ones I've ever personally heard had to do with someone who has either grown up in the church or someone who had some dramatic experience when down on her luck to some degree. If anyone wants to discount my deconversion and present rejection of Christianity because of my experiences, then I could discount the overwhelming number of Christian conversion experiences owing to similar factors like divorce, bankruptcy, jail, addiction, and so forth. Anyone intelligent enough to realize that these factors influence us all will wonder what these factors were for me. So I spell them out here in both my conversion and my deconversion stories. I share these experiences in the attempt to show that my rejection of Christianity is sincere and honest.

I know that some Christians who refuse to deal with the arguments later on in this book will use the personal information I've just shared to attack my character. No doubt you'll hear that I am an adulterer, something that took place eighteen years ago as of this writing, and that I'm divorced. The truth is I have character flaws. I'll be the first one to admit it. However, as a counselor in all of the churches I've served, I learned that every single one of us has some character flaws. It's precisely because I realize this that I can be honest about myself and about my flaws. And this is freeing to me. I can be honest with who I am and what I've done. Christians are in denial and live with guilt because they cannot be honest about themselves outside of the private counseling room. But I know the kind of behavior that leaders in every church I served admitted to doing. I suspect the Christians throwing stones at me are no different than the church people whom I counseled—flawed just like them.

After reading my deconversion story, Dr. Norman L. Geisler wrote to me: "I have just read your book and my heart goes out to you. I think many people would have become atheists, had they gone through what you have. First, I would like to apologize on behalf of the body of Christ for the unloving way in which you were treated. My sympathy is with you. I am so sorry. I wish I knew you better and lived close enough to give you a hug. Just let me say, I love you regardless of what has happened. The legalistic, unkind, and hypocritical way you were treated was simply unchristian and uncalled for. Again, I apologize on behalf of anyone involved who professes the name of Christ. I will be recommending your book to our students. There are many things Christians can learn from it, not the least of which is what Jesus said in John 13:35. Of course, I do not agree with your conclusions, but there is no justification for unloving behavior on the part of Christians."

I don't need any sympathy at this point, and I especially don't want any pity. I very much appreciate Norm's concern and compassion though. On a personal level he's a gracious man whom I consider a friend. But with this recognition comes the next question: Why didn't God do something to avert these particular experiences of mine, especially if he could foreknow that I would eventually write this book and lead others astray?

ADDITIONAL THOUGHTS

While the things I have just written might explain to some degree why my thinking has changed, I want to stress the fact that my thinking has indeed changed. You cannot explain away my present thinking by pointing to these experiences I've had in my life. They may be what provoked my thinking, but they don't answer my arguments. My arguments cannot be dismissed because I had an affair and am divorced, or else we can likewise reject any argument based upon how the proponent lives his life. In talking with me, you will have to deal with my arguments. People believe and doubt for a wide variety of reasons, and that's all there is to it.

For me, it wasn't just my affair with Linda that led me to reject Christianity anyway. I could've gotten beyond the damage that had done to my faith. It was being cut off from the church, of which the affair with her was the catalyst. Taken together with the new way of seeing things that I learned from my cousin Larry that set me on a course of doubt, and the subsequent church experiences I had while teaching at GLCC and in my cousin Jeff's church, I eventually came to reject my former faith. I just couldn't reconcile everything I had experienced and everything I had learned with the Christian faith. Even though I approached Christianity the presumption of faith, my experiences and my studies ended my faith. In the end the skeptics were right all along.

My doubts were simmering for a few years while I was with my wife, Gwen. I didn't think much about them. But when Mel Gibson's movie *The Passion of the Christ* came out, it made me think about them again, intensely. More than anything else this movie put me on a course to finally come out of the closet and tell what I think, for I saw in that movie such an ignorance that I just had to speak out.

I tried as best as I could to be a faithful Christian, and a good minister. Even though I believed it was by grace that I had been saved, I almost always felt guilty that I wasn't doing enough in response to God's purported love. This was something I fully understood only after walking away from the Christian faith. Whether it was spending time in prayer, evangelizing, reading the Bible, tithing, forgiving, or whether it was struggling with temptations of lust, pride, selfishness, and laziness, as I look back, I almost always felt guilty. It may just be because I was so passionate about Christianity that this was the case, and so it just might be my particular temperament. I never could understand how Christian people could come to church every Sunday but never get involved much in the church's programs, because that's what believers should want to do. To be quite frank here, if Christians really believed that God saved them and that the non-Christian was going to hell, how would they really behave? How many true believers are in the churches today?

Today I am guilt free regarding the Christian duties mentioned above. I am so grateful for my present life because I'm living life to the hilt. I just don't think anyone can live a passionate guilt-free Christian life. Think about it; according to Jesus, I should feel guilty for not just what I do but for what I think about—lusting, hating, coveting, and so on. I'd like every person who reads this book to experience the freedom I have found.

I think a former member of my blog named exbeliever best describes how I feel about this whole matter:

> For a long time, I was an ardent admirer of Dr. John Piper. I remember a sermon of
> Dr. Piper's in which he described God as a flowing fountain of delight. The Psalmist

writes, "Taste and see that the LORD is good; blessed is the man who takes refuge in him" (Ps. 34:8). Piper said that we would praise a fountain, not by standing passively by, but by sticking our faces deep inside it to take in its wonderful refreshment. We would stand up and shout, "This is the best water I've ever tasted; come and have some with me!" He invited others to taste and see God's goodness.

But what about those of us who have left the fountain with a horrible taste in our mouths? We came to the fountain and drank as deeply as we could and, for a while, could not get enough of it. We loved reading the Bible and being instructed by it. We believed that it made us wiser than our counselors. We made our bodies our slaves so that they would honor God. We prayed without ceasing. We sought first the kingdom of God. We confessed our sins and believed that God was faithful and just to forgive us our sins. We preached "the Word" in season and out. We attempted to study to show ourselves approved. We fed God's sheep.

But, then, something happened. The fountain became foul to us. We tried to ignore the taste. We went back to it again and again hoping something would change. We opened the Bible and, instead of finding wisdom, we found violence and the justification of immoral acts. We found anti-intellectualism and backward thinking. We found oppression. Our prayers returned to us void. They bounced off of the ceiling. We prayed harder and felt dumber for it. While we could still enjoy the fellowship of Christian people, we discovered that what we liked about them had nothing to do with their Christianity, but rather with their humanity. We found that we simply liked the people for who they were, not because they believed something about a religion.

We weren't trying to "leave the faith." The faith was leaving us. We tried to hold on to the fountain, but something had changed. It wasn't the fountain; it was our taste for it. We realized that the fountain wasn't a being; it was a religion. It was just dogma. It is like we had been drinking from it with our eyes closed and noses plugged. Somehow, though, we opened our eyes and unplugged our noses and discovered that we had been enjoying filth. The fountain was a fountain of blood and other foul things. We realized that we had spent most of our lives consuming a vile concoction.

We would have been happy to have simply left, but we couldn't help but want to pull others away from such a cesspool. We wanted to help them open their eyes and see what we saw. We wanted them to see the trouble the fountain was causing in the world. Quickly, however, we ran into opposition. We found that those still slurping away at the fountain with eyes closed and noses plugged resisted. They said that we were lying about the taste of the fountain or that we had never drunk from it in the first place. We told them to open their eyes, but they responded that the eyes cannot be trusted. We described the filth to them, but even when they accepted that the fountain contained blood and other "foul" things, they insisted that those things were really "good."

With my personal story out on the table, I shall begin my case against Christianity. In the next two chapters I must first deal with some preliminary considerations.

NOTES

1. Thomas V. Morris, *Francis Schaeffer's Apologetics: A Critique* (Chicago: Moody Press, 1976).

2. See *The Jury Is In: The Ruling on McDowell's "Evidence,"* an online book edited by Secular Web founder Jeffery Jay Lowder: http://www.infidels.org.

3. See John Beversluis, *C. S. Lewis and the Search for Rational Religion* (Grand Rapids, MI: Eerdmans, 1985), which has been extensively revised and published by the same title through Prometheus Books, 2007.

4. *Christian Standard*, September 19, 1982.

5. Richard Taylor, *Having Loving Affairs* (Amherst, NY: Prometheus Books, 1982), as quoted in Brooke Noel Moore and Robert Michael Stewart, *Moral Philosophy: A Comprehensive Introduction* (Mountain View, CA: Mayfield, 1994), p. 570.

6. July/August 1995.

7. January/February 1996. Both of these articles can be found on my blog. Just do a search on it for, "Is Baptism Necessary for Salvation?"

8. www.barna.org.

2

THE CHRISTIAN ILLUSION OF RATIONAL AND MORAL SUPERIORITY

I'm going to begin with what many Christians assume about their faith. They assume a certain kind of rational and/or moral superiority over any other system of belief and thought, especially atheism. According to them, their beliefs are rationally superior in the sense that Christianity wins hands down in the marketplace of ideas. They claim that a compelling case can be made for believing in Christianity over any other system of belief and thought. Likewise, according to them, their moral foundation is also superior in the sense that Christianity provides the only sufficient basis for acting morally in life. Other moral systems either do not or cannot do this. Let me offer some criticisms of both of these assumptions, each in turn.

THE ILLUSION OF RATIONAL SUPERIORITY

The way Christians think of atheists in general, and of ex-Christians in particular, is due to what my friend Dr. James F. Sennett calls the *Illusion of Rational Superiority.*[1] Sennett argues against the belief that people who reject Christianity do so because they are ignorant, stupid, or dishonest with the facts. That is, he argues against the idea that a fully rational rejection of Christianity is impossible. This is an illusion, he claims. Although, as a Christian philosopher he argues it is an unnecessary illusion due to the fact that even though his faith is "not rationally compelling to all," it's still "a reasonable faith."

As an example of this illusion, Sennett quotes from Bill Bright, the late founder and president of Campus Crusade for Christ, who wrote: "During my fifty-five years of sharing the good news of the Savior . . . I have met very few individuals who have honestly considered the evidence and yet deny that Jesus Christ is the Son of God and the Savior of men. To me, the evidence confirming the deity of the Lord Jesus Christ is overwhelmingly conclusive to any honest, objective seeker after truth."

As another milder example of this illusion, consider Os Guinness's book titled *In Two Minds: The Dilemma of Doubt and How to Resolve It.*[2] Guinness discusses the main reasons why people, including Christians themselves, have doubts about Christianity: there is doubt from a faulty view of God; doubt from weak intellectual foundations; doubt from a lack of commitment; doubt from lack of growth; doubt from unruly emotions; doubt from fearing to believe; doubt from insistent inquisitiveness; and doubt from impatience or giving up. Since Guinness was arguing on behalf of his Christian faith, he doesn't mention one other major reason to doubt: *doubt from a lack of adequate reasons.* And he fails to note that in the above list of reasons to doubt one could just as well reverse them: believing from the need to be grateful to someone; believing from the need for a God; believing from weak intellectual foundations; believing from the need to be committed; believing in hopes of personal growth; believing because of unruly emotions; believing because of the fear of doubting; believing from not being inquisitive enough; and believing from giving up too soon. While Guinness isn't as blatant as others about the illusion, we still find it here with him. There are some very solid reasons to believe, we're told, so if you doubt, it's because of some fault within you.

But Sennett argues that the Christian cannot overlook "one simple but powerful fact: most of the truly brilliant, deepest thinking, most profoundly influential movers and shakers of the last two hundred years have not been Christians. Neither Albert Einstein nor Bertrand Russell nor Sigmund Freud nor Stephen Hawking nor Karl Marx professed Jesus as lord. And the list goes on. To suggest that these people failed to believe because of ignorance or some rational defect is ludicrous." Of course, the illusion runs both ways, Sennett claims. There is no rational superiority for unbelief, either. Atheist Thomas Nagel is quoted as saying he was made uneasy "by the fact that some of the most intelligent and well-informed people I know are religious believers."

Sennett informs us that "if there is one lesson that modern epistemology has taught us, it is that almost nothing is as rationally certain as '*the illusion*' claims Christianity to be. In other words, almost nothing is so obvious that one could never rationally reject it." Furthermore, it seems possible that "one could rationally deny almost any claim, even if that claim is true." There are plenty of philosophical reasons for Sennett's argument, and many historical examples, not the least of which is the fact that several scholars deny Jesus actually existed at all. The fact is, many scholars have indeed examined the historical evidence for Christianity, and they regard that evidence as flawed.

From the scholarly level to the peon level we disagree about everything there is to disagree about. And this goes especially for religion. There are so many religions and sects within them that if each one was a person, we'd be able to fill up the largest stadium in the world with them. It reveals an incredible amount of chutzpa to claim with complete assurance that Christianity is not only correct, a large claim in and of itself, but also that the others willfully reject the truth.

This book you are reading presents a sustained case against this illusion. It's simply an illusion that Christians have a rationally superior faith and/or those who reject it do so because they are dishonest with the facts. I hope to further show that there are several very strong reasons to reject Christianity.

THE ILLUSION OF MORAL SUPERIORITY

Many Christians maintain they have a superior foundation for knowing and for choosing to do what is good. They claim to have objective ethical standards for being good, based in a morally good creator God, along with the best motivation for being good, which is an eternal reward in the presence of a loving God. These Christians also claim that the atheist has no ultimate justification for being moral, much less a motivation for acting on those morals, especially when they conflict with her own personal self-interest. They claim that atheists do not have a good reason to condemn murder, brutality, and torture, nor do they have an ultimate reason to refrain from murdering, raping, and torturing other people themselves.

Dr. William Lane Craig quotes with approval Fyodor Dostoyevsky's character Ivan Karamazov, who said, "If God doesn't exist, everything is permissible." Craig summed up the moral case against atheism using these words:

> [I]f the existence of God is denied, then one is landed in complete moral relativism, so that no act, regardless of how dreadful or heinous, can be condemned by the atheist. . . . If life ends at the grave, then it makes no difference whether one has lived as a Stalin or as a saint. . . . On this basis, a writer like Ayn Rand is absolutely correct to praise the virtues of selfishness. Live totally for self; no one holds you accountable! Indeed, it would be foolish to do anything else, for life is too short to jeopardize it by acting out of anything but pure self-interest. Sacrifice for another person would be stupid. . . . In a world without God, who is to say which values are right and which are wrong? Who is to judge that the values of Adolf Hitler are inferior to those of a saint? The concept of morality loses all meaning in a universe without God. There can be no right and wrong. This means that it is impossible to condemn war, oppression, or crime as evil. Nor can one praise brotherhood, equality, and love as good. For in a universe without God, good and evil do not exist—there is only the bare valueless fact of existence, and there is no one to say you are right and I am wrong. . . . The world was horrified when it learned that at camps like Dachau the Nazis had used prisoners for medical experiments on living humans. But why not? If God does not exist, there can be no objection to using people as human guinea pigs.[3]

Before we move on to the philosophical arguments for this claim, let's pause and ask first why there is no evidence for what Craig claims. If he is correct, we should see billions of non-Christians acting consistently according to this logic. There should be great mayhem in this world, the likes of which should send the rest of us into the asylum. In other words, why don't non-Christians act consistently? No one says to herself, "this is the reasonable or logical thing to do but I refuse to do it," unless she is mentally challenged. Do theists like Craig want to claim that nearly all non-Christians are mentally challenged . . . that the overwhelming majority of us don't live consistent lives with what we believe? The evidence is overwhelmingly against his claim.

Craig argues that the reason why non-Christians don't act consistently is because we really do have an ultimate standard for morality after all. But it does no good to say there is such a standard when he cannot state what it is and how it should be applied to the specific ethical issues of our day. Christians themselves have changed their minds on these issues down through the centuries and cannot agree about such things today. And such a claim flies in the face of the God we find in the Bible who commanded moral atrocities like genocide, and as we'll see, child sacrifices. To claim there is such an ultimate ethical standard is a mere assertion not backed by the evidence of the moral behavior of billions of non-Christians in the world, the commands of the God of the Bible, and of the history of Christian ethics. I don't know what more needs to be said about this, but there is more to say.

THE ILLUSION OF A SUPERIOR CHRISTIAN ETHICAL STANDARD

There are two philosophical bases for grounding Christian ethical standards. The first is known as the *divine command theory*. I'll deal with this theory first. The second basis is *natural law theory*, which I will dispense with briefly later. I will show that neither of these bases for Christian ethics offers believers a special access to moral truth that unbelievers don't also share. Christian moral foundations are not superior ones.

The divine command theory is stated like this: Morality is based upon what God commands; no other reasons are needed for something to be a moral obligation except that God so commanded it. If God commanded it, then it is right. If God forbids it, then it is wrong. Of this theory Socrates asked a fundamental question: Is conduct right because the gods command it, or do gods command it because it is right? This dilemma is found in Plato's work the *Euthyphro* and known forever since as the *Euthyphro dilemma*.

Ever since Socrates asked this question, every philosopher who has dealt with Christian ethics has commented on it. And most all commentators will admit that the divine command theory has some huge intellectual problems to overcome. If we say, on the one hand, that something is right because God commands it, then the only reason why we should do something is that God commands it. But this makes God's commands arbitrary because there is no reason why God commanded something other than the fact that he did. He just commands what he commands. If this is the case, God could've commanded us to do something horribly evil by simply declaring it good. If God is the creator of morality like he's purportedly the creator of the universe, then he could've declared any act good, and there would be no moral reason above God to distinguish him from the devil. According to John Arthur, this presents us with the "seemingly absurd position that even the greatest atrocities might be not only acceptable but morally required if God were to command them."[4]

William Lane Craig actually bites this bullet when explaining why God allegedly told the Israelites to slaughter the Canaanites. Craig wrote: "the problem isn't that God ended the Canaanites' lives. The problem is that He commanded the Israeli soldiers to end them. Isn't that like commanding someone to commit murder? No, it's not. Rather, since our moral duties are determined by God's commands, it is commanding someone to do something which, in the absence of a divine command, would have been murder. The act was morally obligatory for the Israeli soldiers in virtue of God's command, even though, had they undertaken it on their on initiative, it would have been wrong."[5]

This makes the whole concept of the goodness of God meaningless. If we think that the commands of God are good merely because he commands them, then his commands are, well, just his commands. We cannot call them good, for to call them good we'd have to have a standard above them to declare that they are indeed good commands. But on this theory they are just God's commands. God doesn't command us to do good things; he just commands us to do things. John Arthur argued, "All that could mean is that God wants us to do what he wants us to do." And God isn't a good God either; he is just God. For there would be no standard above God for us to be able to proclaim that God is good. He is just, well, God.

If we say, on the other hand, that God commands what is right because it is right, then there is a higher standard of morality that is being appealed to, and if this is so, then there is a higher standard above God which is independent of him that makes his commands good. Rather than *declaring* what is good, now God *recognizes* what is good and commands us to do likewise. But where did this standard come from that is purportedly higher than God? If it exists, this moral standard is the real God.

The divine command theory is in such disrepute in today's philosophical circles that only modified divine command theories are being discussed. Christian apologist J. P. Moreland actually claims, "I'm not a divine command theorist. . . . [T]his view implies that morality is merely grounded in God's will as opposed to his nature. That's not my view. I think God's will is ultimately expressed in keeping with his nature. Morality is ultimately grounded in the nature of God, not independently of God."[6] Robert M. Adams and Philip Quinn both defend this view.[7] Adams, for instance, claims that God must properly command what is loving, or consistent with that which is loving, because that is his very nature. God is love. Therefore God's commands flow from his loving nature. God can only command what is good and loving. But this difference Adams speaks about makes no difference. It does no good to step back behind the commands of God to his purported nature, for we still want to know whether or not God's nature is good. God's nature cannot be known to be good without a standard of goodness showing that it is. Unless there is a moral standard that shows God is good beyond the mere fact that God declares that his nature is good, we still don't know whether God is good. Again, God is, well, just God.

The basic criticism of Adams's view has been stated adequately enough by the late Louis P. Pojman: "If we prefer the modified divine command theory to the divine command theory, then we must say that the divine command theory is false, and the modified divine command theory becomes equivalent to: God commands the good (or right) because it is good (or right), and the good (or right) is not good (or right) simply because God commands it." Therefore "we can discover our ethical duties through reason, independent of God's command. For what is good for his creatures is so objectively. We do not need God to tell us that it is bad to cause unnecessary suffering or that it is good to ameliorate suffering; reason can do that. It begins to look like the true version of ethics is what we called 'secular ethics.'" "If Adams wants to claim that it is goodness plus God's command that determines what is right," Pojman asks, "what does God add to rightness that is not there simply with goodness. . . . If love or goodness prescribes act A, what does A gain by being commanded by God? **Materially, nothing at all**."[8] It's at this point where both a modified divine command ethic and a secular ethic share the exact same grounding. Why? Because then with Pojman, we must ask what difference it makes whether or not the same ethical principles come from "a special personal authority (God) or from the authority of reason?" For this reason Kai Nielsen argues that the divine command theory in its modified forms "does not meet secular ethics head on," and consequently, "does not challenge . . . secular ethics."[9]

The second philosophical basis for grounding Christian ethics is *natural law theory*. This is the ethical system of Aristotle as adopted by Thomas Aquinas, and it has been the dominant one in the history of the church. It's an antiquated view of morals today, in that it presupposes the world has values built into it by God, such that moral rules can be derived from nature.[10] But if natural law theories are true, then, according to James Rachels, "This means that the religious believer has no special access to moral truth. The believer and the nonbeliever are in exactly the same position. God has made all people rational, not just believers; and so for believer and nonbeliever alike, making a responsible moral judgment is a matter of listening to reason and following its directives."[11]

And this is exactly my point. The foundations of Christian morality are not superior ones to atheistic morality, based upon Christian assumptions. Neither of these two bases for Christian ethics offers believers a special access to moral truth that unbelievers don't share. Christian moral foundations are simply not superior ones. Protagoras was correct, "Man is the measure of all things: of things which are, that they are, and of things which are not, that they are not." This is what all of us do. The only difference is that theists claim their morals come from God. On my blog I devoted several posts to this topic. I argued that "rational self-interest" can account for morality and that the Christian actually operates by the same moral standard (see "An Atheist Ethic").

Besides, there are several ethical systems of thought that do not require a prior belief in God, like social contract theories, utilitarianism, virtue ethics, Kantianism, and John Rawls's theory of justice. Ethical relativism isn't the boogey man that some Christians make it out to be, either, since Michael Martin argues that relativism "is compatible with complete agreement on all ethical matters," whereas "ethical absolutism is compatible with wide-spread disagreement."[12]

Michael Shermer makes an interesting case in his book *The Science of Good and Evil*, where he writes, "morality exists outside the human mind in the sense of being not just a trait of individual humans, but a human trait; that is, a human universal." According to him we "inherit" from our Paleolithic ancestors our morality and ethics, then we "fine-tune and tweak them according to our own cultural preferences, and apply them within our own unique historical circumstances." As such, "moral principles, derived from the moral sense, are not absolute, where they apply to all people in all cultures under all circumstances all of the time. Neither are moral principles relative, entirely determined by circumstance, culture and history. Moral principles are provisionally true—that is, they apply to most people in most cultures in most circumstances most of the time."[13]

CHRISTIAN MORALITY IS LARGELY IN THE SAME BOAT

Even if Christians did have objective moral standards, they cannot be objectively certain that they know them or that they know how they apply to specific real-life cases. Just look at Christianity's past (as we shall look at later) and you'll see what I mean. Believers will still disagree with each other on a multifaceted number of ethical issues, whether they start with the Bible as God's revelation or the morality gleaned from a natural law theory. According to Sam Harris, "People have been cherry-picking the Bible for millennia to justify their every impulse, moral and otherwise." Christians use their "own moral intuitions to authenticate the wisdom of the Bible. . . . We decide what is good in the Good Book."[14]

This cherry-picking from the Bible introduces us to the problem of "the canon within the canon." Which parts of the biblical canon are to be emphasized while others are minimized? If Christians really believed the Bible, they wouldn't let women speak in their churches (1 Cor. 14:34, see 1 Tim. 2:11–12), for the man would be the domineering patriarchal head of the house in which a wife is to "obey" her husband just like Sarah obeyed Abraham (1 Pet. 3:6), even to the point of lying to save his life by having sex with another man (Gen. 12:10–16) and by letting him sleep with another woman so he could have a child (Genesis 16). And yet in order to blunt the force of these passages, today's Christians focus on Paul's principle that "there is neither Jew nor Greek, slave nor free, male nor female, for you are all one in Christ" (Gal. 3:28). Which is it? What Christians stress becomes "the canon within the canon," and this is cherry-picking plain and simple.[15]

This problem forces Christians to specify exactly from where they get their morals. If they can stress one part of the Bible to the neglect of another part, then how do they actually decide which parts to stress and which parts to neglect? I maintain Christians get their morals from the same place I do—from the advancement of a better understanding of who we are and what makes us happy as human beings in society. Christians do not get their morals exclusively from the Bible. Christians have just learned to interpret the Bible differently down through the ages in keeping with our common sense of morality, that's all, as our moral values change with the times.

Since Dr. Craig mentioned Hitler, Auschwitz, and Dachau in his apologetics book, consider this: Germany was a Christian nation—the heart of the Lutheran Protestant Reformation! How could Christian people allow these evil deeds to happen and even be Hitler's willing executioners? How? The Holocaust and the horrible things done to millions of Jews and various minorities is more of a problem for the Christian ethic because it was a Christian nation that did these horrible deeds.[16]

The truth of the matter is that Christian religious moralists are in the same boat as atheists. According to Kai Nielsen: "The religious moralist . . . doesn't have any better or any worse objectivity. Because, suppose he says, 'We should love God,' and then further suppose we ask the religious moralist, 'Why Love God . . . Why obey his commandments?' He basically would have to say, 'Because God is the perfect good, and God with his perfect goodness reveals to us the great value of self-respect for people. He shows that people are of infinite precious worth.' But even if you accept this, you could go on to ask, 'Why should you care? What difference does it make anyway whether people are of infinite precious worth?' Faced with such questioning, you will finally be pushed into a corner, where you say 'It is important to me that people be regarded as being of infinite worth because I just happen to care about people. It means to me that people should be treated with respect.' So the religious moralist as well has to rely finally on his considered convictions. So if that too is subjective ground—that is, grounding things in considered judgments in wide reflective equilibrium—then both the religious person and the secular person are in the same boat."[17]

THE ILLUSION THAT ATHEISTS DO NOT HAVE A MOTIVATION TO BE GOOD

Many Christians will claim that atheists simply do not have an "ultimate motivation" for being good, even if they can grasp what it means to do good for the most part. What motivates an atheist to be a good and kind person? Why should we act morally? Maybe this is the crux of the problem Christians seem to be harping on. J. P. Moreland accepts the fact that atheists can and in fact do good moral deeds, "But what I'm arguing," he says, "is, what would be the point? Why should I do these things if they are not satisfying to me or if they are not in my interests?"[18]

C. Stephen Layman argues in a similar fashion. He points out that the main difference between secular and religious moral views is that "the only goods available from a secular perspective are earthly goods," whereas a religious perspective "recognizes these earthly goods as good, but it insists that there are non-earthly or transcendent goods." Secular ethics, he says, must pay for the individual here on earth. "By way of contrast with the secular view, it is not difficult to see how morality might pay if there is a God of the Christian type."[19]

Before we look at the atheistic motivation for being good, let's first consider the motivation that a Christian has for acting good and not bad. Christians claim that if we disbelieve and disobey God, we'll "fry in hell," as Nielsen describes it. Yet, obeying for this reason "is pure prudence masquerading as morality. . . . [T]hat is hardly a good moral reason for doing anything."[20] If a Christian wants to maintain she obeys God simply because she loves God, all we have to do is ask her if she'd still obey God if he threatened to send her to hell if she refused to steal from and kill people. If in order to escape hell she would obey, as I think she would be forced to do, then it seems evident this is a major motivation for the Christian, whether she admits this or not. This same motive would be akin to obeying a robber who has a gun placed against your head. The carrot-and-stick method of morality due to punishment and reward is, in the end, the same motivation an atheist has, except that the carrots and sticks are those rewards and punishments we receive here on earth, which are social and personal.

Besides, a Christian who desires to do wrong always has an excuse for doing whatever wrong or evil she may want to do. She'll simply say, "God understands; he'll forgive me." This can be the justification for doing anything she wants to do. I know, I've done this, and so has every Christian who has ever knowingly gone against her conscience. Whatever motivation a Christian may have for being good will just fly out the window if she wants to do something against what she believes to be right. How else can so many Christians maintain extramarital love affairs if they consider them to be wrong? The very fact that many of these affairs last for months and years just tells us how long these Christians can act contrary to the Bible and still feel God understands, and that God forgives.

C. Stephen Layman is correct that with the secular view ethical choices must pay for the individual here on earth, so there is no "ultimate motivation" to do good. But it doesn't follow from the lack of an "ultimate motivation" to be a good person that the atheist doesn't have a sufficient motivational grounding for being a good person. There are plenty of motives here on earth to be a good person, and it starts with an overall life plan.

Louis P. Pojman argued that it is reasonable to choose and to act upon an overall "life plan," even though there will be many times where I may have to act against my own immediate or short-term self-interest in keeping with that plan. "To have the benefits of the moral life—friendship, mutual love, inner peace, moral pride or satisfaction, and freedom from moral guilt—one has to have a certain kind of reliable character. All in all, these benefits are eminently worth having. Indeed, life without them may not be worth living." "Character counts," Pojman wrote, and "habits harness us to predictable behavior. Once we obtain the kind of character necessary for the moral life—once we become virtuous—**we will not be able to turn morality on and off like a faucet**." With such an understanding, "there is no longer anything paradoxical in doing something not in one's interest, for while the individual moral act may occasionally conflict with one's self-interest, the entire life plan in which the act is embedded and from which it flows is not against the individual's self-interest."[21]

The bottom line here, states Kai Nielsen, is that "if it is highly implausible to believe in God or immortality, then a secular ethic becomes attractive. . . . [T]here is something to be said for a person who can hold steadily on a course without telling himself or herself fairy tales. Moral integrity, fraternity, and love of humankind are worth subscribing to without a thought to whether or not such virtues will be rewarded in heaven."[22]

NOTES

1. James F. Sennett, *This Much I Know: A Postmodern Apologetic*, unpublished book.

2. Os Guinness, *In Two Minds: The Dilemma of Doubt and How to Resolve It* (Downers Grove, IL: InterVarsity Press, 1976).

3. William Lane Craig, *Apologetics: An Introduction* (Chicago: Moody Press, 1984), pp. 37–51, revised as *Reasonable Faith: Christian Truth and Apologetics* (Wheaton, IL: Crossway Books, 1994). See also Francis Schaeffer's similar comments in *He Is There and He Is Not Silent* (Wheaton, IL: Tyndale House, 1972), pp. 21–27.

4. John Arthur, "Morality without God," in *Contemporary Readings in Social and Political Ethics*, ed. Garry Brodsky et al. (Amherst, NY: Prometheus Books, 1984).

5. Go to his Web site, www.reasonablefaith.org, in the Q & A Archives and see "The Slaughter of the Canaanites."

6. J. P. Moreland and Kai Nielsen, *Does God Exist: The Great Debate* (Nashville: Thomas Nelson, 1990), pp. 130–31; and also in Moreland, *Scaling the Secular City: A Defense of Christianity* (Grand Rapids, MI: Baker Book House, 1987).

7. See Robert M. Adams, "A Modified Divine Command Theory of Ethical Wrongness," in *Religion and Morality: A Collection of Essays*, ed. Gene Outka and John P. Reeder (New York: Anchor Books, 1973); "Moral Arguments for Theistic Belief," in *Rationality and Religious Belief*, ed. C. F. Delaney (Notre Dame, IN: University of Notre Dame Press, 1979); and Phillip Quinn's *Divine Commands and Moral Requirements* (Oxford: Oxford University Press, 1978).

8. Louis P. Pojman, *Ethics: Discovering Right and Wrong*, 5th ed. (Belmont, CA: Wadsworth, 2006), pp. 255–56.

9. Quoted in Moreland and Nielsen, *Does God Exist*, p. 99; for a further critique of the divine command theory see Michael Martin's *The Case against Christianity* (Philadelphia: Temple University Press, 1991), pp. 229–51.

10. Modern virtue ethics are more interesting because these theories are distancing themselves from the older Thomistic view of natural laws.

11. James Rachels, *The Elements of Moral Philosophy* (New York: McGraw-Hill, 1993), p. 53.

12. Michael Martin, *Atheism: A Philosophical Justification* (Philadelphia: Temple University Press, 1990), p. 9.

13. Michael Shermer, *The Science of Good and Evil* (New York: Henry Holt, 2004), pp. 18–23.

14. Sam Harris, *Letter to a Christian Nation* (New York: Knopf, 2006), pp. 18, 49. As far as biblical and Christian ethics go, see Martin, *The Case against Christianity*, pp. 62–196, and Richard Dawkins, *The God Delusion* (Boston: Houghton Mifflin, 2006), pp. 235–72.

15. Granted, Paul does seem to be inconsistent here, which leads Bart D. Ehrman to argue that there are good reasons for thinking that he did not originally write the verses that prohibit women from speaking in the church. See Ehrman, *Misquoting Jesus* (New York: HarperSanFrancisco, 2005), pp. 178–86.

16. As to whether or not Hitler was an atheist, Michael Shermer quotes him in 1938 as saying: "I believe today that I am acting in the sense of the Almighty Creator. By warding off the Jews I am fighting for the Lord's work." Shermer argues that "Hitler and the Nazis were not atheists." See Shermer, *The Science of Good and Evil*, pp. 153–54. However, it can still be argued that Hitler was "just cynically exploiting the religiosity of his audience," according to Richard Dawkins. Nonetheless, the claim that Hitler was an atheist "is far from clear." See Dawkins's discussion in *The God Delusion*, pp. 272–78. For an excellent argument that religion and anti-Semitic racism were the major causes of the Nazi Holocaust, see chapter 12 in Hector Avalos's book *Fighting Words: The Origins of Religious Violence* (Amherst, NY: Prometheus Books, 2005).

17. Moreland and Nielsen, *Does God Exist*, pp. 107–108.

18. Ibid., p. 118.

19. C. Stephen Layman, *The Shape of the Good: Christian Reflections on the Foundations of Ethics* (Notre Dame, IN: University of Notre Dame Press, 1991).

20. Moreland and Nielsen, *Does God Exist*, p. 108.

21. Louis P. Pojman, *Ethics: Discovering Right and Wrong*, p. 188. For defenses of secular morality, see Kai Nielsen, *Ethics without God* (London: Pemberton Books, 1973); Shermer, *The Science of Good and Evil*; Richard Carrier, *Sense and Goodness without God* (2005), pp. 293–48; and Dawkins, *The God Delusion*, pp. 209–33.

22. Moreland and Nielsen, *Does God Exist*, pp. 108–109. To see how atheists do not behave worse than believers go to my blog and do a search for "Godlessness Rare behind Bars," "Does Religiosity Correlate Strongly to Charity?" and "Does Faith or Religious Activity Improve Health?"

3

FAITH, REASON, AND THE CUMULATIVE CASE METHOD

The *philosophy of religion* is a branch of philosophy that attempts to analyze and critically evaluate religious beliefs. It is not a branch of theology (which assumes one religious view as true). It need not be undertaken from a religious standpoint at all. Although, some of the most highly regarded scholars in the field are themselves religious believers.[1]

CHRISTIANITY AND PHILOSOPHY

Many Christians have taken an unenthusiastic view of philosophy because there are dangers in it for their faith. Paul said, "See no one takes you captive through hollow and deceptive philosophy" (Col. 2:8). Jesus purportedly said: "I praise you, Father, Lord of heaven and earth, because you have hidden these things from the wise and learned, and revealed them to little children. Yes, Father, for this was your good pleasure" (Luke 10:21). Paul wrote: "the message of the cross is foolishness to those who are perishing, but to us who are being saved it is the power of God. For it is written: 'I will destroy the wisdom of the wise; the intelligence of the intelligent I will frustrate.' Where is the wise man? Where is the scholar? Where is the philosopher of this age? Has not God made foolish the wisdom of the world? . . . For the foolishness of God is wiser than man's wisdom" (1 Cor. 1:18–25).

Tertullian (160–220 CE) asked: "What has Athens to do with Jerusalem?" In words reminiscent of Søren Kierkegaard, Tertullian wrote of the incarnation of Jesus by saying, "just *because* it is absurd, it is to be believed . . . it is certain *because* it is impossible." Martin Luther called reason "the Devil's whore," and as such, reason "can do nothing but slander and harm all that God says and does." Luther argued against the *magisterial* use of reason, in which reason judges the gospel, and approved of the *ministerial* use of reason, in which reason submits and serves the gospel. William Lane Craig agrees with this viewpoint and argues, "reason is a tool to help us better understand our faith. Should faith and reason conflict, it is reason that must submit to faith, not vice versa."[2]

The truth is that anyone who engages in Christian apologetics will use reason to defend his or her beliefs: the Apostle Paul, Tertullian, Luther, and Craig included. The question here is this one: What role should evidence and reason play in the justification of religious belief systems?[3] There are several proposed answers.

1. WITHOUT SUFFICIENT EVIDENCE WE SHOULD NOT BELIEVE

This is the position of *hard rationalism*. The hard rationalist would say all of our beliefs are either self-evident (true just by understanding them), evident to the senses (based on experience), or incorrigible (the way things appear). The only evidence allowed is either evidence that is provided by direct experience or an argument based upon inferences from experience.

W. K. Clifford best exemplifies this position. He was an English mathematician (1845–1879). His position is summed up with these words: "It is wrong always, everywhere, and for everyone, to believe anything upon insufficient evidence."[4] Take, for example, a ship owner who had brought himself to sincerely believe in the seaworthiness of his ship that was to carry immigrants. He came to believe in part by trusting in God's providence, but it sank to the bottom, killing all aboard. The ship owner was guilty of the deaths of these people, Clifford argued, because he brought himself to believe by stifling his doubts—he did not believe based on sufficient evidence. But there's more: Had the ship not gone down, the ship owner would still not be innocent; he merely wouldn't have been found out! According to him, it is wrong to believe on insufficient grounds, to suppress doubts, or to avoid investigation. It is always right to question all that we believe. It is sinful and unethical to believe on insufficient evidence because the pleasure is a stolen one, which is in defiance of our duty to humankind. When we believe for unworthy reasons, we weaken our powers of self-control, of doubting, and of fairly weighing the evidence. There is a great danger to society here, not just in believing the wrong things, but by losing the habit of testing things, and hence to sink back into savagery by becoming a credulous society. To the objection that we simply cannot check everything out, he replies, then we should not believe anything either. What would be Clifford's opinion about a religious belief system, given the very high standards of proof he demands? Do without them—this is thinly concealed, but there.

Norman Hanson is another hard rationalist who argued there are only two ways to show something does not exist. One way is to offer a logical disproof of such an entity. Since he places the existence of God in the same category of Hobbits and Santa Claus, which are beings that could conceivably exist and are not logically impossible, the only other way to disprove their existence is by carefully looking at the evidence. To those who disagree he says, "if looking and not finding does not constitute grounds for denying the existence of God, then looking and not finding does not constitute grounds for denying the existence of goblins, witches, devils, five-headed Welshmen, Unicorns, mermaids, Loch Ness monsters, flying saucers, Hobbits, Santa Claus . . . etc. *But there are excellent grounds for denying the existence of such entities* . . . these grounds consist largely in the fact that there is no good reason whatsoever for supposing that such creatures do exist."[5]

In what follows I will discuss the merits of the views of Alvin Plantinga, William James, Blaise Pascal, and Søren Kierkegaard on the relationship of faith and reason, ending this chapter by stating what I think the proper relationship is. With Plantinga I will admit there are a few things we believe that are not based upon evidence, contrary to Clifford, however, I claim that the belief in the Christian God is not one of those kinds of beliefs.

2. WE DON'T NEED EVIDENCE TO BELIEVE

Christian philosopher Alvin Plantinga has offered one of the most sustained arguments against W. K. Clifford's position.[6] W. K. Clifford's evidential challenge is this: No religious belief system is capable of meeting the high standards that believing in anything requires, so no reasonable person should accept any religious belief system.

But Plantinga Unveils Two Fatal Flaws Here

First, there are countless things that we believe (and do so properly) without proof or evidence, such as the existence of other minds; that the world continues to exist even when we don't perceive it; that we have been alive for more than twenty-four hours; that the past really happened; that we aren't just brains in a vat; that we can trust our senses about the universe; and so on. Second, the hard rationalist position is self-defeating, for it is neither self-evident, nor evident to the senses, nor incorrigible!

In order to escape the second fatal flaw of the hard rationalist, Anthony Kenny offered some alternative criteria for proper basicality that aren't self-defeating. He argued that a belief is properly basic if it is self-evident, evident to the senses or to memory, or *defensible by argument*.[7] This escapes Plantinga's criticism of the evidentialist criteria since it doesn't demand *evidence* for a belief to be properly basic, but rather it demands an *argument*. Plantinga can respond by claiming he's offering an argument all he wants to, but no atheist or non-Calvinistic Christian is compelled to accept it.

Plantinga Makes Some Distinctions

According to Plantinga *perceptual beliefs* are based on what we perceive through our senses, for example, seeing our hand in front of us. But how would we establish the truth that it's our hand that is in front of us? All of our checking procedures presuppose a more fundamental belief in the general reliability of our senses. So trusting in the reliability of our senses can be seen as a basic belief. *Basic beliefs*, then, are beliefs not inferred from any other beliefs. But they could be wrong: for example, thinking someone is guilty of a crime just by looking at him. *Properly basic beliefs* are basic beliefs that are reasonable to accept even if there is no evidence for them (for example, the past really happened).

Plantinga thinks that the evidentialist challenge places belief in God in the wrong family of beliefs. Belief in God is among those classified as "basic beliefs," he argues, and because this belief comes from God himself, such a belief is a properly basic belief. Belief in God and belief in other minds are in the same family of beliefs. Since belief in other minds is rational without support, so is belief in God, he argues. Religious experience, if it is to count as evidence, "is evidence that is noninferential, nonargumentative, and nonpropositional."[8]

Plantinga argues that "the believer is entirely within his epistemic rights in believing, for example, that God has created the world, even if he has no argument at all for that conclusion. His belief in God can be perfectly rational even if he knows of no cogent argument, deductive or inductive, for the existence of God—indeed, even if there is no such argument."[9] He claims this because he believes God grants innate knowledge of himself to all human beings. The reason why not everyone acknowledges this is due to sin: "God has created us in such a way that we have a strong tendency or inclination toward belief in God. This tendency has been in part overlaid or suppressed by sin. Were it not for the existence of sin in the world, human beings would believe in God to the same degree and with the same natural spontaneity that we believe in the existence of other persons, an external world, or the past."[10]

Clarifications of Plantinga's Position

There is more to Plantinga's epistemology than what I can present, but here are a few clarifications of his position: First, just because the belief in God is a properly basic belief doesn't allow for absurd beliefs to be properly basic, like Linus's belief in the Great Pumpkin. He participates in something called "negative apologetics" by examining and disputing the beliefs of other religious claims. Second, he doesn't deny the possibility that there may be adequate grounds for belief in God. He just claims these things are unnecessary. Third, he asserts that a believer can be rationally justified in claiming to "know" God exists even if others do not agree—even if there are no cogent arguments for this. Proper basicality in no way guarantees the truth of the belief. His discussion is not intended to convince the agnostic or atheist. He thinks whether someone accepts the proper basic belief in God depends upon worldview considerations. "What you properly take to be rational depends upon what sort of metaphysical and religious stance you adopt. And so the dispute as to whether theistic belief is rational can't be settled just by attending to epistemological considerations; it is at bottom not merely an epistemological dispute, but an ontological or theological dispute."[11] Fourth, Plantinga's "reformed epistemology" comes in two forms: *old school* (the version he developed and defended from the end of the 1980s to the early 1990s) and *new school* (the version he developed and defended from the early 1990s to the present). His old-school version was based on an *internalist theory*, and his new-school version is based on an *externalist theory*. Internalism is the view that the factors that render a belief known or justified are internal in a person, in that a belief is rational for a person if that belief is justified for that person based upon her own particular reasons for said belief. By contrast, externalist theories assert that the factors that render a belief known or justified are at least partly external to the agent.[12] In Keith Parsons's words, "Plantinga now holds that a belief is rational if and only if it is 'warranted.' Warrant is an objective matter; it has nothing to do with anyone's subjective awareness of justifying reasons." For the proper functioning of our cognitive faculties in the proper circumstances will sometimes produce warranted beliefs, that is, beliefs that are properly basic, and as such, rational beliefs.[13]

Brief Criticisms

Plantinga faces a strong type of defeater from the results of higher biblical criticism, which, as I will show in this book, is strong and compelling evidence against his faith. If, as he argues, his Christian faith is properly basic and needs no evidence, then what about historical evidence to the contrary? Is he still within his epistemical rights to believe in the face of this evidence against his Christian faith? Plantinga writes, "It could certainly happen that by the exercise of reason we come up with powerful evidence against something we take or took to be a deliverance of the faith. It is conceivable that the assured results of higher Biblical criticism should include such evidence. Then Christians would have a problem, a sort of conflict between faith and reason. However, nothing at all like this has emerged from higher Biblical criticism. . . . What would be the appropriate response if it did happen or, rather, if I came to be convinced that it had happened? Would I have to give up Christian faith? . . . What would be the appropriate response? . . . I don't know the answer to any of these questions. There is no need to borrow trouble, however: we can think about crossing these bridges when (more likely, if) we come to them."[14]

Here we see one major difficulty with Plantinga's epistemology. This should be an easy choice to make for many people, unlike him. If someone became convinced from higher biblical criticism that Christianity is a delusion, then she should not continue to believe. It's that simple. And contrary to his assertion, there is plenty of historical evidence against the Christian faith, as I argue in this book.

About Plantinga's *old school* version, Keith Parsons has argued: "The claim that the theist is within his epistemic rights in believing God is a rather weak claim. . . . If theists want to claim no more than that they are within their epistemic rights in believing in God, atheists should not bother to belabor the point. After all, to say that theists are within their epistemic rights in believing in God in no way indicates that atheists are one wit less rational in not believing in God."[15] In fact, there would be "no reason to prevent the atheist from starting with the *non-existence* of God as obviously properly basic!"[16]

About Plantinga's *new school* version, Keith Parsons tells us "theistic belief is very likely warranted and properly basic, in the external sense, but only if theism is in fact true. This means that believers are in no position to argue that their belief in God is warrant basic unless they can adduce reasons, arguments, or evidence for the existence of God." And so he argues, "the atheist can stand Plantinga's argument on its head and argue that the fact that theistic belief is not warrant basic shows that there probably is no God."[17]

3. CHOOSING TO BELIEVE IN THE ABSENCE OF SUFFICIENT EVIDENCE

William James, in his classic essay "The Will to Believe," took issue with Clifford by espousing a faith-based pragmatism (1842–1910). James makes the following distinctions: A *genuine option* is living, forced, and momentous. *Living*: where we see the alternatives as serious possibilities. *Forced*: where the choice is between two exclusive and exhaustive possibilities where there is no third possibility, such as suspension of judgment. *Momentous*: where the decision matters because it is a unique opportunity and not easily reversed. James: "Our passional nature not only lawfully may, but must decide an option between propositions, whenever it is a genuine option that cannot by its nature be decided on intellectual grounds."

To show this, James first insists, "Our non-intellectual nature does influence our convictions." We have a "passional nature." Second, James maintains that objective certainty is unattainable. Third, James insists that our errors are surely not such awfully solemn things. He regards the pursuit of truth as primary and the avoidance of error as secondary. Clifford's view is the exact opposite, where the avoidance of error is primary and the attaining of truth is secondary. According to James, Clifford's view is like "keeping soldiers out of battle forever rather than risk a single wound." In scientific matters we may suspend judgment because the options are not forced. In moral matters we cannot wait for sensible proof.

How do these things relate to religion? Religion says, first, that the best things are the more eternal things in the universe, and second, that we are now better off if we believe the first affirmation to be true. If someone thinks religion cannot be true by any possibility, then it is not a living option for him or her. But if there is a possibility that religion be true, then this choice is a living option. And as such it is also a momentous option and a forced option.

Turning to skepticism, James faults it for vetoing faith by laying down "agnostic rules for truth-seeking." Skepticism claims "dupery through hope is much worse than dupery through fear." Yet such rules will prevent us from knowing the truth about God, if he exists. Why? "If God exists, then we might have to meet that hypothesis halfway to see whether it is true." If we refused to make religious advances because of the lack of proof, one "might cut himself off forever from his only opportunity of making the god's acquaintance." James claims "a rule of thinking which would prevent me from acknowledging certain kinds of truth, if these kinds of truth were really there, would be an irrational rule."

Brief Evaluation

J. L. Mackie states: "This is a persuasive and powerful case." However, "James claims that in the absence of evidence, 'passion is the tie-breaker.'" Mackie counter claims, "we need a tie-breaker only where there is a tie to be broken." And "if faith is defended as an experiment, it must conform to the general principles of experimental inquiry. . . . [A] favorable result of the experiment would have to be a series of experiences which somehow resisted psychological explanation."[18]

John Hick: "If an idea were true, James would never come to know it by his method, a method that could result only in everyone's becoming more firmly entrenched in his or her current prejudices. . . . It amounts to an encouragement to us all to believe, at our risk, whatever we like."[19] Nicholas Everitt argued that "if the theist can appeal to his passional nature to justify his acceptance of theism, it seems that the atheist can appeal to his passional nature to justify his acceptance of atheism."[20] According to Norman Geisler: "Of course all truth must work, but not everything that works is necessarily true."[21]

Walter Kaufmann argued that James "blurs the distinction between facts which my belief could at least conceivably help to bring about—e.g., that a girl reciprocates my love—and facts which no belief could help to bring about if they were not facts to begin with—e.g., that God exists or that Jesus was resurrected on the third day."[22] Whether God exists is not the kind of fact that faith can bring about.

4. A WAGER IN THE ABSENCE OF SUFFICIENT EVIDENCE

Blaise Pascal lived in France, post-Descartes (1623–1662). His problem was the smug deist, atheist, and skeptic who were indifferent to the spiritual dimension. His goal was to shock these people out of their complacency and deal a blow to the skepticism of his time.[23]

Pascal rejected the premise that reason is equal to the task of a rational defense of faith. He wrote: "I look on all sides and see nothing but obscurity; nature offers me nothing but matter for doubt. . . . A hundred times I have wished that God would mark his presence in nature unequivocally . . . [but] all who seek God in nature find no light to satisfy them. . . . Nature confounds the skeptics, and reason confounds the dogmatists. . . . You can avoid neither skepticism nor dogmatism; but alas, you can live with neither." What then? According to Pascal the strongest proof for the existence of God is the great need felt by human beings for the sustaining presence of God in an otherwise empty universe: "The heart has reasons, which reason knows nothing of." So he is satisfied to argue from our need for God to the existence of God.

He asks what man is in the midst of the infinitely huge universe and the infinitely small microscopic world. "What a chimera is man! Strange! Monstrous! A chaos, a contradiction, a prodigy. Judge of all things, yet a weak earthworm." Compared to the universe, mankind is "nothing." "But were the universe to kill him, man would still be more noble than that which has slain him, because he knows that he dies, and that the universe has the better of him. The universe knows nothing of this. . . . Man is but a reed, weakest in nature, but a reed which thinks. A thinking reed." When Pascal contemplates the blindness and misery of man, he writes: "I fall into terror. . . . My terror is like that of a man who should awake upon a terrible desert island with no means of escape." Given this human condition, Pascal argues that satisfaction can only be found in God: "Man finds his lasting happiness only in God. Without him, there is nothing in nature which will take his place. . . . There is no good without knowledge of God." And yet he realizes that this will not be enough for the skeptic.

Pascal, as the creator of probability theory, applied it to faith and proposed a "wager." He begins by making a distinction among people: (1) Those who have found God and serve him, who are happy and wise. (2) Those who have not found God but diligently seek him, who are unhappy, but wise. (3) Those who have not found God and live without seeking him, who are unhappy and foolish. He has nothing but disdain for the third group. "It is an indispensable duty to seek when we are in doubt." He addresses the following wager to the second group.

Blaise Pascal's Wager (No. 177)

Either (a) there is a God who will send only the religious people to heaven or (b) there is not. To be religious is to wager for (a). To fail to be religious is to wager for (b). We can't settle the question whether (a) or (b) is the case, for if God exists, he is infinitely incomprehensible to us. But (a) is clearly vastly better than (b). With (a) infinite bliss is guaranteed, while with (b) we are still in the miserable human condition of facing death with no assurance as to what lies beyond. We must wager; it is not optional. So (a) is clearly the best wager: if we gain, we gain all; if we lose, we lose nothing. If we have problems in believing, we must bring ourselves to believe against reason by cultivating belief—preparing ourselves morally so that God may give us the faith that we seek by praying and attending church. What do we have to lose?

Now what are the chances that God exists and will reward your faith with an eternal bliss? The payoff is an infinite amount, Pascal argued, so we should wager for faith. According to Richard Swinburne: "A non-religious system would have to be very much more probable than the Christian system for it to be rational to adopt it."[24]

Brief Evaluation

Atheist J. L. Mackie wrote: "It is clear that, given his assumptions, the argument goes through. Everything turns, therefore, on the acceptability of those assumptions." In fact, even if the odds against God's existence are close to, but not quite to, infinity, one would still have the better odds in betting to believe in God's existence, for we would be betting one happy life "free of religious commitments" against an infinity of happy lives. That being said, Mackie proposes that "there might be a god who looked with more favor on honest doubters or atheists who proportioned their belief to the evidence, than on mercenary manipulators of their own understandings."[25] Richard Dawkins wrote, "We are talking about a bet. . . . Would you bet on God's valuing dishonestly faked belief (or even honest belief) over skepticism? . . . Pascal's wager could only ever be an argument for *feigning* belief in God. And the God that you claim to believe in had better not be of the omniscient kind or he'll see through that deception."[26] Nicholas Everitt finds it very strange that Pascal's God is just concerned with whether a person believes in him than in what that person does with her life as a whole: "the idea that we get *infinitely* many merit points just for being theists, no matter what quality the rest of our lives display, or that we get *infinitely* many minus points just for being atheists, no matter what quality the rest of our lives display, portrays God as a megalomaniac simpleton, a kind of cosmic Joseph Stalin."[27]

Pascal's wager can be said to be a form of the adage that less proof is demanded for a higher-risk situation: "The greater the risk, the less proof is required." When a bomb threat is called in, the authorities don't need much evidence to justify evacuating the building. In Pascal's case the risk is hell, isn't it? But the risk factor is based upon the Christian historical claims, is it not? And the Christian claim is a very large one and very hard to defend from historical evidence, as we'll see. So the amount of risk is mitigated by the meager evidence for the large claim. In fact, I argue, unlike Pascal, that there is indeed sufficient evidence not to believe.

Muslims claim that we will go to hell if we don't convert to Islam too, but we cannot be a Muslim and also a Christian. Both religions offer some evidence to believe, but Christians think their faith has more evidence on its behalf than Islam, while one billion Muslims think otherwise. But according to both religions, the other group is going to hell. So choose wisely. The risk is the same because a lot is at stake. Both are calling in a proverbial bomb threat. On the one hand, someone claims if you stay in a building you will die, whereas someone else claims that if you leave the building and go out into the street you will die. This is known as the "many gods" objection. How Pascal's wager helps us with this quandary is itself a quandary.

Those who don't believe either of these religions just think that the historical evidence is below the threshold of proof needed to see any danger or risk in choosing not to believe. It would be comparable to someone claiming "the sky is falling." When it comes to "bomb threats," they've heard too many of them from too many religions. Such claims are the equivalent of someone "crying wolf" way too many times. Besides, according to David Mills, "our earthly life is the only life we're ever going to experience. If we sacrifice this one life in doormat subservience to a non-existent god, then we have lost everything."[28]

5. A LEAP OF FAITH BEYOND THE EVIDENCE

In his book *Concluding Unscientific Postscript*, Søren Kierkegaard (1813–1855) attempted to argue that objective inquiry is totally inappropriate in religious matters. When we approach a question objectively, we treat the truth as an object, whereas if we approach a question subjectively, we treat the truth as a subject to which the knower is related. On which side is the truth to be found, he rhetorically asks.

The objective way to pursue truth rests upon the approximation process, Kierkegaard argued, based upon Gotthold Lessing's argument that historical knowledge is insufficient grounds for the Christian faith (see my chapter 8). For him, historical evidence is only approximate. So he argues we cannot base our eternal happiness on any approximation of the truth since it will never produce the infinite personal interest demanded by religious faith. An infinite personal interest makes the greatest possible sacrifices on the smallest chance of success. Faith for Kierkegaard must be decisive. Belief excludes doubt because the conclusion of belief is a resolution—a decision. This kind of faith requires a "leap" beyond the evidence, a leap that cannot be justified by objective reasoning. "Without risk there is no faith." Moreover, one cannot have an authentic faith without being totally committed to it. On which side is the truth? Who has the greater certainty? Who has the greater faith? One who passionately takes a greater risk based on little evidence, or one who looks into the matter objectively? Kierkegaard's subjective answer is clear.

Kierkegaard used the example of Socrates. Socrates risks his entire life based on *if* there was immortality. Kierkegaard rhetorically asks, "Is there any better proof capable of being given for the immortality of the soul?"

Brief Evaluation

Something is to be said for taking risks and the commitment involved—it is admirable, as in the case of the patriot or the loyalty of a friend when evidence suggests you are guilty. But what about misplaced commitment and loyalty? "Given that faith is a leap, how does one decide which faith to 'jump for'? . . . What would we make of a religious person who calmly informs us that she is well aware that some of her beliefs are logically contradictory, or they conflict with well-known facts, yet she finds this no obstacle to holding these beliefs?"[29] Robert Merrihew Adams asks the crucial question, "whether the maximization of sacrifice and risk are so valuable in religion as to make objective improbability a desirable characteristic of religious beliefs."[30] J. L. Mackie claims: "He seems to be arguing from a position, not to a position." Kierkegaard wants to show what Christianity is, but this means he must show it as he conceives it. Mackie asks whether Kierkegaard thinks the only kind of commitment worthy of the name is one which accepts a paradoxical belief with no objective reasons in its favor. Hence he argues, Kierkegaard advocates "a sort of intellectual Russian roulette."[31] In no other area of knowledge should we do this, so why should we adopt a double standard when it comes to religious knowledge?

6. FAITH, REASON, AND THE CUMULATIVE CASE METHOD

Here I will argue for my approach to evaluating the evidence for Christian truth claims. Let me begin with Christian philosopher William J. Abraham's arguments. He argues: "Religious belief-systems can be rationally evaluated, although conclusive proof of such systems is impossible."[32] As such, religious beliefs should be assessed only as a complete belief system, or worldview, never in stark isolation. What is a worldview? According to James Sire, "A worldview is a set of assumptions or presuppositions which we hold about the basic make-up of our world."[33] Norman Geisler and W. Watkins write, "A world-view is a way of viewing or interpreting all of reality—a world-view is like a set of colored glasses."[34] A more (or less) consistent set of assumptions or presuppositions (what I call control beliefs) forms a worldview. Basic presuppositions answer questions about the existence and nature of God, the world, human beings, our destiny, ethics, history, and so on. About such assumptions A. N. Whitehead wrote, "Some assumptions appear so obvious that people do not know that they are assuming because no other way of putting things has ever occurred to them."[35]

Here are some things to know about worldviews: First, everyone has one. Second, they are pretheoretical—before thought. We don't first get to them by thinking about them. Rather when we come to think about them, we find them already there, already undergirding anything we do. We don't argue to them; we argue from them—although we can argue away from them. Third, they are communal—shared by a community; caught, not taught.[36] Fourth, they are much larger than particular religions, philosophies, and theologies. As such, atheism, per se, is not itself a worldview, since it merely denies God exists (see note).[37] Fifth, while there are major outlines of worldviews that many people share, worldviews themselves include moral and political ways of viewing the world, so there are probably as many worldviews as there are people.

Abraham wrote: "It should be clear that evaluating world-views will never be based on probabilistic arguments, since one cannot simply isolate one presupposition for evaluation. The case must be cumulative—a case must be built slowly." It is based upon cumulative case-type arguments like "jurisprudence, literary exegesis, history, philosophy, and science." "One must be well educated in the relevant moral, aesthetic, or spiritual possibilities." But, "mastering all the relevant data and warrants needed to exercise the required personal judgment seems remote and impractical. . . . This is surely beyond the capabilities of most ordinary mortals. . . . One simply has to proceed, often in an ad hoc fashion, and work through the issues as honestly and rigorously as possible."

This is exactly what I am attempting to do in this book, realizing my limitations as an ordinary mortal. According to Abraham: "The different pieces of evidence taken in isolation are defective, but taken together they reinforce one another and add up to a substantial case. What is vital to realize is that there is no formal calculus into which all the evidence can be fitted and assessed. There is an irreducible element of personal judgment, which weighs up the evidence taken as a whole."

This book is my personal judgment as I reflect on the reasons and pieces of evidence supporting Christianity. My judgment will not necessarily be yours. You may object to certain arguments of mine that are convincing to me, and you may be more informed about that objection than I am. It's just that when I weigh the sum total of all that I know, I believe I'm rational and correct to reject Christianity. It just doesn't make sense to me. Just like any jury has difficulties in assessing the case, we must go with the position that makes the most overall sense of everything that we know.

There are basically four evangelical methods that apologists use to defend Christianity. William Lane Craig defends Christianity by the *classical apologetical approach*, not the *evidential* or the *presuppositional approaches*, as best seen in the book *Five Views on Apologetics*.[38] Craig's classical approach is a continuation of his former mentor, Norman Geisler, best seen in Geisler's two books *Christian Apologetics* and the *Baker Encyclopedia of Christian Apologetics*.[39] It is definitely known as Thomistic, or classical. When it comes to *showing* Christianity true, Craig begins by defending the existence of God through the Kalam cosmological argument. Only after defending the probability that God exists does he then argue for the bodily resurrection of Jesus, which validates the revelation found in the Bible.

Gary Habermas distinguishes his own evidential approach from Craig's classical approach in these words: "Instead of having to prove God's existence before moving to specific evidences (Craig's Classical Approach), the evidentialist treats one or more historical arguments as being able both to indicate God's existence and activity, and to indicate which variety of theism is true."[40] In a way, Craig is a presuppositionalist in that he presupposes that Christianity is true by virtue of a veridical experience of the Holy Spirit. But he is not a presuppositionalist when it comes to his methodology, where he shows Christianity is true. Craig argues that presuppositionalism as an apologetic methodology "commits the informal fallacy of begging the question, for it advocates presupposing the truth of Christian theism in order to prove Christian theism."[41]

As a former apologist I myself wasn't an evidentialist. That apologetic is doomed to failure because evidence can never justify how to view that evidence. Hence, in my opinion, it doesn't even offer an apologetic, that is, an overall defense of the evidence. And a presuppositionalist apologetic assumes what needs to be proved. I am a proponent of the *cumulative case method* of the late Paul D. Feinberg, also a former professor of mine. Even Craig admits that when it comes to showing Christianity true, he finds himself "largely in agreement with the conclusion of Paul Feinberg. A successful apologetic for the Christian faith should be in an appropriate sense a cumulative case."[42] This same cumulative case method is the one I use when debunking Christianity in this book.[43]

There is always reciprocity and dialectic between evidence and assumptions in historical and scientific investigations, so why should it be different in theological investigations? No matter what methodology one claims is the best one for evaluating and arguing on behalf of a religious or metaphysical belief system, the case is always going to be evaluated by people cumulatively, or not at all. This best explains why there is no singular apologetical approach that will cause people to convert, and it best explains why there is no "smoking gun" type of argument that will convince

believing Christians to abandon their faith. Just take a look at the many deconversion stories and you won't see people leaving the fold because of the same reasons.

My particular approach to these issues comes from Dr. James D. Strauss. As a
former student of his I credit much of my approach to three things he drilled into us
as students, but in reverse. When doing apologetics, he said that "if you don't start
with God you'll never get to God." He's not a Van Tillian presuppositionalist
because he doesn't start with the Bible as God's revelation. Just like a scientist who
proposes a hypothesis and then seeks to confirm or disconfirm it, he starts "from
above" by merely supposing a creator God's existence, and then he argues that such
an assumption makes better sense of the Bible and the world than the alternatives.
Again, "if you don't start with God you'll never get to God." Since that's such an
important, central issue, I'll focus on why we should not start "from above" with the
belief in God in the first place, but rather "from below," beginning with the world.
If successful, then my argument should lead us to reject the existence of the God
who is supposed to confirm the biblical revelation.

The second thing Dr. Strauss drilled into us was that "we don't need more data,
we need better interpretive schema." What he meant is that we evaluate the details
of the historical and archaeological evidence through interpretive schema. The need
to come up with more data, or evidence, isn't as important as the need to better evaluate the available data through the lens of an adequate worldview. While the data are
indeed important, the big worldview picture provides the necessary rational support
to the data. We need to be specialists in the *big picture*, not the minutia. I agreed
then, and I agree now, except that the better interpretive schema that supports the
available data is not Christianity, but atheism.

A third thing Dr. Strauss drilled into us is that "all truth is God's truth," and by
this he meant that if something is true, it's of God, no matter where we find it, whether
through science, philosophy, psychology, history, or experience itself. All truth comes
from God wherever we find it. There is no secular/sacred dichotomy when it comes
to truth. There is no such thing as secular "knowledge" at all, if by this we mean
beliefs that are justifiably true. Neither sinful, nor carnal, nor secular, "knowledge"
exists as a category because such "knowledge" isn't true. All truth is sacred and it
comes from God alone, whether we learn it inside the pages of the Bible or outside
of them in the various disciplines of learning. Since not all truth is to be found in the
Bible, it follows that the Christian apologist must try to harmonize all knowledge
since it all comes from God. Strauss argued "from above" that the Christian worldview is what best interprets these other truths—something I now deny. My claim will
be that the lessons learned outside of the Bible in other areas of learning debunk the
Bible by continually forcing believers to reinterpret the Bible over and over until
there is no longer any basis for believing in the Christian worldview.

The Basis for My Control Beliefs

If I have a focus when it comes to debunking Christianity, it is with assumptions,
presuppositions, and control beliefs. Control beliefs are those beliefs that control

how we view the evidence, and so this part of my critique is generally philosophical and epistemological in nature. To see four historic examples of how control beliefs affected how the evidence was viewed, see chapter 1 in Nicholas Wolterstorff's book *Reason within the Bounds of Religion*.[44] I'm interested in how we know what we know. How we view that which we know is what makes all of the difference. I consider my expertise (if I have one) in the area of the big picture. Someone has to stand back from all of the trees to see the forest and describe what it looks like. Since how we each look at the available evidence is controlled to a large degree by certain control beliefs of ours, I want to know how to justify those control beliefs themselves. For me it's all about seeing things differently. It's not just about more and more evidence. It's about viewing that evidence in a different light.

How do we decide which set of control beliefs are preferable when looking at Christianity? That's the biggest question of them all! Why? Because the set of control beliefs we start with when looking at the Bible is usually the same set we will come away with. I think I have better reasons for starting with my control beliefs, presuppositions, and biases, and I share them in this book. I'll argue that I think skepticism (or agnosticism; i.e., "I don't know") about religion in general, and Christianity in particular, is the default position. Anyone who investigates religion in general, or Christianity in specific, must begin with skepticism. Anyone who subsequently moves off the default position of skepticism has the burden of proof, since doing so is making a positive knowledge claim, and in the case of Christianity a very large knowledge claim that cannot be reasonably defended with the available evidence. This best expresses my set of control beliefs from which I derive two others: (1) There is a strong probability that every event is a natural one to be explained by natural causes alone; and, (2) the scientific method is the best (and probably the only) reliable guide we have for gaining the truth, even though I realize there is a fair amount of debate on just what that is (see note).[45] Since I need sufficient reasons and sufficient evidence for what I believe, I have an antidogma, and an antisuperstitious bias. No inspired book will tell me what I should believe. My first question will always be "Why should I believe what this writer wrote?" This doesn't mean that in the end I might not conclude there is a supernatural realm, only that I start out my investigations with such an assumption.

Christians will bristle at these control beliefs and cry "foul." They will argue that if I start out with a predisposition against the supernatural, it predisposes me to reject their religious faith, and they are right. It does. They'll claim that if instead I adopt a supernatural predisposition, I'll be more likely to accept the Christian faith, and that too is correct. The crucial question then is "What reasons are there to justify adopting a skeptical rather than a believing set of control beliefs in the first place?" This first part of my book will deal with this question, but let me introduce it here.

Strauss took his cue from Karl Barth, who spoke of doing theology "from below," in distinction from doing it "from above." If one starts out looking at this natural world and tries to inductively conclude something about God (or the supernatural realm "above"), he cannot do it, Barth would claim. If, however, one starts "from above" in presupposing God (or the supernatural realm) and tries to explain the natural world from that presupposition (for him the Bible as a "witness"), then and only then can it be done. So the biggest question is in trying to justify our starting point. Do we start "from above" or "from below"? Since starting from "above" presupposes what needs to be shown, I start "from below." I am not alone in doing this.

As a Thomist, Norman Geisler's arguments start "from below." His apologetic includes twelve successive steps: (1) Truth about reality is knowable; (2) opposites cannot both be true; (3) the theistic God exists; (4) miracles are possible; (5) miracles performed in connection with a truth claim are acts of God to confirm the truth of God through a messenger of God; (6) the New Testament documents are reliable; (7) as witnessed in the New Testament, Jesus claimed to be God; (8) Jesus' claim to divinity was proven by a unique convergence of miracles; (9) therefore, Jesus was God in human flesh; (10) whatever Jesus (who is God) affirmed as true, is true; (11) Jesus affirmed that the Bible is the Word of God; and (12) therefore, it is true that the Bible is the Word of God and whatever is opposed to any biblical truth is false.[46] The problem with Geisler's twelve apologetical steps is that the probability of his whole case will diminish with each additional step, since each successive step depends on the probability of all previous steps (see note).[47] I will argue against several of these steps in this book. I'm not even so sure of his first step!

Even though I'll present a cumulative case against Christianity, I don't have any successive steps for my control beliefs that are built on any previous ones. Unlike Dr. Geisler, when I start "from below," I begin with several epistemological issues to see which set of control beliefs I should adopt when coming to the Christian faith, and rather than being built on each previous step they are separate arguments that reinforce each other. So let me highlight several reasons for starting with my skeptical control beliefs.

1. *Sociological/Cultural Reasons.* I believe that the control beliefs a person adopts are the ones he or she picks up based on "when and where he or she was born," called the "accidents of birth." Since that is overwhelmingly the case, I am right to be skeptical whenever I examine any religious set of beliefs, including Christianity. (On this see chapter 4.)

2. *Philosophical Reasons.* My chapter 5 examines three of the main arguments for the existence of God. I merely claim that the arguments for God's existence don't prove anything. There are too many holes in them. At best they are all inconclusive. So if I am going to believe in God, a deist kind of God, or a philosopher's god, there had better be other reasons that would tip the scales in favor of believing. But in fact, these other reasons tip the scales away from such a belief.

Another philosophical reason for my control beliefs concerns miracles. Miracles are by definition very improbable based upon natural law. As a result, there isn't any reasonable way to show that a miracle occurred at all, even if one did. That's right. Even if one actually did occur! (On this see my chapter 9. In chapter 10, we don't see a good answer to this problem.)

3. *Scientific Reasons.* Modern science is dealing a fatal blow to the Christian faith in several areas. Science has taught us to assume a natural explanation for every

event based upon methodological naturalism. This method is the foundation of modernity that even Christians use every day. Since this method has produced so many significant results, I think it should equally be used to investigate the Bible, its claims of the miraculous, and the origins of the universe itself. Science provides a great deal of evidence against the Christian faith. (On this see chapter 6.)

4. *Biblical Reasons.* When I look at the Bible itself, I see things in it that are completely barbaric and superstitious to me living in today's world. These things are obvious. So it's more likely to me that biblical people were barbaric and superstitious than that they had good evidence for what they believed. (On this see chapter 7.)

5. *Historical Reasons.* Christianity is a historical religion that says there are certain things that actually happened in history. I'm supposed to believe that these things happened in the past in order to be acceptable to God (like the incarnation and the resurrection). But if God chose to reveal himself in the past, he chose a poor medium and a poor era in the ancient superstitious past to do so. This is especially true when that history is a history of miracles. Since history at best can only give us probabilities, it's a slender reed to hang a supposedly reasonable faith on. (On this see chapter 8.)

6. *Empirical Reasons.* If there was ever an empirical refutation of the Christian belief in an omniscient, omnipotent, and omnibenelovent God, the problem of evil is it. It speaks like a megaphone against the existence of this God. (On this see chapters 11, 12, and 13.)

Christian Responses

In every case when it comes to my reasons for adopting these skeptical control beliefs, the Christian response is pretty much the same. Christians must continually retreat to the position that what they believe is "possible," or that it's "not impossible." Robert M. Price tells us that for Christian apologists "the controlling presupposition seems to be, 'if the traditional view cannot be *absolutely debunked* beyond the shadow of a doubt, if it still *might possibly* be true, then we are within our rights to continue to believe it.'"[48] In my opinion, Christians must repeatedly assert this to defend their faith. Keep in mind that anything that is not logically impossible, is possible. It's possible I'm dreaming right now. It's possible I'm merely recalling an event in the year 2008 in a dream I'm having in the year 2025. It's also possible that Jim Carrey could've gotten the girl of his dreams in the movie *Dumb and Dumber*, too (remember, the girl said he had a "one in a million" chance at doing so).

However, the more Christians must constantly retreat to what is "possible" in order to defend their faith, the more their faith is on shaky ground. Why? Because we want to know what is probable, not what is possible. If we ask Christians to defend a particular belief and they argue such a belief "isn't impossible," then this is a tacit admission that instead of the evidence supporting what they believe, they are actually trying to explain the evidence away. In this book you will see them retreating to the "merely possible" defense far too many times.

My control beliefs are derived from our modern ways of thinking, and I consider this to be the Achilles' heel of Christianity. With these control beliefs I will make a cumulative case against Christianity. I believe I have several good reasons for starting out being skeptical when I examine the Christian evidences for belief. I just don't see how Christians can refute any of these reasons, since they are all practically undeniable (and even obvious) to modern educated scientifically literate people, even if I know Christians will argue against them. How much more is this so when these reasons are taken together as a whole? So it is no surprise that I look at Christianity with the presumption of skepticism. And it is no surprise that I reject it.

Since my skeptical control beliefs don't by themselves tell me what to believe about the evidence of a specific miracle claim, I will also examine the evidence for the foundational miracle claims of Christianity in part 2. I will consider them as the historical claims they are. I will examine them by looking at the *internal evidence* found within the biblical texts themselves. I'll consider what these texts actually say and scrutinize their internal consistency. Wherever relevant, I'll also consider whether the Old Testament actually predicts some of these events. Then I will examine these claims by looking at the *external evidence*. I'll consider any independent confirmation of these events outside of the texts. Last, I will subject these claims to the canons of reason using the control beliefs I have argued for. I will conclude from all of this that Christianity should be rejected. Then I describe why I became an atheist and what it means to live life without God. I present a whole case, a comprehensive case, a complete case, from start to finish, as a former insider to the Christian faith.

As I said, I consider this book to be one single argument against Christianity, with each chapter as a subset of that one argument, and as such it should be evaluated as a whole. Each chapter of this argument depends upon the others for its force since no single one of them alone can bear the whole weight of showing that the Christian worldview is false. In evaluating this one argument of mine, it's proper and fitting to do so as a whole, especially since this is the only way to properly evaluate worldviews.

NOTES

1. Just read *God and the Philosophers*, ed. Thomas V. Morris (Oxford: Oxford University Press, 1994), and *Philosophers Who Believe*, ed. Kelly James Clark (Downers Grove, IL: InterVarsity Press, 1993). But see also the book *Philosophers without Gods: Meditations on Atheism and the Secular Life*, ed. Louis M. Anthony (Oxford: Oxford University Press, 2007).

2. William Lane Craig, *Apologetics: An Introduction* (Chicago: Moody Press, 1984), p. 21.

3. To read a history of the relationship of philosophy to Christian thought, see Colin Brown, *Philosophy and the Christian Faith* (Downers Grove, IL: InterVarsity Press, 1968).

4. W. K. Clifford, "The Ethics of Belief," in *Lectures and Essays* (New York: Macmillan, 1897).

5. Norman Russell Hanson, in *What I Do Not Believe, and Other Essays*, ed. Stephen Toulmin and Harry Wolf (Dordrecht: D. Reidel, 1971), pp. 309–31.

6. See Alvin Plantinga, "Reason and Belief in God," in *Faith and Rationality: Reason and Belief in God*, ed. Alvin Plantinga and Nicholas Wolterstorff (Notre Dame, IN: Univer-

sity Press of Notre Dame, 1983); see also Nicholas Wolterstorff's *Reason within the Bounds of Religion* (Grand Rapids, MI: Eerdmans, 1984).

7. Anthony Kenny, *Faith and Reason* (New York: Columbia University Press, 1983), p. 27.

8. Quoted by Ronald Nash, in *Faith and Reason* (Grand Rapids, MI: Zondervan, 1988), p. 100.

9. Plantinga, "Reason and Belief in God," p. 65.

10. Ibid., p. 66.

11. Plantinga, as quoted in Nash, *Faith and Reason*, p. 91.

12. For details see Plantinga's *Warrant: The Current Debate* (Oxford: Oxford University Press, 1992); *Warrant in Contemporary Epistemology* (New York: Rowman & Littlefield, 1996); and *Warrant and Proper Function* (Oxford: Oxford University Press, 1993).

13. Keith Parsons, "Some Contemporary Theistic Arguments," in *The Cambridge Companion to Atheism*, ed. Michael Martin (Cambridge: Cambridge University Press, 2007), p. 109.

14. Alvin Plantinga, *Warranted Christian Belief* (Oxford: Oxford University Press, 2000), pp. 420–21.

15. Keith Parsons, *Does God Exist: The Great Debate* (Nashville: Thomas Nelson, 1990), pp. 177ff.

16. Keith Parsons, *God and the Burden of Proof* (Amherst, NY: Prometheus Books, 1990), p. 53.

17. Ibid, pp. 110–11.

18. J. L. Mackie, *The Miracle of Theism* (Oxford: Clarendon, 1982), p. 207.

19. John Hick, *Philosophy of Religion*, 4th ed. (Englewood Cliffs, NJ: Prentice-Hall, 1990), p. 60.

20. Nicholas Everitt, *The Non-existence of God* (New York: Routledge, 2004), p. 204.

21. Norman Geisler, *Christian Apologetics* (Grand Rapids, MI: Baker Books, 1976), p. 115.

22. Walter Kaukmann, *Critique of Religion and Philosophy* (Princeton, NJ: Princeton University Press, 1958), pp. 116–20.

23. Blaise Pascal, *Pensees* (LGF Livre de Poche, 2000), pp. 121–26.

24. Richard Swinburne, "The Christian Wager," *Religious Studies* 4 (1969). Pascal's wager is best defended by William G. Lycan and George N. Schlesinger in "You Bet Your Life: Pascal's Wager Defended," in *Reason and Responsibility*, 9th ed., ed. Joel Feinberg (Belmont, CA: Wadsworth, 1996), pp. 119–27.

25. J. L. Mackie, *The Miracle of Theism* (Oxford: Clarendon, 1982), pp. 201–203.

26. Richard Dawkins, *The God Delusion* (Boston: Houghton Mifflin, 2006), p. 104.

27. Everitt, *The Non-existence of God*, p. 198.

28. David Mills, *Atheist Universe* (Berkeley: Ulysses Press, 2006), p. 34.

29. Michael Peterson et al., in *Reason and Religious Belief* (Oxford: Oxford University Press, 1991), p. 40.

30. Robert Merrihew Adams, in "Kierkegaard's Arguments against Objective Reasoning in Religion," *Monist* 60, no. 2 (1977).

31. Mackie, *The Miracle of Theism*, p. 216.

32. William J. Abraham, *An Introduction to the Philosophy of Religion* (Englewood Cliffs, NJ: Prentice-Hall, 1985), pp. 104–13. See also Basil Mitchell, *The Justification of Religious Belief* (Oxford: Oxford University Press, 1981); Peterson et al., *Reason and Religious Belief*, pp. 41–44; and C. Stephen Evans, *Philosophy of Religion* (Downers Grove, IL: InterVarsity Press, 1985), pp. 18–29.

33. James Sire, in *The Universe Next Door* (Downers Grove, IL: InterVarsity Press, 2004).

34. Norman Geisler and William D. Watkins, *Worlds Apart* (Grand Rapids, MI: Baker Books, 1989).

35. A. N. Whitehead, *Science and the Modern World* (New York: Mentor Books, 1948, first published in 1925), p. 49.

36. On this point see Brian J. Walsh and Richard J. Middleton, *The Transforming Vision* (Downers Grove, IL: InterVarsity Press, 1984), pp. 17ff.

37. Atheism is a conclusion about the existence of a God or gods. It is not, itself, a world-view. Zen Buddhists, Taoists, metaphysical naturalists, and Platonic materialists can be described as atheists. Being an atheist does not require a person to subscribe to any one, particular, overall worldview. At the minimum, atheists simply deny the existence of God or gods, and this is how I employ the term in this book. Atheists disagree about economics, politics, art, morality, and science itself. But each atheist has her own particular worldview. While you'll find pockets of atheists who agree with each other on the broad lines of the same worldview, depending on sociological, economic, racial, moral, and political factors, you cannot predict in advance what an atheist believes about other things simply because she is one.

38. Steven B. Cowan, ed., *Five Views on Apologetics* (Grand Rapids, MI: Zondervan, 2000).

39. Norman Geisler, *Baker's Encyclopedia of Christian Apologetics* (Grand Rapids, MI: Baker Books, 1999).

40. Cowan, *Five Views on Apologetics*, p. 92.

41. Ibid., p. 232.

42. Ibid., p. 173.

43. For more on apologetical methods see Bernard Ramm, *Varieties of Christian Apologetics* (Grand Rapids, MI: Baker Books, 1961); Gordon R. Lewis, *Testing Christianity's Truth Claims* (Landham, MD: University Press of America, 1990); R. C. Sproul, John H. Gerstner, and Arthur W. Lindsley, *Classical Apologetics* (Grand Rapids, MI: Zondervan, 1984); Ronald B. Mayers, *Balanced Apologetics* (Grand Rapids, MI: Kregel Academic & Professional, 1996); Avery Cardinal Dulles, *A History of Apologetics* (San Francisco: Ignatious Press, 2005); and Kenneth D. Boa and Robert M. Bowman Jr., *Faith Has Its Reasons: An Integrative Approach to Defending Christianity* (Colorado Springs, CO: Paternoster, 2006).

44. He speaks of the Galileo affair, the concept of ether, Ernst Mach's acceptance of philosophical over scientific notions, and logical positivism. Nicholas Wolterstorff, *Reason within the Bounds of Religion* (Grand Rapids, MI: Eerdmans, 1984).

45. Some thinkers, like Paul Feyerabend, have even argued there is no scientific method, in *Against Method*, 3rd ed. (New York: Verso, 1993). And yet we have a general idea of what it is. In general terms the scientific method depends upon empirical and mathematical evidence coupled with good reasons that can explain the evidence (or lack of evidence). J. P. Moreland and William Lane Craig claim that "there is no such thing as *the* scientific method" (emphasis theirs), but that doesn't mean there aren't distinct scientific methodologies that are better than others for each of the different areas of thought. How someone does theoretical physics will be somewhat different than how he does applied science, and somewhat different when examining the paranormal, or when investigating the claims of history. Craig and Moreland claim that the hypothetico-deductive method advocated by Carl Hempel "does not capture everything that a scientist does," but it is still a correct description, even if it's not a complete one. And even if we cannot offer a total description and justification of the scientific method, Paul Kurtz reminds us that such a requirement is "inappropriate, for science is

implicit in our ordinary ways of thinking. . . . The vindication of scientific methodology is based to a large extent upon an analysis and reflection of what we already do." Kurtz, *Transcendental Temptation* (Amherst, NY: Prometheus Books, 1991), pp. 55–56. In Moreland and Craig's words, Hempel's view "sees scientists as, in one way or another, forming and putting forth a hypothesis, deriving test implications from it, then seeing if observations corroborate with the hypothesis. *Philosophical Foundations for a Christian Worldview* (Downers Grove, IL: InterVarsity Press, 2003), p. 313. Hempel's view is a more than adequate description of the scientific method.

46. Geisler, *Baker's Encyclopedia of Christian Apologetics*, s.v. "Apologetics, Argument of."

47. Alvin Plantinga has argued for something he calls the "Principle of Dwindling Probabilities" against cumulative case–type arguments in general in *Warranted Christian Belief*, pp. 268–80. Plantinga has conceded that his argument fails against Swinburne-type cumulative case arguments, but I think it does apply to Geisler's twelve apologetical steps. If we take Norman Geisler's twelve apologetical steps as our example, we see that if the probability of each one of his twelve steps is 75 percent (being very generous), then the result is a probability of 9 percent for his whole case through to the final step. That's because we simply multiply the percentages to find the probability of the final conclusion ($75\% \times 75\% \times 75\% \ldots$). And while Geisler claims to reject cumulative case arguments as a test for the truth of worldviews, in effect this is what he offers. In any case, Geisler does grant that "at best" a cumulative case can indeed test for the falsity of a worldview, which is what I'm doing in this book. See his *Christian Apologetics*, pp. 117–32.

48. Robert M. Price, *The Incredible Shrinking Son of Man* (Amherst, NY: Prometheus Books, 2003), p. 22.

4

THE OUTSIDER TEST FOR FAITH . . .

There is a great deal of discussion among Christian apologists over Bayesian "background factors," which play a significant role in assessing the truth of Christianity in general, the likelihood of the resurrection of Jesus, the probability of miracles, and the problem of evil. But I want to take a good hard look at the most important background factor of all for cognitively assessing the truth of religious faith—one's sociological and cultural background.

I've investigated my faith from the inside as an insider with the presumption that it was true. Even from an insider's perspective, I couldn't continue to believe. Now from the outside, it makes no sense at all. Christians are on the inside. I am now on the outside. Christians see things from the inside. I see things from the outside. From the inside, it seems true. From the outside, it seems untrue.

There are many religious faiths from which to choose. How does one actually choose to be on the "inside" of any of them if from the "outside" none of them have any plausibility? Unless one is on the *inside* as an adherent of a particular religious faith, she cannot see. But from the *outside*, the adherents of a different faith seem blind. This reminds me of what Mark Twain said: "The easy confidence with which I know another man's religion is folly teaches me to suspect that my own is also." Believers are truly atheists with regard to all other religions but their own. Atheists just reject one more religion.

This whole inside/outside perspective is quite a dilemma and prompts me to propose and argue on behalf of the *outsider test for religious faith*, the result of which makes the presumption of skepticism the preferred stance when approaching any religious faith, especially one's own. The outsider test is simply a challenge to test one's own religious faith with the presumption of skepticism, as an outsider. Test your beliefs as if you were an outsider to your faith. An outsider would begin her journey as a disinterested investigator who didn't think the religious faith in question is true since there are so many different religious faiths in the world. An outsider would be someone who was only interested in which, if any, religious faith is correct and would have no intellectual affiliation with any of them at all. She would have to assume that her culturally inherited religious faith is probably false. To be an outsider would mean she would have nothing at stake in the outcome of her investigations, and hence no fear of hell (however conceived) while investigating them, beginning with her own. Threats of hell could hinder a clearheaded investigation.

When I refer to religious faith here, I'm referring to beliefs that are essential for a member to be accepted in a particular religious community of faith that worships together and/or accepts the same divinely inspired prophetic/revelations and/or those beliefs whereby one's position in the afterlife depends. The reason for this definition will become clear, since the outsider test is primarily a challenge about the religious faith of communities of people. It also applies secondarily in lesser degrees to individual philosophers espousing metaphysical viewpoints who are not guided primarily by communal religious experiences but who are still influenced by the cultural milieu in which they live. Hence the outsider test will have a much greater degree of force against religious faiths of religious communities than on individual philosophers not involved in a religious community.

Surely someone will initially object that this is quite draconian in scope. Why take such an extreme stance? It's because that's how religious people approach all of the other religious faiths but their own. People approach other faiths this way all of the time, so why not do that with one's own religious faith? Why is there this discrepancy in how they evaluate religious faiths? For someone to object that what I'm asking is unfair, she has the burden of proof to show why her inconsistent approach to religious faith is justified in the first place. By contrast, I can offer good reasons why she should adopt such a skeptical presumption. Doing so is based upon some hard, cold sociological facts.

The basis for the outsider test challenge can be found in a statement by John Hick: "[I]t is evident that in some ninety-nine percent of the cases the religion which an individual professes and to which he or she adheres depends upon the accidents of birth. Someone born to Buddhist parents in Thailand is very likely to be a Buddhist, someone born to Muslim parents in Saudi Arabia to be a Muslim, someone born to Christian parents in Mexico to be a Christian, and so on."[1]

Richard Dawkins said the same thing in a much harsher tone: "Out of all of the sects in the world, we notice an uncanny coincidence: the overwhelming majority just happens to choose the one that their parents belong to. Not the sect that has the best evidence in its favour, the best miracles, the best moral code, the best cathedral, the best stained glass, the best music: when it comes to choosing from the smorgasbord of available religions, their potential virtues seem to count for nothing, compared to the matter of heredity. This is an unmistakable fact; nobody could seriously deny it. Yet people with full knowledge of the arbitrary nature of this heredity, somehow manage to go on believing in their religion, often with such fanaticism that they are prepared to murder people who follow a different one. . . . The religion we adopt is a matter of an accident of geography."[2]

Two widely accepted books on persuasive psychology are *Influence: The Psychology of Persuasion*, by Robert B. Cialdini, and *Attitudes and Persuasion: Classic and Contemporary Approaches*, by Richard E. Petty and John T. Cacioppo.[3] Social psychologists refer to these two books to show how people believe and defend their beliefs. Petty and Cacioppo wrote: "Since most of the information that children have about the world comes directly from their parents, it is not surprising that children's beliefs, and thus their attitudes, are initially very similar to their parents." They claim that "social psychologists have well documented that children tend to share their parents' racial prejudices, religious preferences, and political party affiliations."[4]

If you were born in Saudi Arabia, you would be a Sunni Muslim right now. This is an almost undeniable cold, hard sociological and cultural fact. In today's world, if you were born in Iran, you'd be a Shi'a Muslim. If you were born in India, you'd be a Hindu right now. If you were born in Japan, you'd be a Shintoist, and if you lived in Mongolia, you'd be a Buddhist. If you were born in the first century BCE in Israel, you'd adhere to the Jewish faith at that time, and if you were born in Europe in 1200 CE, you'd be a Roman Catholic. These things are as close to being undeniable facts as we can get in the sociological world.

But there's more: Had we lived in ancient Egypt or Babylon, we would have been very superstitious and polytheistic to the core. In the ancient world, we would have sought divine guidance through divination and sought to alter our circumstances through magic. If we were a first-century Christian, we would probably believe God sent illnesses and disasters to discipline and punish people for their sins, and for the first nine hundred years, we would have believed in the *ransom theory* of Jesus' atonement. As Christians in Europe during the Middle Ages, we would probably see nothing much wrong with killing witches, torturing heretics, and conquering Jerusalem from the "infidels" in the Crusades.

There are a whole range of issues that admit of diversity in the moral and political areas as well, based to an overwhelming degree on the "accidents of birth." Caucasian American men would've believed with President Andrew Jackson in *manifest destiny*, our God-given mandate to seize Native American territories in westward expansion. Up through the seventeenth century we would have believed that women were intellectually inferior to men, and consequently, we would not even have allowed them to become educated in the same subjects as men. Like Thomas Jefferson and most Americans, we would've thought this way about black people as well, that they were intellectually inferior to whites, while if we were born in the South, we would have justified slavery from the Bible.

If we were born black in today's America, we would probably still to this day believe O. J. Simpson is not guilty of murder because of our suspicions about racist policemen. If we were born in the Palestinian Gaza strip, we would hate the Jews and probably want to kill them all. If we were born in France, we would have opposed the Iraq war to oust Saddam Hussein. If we were born into a Democratic family in America in the 1980s, we would dislike and distrust George W. Bush and have a strong tendency to believe anything negative about him.

These kinds of moral, political, and religious beliefs, based upon cultural conditions, can be duplicated into a lengthy list of beliefs that we would've had if we were born in a different time and place. For someone to claim he or she wouldn't have believed these same things is what I call *chronological snobbery*, and runs completely counter to the sociological and cultural facts. According to Voltaire: "Every man is a creature of the age in which he lives, and few are able to raise themselves above the ideas of their time."

There are so many moral beliefs we have because of "when and where we were born" that an argument is made by moral relativists based on it and known to ethicists as the dependency thesis (DPT). According to the DPT, "morality is not a matter of independent rational judgment but is causally dependent on cultural conditions." The DPT is one of two legs supporting cultural relativism. The DPT is the second leg supporting it. The first leg is known as the diversity thesis (DVT), which states, "Moral practices and beliefs do in fact vary from culture to culture and at different times in history." Once someone acknowledges the first leg (DVT), then the second leg (DPT) offers a reason for the diversity we find around the globe.[5]

I believe that this same moral cultural relativist argument can be applied to religious faith, qua religious faith, with the exception that I'll not be arguing for complete metaphysical relativism. So let me introduce the *religious diversity thesis* (RDVT), which states, "Religious faith does in fact vary from culture to culture and at different times in history." Based upon the RDVT, the *religious dependency thesis* (RDPT) argues that "religious faith is not merely a matter of independent rational judgment but is causally dependent on cultural conditions to an overwhelming degree." The outsider test is based on the RDVT, which leads us to the RDPT, which in turn leads us to the presumption of skepticism.

No doubt many readers will object that no one can approach any area of learning without some presuppositions, assumptions, or control beliefs, not even scientists, and this is especially true when it comes to religious faiths. So what I'm arguing for is that the sociological and cultural facts strongly suggest the adherent of religious faith should switch her presuppositions. I'm arguing that she should adopt the presumption (or presupposition) of skepticism. If she simply cannot do this, then let me suggest doing what René Descartes did with a methodological (or hypothetical) doubt, although I'm not suggesting his type of extreme doubt. Hypothetically consider your faith from the perspective of an outsider. At the very minimum, a believer should be willing to subject her faith to rigorous scrutiny by reading many of the best-recognized critiques of her faith. For instance, if she is a Christian, she should be willing to read this book of mine. What's more, a church or Christian college should be willing to have small groups and classes where they gather to discuss each chapter of it. (Christian professors, you might as well do this while your students are in your classes because they will have to deal with it anyway.)

The outsider test challenges believers to examine the social and cultural conditions of how they came to adopt their particular religious faith in the first place. That is, believers must ask themselves who or what influenced them and what the actual reasons were for adopting their faith in its earliest stages. Nearly all believers in an overwhelming number of instances simply end up believing what they were taught to believe by their parents. The reason they adopt their faith in the first place is because of social and cultural conditions. Christian, just ask yourself if your initial experiences could be explained by a different, skeptical hypothesis and whether the initial reasons you had for your faith were strong ones. Do what I did in chapter 1. I really didn't have good initial reasons to believe. Very few of us do, as a matter of fact. We just end up believing what we were taught to believe.

Social conditions provide us with the control beliefs that we use from that moment on to incorporate all known facts and experiences. That's why they're called control beliefs. They are like blinders. From the moment you put them on, you only see what your blinders will let you see, because reason is mostly used to serve our control beliefs. Listen to Michael Shermer, a former Christian theist turned atheist, who has done an extensive study of why people believe in God and in "weird things," who concludes: "Most of us most of the time come to our beliefs for a variety of reasons having little to do with empirical evidence and logical reasoning. Rather, such variables as genetic predispositions, parental predilections, sibling influences, peer pressures, educational experiences, and life impressions all shape the personality preferences and emotional inclinations that, in conjunction with numerous social and cultural influences, lead us to make certain belief choices. Rarely do any of us sit down before a table of facts, weigh them pro and con, and choose the most logical and rational belief, regardless of what we previously believed. Instead, the facts of the world come to us through the colored filters of the theories, hypotheses, hunches, biases, and prejudices we have accumulated through our lifetime. We then sort through the body of data and select those most confirming what we already believe, and ignore or rationalize away those that are disconfirming. All of us do this, of course, but smart people are better at it."[6]

According to Robert McKim, "We seem to have a remarkable capacity to find arguments that support positions which we antecedently hold. Reason is, to a great extent, the slave of prior commitments."[7] Hence the whole notion of "an independent rational judgment" is suspect, especially when there are no mutually agreed-upon reliable scientific tests to decide what to believe, even if Christian apologists, for instance, continue to defend their religious faith with reasons. These apologists, if they're good at what they do, will be smart people. But according to Michael Shermer, "smart people, because they are more intelligent and better educated, are able to give intellectual reasons justifying their beliefs that they arrived at for non-intelligent reasons."[8]

Psychiatrist Valerie Tarico describes the process of defending unintelligent beliefs by smart people. She claims, "it doesn't take very many false assumptions to send us on a long goose chase." To illustrate this she tells us about the mental world of a paranoid schizophrenic. To such a person the perceived persecution by the CIA sounds real. "You can sit, as a psychiatrist, with a diagnostic manual next to you, and think: as bizarre as it sounds, the CIA really is bugging this guy. The arguments are tight, the logic persuasive, the evidence organized into neat files. All that is needed to build such an impressive house of illusion is a clear, well-organized mind and a few false assumptions. Paranoid individuals can be very credible."[9] This is what Christians do, and this is why it's hard to shake the evangelical faith, in her informed opinion.

The outsider test is a thought experiment merely to help us see the proper presumption when approaching the faith we were born into. Unlike former atheist Anthony Flew, who argued in favor of the presumption of atheism,[10] I'm arguing in favor of the presumption of skepticism, or agnosticism, which is something even Moreland and Craig admit is more justifiable than the presumption of atheism.[11] Its presumption is that when examining any religious belief, skepticism would be warranted, since the odds are good that the particular one you are investigating is wrong. The outsider test is no different than the prince in the Cinderella story who must question forty-five thousand people to see which girl lost the glass slipper at the ball last night. They all claim to have done so. Therefore, skepticism is definitely warranted. This is especially true when an empirical foot match cannot solve the religious questions we're asking.

For the Christian theist the challenge of the outsider test means there would be no more quoting the Bible to defend the claim that Jesus' death on the cross saves us from sins. The Christian theist must now try to rationally explain it. No more quoting the Bible to show how it's possible for Jesus to be 100 percent God and 100 percent man with nothing left over. The Christian theist must now try to make sense of this claim, coming as it does from an ancient superstitious people who didn't have trouble believing this could happen (Acts 14:11, 28:6). The Christian theist must not assume there is an answer to the problem of evil before approaching the evidence of suffering in our world. And she'd be initially skeptical of believing in any of the miracles in the Bible, just as she would be skeptical of any claims of the miraculous in today's world supporting other religious faiths. Why? Because she cannot start out by first believing the Bible, nor can she trust the people close to her who are Christian theists to know the truth, nor can she trust her own anecdotal religious experiences, since such experiences are had by people of all religious faiths who differ about the cognitive content learned as the result of these experiences. She would want evidence and reasons for these beliefs.

If after having investigated your religious faith with the presumption of skepticism it passes intellectual muster, then you can have your religious faith. It's that simple. If not, abandon it. Any loving God who requires us to believe correctly, when we have this extremely strong tendency to accept what we were born into, especially if he'll punish us if we end up being wrong, should surely make the correct religious faith pass the outsider test.

If your faith doesn't stand after doing this, then the God of your faith is not worthy of being worshiped. Since it's overwhelmingly true that the presumption you begin with will be the one you will end up with, I suspect that if someone is willing to take the challenge of the outsider test, then her religious faith will be found defective and she will abandon it. I also suspect that such a challenge could very well lead her to agnosticism and then onward to a denial of any religious faith, or atheism, like it has me.

If God exists and he doesn't care which religion we accept, then that God might survive the outsider test, but we would end up believing in a nebulous God out there with no definable characteristics, perhaps a deist God or the "god of the philosophers." This God is far and away from any full-blown Christianity or any specific religion though.

ANSWERING FIVE OBJECTIONS

One. It's objected that there are small minorities of people who choose to be Christian theists who were born and raised in Muslim countries and that people can escape their culturally adopted faith. But these are the exceptions. Christian theists respond by asking me to explain the exceptions. I am asking them to explain the rule. Why do religious beliefs dominate in specific geographical areas? Why is that? Furthermore, if the religious dependency thesis (RDPT) is correct, then religious geographical proliferation is exactly what we would expect to find in the world. The exceptions are simply that there are people who think for themselves and in so doing own a particular religious faith, rather than adopt what was taught to them. Then too, there are several social reasons for leaving the faith that a person was born into. If a believer had some bad experiences at the hands of someone who taught her what to believe (victims of Catholic molester-priests, for instance, or abusive fathers, or senseless suffering of any unbearable kind), this believer may leave that faith for another. If the believer just cannot reconcile her faith with what she learns or experiences though life, then she may leave her adopted faith. But when such a believer does decide to leave her faith, and chooses another one, many times that different faith (or sect) will be one that she was already exposed to in her culture. By contrast, atheism can be adopted by a former believer without ever having been exposed to it since it's simply the denial of one more god than what she had previously adhered to.

Two. Someone may argue that even if religious faiths were 100 percent correlated with the "accidents of birth," this wouldn't invalidate any particular one of them, for it could still be possible that theirs is the correct one after all. To this I answer, yes, this is possible. After all, someone can be right if for no other reason than that she just got lucky. But how do you rationally justify such luck? This is why I've developed the challenge of the outsider test in the first place, to test religious faiths against such luck. If the test between religious faiths is based entirely on luck, then what are the chances, based on luck alone, that the particular sect within Christian theism that one adheres to is correct? This still favors the presumption of skepticism.

Three. Someone may ask if my argument is self-defeating. "Do my cultural conditions overwhelmingly 'determine' my presumption of skepticism? If so, then others don't have much of a reason to adopt the skeptical stance. If not, then why do I think I can transcend culture but a Christian theist can't transcend her culture?" In answer I say that if it's the case "the accidents of birth" overwhelmingly determine our religious beliefs, especially in those areas where there is no mutually agreed-upon reliable scientific test to decide between them, then that's a sociological fact everyone must wrestle with when thinking about such matters. Let's say this is the case, that is, that whatever we believe about the origin of this universe is overwhelmingly determined by when and where we are born. I am much more willing to accept the consequences of this than a great majority of people who have religious faith and are so dogmatic about their faith. If this is the case, then we agree that what we believe is based upon when and where we're born.

If true, this does not undercut what I'm saying at all—it supports it. I'm arguing that cultural conditions have an extremely strong influence on us to believe in a given communally shared religious faith in a *primary* sense. And although cultural influences also apply in a *secondary* sense with regard to noncommunal metaphysical beliefs, if I am a skeptic because of these cultural conditions, then I'm right that cultural conditions lead us to believe these things after all. Such an admission doesn't undercut the reason for the outsider test and the skeptical presumption that goes with it based on the RDVT and the RDPT. If cultural factors overwhelmingly cause us to believe what we believe, then we should all become agnostics, which is something I can be quite comfortable with. Agnosticism becomes the default position. So I don't object to being skeptical of my own skepticism. But it's redundant from my perspective, and so it merely reinforces itself.

The truth is that my argument is not self-defeating at all. It strongly suggests we should doubt what we believe. It's not self-defeating to say the odds are that we are wrong. After all, we're talking about the odds here. My argument is based on the facts of religious diversity spread around the globe into separate geographical locations and that Christians evaluate other religions from "the outside." I'm arguing people adopt their religion based upon their culture (to an overwhelming degree), which should cause all of us to subject our beliefs to scrutiny, just like Christians do with other faiths.

J. L. Schellenberg deals with this same criticism of his argument for religious skepticism in these words: "Now this objection can be sound only if my arguments do indeed apply to themselves, and it will not take much to see that they do not." He distinguishes between "bold, ambitious, and risky metaphysical beliefs," on the one hand, which tell us that "active investigation should cease," since "the truth has been discovered," and "the belief that some such bold, ambitious, and risky metaphysical belief is unjustified." The latter belief merely claims that such bold and ambitious metaphysical beliefs "have not successfully made their case; it bides us to continue investigation ... because skepticism is always a position of last resort in truth seeking contexts."[12]

Four. In arguing that one's religious faith is overwhelmingly adopted by "when and where" someone is born, have I committed the informal genetic fallacy of irrelevance? This fallacy is committed whenever it's argued that a belief is false because of the origination of the belief. Applying this to my arguments, it would be objected that just because a particular religious faith is learned from one's culture, it does not make that faith false, for how one first adopts her faith is irrelevant to whether said faith is true.

But I deny this is what I'm arguing. There is no fallacy here unless by explaining how believers first adopt a religious faith I therefore conclude that such a faith is false. I'm arguing instead that the sociological facts provide evidence against religious faiths in general, and the Christian faith in particular. I'm not arguing that they are false because of how believers originally adopt their faith. I'm arguing believers should be skeptical of their religious faith because of how they first adopted it.

Five. One final similar objection asks whether this is all circular. Have I merely chosen a different metaphysical belief system based upon different cultural factors? If it is, it's definitely not viciously circular. I have very good initial grounds for starting out with skepticism in the first place, given the RDVT and the RDPT. Methodological procedures are those procedures we use to investigate something. How we go about investigating something is a separate issue that must be justified on its own terms, and I have done so here. Someone cannot say of the outsider test that I ought to be just as skeptical of it as I am about the conclusion(s) I arrive at when I apply the test, since I have justified this test from the sociological facts. One must first dispute the outsider test on its own terms.

CHRISTIANS HAVE A FEW OPTIONS AT THEIR DISPOSAL HERE

Christians could try to dispute the sociological facts, or they could dispute that they approach other faiths from the outside. These options aren't very promising. Christians could also argue that they shouldn't have to take the outsider test. At that point, I can simply ask them why they apply a double standard here. Why do they treat their own specific faith differently than they do others? That's a double standard. Christians could also take the test and then deny that it leads them to reject their faith. But as I've already said, the conclusion I arrive at when I apply the outsider test to various religious faiths is that they all fail. If a person thinks the outsider test can lead someone to adopt one particular religious faith, then that is still her option. I just doubt that a religious faith can pass the outsider test; that's all.

One other option for the Christian might be to argue that I have not shown there is a direct causal relationship between the RDPT and the RDVT. Just because there is religious diversity doesn't mean that religious views are overwhelmingly dependent on social and geographical factors, they might argue. Reminiscent of David Hume, who argued that we do not see cause and effect, they might try to argue I have not shown it exists between the RDPT and the RDVT. After all, if Hume can say he never sees one billiard ball "causing" another one to move just because they do so after making contact, then maybe there is no direct causal relationship between the RDPT and the RDVT. Is it possible, they might ask, that just because people have different religious faiths which are separated into distinct geographical locations on our planet, that "when and where" people are born has little to do with what they believe? My answer is that if this is possible, it is an exceedingly small possibility. Do Christians really want to hang their faith on such a slender reed as this? I've shown from sociological, geographical, and psychological studies that what we believe is strongly influenced by "the accidents of history." That's all anyone can ask me to show.

Christians have still another option. They can try to reasonably explain why there is such a geographically situated religious diversity. The adherents of the various religions all have their explanations for religious diversity. These explanations are similar in kind to each other, if not exactly the same. Adherents will argue that those who don't accept their particular religion are either ignorant of the truth (or willfully ignorant), unenlightened, deceived by Satan, or that God has good reasons for permitting this state of affairs. Cultural factors are either downplayed or ignored, even though I have shown they play an overwhelming role in what a person believes.

Some Christians simply argue that everyone in the world will be saved in the end, known as "universalism," and so religious diversity presents no serious problem. But such a view has several Bible passages to explain away, and it undermines any need for people to accept the Christian faith in the first place, or for evangelism.[13]

Now consider William Lane Craig's explanation for religious diversity. He claims, "it is *possible* that God has created a world having an optimal balance between saved and lost and that God has so providentially ordered the world that those who fail to hear the gospel and be saved would not have freely responded affirmatively to it even if they had heard it."[14] Craig argues that if this scenario is even *possible*, "it proves that it is entirely consistent to affirm that God is all-powerful and all-loving and yet that some people never hear the gospel and are lost." However, there are many things that might be possible, and apologists like Craig seem to resort to that standard way too many times, in my opinion. The probability that not one of the billions of people who have never heard the gospel would respond if they did hear it can probably be calculated, if missionaries kept records of their efforts. To claim what he does against the overwhelming evidence of missionary efforts belies the facts. Contrary to Craig, when we look at the billions of people who have never been given a chance to be "saved" because of "when and where they were born," his scenario seems extremely implausible, to say the least, and depends upon God not only having the capability to foreknow future free-willed contingent human actions, but also that God knows what the future would've been like if every single free choice had been different for every single human being throughout history (something I dispute in chapter 16).[15] No wonder he only wants to talk about what is possible.

When religious believers actually do grapple with the cultural basis of religious faith, they will all respond in the same manner against what I have been arguing for here. Whether they are Buddhist, Muslim, Hindu, Jew, or Christian, they will all argue that I have not shown their particular religious faith to be false simply because it's an overwhelming sociological fact that we believe based upon when and where we were born. William Lane Craig responds, just as most every defender of a different religion might do, when he asks, "Why could not the Christian worldview be objectively true? How does the mere presence of religious worldviews incompatible with Christianity show that distinctively Christian claims are not true? Logically, the existence of multiple, incompatible truth claims only implies that all of them cannot be (objectively) true; but it would be obviously fallacious to infer that not one of them is (objectively) true."[16] Craig is correct about this. But most every defender of every religion could argue the same exact thing, just by inserting her own particular religion into Craig's words. Then after making such a statement, each believer could proceed all over again to argue that she has the true faith, just like Craig does. Whether or not people accept these apologetical arguments will depend upon whether or not they are already *insiders* to that particular faith in the first place. Is this not circular? The bottom line is that there is a huge difference between having the evidence of religious diversity separated into separate geographical locations on my side, which I'm claiming that it is, and trying to explain away the evidence, which is what Dr. Craig is forced to do.

Skepticism (or agnosticism) becomes the favored (or default) position as a result of the initial presumption—a presumption that is justified by the religious diversity around the globe. I believe skepticism of all religious and metaphysical positions leads one inexorably to agnosticism, and agnosticism can lead someone inexorably to atheism. And atheism, in the end, is a denial of all religious faiths.

NOTES

1. John Hick, *An Interpretation of Religion* (Hartford, CT: Yale University Press, 1989), p. 2.

2. *Nullifidian*, December 1994.

3. Robert B. Cialdini, *Influence: The Psychology of Persuasion* (New York: William Morrow, 1993); Richard E. Petty and John T. Cacioppo, *Attitudes and Persuasion: Classic and Contemporary Approaches* (Dubuque, IA: William C. Brown, 1981).

4. Petty and Cacoippo, *Attitudes and Persuasion*, p. 184.

5. Arthur F. Homes, *Ethics: Approaching Moral Decisions* (Downers Grove, IL: Inter-Varsity Press, 1984), pp. 15–21.

6. Michael Shermer, *Why People Believe Weird Things*, 2nd ed. (New York: Henry Holt, 2002), pp. 283–84.

7. Robert McKim, *Religious Ambiguity and Religious Diversity* (Oxford: Oxford University Press, 2001), p. ix.

8. Shermer, *Why People Believe Weird Things*, p. 299.

9. Valerie Tarico, *The Dark Side: How Evangelical Teachings Corrupt Love and Truth* (Seattle: Dea, 2006), pp. 221–22.

10. Antony Flew, *The Presumption of Atheism* (Amherst, NY: Prometheus Books, 1976).

11. As J. P. Moreland and William Craig remind us, "The assertion 'God does not exist' is just as much a claim to knowledge as the assertion 'God exists,' and therefore the former requires justification just as the latter does. . . . If anything, then, one should speak at most of a presumption of agnosticism." *Philosophical Foundations for a Christian Worldview* (Downers Grove, IL: InterVarsity Press, 2003), p. 156.

12. J. L. Schellenberg, *The Wisdom to Doubt: A Justification of Religious Skepticism* (Ithaca, NY: Cornell University Press, 2007), pp. 47–48.

13. John Hick defends universalism in *More Than One Way: Four Views on Salvation in a Pluralistic World*, ed. Dennis L. Okholm and Timothy R. Phillips (Downers Grove, IL:

InterVarsity Press, 1995), but the respondents attack him on these very points.

14. See Craig's "Politically Incorrect Salvation," in *Christian Apologetics in the Post-Modern World*, ed. T. P. Phillips and D. Ockholm (Downers Grove, IL: InterVarsity Press, 1995), pp. 75–97.

15. This view is known as Molinism. This is disputed by evangelicals themselves. See *Divine Foreknowledge: Four Views*, ed. James K. Beilby and Paul R. Eddy (Downers Grove, IL: InterVarsity Press, 2001), where Craig defends his view against three other evangelicals.

16. See Craig, "Politically Incorrect Salvation."

5

DOES GOD EXIST?

When it comes to why something—anything—exists, our choices can be reduced to these: (1) Something—anything—has always existed, or (2) something—anything—popped into existence out of absolutely nothing. Either choice seems extremely unlikely—or possibly even absurd. There is nothing in our experience that can help us grasp these two possibilities. But one of them is correct and the other false. We either start with the "brute fact" that something has always existed or the "brute fact" that something popped into existence out of nothing. A third view is that (3) our existence in the universe is absurd to the core.

Dr. William Lane Craig used the word "bizarre" to describe our choices about the existence of the universe when he wrote, "I well recall thinking, as I began to study the *Kalam Cosmological Argument*, that all of the alternatives with respect to the universe's existence—the infinitude of the past, creation *ex nihilo*, spontaneous origination *ex nihilo*—were so **bizarre** that the most reasonable option seemed to be that nothing exists! Since our existence is, however, undeniable, we must settle, however uncomfortably, on one of the above three."[1]

The Christian maintains that a good personal triune Creator has always existed. The atheist maintains that the material universe either popped into existence out of nothing, has always existed, is self-caused, or it's just a brute fact. Many atheists believe there may be other universes, which have each come into existence by their own big bangs. Atheist philosopher Quentin Smith claims that our universe came "from nothing, by nothing, and for nothing." He even argues that the universe caused itself to exist.[2]

So we can understand why G. W. Leibniz claimed the fundamental metaphysical question is this: "Why is there something rather than nothing at all?" He argued we should expect that nothing at all exists—nothing. Why? Because such a state of affairs seems to require no explanation. The fact that something exists demands an explanation for why it exists, he argued.

Why do atheists disbelieve in God? Many of us begin by attacking the notion of God as incoherent. For instance, we claim that there is simply too much intense suffering in this world for there to be a good creator. Atheists generally think Christian theism inhibits scientific progress, creates class struggles, sexism, racism, mass neurosis, intolerance, and environmental disasters. Christian thinkers, however, respond that atheism cannot give sufficient reasons why human beings experience consciousness or why people should be morally good. Christians also charge atheists with not being able to sufficiently answer what Albert Camus claimed was the fundamental philosophical question. It is this: "Why not commit suicide?" That is, if we cannot find meaning in our existence, then why not just end it all? Because of this conundrum, Leo Tolstoy chose to believe in God "contrary to reason," and in so doing was "saved from suicide."[3]

Atheists have also offered suggestions as to why people turn to religion. Sigmund Freud claimed that religion is an expression of the longing for a father figure. Ludwig Feuerbach claimed that God didn't make man in his image, but rather human beings made God in their image. Karl Marx taught that religion is the opium of the working-class people. It is funded and pushed by the rich class in order to numb the working class from trying to right the injustices put on them by the rich class. Religion keeps the working class focused on a hope of bliss in the hereafter. Friedrich Nietzsche claimed that religion endures because weak people need it. For Jean-Paul Sartre, God represented a threat to authentic morality. If God is autonomous, in the Calvinistic sense, then human beings cannot be responsible for themselves. He argued that the rejection of God makes morality and freedom possible, for only then can people take responsibility for their own choices.

Christians have their own explanations for why people become atheists. Psychologist Paul Vitz, for instance, claims the reason why people become atheists is because of bad father figures.[4] They'll further claim that if God does indeed exist, then we need him. Christianity may be a crutch for the weak, but if it is true, then they need a crutch because they're crippled. And if God exists, then Sartre's admonition of autonomous freedom is nothing short of rebellion against God.

These explanations on both sides of this debate depend upon whether or not God exists though. So what reasons do Christians have for preferring to believe God has always existed and created the universe? There are three main categories of arguments for God's existence that I'll mention. There are *ontological arguments*, *cosmological arguments*, and *teleological (or design) arguments*.[5]

ONTOLOGICAL ARGUMENTS

Here's a very brief history of the ontological argument for the existence of God: Italian Anselm originated it around the eleventh century. Duns Scotus and St. Bonaventure accepted the argument, but William of Ockham did not. Italian Thomas

Aquinas rejected it in the thirteenth century. Frenchman René Descartes resurrected it in the early seventeenth century, and then Baruch Spinoza and Leibniz added their own versions of it. Scotsman David Hume rejected it as did Prussian/German Immanuel Kant, who offered a refutation of it in the latter half of the seventeenth century. German Idealist G. W. F. Hegel argued for it in the nineteenth century. Then in the past several decades Americans Norman Malcolm, Charles Hartshorne, and Alvin Plantinga have all defended it. Criticisms and debate about it abound in almost every philosophy of religion textbook.[6]

It is generally agreed that the ontological argument never converted anyone (even though Bertrand Russell once thought it was correct, but later changed his mind). It is an amazing argument—a philosopher's delight! According to Robert Paul Wolff, this is the "most famous, the most mystifying, the most outrageous and irritating philosophical argument of all time. . . . It remains as one of the most controversial arguments in all of philosophy." Yet, "whenever I read the Ontological Argument, I have the same feeling that comes over me when I watch a really good magician. Nothing up this sleeve, nothing up the other sleeve; nothing in the hat; presto! A big fat rabbit. How can Anselm pull God out of an idea?"[7]

Anselm's Ontological Argument for the Existence of God

(1) On the assumption that that than which nothing greater can be conceived is only in a mind, something greater can be conceived, because

(2) Something greater can be thought to exist in reality as well.

(3) The assumption is therefore contradictory: either there is no such thing even in the intellect, or it exists also in reality;

(4) But it does exist in the mind of the fool (see Ps. 14:1);

(5) Therefore that than which nothing greater can be conceived exists in reality as well as in the mind.

Anselm argued that even those who doubt the existence of God would have to have some understanding of what they were doubting—namely, they would understand God to be a being than which nothing greater can be thought. Given that it is greater to exist outside of the mind rather than just in the mind, a doubter who denied God's existence would be caught in a contradiction, he argued, because he or she would be saying that it is possible to think of something greater than a being than which nothing greater can be thought. Hence, God exists necessarily.

David Hume criticized this argument using his distinction between the *relations of ideas* and *matters of fact*. The former has to do with abstract ideas, logic, and math that are deductively known, while the latter has to do with what exists in the world inductively known through experience. Hume argued that the question of the existence of God is about matters of fact, which can be known from experience. Since matters of fact are either true or false, we can also entertain the idea that a necessary being such as God supposedly is, does not exist, so the argument fails. For the ontological argument uses the evidence of the relations of ideas to show the existence of a matter of fact, and that's something Hume would not allow. As Todd M. Furman tells us, a question about matters of fact is "a claim that requires empirical evidence for any sort of justification it might ever have."[8] Or, in the words of J. C. A. Gaskin, "No assertion is demonstrable unless its negation is contradictory. No negation of a matter of fact is contradictory. All assertions about existence of *things* are matters of fact. Therefore no negation of an assertion that some *thing* exists is contradictory. Hence, there is no *thing* whose existence is demonstrable."[9]

The basic Kantian criticism of Anselm's argument is that someone cannot infer the extramental existence of anything by analyzing its definition. Yet defenders reply that Anselm is not defining God into existence. He's merely asking whether we can reasonably suppose that something than which nothing greater can be conceived exists only in the intellect.

Another major criticism of this argument comes from whether our conceptions of the greatest conceivable being might entail attributes that involve unrecognized inconsistencies or even contractions. Anthony Kenny examined the principal attributes traditionally ascribed to theistic God, particularly omniscience and omnipotence, and argued that there can be no such being as the God of traditional natural theology.[10] A lot of ink has been spilled over these kinds of issues.

Take for instance the present debate over *open theism*, among evangelicals. They're debating whether God exists in time in some sense, or whether God exists outside of time.[11] Paul Helm has claimed that "the arguments used to show that God is in time, in effect support the view that God is finite." There is such a close connection between the timelessness of God and the spacelessness of God, Helm argued, that a denial of God's timelessness is also a denial of God's spacelessness. Therefore, he claims it's possible that "the belief in God is even more incoherent than previously thought, in that it requires unintelligibilities such as a timeless and spaceless existence." Helm concludes by laying out the three theistic options: Someone can either accept the unintelligible existence of both a timeless and spaceless God, accept the consequences of a God who is both in time and finite, or supply other arguments on behalf of a God who is in time which do not also deny God's spacelessness.[12] To this date, option three has not been adequately met in my opinion. I think this whole debate indicates God's existence is unintelligible, regardless of what we might conceive him to be, and hence ontological arguments can't even get off the ground.[13]

According to Toni Vogel Carey, rather than the ontological argument being "a proof of God's existence, what emerges is a reason for doubt about claiming we have any understanding of the nature and existence of God. To see this, take a closer look at the role played by the fool. What a fool can understand, anyone can understand, fools being, by definition, deficient in candlepower and wisdom. Why should we suppose, then, that a being than which none greater can be conceived by the fool is as great as a being than which none greater can be conceived, say, by a smart *Philosophy Now* reader? And by the same reasoning, why should we suppose that a being than which none greater can be conceived by you, with all due respect, is as great as a being than which none greater can be conceived by a genius like Einstein or a saint like Anselm? Finally, why should we suppose that a being than which none greater can be conceived by Einstein or Anselm is as great as a being than which none greater can logically possibly be conceived—than which none greater could be conceived even by God? For plainly this, and not merely the greatest concept of which the fool is capable, is what Anselm's argument requires."[14]

Likewise, if we asked an Easterner what she conceives to be the greatest conceivable being, her conception will start off being different from those of Westerners from the get-go. I think Anselmian arguments, including those of Hartshorne, Plantinga, and Malcolm, all begin with Occidental not Oriental conceptions of God, and their Western conceptions of God are theirs by virtue of the prevalence of the Christian gospel in the West. If ontological argumentation is sound, then the Eastern conceptions of God will entail that their God (or the One) also exists. Since these two conceptions of God produce two mutually exclusive conclusions about which kind of God exists, then the ontological argument itself does not lead us to believe in the Christian God alone. An Easterner might even start off by saying that the greatest conceivable being is the ONE, which cannot be conceived. Where do you go with the ontological argument from here?[15]

COSMOLOGICAL ARGUMENTS

Cosmological arguments begin with some fact of the world and argue to a transcendent God as the best explanation of it. In the Bible there isn't a philosophical argument for God's existence. It was assumed that there was a God. The problem they faced wasn't atheism. It was polytheism.

There are three types of cosmological arguments:

1. *The Thomistic "Five Ways" Arguments.* For the first thousand years Christian thinkers found the most useful philosophical framework within the philosophy of Plato. Most of the works of Aristotle were lost to Western scholars, except as known through Arabic commentators. In the minds of most Christian thinkers in the thirteenth century, Plato was *the* Christian philosopher, while Aristotle was considered a pagan philosopher. But with the discovery of Aristotle's works, Thomas Aquinas (1225–1275 CE) almost single-handedly transformed the perceptions of Aristotle as a pagan philosopher into *the* Christian philosopher, such that Aristotelian thought became the official doctrinal framework for the Roman Catholic Church down to our own century. Nothing comparable to this intellectual feat has been done before or after.[16]

Aquinas attempts to show that (1) our world is dependent upon an unmoved mover for the fact of motion, (2) there is an uncaused cause for our very existence, (3) there is a necessary being for the universe of contingent beings, (4) there is an absolutely perfect being to account for limited perfection, and (5) there is a cosmic designer to account for ordered design in the universe. These five arguments all assume the eternity of the universe. Even an eternal universe needs a God, Aquinas argued. He did believe that the universe began at some point in time. He just figured if he could show that God exists even when granting the assumption of an eternal universe, then how much more would it be true that God must exist if the universe had a beginning in time. When Aquinas argues against an infinite series of causes, he's not talking about a temporal series, one that stretches backward in time, but a series stretching hierarchically, up some sort of great chain of being. For him, "every moment in the universe, even if the universe has always been here, is dependent for its existence, at that moment, upon an ultimate cause."[17] Thus "the cause to which the argument concludes might best be termed a sustaining cause rather than a first creative cause,"[18] an unmoved Mover.

According to Ed L. Miller, "St. Thomas really thought of his 'Five Ways' as variations on a single idea, which is the substance of all of them: We know from experience that the world is contingent, that is, it depends on something outside itself for its existence. And this would be true even if the world has always been here, for an infinite collection of contingent things is no less contingent than a finite one. But there must be some unconditional, ultimate being upon which the world depends, otherwise it would have no final basis for existence."[19]

There are many things that could be said in criticism of Aquinas's five ways, especially in light of the big bang theory, which has shown our universe began to exist, along with the concept of inertia, which does away with the need to explain motion as requiring either a regress of causes, or an unmoved mover. Nonetheless, Michael Martin argues that "Aquinas gives us no non-question-begging reason why there could not be a nontemporal infinite regress of causes." A first cause, or unmoved mover, is merely assumed as self-evident in his argument, since "it finds no support in experience." Martin offers a history lesson as an analogy: "any appeal to obvious or self-evident evidence must be regarded with suspicion, for many things that have been claimed to be self-evidently true—for example, the divine right of kings and the earth as the center of the universe—have turned out not to be true at all."[20] J. L. Mackie wrote, "The greatest weakness of this otherwise attractive argument is that some reason is required for making God the one exception to the supposed need for something else to depend on: why should God, rather than any-thing else, be taken as the only satisfactory termination of the regress?"[21] According to John Hick, the family of cosmological arguments "does not compel us to believe that there is a God. For one may opt instead to accept the universe as a sheer unex-plained fact." Because "we are accordingly faced with the choice of accepting God or accepting the existence of the physical universe itself as a given unintelligible and mysterious brute fact." Hick rhetorically asks, "Why, however, should we not take the physical universe itself to be the ultimate unexplained reality?"[22]

2. *The Kalam Argument.* This argument attempts to show that the physical uni-verse must have begun at some point, which requires a timelessly existing personal God as the explanation for such a beginning. This argument states that a beginning-less series of events in time is impossible. We can never have an infinite collection of anything, much less events in time, it's argued. Therefore the physical universe began to exist. And since it could not come about by nonpersonal events in time, it requires a personal agent, God, who is outside of time to create it when it began. William Lane Craig is this argument's leading defender today.[23]

While the Kalam argument is fascinating, several scholars have offered critiques of it, beginning with J. L. Mackie and Michael Martin.[24] Book-length treatments of it have been written by Quentin Smith (with William Lane Craig) and Mark R. Nowacki.[25]

For this argument, Professor Craig offers a simple structure:

1. Everything that begins to exist has a cause of its existence.
2. The universe began to exist.
3. Therefore, the universe has a cause of its existence.

In a published exchange with Wes Morriston, Craig claims the first premise is an obvious "metaphysical intuition."[26] But Craig is trying to explain more than the origins of space/matter/energy, for along with it he's also trying to explain the beginning of time itself. And it simply is not an obvious intuition to conceive of an event prior to the first event in time. It seems a better intuition would be that the universe has always existed since time now exists, for there would be no "time" at which the universe began to exist independently of the time that originates with the universe.

Craig claims God is outside of time before creation and that he becomes inside of time afterward when time begins with the universe. Graham Oppy tells us the problem with his view of God (via e-mail): "If there is a dimension analogous to time that can be used to measure God's existence outside of time, then either (1) God has a beginning in that dimension, or else (2) God has always existed in that dimension. Following the lead of Craig's remarks in connection with the universe, it seems that the first option leads to the suggestion that there is a cause of God's existence, and the second option leads to infinite regress. But, if there is no dimension analogous to time that can be used to measure God's existence outside of time, then it seems to me to be doubtful that we even understand the suggestion that God existed outside of time."

By analogy Craig argues on behalf of this so-called metaphysical intuition that people don't imagine tigers "springing into existence uncaused," but Wes Morriston rightly responds that "the First Moment in the history of our universe is unlike all others because that is when the whole natural order comes into being." Morriston continues: "We have no experience of the origin of worlds to tell us that *worlds* don't come into existence like that. We don't even have experience of the coming into being of anything remotely analogous to the "initial singularity" that figures in the Big Bang theory of the origin of the universe. That is why the absurdity of tigers and the like popping into existence out of nowhere tells us nothing about the utterly unique case of the Beginning of the whole natural order."

Morriston goes on to argue that Craig's view of "*creation out of nothing* is at least as counterintuitive as is [the idea of] *beginning to exist without a cause.* . . . If someone insists it is just 'obvious' that God could create a world without any preexisting material stuff to work with, on the ground that there is no *logical contradiction* in the idea of such a feat, then the proper reply is that there is *also* no *logical contradiction* in the idea of the universe beginning without a cause."

Craig's second premise is that the universe began to exist. It too has difficulties. When it comes to scientific discussions about time, relativity, cosmic singularities, and quantum mechanics, this gets pretty deep. Graham Oppy (via e-mail) simply notes that "Craig endorses a theory of space and time that is almost universally rejected by contemporary physicists." Richard Carrier agrees (via e-mail) that "though there are a few philosophers and scientists on his side, Craig's theory of time still goes against the current scientific consensus, and is far from being established."[27] David Ramsay Steele reminds us that according to quantum mechanics "things begin to exist without any cause all the time."[28] So if some things can begin to exist without a cause, the universe could be one of them, which does not require a creator at all.

Craig begins his philosophical arguments by making the distinction between an actual infinite collection of things (which is numerically infinite) and a potential infinite collection of things (which is merely "indefinite," having the potential of being numerically infinite). Using several thought experiments Craig argues that an actual infinite collection of things is impossible. In one of them Craig tries to show that an actual infinite cannot be formed (or traversed) by adding one number after another successively. This is impossible, he says. If someone began the task of counting in the distant past, she could never count to infinity no matter how high she counted, for there would always be one number higher to count. But this is irrelevant to the case Craig wants to make if he intends to show by it that the physical universe couldn't have always existed. Because it says nothing against the possibility of an immortal being counting to infinity *if she has always been counting*, which is what he must argue against if he intends to claim an actual infinite series of events could not exist.

Craig's favorite thought experiment is about Hilbert's Hotel. This hypothetical hotel has an infinite number of guests each in their own separate rooms. Absurdities set in at this point, Craig argues. For even though we already had an infinite number of guests in the hotel, we could repeatedly add more and more guests by simply moving all the present guests down one room and then adding the newest guest to room number one. We could potentially add an infinite number of new guests without the actual number of guests increasing. Furthermore, an infinite number of guests could check out of the odd numbered rooms leaving an infinite number of guests in the even numbered rooms. Craig claims this is absurd. Therefore he concludes that an actual infinite collection of things is impossible, and by analogy, there cannot be an actual infinite series of events in time either.

Craig argues that the universe had a beginning since it leads to absurdities to suppose that it didn't. For example, he claims that if an immortal being traversed an infinite in the distant past by counting an infinite number of events down from negative infinity to zero ($\ldots -3, -2, -1, 0$), then we could never travel back in time to see her counting events, for no matter how far back we go she would already be finished counting them. That's absurd, Craig claims. But he cannot have it both ways. He cannot say she has always been counting and that she has never been counting! If we cannot go back in the infinite timeless past to find her counting, then she was never counting at all, for we have gone as far back in time as possible. But if we can, then there must be a last event that she counts. And if that's so, what reason does Craig have for thinking the immortal being must be finished counting events? It could be that the immortal being is nowhere close to finishing her count.

Craig's basic problem is that he conflates counting an infinite number of events with counting all of them. An immortal being could finish her beginningless task (... −5, −4,−3) and yet not count all events (−2, −1, 0). Let's face it; a set of an infinite number of events is not to be regarded as the same thing in every respect as an infinite number of sets each containing an infinite number of events, unless he's equivocating on the notion of what an infinite set of events means (see note).[29]

Besides, even though Craig claims his God is outside of time prior to creation, there is still no conceptual improbability with an infinite God eternally creating the universe from the beginningless past. I don't see how Craig can reasonably argue that his God could not have done this if he had chosen to do so, just as Aquinas saw no problem with an eternal universe and even supposed it for the sake of his arguments.

Craig concludes the Kalam argument by claiming the universe must have had a personal cause of its existence. He claims that a nonpersonal cause from all eternity would've already produced the universe no matter how far back in time we go, since all of the nonpersonal factors that would've given rise to the universe had already been in place from all eternity. However, Wes Morriston counters that if God is timelessly eternal there was never a moment in time when God did not will into existence this universe. Since Craig must affirm that God's intention to create our world is an eternal decision, then God's "decision to create a universe must surely be causally sufficient for the existence of that world." Either "a timeless personal agent timelessly wills to create a world with a beginning, or else it does not so will. There can be no *temporal gap* between the time at which it does the willing and the time at which the thing willed actually happens. In this respect a *timeless* personal cause is no different from a nonpersonal cause." So the Kalam argument fails.

But even if the Kalam argument is sound, I still don't see how it follows that this universe was caused to come into existence by the Trinitarian Christian God of the Bible. And there is nothing about the Kalam argument that tells us anything about this God, if he exists, other than that he caused it to spring into existence. There is equally nothing about the argument that leads me to think that this God is all powerful, either, or loving. The argument at its very best may only lead us to believe that a deistic "god" merely had the power to create what Edward Tryon and Stephen Hawking both describe as a "quantum wave fluctuation," [30] and that's a far different kind of God than the one Craig believes in. Contrary to James F. Sennett, moving from the God of the theistic arguments to the Christian God is like trying to fly a plane to the moon (see note).[31]

3.*The Leibnizian Argument.* G. W. Leibniz's (1646–1716) cosmological argument attempts to show that the principle of sufficient reason, when applied to a contingent universe, leads us to believe in a self-explanatory being. The principle of sufficient reason (PSR) states: "There is some explanation for the existence of anything whatever, some reason why it should exist rather than not." The argument begins by supposing that nothing existed—which is what we should expect to find.

The existence of nothing would not require an explanation, it's argued. But the existence of something—of anything—does force us to ponder the question, why? We would need no reason to explain the nonexistence of the world. But given the fact that the world exists, we are driven to wonder why it exists.

Richard Taylor explains the Lebnizian argument with an easy-to-understand thought experiment, from which I will use in what follows.[32] Suppose you were walking in the woods and you found a perfectly smooth transparent ball about your own height. This would puzzle you greatly.

Lesson 1. If you were quite accustomed to such objects of various sizes but had never seen an ordinary rock, then upon finding a large ordinary rock in the woods you would be just as puzzled. Thus, something that is puzzling ceases to be so by its accustomed presence. Likewise, it is strange indeed that our universe exists; yet few are very often struck by this strangeness.

Lesson 2. You might not know why it is there, but you would hardly doubt that it did not appear there all by itself. Few people would entertain the idea that it might have come from nothing at all—that it has no explanation for its existence. Likewise existence seems to require a reason, whereas nonexistence does not.

Lesson 3. It is not the fact of its having been found in the forest rather than elsewhere that renders an explanation necessary, for our question is not how it happens to be there but how it happens to exist at all. If we annihilate the forest and everything else as well, leaving this ball to constitute the entire physical universe and that no other reality has ever existed or will exist, we cannot for a moment suppose that its existence has been explained. Likewise, it doesn't matter what the thing in question is, or how large it is, or how complex it is—it could be a grain of sand. We do not avoid the necessity of a reason for the existence of that which exists.

Lesson 4. It is no answer to the question why a thing exists to state how long it has existed, for the question was not one concerning age but its existence. Likewise, if the universe had no beginning at all, it can still be asked why there is a world, why there is something rather than nothing.

Some Criticisms

First, when it comes to the PSR, atheists simply argue that the universe is just a brute fact—we deny the PSR when applied to the existence of the universe. Bertrand Russell said, "The universe is just there, and that's all." Maybe reason isn't something that can answer the question of our origins. After all, those who believe that God created the universe cannot offer any reasons why there should be a self-existent being that has always existed, either. For them, God is their brute fact, just like the physical universe is a brute fact for atheists. And since that's so, then the PSR must be equally applied to God. What is the sufficient explanation for the existence of God?

Second, could we suppose that the universe itself contains the reason for its existence—that it is a necessary being? The Christian can reply that we find nothing about the world to suggest that it exists by its own nature, and many things that suggest that it doesn't. Every part of it suggests that it is not indestructible—that it has a finite duration. Suppose that a single grain of sand has forever constituted the whole universe. It seems quite impossible to suppose that it exists by its own nature and could never have failed to exist. The same should be true if the world consisted not of one or two, but a million grains of sand. However, what seems to be the case from our perspective and what is actually the case might be two different things. Humans just might have the tendency to suppose these things. When it comes to the origins of reality itself, we must start with a brute fact either way we look at it, and so we may have to throw all our normal suppositions out the window.

Third, the main objection is that this argument is based upon the *fallacy of composition*—reasoning fallaciously from the properties of the parts to the properties of the whole. The truth is that the whole is greater and can even be different than the sum of its parts. Christian theists argue that the things we experience all have causes; therefore they conclude the whole universe needs a cause. Sometimes we can reason this way and sometimes we can't. Here are some legitimate examples of this way of reasoning: Each block in this wall is a brick; therefore, this wall is made of bricks. All the states in the United States are located in the Northern Hemisphere; therefore, the United States is in the Northern Hemisphere. But consider instead these arguments: Each drink is good; therefore, a drink made of all drinks would be good. Or, individual basketball players are good; therefore, a team of them would be good. Or, every person here weighs less than three hundred pounds; therefore, together we weigh less than three hundred pounds. The point is that sometimes we can reason from the parts to the whole, and sometimes we can't. But there is no independent way to decide how we should view the universe. Is it more like a wall made of bricks, or a drink composed of all drinks?

In any case Felipe Leon informs us (via e-mail) "the PSR assumes that dependent beings must have their ultimate explanation in terms of 'necessarily existent' independent beings (who exist in all possible worlds), when in fact 'essentially' independent beings (who exist in all possible worlds 'in which they exist') are all that is needed to do the requisite explanatory work. The PSR entails that this isn't enough: if there are any essentially independent, indestructible, free-standing beings, then these beings must be further explained in terms of a necessarily existent being. But surely this is explanatory overkill, and since the PSR entails that a further explanation is required for the necessarily existent being, this epistemic possibility is an undercutting defeater for the PSR."

THE TELEOLOGICAL (OR DESIGN) ARGUMENT

Stated simply, the teleological (or design) argument argues that a designed universe demands a designer. We'll look at two areas: *cosmology* and *biochemical complexity*.[33]

First we'll look at cosmology and the anthropic principle. The anthropic principle states the fact that if the initial conditions at the big bang had been different from what they were, life as we know it could not have arisen. That is, human beings would not be here to wonder why it is the way it is, and that explains why we see the order that we do.[34]

If gravity were significantly stronger than it is, stars would exhaust their hydrogen fuels much faster, and human life could not appear where stars die young. Or if the strong force, which binds the nuclei of atoms together, were stronger, helium nuclei would dominate the universe, and no hydrogen would be left over. Without hydrogen there would be no water, and no life, as we know it. Had the rate of expansion of the big bang been different by one million millionths no life would have been possible. If the mass of a proton were increased by 0.2 percent, hydrogen would be unstable and life would not have formed. The earth is just the right distance from the sun, just the right size, with the right rotational speed, and with a special atmosphere allowing for life. The earth contains the proper amounts of metals and water-forming compounds. Other constants in the universe include the speed of light, the charge of the proton, the gravitational constant, Plank's constant, and so on. These examples can be multiplied, but the point is that "with a change in any one of a number of factors," then the "universe would have evolved as a lifeless, unconscious entity." Don Page of the Institute for Advanced Study in Princeton, New Jersey, calculated the odds against the formulation of our universe. "His exact computation was 10,000,000,000 to the 124th power, a number so large that to call it 'astronomical' would be to engage in a wild understatement."

Atheists object that there is nothing surprising at all about the fact that we find order in the universe, for if there wasn't, then we wouldn't be around to comment on it—we could not possibly find anything else. But theists like Richard Swinburne counter that the problem is "not that we perceive order rather than disorder, but that order rather than disorder is there. Maybe only if order is there can we know what is there, but that makes what is there no less extraordinary and in need of explanation."[35]

This fine-tuning argument, however, "has at least one fatal flaw," according to Victor J. Stenger. "It makes the wholly unwarranted assumption that only one type of life is possible—the particular form of carbon-based life we have on Earth. Even if this is an unlikely result of chance, some form of life could still be a likely result. It is like arguing that a particular card hand is so improbable that it must have been preordained."[36]

Richard Dawkins thinks it's strange that religious apologists love the anthropic principle. "For some reason that makes no sense at all, they think it supports their case. Precisely the opposite is true. The anthropic principle is the better alternative to the design hypothesis. It provides a rational, design-free explanation for the fact that we find ourselves in a situation propitious to our existence. What the religious mind fails to grasp is that two candidate solutions are offered to the problem. God is one. The anthropic principle is the other. They are *alternatives*. . . . It has been estimated that there are between 1 billion and 30 billion planets in our galaxy, and about 100 billion galaxies in the universe," so "a billion billion is a conservative estimate of the number of available planets in the universe." Therefore "even with such absurdly long odds, life will still have arisen on a billion planets—of which Earth, of course, is one." Once life has arisen, the principle of natural selection takes over, and "natural selection is emphatically not a matter of luck.[37]

The theistic answer to this objection posits a fully formed and completely ordered God as the answer to this ordered universe. This is an equally troublesome view. According to Richard Carrier, "Who rolled the dice that gave us our god, rather than some other god, or no god at all? Basically theism posits an extremely orderly being that just 'exists' for no reason at all." He goes on to explain how order comes from chaos, because when we roll the dice enough times, "the odds become very good that you will roll the exact orderly sequence of 1, 2, 3, 4, 5, 6. The odds against such a sequence are something like one in fifty thousand." So, he argues, "it follows that from chaos we can predict order, even incredibly complex order. But we have no comparable explanation for where an orderly god would come from, or why such an innate order would exist at all in a god, rather than a different order, or a chaos instead."[38] We'll come back to this argument later on when Dawkins says something stronger than this.

Have you ever stopped to think what exists outside of our universe, that is, what is beyond the known order of our universe? Presumably there can be no end to that which lies beyond our universe, if we can even speak of it this way. There are many conceptual problems in understanding what "nothing" is. The VOID is the area beyond space and time itself, and therefore any verbal description or mental image of it will be a terribly imperfect analogy at best. But for a lack of a better term, I'll call this nothingness the VOID (with capitals). How the VOID behaves is simply not known at all since it is nothing. We know it "exists," whatever that might mean, when speaking of nothing. But it is a well-founded supposition that the VOID is infinite—it has to be. How could it end, if we can even speak of it beginning? That thought is mind-boggling to me, and if you'll take a moment to think about it, then you too will be boggled by it. Never ending VOID! Infinite nothingness!

We do know about the laws of our universe. But what about the VOID? Is there any law in the VOID that prohibits something coming from nothing, or prohibiting a multitude of universes from existing without beginning? Who knows? If the VOID is "infinite," and we do not know its properties, then perhaps there may be up to an infinite number of universes. With such a number of universes (called a *multiverse*), other universes may have arisen just like ours inside black holes, although we are the only ones puzzled by this because it indeed looks initially improbable to have arisen out of blind chance, given one try. What is the possibility of our particular universe having arisen out of an infinite VOID where there may be up to an infinite number of universes each arising out of the VOID, and where there may be no ordered laws prohibiting something coming from nothing, or something existing without beginning? Who knows?

Some philosophers are now arguing that the answer to the age-old question "why is there something rather than nothing at all" can be answered scientifically. David Ramsay Steele questions why nonexistence is the default view. When it comes to explaining why there is something rather than nothing, he wrote: "It's unwarranted to suppose that nonexistence is more natural than existence. No good theory, physical or metaphysical, tells us to expect there to be nothing."[39] To be sure, there are some good arguments to suggest otherwise. Bede Rundle argues that "there had to be something."[40] Frank Wilczek answers that the reason why something exists is because "'nothing' is unstable."[41] Victor J. Stenger explains: "Since nothing is as simple as it gets, we cannot expect it to be very stable." Given the laws of nature, "the probability for there being something rather than nothing can actually be calculated; it is over 60 percent."[42] As such, "only by the constant action of an agent outside the universe, such as God, could a state of nothingness be maintained. The fact that we have something is just what we would expect if there is no God."[43]

In *Reason for the Hope Within*, Robin Collins lists and defends five independent reasons to reject any kind of many-universes hypothesis."[44] But to people like Collins, Dawkins simply says they "have not had their consciousness raised by natural selection."[45] Stenger argues that the existence of multiple universes "is consistent with all we know about physics and cosmology. . . . In fact, it takes an added hypothesis to rule them out—a super law of nature that says only one universe can exist. But we know of no such law." He continues, "The hundred billion galaxies of our visible universe, each with a hundred billion stars, is but a grain of sand on the Sahara that exists beyond our horizon, grown out of that single, original bubble of a false vacuum. An endless number of such bubbles can very well exist, each itself nothing but a grain of sand on the Sahara of all existence. On such a Sahara, nothing is too improbable to have happened by chance."[46] If this supposition is correct, the whole notion of God as an explanation of the universe isn't needed because there are a potentially infinite number of universes, and ours just happened to be the lucky one that resulted in us being here to wonder why we exist at all.[47]

We turn now to *biochemical complexity*. Fred Hoyle and N. C. Wickramasinghe maintain that the "usual theory of mutation and natural selection cannot produce complex biomolecules from random association of atoms." They point out that there are "ten to twenty distinct amino acids which determine the basic backbone of the enzyme" and that for the enzyme to form, these acids "must be in the correct position." They calculate the odds of creating one enzyme at 10^{20}. "The trouble," they argue, "is that there are about 2000 enzymes, and the chance of obtaining them all in a random trial is only one part in $10^{40,000}$, an outrageously small probability that could not be faced even if the whole universe consisted of organic soup." But this is only the beginning, for "nothing has been said of the origin of DNA itself, nothing of DNA transcription to RNA, and so on. These issues are too complex to set numbers to." But the chance for these biological systems being formed "through random shufflings of simple organic molecules is exceedingly minute, to a point where it is insensibly different from zero."[48]

The earlier defender of intelligent design was law professor Phillip E. Johnson.[49] Today there is Michael J. Behe and William A. Dembski, along with some others whose arguments have had no success in the scientific community.[50] There are several writers who are answering them, including Richard Dawkins, Daniel C. Dennett, Philip Kitcher, Matt Young, Taner Edis, Michael Shermer, and Mark Perakh, to name a few.[51] Victor J. Stenger simply argues that "DNA did not assemble purely by chance. It assembled by a combination of chance and the laws of physics."[52]

Michael J. Behe has argued that there is an irreducible element to even the simplest bodily functions. He compares complex biological phenomena like blood clotting to a mousetrap. If we take away any piece, like the spring or the baseboard, the mousetrap will not work. Similarly, if any one of the more than twenty proteins involved in blood clotting is missing or deficient, clots will not perform properly. Such all-or-nothing systems could not have arisen incrementally but had to be there all at once, so there must be an intelligent designer.

But according to H. Allen Orr, "Behe's colossal mistake is that, in rejecting these possibilities, he concludes that no Darwinian solution remains. But one does. It is this: An irreducibly complex system can be built gradually by adding parts that, while initially just advantageous, become—because of later changes—essential. The logic is very simple. Some part (A) initially does some job (and not very well, perhaps). Another part (B) later gets added because it helps A. This new part isn't essential, it merely improves things. But later on, A (or something else) may change in such a way that B now becomes indispensable. This process continues as further parts get folded into the system. And at the end of the day, many parts may all be required."[53] Dr. Joshua Sharp, an assistant research scientist at the University of Georgia, reminded me of the similarity of this process to scaffolding (via e-mail): "Much like building an arch, different parts are added with a scaffolding to hold them together and help them do their job. However, when a particular part is added, the scaffolding parts become unnecessary and are removed to save energy, much like the scaffolding of an arch can be removed after the keystone is placed."[54]

Natural selection is the organizing principle for evolution, where the environment selects those species and mutations that can survive in their given environment. Cesare Emiliani illustrates how efficient natural selection can be: "Imagine that you want to have the entire Bible typed by a wild monkey. What are the chances that such a monkey, typing at random, will come up with the Bible neatly typed without a single error? The English Bible (KJV) contains about 6 million letters. The chances of success, therefore, are 1 in 26 to the 6 millionth power, as there are 26 letters in the English alphabet. This is equal to 10 to the minus 8,489,840. I wouldn't exactly wait around. Suppose, however, that I introduce a control (the environment) that wipes out any wrong letter the monkey may type. Typing away at one letter per second and assuming an average of 13 errors per letter (half of 26), the monkey will produce the Bible in 13 x 6,000,000 seconds = 2.5 years. Not only that, but you are mathematically sure that the monkey will produce the Bible within that time and without a single error. What is utterly impossible has suddenly become not only possible but certain."[55]

Stating the odds as intelligent design (ID) theorists do is highly misleading since they presume that life *must* have turned out exactly as it has. All we are left with is rarity. But "rarity by itself shouldn't necessarily be evidence of anything. When one is dealt a bridge hand of thirteen cards, the probability of being dealt that particular hand is less than one in 600 billion. Still, it would be absurd for someone to be dealt a hand, examine it carefully, calculate that the probability of getting it is less than one in 600 billion, and then conclude that he must not have been dealt that very hand because it is so very improbable."[56]

The bottom line, according to John Hick, is that "when we look past ANY event into its antecedent conditions, their improbability multiplying backwards exponentially towards infinity, the event appears as endlessly improbable."[57] Whether or not such an event is improbable is purely notional, not objective. "There is no objective sense in which this is either more or less probable than any other possible universe. The only reality is the actual course of the universe, with ourselves as part of it." Given any event, it is improbable that it occurred at all when one considers the antecedent conditions required for its occurrence. "The antecedent improbability of an individual being conceived who is precisely me is thus already quite staggering— truly astronomical." My great-great-grandparents had to meet and marry, and one sperm penetrated one egg to form one of my parents, who met and married a spouse, who raised me the way they did plus all of the experiences and thoughts that make up who I am today. According to Hick, "And the same kind of calculation applies to everyone and everything else in the universe." So for any two people who meet and have a conversation, the odds of them meeting and speaking the exact words they do to one another, being dressed as they are, is quite literally impossible from the standpoint of just one hundred years ago. But it happened!

Furthermore, Sam Harris reminds us that "examples of unintelligent design in nature are so numerous that an entire book could be written simply listing them."[58] I consider all of the natural evils in our world to be evidence of unintelligent design (these are spelled out in chapters 12 and 13 in this book). Karen Bartelt specifies a few of them with regard to the design of the human body by saying, "If we assume that Behe is correct, and that humans can discern design, then I submit that they can also discern poor design (we sue companies for this all the time!). In *Darwin's Black Box*, Behe refers to design as the 'purposeful arrangement of parts.' What about when the 'parts' aren't purposeful, by any standard engineering criteria? When confronted with the 'All-Thumbs Designer'—whoever designed the spine, the birth canal, the prostate gland, the back of the throat, etc.—Behe and the ID people retreat into theology. That God can do whatever he wants, or we're not competent to judge intelligence by God's standards, or being an intelligent designer does not mean being a good or perfect designer."[59]

Richard Swinburne claims that in a typical argument there are certain phenomena that call for an explanation. If a scientific (nonpersonal) explanation fails to do justice to the phenomena, it is natural to conclude that we must seek an explanation in terms of the intentional action of some rational agent; that is, God in this case.[60] But a personal explanation in a self-existent eternal triune God of the Bible doesn't do justice to the phenomena in question at all.

Divine Simplicity, Necessity, and the Nature of God

My aim here is to poke holes in the arguments that show God exists, and I've done that. But I'm not certain God doesn't exist. Some kind of designer God might possibly exist. I just don't think so. As James F. Sennett has said, "If you don't believe in God and the Argument from Design doesn't keep you up at night, then you don't understand it."[61] After all, this was the same argument that had convinced an Alzheimer's affected Antony Flew to become a deist after being the leading atheist thinker of the last century.

Dawkins, however, thinks he can do better than merely to say it's improbable that God exists. In his bestselling book *The God Delusion*, he offers his Ultimate Boeing 747 gambit, which, if "properly deployed, comes close to proving that God does not exist." He writes, "however statistically improbable the entity you seek to explain by invoking a designer, the designer himself has got to be at least as improbable. God is the Ultimate Boeing 747."[62]

Alvin Plantinga explains what Dawkins means in these words: "Dawkins says a designer must contain at least as much information as what it creates or designs, and information is inversely related to probability. Therefore, he thinks, God would have to be monumentally complex, hence astronomically improbable; thus it is almost certain that God does not exist."[63] Plantinga faults Dawkins for thinking evolution by natural selection disproves God's existence, when what Dawkins has actually done is to argue that God doesn't exist because he thinks evolution is unguided. Dawkins argues that even if God existed, he could not guide the process of evolution. Of course, if evolution is unguided, then God doesn't exist. Whether or not God exists needs to be argued philosophically, Plantinga argues, and that's something I've done here. I've concluded the arguments are inconclusive at best.

Contrary to Dawkins, Plantinga argues that God is not a complex being. He argues that God is a simple being. Plantinga wrote *Does God Have a Nature*, in which he examines the issue in scholarly detail.[64] What can be said about Plantinga's argument? In the first place, it's very difficult to see how a triune God is not a complex being since we're talking about Christian theism here. Richard Swinburne has admitted that "all arguments to the existence of God derive their force, in my view, from their ability to explain the orderly complexity of our world as deriving from a single source of being. To suppose that there were two or more sources of being, neither of which was dependent on the other, would deprive such arguments of their force." In order to meet this problem head on, Swinburne argues for the Nicene subordination doctrine of the Trinity.[65] He claims that a first God could eternally "create" a second and even a third God, who "proceeds" from the first God, but that there was no reason to eternally create any other Gods since love would be complete in three Gods and no more. He concludes that "if there is at least one God, then there are three and only three Gods" since "there is something profoundly imperfect and therefore inadequately divine in a solitary God." Swinburne's view is but one form of the "social Trinitarian model" of the Trinity. I don't think any account of the Trinity is plausible for the Christian, and that includes Swinburne's understanding (see note).[66] I find Swinburne's scenario wildly implausible and guided more by what he thinks the Bible says than by any philosophical reasoning. The bottom line is that no matter how an orthodox triune God is conceived, this is not a simple being.

The doctrine of divine simplicity is one that has been hotly disputed over the centuries by theologians who argue anywhere from extreme realism to nominalism.

As Plantinga admits, discussions about such a doctrine get "pretty complicated, not to say arcane." The full-blown doctrine of divine simplicity states that God is not divisible into separate parts. The attributes of God are not parts that together make up who God is, for God has no parts. For instance, God does not have properties like goodness or truth. Rather, God is goodness and truth. But since God's nature is described in the Bible as having various attributes, or properties, like love, goodness, justice, knowledge, and wisdom, such a view is problematic. The first problem is how human beings could ever know such a being. We could never know an absolutely simple essence since the finite cannot comprehend the infinite. The Christian answer is that through revelation God divides himself into parts so we can understand him. However, this answer still means we cannot know who God really is. He may actually be like the ineffable god of Eastern thinkers, which Huston Smith argues for.[67] Other problems arise. On the one hand, if God is identical to his properties, then God must be a property. On the other hand, if God isn't identical with his properties, then he is either bound by these independently existing properties (extreme realism) or he doesn't have a nature and can change his properties at will (nominalism). There are several Christian attempts to escape these extremes, notably René Descartes, who argued that although God has properties he does not possess them essentially; contemporary nominalists, who argue that God doesn't have a nature simply because there are no properties (that is, there is no such thing as the property of omniscience); and especially Thomas Aquinas's classic answer that God is identical with his nature.

Plantinga takes issue with these attempts to understand divine simplicity. Against Aquinas, for instance, if each of God's properties is identical with all of the rest of God's properties, then God has only one property (God's knowledge is the same as God's goodness, for instance). And if that's so, how can God be a person? Plantinga's answer to this problem is to say that all abstract properties exist necessarily and yet they are dependent upon God because God eternally affirms these properties. Plantinga doesn't claim to have solved this particular problem, but he thinks he's pointing people in the right direction. I, however, don't see how his answer solves anything at all, for it just creates a different dilemma. What if God chose not to affirm these properties? Then what? Would they still exist necessarily? Can he choose not to affirm them? If he cannot, then he is bound by them. If he can, then he has no nature.[68]

For these reasons J. P. Moreland and William Lane Craig reject "a full blown doctrine of divine simplicity," and favor instead a "modified doctrine," in two ways.[69] In the first way, with Plantinga, they think God is simple in that he "is pure mind." That indeed is simpler if we could just understand what a "pure mind" is, and it still leaves the problem of the Trinity unresolved. In the second way, God is simple in the sense that God has "a simple intuition of all reality, which we human cognizers represent to ourselves propositionally. . . . We finite knowers break God's undivided intuition into separate ideas." But if this is the case, we are back to square one, for how can we claim to know God? Moreover, now we have the problem of what it means for God not to have propositional "knowledge." So we still have no reason to think we understand God since he purportedly revealed himself propositionally in the Bible. Craig and Moreland admit that such a view "deserves further exploration by Christian thinkers," which simply means there isn't yet a satisfactory answer to understanding God as a simple being.

Besides, when it comes to human minds, there are brilliant, knowledgeable minds and childish or simplistic minds. Complex minds have a great deal of knowledge, while simple minds have little by comparison. This is primarily what we're talking about here anyway. How did God gain his knowledge? Where did he learn it? Does he know everything about himself as well?

Continuing on, Plantinga next concedes for the sake of argument the possibility that God isn't simple. Even if this is so, Plantinga informs us that God is a necessary being according to classical theology. Therefore, "if Dawkins proposes that God's existence is improbable, he owes us an argument for the conclusion that there is no necessary being with the attributes of God. . . . Dawkins doesn't even seem to be aware that he needs an argument of that sort." Here Plantinga makes a good point. Whether Dawkins is aware of this I cannot say.

The idea that God is a necessary being expresses the notion that God cannot not exist. It is impossible for God not to exist. There are discussions about whether God is a *logically necessary being*, who exists in every possible world, or a *factually necessary being*, who does not exist in every possible world but who exists eternally as an uncaused, eternal, and independently existing being in this particular world, in which everything else is dependent upon him. The idea of a necessary being is the conclusion of the ontological argument, which I've addressed briefly earlier. This argument doesn't appear to succeed at all. If none of the arguments for the existence of God succeed, then neither is it true that God exists, no matter what one thinks about him or how one defines him. I have concluded that at best the arguments are inconclusive, and at worst they are wrong. Furthermore, it probably does no good to think necessary existence is something that defines God, a person, since necessary existence may only apply to abstract concepts, not concrete objects. Abstract concepts, like truth, goodness, and justice, seem to be entirely different. In any case, the debate rages on.[70]

If the arguments for the existence of God are indeed inconclusive, then we have every right to consider how it is that a being such as God might exist. We must start with what we know. And we know that order arises out of chance. This is what we see. This is what we know. Based upon what we know and denying the validity of the arguments for the existence of God, we can ask how it is that God exists. It is difficult to see how positing the existence of God is any better as an answer for our existence.

Who Made God?

My friend Dr. Paul Copan, a former student of Dr. Craig's, tries to answer the million-dollar question, "If God Made the Universe, Who Made God?"[71] Let's take a brief look.

Copan argues that "the theist does not claim that whatever exists must have a cause, but whatever begins to exist must have a cause. . . . We must begin with a non-question-begging starting point" and this "does just that." Such a starting point, he says, "does not automatically entail that God created the universe," for then the question to explore is "whether the cause is personal or impersonal." But without such a starting point, he argues, the skeptic is "assuming what one wants to prove." It's like arguing that "all reality is physical; therefore God can't exist." Furthermore, Copan argues that God is in a different category than the universe. God is "the self-existent, uncaused Cause, who is by definition unmakeable," and so the answers that the Christian provides for such a God do not apply to the universe. In other words, the "brute fact" of the universe needs some explaining that God, being eternal and uncreated, does not need.

There are at least three responses to his argument. First, it's question begging to assume God is in a different "category" than the universe as the one exception to that which needs explaining, especially one who never had a beginning as a fully formed eternally uncaused self-existent personal three-in-one being. Such a Christian concept of God has its own problems as I'm arguing. Christians like Copan say the universe needs an explanation. I say their explanation has insurmountable problems on its own terms. Second, even if I agree with Copan's non-question-begging starting point, I can still turn around and argue with Lee Smolin that baby universes are born out of black holes within other universes in a process that stretches back into infinity.[72] Lastly, it can be argued that this is an odd argument. Whenever it comes to unexplainable "brute facts," we reach an impasse. We all must begin with something that exists as a "brute fact." Since this is the case, agnosticism is the default intellectual position. When leaving the default position, Christians must have reasons for struggling up the ladder to a full-blown Christianity, past pantheism, deism, Judaism, and Islam. Me? It's just easier to move in the direction agnosticism already pushes me toward, atheism.

In a video on YouTube ("Dr. William Lane Craig Responds to Dawkins' Book"), Dr. Craig answers the question "Who designed the designer?" He did so in the following manner: "In order to recognize an explanation is the best you don't have to have an explanation of the explanation." He gave the example of archaeologists who found some arrowheads and inferred someone made them. This is a reasonable conclusion, Craig said, even though the archaeologists may not be able to explain who made the arrowheads or how they got there. But his example is a nonanalogous one, for as I've just argued, rarity, by itself, doesn't prove design when it comes to why something—anything—exists. And it doesn't follow that the archaeologists need not explain who or what made the arrowheads, either. They aren't done with their job until they do. So, even if we grant Craig his example, the default position is still agnosticism concerning who made them unless there is evidence to prefer one explanation over another.

Christians claim the upper hand by definition, but that's all they're doing. They define God in such a way that the definition solves problems that the alternative theory doesn't have. But just by defining such a supreme being as one who necessarily exists doesn't mean such a being actually exists. There isn't much by way of evidence that he does. We know this universe exists. Ockham's razor tells us the simplest explanation is the better one. God needs an explanation despite the definition.

The God of the Bible

The arguments for God's existence are supposed to lead us to a supreme being, known as God. But as I've suggested, even if the arguments have some force to them, and there is plenty of room for doubting this, then such a conclusion doesn't lead us to the specific view of the Trinitarian God of the Bible. Such a God may have gone out of existence after creating this as his last act. This God might be composed of a committee of intelligences, as David Hume wondered. He may not have much power. He may not be very smart. He might not even care about us.[73] This God would be known as the philosopher's god. He would be an explanation for the existence of this world; that's all. A distant God. But if that's all these arguments lead us to, then a distant God is not much different than no God at all!

One thing is sure to me. The Triune God in the Bible simply cannot be describing the God who exists. I find it implausible to believe that a Triune (3 persons in 1?) God has always and forever existed (what's the likelihood of even one eternal God-person?) and will always and forever exist (even though our entire experience is that everything has a beginning and an ending) as a fully formed being (even though our entire experience is that order grows incrementally) who knows all true propositions (and consequently never learned any new ones), with all power (but doesn't exercise it like we would if we saw a burning child), and who is present everywhere (who also knows what time it is everywhere in our universe even though time is a function of movement and bodily placement, and if timeless, God cannot act in time). How is it possible for this being to think (thinking involves weighing alternatives), make choices, take risks, or even freely choose who he is and what his values are?

Most Christians do not believe in the God of the Bible anyway, despite what they claim. Instead, they believe in the perfect being of St. Anselm in the eleventh century after centuries of theological gerrymandering. The Bible isn't consistent in describing its God, but one probable description is as follows: Rather than creating the universe ex nihilo, God fashioned the earth to rise out of the seas in divine conflict with the dragon sea god sometimes called Rahab (in Job 26:9–12). This God is merely the "god of the gods," who like the other gods had a body that needed to rest on the seventh day and was found walking in the "cool of the day" in the Garden of Eden. Yahweh, the god of Israel, probably emerged out of a polytheistic amalgamation of gods known in the ancient Near East in prebiblical times. In the ancient Near East, all pantheons were organized as families, and Yahweh was simply one of the members of that family. Some biblical authors consider Yahweh, the god of Israel, as one of many gods fathered by Elyon whose wife was Asherah,[74] to whom was given the people and land of Israel to rule over (Deut. 32:8).[75] This God was responsible for doing both good and evil, sending evil spirits to do his will and commanding genocide. As time went on, Yahweh was believed to be the only God that existed. Still later, Satan was conceived as an evil rival in order to exonerate Yahweh from being the creator of evil. Still later, in the New Testament the God of the Bible was stripped of physical characteristics and known as a spiritual being. As later theologians reflected on their God, they came to believe he created the universe ex nihilo. Anselm finally defined him as the "greatest conceivable being." But Anslem's God is at odds with what we find in most of the Bible.

Regardless, the biblical God is a hateful, racist, and sexist God. Consider the following things: In the Flood story we're told God wanted to destroy all mankind. In Moses's day God wanted to destroy all of the Israelites. In Joshua's day God wanted the Israelites to kill all of the inhabitants of the Promised Land. Saul was purportedly told by God to obliterate the Amalekites (1 Sam. 15:3), while later we find God is pleased with anyone who would dash Babylonian babies against the rocks (Ps. 137:9). According to Jonah, God was going to destroy the people of Nineveh. God also destroyed and scattered the northern tribes of Israel because he was displeased with them. God allowed Satan, the accuser, to destroy Job's health and family life just to win a "bet." In the New Testament, God will destroy all unbelievers in the lake of fire. He's a pretty barbaric God, if you ask me. This God is simply the reflection of ancient barbaric peoples.

God decreed that a man who picked up sticks on the Sabbath day was to be stoned to death (Num. 15:32–36). God commanded that anyone who curses his father or mother was to be put to death (Exod. 21:17). Witches, and those of differing religious views, were to be killed (Exod. 22:18, 20). These are pretty stiff punishments, eh? Christians think militant Muslims are wrong for wanting to kill free-loving people in the world, and they are. But the only difference between these Muslims and the biblical God is that they simply disagree on who should be killed. They both agree people should be killed; they just disagree on who should die.

This God declared that a slave is the property of another man (Exod. 21:21). A female captive in war was forced to be an Israelite man's wife (Deut. 21:10–14). If a virgin who was pledged to be married was raped, she was to be stoned along with her rapist (Deut. 22:23–24), while if a virgin who was not pledged to be married was raped, she was supposed to marry her rapist (Deut. 22:28–29). God commanded men to divorce their foreign wives for no other reason but that they were not God's people (Ezra 9), and women were helpless if they weren't married in those days.

God asked Abraham to kill and sacrifice his son Isaac. If we heard a voice today telling us to do that, we would not think this voice was God's, although Abraham wasn't horrified at the suggestion. *Enough!* According to Sam Harris, "it is only by ignoring such barbarisms that the Good Book can be reconciled with life in the modern world." (see note)[76]

As Thomas Paine wrote in his classic *The Age of Reason*: "Are we sure that the Creator of man commissioned these things to be done? And are we sure that the books that tell us so were written by His authority? . . . To believe, therefore, the Bible to be true, we must unbelieve all our belief in the moral justice of God; . . . And to read the Bible without horror, we must undo everything that is tender, sympathizing, and benevolent in the heart of man. Speaking for myself, if I had no other evidence that the

Bible is fabulous than the sacrifice I must make to believe it to be true, that alone would be sufficient to determine my choice."[77]

Ludwig Feuerbach is surely right. God did not make us in his image; human beings made God in their image.

NOTES

1. William Lane Craig, "Must the Beginning of the Universe Have a Personal Cause? A Rejoinder," *Faith and Philosophy* 19, no. 2 (April 2002).

2. Quentin Smith, "The Reason That the Universe Exists Is That It Caused Itself to Exist," *Philosophy* 74 (1999): 579–86.

3. See, Leo Tolstoy, *A Confession and the Gospel in Brief*, trans. Aylmer Maude (Oxford: Oxford University Press, 1921).

4. Paul Vitz, *Faith of the Fatherless: The Psychology of Atheism* (Dallas: Spence, 2000).

5. Besides other books that I quote from in this chapter, see also the following three books: Richard Gale, *On the Nature and Existence of God* (Cambridge: Cambridge University Press, 1993); Graham Oppy, *Arguing about Gods* (Cambridge: Cambridge University Press, 2006), and especially Nicholas Everitt, *The Non-existence of God* (New York: Routledge, 2003).

6. For a detailed survey and critique of the various ontological arguments, see Graham Oppy, *Ontological Arguments and Belief in God* (Cambridge: Cambridge University Press, 1995).

7. Robert Paul Wolff, *About Philosophy*, 7th ed. (Upper Saddle River, NJ: Prentice-Hall, 1998), pp. 284ff.

8. Todd M. Furman, "In Praise of Hume," in *In Defense of Natural Theology: A Post Humean Assessment*, ed. James F. Sennett and Douglas Groothuis (Downers Grove, IL: InterVarsity Press, 2005), p. 45.

9. Quoted from Furman, "In Praise of Hume," p. 45. Paul Copan deals with what is known as "Hume's fork" by arguing that Hume's distinction between "relations of ideas" and "matters of fact" is "self-referentially incoherent" in "Hume and the Moral Argument," later in that same book (p. 208), although Furman claims Hume's criticism of Anselm's argument "seems to me to be right on target."

10. Anthony Kenny, *The God of the Philosophers* (Oxford: Oxford University Press, 1987).

11. See Clark Pinnock et al., *The Openness of God* (Downers Grove, IL: InterVarsity Press, 1994). See also my chapter 16.

12. Paul Helm, "God and Spacelessness," *Philosophy* 55 (1980).

13. To see the problems inherent in some of the divine attributes, see Joshua Hoffman and Gary S. Rosenkrantz, *The Divine Attributes* (London: Blackwell, 2002).

14. Toni Vogel Carey, "The Ontological Argument and the Sin of Hubris," *Philosophy Now*, December 2005.

15. When it comes to Alvin Plantinga's formulation of the ontological argument, John Hick argues that "the reasoning looks suspiciously like an attempt to prove divine existence by definitional fiat," and he believes that the suspicion is justified. "Plantinga's argument for a maximally excellent being, if valid, would also work for a maximally evil being." But since the ontological argument can be used to prove that two mutually exclusive beings both exist, the reasoning itself is faulty. John Hick, *An Interpretation of Religion* (New Haven, CT: Yale University Press, 1989), pp. 78–79.

16. To trace the history of cosmological arguments see W. L. Craig, *The Cosmological Argument from Plato to Lebniz* (New York: Macmillan, 1980). In the atheist literature there are actually cosmological arguments *against* the existence of God, which are compiled in part 1 of the book *The Improbability of God*, ed. Michael Martin and Ricki Monnier (Amherst, NY: Prometheus Books, 2006).

17. Ed L. Miller, *Questions That Matter: An Invitation to Philosophy*, 4th ed. (New York: McGraw-Hill, 1984), p. 285.

18. Michael Peterson et al., *Reason and Religious Belief* (Oxford: Oxford University Press, 1991), p. 76.

19. Miller, *Questions That Matter*, p. 286.

20. Michael Martin, *Atheism: A Philosophical Justification* (Philadelphia: Temple University Press, 1990), pp. 97–100.

21. J. L. Mackie, *The Miracle of Theism* (Oxford: Clarendon, 1982), p. 92.

22. Hick, *An Interpretation of Religion*, p. 80. Thomistic type arguments are defended by Brian Davies in *An Introduction to the Philosophy of Religion* (Oxford: Oxford University Press, 1993), pp. 80–93; Norman Geisler in *Christian Apologetics* (Grand Rapids, MI: Baker Book House, 1976), pp. 237–58; and Bruce Reichenbach in *The Cosmological Argument: A Reassessment* (Springfield: Charles Thomas, 1972).

23. See William Lane Craig, *The Kalam Cosmological Argument* (London: Macmillian, 1979); J. P. Moreland, *Scaling the Secular City: A Defense of Christianity* (Grand Rapids, MI: Baker Book House, 1987); and Paul Copan and William Lane Craig, *Creation Out of Nothing: A Biblical, Philosophical, and Scientific Exploration* (Grand Rapids, MI: Baker Academic Books, 2004).

24. Mackie, *The Miracle of Theism*, pp. 92–95; and Martin, *Atheism: A Philosophical Justification*, pp. 101–106.

25. William Lane Craig and Quentin Smith, *Theism, Atheism, and Big Bang Cosmology* (Oxford: Oxford University Press, 1993); and Mark Nowacki, *The Kalam Cosmological Argument for God* (Amherst, NY: Prometheus Books, 2007).

26. See Wes Morriston, "Must the Beginning of the Universe Have a Personal Cause? A Critical Examination of the Kalam Cosmological Argument," *Faith and Philosophy* 17, no. 2 (2000): 149–69; Craig's reply: "Must the Beginning of the Universe Have a Personal Cause? A Rejoinder"; and Morriston's counterreply, "Causes and Beginnings in the Kalam Argument: Reply to Craig," *Faith and Philosophy* 19, no. 2 (April 2002): 233–44. All three essays can be found on the Web.

27. Carrier reports that even Craig acknowledges this point, and thus attempts to reinterpret relativity theory against the usual scientific consensus in his book *Time and the Metaphysics of Relativity* (Boston: Kluwer Academic, 2001). Craig has recently recruited atheist Quentin Smith and a few other philosophers (and even some theoretical physicists) in attempting to defend his reinterpretation of relativity theory in *Einstein, Relativity and Absolute Simultaneity* (New York: Routledge, 2008), though they all acknowledge they are arguing against the current scientific consensus. For more on Carrier's views he has an interesting discussion of time found in his book *Sense and Goodness without God* (Bloomington, IN: Authorhouse, 2005), pp. 84–95. Also go to www.richardcarrier.blogspot.com and do a search for "The Ontology of Time."

28. David Ramsay Steele, *Atheism Explained: From Folly to Philosophy* (Peru, IL: Open Court, 2008), p. 76.

29. Richard Gale explains by distinguishing between the numerical sense of infinity, where "a set is bigger than another if it has a greater number of members," and the part-to-

whole sense of infinity, where "a whole is bigger than any proper part." He writes: "When dealing with finite quantities, anything that is bigger in the part-to-whole sense is also bigger in the numerical sense. But this is not so in the case of infinite quantities. Although in the part-to-whole sense there are more people in (Hilbert's) hotel after a new guest arrives . . . in the numerical sense there are not. Indeed, mathematicians take the failure of the part-to-whole sense . . . to imply the numerical sense to be the defining feature of infinity." Richard M. Gale, in "The Failure of Classical Theistic Arguments," in *The Cambridge Companion to Atheism*, ed. Michael Martin (Cambridge: Cambridge University Press, 2007), p. 93. See also Wes Morriston, "Must the Past Have a Beginning?" *Philo* 2, no. 1 (1999): 5–19; his "Craig On the Actual Infinite," *Religious Studies*, no. 38 (2002): 147–66; and Paul Draper, "A Critique of the Kalam Cosmological Argument," in *Philosophy of Religion: An Anthology*, 4th ed., ed. Louis P. Pojman (Belmont, CA: Wadsworth, 2002). Craig is aware of these kinds of problems, but I don't think he successfully answers them.

30. Edward Tryon in *Nature* (December 1973), and Stephen Hawking in *Physical Review* (December 1983).

31. James F. Sennett describes my type of objection as "Hume's Stopper," in "Hume's Stopper and the Natural Theology Project," in Sennett and Groothuis, *In Defense of Natural Theology: A Post Humean Assessment*, pp. 82–104. Sennett basically argued against this move of mine, as I follow Hume, by utilizing a cumulative case for the existence of a theistic God based upon the conclusions of the various theistic arguments for the existence of God. He suggests these separate theistic arguments, assuming they are all correct, lead to several candidate gods, and that the theistic God is the best candidate when these gods are compared, contrasted, and scrutinized. But there is something I think Sennett fails to realize about the theistic concept of God. I believe this particular concept of God evolved over time beginning with an embodied god from polytheism, to a spiritual being who has all the perfections of Anselmian theology. As this concept of God evolved, it picked up the best ideas Western people could conceptualize. So it's no surprise that these Western theistic arguments cumulatively lead to that very conception of God, the best one that they could imagine. And it's no surprise what they conclude, if we grant that they all work, which I don't! Theistic arguments are conceived for the express purpose of concluding that such a God exists in the first place. Oriental conceptions of a deity are excluded by Sennett out of hand because they are not personal beings. Yet, as I'm arguing here, there is nothing about theistic arguments that necessarily lead us to think a personal God follows from these arguments. Still, my main point is that even if we grant that a designing creator exists, this at best leads to the "god of the philosophers," the deistic God, and that God is far removed from the Christian God of the Bible.

32. Richard Taylor, *Metaphysics*, 4th ed. (Englewood Cliffs, NJ: Prentice-Hall, 1992).

33. I have been helped extensively here by L. Stafford Betty with Bruce Cordell, "The Anthropic Teleological Argument," *International Quarterly* 27, no. 4 (December 1987), who argued on behalf of a designer God.

34. On this see John D. Barrow and Frank J. Tipler, *The Anthropic Cosmological Principle* (Oxford: Oxford University Press, 1988). This principle comes in several varieties and is difficult to grasp and to understand, as seen in Martin Gardner's essay, "WAP, SAP, FAP and PAP," *New York Review of Books*, May 8, 1987. He distinguishes the *Weak Anthropic Principle* (WAP), the *Strong Anthropic Principle* (SAP), the *Future Anthropic Principle* (FAP), the *Participatory Anthropic Principle* (PAP), and the *Completely Ridiculous Anthropic Principle*.

35. Richard Swinburne, *The Existence of God* (Oxford: Oxford University Press, 1979), p. 138.

36. Victor J. Stenger, "Anthropic Design," in *Science and Religion: Are they Compatible?* ed. Paul Kurtz (Amherst, NY: Prometheus Books, 2003), p. 43.

37. Richard Dawkins, *The God Delusion* (Boston: Houghton Mifflin, 2006), pp. 134–41.

38. Carrier, *Sense and Goodness without God*, pp. 86–87.

39. Steele, *Atheism Explained: From Folly to Philosophy*, p. 86.

40. Bede Rundle, *Why Is There Something Rather Than Nothing?* (Oxford: Clarendon, 2004).

41. Frank Wilczek, "The Cosmic Asymmetry between Matter and Antimatter," *Scientific American* 243, no. 6 (1980): 82–90.

42. Stenger, *God: The Failed Hypothesis*, pp. 132–33. See also Stenger's *The Comprehensible Cosmos: Where Do the Laws of Physics Come From?* (Amherst, NY: Prometheus Books, 2006), supplement H.

43. Ibid.

44. Collins claimed we should have independent evidence for it; the "many-universes generator" still needs a designer; it still doesn't explain how the laws of physics came about randomly; it cannot explain the design of things like beauty; and it goes against the law of entropy. Michael J. Murray, ed., *Reason for the Hope Within* (Grand Rapids, MI: Eerdmans, 1999), pp. 60–64.

45. Dawkins, *The God Delusion*, p. 146.

46. Stenger, "Anthropic Design," p. 45.

47. Paul Davies argues for this in *God and the New Physics* (New York: Pelican Books, 1984); see also Carrier's book *Sense and Goodness without God*, pp. 71–95.

48. Fred Hoyle and N. C. Wickramasinghe, *Evolution from Space: A Theory of Cosmic Creationism* (New York: Simon & Schuster, 1981), p. 24.

49. Philip Johnson, *Darwin on Trial* (Washington, DC: Regnery, 1991). But see what Nancey Murphy said about his lame arguments in "Phillip Johnson on Trial: A Critique of His Critique of Darwin," *Perspectives on Science and Christian Faith* 45, no. 1 (March 1993): 26–36.

50. Michael Behe, *Darwin's Black Box: The Biochemical Challenge to Evolution* (New York: Simon & Schuster, 1996); William A. Dembski and Michael Ruse, eds., *Debating Design: From Darwin to DNA* (Cambridge: Cambridge University Press, 2004); and William A. Dembski, *The Design Revolution: Answering the Toughest Questions about Intelligent Design* (Downers Grove, IL: InterVarsity Press, 2004); For a theological debate over intelligent design and creationism, see J. P. Moreland and John Reynolds, eds., *Three Views on Creation and Evolution* (Grand Rapids, MI: Zondervan, 1999).

51. Richard Dawkins, *The Blind Watchmaker: Why the Evidence of Evolution Reveals a Universe without Design* (New York: Norton, 1996); Richard Dawkins, *Climbing Mount Improbable* (New York: Norton, 1997); Daniel C. Dennett, *Darwin's Dangerous Idea: Evolution and the Meanings of Life* (New York: Simon & Schuster; 1996); Philip Kitcher, *Living with Darwin: Evolution, Design, and the Future of Faith* (Oxford: Oxford University Press, 2006); Matt Young and Taner Edis, *Why Intelligent Design Fails: A Scientific Critique of the New Creationism* (New Brunswick, NJ: Rutgers University Press, 2004); Michael Shermer, *Why Darwin Matters: The Case against Intelligent Design* (New York: Times Books, 2006); Mark Perakh, *Unintelligent Design* (Amherst, NY: Prometheus Books, 2003).

52. Victor J. Stenger, at www.talkorigins.org. Stenger has several books that are must reading on these topics. See his book *God: The Failed Hypothesis*.

53. H. Allen Orr, "Darwin v. Intelligent Design (Again)," *Boston Review* (December 1996/January 1997). See also http://bostonreview.mit.edu/.

54. In personal correspondence. He didn't originate this argument. He has helped me with this section of my chapter, for which I'm grateful. Any errors are mine.

55. Cesare Emiliani, *The Scientific Companion: Exploring the Physical World with Facts, Figures, and Formulas* (New York: Wiley, 1995), p. 149.

56. John Allen Paulos, *Innumeracy: Mathematical Illiteracy and Its Consequences* (New York: Hill and Wang, 2001).

57. Hick, *An Interpretation of Religion*, p. 89.

58. Sam Harris, *Letter to a Christian Nation* (New York: Knopf, 2006), p. 78.

59. In Karen Bartlet, "A Central Illinois Scientist Responds to the Black Box," http://www.reall.org/newsletter/v07/n12/index.html. On unintelligent design, see also S. Jay Olshansky, Bruce Carnes, and Robert N. Butler, "If Humans Were Built to Last," *Scientific American*, March 2001.

60. See Swinburne, *The Existence of God*, p. 20.

61. James F. Sennett, *This Much I Know: A Postmodern Apologetic* (unpublished).

62. Dawkins, *The God Delusion*, pp. 113–14, 147.

63. Alvin Plantinga, "The Dawkins Confusion: Naturalism ad Absurdum," *Books and Culture* (March/April 2007), http://www.christianitytoday.com:80/bc/2007/002/1.21.html.

64. Alvin Plantinga, *Does God Have a Nature?* (Milwaukee: Marquette University Press, 1980).

65. Richard Swinburne, "Could There Be More Than One God? *Faith and Philosophy* 5, no. 3 (July 1988): 225–41. Reformed thinkers like John Calvin and Benjamin Warfield argued for Trinitarian *autotheos*, in that the Son and the Spirit do not derive their being from the Father but are God in and of themselves. See Paul Helm, *John Calvin's Ideas* (Oxford: Oxford University Press, 2006), pp. 35–57.

66. Social trinitarianism stresses the diversity of persons within the Trinity, while anti–social trinitarianism stresses the unity of the Godhead. According to William Lane Craig and J. P. Moreland, "Social trinitarianism threatens to veer into tritheism (three gods); anti–social trinitarianism is in danger of lapsing into unitarianism (one God with no distinct persons in the Godhead)." *Philosophical Foundations for a Christian Worldview* (Downers Grove, IL: InterVarsity Press), p. 583. Craig and Moreland criticize Swinburne's view by arguing that "the Father's begetting the Son amounts to creation *ex nihilo* (creation out of nothing), which . . . makes the Son a creature." However, without this causal dependence of the Father to the Son and Holy Spirit, "then we are stuck with the surprising and inexplicable fact that there just happen to exist three divine beings all sharing the same nature, which seems incredible" (p. 588).

A second form of social trinitarianism is known as the "group mind" theory, in which the Trinity is "a mind that is composed of the minds of the three persons in the Godhead." Craig and Moreland tell us the specific problem they attempt to deal with: "if such a model is to be theologically acceptable, the mind of the Trinity cannot be a self-conscious self in addition to the three self-conscious selves who are the Father, the Son, and Holy Spirit, for otherwise we have not a Trinity but a Quaternity, so to speak" (p. 588).

The third form of social trinitarianism is called "Trinity monotheism," Moreland and Craig inform us, which "holds that while the persons of the Trinity are divine, it is the Trinity as a whole that is properly God." The problem with this view they attempt to deal with is that if it is to be considered as "orthodox," "it must hold that the Trinity alone is God and that the Father, Son, and Holy Spirit, while divine, are not Gods" (p. 589). For an excellent critique of social trinitarianism, which has become the dominant evangelical model for trinitarian models, see Brian Leftow's "Anti-social Trinitarianism," in *The Trinity*, ed. Stephen T. Davis, Daniel Kendal, and Gerold O'Collins (Oxford: Oxford University Press, 1999). Leftow's main point is that social trinitarianism "cannot be both orthodox and a version of monotheism" (p. 203). Moreland and Craig argue that anti–social trinitarianism reduces to unitarianism. I agree with both of these criticisms, leaving us with no plausible understanding of the Trinity.

67. Huston Smith, *Why Religion Matters* (New York: HarperSanFranscisco, 2001), pp. 213–33.

68. For helpful nontechnical discussions of divine simplicity, see Ronald Nash, *The Concept of God* (Grand Rapids, MI: Zondervan, 1983), pp. 85–98, and Thomas Morris, *Our Idea of God* (Downers Grove, IL: InterVarsity Press, 1991), pp. 113–18. Both Nash and Morris have a great difficulty even accepting the doctrine.

69. Moreland and Craig, *Philosophical Foundations for a Christian Worldview*, pp. 525–26.

70. For one Christian discussion of these issues see Joshua Hoffman and Gary S. Rosenkrantz, *The Divine Attributes* (London: Blackwell, 2002).

71. Paul Copan, *"That's Just Your Interpretation"* (Grand Rapids, MI: Baker Book House, 2001), pp. 69–73.

72. See his book *The Life of the Cosmos.* One plausible mechanism for this possibility comes from inflationary cosmology, which supports the view that our universe is a "pocket universe" within a vastly larger universe, or multiverse. This is defended by Alexander Vilenkin, in his book *Many Worlds in One: The Search for Other Universes* (New York: Hill and Wang, 2006).

73. For my answers to James F. Sennett's objections to this be sure to read note 31.

74. On this see William G. Dever, *Did God Have a Wife?* (Grand Rapids, MI: Eerdmans, 2005).

75. On this point see Hector Avalos, *The End of Biblical Studies* (Amherst, NY: Prometheus Books, 2007), pp. 44–47.

76. Sam Harris, *The End of Faith: Religion, Terror, and the Future of Reason* (New York: Norton, 2004), p. 18. In a major article for *Philosophia Christi* Paul Copan attempts to answer the question, "Is Yahweh a Moral Monster? The New Atheists and Old Testament Ethics" (10, no. 1 [2008]). I wish I had the space to devote a critique of it here, but I don't. What we see in that article is a prime example of the mental gymnastics of a gerrymanderer. Notice how often Copan says things like: "On the surface . . ."; ". . . appears to suggest . . ."; "If such a reading is correct. . . ." As Harry McCall said on my blog: "Copan's article is simply an apologetic defense based on the selective and manipulative use of the data drawn from conservative authors published by very conservative to moderate church presses. The anachronistic use of ancient material in relationship to the Bible is extremely disappointing." For a rebuttal of Copan's article, do a search on my blog for Hector Avalos's post: "Paul Copan's Moral Relativism: A Response from a Biblical Scholar of the New Atheism."

77. Thomas Paine, *The Age of Reason* (Radford, VA: Wilder Publications, 2007), part II, chap. 1, p. 71.

6

THE LESSONS OF GALILEO, SCIENCE, AND RELIGION

The French *philosophes*, or social critics of the eighteenth century, used the trial of Galileo for propaganda purposes to show the conflict between science and Christianity, and it was. It was a conflict of sciences that the church as an *institution* got caught up in. The church had taken a stand on Aristotelian science and was not prepared to let the new science progress. And yet there was more to it.[1]

The problem for astronomers in this era was to explain the retrograde motion of the planets. The word "planet" in the Greek literally means "wanderer," and in the New Testament the word means "deceiver." In the night sky the planets seem to back up and then go forward again as the weeks go by, rather than move in one direction across the sky. This observed motion is actually because the earth revolves around the sun along with the other planets. All of the planets pass each other in their yearly cycles. But since "the ancients viewed the celestial realm as the residence of the gods,"[2] the planets were defying the perfect symmetry of the heavenly realm. The retrograde motion of the planets seemed to contradict the perfect divine order of the universe, thus endangering human faith in the divine creator of the universe.

The philosopher's task, in Plato's words, was to "save the phenomena"—to redeem the apparent disorder of the empirical heavens. The Pythagoreans actually suggested a stationary sun, and Aristarchus posited a heliocentric theory. Yet the obstacles were formidable to these viewpoints: there was no observable *stellar parallax* (described later) because they lacked a telescope. There was also the commonsense notion that a moving earth would force people on earth to be knocked about. Plus the ancients believed in the terrestrial-celestial separation between the realm of the gods and of humans. They believed that the heavens operated by a different set of laws than on earth.

The reason this was a problem is because Aristotelian cosmology led to the con-

clusion that the earth was the center of the universe. Aristotle's viewpoint is teleological. He concluded there were four causes for everything that exists: (1) the formal
cause, "What is its form?"; (2) the material cause, "What is it made of?"; (3) the efficient cause, "What made it?"; and (4) the most significant: *the final cause*, that is,
"What purpose does it serve?" According to Aristotle, rocks fall to earth because they
seek their rightful place. And heavier ones fall faster because they have more potentiality, he said. This is a purpose-oriented answer, but it is completely untrue when
falling in a vacuum. Aristotle believed hot water froze faster than cold water because
hot water has more potentiality. But it doesn't freeze faster! "Why is there wind?"
Aristotle claimed the wind is the result of the earth breathing. These are purpose-oriented answers. He talked as though nature is a consciously operating organism. This
teleological viewpoint led to the idea that the earth was the fixed center of the universe. Why? Because all objects fall to earth, their rightful place. Therefore the earth
is the center of the universe. According to Aristotle, teleological explanations are ultimate explanations for why something happens.

Ptolemy (100–178 CE) outlined the answer to the problem of the planets that
held sway until Copernicus. It was very complicated and involved the notion that
planets revolved around certain circular points in the universe called *epicycles*, thus
explaining why the planets were brighter during the retrograde cycle. (By the way,
Ptolemy argued convincingly for a spherical earth!)

Nicholas Copernicus had come to regard the Ptolemaic system as a "monster,"
which still failed to account for or to predict observed planetary positions with reliable accuracy. Copernicus believed that "the divine creator, whose works were
everywhere good and orderly, could not have been slipshod with the heavens." With
him the appearances were saved with greater conceptual elegance. He saw his work
fully published on the last day of his life, 1543 CE, titled *The Revolutions of the
Heavenly Spheres*. Yet "for most who heard of it, the new conception was contrary
to experience and so patently false, as to not require serious discussion."[3]

THE TRIAL OF GALILEO (1633 CE)

By Galileo's day in the early seventeenth century, the Catholic Church felt compelled to take a definite stand against the Copernican hypothesis for various reasons
(the Protestants had done this earlier). One major reason was that Dante harmonized
the Christian religion with the science of his day. When the Aristotelian-Ptolemaic
cosmology was embraced by the Christian poet Dante (1265–1321 CE) in his
extremely popular *Divine Comedy*, the ancient cosmological view "fully reentered
the Christian psyche."[4] Dante did this, according to Richard Tarnas, by "poetically
uniting the specific elements of Christian theology with the equally specific elements
of classical astronomy. . . . The Aristotelian geocentric universe thus became a massive symbolic structure for the moral drama of Christianity . . . all of the Ptolemaic
planetary spheres now took on Christian references, with specific ranks of angels
and archangels responsible for each sphere's motions. . . . Every aspect of the Greek

scientific scheme [was] now imbued with religious significance." If, for example, a moving earth were to be introduced into that system, "the effect of a purely scientific innovation would threaten the integrity of the entire Christian cosmology."[5]

Tarnas again: "If the earth truly moved then no longer could it be the fixed center of God's Creation and his plan of salvation. Nor could man be the central focus of the cosmos. The absolute uniqueness and significance of Christ's intervention into human history seemed to require a corresponding uniqueness and significance for the Earth. The meaning of redemption itself, the central event not just of human history, but also of universal history, seemed at stake. *To be a Copernican seemed tantamount to atheism.*"[6]

According to Christian philosopher Diogenes Allen, the Aristotelian/Ptolemy view "included values as part of the very fabric of the universe. . . . Obligations and rights . . . are confirmed and supported by the physical order of the cosmos itself. . . . It seemed to threaten the very foundations of the social, political, and moral order."[7]

The invention of the telescope changed the debate. It destroyed several Ptolemaic conceptions: (a) They believed that the spheres of the universe were perfect, yet Galileo noticed the moon has craters; (b) they believed everything rotates around the earth, yet Galileo discovered Jupiter had four moons; and (c) they believed the heavenly bodies were eternal, yet Galileo discovered sun spots indicating that the sun was decaying. He defended the Copernican system with observations, and thus began the rise of modern experimental science. He showed by experiment how heavier rocks do not fall faster than lighter ones (contrary to Aristotle). He conceptualized tying a string from a heavier rock to a lighter one, thus making them one object. But would the combined rock now fall faster than either one, or would the lighter one drag? Such problems plagued the older view.

But look at how Galileo's views were answered purportedly by a Florentine astronomer named Francesco Sizzi: "There are seven windows in the head: two nostrils, two eyes, two ears, and a mouth. So also in the heavens there are two favorable stars, two unfavorable, two luminaries, and Mercury alone undecided and indifferent. From all this, and from other such natural phenomena, such as seven metals, etc., all too pointless to enumerate, we can conclude that the number of planets is necessarily seven. . . . Furthermore, the alleged satellites of Jupiter are invisible to the naked eye, and therefore can have no influence on earth, and therefore would be useless, and therefore do not exist. . . . Besides all this, the Jews and other ancient peoples as well as modern Europeans have always divided the week into seven days and have named them after the seven planets. Now if we, like Galileo, increase the number of planets, this whole and beautiful system falls to the ground."[8]

What must be understood about the trial: First, there was real debate about the geocentric system—but it was to be regarded as a "hypothesis not fact." Second, Copernicus's and Galileo's systems contained ideas that were "hopelessly inaccurate," and there was no evidence yet for things that should be noticed. For instance, the proper planetary orbits were not known yet—they were arguing for more complete circles revolving around the sun; and there was "no observable stellar parallax"—individual stars should appear at different points in the sky when the earth is at its two farthest distances in its cycle around the sun. Either the stars were immensely more distant, which we now know is the case, or the earth didn't move. Thus, the Copernican system was not yet established on scientific grounds. Third, the pope, Urban VIII, felt personally betrayed by Galileo, a former friend, because he thought one of the incompetent speakers in Galileo's book *Dialogue of Two Chief World Systems* was intended to represent him.

Regardless, with the success of the Copernican revolution the belief that the universe operates uniformly by the same consistent pattern of laws is firmly established as fact. Scientists will not, cannot, and should not give in on this. Any theory that contradicts this viewpoint should be judged on scientific grounds to be in gross error, like biblical literalism, which places the earth ten thousand years old at the center of the universe.

THE RELATIONSHIP OF SCIENCE TO RELIGION

Ian Barbour presents four ways of relating science and religion.[9] Let me briefly comment on them.

1. Conflict. Scientific Materialism ("Scientism") vs. Biblical Literalism

Scientific materialism ("scientism") makes two claims: the scientific method is the only reliable path to knowledge; and matter is the fundamental reality of the universe. The first one is an epistemological claim. The second one is a metaphysical claim. Yet the second claim is based upon the first one, which has been shown to be very reliable through the centuries. *Biblical literalism* claims that a literal interpretation of the Bible sets the limits for science. It claims that a universal flood explains geology, and a six-day creation explains the origin of the universe.

J. P. Moreland and William Lane Craig make a distinction here between *strong scientism* and *weak scientism*. Strong scientism states, "There are no truths apart from scientific truths, and even if there were, there would be no reason whatever to believe them." Weak scientism, in their words, will "allow for the existence of truths apart from science and are even willing to grant that they can have some minimal, positive rationality status without the support of science. But advocates of weak scientism still hold that science is the most valuable, most serious, and most authoritative sector of human learning . . . fields outside science gain if they are given scientific support and not vice versa." Accordingly, if weak scientism is true, "then the conversation between theology and science will be a monologue with theology listening to science and waiting for science to give it support."[10] I'm an advocate of weak scientism. In the words of Steven Pinker, during an interview when he was asked if something was possible, said, "That's an interesting hypothesis; I hope someone tests it."

Biblical literalism was one of the problems in Galileo's day. It is a very untrustworthy approach to science, and so it is rejected by scientifically educated people today. According to Neil DeGrasse Tyson, the argument against biblical literalism is "simple." "I have yet to see a successful prediction about the physical world that was inferred or extrapolated from the content of any religious document. Indeed, I can make an even stronger statement. Whenever people have used religious documents to make detailed predictions about the physical world they have been famously wrong. By a prediction I mean a precise statement about the untested behavior of objects or phenomena in the natural world that gets logged before the event takes place."[11]

2. Independence

This view can be summed up in these words: Science and religion are totally independent enterprises and separated into watertight compartments. They have contrasting methods and differing languages. The rest is merely deciding who reigns over which area—turf wars. However, Barbour reminds us, "if religion deals with God and the self, and science deals with nature, who can say anything about the relationship between God and nature, or between the self and nature?"[12] Furthermore, if religious beliefs have an independent status, there must be ways of establishing religion on its own grounds, and that is something I'm arguing against in this book. Unless someone can propose a mutually agreed-upon reliable scientific test to show that religion is a legitimate domain of knowledge on its own merits, it doesn't have any independent status.

3. Dialogue

This view can be summed up in these words: There are some methodological parallels between science and religion as well as some differences. Religious beliefs interpret and correlate experience, much as scientific theories interpret and correlate experimental data. All our beliefs can be tested by the criteria of consistency with experience. But personal involvement is more total in the case of religion, since the primary goal is the reformation of the person. Science sets limits within which accounts of meaning can work. Science explains but religion reveals, science informs but religion reforms.

Donald MacKay advocates this viewpoint: "both science and theology give different kinds of explanations—with different methods and aims—about the same objects. Both explanations of the same event can be true and complete on their own levels. But the methods differ greatly." Both of these explanations can be correct and are not mutually exclusive. Compare how an artist, poet, theologian, or astronomer might view a sunset. They can all be correct from their perspective, even if they disagree with one another. MacKay would argue that there is no incompatibility in claiming that the formation of the universe as we know it is the result of natural processes, and that "the cosmos is God's creation." Each explanation is from a particular conceptual framework and can be true from that framework.[13]

Howard Van Till argues in a like manner by setting the limits of the dialogue: "When scientists make statements concerning matters of origin, governance, value or purpose of the cosmos, they are necessarily stepping outside the bounds of scientific investigation and drawing from their religious or philosophical perspectives. . . . [Similarly] . . . when theologians make statements or conjectures about geological processes or thermodynamic phenomena or cosmic chronology, they are necessarily stepping outside the bounds of scriptural exegesis and into the domain of modern natural science."[14]

However, unless someone can propose a mutually agreed-upon reliable scientific test to distinguish between competing religious claims, scientists don't know which one of them to dialogue with. Richard Dawkins makes a passionate and thoughtful case that science does not need to dialogue with religious views since they don't have a reliable method like scientists do. He writes: "Why shouldn't we comment on God, as scientists? And why isn't Russell's teapot, or the Flying Spaghetti Monster, equally immune from scientific skepticism? . . . A universe with a creative superintendent would be a very different kind of universe from one without. Why is that not a scientific matter?" It is said that "science concerns itself with *how* questions, but only theology is equipped to answer *why* questions. What on Earth *is* a why question? Not every English sentence beginning with the word 'why' is a legitimate question. Why are unicorns hollow? . . . What is the color of abstraction? What is the smell of hope? The fact that a question can be phrased in a grammatically correct English sentence doesn't make it meaningful, or entitle it to our serious attention. . . . Perhaps there are some genuinely and meaningful questions that are forever beyond the reach of science. . . . But if science cannot answer some ultimate question, what makes anybody think that religion can?"[15]

Religion is used by people of faith to explain the gaps in our knowledge, but science has been filling those gaps one by one. There is becoming less and less room for God, as we explain more and more. Call it the *God of the Gaps* if you want to (see note),[16] but we are less religious today because of science. After surveying several times when theologians have retreated in the face of the progress of science, Richard Carrier wrote, "theologians have been wrong every time so far. Why keep betting on them?"[17] I just don't see why we should.

4. Integration

The content of theology and science can be integrated. 1) *Natural theology* asserts "from below" that understanding nature can give rise to and support theology, as argued by Thomas Aquinas, Norman Geisler, and Richard Swinburne. 2) The *theology of nature* asserts that our understanding of the general characteristics of nature will affect our models of God's relation to nature. Religious beliefs and scientific theories should be in harmony, such that some adjustments or modifications are called for. Arthur Peacocke and Teilhard de Chardin advocate this view. Chardin argues from evolution to the existence of God, and that at some point humans will achieve convergence to an "Omega Point."[18] 3) Then there is *panentheism*, or *process theology*, which is defended by Paul Davies, Alfred North Whitehead, and Charles Hartshorne. "The World Is God's Body." 4) *Deism* is an integrative approach that went through four different stages and traveled from England to America and France. The last stage merely affirmed that God created the universe and that's it. Deism basically rejects revealed religion and instead affirms that reason must support any theological belief. If it can't, then that religious belief is to be jettisoned.[19]

However, if there is any integration taking place, religious beliefs are always the ones that have been forced to integrate with science and not the other way around, so why not just admit science sets the boundaries for what we believe? Science and its theories can be tested empirically in a dialectical manner, whereas there is no mutually agreed-upon reliable test to establish religious beliefs. Scientific tests on prayer have actually shown the opposite. I suspect that with scientists who have tried to integrate science and religion, the integration has become complete for some of them. For them, science swallows up religion with nothing left over.

HERE IS SOME SCIENTIFIC EVIDENCE AGAINST THE CHRISTIAN BELIEF IN THE GOD OF THE BIBLE

Astronomy tells us the universe is thirteen to fifteen billion years old and arose out of a cosmic singularity. No account of the development of this universe can be harmonized with the creation accounts in Genesis except that these accounts were pure mythic folklore. Archaeology shows us there isn't any evidence for Israelites being slaves in Egypt for four hundred years, or that they wandered in the wilderness for forty years, or that they conquered the land of Canaan. Geology confirms the slow evolutionary development of life in the sedimentary rock layers on a planet nearly five billion years old, just as astronomy confirms the slow evolutionary development of galaxy, star, and planet formation. Geology also disconfirms that there was a universal flood that covered the earth. Neurology confirms that strokes, seizures, and other illnesses stem from a brain malfunction and hence disconfirms that there is something called a mind or soul. Sam Harris points out that if God created us with minds, then there is no reason to expect that he also created us with brains. Modern medicine has achieved astounding results that such superstitious practices like exorcisms, bloodletting, and supernatural healings are delusional. Psychology confirms that who we are and how we behave are determined to an overwhelming degree before we reach the age of accountability. People are not evil so much as much they may be sick. People are born with different propensities for evil based on their genes, and these propensities are acted upon by upbringing and environment. There is no rebellion against God. If God is omniscient, then like the ultimate psychotherapist he knows why we do everything we do, and since this is the case, there can be no wrathful God.

SCIENCE HAS ALSO DISPLACED GOD

There are four cosmological displacements:

1. The Copernican theory of the heliocentric universe defended by Galileo (1600s). Man was no longer the center of our particular solar system.

2. The discovery that our solar system is not central to the Milky Way galaxy, but located on the periphery, out on a spiral arm (c. 1900). Man was not even central in his own galaxy.
3. The discovery that our galaxy is only one of billions of galaxies (c. 1930s). Man isn't even central to the universe as a whole. We are insignificant.
4. The possibility that there are an infinite number of universes, called a *multiverse*. God is no longer needed.

THE ORIGINS OF EXPERIMENTAL SCIENCE

Christians claim that "the fully amplified Judeo-Christian view of creation was, historically, a very significant factor in the rise of science. . . . Furthermore, it appears that no other historic view had the same fruitful logic and suggestiveness that could give science momentum. . . . Science makes sense only in a certain kind of world—the kind that was in fact first envisioned by Christian theism."[20]

What motivated Newton to quantify the movements of objects? The history of scientific notions about motion itself reveals various ideas, depending a great deal upon religious and philosophical views, beginning with Parmenides and Zeno, who denied there was motion. Ockham simply believed there was no need to posit the existence of motion since the simpler explanation is that things just reappear in a different place. And yet Ockham, Zeno, and Parmenides all saw the same things we do today. So for them to see things differently, people had to adopt different philosophical assumptions. Without a change in these assumptions, science would never have arisen; this is true. The question is whether they came from Christian theism or not, and even if they did, whether this proves anything at all.

Michael Polanyi, Ian Barbour, Thomas Kuhn, and Karl Popper all examine the art of scientific discovery and what it takes to understand science.[21] It's more than just one fact built upon another. On the one hand the philosophical foundations had to be in place for there to be some initial discoveries, although on the other hand, it must be acknowledged that surprise discoveries caused a change in their assumptions. I maintain that this whole process of discovery is just a two-way street, both changing the other in tandem, dialectically.

It's claimed there are four foundations, or bases of science. Let's take a very brief look at them: (1) Einstein said, "The belief in an external world independent of the perceiving subject is the basis of all natural science."[22] While this may be true, for all I know, if so, it doesn't say anything about Christianity per se, and it doesn't say whether there is an external world independent of the perceiving subject, nor that this cannot be defended from a naturalistic standpoint, either. It would only support the claim that such a belief helped to establish science. Historically, even false beliefs have caused science to advance, as Karl Popper has shown. For that's how science progresses, he argued, by informed conjectures and guesses, which in turn are refuted for better ones, and so on. Does anyone want to say that just because Galileo had a false understanding of the way planets revolve around the sun that his model of the universe didn't help science progress? Newton's theory of gravitation helped science progress too, and while it is still close enough to be used in contexts that only require a close approximation, it was wrong and eventually superseded by Einstein's relativity theory. As we shall see shortly, the Greek philosopher/scientist Thales was wrong to suggest water is the source of all things, but his naturalistic method was probably more important to the advancement of science, which excluded supernatural explanations. Besides, the fact is that Einstein probably did not believe in the supernatural anyway.[23]

(2) The intelligibility of nature—that we can understand nature to some degree. Immanuel Kant is reported to have said, "the eternal mystery of the world is its comprehensibility." This seems strange coming from Kant, who did not think we see reality itself, the "things in themselves." That being said, many aspects of the world still defy our comprehension or ability to describe them. Does anyone truly understand quantum mechanics?

(3) The uniformity of nature—that nature is ordered according to patterns we generalize into laws, and that these laws operate uniformly throughout the whole universe. Let me elaborate here. The notion of the uniformity of nature presents us with the "riddle of induction." What justifies the belief in the uniformity of nature such that scientists can be confident in induction as a scientific method? When speaking of this problem, Paul Kurtz argued, "All other positions face a quandary similar to that hurled at the scientific humanist—though compounded. It is unfair to burden the scientific humanist with the 'riddle of induction,' for there is a 'riddle of intuition' or a 'riddle of subjectivism' or a 'riddle' for any other method. The intuitionist, mystic, or subjectivist can only justify his position by assuming his method to do so, thus committing a *petito principi* (begging the question). The burden of proof rests with these alternative positions. . . . If all positions involve some question begging and are on the same ground in this regard, we may ask: 'Which is the least self-defeating?'"[24]

In truth, the uniformity of nature is a good model for understanding the universe, which has a great deal of support that is continually being tested in light of observations from distant galaxies, and that may be all we can claim. Philosopher of science Bas Van Fraassen has gone farther in a detailed argument that there are no natural laws. While he agrees there are "regularities," he argues that no metaphysical account of laws can succeed. He develops an empiricist view of science as a construction of models to represent the phenomena. Van Fraassen argues that no adequate account of the concept of natural laws has been given, although science can continue without recourse to such laws. I'm certainly no expert in this area, but we should hesitate before claiming that nature operates by uniform natural laws.[25] Victor J. Stenger, who agrees with Van Fraasen, has argued that "the laws of physics are not restrictions on the behavior of matter. Rather they are restrictions on the way physicists may describe that behavior."[26]

(4) The adequacy of scientific language and mathematics to adequately describe the world. It has been said that "humans invent abstract mathematics; basically making it up out of their imaginations, yet math magically turns out to describe the

world."[27] But science works as a way of investigating the world because the world behaves in a manner that can be investigated and can be described (in part) by formal mathematical language. Mathematics was not made up. It came as the result of empirical observations. Before people decided $2 + 2 = 4$, they took two sets of two, put them together, and counted the result. This is just part of the whole anthropic principle as applied to science. If the world didn't behave regularly, then we wouldn't even be here to learn about it in the first place.

Science is a joint effort, performed in various fields of specialized research, where discoveries of the past become stepping-stones for progress in the future. Science proceeds on the basis of past research in a multifaceted array of separate specializations. Scientists don't have to continually "reinvent the wheel," for instance. There is little room in science for very many fundamental assumptions. The main exception is the philosophical notion that our senses reliably reflect a mutually shared experience of this world. But that's an assumption we all make precisely because without it we cannot live a normal life.

Dr. Joshua Sharp, assistant research scientist at the University of Georgia, described it to me (via e-mail) like this: "The assumption of science is that the universe that appears to exist actually exists, and that our observations of the universe relate to the actual universe in some repeatable way. This assumption can only be supported by circumstantial utilitarian evidence (with it, we can predict the future), but we have acquired mountains of utilitarian evidence for it! This assumption has led us to certain mathematical models, including logic. Science can present no evidence for or against solipsism or the Matrix; assuming that what we observe in some way approximates a universe that actually exists. But we can justify a belief in logic. We did not assume logic; we assumed the universe and developed logic by observing how the universe works."

With modern science we simply don't need metaphysical assumptions, since a good scientist could be an atheist, a pantheist, a deist, or a Muslim. The bottom line, if nothing else, is that science justifies itself pragmatically. We needed some assumptions to help get science off the ground and to jettison the superstitions that held us back from discovering it. But those beliefs which we might have called assumptions in a prior era are now known as the bedrock facts of science because, if for no other reason, they produce solid results. The assumption for Galileo was that the universe operates by the same set of laws. Now this is no longer considered an assumption at all. It is a well established fact! So pragmatic justification alone is all we need. It's surely all that anyone has to go on. To reach the moon we must do *thus and so*. We did *thus and so* and we reached the moon. Therefore doing *thus and so* gets us to the moon. As Stenger writes, "The validity of the scientific method is justified by its immense success."[28] Why would we need a worldview to see this? According to Karl Popper scientific knowledge progresses based upon "conjectures" or "guesses," which are falsified and replaced by better "conjectures" or "guesses." I see no good reason to suppose this body of knowledge is dependent on any worldview considerations. Moreover, the results of science are breaking down superstitions around the globe too. So in a way, as science progresses it's tearing at the heart of religious beliefs everywhere by providing the answers that religion always promised but failed to deliver.

Paul Kurtz sums up what the pioneers of modern science did by telling us they actually "abandoned tradition, mysticism, revelation, and faith, and proceeded directly to the Book of Nature. They eschewed hidden occult explanations for natural causes. They rejected purely speculative metaphysics and sought hypotheses and theories that were verified by empirical observation, experimental prediction, and the precision and power of mathematics. Scientific progress could only occur when the theological and philosophical authorities of the past were discarded, and a fresh bold approach to nature was adopted."[29]

Richard Carrier is doing his doctoral dissertation on science and early Christianity, which will be published when he's done. According to him, to say "'our concept of science is an outgrowth of Christian theology' is no more true than 'our concept of science is an outgrowth of pagan theology.' Modern science grew up in a Christian context, but only by re-embracing ancient scientific values against the grain of the original Christian mind-set. In turn, those ancient scientific values grew up in a pagan context. As with Christianity, that's not causality, it's just circumstance." Moreover, "most Christians were uniformly hostile to the whole system of scientific values, condemning them as vain, idolatrous, arrogant, and unnecessary, if not outright dangerous. It took a long, gradual process to finally change minds on that score." In the end, Carrier argues, "Christianity was bad for science. It put a stop to scientific progress for a thousand years, and even after that it made science's recovery difficult, painful, and slow."[30] And I think history would bear this out. Every major innovative scientific advance was made difficult by the Church, and still is today.

Let me put it this way. Christians claim their faith gave rise to modern science even though the Bible literally contains talk of a six day creation, a three-tiered universe, a worldwide flood let loose from the firmament above, nine-hundred-year-old men, talking snakes and donkeys, a sun that stood still, and a hell in the deepest parts of the earth, and they still want to claim their faith gave rise to science? That's balderdash (sorry, I can't resist)! Science itself has completely undermined these views, forcing thoughtful Christians to reinterpret their Bibles over and over again. Furthermore, if Christianity gave rise to modern science then why are these apologists silent about the fact that it didn't begin among Christianities that existed in the Byzantine Empire, Russia, or Egypt? This fact alone helps us see that cultural factors were the dominant ones.

METHODOLOGICAL NATURALISM

Methodological naturalism best describes the method I use to evaluate any claim, which is the basis for my skeptical control beliefs. The phrase "methodological naturalism" is believed to have been coined by the philosopher Paul de Vries, then at Wheaton College, who introduced it at a conference in 1983 in a paper subsequently published as "Naturalism in the Natural Sciences." De Vries distinguished between what he called "methodological naturalism," a disciplinary method that says nothing about God's existence, and "metaphysical naturalism," which "denies the existence of a transcendent God."[31]

This method assumes that for everything we experience there is a natural explanation.[32] Paul Kurtz defined it as well as anyone when he wrote that it is a "principle within the context of scientific inquiry; i.e., all hypotheses and events are to be explained and tested by reference to natural causes and events. To introduce a supernatural or transcendental cause within science is to depart from naturalistic explanations." It is further argued that methodological naturalism leads to philosophical (or ontological) naturalism, whereby it's claimed all that exists is nature. Again in Paul Kurtz's words, philosophical naturalism is "a generalized description of the universe. According to the naturalists, nature is best accounted for by reference to material principles, i.e., by mass and energy and physical-chemical properties as encountered in diverse contexts of inquiry."[33]

The ancient Greek philosopher/scientist Thales was probably the first person known to adopt a methodological naturalist standpoint. He asked the significant question, "What is the source of all things?" His answer was that water was the source of all things. His question led to the beginnings of Western philosophy as we know it and with it provided probably the most important basis for science itself. His answer was a naturalistic one that did not rely on any supernatural explanation. He assumed a natural explanation for the source of all things, even if today with the periodical table of the elements we know his answer was faulty.

We who live in the modern world operate on this method ourselves every day. This method is the foundation of modernity. It is what defines us as modern people. In today's world all modern educated people base their deductions on the method of naturalism in a vast number of areas. Before the advent of science, in previous centuries people either praised God for the good things that happened to them or they wondered why God was angry when bad things happened. If someone got sick, it was because of sin in his or her life. If it rained, God was pleased with them; if there was a drought, God was displeased, and so on, and so on. Science wasn't content to accept the notion that epilepsy was demon possession or that sicknesses were sent by God to punish people. Nor was science content with the idea that God alone opens the womb of a woman, nor that God was the one who sent the rain. Now we have scientific explanations for these things, and we all benefit from those who assumed there was a natural cause to everything we experience. Because of this, we have some control over the natural processes of life. Because we seek to understand the forces of nature, we know how to make life easier for ourselves, with fewer diseases. We can predict the rain. We know how babies are conceived, and how to prevent a host of illnesses. There is no going back on this progress, and it is ongoing.

Christians themselves usually assume a natural explanation when they hear a noise in the night. They usually assume a natural explanation for a stillborn baby, or a train wreck, or an illness. Even a Christian police detective assumes a natural cause when investigating a crime. If Christians were placed back in time with the same modern mind-set they have today, they themselves would ask for evidence if someone claimed that an ax head floated or a donkey talked. But because it's in the Bible, they adopt it unquestionably, and I find that to be holding to a *double standard*. Why do they operate on a double standard like this? Ancient people didn't even have a firm conception of natural law. For all they knew, anything could happen in nature when acted upon by God, gods, or goddesses. Ancient people just didn't have the required scientific understanding of natural laws we do today in order for them to question a miraculous story when they heard one. Scientifically literate people today are simply not gullible enough to believe any such story. All of us ask whether an unusual event can be explained naturalistically, unlike ancient people.

In scientific disciplines methodological naturalism is a way to gain the truth about nature, and it has astounding results. Many scientists go so far as to claim that since it works, then nature must be ultimate, but that doesn't follow as a scientific claim, for the latter conclusion is beyond the scope of science; it is a metaphysical claim. Although, as Barbara Forrest argues, it's a conclusion that makes a great deal of sense. Forrest examines the question whether methodological naturalism entails philosophical (or ontological or even metaphysical) naturalism. In her own words, "I conclude that the relationship between methodological and philosophical naturalism, while not one of logical entailment, is the only reasonable metaphysical conclusion given (1) the demonstrated success of methodological naturalism, combined with (2) the massive amount of knowledge gained by it, (3) the lack of a method or epistemology for knowing the supernatural, and (4) the subsequent lack of evidence for the supernatural. The above factors together provide solid grounding for philosophical naturalism, while supernaturalism remains little more than a logical possibility."[34]

Scientists believe that methodological naturalism has had so many successes in the past that it will prove fruitful in understanding how we humans got here on planet earth too—that there is a natural explanation for it all—even if there are several problems to work out yet. Creation scientists believe that there are too many problems to work out and that a supernatural explanation is needed to explain human life. Mainstream scientists think that creation scientists have given up way too early in the game on a method that is rock solid throughout history. Creation scientists stress that methodological naturalism is not a final statement on how the world works, whereas many mainstream scientists think that the reason the method works so well is because nature alone must be the final reality. This naturalistic method has brought in modernity and jettisoned superstition. It is what defines us as modern people. And while it seems to me that as yet there is no repeatable experiment that can show that nature is ultimate, it isn't beyond the realm of possibility, and there are some very good conceptual schemes for how it may have taken place.[35]

To see why admitting supernatural claims into scientific discussions should be prohibited, consider David A. Shotwell's conjectural hypothesis that "each subatomic particle is inhabited by a ghostly little gremlin." According to this hypothesis, "each gremlin maintains the existence of its particle by a continuous creative act and is in instantaneous telepathic communication with all the others. By this means they cooperate to produce the universe and its lawful behavior. This hypothesis 'explains' everything that exists and every event that occurs." The reason he advances this hypothesis is to show that "if you admit the supernatural into your calculations, anything goes. That is why a supernatural explanation is useless to a scientist. . . . It provides no direction for research, suggests no testable hypotheses, and gives no reason to expect one result rather than another from any observation or experiment."[36]

Christians like Plantinga object to the use of methodological naturalism in many areas related to their faith. They cry foul. They argue that their faith provides them with the control beliefs to interpret the evidence regarding the origins of the universe and of the human race. And they cry foul when it comes to the strict adherence to that method when analyzing the claims of biblical miracles. Robert T. Pennock tried to address their concerns in chapter 4 of his book *Tower of Babel: The Evidence against the New Creationism*.[37] The author argues against the new creationists for failing to realize that science is committed to methodological naturalism and not philosophical (or ontological) naturalism. Methodological naturalism is a much weaker position, he argues. It does *not* deny the existence of supernatural entities, per se. It simply assumes for the purpose of inquiry that they don't exist. It operates on the assumption that in the context of scientific inquiry only natural processes and events happen. He wrote: "The methodological naturalist does not make a commitment directly to a picture of what exists in the world, but rather to a set of methods as a reliable way to find out about the world—typically the methods of the natural sciences, and perhaps extensions that are continuous with them—and indirectly to what those methods discover."[38]

According to Pennock, adopting methodological naturalism would prevent biblical creationists from appealing to divine causes as an alternative to evolutionary ones. He points out that just as Christians shouldn't do this when it comes to the scientific study of the origins of language because of the Tower of Babel story, they shouldn't do it when it comes to the scientific study of our origins because of the Creation stories, either. The adoption of methodological naturalism, he argues, would rule out these kinds of explanations without at the same time preventing religious beliefs in nonscientific faith contexts. Therefore, Pennock claims methodological naturalism, in contrast to ontological naturalism, is compatible with the belief in God. As such, believers should have nothing to fear from it. Doing so keeps science free of God, and as such, science can continue to progress unhindered by these religious beliefs.

Surely this will not satisfy Christian theists like Plantinga, who wrote, "a Christian academic and scientific community ought to pursue science in its own way, starting from and taking for granted what we know as Christians." He continues, "What the Christian community really needs is a science that takes into account what we know as Christians. Indeed, this seems the rational thing in any event; surely the rational thing is to use all that you know in trying to understand a given phenomenon." But do you notice what he's doing here? Plantinga is forced into retreating to Bayesian background factors to support a weak position. He's trying to explain the evidence away. He's retreating to what is merely possible; that while methodological naturalism has worked very well in understanding our world, it's possible that it doesn't apply across the board into the Christian set of beliefs he's adopted from the Bible. And he's right. It is possible. But again, how likely is it that it works so well on every other area of investigation but that it shouldn't be used in investigating the claims we find in the Bible, which form his background beliefs? I will argue later, when it comes to the distinctive miraculous claims that a Christian firmly holds to, that they are believed based upon the evidence found in history, and history can at best show us probabilities. To be blunt here, many claims can be rationally denied in history, even if they happened. That's right. Even if they happened! And of those events in the past which we are confident took place, they still leave room for a lot of doubt about the specifics. There are always additional unanswered questions. As such, history is a slender reed to lean on in the face of the onslaught of science (see my chapter 8).

Michael Martin sifts through this whole issue and tries to find a justification for methodological naturalism that doesn't commit the Christian believer to ontological naturalism.[39] Martin asks, "If you reject *Ontological Naturalism* and yet believe that *Methodological Naturalism* is an appropriate stance in the context of science, how can *Methodological Naturalism* be justified?" As I understand him to say, after surveying several possible justifications for this, Martin suggests this one: "Do not use explanations in science that cut off further inquiry unless inquiry-blocking explanations are the only plausible ones that can be thought of . . . in the long run!" This, Martin argues, "is compatible with scientists acting for long periods of time as if certain explanations are ultimate relative to their evidence and background theories. But such a practice would not block inquiry because in contrast to explanations in terms of God, it would be possible for these explanations themselves to be explained as science progresses." Then he concludes by saying, "Although the prospects of a metaphysically uncontroversial science are not encouraging, I see no reason why science cannot be conducted in a way that does not block inquiry, and I suggest that *Methodological Naturalism* should be justified in terms of not blocking inquiry." And as such, according to Victor J. Stenger, "methodological naturalism can still be applied without implying any dogmatic attachment to metaphysical naturalism."[40] That being said, Dr. Joshua S. Sharp, told me (via e-mail): "Since no one can precisely determine what 'the long run' means, it is impossible to predict which areas will always prove resistant to future non-inquiry-blocking explanation. Therefore, supernatural explanations can never be justified for scientific phenomena."

NOTES

1. See Diogenes Allen, *Christian Belief in a Postmodern World* (Louisville, KY: Westminster Press, 1989), pp. 26–49; Mario Biagioli, *Galileo, Courtier: The Practice of Science in the Culture of Absolutism* (Chicago: University of Chicago Press, 1993); and Timothy Moy, "The Galileo Affair," in *Science and Religion: Are They Compatible?* ed. Paul Kurtz (Amherst, NY: Prometheus Books, 2003), pp. 139–43. To read the primary documents of the Galileo trial and aftermath in order to decide for yourself on this issue, see Maurice A. Finocchiaro, *The Galileo Affair: A Documentary History* (Berkeley: University of California Press, 1989) and his *Retrying Galileo* (Berkeley: University of California Press, 2005). I maintain that for the medieval person influenced by Dante's *The Divine Comedy*, the Copernican theory

was a very serious threat to the faith. I also maintain that the Church had no business telling Galileo what he could think or write. It's appalling to me that the Church ever had that much power to stifle science and freethinking like this.

2. Richard Tarnas, *The Passion of the Western Mind* (New York: Ballantine Books, 1991), p. 49.

3. Ibid., p. 251.

4. Ibid, pp. 248ff.

5. Ibid., pp. 195–96.

6. Ibid., pp. 253–54.

7. Allen, *Christian Belief in a Postmodern World*, pp. 41, 42.

8. Francesco Sizzi, *Dianoia Astronomica*, 1611.

9. Ian Barbour, *Religion in an Age of Science* (New York: Harper & Row, 1990); and Ian Barbour, *When Science Meets Religion: Enemies, Strangers, or Partners?* (New York: HarperCollins, 2000).

10. J. P. Moreland and William Lane Craig, *Philosophical Foundations for a Christian Worldview* (Downers Grove, IL: InterVarsity Press, 2003), p. 347.

11. Neil DeGrasse Tyson, "Holy Wars," in Kurtz, *Science and Religion: Are They Compatible?* pp. 74–75.

12. Barbour, *Religion in an Age of Science*, p. 16.

13. See Donald McKay, *Brain, Machines and Persons* (Grand Rapids, MI: Eerdmans, 1980), pp. 19ff.

14. See Howard Van Till, *The Fourth Day* (Grand Rapids, MI: Eerdmans, 1986), pp. 197–98; and Howard Van Till, Davis A. Young, and Clarence Menninga, *Science Held Hostage* (Downers Grove, IL: InterVarsity Press, 1988).

15. Richard Dawkins, *The God Delusion* (New York: Houghton Mifflin, 2006), pp. 55–56.

16. I can agree with Robert Larmer that there isn't anything wrong with arguing from the gaps in our knowledge to the existence of a God. See his "Is There Anything Wrong with 'God of the Gaps' Reasoning?" *International Journal for Philosophy of Religion* 52 (2002): 129–42. However, if he's correct, then I can legitimately argue from the fact that science is closing these gaps to the nonexistence of God. It's not a large step to take. Since it's reasonable to think there will always be gaps in our understanding, the only question left is which set of control beliefs best explains why these gaps are being closed. The point is that Christians must admit that the scientific method is indeed extremely fruitful, but then deny it should be applied to an investigation of the Bible and its claims of miracles, including the origin of the universe. They have to deny what seems to scientifically literate people undeniable, or at the very minimum, most probable. They must apply a double standard here, for while they accept it in all other areas of their lives they deny it when it comes to the Bible. Why the double standard?

Christian philosopher W. Christopher Stewart objects to the "god of the gaps" reasoning because, as he says, "natural laws are not independent of God. For the Christian theist, God upholds nature in existence, sustaining it in a providential way." From his perspective this is true. But his rationale for objecting to the god of the gaps reasoning is a bit strange. He says, "To do so is to make religious belief an easy target as the gaps in scientific understanding narrow with each scientific discovery." "Religion and Science," in *Reason for the Hope Within*, ed. Michael Murray (Grand Rapids, MI: Eerdmans, 1999), pp. 321–22. Now why should he be concerned with this unless science truly is leaving less and less room for the supernatural? He's admitting the evidence does not favor his faith. He's trying to explain away the evidence. I dare say that if he still lived in a prescientific era before science could explain so much he'd be arguing this is evidence that God exists!

17. In Richard Carrier, *Sense and Goodness without God* (Bloomington, IN: Author-house, 2005), pp. 87–88.

18. Arthur Peacock, *Theology for a Scientific Age* (Minneapolis: Fortress Press, 1993); Pierre Teilhard de Chardin, *Phenomenon of Man* (New York: Harper Perennial, 1976).

19. J. O'Higgins distinguishes between four types of Deism in "Hume and the Deists: A Contrast in Religious Approaches," *Journal of Theological Studies* 23, no. 2 (October 1971): 479, 480, which is summarized in Norman L. Geisler and William D. Watkins, *World's Apart: A Handbook on Worldviews* (Grand Rapids, MI: Baker Book House, 1989), pp. 148–49.

20. Michael Peterson et al., *Reason and Religious Belief* (Oxford: Oxford University Press, 1991), pp. 212, 214. See also the works by Stanley Jaki, *Science and Creation* (Edinburgh: Scottish Academic Press, 1974); *The Origin of Science and the Science of Its Origin* (South Bend, IN: Regnery, 1978); and *The Road of Science and the Ways to God* (Chicago: University of Chicago, 1978); J. P. Moreland's *Christianity and the Nature of Science* (Grand Rapids, MI: Baker Book House, 1989); Rodney Stark, *For the Glory of God: How Monotheism Led to Reformations, Science, Witch-Hunts, and the End of Slavery* (Princeton, NJ: Princeton University Press, 2004); and recently by Dinesh D'Souza, *What's So Great about Christianity* (Washington, DC: Regnery, 2007), pp. 83–111.

21. Michael Polanyi, *Personal Knowledge* (Chicago: University of Chicago Press, 1958); Barbour, *Religion in an Age of Science*; Thomas S. Kuhn, *The Structure of Scientific Revolutions*, 2nd ed. (Chicago: University of Chicago Press, 1970); Karl Popper, *The Logic of Scientific Discovery* (New York: Basic Books, 1959), and his *Conjectures and Refutations* (London: Routeledge, 1994).

22. Albert Einstein said this in an essay titled "Maxwell's Influence on the Development of the Conception of Physical Reality" (1931).

23. On this, see Dawkins, *The God Delusion*, pp. 13–19.

24. Paul Kurtz, *The Transcendental Temptation* (Amherst, NY: Prometheus Books, 1991), pp. 57–58.

25. Bas van Fraassen, *Laws and Symmetry* (Oxford: Oxford University Press, 1989).

26. Victor J. Stenger, *God: The Failed Hypothesis* (Amherst, NY: Prometheus Books, 2007). See his book *The Comprehensible Cosmos: Where Do the Laws of Physics Come From?* (Amherst, NY: Prometheus Books, 2006).

27. "Science Finds God," *Newsweek*, July 20, 1998.

28. Stenger, *God: The Failed Hypothesis*, p. 37.

29. Paul Kurtz, "An Overview of the Issues," in *Science and Religion: Are They Compatible?* p. 11.

30. http://richardcarrier.blogspot.com/2006/science-and-medieval-christianity.html. John Hick argues for the same thing in *An Interpretation of Religion* (New Haven, CT: Yale University Press, 1989), pp. 327–29.

31. Paul de Vries, "Naturalism in the Natural Sciences," *Christian Scholar's Review* 15 (1986): 388–96.

32. For discussions of this see Alvin Plantinga's essay "Methodological Naturalism?" parts 1 and 2, which can be found at www.arn.org and in the journal *Perspectives on Science and Christian Faith* (49 [1997]). Barbara Forrest's "Methodological Naturalism and Philosophical Naturalism: Clarifying the Connection," *Philo* 3, no. 2 (Fall–Winter 2000): 7–29, along with Michael Martin's "Justifying Methodological Naturalism," can both be found at www.infidels.org/library.

33. Paul Kurtz, "Darwin Re-Crucified: Why Are So Many Afraid of Naturalism?" *Free Inquiry* (Spring 1998): 17.

34. Forrest, "Methodological Naturalism and Philosophical Naturalism: Clarifying the Connection," pp. 7–29.

35. For a naturalistic account of the beginning of this universe, see chapter 12 of Paul Davies, *Superforce: The Search for a Grand Unified Theory of Nature* (New York: Touchstone, 2002).

36. David A. Shotwell, "From the Anthropic Principle to the Supernatural," in Kurtz, *Science and Religion: Are they Compatible?* p. 49.

37. Robert T. Pennock, *Tower of Babel: The Evidence against the New Creationism* (Cambridge, MA: MIT Press, 2000).

38. Ibid., p. 191.

39. Martin's "Justifying Methodological Naturalism," as found at www.infidels.org/library.

40. Stenger, *God: The Failed Hypothesis*, p. 29.

7

THE STRANGE AND SUPERSTITIOUS WORLD OF THE BIBLE

I n the Bible we find a strange world. Karl Barth wrote an essay titled "The Strange New World Within the Bible." To the question of what lies within the world of the Bible, Barth gives this answer: "Within the Bible, there is a strange, new world, the world of God."[1] And it is indeed strange to us today—very strange.

We find a world where a snake and a donkey talked, where giants lived in the land, where people could live to be nine-hundred-plus years old, where a woman was turned into a pillar of salt, where a pillar of fire could lead people by night, where the sun stopped moving across the sky or could even back up, where an ax head could float on water, where a star could point down to a specific home, where people could instantly speak in unlearned foreign languages, and where someone's shadow or handkerchief could heal people. It is a world where a flood could cover the whole earth, and where a man could walk on water, calm a stormy sea, change water into wine, or be swallowed by a "great fish" and live to tell about it. It is a world populated by demons that could wreak havoc on earth and also make people very sick. It is a world of idol worship, where human and animal sacrifices pleased God. In this world we find visions, inspired dreams, prophetic utterances, miracle workers, magicians, diviners, and sorcerers. It is a world where God lived in the sky (heaven) and people who died went to live in the dark recesses of the earth (*Sheol*).

New Testament scholar Rudolph Bultmann just calls them "myths" and gets his point across by exaggerating his case: "The cosmology of the N.T. is essentially mythical in character. The world is viewed as a three-storied structure, with the earth in the center, the heaven above, and the underworld beneath. Heaven is the abode of God and of celestial beings—angels. The underworld is hell, the place of torment. Man is not in control of his life. Evil spirits may take possession of him. Satan may inspire him with evil thoughts. It is simply the cosmology of a prescientific age. To modern man

. . . the mythical view of the world is obsolete. It is no longer possible for anyone seriously to hold the N.T. view of the world. We no longer believe in the three-storied universe. No one who is old enough to think for himself supposes that God lives in a local heaven. There is no longer any heaven in the traditional sense. The same applies to hell in the sense of a mythical underworld beneath our feet. And if this is so . . . we can no longer look for the return of the Son of Man on the clouds of heaven. It is impossible to use the electric light and the wireless and to avail ourselves of modern medical and surgical discoveries, and at the same time to believe in the N.T. world of spirits and miracles. The same objections apply to the doctrine of the atonement. How can the guilt of one man be expiated by the death of another who is sinless?"[2]

On the one hand, we have the ancient world as expressed in the Bible, and on the other hand, we have the one with gods and goddesses expressed in Homer's *The Iliad* and *The Odyssey*. These worlds look very similar to me, and very superstitious to the core. Today's Christians believe the Bible accurately describes the ancient world of the Israelites and that the events depicted in it really happened, depending on how they interpret it all. However, today's Christians reject the world of the gods and goddesses described by Homer as superstitious to the core. Nonbelievers like me just think both books describe worlds so strange to our ears that they both must be mythical reflections of very superstitious people.

It's very interesting to me that Christians will believe in the miracles recorded in the Bible, simply because they are recorded in the Bible, but if I claimed I saw one of these miracles yesterday, they would not believe me. I dare say that if an evangelical Christian with her present modern mind-set would step back into the ancient world and hear someone tell a tale that a woman turned into a pillar of salt, she wouldn't believe it unless she saw evidence. If someone told her a snake or a donkey talked, she would scoff. But simply because these things are told in the Bible, she believes they happened. What I want to know is why the Christian maintains a double standard. Why does she believe the world of the Bible but reject the world of Homer? Why does she believe the biblical claims of miracles but would reject similar claims of a miracle today? Why does she believe the biblical stories but would reject those stories if she lived in that era?

Sam Harris makes this point very vivid in these words: "Tell a devout Christian that his wife is cheating on him, or that frozen yogurt can make a man invisible, and he is likely to require as much evidence as anyone else, and to be persuaded only to the extent that you give it. Tell him that the book he keeps by his bed was written by an invisible deity who will punish him with fire for eternity if he fails to accept its every incredible claim about the universe, and he seems to require no evidence whatsoever."[3]

ANCIENT PEOPLE WEREN'T STUPID, JUST SUPERSTITIOUS

Ancient people were not stupid people. After all, they built great walls, roads, buildings, cities, temples, and empires, along with weapons and military strategies to defend themselves. But many Christians think ancient people were just as skeptical as we are today, and/or that modern people today are just as superstitious as the ancients were. The main difference, according to them, is that the events described in the Bible really happened, that's all. However, if the biblical people were very superstitious in comparison to us, it would greatly weaken their claims, because then it could be claimed by skeptics that ancient people did not have solid evidence to believe. It could then be argued that extremely superstitious people will tend to believe most any wondrous story if it is told by a sincere and devoted person. This will be my point here.

My contention is that ancient people weren't stupid, just very superstitious. Christopher Hitchens puts it this way: "One must state it plainly. Religion comes from the period of human prehistory where nobody had the smallest idea what was going on. It comes from the bawling and fearful infancy of our species, and is a babyish attempt to meet our inescapable demand for knowledge."[4] While I'll admit that our day and age still contains a lot of superstitious people, more thoughtful and scientifically literate people in today's world have different standards—higher standards—for the evidence needed to believe. Carl Sagan was right when he subtitled his book *The Demon Haunted World* with these words: *Science as a Candle in the Dark*. Our standards have been adopted as the results of modern science, where we know how babies are born, what makes it rain, why nations win wars, and what makes people sick, for the most part. Even Christians look for natural causes for these things, for the most part. Why else would they go to fertility doctors, or any doctors at all? Why would they listen to the weatherman on TV? Or why seek guidance from American generals about Iraq and Afghanistan? It's because even Christians today have accepted the same standards from modern science as the rest of us.

Let's define *superstition*, using *Microsoft Encarta*:

> Superstition, a belief or practice generally regarded as irrational and as resulting from ignorance or from fear of the unknown. It implies a belief in unseen and unknown forces that can be influenced by objects and rituals. Magic or sorcery, witchcraft, and the occult in general are often referred to as superstitions. Examples of common superstitions include the belief that bad luck will strike the person in front of whom a black cat passes or that some tragedy will befall a person who walks under a ladder. Good luck charms, such as horseshoes, rabbits' feet, coins, lockets, and religious medals, are commonly kept or worn to ward off evil or to bring good fortune.
>
> **The question of what is or is not superstitious, however, is relative. One person's beliefs can be another's superstitions. All religious beliefs and practices may be considered superstition by unbelievers, while religious leaders often condemn unorthodox popular practices as a superstitious parody of true faith.** (Emphasis mine)

As the last paragraph indicates, there are problems in defining *superstition*. But this is true of many words. Would you please define *pornography*? What is a *normal* human being? What is *beautiful*? We may not always be able to specify what we mean, but "we know it when we see it," don't we? And this is usually an acceptable answer, even though it's a person-related answer too. All I'm arguing here is that ancient people believed a great many things that modern educated people today would say are superstitious, and that's good enough.

I can propose scientific tests for what I consider superstitions. I can compare what a meteorologist says about the weather with someone who plans to do a rain dance, and test to see who's right more often. That's science. The results of reason and science have jettisoned a great many superstitions. Testing and comparing results—that's science. I can do the same for the superstitious practice of bloodletting, for exorcisms, for people who claim to predict things based on palm reading, or tea leaves, or walking under a ladder, or breaking a mirror, or stepping on a sidewalk crack. I can even test the results of someone who gets a shot of penicillin when sick with the person who refuses this and prays instead. That's science. And we modern people are indebted to science for these things. It's what makes us different from ancient people.

ANCIENT PEOPLE DEFINITELY WERE VERY SUPERSTITIOUS

One way to examine whether or not ancient people were very superstitious is to examine historical documents and archeological records to see what these people were doing and thinking at that time. Richard Carrier did this in "Kooks and Quacks of the Roman Empire: A Look into the World of the Gospels."[5] According to him, the ancient New Testament age was one "of fable and wonder, where magic, miracles, ghosts, and gods were everywhere and almost never doubted."[6] Tim Callahan has examined the biblical stories for precursors in the ancient superstitious world, and he makes an excellent case that many of the biblical stories themselves come from early superstitious myths of their pagan neighbors.[7]

But I think there is another way to see how superstitious the ancients were. I decided to reread portions of the Bible just like fundamentalist and evangelical Bible-believing Christians do. That is, I took the Bible at face value without utilizing the results of higher critical biblical scholarship regarding the true nature of the dates, sources, and time periods of the biblical documents. What I wanted to find out is whether the Bible, taken at face value, leads us to think other surrounding cultures were superstitious by our standards today. If the Bible is believed to be the word of God, and the Bible tells us that the peoples of that time were superstitious, then it will lead us to think that even the Israelites and Christians were superstitious too, especially if it shows that they regularly were "led astray" to practice the same beliefs. After all, according to Voltaire, "Every man is a creature of the age in which he lives, and few are able to raise themselves above the ideas of their time."

What I found was that there were so many superstitious beliefs by the Gentile nations at every period of time in the Bible that superstition reigned in those ancient days. I don't think any modern person should be able to conclude anything other than that. The beliefs of these nations were so prevalent that God's people in the

Bible regularly joined in the same practices and worship of these gods and goddesses. So my question here will be this: If these nations were so superstitious that Israel regularly joined them in their beliefs, then how do we know that the beliefs of the Israelites, and later the Christians, weren't based upon superstitions too?

Every surrounding culture had a plethora of gods and goddesses, along with priests, magicians, sorcerers, astrologers, and diviners. This is very easily documented.[8] These myths of gods and goddesses were believed by the peoples of those days, and these people had a great deal of contact with the Jews of the Old Testament and the Christians in the New Testament. After all, if Abraham came from the Babylonian area then he was brought up by his father who served other gods (Josh. 24:2). Abraham purportedly traveled to Palestine by means of the Fertile Crescent, and he lived in Egypt for a time during a famine. The Fertile Crescent was used as a heavily traveled trade route for the Near Eastern peoples of Assyria, Babylonia, Asia, and Egypt, which met midway in Palestine. So they had to have a great deal of contact with other cultures throughout biblical times.

Furthermore, the Israelites purportedly lived in Egypt, the Bible says, for about four hundred years, and then they settled in and among the Canaanites. Later the tribe of Judah was carried away into Babylonian captivity for seventy years, before being able to return home. First-century CE Jews and Christians lived under Roman rule. How could they not be influenced by these great cultures, is the question I pose. And since people of every era are unavoidably "children of their times," the burden of proof is on those who say that the Jews and Christians are the exceptions to this rule. Even though it can be shown they had distinctive beliefs and practices, whereby every culture distinguished itself from the others, they all shared a fundamental superstitious outlook on the world.

We who live in the modern world of science simply don't believe in a god of the sun, or moon, or harvest, or fertility, or rain, or the sea. We don't see omens in an eclipse, or in flood, a storm, a snakebite, or a drought, either. That's because we understand nature better than they did, by using science. We don't see sickness as demon possession, nor do educated thinking people believe in astrology to get an insight into the future. Nor do we think we are physically any closer to God whether we're up on a mountaintop rather than down in a valley. But every nation did in ancient days. Most all of the kings of those days believed these things, even if it can be accurately pointed out that there were many people who did not believe in the myths of their day. For example, Socrates (fifth century BCE) was charged with not believing the Greek gods and consequently condemned to die for corrupting the youth. But remember, he was condemned to die by the superstitious people of his day, too, so he's merely an exception.

OLD TESTAMENT EXAMPLES

The first thing we notice is that the Hebrew God is pictured with a body, just like the gods of their polytheistic neighbors. The gods of surrounding cultures had human and physical characteristics. There is no reason to suppose the Hebrews thought differently about their God from what we read in the early parts of the Old Testament. What we have in the Bible is an evolving understanding of the nature of God, so we find later statements to the contrary, that is, that "God is a Spirit" (John 4:24). But in the early portions of the Old Testament we see God with a body.

The Bible states that man and woman are to have been created in the image/likeness of God in three passages in the early chapters of Genesis (Gen. 1:26–28; 5:1–3; 9:6)—for instance: "God created man in His own image, in the image of God He created him; male and female He created them" (Gen. 1:27).

About this image, listen to *The Anchor Bible Dictionary* ("Image of God'), which tells us: "Gen. 5:1–2 makes it clear that both male and female are included under the designation *adam* who was made in God's image. Gen. 5:3 reports that Adam fathered a son 'in his likeness, according to his image,' and the verse employs the same nouns used in Gen. 1:26–27, though the order of the nouns and the prepositions used with each are reversed in comparison to Gen. 1:26. This suggests that the way in which a son resembles his father is in some sense analogous to the way in which the human is like God."

Harper's Bible Dictionary ("Image of God") is more to the point: "To speak of human beings ('Adam') as created in the image of God apparently refers primarily to the bodily form (the Hebrew term for 'image' usually denotes a concrete likeness) but also to the spiritual attributes the physical body symbolizes."

If we want to know just what that image is, we should consider some of the passages that describe God with a human form. Genesis 2:2: "And on the seventh day God ended his work which he had made; and he rested on the seventh day from all his work which he had made." But only a physical being needs to rest. Genesis 3:8: "They heard the sound of the LORD God walking in the garden at the time of the evening breeze, and the man and his wife hid themselves from the presence of the LORD God among the trees of the garden." Shouldn't this verse settle the whole issue?

From Exodus 33:18–23: "Then Moses said, 'Now show me your glory.' And the Lord said, 'I will cause all my goodness to pass in front of you, and I will proclaim my name, the Lord, in your presence. But,' he said, 'you cannot see my face, for no one may see me and live.' Then the Lord said, 'There is a place near me where you may stand on a rock. When my glory passes by, I will put you in a cleft in the rock and cover you with my hand until I have passed by. Then I will remove my hand and you will see my back; but my face must not be seen.'" This is strange if God wasn't viewed as having a body, especially since God purportedly said, "there is a place near me."

According to the Bible, God has arms. God has ears. God has eyes. God has hands. God has a footstool. God has a scepter. God sits on a throne. God has a heavenly court. God even has nostrils. The burden of proof is upon the conservative Christian to show why the ancient Hebrews didn't think of God in a human form. Mormons today take these statements literally and believe God has the shape of a human being, so if modern people like Mormons think this way, then it's even more likely that ancient Hebrews did. Christians will argue that passages in the Bible about God having a body are merely anthropomorphic, that is, they are not to be taken literally. However, where is the word *anthropomorphic* in the Bible such that we'll know how to interpret a passage properly when it is "red flagged" with that word? I don't have such a Bible, do you? Christians will also claim these are "theophanies" where God appeared in a human form, or where Jesus himself appeared in a pre-incarnate bodily form. The only reason they call these things anthropomorphic (or theophanies of Jesus) is because they are reading the texts in their original settings anachronistically based upon later or hindsight Christian understandings. Later I will question the nature of the incarnation of Jesus, and will suggest that visions can account for the purported sightings of Jesus' resurrected body, so I see no reason to accept these explanations for what we see here in the Old Testament text itself. For now I just want to note that the early Hebrews thought of God as having a body, just like their superstitious polytheistic neighbors thought of the gods and goddesses with bodies.

I'll skip the creation accounts, the Garden of Eden story, and Noah's Flood, since I'll cover them in detail later.

The "Sons of God" Sire Children Called Nephilim (Gen. 6:1–4)

Genesis 6:1–4 opens up with a description of the evils that had finally taken place on earth. There is a new and horrible evil. The divine "sons of god" were having sex with the "daughters of men" and producing semi-divine offspring giants called Nephilim. This biblical text tells us that there were divine beings (later known as angels) who had genitalia and produced offspring. Moreover, according to Gordon J. Wenham, the text implies "that the divine-human intercourse was, like eating the tree of life, intended to procure eternal life for man," and as such, was an "attempt to usurp what belongs to God alone."[9] This was a deliberate act of rebellion that Donald Gowan tells us was understood by early Jewish commenters to be "more important than the story of the sin of Adam and Eve. . . . For several authors this was the true 'Fall Story,' the account of how evil came into the world by means of the descent of certain rebellious angels."[10]

For Christians to say that the "sons of god" are the descendants of Seth, or that they are kings, belies the facts for so many convincing reasons that the main motivation to claim these things is to rid the Bible of obvious mythic elements. Gleason Archer grabs a text from the New Testament that says angels are "spirits" (Heb. 1:14) and claims they are "utterly incapable of carnal relations with women," which leads him to conclude Genesis 6 must record "the first occurrence of mixed marriage between believers and unbelievers."[11] But this view goes against the natural reading of the text. The word for "men" in verse 1 should have the same meaning as in verse 2, describing the human race and then their daughters. The exact phrase, "sons of god," always meant supernatural beings (Job 1:6; 2:1; 38:7; Ps. 29:1; 89:6). And the text itself says nothing about believers and unbelievers, nor can one assume that all of the male descendants of Seth were godly and all of the female descendants of Cain were ungodly. Besides, as we'll see with the evolving notions of God, and as we shall see later with the notions of Satan and hell, notions about angels evolved as well.

The "sons of God" in Genesis 6 were understood "without exception" by Jewish and Christian writers up until Augustine (fourth century CE) to be supernatural fallen beings, admits the conservative F. B. Huey Jr.[12] The fact is that "marriages between men and gods are a well-known feature of Greek, Egyptian, Ugaritic, Hurrian, and Mestopotamin theology," says the conservative Gordon Wenham. As such, even Wenham admits this Genesis text "comes closer to myth than anywhere else, for it is describing acts of godlike figures."[13]

There Is the Purported Tower of Babel (Gen. 11:3–9)

They said to each other . . . "Come, let us build ourselves a city, with a tower that reaches to the heavens, so that we may make a name for ourselves and not be scattered over the face of the whole earth." But the LORD came down to see the city and the tower that the men were building. The LORD said . . . "Come, let us go down and confuse their language so they will not understand each other." So the LORD scattered them from there over all the earth, and they stopped building the city.

The implication here, although not expressly stated, is that God wanted to stop them from building a tower to "heaven." Among the ancients this would be clearly understood that God didn't want these people to approach him where he lived, so God stopped them from doing so. Gordon Wenham states: "It was a commonplace of Babylonian thought that temples had their roots in the netherworld and their tops reached up to heaven. . . . It seems likely that Genesis views it as a sacrilege. For the sky is also heaven, the home of God, and this ancient skyscraper may have been another human effort to become like God from what is said here (cf. 3:5; 6:1–4)."[14]

Furthermore, ancient people would also consider that this God, like the other gods, had a pantheon of gods with him who helped him (hence the words "let us"). No one would have considered the idea of a triune God here. It was something Christians read back into the Old Testament stories of Creation and the Tower of Babel. According to Wenham: "Christians have traditionally seen this verse as adumbrating the Trinity. It is now universally admitted that this verse was not what the plural ('let us') meant to the original author."[15]

There Are Mythical Creatures

There is "Rahab." According to *Harper's Bible Dictionary*: This is "the mythical chaos dragon whom God killed in battle and thus made an orderly creation possible (Job 26:7–14; Isa. 51:9; Ps. 89:10)." *There is "Leviathan."* According to *Harper's Bible Dictionary*: "Leviathan is a great, mythological monster. In Ugaritic mythology, Leviathan (appearing by the name 'Lothan') is one of the primeval sea monsters who battles against Baal on the side of Mot (the god of the underworld) and who is ultimately defeated. This mythological tradition was adopted and transformed in the Bible where God appears as the victor over the sea monsters (Ps. 74:13–14, cf. Job 3:8; 26:12–13; 41:1–34; Ps. 104:26). The references to God 'playing' with Leviathan (Ps. 104:26; Job 41:5) are explainable on the basis of God's omnipotence which reduces this mighty rebellious dragon to a plaything. . . . The future and final destruction of Leviathan becomes a symbol in Isaiah (27:1) for the death of the wicked, to be succeeded by the redemption of Israel (26:20–21; 27:2–13)." My question is how can God defeat mythical beasts that do not exist? *There is also "Behemoth"* (Job 40:15). According to *The Anchor Bible Dictionary*, it has been claimed, "Behemoth and Leviathan denote respectively the hippopotamus and the crocodile. However, they are probably instead chaos monsters. The description of neither Behemoth nor Leviathan corresponds to any known creature, and certainly not the hippopotamus and crocodile. It seems fundamental to the argument in Job 40–41 that the beasts in question can be captured by God alone, otherwise Job might have replied that he could have captured them, and then God would lose the argument!"

The King James translators used the word *unicorn* to refer to a beast in the Bible having one horn (Num. 23:22; 24:8; Deut. 33:17; Job 39:9–10; Ps. 22:21, 29:6; 92:10; Isa. 34:7). If that's not the proper English word to translate the Hebrew word, then at the very minimum, the King James translators were themselves believers in mythical beasts. Marco Polo himself searched for a unicorn! The same thing can be said for the other mythical beasts we find in the Bible, like *dragons* (Deut. 32:33; Isa. 34:13; Ps. 74:13; 91:13; Mic. 1:8). According to David Mills, "The Bible contains innumerable other references to fanciful creatures, such as the Cockatrice—a serpent hatched from the egg of a cock whose mere glance could kill its enemies (Isa. 11:8; 14:29); Satyrs—creatures that were half man and half goat or horse (Isa. 13:21); Fiery serpents (Deut. 8:15), and Flying serpents (Isa. 30:6)."[16]

A BRIEF HISTORY OF SUPERSTITION IN ISRAEL

When Moses confronted the Egyptian pharaoh of his day, we read: "Aaron threw his staff down in front of Pharaoh and his officials, and it became a snake. Pharaoh then summoned wise men and sorcerers, and the Egyptian magicians did the same things by their secret arts: Each one threw down his staff and it became a snake" (Exod. 7:10–12). Never mind for the moment that we're told that Aaron's staff swallowed up their staffs, because whether or not this happened is in question. We're told that the Egyptian magicians were able to turn a staff into a snake, turn water into blood (Exod. 7:19–22), and duplicate the plague of frogs (Exod. 8:18), just as Moses did. And the Egyptian sorcerers weren't surprised at doing so. They weren't surprised at all? Not even Moses nor Aaron were surprised by this, nor was the writer of this account, nor the ancient people who believed such a story. That's very strange to modern ears, that these sorcerers even attempted to do this, much less weren't surprised at the results. But we would be if we heard such a tale.

After just being rescued out of Egyptian slavery, we read, that the people "have made themselves an idol cast in the shape of a calf. They have bowed down to it and sacrificed to it and have said, 'These are your gods, O Israel, who brought you up out of Egypt'" (Exod. 32:7–9).

This took place "on the third month after the Israelites left Egypt," plus forty days and nights (Exod. 19:1; 24:18). So four months and ten days later these people ("all the people," Exod. 32:3) wanted to worship a golden calf that Aaron said, "brought you out of Egypt." How could they so quickly abandon the God of Moses? If the events all took place as described in Exodus, I doubt very much if anyone would dare take the risk to worship this calf against the God of Moses. If I was there, I know I wouldn't! This leads me to the conclusion that the reason they could so quickly abandon the biblical God of Moses is that their history was itself built upon nonhistorical myths. But because they did, Moses had the Levites kill "his brother and friend and neighbor," three thousand of them (Exod. 32:27–29)! It looks like Moses just intimidated the people to believe against their wills. They knew who delivered them out of Egypt—it was the gods of Egypt who revolted against the Egyptians themselves, allowing the Israelites to escape.

It just seems more likely to me, from the story itself, that the pharaoh of Egypt was himself superstitious. And because there were some strange natural phenomena going on in the land at the time, which he would have viewed as omens, he would've sent these foreigners away, while Moses received the credit for it all. So when Moses didn't come down from Mt. Sinai, the Israelite people simply gave credit to the true god who had given them their freedom, in their minds. "The calf was probably similar to representations of the Egyptian bull-god Apis."[17] They knew who had released them from Egypt, but Moses threatened them with death if they disagreed.

The Bible records that the Israelites lived in the wilderness for forty years, where manna from heaven fed them, they got water out of a rock, they were directed by a pillar of fire at night and a pillar of cloud by day, and their clothes never wore out during these years. You'll just have to pardon my complete and utter skepticism here, especially in light of the fact that there is no independent confirmation or evidence to believe this except that some ancient biblical writer told this story. This is simply unbelievable, and I'll just pass on this with a laugh (sorry).

During a particular battle the Israelites fought, we read that "Joshua fought the Amalekites as Moses had ordered, and Moses, Aaron and Hur went to the top of the hill. As long as Moses held up his hands, the Israelites were winning, but whenever he lowered his hands, the Amalekites were winning. When Moses' hands grew tired, they took a stone and put it under him and he sat on it. Aaron and Hur held his hands up—one on one side, one on the other—so that his hands remained steady till sunset" (Exod. 17:10–12). In the New Testament Jesus purportedly commended the Centurion in his day for having the faith that Jesus could merely speak the word and his servant would be healed (Matt. 5:5–10). But apparently God required Moses to raise his hands to defeat the enemy. This is a case of *magic*, which I'll explain later. But just imagine standing there watching this scenario play out in front of your eyes and you'll see the utter foolishness of these grown men. There would be no evidence as the army advances that it's because the hands of Moses were raised they were winning, just like there would be no evidence as the battle reversed itself. Just because the Israelites gained the victory would not be any evidence that what Moses did worked, either. But we would watch and just shake our heads at what they were doing while men were being killed on both sides, as they claimed what they were doing provided the victory.

When the Israelites were camped along the Jordon River before entering the Promised Land, we read: "Balak son of Zippor, who was king of Moab at that time, sent messengers to summon Balaam son of Beor, who was at Pethor, near the River, in his native land. Balak said: 'A people has come out of Egypt; they cover the face of the land and have settled next to me.   Now come and put a curse on these people, because they are too powerful for me. Perhaps then I will be able to defeat them and drive them out of the country. For I know that those you bless are blessed, and those you curse are cursed'" (Num. 22:4–7, 24:1). And even though Balak took Balaam to three "high places," which were believed closer to where God lived in heaven, we're told Balaam couldn't curse the Israelites.

Ancient people like Balak and Balaam believed that curses could actually help defeat an enemy. And it's recorded in the Bible because we're told God would only allow Balaam to bless the Israelites. Blessings cause good events to happen. The biblical author believed the same thing as Balak did about curses and blessings; it's just that Balaam couldn't curse the Israelites. So let me ask you this: How would that go over today if our president did that with the approval from the House and Senate to curse the militant Muslims? What would the media say about doing this? What would you say?

The reason the story about Balak is even recorded here is because of the importance the Israelites placed on blessings and curses—something we find throughout the Old Testament. (Note especially Gen. 12:2–3; 27–28, 49; Deut. 27–28, 33; and Judges 5). The patriarchs blessed their children, but notice that Isaac cannot reverse what he has promised to Jacob (Gen. 27:33–37). Notice also that when Jesus cursed a fig tree, it withered and died (Mark 11:12–23). Curses were even believed to cause the thighs of adulterous women to rot (Num. 5:12–21)!

Even though Balaam couldn't curse Israel but blessed them instead, some of the Israelites were seduced by Moab: "While Israel was staying in Shittim, the men began to indulge in sexual immorality with Moabite women, who invited them to the sacrifices to their gods. The people ate and bowed down before these gods. So Israel joined in worshiping the Baal of Peor. And the Lord's anger burned against them. So Moses said to Israel's judges, 'Each of you must put to death those of your men who have joined in worshiping the Baal of Peor'" (Num. 25:1–5). More people died who disagreed with Moses. It would seem that many people followed their cult hero, Moses, out of fear, not true belief.

After Israel settled in the land promised, we're told, "the LORD raised up judges, who saved them out of the hands of these raiders. Yet they would not listen to their judges but prostituted themselves to other gods and worshiped them. Unlike their fathers, they quickly turned from the way in which their fathers had walked, the way of obedience to the LORD's commands. Whenever the LORD raised up a judge for them, he was with the judge and saved them out of the hands of their enemies as long as the judge lived. . . . But when the judge died, the people returned to ways even more corrupt than those of their fathers, following other gods and serving and worshiping them" (Judg. 2:16–19; 10:6). It just didn't take the people of Israel very long at all to worship other gods, especially if God provided miraculous manna to eat, gave them water from rocks, and didn't let their shoes wear out for forty years.

Judge Jephthah sacrificed his daughter to "God" (Judg. 11:39). Was God pleased at that? Micah had a shrine, some idols, and even a priest (Judg. 17:5, 10). When Samson lost his strength, the Philistines praised their god for this (Judg. 16:24). Yep, the Philistines believed their god helped them. But when we subject the Samson story itself to a detailed analysis, "the logistics here just don't add up," argues former preacher Joe E. Holman (see note).[18]

The people of God were tempted with the religious beliefs and practices of their neighbors throughout all of the Old Testament. The first King of Israel, King Saul, resorted to necromancy when "the Lord did not answer him, either by dreams, or by Urim, or by prophets," and he had to consult the medium of Endor to bring up Samuel for him (1 Samuel 28).

At the beginning of King Solomon's reign we find that "The people . . . were still sacrificing at the high places, because a temple had not yet been built for the Name of the Lord.   Solomon showed his love for the Lord by walking according to the statutes of his father David, except that he offered sacrifices and burned incense on the high places" (1 Kings 3:2–3). Even though Solomon built a temple to the God of Israel, he married seven hundred foreign wives for political gain, but these foreign marriages brought foreign religions. So we read, "As Solomon grew old, his wives turned his heart after other gods, and his heart was not fully devoted to the Lord his God, as the heart of David his father had been. He followed Asherah the goddess of the Sidonians, and Molech—the detestable god of the Ammonites. So Solomon did evil in the eyes of the Lord; he did not follow the Lord completely, as David his father had done. On a hill east of Jerusalem, Solomon built a high place for Chemosh the detestable god of Moab, and for Molech the detestable god of the Ammonites. He did the same for all his foreign wives, who burned incense and offered sacrifices to their gods" (1 Kings 11:1–8).

After the kingdom divided between Israel to the north and Judah to the south, we see little change. In the northern kingdom of Israel we are told that King Ahab "did more evil in the eyes of the Lord than any of those before him. He not only considered it trivial to commit the sins of Jeroboam son of Nebat, but he also married Jezebel daughter of Ethbaal king of the Sidonians, and began to serve Baal and worship him. He set up an altar for Baal in the temple of Baal that he built in Samaria. Ahab also made an Asherah pole and did more to provoke the Lord, the God of Israel, to anger than did all the kings of Israel before him" (1 Kings 16:30–33). Queen Jezebel herself practiced sorcery (2 Kings 9:22), and had a personal war with Israel's prophets by attempting to kill them off (1 Kings 18:4).

At times Judah to the south ended up being worse than the nations they destroyed when possessing their land: "Manasseh led Judah and the people of Jerusalem astray, so that they did more evil than the nations the LORD had destroyed before the Israelites" (2 Chron. 33:1–9). Listen to the prophet Isaiah here: "O house of Jacob, come, let us walk in the light of the LORD. For thou hast rejected thy people, the house of Jacob, because they are full of diviners from the east and of soothsayers like the Philistines, and they strike hands with foreigners. Their land is filled with idols; they bow down to the work of their hands, to what their own fingers have made" (Isa. 2:6–8). Filled with idols? That's what it says.

When Israel was destroyed by Babylonia, here are the stated reasons why: "They followed worthless idols and themselves became worthless. They imitated the nations around them although the LORD had ordered them, 'Do not do as they do,' and they did the things the LORD had forbidden them to do. They forsook all the commands of the LORD their God and made for themselves two idols cast in the shape of calves, and an Asherah pole. They bowed down to all the starry hosts, and they worshiped Baal. They sacrificed their sons and daughters in the fire. They practiced divination and sorcery and sold themselves to do evil in the eyes of the LORD, provoking him to anger. So the Lord was very angry with Israel and removed them from his presence" (2 Kings 17:14–18). "Only the tribe of Judah was left, and even Judah did not keep the commands of the Lord their God. They followed the practices Israel had introduced" (2 Kings 17:18–19).

When it comes to child sacrifice, it was actually commanded by God. In Exodus 22:29–30 we read: "You shall not delay to offer from the fullness of your harvest and from the outflow of your presses. The first-born of your sons you shall give to me. You shall do likewise with your oxen and with your sheep: seven days it shall be with its dam; on the eighth day you shall give it to me." Later on God admitted he did this in Ezekiel 20:25–26 where he purportedly said: "Moreover I gave them statutes that were not good and ordinances by which they could not have life; and I defiled them through their very gifts in making them offer by fire all their first-born, that I might horrify them; I did it that they might know that I am the LORD" (see note).[19]

The context of the Exodus passage just quoted above concerns offerings and sacrifices, and it says God requires that firstborn sons are to be literally sacrificed to him. Hence, unlike other passages where there is the possibility of redemption with a substitute sacrifice (cf. Exod. 13:13; 34:10–20), none is stated there. The concept of "redemption" is an interesting one that goes hand in hand with child sacrifice, because animals were substituted for the firstborn. Yet that says nothing against the idea that a better sacrifice was the firstborn child himself, and many people in the Old Testament did just that. Circumcision was probably a substitutionary child sacrifice (Exod. 4:24). Child sacrifice was probably only considered evil when it was done in the name of a foreign god, and doing so was punishable by death precisely because it was offered to another deity (Lev. 20:2, 18:21; Deut. 12:31, 18:10; 2 Kings 17:17, 23:10; 2 Chron. 28:3, 33:4–10; Ps. 106:38; Isa. 57:5, 6; Jer. 7:31, 32:35; Ezek. 16:20, 21, 20:26, 31, 23:37, 39; Acts 7:43).

Child sacrifice was something that several biblical people either did, or assisted others in doing so. Abraham was not morally repulsed by the command itself and there is no command against this practice there by God (Genesis 22). Then there is Jepthah who sacrificed his daughter because of a stupid vow (Judges 11); David (2 Sam. 21:7–9); Solomon and his wives (1 Kings 3:16); Ahab (1 Kings 16:33–34); Ahaz (2 Kings 16:2–3); Hoshea (2 Kings 17:7); and Manasseh (2 Kings 21:6; 2

Chron. 33:6). It was a problem for King Josiah (2 Kings 23:10), for Jeremiah (Jer. 7:30–31; 19:35; 32:35), and Ezekiel (Ezek. 16:20–21; 20:25–26, 30–31). The prophet Micah wonders if he should sacrifice his oldest son "as a sin offering" (6:6–8). It was a practice so prevalent when offered to foreign gods, that it is named as one of the reasons God sent the Babylonians to conquer Israel and forcibly take many of them as captives (2 Kings 17:16–18). We even read where the King of Moab sacrificed his son, which caused the Israelites to retreat in defeat. Moab's sacrifice created a great "wrath" (*ketzef*), which was an external force to the warriors in the story, indicating that his sacrifice caused some divinity to act on behalf of Moab (2 Kings 3:26–27). In the New Testament God the Father sacrifices his only son (Jesus) as the central redemptive act of Christianity, and God still seeks to fulfill his lust for human sacrifice by burning humans forever in the lake of fire.

Nonetheless, according to Robin Lane Fox, when the Jews were defeated by Babylonia in 587 BCE, "a realistic response to the fall of Jerusalem would have been to accept that the God of the Jews was in fact less strong than his neighbors." But the "Jews whose writings survive did not take that route: they interpreted events in defiance of the facts. The authors do not blame Yahweh; they blame the Jews' own sins." They "had brought ruin on themselves." [20]

When we look at Israel's history, we see how quickly Israel can follow the God of Moses during the lifetime of a "good" king, and then when an "evil" king arises, turn and follow other gods and goddesses and their worship practices. This happened in both the divided monarchies of Israel and Judah. How could they so easily reject their "history," unless there was no real history to reject? I'm suggesting that much of their history rested on the same foundations as all the other nations. It rested on myths, legends, and superstitions.

Take for instance, the development of the Hebrews' notion of God. Isaiah 40–55 most likely shows the culmination of God's teaching to the Israelites that he alone is God (monotheism vs. henotheism). However, the word for God, *elohim*, is plural, "gods." And, in Genesis 1:26, God says: "Let *us* make man in our image." Christians were able to use this to argue for the doctrine of the trinity, but as Alan Hauser argues, "the concept of the trinity could not have been in the mind of the writer or the writer's audience." And, "'wind,' not 'spirit,' is the best translation of *ruah* in Genesis 1:2." [21] In some of the Psalms we read only that he is the "God of the gods" (Ps. 86:8; 95:3; 96:4,9; 135:5; 136:2; 138:1). Why didn't the text deny the existence of any other gods at this point? It certainly looks as if the Hebrews started out believing in a plurality of gods, which was progressively brought down to the belief in just one God. [22]

Christians might object that America has changed drastically in two hundred plus years, too. Someone might say, "If we observed just the last two hundred plus years of our history in this part of the world, we'd be a different nation." But consider this. Look for yourself how long a judge ruled in the book of Judges to see how quickly, in terms of a few short years, the people of Israel went back and forth between gods. The same thing goes for "good" kings and "evil" kings throughout the monarchies of both Israel and Judah. And yes, we've changed in America in the last two hundred plus years, but some things we still all agree on, like democracy is the worst form of government until you compare it with all the others. Our changes have been significant because of the rise of globalization and the results of science and the electronic media. A better comparison would be the minimum changes in the medieval society lasting over a thousand years before the rise of science. The medieval world didn't change that much, so why did biblical Israel change back and forth and back and forth between the God of Moses and the gods and goddesses of the neighboring nations?

MAGIC, DIVINATION, AND DREAMS

When the Jews were held in captivity in Babylonia, King Nebuchadnezzar had a dream. Never mind for a minute that it's claimed Daniel told him the dream and he also interpreted it, because whether he did this or not is what's in question here. I want us to consider the religious culture surrounding the ruler of a great empire. We read, "In the second year of his reign, Nebuchadnezzar had dreams; his mind was troubled and he could not sleep. So the king summoned the magicians, enchanters, sorcerers and astrologers to tell him what he had dreamed. When they came in and stood before the king, he said to them, 'I have had a dream that troubles me and I want to know what it means'" (Dan. 2:1–3). Nebuchadnezzer believed that dreams came from the gods as divine communication. And he had magicians and sorcerers who he depended upon to advise him and help run his whole country (see Dan. 5:7). How would that go over today, if the president had such advisers? But it was acceptable to the ancient people whom Nebuchadnezzer ruled over. And to treat our president's advisers as if they were the equivalent of magicians and sorcerers is historical nonsense. Modern presidential advisers think through the problems and try as best as possible to come up with reasoned answers. But what if one adviser were to say, "I read my tea leaves today and they say we should attack Iraq"?

Since Daniel himself was appointed by king Nebuchadnezzer to be in charge of his "wise men" (Dan. 2:48), which included the magicians, enchanters, astrologers, and diviners (Dan. 5:11), let's take a look at two of these practices and ask ourselves how he could be in charge of them when they practiced the arts of *magic* and *divination*.

Magic

According to *Harper's Bible Dictionary*, "**Magic** is the means by which humans attempt to secure for themselves some action or information from superhuman powers. Magic is an attempt by human beings to compel a divinity, by the use of physical means, to do what they wish that divinity to do."

"A host of intermediary beings called demons exist between gods and humans. Depending on their proximity to the gods, demons possess divine power in diminishing measures. Those closest to the gods have bodies of air; those closest to humans, bodies of steam or water. Because of this descending order, the unity of the

cosmos can be preserved. Otherwise, human and divine would be irreparably separated and no communication between the two would be possible. Everything is connected through the demons who mediate between the divine and the material. Magic
rests upon the belief that by getting hold of demons in physical objects, the divinity
can be influenced. The magician's art is to find out which material (metal, herb,
animal, etc.) contains which divinity and to what degree. Thus magic can achieve
either blessing or curse. The magician knows the secret and knows how to use it in
the correct way with the best results."

Biblical people themselves practiced magic. Rachel used mandrake plants in
order to bear a child (Gen. 30:14–24), and the text doesn't say they didn't help her
to conceive. Jacob made his flock of speckled or spotted sheep to increase over
Laban's sheep by pealing branches from poplar and almond trees and placing them
in the water troughs so that when the flocks mated in front of the branches they bore
young that were speckled or spotted (Gen. 30:25–43). What? How? Where is the science in that? Samuel's pouring out water to induce a storm in 1 Samuel 7:6 is often
thought to denote sympathetic magic. Samson's long hair supposedly gave him
strength. There are some stories from all parts of the world in which the soul or the
strength of someone resided in his hair. Job asked that the day of his birth should be
cursed by those who curse the day, who are ready to rouse up Leviathan, a mythical
beast (Job 3:8). Here might be a reference to magicians who were thought to rouse
up a dragon to swallow the sun at an eclipse. Then there is the magical power of
blessings and curses, already mentioned when we discussed Balaam.

According to *Harper's Bible Dictionary*, under the "Magic and Divination"
entry: "It was believed that great power rested in those holy men who were in close
proximity to God. Physical contact with such a person would have beneficial consequences." We see this with Elijah (1 Kings 17:17–24); Elisha (2 Kings 4:31–37);
and Jesus (Matt. 8:14–15; 9:29). "Anything in connection with such holy men
absorbed and transmitted a portion of their power. Elijah's mantle parted the waters
of the Jordan, and when Elisha put it on, Elijah's spirit rested on him (2 Kings
2:8–15). The garment of Jesus radiated and transmitted healing power (Mark
5:28–29), as did the handkerchiefs and aprons that people carried away from the
body of Paul (Acts 19:11–12). Some believers even attributed beneficial properties
to the shadow of Peter (Acts 5:15)."

Divination

What about *divination?* Pagan diviners are mentioned in 1 Samuel 6:2, Isaiah 44:25,
Ezekiel 21:22, and Acts 16:16, where a girl has a spirit of divination. According to
Harper's Bible Dictionary, under "Divination": "With divination, in contrast to
magic, one does not seek to alter the course of events, only to learn about them. The
ancient world developed many devices by which the veil of secrecy covering future
events could be lifted." Divination may take many forms. According to the *New
Bible Dictionary*, also under "Divination", the following forms are mentioned in the
Bible: "One) **Rhabdomancy.** Ezek. 21:21. Sticks or arrows were thrown into the air,

and omens were deduced from their position when they fell. Two) **Hepatoscopy.** Ezek. 21:21. Examination of the liver or other entrails of a sacrifice was supposed to give guidance. Three) **Teraphim**. Household gods associated with divination in 1 Sam. 15:23; Ezek. 21:21; Zech. 10:2. Four) **Necromancy**, or the consultation of the departed (Deut. 18:11; 1 Sam. 28:8; 2 Kings 21:6). Five) **Astrology** draws conclusions from the position of the sun, moon and planets in relation to the zodiac and to one another. The wise men (Magi) who came to the infant Jesus (Mt. 2:9) were probably trained in Babylonian tradition which mixed astronomy with astrology. Six) **Hydromancy,** or divination through water. Here forms and pictures appear in the water in a bowl, as also in crystal-gazing. The gleam of the water induces a state of light trance, and the visions are subjective (Gen. 44:5, 15)."

Even among God's people we see divination through the *casting of lots.* In the Old Testament the lot was cast to discover God's will for the allocation of territory (Josh. 18–19, etc.), the choice of the goat to be sacrificed on the Day of Atonement (Leviticus 16), the detection of a guilty person (Josh. 7:14; Jon. 1:7), the allocation of Temple duties (1 Chron. 24:5), and the discovery of a lucky day by Haman (Esther 3:7). The Urim and the Thummim are lots used to make important decisions where the answer was either yes or no (1 Sam. 14:41; 28:6; Exod. 28:29; Deut. 33:8; Lev. 8:7; Num. 27:21). In the New Testament Christ's clothes were allocated by lot (Matt. 27:35). The last occasion in the Bible on which the lot is used to divine the will of God is in the choice of Matthias to replace Judas Iscariot (Acts 1:15–26). Can you imagine any judges today casting lots to divide up land or to make any decisions?

Dreams

Dreams in the ancient world were believed to be communication from God.[23] Dreams were thought to convey messages from God or the gods. (See Genesis 20; 21:32; 24; 31:24; 40–41; Judg. 7:13–14). Pharaoh had two dreams and demanded that someone interpret them, and it's claimed Joseph accurately interpreted them for him (Genesis 41); Solomon had a dream where he asked and received his request for wisdom (1 Kings 3:5–15); the gospel of Matthew records five dreams in connection with the birth and infancy of Jesus, in three of which an angel appeared with God's message (Matt. 1:20; 2:12–13, 19, 22; 27:19), and one records the troubled dream of Pilate's wife that Jesus is innocent, and this dream was considered as at least enough evidence of Jesus' innocence to mention it. On occasions there is virtually no distinction between a dream and a vision during the night (Job 4:12ff.; Acts 9:10; 10:10, 30; 16:9; 18:9ff.). There is a very close connection between dreams and visions and prophecies: "And afterward, I will pour out my Spirit on all people. Your sons and daughters will prophesy, your old men will dream dreams, your young men will see visions" (Joel 2:28; Acts 2:17, cf. Num. 12:6).

Today's modern educated people simply don't accept that view of magic, divination, blessings, curses, or dreams. Dreams, for instance, are the combined product of memory and sensation running wild, as the rational part of our brains is unconscious. CAT scans and probes tell us which parts of our brains are "asleep" and which parts are awake when we are sleeping. Dreams open the window of the mind. Dreams give us a glimpse of a person's unconscious self. The Bible contains far too many things that people living in our day and age simply cannot accept any longer. It is unreasonable and superstitious, in the light of brain science, to consider dreams as any communication from God, gods, or the dead.

THE OLD TESTAMENT PROPHETS

The Old Testament prophets had to battle with the Israelite tendency to worship other gods, spoken of earlier, in both the northern and southern kingdoms (Isa. 47:11; Jer. 27:16–16; 29:8–9; Ezek. 13:2–9; 14; 22:28; Mic. 3:6–7; Zech. 10:2; Mal. 3:5), and beyond to other nations.

For what I consider a typical look at the evidence of a prophetic word, take a look at the prophetic story in Jonah. Although I do not believe there is a shred of historical evidence for this story, let me treat it as if it were historical in every detail. Try to put yourself in the shoes of each of the characters involved, including Jonah, the sailors, the police in Tarshish, the king of Ninevah, and his people. Read the story as if you are each of these characters, respectively. What would you think and do?

Prophets received their prophecies by means of dreams and visions (Num. 12:6). Several of the prophetic books claim to be based upon visions (Isa. 1:1; Ezek. 1:1; Obad. 1:1; Nah. 1:1), while most all of the rest of them start out either with "the word of the Lord came to me" (Jon. 1:1), or simply, this is "an oracle." I have known Christian people in the Pentecostal tradition who will claim a word from God too. One lady "prophesied" to a group of us that we'd start a Christian rock band (I played the drums) and we'd name it "Walk by Faith Not Sight." Such a band never came about. (Maybe it could still happen?) She was wrong.

In the Old Testament there were many prophets (1 Sam. 10:10–13), and they sought guidance from God in dreams and visions. So how did any of them know for sure their prophecies were truly from God? They had a dream. They saw a vision (which probably is indistinguishable from a dreamlike state anyway). The tests of the prophet laid down in Deuteronomy 13 and 18 merely demand that they spoke in God's name, and if they prophesied about the future, the things prophesied should come to pass. I take it that Jonah was upset at the corruption in Ninevah, much like Christians today are upset at the corruption in America, had a dream about it, and just felt certain about it.

When God purportedly called Jonah to preach against the city of Nineveh, he tried to flee from God by sailing to some place called Tarshish (v.3). Even though Jonah felt certain about the prophecy, he didn't like it, because he didn't want to warn the Ninevites of their impending destruction, because as later explained, he thought they might repent and escape God's judgment. But the kind of God he believed in when he fled was a tribal, localized god, and certainly not the later monotheistic omnipotent creator God.

Then the LORD sent a great wind on the sea, and such a violent storm arose that the ship threatened to break up. All the sailors were afraid and each cried out to his own god. And they threw the cargo into the sea to lighten the ship. (Jon. 1:4–5)

Of course, any sailor back then would blame the gods for the wind and the storm, but this is also Jonah's belief, since this is supposedly his writing, that his God sent this storm because he was running away from him. Is that what we do today? . . . blame ourselves or someone else for a storm?

But Jonah had gone below deck, where he lay down and fell into a deep sleep. The captain went to him and said, "How can you sleep? Get up and call on your god! Maybe he will take notice of us, and we will not perish." (Jon. 1:5–6)

The captain didn't care which god Jonah prayed to, so long as no god was left out of their prayers. This is true polytheism.

Then the sailors said to each other, "Come, let us cast lots to find out who is responsible for this calamity." (Jon. 1:7)

They cast lots and the lot fell on Jonah. This is a form of divination. Do you want to cast lots to see who's to blame for any hurricanes that come our way? Jonah accepted the results too.

So they asked him, "Tell us, who is responsible for making all this trouble for us? What do you do? Where do you come from? What is your country? From what people are you?" He answered, "I am a Hebrew and I worship the LORD, the God of heaven, who made the sea and the land." This terrified them and they asked, "What have you done?" (Jon. 1:8–10) (They knew he was running away from the LORD, because he had already told them so.)

Jonah expresses a view of God here that is at odds with his running away from God earlier. It's hard to reconcile the fact that he thought he could run away from God with his belief that the God is a "God of heaven, who made the sea and the land," except that Jonah may have truly realized this for the first time in the storm itself. But he states it as if he thought this all along.

With the casting of lots and the fact that he was running away from this kind of God, it terrified these sailors. These things would not terrify us today. Does God zap people who disobey him today? Like Ananias and Sapphira? Uzzah? Lot's wife? What if the lot had instead fallen on some follower of Zeus who was running away from him, or fighting against him, like Odysseus in *The Odyssey*? These sailors would still respond in the exact same way, because the proof was in the casting of lots, and the storm, and the story. They didn't need any other proof or evidence. Does this type of gullibility describe any thinking person today?

The sea was getting rougher and rougher. So they asked him, "What should we do to you to make the sea calm down for us?" "Pick me up and throw me into the sea," he replied, "and it will become calm. I know that it is my fault that this great storm has come upon you." (Jon. 1:11–12)

Yep, that's what Jonah concluded. Kill me and it'll be okay for you. We learn at the end of this book that he was suicidal anyway, so there's no difference expressed in this attitude of his. Jonah believes the storm is his fault. Have you ever blamed yourself because of a storm? Does God or nature act that way?

Instead, the men did their best to row back to land. But they could not, for the sea grew even wilder than before. Then they cried to the LORD, "O LORD, please do not let us die for taking this man's life. Do not hold us accountable for killing an innocent man, for you, O LORD, have done as you pleased." (Jon. 1:13–14)

Here they faced an ethical decision. They "know" Jonah is to blame for the storm, but does Jonah's God really demand they kill him? If they kill him, will Jonah's God be more upset with them for doing so? But Jonah eased their minds, because he himself says that's what they should do.

Then they took Jonah and threw him overboard, and the raging sea grew calm. At this the men greatly feared the LORD, and they offered a sacrifice to the LORD and made vows to him. (Jon. 1:15–16)

These sailors should be tried for attempted murder. Surely they had a list of the people on board. And when they docked to a port, someone would notice him missing. What would the police in Tarshish do then? Anything comparable to what our police would do? What would these men say to the police? Would their story hold up in today's courts? Absolutely not!

—But the LORD provided a great fish to swallow Jonah, and Jonah was inside the fish three days and three nights. (Jon. 1:17)

Hmmm. With a person like that telling the first part of this story, I doubt that he can be trustworthy telling the rest of the story. And if people were superstitious enough to believe God caused a storm to stop Jonah in his tracks without any evidence but nature and the story itself, then they would also believe he was swallowed by a fish simply because he told them it happened. If no evidence is required to believe the first part of the story, then no evidence is required to believe the last part.

At the end after the fish puked him up we read:

Then the word of the LORD came to Jonah a second time: "Go to the great city of Nineveh and proclaim to it the message I give you." Jonah obeyed the word of the LORD and went to Nineveh. Now Nineveh was a very important city—a visit required three days. On the first day, Jonah started into the city. He proclaimed: "Forty more days and Nineveh will be overturned." The Ninevites believed God. They declared a fast, and all of them, from the greatest to the least, put on sackcloth. (Jon 3:1–5)

Jonah obeyed his vision or dream, and preached the message he felt certain about, that "Forty more days and Nineveh will be overturned." That's what he said. Remember this.

When the news reached the king of Nineveh, he rose from his throne, took off his royal robes, covered himself with sackcloth and sat down in the dust. Then he issued a proclamation in Nineveh: "By the decree of the king and his nobles: Do not let any man or beast, herd or flock, taste anything; do not let them eat or drink. But let man and beast be covered with sackcloth. Let everyone call urgently on God. Let them give up their evil ways and their violence. Who knows? God may yet relent and with compassion turn from his fierce anger so that we will not perish." (Jon. 3:6–9)

In the first place, what evidence did the king of Ninevah have for believing Jonah? We are simply not told. Presumably none was needed because of the supposed fame of the Hebrew God. But if that's the case, then why didn't they already believe in this God? Even with the supposed fame of the Hebrew God, how would the king know that Jonah was his true prophet? That's a fair question, isn't it? Even Moses supposedly had wondered how the pharaoh would know he was sent from God, didn't he?

Still, how would America react to the same prophetic message by none other than Billy Graham: "Forty more days and America will be overturned." The laughter would be constant. Jay Leno and David Letterman would have a field day with this. That's because we today would demand some evidence. And there have been some prophets of doom in America too. Just listen to Jack Van Impe. But for the last thirty years or more Van Impe has always been wrong, and he's still getting donations to stay on the air!

I just don't see Ninevah repenting simply because the Ninevites probably didn't think they were doing that much wrong. And I see no further reason to suggest that at Jonah's preaching they would've turned and believed in the Hebrew God either, since they were polytheistic to the core.

When God saw what they did and how they turned from their evil ways, he had compassion and did not bring upon them the destruction he had threatened. (Jon. 3:10)

WHAT? I'm sure I read somewhere that the test of a prophet was that what he said was to come to pass (Deut. 18:22). Didn't he say Nineveh would be destroyed? Did he or didn't he? Answer the question. But it wasn't destroyed after all, was it? What if Billy Graham used this excuse to explain why America wasn't destroyed? Laughter again. What would you say about Jonah then? After all, there were a great many prophets running around proclaiming that God spoke to them too. If what he prophesied didn't come to pass, then is there any evidence at all that he was really called to speak God's word? And how should we now think about Jonah? After all, his prophecy failed the test of a true prophet! But yet his book is in the Bible. (For more on this see my chapter 16.)

What's missing in this story is evidence. No evidence was offered for any claim, except that Jonah said it was true. Without a doubt no Christian today would believe the same type of story told in the modern era, unless there was some pretty hard evidence.

Is there any evidence that Nineveh became monotheistic and righteous? If the Ninevites remained polytheistic and failed to worship the Hebrew God, that wouldn't be enough for Jonah's God, would it? If it was just about their moral behavior, then cities and countries all go through some cycle of "revival" from time to time, so it might be that Jonah was taking credit for something that happened on its own anyway. And where's this purported fish, anyway? The ancients had the superstitious belief that mythical beasts and fish lived in the seas, likened to the Loch Ness monster, like Rahab, Behemoth, and Leviathan.

This is what I mean by superstition. Little or no evidence is required, just a good story, based in fear, along with the storms of life.

Who Spoke for God?

The Old Testament prophets argued for their God over the gods and goddess worship that vied for the attention of the Israelites. Christians claim that anyone who worshiped these other gods was just doing wrong. After all, Moses and the prophets warned Israel to stay away from these beliefs and the practices that went with them, like sorcery, magic, witchcraft, and divination (e.g., Lev. 19:26; 20:27; Deut. 18:10–14). However, my question is that if God condemned these things over and over again, why did the people practice them over and over again? Why did they? My suggestion is that with a history mixed with so many myths, Israel was engaged in a battle over the correct message of the divine will and the correct methods for discovering it. It was a constant battle over the hearts and minds of the people, precisely because the so-called history from Genesis through Joshua contained far too many nonhistorical myths to be reliable enough evidence as to their origins. On the one side, you had magicians, sorcerers, and diviners, and on the other, you had the prophets, all vying for the people's hearts. Even among the prophets themselves there were many who were called false prophets by the other group of prophets.

Who said idol worship and sorcery were wrong in the first place? The prophets said so, whom the so-called faithful believed, from Moses, to Samuel, to Isaiah, to Malachi. In my opinion the biblical prophets simply forbad all other methods but their own for knowing God and his will. They gained their prophecies by means of "visions" and "dreams" (Num. 12:6) being formerly called "seers" (1 Sam. 9:9), and they forbad all other ways of gaining divine knowledge, because that's how they did it. There is power in advocating that how you do things is the only way they should be done, isn't there? No wonder then, that Queen Jezebel attempted to kill off the prophets (1 Kings 18:4; cf., Jer. 20:1–2). It was a power struggle over who could know the divine will and which methods were appropriate for this, since she practiced sorcery (2 Kings 9:22), and she worshiped Baal.

There were many prophets in the land (1 Sam. 10:5), as I've said, but only the ones who gained a following were highly regarded (e.g., Samuel was highly regarded as such, 1 Sam. 3:20). The other ones were just regarded as false prophets by the others. One person's false prophet was another person's true prophet of God, and vice versa (Jer. 23:9–40; 26:7–9). There were also many challenges between prophets to see who was a true prophet of God (1 Kings 18; Jeremiah 28). The reason was because people didn't automatically know the true ones from the false ones.

Elijah on Mt. Carmel—1 Kings 18:16–40

So Obadiah went to meet Ahab and told him . . . summon the people from all over Israel to meet me on Mount Carmel. And bring the four hundred and fifty prophets of Baal and the four hundred prophets of Asherah, who eat at Jezebel's table." *(18:16)*

Jezebel was Ahab's wife, who was the "daughter of Ethbaal king of the Sidonians." It was a political marriage done to stave off war and to save lives. Ahab "began to serve Baal and worship him. He set up an altar for Baal in the temple of Baal that he built in Samaria. Ahab also made an Asherah pole and did more to provoke the Lord, the God of Israel, to anger than did all the kings of Israel before him" (1 Kings 16:30–33). Queen Jezebel practiced sorcery (2 Kings 9:22). She amassed herself with many prophets of Baal and Asherah. They had 850 prophets. Why so many? Where did they work and live? They practiced sorcery, magic, divination, and probably astrology. That's a great number of prophets, and for each one of them there were many people who went to them for guidance and knowledge. I'm sure these prophets would've warned the people not to be misled by the other prophets, so the people had a great deal of difficulty knowing whom to believe, didn't they? Most Christians would say they wouldn't have had a hard time with this at all; they would've just rejected Baal. But that's claiming to be more intelligent than these ancient people were, and I never said they were stupid, just superstitious. It's always easier to decide which prophet was the true prophet after the war is over—that is, if you consider success the key characteristic of which god was the true god like they did, and that's probably all they had to go on.

Just think if our president did what Ahab did, and amassed for himself prophets who practiced sorcery in Christian America? Wouldn't the Christian majority rise up against such a thing as one, both liberals and conservatives of every shape and size? That's because Christians claim to have evidence for their beliefs—whether they do or not is the question here.

Who are these gods that Ahab accepted? According to *Harper's Bible Dictionary*: "Baal is a weather god associated with thunderstorms. Baal was said to appoint the season of rains. Clouds were thought to be part of his entourage. Lightning was his weapon, and it may have been his invention. The windows of Baal's palace were thought to correspond to openings in the clouds through which rain flowed. Rain was important to Canaanite agriculture, and Baal was consequently a god of fertility—a prodigious lover as well as the giver of abundance. . . . The gods are regarded as the children of Asherah and El. Her relationship with Baal is perplexing. Baal's assault on the offspring of Asherah is once narrated, yet Asherah advocates for Baal the role of king and judge among the gods."

And here we have many people in Israel believing this? Was there any evidence for this? I cannot think of any since we know something about rain, and lightning and thunderstorms. So why did they believe this? If there was any solid evidence for the God of Moses and what he supposedly had done, then why would the Israelites so easily believe these other myths? Unless, of course, as is my contention, the stories told about the God of Moses were on an equal playing field—that there was no evidence for believing those stories either.

So Ahab sent word throughout all Israel and assembled the prophets on Mount Carmel. Elijah went before the people and said, "How long will you waver between two opinions? If the LORD is God, follow him; but if Baal is God, follow him." But the people said nothing. Then Elijah said to them, "I am the only one of the LORD's prophets left, but Baal has four hundred and fifty prophets. Get two bulls for us. Let them choose one for themselves, and let them cut it into pieces and put it on the wood but not set fire to it. I will prepare the other bull and put it on the wood but not set fire to it. Then you call on the name of your god, and I will call on the name of the LORD. The god who answers by fire—he is God." Then all the people said, "What you say is good." (18:20–24)

Now let's think about some challenge like this occurring in the modern world. Would anyone even show up to see it? Would any Christian issue such a challenge? If challenged, would any Christian accept this challenge? Not at all. So I ask why?

Elijah said: "I am the only one of the LORD's prophets left." Boy that sure sounds like a minority of one here. So again, how is it possible that the people of Israel had so fully rejected the God of Moses to the point where there was only one faithful prophet of God in the northern kingdom of Israel? The answer is that they were a very superstitious people who were swayed very easily to believe stupendous mythical stories that lacked evidence. That is, there was no evidence either way, just religious experiences and stupendous stories. These stories competed for the hearts and minds of the people because there was no historical evidence either way between them.

Elijah said to the prophets of Baal, "Choose one of the bulls and prepare it first, since there are so many of you. Call on the name of your god, but do not light the fire." So they took the bull given them and prepared it. Then they called on the name of Baal from morning till noon. "O Baal, answer us!" they shouted. But there was no response; no one answered. And they danced around the altar they had made. At

noon Elijah began to taunt them. "Shout louder!" he said. "Surely he is a god! Per-
haps he is deep in thought, or busy, or traveling. Maybe he is sleeping and must be
awakened." So they shouted louder and slashed themselves with swords and spears,
as was their custom, until their blood flowed. Midday passed, and they continued
their frantic prophesying until the time for the evening sacrifice. But there was no
response, no one answered, no one paid attention. (18:25–29)

Apparently these prophets thought they were up to the challenge, so they tried
and they tried. That's what it says. These prophets really believed they could do it,
so they tried. Would you have tried? And even if it was for show, to save face, how
long would you try? And look how they tried, by shouting and slashing themselves
"as was their custom" and prophesying. There is every indication here that they
thought they could do it. If I was back then and I was challenged by Elijah, I would
simply say, "I don't think it will work, so you go ahead and show me." That's
because I am not superstitious by their standards. I live in the modern world of science where lightning is a meteorological event produced in a thunderstorm.

Then Elijah said to all the people, "Come here to me." They came to him, and he
repaired the altar of the LORD, which was in ruins. . . . Elijah stepped forward and
prayed: "O LORD, God of Abraham, Isaac and Israel, let it be known today that you
are God in Israel and that I am your servant and have done all these things at your
command. Then the fire of the LORD fell and burned up the sacrifice, the wood, the
stones and the soil, and also licked up the water in the trench. When all the people
saw this, they fell prostrate and cried, "The LORD—he is God! The LORD—he is
God!" (18:30–39)

If this truly happened, then I would fall on my face and worship God as well.
But I'm trying to establish that such an age as theirs was highly superstitious, and
hence unreliable as a testimony to understand what actually happened. Christian
thinker Clark Pinnock admits that "the problem for us is that the Bible was written
long before the time when a clear line was drawn between strictly historical and sto-
rylike narrative. Whereas we are eager to distinguish the factual from the nonfactual,
it cannot be said that the Biblical writers always were."[24] Just look at any introduction to 1 Kings and you'll know that, at best, this account was compiled no earlier
than 180 years after it supposedly happened. Even in a modern society we have
developed myths surrounding our heroes, like Paul Revere's ride, George Washington and the cherry tree, or Abe Lincoln walking for a mile to return someone's
penny. These myths are small ones among less superstitious people, but think about
the myths that could be generated in 180 years surrounding the Mt. Carmel event by
superstitious people. Probably the same kind of myths that surrounded Samson and
his great strength. Remember here, we're dealing with a superstitious people who
may just believe any good story and embellish it as it goes, adding to it some very
stupendous things.

David L. Edwards wrote that when it comes to Elijah and Elisha, "the storytelling has become fanciful . . . the stories are so colorful that we cannot tell exactly what took place in the time of Elijah and Elisha."[25]

Then Elijah commanded them, "Seize the prophets of Baal. Don't let anyone get away!" They seized them, and Elijah had them brought down to the Kishon Valley and slaughtered there. (18:40)

It's no wonder that Jezebel waged war against the other prophets who claimed to speak for the God of Moses. A lot of killing was going on, depending on which religion you practiced. It was indeed a war; the war of the prophets. And this story ends with 850 prophets dying at the hands of Elijah's new converts.

Furthermore, since 1 Kings was compiled either at the time of Jerusalem's demise or afterward, the people finally concluded that the prophets of Baal and Asherah were the false prophets, so their whole history was written and compiled from hindsight with this lesson in mind. Why did they conclude that those "false" prophets were wrong? Here's why: since the worship of these other gods was blamed by the "true" prophets for why they were destroyed as a people and sent into captivity, then those gods were the false gods and those prophets were the false prophets. Nations believed in the gods that brought them victory, and rejected the gods that didn't. History would have been written differently, from the perspective of the prophets of Baal and Asherah, had it turned out differently.[26]

THE NEW TESTAMENT PERIOD

Now we turn to the various events and superstitions we find in the New Testament. I'll skip over several superstitious beliefs like the virgin birth, incarnation, atonement, and resurrection of Jesus, along with the belief in Satan and hell, since I'll cover them in detail later. In the New Testament, miracles themselves are sometimes seen as the result of magic. The pagan world certainly regarded many miracles as magic (Acts 8:9–11), and on at least one occasion Jesus used magic when he put mud in a man's eyes to heal him of blindness. In John 9:6–7 (from the New American Standard Bible) we read: "Having said this, he spit on the ground, made some mud with the saliva, and put it on the man's eyes. 'Go,' he told him, 'wash in the Pool of Siloam' (this word means Sent). So the man went and washed, and came home seeing." For the magical properties of the "pool of Siloam" look at John 5:1–7: "Now there is in Jerusalem by the sheep gate a pool, which is called in Hebrew Bethesda, having five porticoes. In these lay a multitude of those who were sick, blind, lame, and withered [waiting for the moving of the waters; for an angel of the Lord went down at certain seasons into the pool and stirred up the water; whoever then first, after the stirring up of the water, stepped in was made well from whatever disease with which he was afflicted.] A man was there who had been ill for thirty-eight years. When Jesus saw him lying there, and knew that he had already been a long time in that condition, He said to him, 'Do you wish to get well?' The sick man answered Him, 'Sir, I have no man to put me into the pool when the water is stirred up, but while I am coming, another steps down before me.'" The part in brackets was pseudonymously added by a later Christian to explain why these people were there. A "multitude" of them believed in the magical properties of this pool, when it's stirred. Where is a pool like that today? Although archaeology has found this pool in Jerusalem, it doesn't have any magical properties. It sounds to us just like the mythical "fountain of youth."

Speaking of magical properties, the New Testament writers held to the ancient superstitious belief in the "evil eye." Are we to actually believe that people have a powerful "evil eye"? In Matthew 6:22 (and Luke 11:34–36) Jesus says, "The eye is the lamp of the body. So, if your eye is generous, your whole body will be full of light; but if your eye is evil, your whole body will be full of darkness. If then the light in you is darkness, how great is the darkness!" Later, Jesus mentions the evil eye in the parable of the laborers in the vineyard (Matt. 20:15). The landowner asks the worker, "Do you have the evil eye because I am generous?" In a dispute with the Pharisees over the issue of purity (Mark 7:1–23), Mark's Jesus lists the evil eye among several evil things that emerge from the human heart which contaminate a person. Paul writes: "O foolish Galatians! Who has put the evil eye on, you before whose eyes Jesus Christ was proclaimed crucified?" (Gal. 3:1).

Bruce Malina and Richard Rohrbaugh describe what the ancients believed about the evil eye. Here is an excerpt: "Fear of the evil eye was widespread in classical antiquity. Because the eye was considered the 'window of the soul' (Plato), it could act as a conduit through which internal feelings and desires could be (voluntarily or involuntarily) projected onto the external world. As Plutarch explains it, odor, voice, and breath are all caused by streams of particles emanating from the physical body. When these emanations encounter another physical body, they excite the sense organs and produce a real physical effect. In the same way, he argues, an actual (the most active) stream of emanations comes from the eyes, and like other bodily emanations can produce actual physical effects, in whatever they happen to strike. Thus envy, greed, covetousness, jealousy, and any of the other negative attitudes that originate in the heart, when projected outward through the eye and onto other persons or things, could do real physical damage. . . . In essence it is the belief that certain individuals have the power to physically damage whatever they look upon. Avoiding the glance of those possessing the evil eye is thus a very serious matter. 'Fascinators,' persons possessing the evil eye, come from all stations in life, including both genders, all ages, all social classes, all occupations, all cultural and ethnic groups. Often rivals or enemies, strangers, the physically deformed, or persons deemed socially deviant were considered like possessors. And one motivated by envy or greed would be especially suspect."[27] This brings me to demonology in the New Testament.

Demon Possession in the New Testament

There were many exorcists in Jesus' day: "Some Jews who went around driving out evil spirits tried to invoke the name of the Lord Jesus over those who were demon-possessed. They would say, 'In the name of Jesus, whom Paul preaches, I command you to come out.' Seven sons of Sceva, a Jewish chief priest, were doing this'" (Acts 19:13–16). There were many sorcerers too. We find them in Samaria (Acts 8:9–11), and in Paphos on the island of Cyprus, there was a sorcerer "who was an attendant of the proconsul, Sergius Paulus" (Acts 13:6–8; see also Rev. 21:8; 22:15).

In the gospels we often read that Jesus' opponents say he is demon possessed: (cf. Matt. 9:32–34; Matt. 12:24). Sometimes Jesus is called demon possessed simply because he says things that seemed to his hearers just plain crazy: "'Has not Moses given you the law? Yet not one of you keeps the law. Why are you trying to kill me?' 'You are demon-possessed,' the crowd answered. 'Who is trying to kill you?'" (John 7:20). "At these words the Jews were again divided. Many of them said, 'He is demon-possessed and raving mad. Why listen to him?'" (John 10:19–20; 8:48–51). Even John the Baptist was thought to be demon possessed (Matt. 11:18). It was easy to claim someone was possessed in those days. Whenever Jesus acted contrary to what was normally expected, or his teaching sounded strange or weird, they concluded he was a demon-possessed person, much like someone today might say, "you're crazy."

Look how Jesus responded to these charges: "Jesus knew their thoughts and said to them, 'if I drive out demons by Beelzebub, by whom do your people drive them out? So then, they will be your judges'" (Matt. 12:27). There were lots of Jewish exorcists and lots of demon-possessed people in those times, and Jesus didn't deny what these exorcists could do. "'Teacher,' said John, 'we saw a man driving out demons in your name and we told him to stop, because he was not one of us.' 'Do not stop him,' Jesus said. 'No one who does a miracle in my name can in the next moment say anything bad about me, for whoever is not against us is for us'" (Mark 9:38–40).

Look at the close connection between healing and exorcism: "The Twelve were with him (Jesus), and also some women who had been cured of evil spirits and diseases: Mary (called Magdalene) from whom seven demons had come out" (Luke 8:1–2). "Jesus said, 'Go tell that fox, "I will drive out demons and heal people today and tomorrow, and on the third day I will reach my goal"'" (Luke 13:32). "Philip went down to a city in Samaria and proclaimed the Christ there. When the crowds heard Philip and saw the miraculous signs he did, they all paid close attention to what he said. With shrieks, evil spirits came out of many, and many paralytics and cripples were healed. So there was great joy in that city" (Acts 8:5–8).

Today we just don't think sick people are demon possessed. With the advent of modern medicine we treat the physical causes, and with psychology we treat the mental causes of illnesses the best that we can. And while it can be argued that Luke was a "physician" (Col. 4:14) and that he knew the difference, we simply have to consider how much of the science of medicine he knew in his day. As a child of his times, it would seem reasonable to suppose that those illnesses he couldn't cure with the medicine he had at his disposal would be thought of by him as demon possession too. According to *Harper's Bible Dictionary*, under "Physicians": "As with other ancient cultures, there was in Israel no necessary conflict between belief in divine, demonic, and/or human causation of illness or between requests for divine assistance and the application of practical therapy."

All I can say here is what a mixed-up world it must have been to live in such a superstitious age as the first century! Formerly epilepsy was viewed as demon possession. But now we know some of the causes and can minimize the effects. Mental disease also has its known causes, and some specialists can help with brain surgery. So there is a whole lot less demon possession today simply because of modern science.

Some Christians will argue from the book of Revelation (20:1–10) that Satan is bound and cannot hurt us like that anymore. But if Christians believe this, then it also says that Satan will be bound for a one thousand years. When did those thousand years start so that I may know when they end? If they say that the thousand years is not literal, then how can they take a literal view of Satan being bound at all? (As far as Satan and the demons go, see my chapter 21.)

Is the Heart the Seat of the Mind?

The Bible is filled with claims that a few of our bodily organs are the seat of emotions. The Old Testament understands the liver, bowels, and heart as emotional seats for mental states that were later reduced in the New Testament to the heart. What Jesus said is typical: "For out of the heart comes forth evil thoughts, murders, adulteries, sexual sins, thefts, false testimony, and blasphemies" (Matt. 15:19).

One scholarly reference tells us: "There is in the New Testament a rich usage of heart (*kardía*) for a. the seat of feelings, desires, and passions (e.g., joy, pain, love, desire, and lust; cf. Acts 2:26; John 16:6; 2 Cor. 7:3; Rom. 10:1; 1:24); b. the seat of thought and understanding (cf. Matt. 7:21; John 12:40; Acts 8:22; Mark 11:23; Rev. 18:7; Rom. 1:21); c. the seat of the will (e.g., Acts 11:23; 2 Cor. 9:7; Luke 21:14); and d. which determines moral conduct (e.g., Luke 16:15; Rom. 5:5; 8:27; Eph. 3:17; Heb. 8:10; 2 Pet. 1:19; as the heart of the sinner, Mark 7:21; John 12:40; Eph. 4:18; James 1:26; as the heart of the redeemed, Matt. 11:29; 1 Tim. 1:5; 1 Thess. 3:13; Coloss. 3:22; 1 Pet. 3:15; James 4:8, etc.)."[28]

Most prescientific ancient cultures believed the heart was the seat of emotions simply because it beat faster or slower depending on the emotional state of people. They concluded that a person used it to feel and to think. The process of mummification by ancient Egyptian priests, for instance, involved saving all the major internal organs in urns (including the heart) but removing the brain through the nasal cavity and throwing it away as totally useless.[29] We now know that our brain is the seat of thinking and of our emotions. Modern artificial heart transplants now adequately debunk these beliefs, for we can do just fine without our own hearts. Therefore, it is nonsensical to believe in a "sinful heart" or in asking Jesus "into our hearts."

Visions in the New Testament

From the *New Bible Dictionary*: "**VISION**. The borderline between vision and dream or trance is difficult, if not impossible, to determine. This is reflected in the biblical vocabulary of 'vision.' The NT uses two words in this connection: *horama* (Acts 9:10, 12; 10:3, 17, 19) and *optasia* (Luke 1:22; Acts 26:19; 2 Cor. 12:1). They signify 'appearance' or 'vision.' [Later on this will have some significance with the resurrection appearances of Jesus.] The circumstances in which the revelatory visions came to the seers of the Bible are varied. They came in men's waking hours (Dan. 10:7; Acts 9:7); by day (Acts 10:3) or by night (Gen. 46:2). But the visions had close connections with the dream-state (Num. 12:6; Job 4:13). . . . In the NT Luke manifests the greatest interest in visions. The supreme set of visions in the NT is that in the book of the Revelation."

Luke's usage of the word group for "vision." Zechariah, John the Baptist's father, didn't actually see angels; he saw a vision (Luke 1:22). The women who went to the tomb of Jesus said they didn't see angels, just a vision (Luke 24:23). Ananias saw visions and followed them to speak to Saul/Paul: "In Damascus there was a disciple named Ananias. The Lord called to him in a vision, 'Ananias!'" (Acts 9:10). "So Ananias departed and entered the house, and after laying his hands on him said, 'Brother Saul, the Lord Jesus, who appeared (i.e., gave a vision) to you on the road by which you were coming, has sent me so that you may regain your sight and be filled with the Holy Spirit'" (Acts 9:17).

At Caesarea there was a man named Cornelius who was "a centurion in what was known as the Italian Regiment." He received a vision "one day at about three in the afternoon," and followed it (Acts 10:1–3). Then the Apostle Peter himself has one and learns from it that "God has granted even the Gentiles repentance unto life" (Acts 11:5–6,18). That's an educated way to learn something, isn't it?

Luke also tells us Peter received his "vision" while "in a trance." A trance? Paul himself received a vision while in a trance (Acts 22:17). Ancient people, especially those considered prophets and priests (and apostles too), would put themselves in a trance to gain divine knowledge. How often did Peter and Paul do that? The *Enhanced Strong's Lexicon* tells us that "Trance" equals "ecstasy . . . throwing of the mind out of its normal state, alienation of mind, whether such as makes a lunatic or that of a man who by some sudden emotion is transported as it were out of himself, so that in this rapt condition, although he is awake, his mind is drawn off from all surrounding objects and wholly fixed on things divine that he sees nothing but the forms and images lying within, and thinks that he perceives with his bodily eyes and ears realities shown him by God." (On "trance" in the Old Testament, see also Dan. 8:18; 10:9.)

Paul's missionary journeys are said to be directed by visions, which happened in the night (hence, dreams). "And a vision appeared to Paul in the night; There stood a man of Macedonia, and prayed him, saying, Come over into Macedonia, and help us. And after he had seen the vision, immediately we endeavored to go into Macedonia, assuredly gathering that the Lord had called us for to preach the gospel unto them" (Acts 16:9–10).

In Acts 18:9 it is said that Paul was once again in a trance. Paul even seems to equate his Damascus Road conversion experience to a vision, "So, King Agrippa, I did not prove disobedient to the heavenly vision" (Acts 26:19). Was his vision of Jesus just another dream? Maybe so.

Paul in Lystra of the Galatians—Acts 14:8–20

In Lystra there sat a man crippled in his feet, who was lame from birth and had never walked. He listened to Paul as he was speaking. Paul looked directly at him, saw that he had faith to be healed and called out, "Stand up on your feet!" At that, the man jumped up and began to walk. (14:8–10)

I know that this is difficult to dispute, since the story is written by Luke, "the Physician." What I do know is that such things are claimed by Benny Hinn's followers all of the time, as well as Oral Roberts. I also know that Luke was a believer and he wanted to tell a story that would cause other people to believe. So I reflect back and remember how Christians would regularly inflate their claims of healing too, and wonder if this is what Luke did. But the bottom line is that I require more evidence to believe something like this than a mere report by someone in the past who lived and breathed among people who were wildly superstitious. Anyway, are there any other clues here?

When the crowd saw what Paul had done, they shouted in the Lycaonian language, "The gods have come down to us in human form!" Barnabas they called Zeus, and Paul they called Hermes because he was the chief speaker. The priest of Zeus, whose temple was just outside the city, brought bulls and wreaths to the city gates because he and the crowd wanted to offer sacrifices to them. (14:11–13)

The crowd? Greek: $o\chi\lambda o\iota$ noun, masculine, plural, nominative, "a multitude, the common people." Not the educated classes, but we are hardly ever talking about the educated classes in the New Testament. It's almost always, unless specified, the common average classes or lower classes that Jesus and Paul reached. And so far, those classes of people seemed overwhelmingly superstitious.

Wait a minute? "The gods have come down to us in human form!" What? They believed it was possible for the gods to come down in the human forms of Paul and Barnabas? Isn't that also what Paul and Barnabas believed about Jesus? Hmmm. And they wanted to offer sacrifices to Paul and Barnabas? This is all so strange to us today.

But when the apostles Barnabas and Paul heard of this, they tore their clothes and rushed out into the crowd, shouting: "Men, why are you doing this? We too are only men, human like you. We are bringing you good news, telling you to turn from these worthless things to the living God, who made heaven and earth and sea and everything in them. . . . Even with these words, they had difficulty keeping the crowd from sacrificing to them. (14:14–18)

Paul did a great miracle and yet the people had a hard time believing what these two gods said? That too is very strange. If I thought someone was god, I'd listen to what he said. But they were in a frenzy.

Then some Jews came from Antioch and Iconium and won the crowd over. They stoned Paul and dragged him outside the city, thinking he was dead. But after the disciples had gathered around him, he got up and went back into the city. The next day he and Barnabas left for Derbe. (14:19–20)

How would it be possible for the Jews to have "won the crowd over" after what Luke just told us that Paul had done? The usual response of rational people would be to reject what the Jews said, rather than what Paul said, since they already believed Paul was a god. And Jews? This polytheistic crowd listened to Jews? My, how quickly they were swayed back and forth and back and forth, according to Luke's own account. And Luke wants us to believe him? That's very strange too.

They stoned Paul? The only reason they might have listened to what the Jews said is that they claimed Paul and Barnabas were demons or demon possessed. But Paul and Barnabas would be right there denying it. So whom would you believe? Paul supposedly did a great miracle, and the next moment they stoned him. Maybe the miracle wasn't so great after all? And it shows once again that the people Paul spread the gospel to were superstitious to the core. No evidence was needed. They just believed the person who had the best story. And they were ready to kill Paul too.

Why would they turn Paul over to the Jews to kill him or attempt to kill him themselves? Again, it's because they were fearful that with these two demons in their midst, the gods would be displeased with them and not send rain, or not allow their women to bear children, or send fire from the sky instead. No wonder the message of Paul spread. It was quite literally the best story out there. Nothing could top it. But the evidence? Who needs that when you're dealing with superstitious people like this? All you had to be concerned about was being stoned.

Paul in Athens—Acts 17:16–31

While Paul was waiting for them in Athens, he was greatly distressed to see that the city was full of idols. (17:16)

Athens was full of idols? These people were overwhelmingly superstitious people. There are rites and sacrifices that go with each idol. There are priests and diviners, sorcerers and magicians that go with each one, and there are even temples that go with each one.

So he reasoned in the synagogue with the Jews and the God-fearing Greeks, as well as in the marketplace day by day with those who happened to be there. A group of Epicurean and Stoic philosophers began to dispute with him. Some of them asked, "What is this babbler trying to say?" Others remarked, "He seems to be advocating foreign gods." They said this because Paul was preaching the good news about Jesus and the resurrection. (17:17–18)

Of course, whoever writes the story frames the discussion. Paul "reasoned" with them, it says. Did they not reason with him too? They had to. It's just that the author considered Paul's arguments much more reasonable. But look at how some of them responded: "He seems to be advocating foreign gods." They were referring to the god "Jesus" and the god "Resurrection" here. They were so polytheistic that they couldn't understand what Paul was even talking about. But they were concerned about these two "foreign gods." They liked their own gods and may have felt threatened by the missionary who wanted to advocate other foreign gods.

Then they took him and brought him to a meeting of the Areopagus, where they said to him, "May we know what this new teaching is that you are presenting? You are bringing some strange ideas to our ears, and we want to know what they mean." (All the Athenians and the foreigners who lived there spent their time doing nothing but talking about and listening to the latest ideas.) (17:19–21)

By the way, verse 21 has to be such an exaggeration that it's quite simply false, and hence a lie. "All the Athenians . . . spent their time doing nothing but talking." What? They didn't work, or wash clothes, or cook? Such a demeaning attitude toward Athens is just that, demeaning. And even taking into consideration that it is an exaggeration, which we would quite naturally do, as an exaggeration it's still false, stupid, and a lie. What if the your local newspaper prints: "All the people in Chicago and all of its visitors spend their time doing nothing but talking about and listening to the latest ideas"? At first glance we'd shake our heads. Then we'd read the story and ask ourselves what the people of Chicago would say in response, because the story is obviously biased. Then we'd say that such a report is so grossly unfair and exaggerated that the editor should be fired. Since we already know this report in Acts is a gross exaggeration, we have to start asking what would the people in Athens say in response to this account, as well as the rest of the book of Acts.

Paul then stood up in the meeting of the Areopagus and said: "Men of Athens! I see that in every way you are very religious. For as I walked around and looked carefully at your objects of worship, I even found an altar with this inscription: TO AN UNKNOWN GOD. Now what you worship as something unknown I am going to proclaim to you." (17:22–23)

This was the milieu of Athens. The King James Version uses the words "very superstitious" instead of "very religious" here. "Very religious" or "Very superstitious", it doesn't matter. They were so superstitious that they even had an idol "TO AN UNKNOWN GOD." Apparently they didn't want to offend any god at all!

The God who made the world and everything in it is the Lord of heaven and earth and does not live in temples built by hands. And he is not served by human hands, as if he needed anything, because he himself gives all men life and breath and everything else. From one man he made every nation of men, that they should inhabit the

whole earth; and he determined the times set for them and the exact places where
they should live. God did this so that men would seek him and perhaps reach out for
him and find him, though he is not far from each one of us. "For in him we live and
move and have our being." As some of your own poets have said, "We are his off-
spring." (17:24–28)

Of course, Paul here really misunderstands the nature of idols. The truth is that
these idols *represent* the gods. They are images of the gods. This analysis can be
borne out, I think. But still, look at what their own poet said: "We are his offspring."
Very religious, and very superstitious.

Therefore since we are God's offspring, we should not think that the divine being is
like gold or silver or stone—an image made by man's design and skill. In the past
God overlooked such ignorance, but now he commands all people everywhere to
repent. For he has set a day when he will judge the world with justice by the man he
has appointed. He has given proof of this to all men by raising him from the dead.
(17:29–31)

The ignorance Paul refers to may be his own, about the divine nature being like
gold or silver or stone—an image made by man's design and skill. I grant that any
image of any god can be mistakenly worshiped, and Paul's point here isn't that far
off the mark. Those adherents who were educated about their idol worship would
know the difference. But the fact that many people in Athens may not have is itself
telling on their level of understanding. How much more superstitious are these
people who think the man made idol is itself the god.

All I point out here is the nature of the people in Athens at the time of the
spreading of Paul's gospel. Superstitious people like the ones described here in Acts
do not need evidence for their beliefs. They just need to hear a believable story by
sincere people, and have some corresponding religious experiences.

The Riot in Ephesus—Acts 19:23–41

About that time there arose a great disturbance about the Way. A silversmith named
Demetrius, who made silver shrines of Artemis, brought in no little business for the
craftsmen. He called them together, along with the workmen in related trades, and
said: "Men, you know we receive a good income from this business. And you see and
hear how this fellow Paul has convinced and led astray large numbers of people
here in Ephesus and in practically the whole province of Asia. He says that man-
made gods are no gods at all. There is danger not only that our trade will lose its
good name, but also that the temple of the great goddess Artemis will be discredited,
and the goddess herself, who is worshiped throughout the province of Asia and the
world, will be robbed of her divine majesty." (19:23–27)

Who's Artemis, anyway? While it's probably an exaggeration to say that this goddess "is worshiped throughout the province of Asia and the world," certainly most
all people in and around Ephesus did. There were undoubtedly many people
throughout the known world who did. *Microsoft Encarta* tells us: "Artemis, in Greek
mythology, one of the principal goddesses, counterpart of the Roman goddess
Diana. She was the daughter of the god Zeus and Leto and the twin sister of the god
Apollo. She was chief hunter to the gods and goddess of hunting and of wild animals, especially bears. Artemis was also the goddess of childbirth, of nature, and of
the harvest. As the moon goddess, she was sometimes identified with the goddesses
Selene and Hecate. . . . Although traditionally the friend and protector of youth,
especially young women, Artemis prevented the Greeks from sailing to Troy during
the Trojan War until they sacrificed a maiden to her. According to some accounts,
just before the sacrifice, she rescued the victim, Iphigenia. Like Apollo, Artemis was
armed with a bow and arrows, which she often used to punish mortals who angered
her. In other legends, she is praised for giving young women who died in childbirth
a swift and painless death."

*When they heard this, they were furious and began shouting: "Great is Artemis of
the Ephesians!" Soon the whole city was in an uproar. The people seized Gaius and
Aristarchus, Paul's traveling companions from Macedonia, and rushed as one man
into the theater. Paul wanted to appear before the crowd, but the disciples would not
let him. 31 Even some of the officials of the province, friends of Paul, sent him a message begging him not to venture into the theater. (19:28–31)*

Even though the text attributes financial motive to Demetrius, the overwhelming reaction is that the initial crowd believed in Artemis.

*The assembly was in confusion: Some were shouting one thing, some another. Most
of the people did not even know why they were there. The Jews pushed Alexander to
the front, and some of the crowd shouted instructions to him. He motioned for
silence in order to make a defense before the people. But when they realized he was
a Jew, they all shouted in unison for about two hours: "Great is Artemis of the Ephesians!" (19:32–34)*

Even if some of these Ephesians hadn't known why they were there, they did
know what they believed—with fanaticism. Two hours!

*The city clerk quieted the crowd and said: "Men of Ephesus, doesn't all the world
know that the city of Ephesus is the guardian of the temple of the great Artemis and
of her image, which fell from heaven? Therefore, since these facts are undeniable,
you ought to be quiet and not do anything rash. You have brought these men here,
though they have neither robbed temples nor blasphemed our goddess. If, then,
Demetrius and his fellow craftsmen have a grievance against anybody, the courts
are open and there are proconsuls. They can press charges. If there is anything fur-*

ther you want to bring up, it must be settled in a legal assembly. As it is, we are in danger of being charged with rioting because of today's events. In that case we would not be able to account for this commotion, since there is no reason for it." After he had said this, he dismissed the assembly. (19:35–41)

Here's a pragmatic clerk in the midst of fanaticism. But can you imagine any town clerk in America dealing with the same problem—and admitting the things he did: "these facts are undeniable." That's the difference between them and us today, I think. These people were definitely overwhelmingly superstitious, and had no evidence for the existence of Artemis, except religious experiences that can be interpreted according to their own beliefs. These people would believe any good story if told sincerely, wouldn't they? And so it would seem that the competition among religious truth claims would be in who had the best story, wouldn't it, even if old beliefs die hard, like in Ephesus. The Christian story had to win, because it couldn't be topped. And Paul established a church there.

Paul in Malta—Acts 28:1–6

Once safely on shore, we found out that the island was called Malta. The islanders showed us unusual kindness. They built a fire and welcomed us all because it was raining and cold. Paul gathered a pile of brushwood and, as he put it on the fire, a viper, driven out by the heat, fastened itself on his hand. When the islanders saw the snake hanging from his hand, they said to each other, "This man must be a murderer; for though he escaped from the sea, Justice has not allowed him to live." (28:1–4)

I don't think the incident occurred as reported. "Fastened on his hand"; later he "shook it off." Most snakebites are very quick. And if it was quick, maybe the venom wasn't enough to kill or even hurt Paul? Even if otherwise, who actually was there to see it happen? How many actually saw it? Maybe Paul merely told them what happened? Or maybe one other person saw something and told the others. So when it says the "islanders" saw it, how many people does that mean? And if it actually means most or all of them, then the rest of the islanders believed it because it was merely told to them. And if the snake fell into the fire afterward, who knew exactly which kind of snake it was that bit him?

They concluded that Paul was a murderer and that the god "Justice" has not allowed him to live. A murderer? Why not a rapist? Or a thief? I tell ya, I could get these people to buy a piece of property in the Land of Oz. Bad things happen because of the gods. That's just stupid.

But Paul shook the snake off into the fire and suffered no ill effects. The people expected him to swell up or suddenly fall dead, but after waiting a long time and seeing nothing unusual happen to him, they changed their minds and said he was a god. (28:5–6)

They changed their minds? All of them? Back and forth and back and forth. If a bad thing happened, then god was angry. If a good thing happened, a god was pleased, or the person himself was a god. This is much too fickle for me, and we've seen this before. But my point is to see how these people reached conclusions that few educated modern people today would reach. I tell you I could go back in time and with a sleight bit of hand, I could convince them I was a god and have a pampered life. I could also convince them that Jesus arose from the dead too.

The New Testament "War of the Teachers"

In the New Testament, like the Old Testament we see numerous warnings against false prophets, teachers, and ministers The following warning comes from Jude:

Dear friends, although I was very eager to write to you about the salvation we share, I felt I had to write and urge you to contend for the faith that was once for all entrusted to the saints. For certain men whose condemnation was written about long ago have secretly slipped in among you. They are godless men, who change the grace of our God into a license for immorality and deny Jesus Christ our only Sovereign and Lord. (1:3–4)

This warning is from 2 Peter 2:1–3:

But there were also false prophets among the people, just as there will be false teachers among you. They will secretly introduce destructive heresies, even denying the sovereign Lord who bought them—bringing swift destruction on themselves. Many will follow their shameful ways and will bring the way of truth into disrepute. In their greed these teachers will exploit you with stories they have made up. Their condemnation has long been hanging over them, and their destruction has not been sleeping.

The author says, "with stories they have made up." This is spoken from the author's perspective, of course. But apparently many people did make up stories back then, didn't they?

My questions here are threefold: First, since we already know that prophets received their prophecies by means of dreams and visions (Num. 12:6), how did any of them know for sure their prophecies were truly from God?

Just go back and read Jonah. The only way they could tell whether a "vision" was from God or not was whether something they did afterward corresponded to it, much like self-fulfilled prophecies, or horoscope reading, or Chinese fortune cookies. If something didn't correspond with their vision, they merely concluded they misunderstood it, or this particular vision wasn't from God after all. But it wouldn't stop them from considering future dreams and trancelike states as visions. And given the numbers of superstitious people in the ancient world, many people considered their dreams as visions, so some of these "visions" will turn out to be true, if for no other reason but the odds themselves.

Second, why are there so many warnings about false teachings in the New Testament if these people had solid evidence to base their faith upon and they were not like their contemporaries who would believe most any good story? Why the many warnings? Along with the threats? It seems obvious that many Christians were led astray. Many in the Corinthian church rejected Paul's apostleship, tolerated immorality in the church, doubted the resurrection of Jesus, accepted "false apostles," and the list goes on and on. They doubted the resurrection of Jesus? That's right! (1 Cor. 15).

And if we have trouble with these questions, then, third, how did the authors of the Bible know they themselves were teaching divine truths? As we shall see later, there are many apocryphal and pseudonymous books that were written back then. But again, the winner of the New Testament "war of the teachers" decided which books went into the canon.

When an outsider looks at Christian history, she will find so many disagreements down through the years between different denominations and inside of each one of them that it becomes quite a tangled mess to figure out which branch of Christianity adheres faithfully to the spirit and/or beliefs of the first Christians. Even the earliest Christians, including the apostles themselves, had internal debates about what beliefs and practices were truly Christian ones, along with who their true leaders were.

According to James D. G. Dunn, "earliest Christianity was quite a diverse phenomenon. The Christianity established by the first apostles was little different from Christianity since then—the same sorts of tensions and differences, even divisions, such as we know all too well today!" There were three branches of early Christianity that vied for dominance: Catholic, Jewish, and Gnostic. Concerning Gnostic Christianity, Dunn acknowledges that "much of the 20th century scholarly debate about Christian beginnings has focused on the question of whether Gnosticism was already in full flower before Christianity and whether Christianity borrowed its ideas about Christ as heavenly redeemer from Gnosticism, rather than the other way around."[30] One thing seems likely, according to Dunn, most of the evidence and documents from Gnostic churches were suppressed and/or destroyed as Catholic Christianity gained in popularity.[31]

Bart D. Ehrman concurs that the theological diversity in the second and third centuries "was so extensive that groups calling themselves Christian adhered to beliefs and practices that most Christians today would insist were not Christian at all." He enumerates several of these disputed beliefs and then asks, "Why didn't these other groups simply read their New Testament to see that their views were wrong? It is because there was no New Testament . . . there was no agreed-upon canon—and no agreed upon theology. Instead, there was a wide range of diversity: diverse groups asserting diverse theologies based upon diverse written texts, all claiming to be written by apostles of Jesus." Eventually, one group won out over the others, and it was "this group that decided what the Christian creeds would be" and "which books would be included in the canon of Scripture."[32]

FOUR LAST OBJECTIONS.

Objection 1

Someone might claim that modern people are just as superstitious as the ancients, with the major exception that we have less to be superstitious about because of modern knowledge. That is to say, some modern people still read their horoscopes, have a lucky rabbit's foot, or are worried about seven years of bad luck if they break a mirror.

Okay, so let's assume that there were ten thousand things to be superstitious about in the ancient world, but because the ancients lacked accessible scientific knowledge, the most superstitious among them believed in all ten thousand of them, while the more knowledgeable believed in only nine thousand of them. Among modern educated Westerners let's say there are now only one hundred things to be superstitious about, and the more superstitious among us will believe all one hundred of them, while the more knowledgeable will believe five to ten of them. This describes the "god of the gaps" epistemology, and there are far fewer gaps with our knowledge today.

But my whole point is about the number of superstitious beliefs ancient people had when compared to ours. If someone wants to maintain that modern people are just as superstitious as the ancients, with the major exception that we have less to be superstitious about because of modern knowledge, then what does that gain her in terms of what I'm claiming here? The whole reason I'm discussing this is because I'm questioning the knowledge claimed by the biblical writers and early Christians. I'm saying that their knowledge was largely based upon ancient superstitions, which even modern Christians would reject if those same things were claimed by someone today. I'm arguing that Christians have a nonhistorical double standard when they evaluate the superstitious knowledge claims of people in our day in comparison to how they evaluate the knowledge claims of biblical writers.

Objection 2

A second objection is that modern scientifically educated people have their own myths: rationality comes from irrationality, order comes from chaos, morality comes from amorality, life comes from nonlife, complexity comes from simplicity. But these beliefs are the result of weighing all of the religious and nonreligious alternatives—these beliefs are the result of the process of thinking and weighing evidence, not from reading tarot cards.

A point of clarification might help here. There are several different ways to view modern science and it's relationship with philosophy and/or theology. There are several branches of scientific study. The philosophy of science is the area where science and philosophy interact the very most, because in this branch of study, the whole question is this: What constitutes science? There is a branch of science called theoretical physics, which is almost completely mathematics. But the branch of science I'm mostly referring to here is applied science, along with its implications for modern people. We can see how applied science has impacted us (in no particular order) in the areas of medicine, biology, earth science, computer science, engineering technology, zoology, geology, electricity, botany, genetics, dental technology, rocket science, astronomy, forensics, meteorology, chemistry, laser surgery, hydraulics, x-rays, and plasma physics. It has increased the number of elements in the periodic table of elements, as well as aided our understanding the nervous and muscular system, brain science, the whole notion of friction, and so on.[33]

Compare the above scientific disciplines with such things as divination, casting of lots, dreams, visions, trances, magic, exorcisms healing people, astrology, necromancy, sorcery, prophets for every religion, idol worship, gods and goddesses for every natural phenomenon, human and animal sacrifices, priests, omens, temples, festivals, sacred writings, and the Pseudepigrapha. We live in a much different world than the ancients, primarily because of Newtonian science.

Objection 3

It's claimed from original letters and the writing of the educated classes that Rome was not that superstitious in Paul's day. The Roman government (and usually Rome itself) was "atheistic" in that the gods were used in order to manipulate those either in Rome or outside of Rome (typically the latter). Roman (not Greek) religion was all about enhancing the power of the state. Belief was irrelevant as long as one sacrificed to the statue of *Roma*, which was done to show or maintain citizen status. Thus what mattered was an outward action that showed service to the state. Many of the different Greek gods were adopted (under Latin names) into the Roman pantheon for the purpose of conquering through diplomacy rather than arms. If a cultural group joins the Roman Empire, the group's god(s) were often honored by adoption under a different name into the Roman gods. Then the goddess *Roma* would be added to their major temple.

So what does this prove? Rome was adoptionistic in practice, and as a political system among superstitious people, it worked very well. How is that exactly different than in America, with the so-called separation of church and state? American people are very religious, but our government is democratic, allowing us all to practice our faith as we may. This doesn't automatically make Rome atheistic any more than it makes America atheistic. We are just not a theocracy. I don't see how the political structure of Rome and how the Romans handled the various religions shows anything nonsuperstitious about the nature of the ancient people of that day whom Paul reached with his Christian message. It only reveals the Roman political system, which dealt with superstitious people. Christianity initially converted mostly the lower classes of people anyway, and they are the ones who were overwhelmingly superstitious.

Objection 4

Some might say that I am intolerant when I harshly judge superstitious thinking people. In reply, let me mention just one example. Consider the witch trials the church "investigated."[34] Once accused by some priest who should know, there was nothing that could get the accused off the hook. And they looked for the "signs" of a witch, like a birthmark, that was unusual (put there as Satan's brand mark). And the woman was stripped and examined by "celibate" priests who could rape her and claim she was lying when she told anyone about it. Anything she claimed differently was meant to deceive the "investigators." And anyone who came to her defense was being deceived by her. So the only thing to do was to force her to confess and burn the demon out of her.

This kind of superstitious thinking is very dangerous. It is what I strongly object to. Since I believe this is the kind of thinking the Bible is based upon, this is the stuff I reject. So I don't feel maligned when someone calls me intolerant, if being intolerant is condemning superstitious ways of thinking that can be used to convict people of crimes they didn't commit without any evidence. It goes against educated, logical, and scientific reasoning.

CONCLUSION

Throughout this brief study we find that the Gentile pagans believed and practiced many superstitious things. This is undeniable from the Bible itself. My contention here is that ancient people weren't stupid, just very superstitious. Much of Israel's history rested on the same foundations as all the other nations; it rested on myths, legends, and superstitions. This explains how they could so easily reject their "history"—there just wasn't a real history to reject. Most superstitious people like the ones described in the Bible would probably believe any good story if told sincerely.

The Christian big picture assumes that ancient people were just as superstitious as people are in our day, and yet that flies in the face of the results of modern science. Moreover, their big picture has a double standard when looking at the ancients, too. Their big picture assumes that the "faithful" people in the Bible were different than their contemporaries—that they were not as superstitious as their contemporaries. Their big picture acknowledges how many people in the ancient past claimed divine knowledge, and yet they arbitrarily choose to accept the divine knowledge claims of the "faithful" people in the Bible. I merely want to know why they apply a double standard here.

From what I've argued in this chapter, I can legitimately and rationally ask whether I should believe the things claimed in the Bible if the people in biblical times were superstitious to the core like their neighbors. Why should I believe what they believed?

NOTES

1. Karl Barth, *The Word of God and the Word of Man* (New York: Harper & Row, 1928), p. 33.

2. R. Bultmann, in *Kerygma and Myth: A Theological Debate*, ed. Hans Werner Bartsch (New York: Harper & Row, 1961), pp. 1–7.

3. Sam Harris, *The End of Faith: Religion, Terror, and the Future of Reason* (New York: Norton, 2004), p. 19.

4. Christopher Hitchens, *God Is Not Great: Why Religion Poisons Everything* (New York: Twelve, 2007), p. 64.

5. This can be found at www.infidels.org/library, or see his *Sense and Goodness without God*, part 4, "Not Much Room for the Paranormal" (Bloomington, IN: Authorhouse, 2005), pp. 209–52.

6. Robert M. Price and Jeffery Jay Lowder, eds., *The Empty Tomb* (Amherst, NY: Prometheus Books, 2005), p. 171.

7. Tim Callahan, *Secret Origins of the Bible* (Altadena, CA: Millennium Press, 2002).

8. On Canaanite divinities, see the entry in *The Baker Encyclopedia of the Bible* (Grand Rapids, MI: Baker Book House, 1988). On Egyptian mythology see Anthony S. Mercatante, *Who's Who in Egyptian Mythology* (New York: Crown, 1978). On Babylonian and Assyrian mythology, see Gwendolyn Leick, *A Dictionary of Near Eastern Mythology* (London: Routledge, 1991). On Greek and Roman mythology, see Catherine Avery, *The New Century Handbook of Greek Mythology and Legend* (New York: Appleton, 1972); and Michael Grant, *Myths of the Greeks and Romans* (New York: Meridian, 1995).

9. Gordon Wenham, *Genesis 1–15* (Dallas, TX: Word Incorporated, 1987), p. 141.

10. Donald E. Gowan, *From Eden to Babel* (Grand Rapids, MI: Eerdmans, 1988), p. 82.

11. Gleason Archer, *The Encyclopedia of Bible Difficulties* (Grand Rapids, MI: Zondervan, 1982), pp. 79–80.

12. F. B. Huey Jr. "Are the 'Sons of God' in Genesis 6 Angels?" in *The Genesis Debate*, ed. Ronald F. Youngblood (Grand Rapids, MI: Baker Book House, 1990), pp. 188–91. On this see also 1 Enoch 6–11; 2 Enoch 18; Jub. 5:1–11; *Testaments of the Twelve Patriarchs*; *Genesis Apocryphon*; Philo; Josephus; Justin Martyr; Clement of Alexandria; Tertullian; Irenaeus; Cyrian; Ambrose, etc.

13. Gordon Wenham, *Genesis 1–15* (Dallas, TX: Word Incorporated, 1987), p. 138.

14. Ibid., pp. 237–39.

15. See his discussion of this in ibid., pp. 27–29.

16. David Mills, *Atheist Universe* (Berkeley, CA: Ulysses Press, 2006), p. 150.

17. Ronald Youngblood and Gleason Archer, in the *NIV Study Bible*.

18. Holman argues: "In every area, Samson would have needed the physical abilities of Superman to accomplish what the scriptures say he did." According to the Bible he slew one thousand Philistine soldiers in one battle all by himself, using only the jawbone of an ass. In order to take on these fully armored sword wielders, pole-bearers, and archers, all at the same time, Samson would've needed speed beyond what any human body can possibly achieve. Can you picture the speed which was required for Samson to shield himself from fifty arrows shot at him at the same time with that jawbone, for instance? In doing so Samson would've had to "swing the bone three or four times the speed of sound," and "if someone could swing this makeshift club that fast, the club would break from the sheer force of the air opposing it." Furthermore, even if it was a fresh jawbone, "the density of it would only be good for a few hits to any well-crafted steel body armor before the jawbone broke." Joe E. Holman, *Project Bible Truth* (forthcoming, 2008), pp. 225–31.

19. Hector Avalos tells us that, "For most of biblical history, Yahweh was not against child sacrifice per se, but rather against child sacrifice to other gods." See his "Creationists for Genocide" found at http://www.talkreason.org/. Jon D. Levenson states that "only at a particular stage rather late in the history of Israel was child sacrifice branded as counter to the will of YHWH and thus ipso facto idolatrous." *The Death and Resurrection of the Beloved Son*

(New Haven, CT: Yale University Press, 1993), p. 5. Susan Niditch, in *War in the Hebrew Bible: A Study in the Ethics of Violence* (Oxford: Oxford University Press, 1993) says, "While there is considerable controversy about the matter, the consensus over the last decade concludes that child sacrifice was a part of ancient Israelite religion to large segments of Israelite communities of various periods," p. 47. S. Ackerman argues that within the ancient Israelite community, "the cult of child sacrifice was felt in some circles to be a legitimate expression of Yawistic faith." *Under Every Green Tree: Popular Religion in Sixth-Century Judah* (Atlanta: Scholars Press, 1992), p. 137. See also Francesca Stavrakopoulou, *King Manasseh and Child Sacrifice: Biblical Distortions of Historical Realities* (New York: Walter De Gruyter, 2004).

20. Robin Lane Fox, *The Unauthorized Version: Truth and Fiction in the Bible* (New York: Knopf, 1992), p. 71.

21. See Ronald Youngblood, ed., *The Genesis Debate* (Grand Rapids, MI: Baker Book House, 1990), pp. 110–29.

22. See Jonathon Kirsch, *God against the Gods: The History of the War between Monotheism and Polytheism* (New York: Viking Compass, 2004).

23. A. L. Oppenheim, *The Interpretation of Dreams in the Ancient Near East* (Philadeplia: American Philosophical Society, 1956).

24. Clark Pinnock, *The Scripture Principle* (New York: Harper & Row, 1984), p. 119.

25. David L. Edwards and John Stott, *Evangelical Essentials: A Liberal-Evangelical Dialogue* (Downers Grove, IL: InterVarsity Press, 1988), p. 179.

26. For more on this see Frank M. Cross, *Canaanite Myth and Hebrew Epic* (Cambridge, MA: Harvard University Press, 1997); and Hershel Shanks, *Ancient Israel* (Englewood Cliffs, NJ: Prentice-Hall, 1999).

27. Bruce Malina and Richard L. Rohrbaugh, *Social Science Commentary on the Synoptic Gospels*, 2nd ed. (Minneapolis, MN: Augsburg Fortress, 2003), pp. 357–59. See also Bruce Malina, *The New Testament World: Insights from Cultural Anthropology* (Louisville: Westminster John Knox Press, 2001). Once again, I thank Matthew J. Green for this insight.

28. G. Friedrich Kittel and G. W. Bromiley, eds., *Theological Dictionary of the New Testament* (Grand Rapids, MI: Eerdmans, 1995), p. 416.

29. I thank Harry McCall for this analogy and for pointing this whole issue out to me.

30. James D. G. Dunn, *Evidence for Jesus* (Louisville, KY: Westminster Press, 1985), pp. 97–99.

31. For more on this see, James D. G. Dunn, *Unity and Diversity in the New Testament: An Inquiry into the Character of Earliest Christianity*, 3rd ed. (London: SCM, 2006); and Bart Ehrman's, *Lost Christianities: The Battles for Scripture and the Faiths We Never Knew* (Oxford: Oxford University Press, 2005).

32. Bart Ehrman, *Misquoting Jesus: The Story behind Who Changed the Bible and Why* (New York: HarperCollins, 2005), pp. 152–53. See also Ehrman's book *Lost Christianities: The Battles for Scripture and the Faiths We Never Knew*.

33. See Ian Barbour, *Religion in an Age of Science* (New York: Harper & Row, 1990), who deals with these relationships. See also the popular treatments in *New York Public Library's Science Desk Reference* or the *Encyclopedia of Science and Technology*, general ed. James Trefil (New York: Routledge, 2001).

34. On this see Brian Levack, *The Witch-Hunt in Early Modern Europe* (London: Pearson Educated, 2006).

PSEUDONYMITY IN THE BIBLE

I f I'm correct that there was a war of the prophets and that the history of Israel and of Christianity was written and rewritten from the perspective of the winners of each of these wars, then we'd expect to see some evidence of this in the Bible itself. This is where biblical criticism comes into play. Later we'll see where there are two separate creation accounts in Genesis 1–2 (with the first one written much later to reflect more of a monotheistic belief), how the story of Cain was originally a self contained folk story, and how the Flood story in Genesis 6–9 has several sources from which it was drawn. For now I just want to indicate that there is indeed evidence of rewriting in the Bible itself, that is, up until the canon of each testament was declared "closed."

Scholarship has shown that Moses did not write what is now known as the first five books of Moses, known as the Pentateuch. According to James D. G. Dunn, "it would be flying in the face of too much evidence and good scholarship to deny this basic affirmation: that the Pentateuch is the product of a lengthy process of tradition."[1] Here's just some of the evidence:[2]

(1) Deuteronomy (34:6) tells us that Moses was buried and states "no one knows his burial place to this day." This indicates that this was written some time after Moses's death because it is remarkable that no one knows to this day—that is, in a time far removed from his death. Even conservatives admit that Moses didn't write this. Usually, they say it is Joshua, but that really wouldn't make sense of the "to this day" comment. (2) Genesis 14 states that Abraham chased his nephew's captors to the city of Dan. The problem is that Dan was not the name of that city until the time of Samson (Judg. 18:27–31) three centuries after Moses died. In Moses' day the city was named Laish, not Dan. The Danites named it after their forefather Dan. (3) Genesis 36:31 lists some kings of the other countries "before any king reigned over the

Israelites." In Moses's life there were no kings in Israel. This didn't happen until Saul became the first king, hundreds of years after Moses died. And the fact that the passage says "any king" implies that there had to have been at least more than one king before this passage was written. Moses couldn't have written this. Sure, Moses was a prophet, but the fact that this statement is said so matter-of-factly is notable. One wonders why Samuel wouldn't have brought it up when the people were calling for a king hundreds of years later. (4) Exodus 16:35 reads, "The Israelites ate manna forty years, until they came to a habitable land; they ate manna, until they came to the border of the land of Canaan." Moses was dead before the Israelites reached the border. Besides, ancient political leaders involved in the daily activities of ruling a nation don't generally write their own history anyway. If the events actually happened as described, then the time to write this history would've been after the Israelites settled in Canaan. (5) In trying to prove the existence of giants, Deuteronomy 3:11 says, "Now only King Og of Bashan was left of the remnant of the Rephaim. In fact his bed, an iron bed, can still be seen in Rabbah of the Amorites." In this passage, this bed is already an ancient relic that can still be seen in the city of Rabbah, which was not even conquered until King David ruled over Israel (see 2 Sam. 12:27–30).

There is the added difficulty of Jeremiah 7:22–23, where God purportedly said: (KJV): "For I spake not unto your fathers, nor commanded them in the day that I brought them out of the land of Egypt, concerning burnt offerings or sacrifices: But this thing commanded I them, saying, Obey my voice, and I will be your God, and ye shall be my people: and walk ye in all the ways that I have commanded you, that it may be well unto you." Burton Scott Easton tells us, "The problem presented in Jeremiah 7:22 is a very serious one." Jeremiah (ca. 626–586 BCE) "denies categorically that a command to offer sacrifices WAS PART OF THE DIVINE LAW AT ALL," even though in the book of Leviticus, Moses supposedly gives instructions about who were to offer sacrifices, where they were to do so, and how.[3] Easton argues from this that the Old Testament incorporated laws belonging to different periods of Israel's history. How and when this was done is a matter of scholarly discussion. (seen note)[4]

When could the majority of the Pentateuch have been written? In 2 Kings 22:8–13, there is an interesting story. Israel had long been divided into two kingdoms. Josiah had just come to be king of Judah. He wanted to repair the temple and told the priest to go through all the stuff and see how much money they had. While the high priest was looking, he found the "Book of the Law" and gave it to a secretary who read it to Josiah. When Josiah heard it, he tore his clothes because he realized that they had not been obeying God.

Scholars think that instead of "finding" the Law (another way of saying the first five books of the Bible) here, this is when it was actually compiled and/or much of it written. Most of the Hebrew Bible was actually written at a time in the divided kingdom of Israel when Josiah wanted to control the people he was ruling. It was written to keep a crumbling kingdom together as a system of control, and it was claimed that Moses wrote it. It's also suggested that since Jeremiah's prophetic ministry took place during Josiah's reign (seventh century BCE), he may have been the pseudonymous author of a large part of Deuteronomy. Richard Elliot Friedman tells us the book of Jeremiah "seems to be written, at several points, in the same language and outlook as Deuteronomy. Parts of Jeremiah are so similar to Deuteronomy that it is hard to believe that they were not written by the same person."[5] That's what scholarship leads us to think.

This may explain why the Bible tells us the Passover meal was not celebrated for hundreds of years before King Josiah's time. In 2 Kings 23:21–23, Josiah commanded the people to celebrate the Passover. And there we read, "Not since the days of the judges who led Israel, nor throughout the days of the kings of Israel and the kings of Judah, had any such Passover been observed. But in the eighteenth year of King Josiah, this Passover was celebrated to the Lord in Jerusalem." It's likely that the Passover meal was first celebrated during his reign.[6]

But there is more. Take a look at the book of Isaiah. It has been long accepted that the present book of Isaiah was compiled by at least two authors, and probably three. From the *Anchor Bible Dictionary* ("Isaiah"): "The historical context of chaps. 40–55 differs entirely from that of chaps. 1–39. The enemy of Israel is the Neo-Babylonian Empire (626–539 B.C.; cf. chaps. 46; 47; 48:20–21), not the Neo-Assyrian Empire of Isaiah (935–612 B.C.; cf. chaps. 10; 14:24–27), which collapsed with the destruction of Nineveh in 612 B.C. The gentile king in chapters 40–55 is Cyrus of Persia (fl. 560–530 B.C.; cf. 41:2–3, 25; 44:24–45:13; 48:14), not the Assyrian king of Isaiah (10:5–19). The people are in Babylon, not in Isaiah's 8th-century Jerusalem; the message is to leave Babylon, cross the desert, and return to Zion. . . . That a 6th-century author, name unknown, wrote chaps. 40–55, and another author or authors, also anonymous, wrote chaps. 56–66, is now accepted by all but a scholarly minority, who hold out for the unity of Isaiah."

Conservative professor R. K. Harrison wrote, "Whereas the earlier sections of the prophecy [of Isaiah] spoke of the divine majesty, later chapters described His uniqueness and eternity. As contrasted with the emphasis found in the first thirty-nine chapters, where Jehovah was exalted above all other gods, the remaining chapters of the prophecy denied their very existence, and instead discussed the concept of God as the sole deity. In the first portion of Isaiah, the remnant was held to constitute the faithful left behind in Jerusalem, whereas in the later part of the work it was thought of as the faithful exilic group about to be brought back to Palestine. Finally, the messianic king of chapters 1–39 was to have been replaced by the concept of the Servant in chapters 40–66."[7]

The main reason why the unity of Isaiah was accepted for so long despite the problems with the different historical contexts was because of a predisposition to believe in the verbal inspiration of the Bible as a whole, modeled on the prophetic paradigm (for which see my chapter 16). But eventually, with the rise of historical consciousness, scholars challenged this assumption with the facts of Isaiah itself. Professor James D. G. Dunn argues: "we can speak of an overwhelming consensus of biblical scholarship that the present Isaiah is not the work of a single author. . . . **It is not simply a question of whether predictive prophecy is possible or not. It is rather that the message of Second Isaiah would have been largely meaning-**

less to an 8th century Jerusalem audience. It is so clearly directed to the situation of exile. Consequently, had it been delivered a century and a half before the exile, it would be unlike the rest of Jewish prophecy."[8]

This rewriting is true of many, if not most, of the books in the Bible. The book of Daniel clearly had pseudepigraphal additions to it. The book contains sections of Hebrew and sections of Aramaic languages. According to the *Anchor Bible Dictionary*, under "Daniel": It is probable that "the two languages reflect the history of composition. Chapters 2–6 (and probably chap. 1) were composed in Aramaic and chap. 7 was added in the time of Antiochus Epiphanes (c.a. 175–164 B.C.). Then either the same author or others of the same circle composed chaps. 8–12 in Hebrew (possibly because of nationalistic fervor). Chapter 1 was either translated from Aramaic or composed in Hebrew in order to form a Hebrew inclusion around the Aramaic chapters."

There were clear additions to Daniel. The *Anchor Bible Dictionary* states: "**The Additions to Daniel (Adds)** consist of three extended passages in the Greek Septuagint which have no counterpart in the canonical text of Daniel: (1) '**The Prayer of Azariah and the Hymn of the Three Young Men**,' consisting of 66 verses and located between what would correspond to vv 23 and 24 of the third chap. of canonical Daniel; (2) '**Susanna**,' consisting of 64 verses; and (3) '**Bel and the Snake**,' consisting of 42 verses, the latter two Adds usually appearing after the canonical chapters of Daniel. All three Adds have their setting in Babylon and describe how some Jew who trusted in the Lord God of Israel was delivered from certain death through the intervention of an angel. . . . Evidently never a part of the Jewish canon (the one probably established by ca. 150 B.C.) nor as it existed in Josephus' day in the 1st century A.D., the Adds were regarded as part of the Christian canon of the Western Church until the time of the Protestant and Catholic movements, at which time they were rejected by Protestants and were termed 'apocryphal' while the Roman Catholic Church at its Council of Trent in 1546 reaffirmed them and termed them 'deuterocanonical.'"

THE PREVALENCE OF PSEUDONYMITY

That there might be more than one author of the Pentateuch, Isaiah, Daniel, or many of the books in the Bible itself introduces us to the whole idea of pseudonymity in the Bible, and the Pseudepigrapha. The books known as pseudepigraphal are considered by scholars to be works that are false, by today's standards. They are either purported to be authored by a famous person of the past or they contain material claimed to have been from a famous person of the past. Bart D. Ehrman simply calls them what they truly are, "forgeries." And there are many such Old Testament examples: 1 Enoch, Questions of Ezra, 2 Enoch, Revelation of Ezra, 3 Enoch, 2 Baruch, Treatise of Shem, 3 Baruch, Apocryphon of Ezekiel, Apocalypse of Abraham, Apocalypse of Zephaniah, Apocalypse of Adam, the Fourth Book of Ezra, Apocalypse of Elijah, Greek Apocalypse of Ezra, Apocalypse of Daniel, Vision of Ezra, Testaments of the Twelve Patriarchs, Testament of Moses, Testament of Job, Testament of

Solomon, Testaments of the Three Patriarchs (Abraham, Isaac, and Jacob), Testament of Adam, More Psalms of David, Prayer of Joseph, Prayer of Manasseh, Prayer of Jacob, Psalms of Solomon, Odes of Solomon, and so on.

Some of the New Testament examples are: *documents falsely attributed to Paul,* such as 3 Corinthians, the Epistle to the Alexandrians, the Epistle to the Laodiceans, the Epistles of Paul and Seneca, the Apocalypse of Paul, the Vision of Paul, the Acts of Paul, the Martyrdom of Paul, and the Martyrdom of Peter and Paul; *documents falsely attributed to Peter*, such as the Apocalypse of Peter, the Gospel of Peter, the Preaching of Peter, the Acts of Peter, the Acts of Andrew and Peter, and the Martyrdom of Peter (also 2 Peter); and also *documents falsely attributed to Mary* the mother of Jesus, such as the Birth of Mary, the Gospel of the Birth of Mary, the Passing of Mary, the Questions of Mary, the Apocalypse of the Virgin, the Assumption of the Virgin, and the Coptic Lives of the Virgin.

THE MEANING OF PSEUDEPIGRAPHA AUTHORSHIP

According to pseudepigraphal scholar James H. Charlesworth: "The Pseudepigrapha poses a perplexing problem for many readers: Why did the authors of these writings attribute them falsely to other persons? These authors did not attempt to deceive the reader. They, like the authors of the Psalms of David, the Proverbs of Solomon, the Wisdom of Solomon, and the additions to Isaiah, attempted to write authoritatively in the name of an influential biblical person. Many religious Jews attributed their works to some biblical saint who lived before the cessation of prophecy and who had inspired them. Also, the principle of solidarity united early Jews with their predecessors who, in their eyes, had assuredly been guided by God himself. It is also conceivable that some of the apocalyptic writers had dreams or visions in which they experienced revelations given to Enoch, Abraham, Elijah, Ezra, Baruch, and others."[9]

James D. G. Dunn argues: "Here we see a willingness to make substantial additions to earlier writings. There was evidently no sense that a document once written was complete and closed, that no additions to it would violate its character or the integrity of the original author. And certainly talk of deception and forgery would be inappropriate. What we have rather is a sense that earlier traditions can be expanded and elaborated in a way wholly appropriate to that tradition, so that the elaborations and expansions can be retained within that tradition, continuous with it, part of a larger integrated whole which can be regarded as belonging to the original author's corpus without impropriety." Dunn goes on to argue this happened with regard to the Pentateuch, the Psalms, 1 Samuel through 2 Chronicles, and New Testament writings like the Pastoral letters and 2 Peter.[10]

Richard Carrier argues that the empty tomb story of Matthew and Luke was a legendary expansion of Mark's original metaphorical empty tomb. But Carrier says, "This does not mean these authors must be considered liars. Just as Paul can find 'hidden meaning' in the Old Testament Prophets . . . so could the Gospel authors *CREATE* narratives with deeper, hidden meanings under a veil of history. It was honest work then, even if it disturbs us today."[11]

Charlesworth, Dunn, and Carrier have a point. However, if this was in fact the way these writers thought, it reveals something significant about them. When they wrote their pseudepigraphal works or placed pseudonymous comments inside other books, the authors may have thought that the spirit of Isaiah, Moses, Ezra, Baruch, Solomon, or David, and so on, was speaking through them, or more than likely, they believed historical and prophetic truth could be revealed directly to them by God. That's what many of them may have thought, whether the whole book was purportedly written by those men of antiquity or they quoted them within their own works. That's why the second author of Isaiah may have had no problem adding and reworking the original Isaiah's work. God was still speaking Isaiah's message, or rather, that the second author was a prophet "like unto" Isaiah—a "second Elijah."

My point here is about the very presence of the pseudonymous writings and what they tell us about ancient Jewish thinking. It tells us that the written product was able to be amended, because, according to Dunn, the authority was not "a closed authority, but a living authority which could be and WAS (his emphasis) expanded and elaborated as new insights emerged and which could be and evidently was adapted and modified as circumstances changed."[12] They just wrote and rewrote their history from the conclusions of hindsight.

Even if this is what they thought, it does nothing to change how we should view them by today's standards. Bart D. Erhman argues that to call these writings "pseudonymous" is perhaps "a more antiseptic term. But it does little to solve the problem of a potential deceit, for an author who attempts to pass off his own writing as that of some other well-known person has written a forgery." What's more, the ancient world deplored forgeries as well. Erhman tells us: "People in the ancient world did not appreciate forgeries any more than people do today. There are numerous discussions of forgery in ancient Greek and Latin sources. In virtually every case the practice is denounced as deceitful and ill-spirited, sometimes even in documents that are themselves forged."[13] Still, not to offend Christians too much I've chosen the antiseptic term "pseudonymity" for this chapter, even though Ehrman has made his point well.

CLEAR EXAMPLES OF PSEUDONYMITY APPEARING IN THE NEW TESTAMENT

First, let's consider the most obvious examples of pseudonymity in the New Testament. The most obvious cases are Mark 16:9–20; John 5:3–4; Acts 8:37; John 7:53–8:11; and 1 John 5:7–8. Just compare these passages in the King James Version (KJV) and later translations. Notice them missing in the later ones? These are obvious cases. How did they get in the text in the first place? Who wrote them? Why were they accepted as scripture for way too long? Revelation 1:11: the phrase "I am Alpha and Omega, the first and the last" (KJV) was not in the original Greek texts. The Alpha Omega phrase "is not found in virtually any ancient texts" nor is it even mentioned in a footnote in modern versions.[14] There are several others I'd like to highlight below.

Jude 14

"Enoch, the seventh from Adam, prophesied about these men: 'See, the Lord is coming with thousands upon thousands of his holy ones.'"

Enoch, the "seventh from Adam," didn't say this, because the book of Enoch was written in the second century BCE and couldn't have come from Enoch himself! About this text, listen to what James Barr said: "The letter of Jude quotes from the Book of Enoch with all the air of accepting it as a fully authoritative religious book. It is clearly intended to carry the strongest weight within the argument of the letter. . . . Enoch is regarded as having 'prophesied,' just as Moses or Elijah or Isaiah had done. As all true prophets were, he must have been inspired. The citation of Enoch had, for the purposes of Jude's argument, just the same validity and the same effect as the citation of the scriptures which came later to be deemed canonical. To say Enoch's book 'was not scripture' would have been unintelligible to Jude."[15]

While Jude's use of Enoch is an explicit quotation, there is a great deal of implicit acceptance of the Old Testament apocryphal and pseudepigraphal writings in the New Testament. According to Barr: "Much of the impact of ancient authoritative writings on the New Testament comes not through explicit quotation but through tacit or implicit acceptance of their doctrine or their emphasis. In this respect the thinking of a book like the *Wisdom of Solomon* can be traced with high probability in various parts of the New Testament: in fact such a book, though it counts as 'apocryphal' in Protestantism, very likely exercised more influence than some portions of the now canonical Old Testament."[16] About the Wisdom of Solomon, Marcus Borg informs us: "This remarkable book has been more important in the history of Christianity than the non-canonical status given it by Protestants would suggest. Augustine, for example, refers to it almost 800 times."[17]

Consider, for example, the Pauline argument from sin and death (Rom. 5:12): "Therefore as sin came into the world through one man and death through sin, and so death spread to all men because all men sinned," which clearly places a stress on sin and death much greater than we actually find in the story of the supposed Fall of Adam and Eve (Genesis 2–3). The truth is that the origin of sin is never traced back to Adam and Eve in the Old Testament. It was only interpreted to be so during the intertestamental period, especially in the apocryphal and the pseudepigraphal literature. It is there where we first find this stressed as the point of the story. We find such a viewpoint expressed in noncanonical writings like the Wisdom of Solomon (2:23f.), where we read, "For God created man for incorruption, and made him in the image of his own eternity, but through the devil's envy death entered the world, and those who belong to his party experience it." Claus Westermann similarly argues: "the teaching of the Fall and of original sin rests on the late Jewish interpretation (of Esd. 7:118). It has no foundation at all in the (Genesis) narrative."[18]

2 Timothy 3:8-9

"Now as Jannes and Jambres withstood Moses, so do these also resist the truth: men of corrupt minds, reprobate concerning the faith. But they shall proceed no further: for their folly shall be manifest unto all men, as theirs also was."

James H. Charlesworth tells us: "Though the Jannes and Jambres tradition probably arose on Palestinian soil and in a Semitic-speaking environment, there is no indication that the original language of the book was other than Greek. The date of origin of the tradition can hardly be much later than the 2nd century B.C.E., while the book was written probably at least as early as the 2nd century C.E."[19]

Other Examples

There is the detail that the prophets "were sawn in two" in Hebrews 11:37, which is probably from the Martyrdom of Isaiah, and the story that: "the archangel Michael, contending with the devil, disputed about the body of Moses," in Jude 9, which is not to be found anywhere in the Old Testament, but once again, a Jewish legend, and used by Jude as a matter of fact to make an important point.

The whole Gospel of Matthew itself is a work finished by a pseudonymous author (or a school of authors). "All scholars now admit that the author of this gospel simply cannot have been an eyewitness of the ministry of Jesus, since he employs secondary sources (Mark & Q), themselves patchworks of well-worn fragments. It is inconceivable that an eyewitness apostle would not have depended upon his own recollections."[20] This is especially true when this gospel tells of the calling of Matthew by Jesus into discipleship. Why would he copy almost word for word Mark's account of this calling if the author were actually the disciple Matthew (Matt. 9:9–13; Mark 2:14–17)?

2 Peter is also pseudonymous. According to the *Anchor Bible Dictionary*: "The strong consensus among scholars is that 2 Peter is also pseudonymous and may well be the last NT book to be composed, perhaps in the first decades of the 2nd century." According to James D. G. Dunn, "If any document in the NT is pseudonymous it is this one. Its language and style is so very different from that of I Peter. It is clearly post-Pauline and reflects an anxiety over the delay of the *parousia* which would be unlikely were Peter himself still alive. And its difficulty in gaining acceptance into the canon points firmly to the same conclusion."[21]

So in the war of the Old Testament prophets, and even in the war of the New Testament teachers, we find that not even the inspired writers themselves knew what a true prophetic voice from God was! And we can see this in the continued early church discussions of the canon, which can be called the "war over the canon."[22]

There is also a widely recognized pseudonymous interpolation in Josephus's work by a later Christian author, which claims Jesus was the Christ and that he arose from the dead, found in the Antiquities of the Jews (18:3, 3) known as the *Testimo-*

nium Flavianum. It reads, "Now there was about this time Jesus, a wise man, if it be lawful to call him a man, for he was a doer of wonderful works, a teacher of such men as receive the truth with pleasure. He drew over to him both many of the Jews, and many of the Gentiles. He was the Christ; and when Pilate, at the suggestion of the principal men amongst us, had condemned him to the cross, those that loved him at the first did not forsake him, for he appeared to them alive again the third day, as the divine prophets had foretold these and ten thousand other wonderful things concerning him; and the tribe of Christians, so named from him, are not extinct to this day." Not even conservative scholars think Josephus made these claims, because he was not a Christian.[23] According to Christopher Price, "The passage contains some obvious Christian glosses that no Jew like Josephus would have written, such as Jesus being 'the Christ' and 'he appeared to them alive again the third day.'" Although, as Price continues to argue, the question is how much of it is authentic, and parts of it may very well be, but my point here is to show that early Christians doctored up texts like this.[24]

NOTES

1. James D. G. Dunn, *The Living Word* (Philadelphia: Fortress Press, 1987), p. 71.

2. Points 1–5 are summarized by exbeliever from my blog.

3. Emphasis is his. "Criticism (The Graf-Wellhausen Hypothesis)," in *The International Standard Bible Encyclopedia*, vol. 2, general ed. James Orr (Grand Rapids, MI: Eerdmans, 1956), pp. 753–60.

4. Evangelicals attempt to explain this problem away. David K. Stabnow claims: "It was not literally the case that the Lord said nothing about sacrifices and offerings when He brought Israel out of Egypt; His words here were meant as sarcasm." *The Apologetics Study Bible*, general ed. Ted Cabal (Nashville: Holman Bible, 2007), p. 1099. But how does he know this? Even if this is the case, was God also being sarcastic when he commanded his people to love him and obey his commands? Hardly. Gleason Archer claims, "God never said anything to them at the beginning—*'in the day that I brought them out of the land of Egypt'*—about offerings or sacrifices," since it wasn't until Exodus 20:24 God said something about it. *The Encyclopedia of Bible Difficulties* (Grand Rapids, MI: Zondervan, 1982), p. 272. But Easton argues such a solution is "quite unsatisfactory," because "this would make Jeremiah quibble," just as Archer is doing. And it doesn't do justice to the textual data that shows Jeremiah was a major contributor to the book of Deuteronomy as I show.

5. Richard Elliot Friedman, *Who Wrote the Bible?* (New York: Harper & Row, 1997), pp. 126–27. Just compare Deut. 28:1 and Jer. 17:24; Deut. 10:16 with Jer. 4:4; Deut. 4:19 with Jer. 8:2; Deut. 4:20 with Jer. 11:4; and Deut. 13:4 with Jer. 32:41. See also Friedman's book *The Bible with Sources Revealed* (New York: HarperOne, 2005).

6. It's even doubted whether or not there was a united monarchy under the reigns of King David and Solomon. Some scholars suspect that the figure of King David, for instance, is about as historical as that of King Arthur. See Hector Avalos, *The End of Biblical Studies* (Amherst, NY: Prometheus Books, 2007), pp. 154–64. See also Israel Finkelstein and Neil Asher Silberman, *David and Solomon: In Search of the Bible's Sacred Kings and the Roots of the Western Tradition* (New York: Free Press, 2006).

7. R. K. Harrison, *Introduction to the Old Testament* (Grand Rapids, MI: Eerdmans, 1969), p. 775.

8. Dunn, *The Living Word*, pp. 73–74, emphasis mine.

9. James Charlesworth, "Pseudepigrapha," in *The Anchor Bible Dictionary*. See James Charlesworth, *The Pseudepigrapha and Modern Research with a Supplement* (Chico, CA: Scholars Press, 1981); and *The Old Testament Pseudepigrapha and the New Testament* (Cambridge: Cambridge University Press, 1985).

10. Dunn, *The Living Word*, pp. 69–70. For further treatment Dunn recommends David G. Meade, *Pseudonymity and Canon* (Tübingen: J. C. B. Mohr, 1986).

11. Robert M. Price and Jeffery Jay Lowder, eds., *The Empty Tomb: Jesus beyond the Grave* (Amherst, NY: Prometheus Books, 2005), p. 156. Emphasis is his.

12. Dunn, *The Living Word*, p. 71.

13. See Bart Ehrman, *Lost Christianities: The Battles for Scripture and the Faiths We Never Knew* (Oxford: Oxford University Press, 2003), pp. 9–10.

14. For a discussion of these and other texts, see Bruce Metzger's, *A Textual Commentary on the Greek New Testament*, 2nd ed. (London: United Bible Societies, 2005). See also Bart Ehrman, *Misquoting Jesus: The Story behind Who Changed the Bible and Why* (New York: HarperCollins, 2005).

15. James Barr, *Beyond Fundamentalism* (Philadelphia: Westminister Press, 1984), pp. 42–50.

16. Ibid., p. 44.

17. Marcus Borg, *Meeting Jesus Again for the First Time* (New York: HarperSanFrancisco, 1994), p. 113, n. 21.

18. Claus Westermann, *Creation* (Minneapolis, MN: Fortress Press, 1974), pp. 108–109.

19. James H. Charlesworth, "Pseudepigrapha," in *Anchor Bible Dictionary*.

20. Price and Lowder, *The Empty Tomb*, p. 88.

21. Dunn, *The Living Word*, p. 83.

22. For which see James Barr, *Holy Scripture: Canon, Authority, Criticism* (Philadelphia: Westminster Press, 1983); and Bruce Metzger, *The Canon of the New Testament: Its Origin, Development, and Significance* (Oxford: Oxford University Press, 1997). For a good accessible work on the writing and rewriting of the biblical accounts, see Robin Lane Fox, *The Unauthorized Version: Truth and Fiction in the Bible* (New York: Knopf, 1992).

23. Even Josh McDowell thinks this statement was not made by Josephus. See *He Walked among Us: Evidence for the Historical Jesus* (San Bernadino, CA: Here's Life Publishers, 1988).

24. See "A Response to Ken Olson on Josephus and Eusebius" at http://christian cadre.org.

ARCHAEOLOGY, EXODUS, AND THE CANAANITE CONQUEST

A ssuming the story of the Exodus is correct, there should be some archaeolog-ical evidence for the Exodus, the crossing of the Red Sea, the Israelites' camping at Sinai, their wilderness wanderings, and their Canaanite conquest that should correspond to the biblical account. After all, the plagues described in Exodus would have wiped that nation out, given the numbers of slaves they lost (over 3–4 million of them!), as well as the loss of crops, cattle, soldiers, and firstborn children. But what we find instead is an almost complete lack of it, and the story itself doesn't make a great deal of sense.

The plagues would have devastated the Egyptian country (cf. Exod. 8:20; 9:6, 25; 10:7, 15; 12:29–30). This is actually what we are led to believe from the text. The crops had all been destroyed, their cattle were all killed (on three separate occa-sions: 9:6; 9:25; 11:5), and the infrastructure was severely damaged, culminating in the death of every firstborn male in the country. Finally, we're told that the entire army had perished in the Red Sea. We should expect to find some indication of this in archaeological digs and in the Egyptian hieroglyphic texts, no matter how embar-rassing it may have been to their pride.

But according to William G. Dever, professor of Near Eastern archaeology and anthropology at the University of Arizona, Tucson, "there is no direct archaeolog-ical evidence that any constituents of later Israel were ever in Egypt."[1] Dever argues there is "absolutely no trace of Moses, or indeed of an Israelite presence in Egypt."[2] Archeologists Israel Finkelstein and Neil Asher Silberman argue that there is no archaeological evidence for an Israelite presence in Egypt prior to the thirteenth cen-tury BCE, when most Christian scholars think the Exodus took place. Before that time "not a single campsite or sign of occupation . . . has been identified in Sinai" even though they show how archaeology has detected the smallest of such sites elsewhere around the world. Their "irrefutable" conclusion is that "the Exodus did not happen at the time and in the manner described in the Bible."[3]

IF GOD ACTUALLY DID DO WHAT
THE BOOK OF EXODUS CLAIMS,
THEN WHY IS IT SO HARD TO EVEN DATE THE EXODUS?

There should be some archaeological evidence for this cataclysmic event that would show one date over the other. According to K. A. Kitchen, professor of Egyptology and Oriental Studies at the University of Liverpool, in Liverpool, England, "The lazy man's solution is simply to cite the 480 years ostensibly given in 1 Kings 6:1 from the Exodus to the 4th year of Solomon (ca. 966 B.C.) and so to set the Exodus at ca. 1446 B.C. However, this too simple of a solution is ruled out by the combined weight of all the other biblical data plus additional information from external data." Kitchen concludes by saying, "the Exodus, the sojourn in the wilderness, and the entry into Canaan can reasonably be limited to within ca. 1279–1209 B.C., a maximum of 70 years; or if within about 1260–1220 B.C., very nearly 300 years before the 4th year of Solomon (966 B.C.)." Of course, that's if it happened at all.[4]

WHY IS IT SO HARD TO IDENTIFY
THE RED SEA THAT THESE
3–4 MILLION PEOPLE CROSSED ON DRY LAND?

The Egyptian soldiers with their armor and chariots all died there, so where is this evidence? Surely there should be chariots and shields and spears to find. Scholars are debating the actual place of the crossing, but there is not a shred of evidence for any conclusion.[5] A film titled *The Exodus Conspiracy* will be released as my book is going to press, attempting to show that there is a conspiracy to keep the evidence of the Exodus hidden. Edward T. Babinski has an initial critique of its sources to be found at my blog. Go there and do a search for "The Exodus Conspiracy." He takes issue with Ron Wyatt's photo of a "gilded chariot wheel" allegedly from the Egyptian army that chased the Hebrews as they fled during the supposed Exodus, as a fraud.

THE UNHEARD-OF NUMBERS OF ISRAELITES
WHO SUPPOSEDLY WERE LET GO FROM EGYPT
PRESENTS ALL SORTS OF PROBLEMS

The Israelites emerged from Egypt numbering three to four million. Using only the biblical text, which was all that was available to him, Hermann Samuel Reimarus (1694–1768) made a number of interesting calculations.[6]

The livestock to support the Israelites would have been numerous. They lived in Goshen because they raised livestock (Gen. 46:31–34). Their cattle were said not to suffer from the plague that killed the Egyptian cattle (Exod. 9:1–7). When they supposedly left Egypt, Moses had wanted Pharaoh to allow them to take all of their livestock (Exod. 10:24–26; 12:32, 38; cf. Num. 11:21–22).

Dr. Lester L. Grabbe of the University of Hull wrote a detailed essay about this in which he tells us that Reimarus asked some tough questions about the text. He asked "about the amount of time required for such a large group to exit the country. Taking the figures of three million people, 900,000 animals (300,000 beef cattle and 600,000 sheep and goats, based on Exod. 9:1–7; 10:24–26; 12:32, 38; cf. Num. 11:21–22) and 10,000 wagons (Num. 7:3, 6–8), he calculated how long the traveling column would be. Naturally, that would depend on how wide the column was. He estimated fifty people marching abreast (which he thought was too many), with the space of three steps taken up by each row of people. . . . It would surely have taken at least a week to cross the 'Red Sea!'"[7]

The crucial issue is "the refusal of cooperation by the Edomites and the Transjordanian tribes, and the resistance by the Canaanites," which "are practically inexplicable. They make little sense, for two reasons: first, the size of the Israelite forces, and, second, the reputation that must have accompanied this group which had lived in the wilderness for 40 years. Suppose you are king of a small nation, such as Edom or Midian, which can be defeated by an army of 12,000 (d. Num. 31:6–8). So when a nation with a potential army of 600,000 men in their prime, who have been living on miraculous provisions falling from heaven, asks to move peacefully through your land, you say no?"

WHEN THE BIBLE SPEAKS OF THE CONQUEST OF CANAAN, ARCHAEOLOGY PRESENTS A DIFFERENT PICTURE

William Dever argues that, "the external material evidence supports almost nothing of the biblical account of a large-scale, concerted Israelite military invasion of Canaan."[8] There are, for instance, no indications of a massive increase in population in Canaan. When explaining what might actually have happened, Dever concludes: "Clearly, from our discussion the conquest model is ruled out. The founders of the Iron I villagers do not appear to have been newcomers to Palestine, much less settlers displacing Canaanites in the urban centers by military force. The few sites actually destroyed ca. 1200 B.C. were destroyed either by the Philistines, or by unknown agents; and none is resettled within a reasonable time by people who could be implicated in the destruction, or could otherwise be identified as 'Israelites.'" According to Dever, who is known as a maximalist: "The peasants' revolt (or 'internal conquest') model seems more compatible with current archaeological data and theory than any other. This model presumes that the early Israelite movement was made up of various dissident elements of late bronze age Canaanite society, mostly dispossessed peasant

farmers, who colonized new areas in the hinterland and there adopted a less strat-
ified social order better suited to an agrarian economy."[9]

Israel Finkelstein and Neil Asher Silberman who are minimalists, agree with
Dever that "a lightning invasion" by the Israelites "would have been impractical and
unlikely in the extreme." But they go on to argue that a peasant revolt doesn't accord
with the evidence. According to them, "the archaeological evidence indicates that
the destruction of Canaanite society was a relatively long and gradual process." The
destruction of Hazor, Aphek, Lachish, and Mediggo, four cities mentioned as being
destroyed in Joshua's military campaign, "took place over a span of more than a century. The possible causes include invasion, social breakdown, and civil strife. No
single military force did it, and certainly not in one military campaign."[10] In either
case, the archeological evidence for an Exodus from Egypt and Conquest of Canaan
simply is not to be found.

NOTES

1. William Dever, "Archaeology and the Israelite Conquest," in *The Anchor Bible Dictionary*, ed. David Noel Freedman (New York: Doubleday, 1992).

2. William Dever, *Recent Archaeological Discoveries and Biblical Research* (Seattle:
University of Washington Press, 1990), p. 25.

3. Israel Finkelstein and Neil Asher Silberman, *The Bible Unearthed: Archaeology's New
Vision of Ancient Israel and the Origin of Its Sacred Texts* (New York: Free Press, 2001), pp.
62–63.

4. *The Anchor Bible Dictionary*, s.v. "Exodus, The."

5. Ibid., s.v., "Red Sea."

6. "Uber den Durchgang der Israeliten durch das Rohte Meer," in *Apologie* (Frankfurt
am Main: Insel Verlag, 1972), book 3, chap. 2.

7. Lester L. Grabbe, *Biblical Interpretation, 8½* (Leiden, Netherlands: Koninklijke Brill
NV, 2000).

8. William Dever, *Who Were the Early Israelites and Where Did They Come From?*
(Grand Rapids, MI: Eerdmans, 2003), p. 71.

9. Dever, "Archaeology and the Israelite Conquest."

10. Finkelstein and Silberman, *The Bible Unearthed*, p. 90.

8

THE POOR EVIDENCE
OF HISTORICAL EVIDENCE

In this chapter I'll examine whether or not the historical evidence for Christianity is enough to lead someone in today's world to believe. I will claim that it isn't. If God revealed himself in the past, then he chose a poor medium and a poor historical era to do so. I'll start with German critic Gotthold Lessing's (1729–1781 CE) argument with regard to historical knowledge, personal experience, and the necessary truths (or conclusions) of reason when it comes to the Christian faith: "Miracles, which I see with my own eyes, and which I have opportunity to verify for myself, are one thing; miracles, of which I know only from history that others say they have seen them and verified them, are another." "But . . . I live in the 18th century, in which miracles no longer happen. The problem is that reports of miracles are not miracles. . . . [They] have to work through a medium which takes away all their force. . . . Or is it invariably the case, that what I read in reputable historians is just as certain for me as what I myself experience?"[1]

Lessing, just like G. W. Leibniz before him, distinguished between the contingent truths of history and the necessary truths of reason and wrote: Since "no historical truth can be demonstrated, then nothing can be demonstrated by means of historical truths." That is, "the accidental truths of history can never become the proof of necessary truths of reason."

He continued: "We all believe that an Alexander lived who in a short time conquered almost all Asia. But who, on the basis of this belief, would risk anything of great permanent worth, the loss of which would be irreparable? Who, in consequence of this belief, would forswear forever all knowledge that conflicted with this belief? Certainly not I. But it might still be possible that the story was founded on a mere poem of Choerilus just as the ten-year siege of Troy depends on no better authority than Homer's poetry."

Someone might object that miracles like the resurrection of Jesus from the dead are "more than historically certain," because these things are told to us by "inspired historians who cannot make a mistake." But Lessing counters that whether or not we have inspired historians is itself a historical claim, and only as certain as history allows. This, then, "is the ugly broad ditch which I cannot get across, however often and however earnestly I have tried to make the leap. . . . Since the truth of these miracles has completely ceased to be demonstrable by miracles still happening now, since they are no more than reports of miracles, I deny that they should bind me in the least to a faith in the other teachings of Christ."

Christianity is a historical religion, unlike most Eastern religions. It asks the faithful to believe certain historical events took place, like the prophesied virgin birth of Jesus, his reputed miracles, his teachings as told to us by "inspired historians," his death on the cross, his resurrection from the dead, and his ascension into heaven. From these historical claims we are further asked to believe he was God incarnate, that he died on the cross "for our sins," that he will physically return to earth, and that he will reward the faithful and punish the unfaithful eternally. With this belief we are asked to surrender everything we have in service to the demands of such a faith and to "forswear forever all knowledge that conflicted with this belief."

Lessing asks us to consider whether Christianity should be believed based upon history alone, over and against his own personal experiences. That is, can this history be demonstrated in the same way that his own experiences can be demonstrated? And his answer is an emphatic "No!" Why? Because just like it might be false that Alexander conquered almost all of Asia, then it might also be false that the aforementioned historical events in the life of Jesus didn't happen either. And if these supposed events in the life of Jesus cannot be historically demonstrated, then even more so it cannot be demonstrated he is God incarnate who died for our sins and will reward or punish us in the hereafter, either. This then, he says, is the "ugly broad ditch which I cannot get across, however often and however earnestly I have tried to make the leap."

Lessing did, however, claim to believe in the faith of Jesus based upon other grounds. He believed, he said, because of the teachings of Jesus themselves. But, of course, today there are many historical questions about what Jesus actually taught. So Lessing's faith is actually undercut by his own skepticism over historical knowledge. Since history teaches us about what Jesus taught, then Lessing too had no basis to believe—but he probably saw that. According to Henry Chadwick: "In one sense, it could be said that Lessing spent his life hoping that Christianity was true and arguing that it was not."[2]

Lessing's argument influenced existentialist Søren Kierkegaard, who regarded historical knowledge as completely insufficient grounds for the Christian faith. In C. Stephen Evan's words, Kierkegaard believed that "there is an incommensurability between the evidence supplied by historical research and the decision to become a Christian. The historical evidence attains at most a certain level of probability. The decision which I must make on the other hand carries with it an infinite risk—eternal happiness or eternal damnation may be the result. No amount of probability could be sufficient to base such a decision upon."[3]

THE PROBLEMS OF HISTORICAL RESEARCH

Any historian will tell you the problems she faces when researching into the past. The historian attempts to write an accurate report of what happened in the past given the hindsight implications of that past for her day and age. That's the goal. Writing this historical record cannot be divorced from the hindsight implications for her era, for some events in the past may not have been viewed by the people of the past as importantly as they are viewed in her own day. Conversely, the people of the past may have viewed other events more importantly than they are considered at the time of the historian. That's why historians have to continue reexamining the past to see how it needs to be rewritten. History is written from the perspective of the historian, and it's unavoidable to do otherwise. The question here is whether or not the perspective of the people in the past is preferable to the perspective of the present-day historian. This is where the historian's values unavoidably enter into the picture.

Consider the claim that Columbus "discovered" America. Certainly that was big news to the European people of the past, and likewise to present people today, for it did change the world to a very large degree. But depending on your perspective, the change may not have been good. Columbus called the inhabitants of the Americas "Indians" because he thought he had reached the coasts of India. This on hindsight we know to be false. But it took a hindsight perspective to see this, so history has a way of correcting how we view the past. Another claim is that he "discovered" the Americas. Did he? Well it depends upon your perspective, doesn't it? If Native Americans were writing that history, they would say he didn't discover America. They did! Europeans wrote about that great "discovery" and what it gained for them by bridging the two worlds, but Native Americans would have described how it destroyed their civilization with diseases, land grabbing, massive buffalo slaughter, and the subsequent westward expansion of these foreigners.

Christian professor of history D. W. Bebbington describes the problem of the historian: "The historian's history is molded by his values, his outlook, and his worldview. It is never the evidence alone that dictates what is written. The attitudes that a historian brings to the evidence form an equally important element in the creation of history. The bias of a historian enters his history. The historian himself is part of the historical process, powerfully influenced by his time and place. The problem of the historian himself nevertheless dictates that two historians presented with the same evidence are likely to reach different conclusions. This is true of people living in the same period; it is more true of people living in different periods. That is why each age writes history that reflects its own concerns."[4]

According to E. Schillebeeckx, "Historical objectivity is not a reconstruction of the past in its unrepeatable factuality, it is the truth of the past in the light of the present."[5] Albert Nolan has argued this point with regard to Jesus: "To imagine that one can have historical objectivity without a perspective is an illusion. One perspective, however, can be better than another, [but] the only perspective open to us is the one given to us by the historical situation in which we find ourselves. If we cannot achieve an unobstructed view of Jesus from the vantage point of our present circumstances, then we cannot achieve an unobstructed view of him at all."[6]

Of course, this historical problem is compounded when we understand that the evidence the historian considers is the stuff of the past, and the past is not immediately available for investigation. Time separates the historian from her subject matter. The historian "cannot conduct opinion polls on the dead." And there is a "paucity of evidence" for a great part of the past. According to Bebbington, "Our knowledge of the earlier middle ages depends on a tiny number of written sources that can be eked out by such supplementary material as place-names and coinage." Furthermore, the evidence is not always reliable. According to Bebbington, "forgeries and misrepresentations, whether from good or bad motives, litter the world's archives. The historian, therefore, develops a skeptical turn of mind. Original documents may themselves mislead; and what books about the past claim is much more likely to be wrong. History demands a critical frame of mind." Because of these problems Bebbington states the obvious: "Written history cannot correspond precisely with the actual past. . . . To write a value-free account of the past is beyond the historian's power.[7]

One school of thought headed up by Leopold Von Ranke actually sought to do this. Their goal was to write history "free from prejudices," and in so doing write the events of the past "as they actually happened." But most all modern historians think this is impossible to do. Harry Elmer Barnes argues against this possibility. In the first place, modern psychology has completely undermined total historical objectivity by showing that "no truly excellent piece of intellectual work can be executed without real interest and firm convictions." In other words, total objectivity in a subject is impossible. Second, Barnes reminds us that each historical event is essentially unique never to be repeated in its entirety. Hence, "no one can ever entirely recreate this historical entity. . . . It is manifestly impossible to create the past 'as it actually happened.'"[8]

Karl Popper has argued that verifying the assassination of Caesar is impossible because verification would require an "infinite regress" of documentation. For example, to verify it, we would have to verify the source leading us to that conclusion. But then we'd also need to verify the source that verifies that Caesar was assassinated, which would need to be verified, and so on, and so on. Maybe Popper seeks too strict of a verification process. Nonetheless, with each independent source used to verify the previous source, the probability diminishes for the original event we seek to verify.[9] Some thinkers like Carl Becker have gone so far as to deny that we can know the past with any objectivity at all—that historical facts only exist in the mind, and they advocate a historical relativism with regard to the events of the past.[10]

Several Christian apologetics books address this issue.[11] William Lane Craig dealt with this issue in *Reasonable Faith: Christianity and Apologetics*, and Norman Geisler dealt with it in his book *Christian Apologetics*.[12] Yet the meager conclusion from reading Craig's and Geisler's chapters is that objective knowledge of history is possible. According to Craig, "first, a common core of indisputable historical events exists; second, it is possible to distinguish between history and propaganda; and third, it is possible to criticize poor history." Craig concludes: "neither the supposed problem of lack of direct access to the past nor the supposed problem of the lack of neutrality can prevent us from learning something from history." The goal is to "obtain probability, not mathematical certainty."[13] But such a conclusion is indeed a meager one; that knowledge of the past is possible. Even though I think this is true, there is a lot of doubt about many, if not most historical claims, especially those that involve the miraculous.

Consider the following historical questions: How were the Egyptian pyramids made? Who made them? Why? Was Shakespeare a fictitious name for Francis Bacon? Exactly how was the Gettysburg battle fought and won? What was the true motivation for Lincoln to emancipate the slaves? What happened at Custer's last stand? Who killed President John F. Kennedy? Why? Who knew what and when during the Watergate scandal that eventually led to President Nixon resigning? Why did America lose the "war" in Vietnam? Did George W. Bush legitimately win the 2000 election? Did President Bush knowingly lead us into a war with Iraq on false pretenses? What about some high-profile criminal cases? Is O. J. Simpson a murderer? Who killed JonBenet Ramsey? Is Michael Jackson a pedophile?

There are also many problems inside the Bible itself that biblical scholars are trying to figure out. Where was Jesus actually born? What did Jesus actually say? Did he himself claim to be God's unique son? What best describes his message? What day was Jesus crucified on? What was Paul's relationship to the Christian leadership in Jerusalem? How many times did Paul visit Jerusalem? Who wrote each book in the Bible? What is the date of any specific book in the Bible? What theory best describes the relationship of the synoptic Gospels? And so on.

THE HISTORIAN AND MIRACLES

Is it any wonder, then, why Lessing and Kierkegaard both questioned the reliability of historical knowledge to lead one to believe in Christianity with its miraculous claims? History itself is fraught with many difficult problems when one comes to understand the events of the past. According to Bebbington again, "Any historical account is, in strict logic, open to doubt. It is not just remarkable events long ago like Biblical miracles that are not logically certain."[14] But if nonsupernatural events in the past are open to doubt, then how much more so is it the case with supernatural claims of events in the past, like biblical miracles.

One of the claims made by William Lane Craig is that both the historian and the scientist seek systematic consistency by using the "hypothetical-deductive model": "we should accept the hypothesis that provides the most plausible explanation of the evidence."[15] Since he brings up science as an analogy to historical understanding, please recall what I said in chapter 6 when it came to methodological naturalism. When looking into the past, modern historians (qua historians) must operate on that same method and assume a natural causal explanation for every event in history. If that method has had so many successes in science, then why not apply that method to history as well? And modern historians have done just that. They are taught to be critical of the past, as we've just mentioned. As historians they must. That is the standard for what they do as historians, to be skeptical of the past record, especially claims of the miraculous. If historians weren't skeptical of the miraculous, then as Robert M. Price warns us, they "would be at the mercy of every medieval tale, every report that a statue wept, or that someone changed lead into gold or turned into a werewolf."[16]

According to I. Howard Marshall, "many historians—the great majority in fact—would say that miracles fall outside their orbit as historians. For to accept the miraculous as a possibility in history is to admit an irrational element which cannot be included under the ordinary laws of history. The result is that the historian believes himself justified in writing a 'history' of Jesus in which the miraculous and supernatural do not appear in historical statements. The 'historical' Jesus is an ordinary man. To some historians he is that and no more. To others, however, the possibility is open that he was more than an ordinary man—but this possibility lies beyond the reach of historical study as such."[17] Marshall defends Christianity, but he has an excellent summary of the problems of the modern historian for his faith, from which I use in what follows.

Three lines of evidence incline "the great majority" of historians to take this stance. First, our knowledge of Jesus comes almost exclusively from those who believed Jesus was the one and only savior of the world, and they were convinced he was God's Messiah. They sought to convert others to this same belief. They were committed men. But the historian asks how reliable their record can be when they wrote the books of the New Testament? They were simply not impartial with regard to what they wrote. And if these authors were dependent upon other committed believers for their information, doesn't this call into question their reliability? It does in every other area of historical research. According to Marshall, "How can we be sure that the whole story has not been colored by the pious imagination of the earliest Christians who saw the story of Jesus in the light of the religious position which they ascribed to him after his death? If the Evangelists had been scientific historians, disinterested recorders of what happened, then there is some chance that they might have avoided displaying such bias. But this is not what they were. They were writers of Gospels, works intended to convert the outsider and strengthen the believer. They were not writing history but religious *propaganda* (emphais mine)."[18] Did they check their sources? Did they cross-examine their witnesses? Or did they have a predisposition to believe what was told to them?

Second, it can be pointed out that many similar stories of the miraculous were told by all kinds of respected people in ancient times. According to R. Bultmann, an impressive list of miraculous stories can be found from the same age and environment of Jesus and first-century Christians.[19] The Jews had similar stories about some of their rabbis that claimed they had the power to heal. It was also claimed that the Roman Emperor Vespasian had the ability to heal. Richard Carrier has documented these stories in "Kooks and Quacks of the Roman Empire: A Look into the World of the Gospels." Here is what he concluded: "From all of this one thing should be apparent: the age of Jesus was not an age of critical reflection and remarkable religious acumen. It was an era filled with con artists, gullible believers, martyrs without a cause, and reputed miracles of every variety. In light of this picture, the tales of the Gospels do not seem very remarkable. Even if they were false in every detail, there is no evidence that they would have been disbelieved or rejected as absurd by many people, who at the time had little in the way of education or critical thinking skills. They had no newspapers, telephones, photographs, or public documents to consult to check a story. If they were not a witness, all they had was a man's word. And even if they were a witness, the tales above tell us that even then their skills of critical reflection were lacking. Certainly, this age did not lack keen and educated skeptics— it is not that there were no skilled and skeptical observers. There were. Rather, the shouts of the credulous rabble overpowered their voice and seized the world from them."[20]

So the modern historian can ask two lines of questions about these similar kinds of stories. (1) To today's Christians who believe in miracles, she will ask whether the other miraculous stories about other great men in the first century occurred. Why should we believe one set of miraculous stories and not another set? The evidence for both kinds of stories seems to be the same, so why do Christians just accept one set of stories and reject the other set? (2) If miraculous stories were being told about other great men during their day, then wouldn't early Christians be tempted to tell similar kinds of stories—and even greater stories—about Jesus, to prove he was greater than the others? In an environment where a great man is known by his great and even miraculous deeds, then early Christians would be faced with the choice of telling even bigger deeds for their Jesus, or not gaining the attention of those who believed Jesus wasn't that great of a man.

Third, the modern historian lives in the modern world, a world where miracles and supernatural events simply don't take place. At least that is her experience, as well as my own experience. I have never personally seen a miracle even in my days as a former Christian and minister in the Christian faith. But if this is true for us, then it must be true among ancient people as well. As historians it's extremely difficult, if not impossible, to step outside what one has learned and experienced in one's own day and time, and not see the past from that same perspective. There should be no reason to suppose that ancient historical people experienced anything different than what we experience today. They were perhaps just superstitious, that's all, and they lived in a world where there was nothing known about nature's fixed laws—just their belief in a God who expresses his will in all events. So when confronted with a miraculous story, the modern historian assumes a natural explanation, or that the story became exaggerated in the telling, or the cure was a psychological one, or it may simply be a legend to enhance the reputation of the miracle worker.

THE CHRISTIAN FRAMEWORK FOR VIEWING HISTORY

Ronald A. Wells, who teaches history at Calvin College, wrote a book that provides the meaning of history through the eyes of Christian faith, he says, starting with Jesus and Christianity down through to the twentieth century. It's history as interpreted by means of the Christian framework. In the first chapter he admits that "the facts of history simply do not speak for themselves; historians speak for them from an interpretive framework of the ideas they already hold." He merely suggests that over and against the secular view of history as a two-dimensional world (space and time) Christians "insist that there is a third dimension—spirit—and that a whole view of the world must be three dimensional." This, he claims, is the proper way to view history.[21]

But this isn't the only framework for viewing history. David Bebbington speaks of five different philosophies of history, Christianity being just one of them. The other four are briefly as follows: the ancient and oriental cyclical view of history in which history is a pattern of cycles; the idea of progress, in which there was confidence that the future will be better than the past with human beings as the sole actors, not God; historicism, which regards each nation as having a distinctive culture, and that history is the story of the growth of each culture from within each culture; and Marxism, in which the historical process is created by man as he labors to satisfy his basic needs, with ideas about God hindering that process.[22] There are also feminist views of history.

Which framework should we adopt? In arguing for the Christian view of history, Norman Geisler admits that "unless one can settle the question as to whether this is a theistic or nontheistic world on grounds independent of the mere facts themselves, there is no way to determine the objective meaning of history. If, on the other hand, there are good reasons to believe that this is a theistic universe, then objectivity in history is a possibility. For once the overall viewpoint is established, it is simply a matter of finding the view of history that is most consistent with that overall system."[23] In other words, in order to read history in light of Christianity, one must first have sufficient reasons for this Christian framework. But where does Geisler propose that we find these reasons? Whether or not we can view biblical history through the eyes of the Christian framework, for instance, depends upon that history, since it is a historical religion. It asks us to believe certain foundational miraculous events occurred, like the virgin birth and resurrection of Jesus. No one can defend these so-called historical events via philosophy. They must be defended historically. Otherwise, doing so is circular.

The Christian looks at history using the Christian framework (or worldview) to do so. The question is whether or not that framework is the proper way to view all of history, especially Bible "history." Think about the circular nature of this for a while. Using the Christian framework, the Christian views all of history from that perspective. So when the Christian examines biblical "history," he or she will more than likely believe its miraculous claims, because that's what the Christian framework dictates in the first place. And yet, Christians claim that this same biblical "history" provides them with the framework to view that "history" as believable in the first place. What? How is it possible to gain the Christian framework for viewing biblical "history" from that same "history," unless there are reasons for viewing it as such? Conversely, how is it possible to view biblical "history" as real history unless one already approaches it with the Christian framework for viewing it as real history?

It's this conundrum that forces me to ask for more evidence to believe today, like Lessing. I need evidence to believe for today. Yesterday's evidence no longer can hold water for me, for in order to see it as evidence, I must already believe in the framework that allows me to see it as evidence. In other words, in order to see yesterday's evidence as evidence for me, I must already believe the Christian framework that allows me to see yesterday's evidence as evidence.

I. Howard Marshall's answer to this vexing problem is to argue that our particular framework (worldview, or set of presuppositions) and the historical evidence "stand in a dialectical relationship to one another. . . . We interpret evidence in light of our presuppositions, and we also form our presuppositions in the light of the evidence. It is only through a 'dialogue' between presuppositions and evidence that we gain both sound presuppositions and a correct interpretation of the evidence. The process is circular and unending. It demands openness on the part of the investigator. He must be prepared to revise his ideas in the light of the evidence, for ultimately it is the evidence which is decisive." Now I don't deny that he's right about this. This is the best that a human being can do. But even Marshall admits that while the Christian should be prepared to let his worldview be altered by the evidence, "his worldview is part of the evidence, and cannot be simply laid aside." And while he argues that a modern-day personal experience of "the risen Lord" is a "relevant factor" in assessing the historical facts regarding the resurrection of Jesus, he also admits that "if a person fails to have a personal experience of the risen Lord, this may prove to him that the biblical evidence does not support belief in the resurrection of Jesus."[24]

HISTORICAL KNOWLEDGE AND OUR ETERNAL DESTINY

Let me ask one final question. It's this: How can our eternal destiny be at stake if it is based upon historical knowledge? Let's say, for instance, that in order to gain an eternal reward in heaven, you must know what the primary cause was for the Protestant Reformation in the sixteenth century, or why America lost the "war" in Vietnam, or whether or not Michael Jackson is a pedophile. These are all historical questions. If our eternal destinies were at stake, then we'd certainly study such things, as much as possible, because our lives would be at stake. However, even if this were the eternal threat, there would still be people who disagreed with each other on these issues. The main reason isn't because we wouldn't want to know the truth for fear of a lifestyle change, because we would be desperate to know the truth. It would be because we have different ways of looking at the facts. We have different presuppositions about what is even considered a fact. That's the nature of human understanding, and that's the nature of historical investigations.

But if we ended up being wrong, God would be heard to say, "I'm sorry, you got it wrong. Off you go into eternal damnation." That wouldn't be fair, would it? That is, unless there was an overwhelming case on behalf of any of these issues, and even that wouldn't be fair, because an overwhelming case is still not a case that is certain, is it? A sufficient, but not certain case, is insufficient when our eternal destiny is at stake, wouldn't you think? But that's exactly the situation we face when it comes to believing the truth about Christian history. People who get it wrong will be punished forever, according to the Christian faith. Now I know that Christians will respond that getting biblical history wrong isn't what condemns people to hell—their sins send them to hell. But the way to be saved from eternal condemnation, according to them, is to get biblical history right—that is, they must believe certain biblical historical claims.

When it comes to history, especially the miraculous "history" represented in the Bible, there can never be a sufficient case for accepting it—much less a certain one—because it depends on the particular framework we use to view history in the first place. This is, in my opinion, circular reasoning. There is simply no way to tell for sure that a historical religion like Christianity is true based upon history, and there is likewise no way God can judge us for all of eternity if we get it wrong. Lessing is surely right. What we need is some incontrovertible evidence for Christianity for us living in today's world.

FIVE OBJECTIONS TO THIS CONCLUSION

Let me mention and briefly argue with five anticipated objections to what I've written.

1. *The origin and the historical continuity of the church from the earliest days up until now, even if somewhat fragmented, provides sufficient evidence for the claims made about Jesus. That is, the history of the church provides sufficient evidence to believe in the New Testament documents of the church.*

But how can the history of the church provide sufficient evidence for the history about Jesus? History provides evidence for how we should view history? Lessing would say whether or not we have an accurate history of the earliest days of the church is itself a historical claim and is only as certain as history allows. How one sees the origin of the church is a historical question fraught with all of the same problems mentioned earlier in this chapter. Quite simply there are various accounts of the origins of the church.[25] It's just false to say that history provides the justification for viewing history. Islam, another historical religion, has a long history to it too. Does that history justify the Muslim faith? Well, it depends upon whether you were born into the Muslim faith and approach Muslim history from a Muslim framework, doesn't it? The Mormons have a history to their faith too. Does their history justify their faith? Again, it depends on whether you were born into the Mormon faith and approach the Mormon history from a Mormon framework.

2. *Jesus purportedly said that some people wouldn't believe even if God raised a man from the dead. Even after Jesus was raised from the dead, they still didn't believe. Likewise, some people today would not believe even if God provided a glowing cross in the sky for all to see.*

The word *some* here needs to be unpacked when it is said, "some people today still would not believe." How many does the word *some* mean? Who knows? But let's think about the numbers of others who would believe. That's the whole point. Millions of people would believe if there was a glowing cross in the sky, and yet all that some Christians can do is to object that there will still be "some" who don't believe? Every Christian cares more for the lost than God purportedly does, for they would do whatever they could to see that the lost were saved. And if a Christian had died for the sins of the world (the greater deed), she would certainly do other things to help people accept that salvation by providing more evidence to believe (the lesser deeds).

Let's say I die and I go to hell. Then God grants me my wish to come back and tell my friends and relatives to avoid hell. They were at my funeral, and they got stuck with all of my funeral bills. I would be able to convince everyone who was at my funeral and anyone who saw me die, for starters. And so this is the whole reason God doesn't raise anyone else up from the grave to warn others today? He doesn't do this because he proclaims it wouldn't do any good? That's a lame excuse if I ever heard one.

J. P. Moreland and William Lane Craig claim that "we have no way of knowing that in a world of free creatures in which God's existence is as obvious as the nose on your face that more people would come to love him and know his salvation than in the actual world."[26] But I think it's demonstrably false to say that most people wouldn't believe if the evidence were overwhelming, because God carries a big stick—he'd send you to hell if you don't believe. With that big stick God carries around, coupled with the overwhelming evidence of a glowing cross in the sky, people would turn to Christianity by the millions. How could one say otherwise? People all over the world are looking for answers, in every continent across the globe. Most of them agonize over the truth. It's frustrating not to know who they are, why they are here, and where they are going. They would be greatly relieved to find the answer. And the answer Christianity gives, that God loves them and sent his son to die for them, is the most wonderful story of them all. There is no other story to compare with that one—none. It is such a fulfilling and satisfying answer to the perplexity of life that with overwhelming evidence, and the threat of hell, there would only be a small minority of people who refused to believe.

3. *The reason people don't believe the historical evidence is because most people reject the gospel for the same reasons people rejected Jesus during his ministry: pride and pleasure. People want answers that won't cost them anything—as in repentance.*

Really? People all over the world in various non-Christian religions are taking Draconian measures to live up to their faith. In some of them it costs them everything, as in a Tibetan monk. And what about militant Muslims who are willing to become suicide bombers to kill American infidels? And they don't believe in Christ because it'll cost them something? Just study these other religions. It costs them as much or more to believe what they do than Christianity does, as evidenced by even the most committed Christian. People will commit everything they have for something they can really believe in, Americans included, although I think Americans are just soft on commitment with regard to any faith they believe in. People want something big enough to commit themselves to. It's just that few people find something they can believe in that will cause them to be totally committed. And how do Christians first convert? They are relieved to find the answers that Christianity offers. It was grand to believe in a God who loves and forgives me. Surely that's enough motivation to change lifestyles. Repentance isn't too hard to try when you come to believe in the Christian message. Repentance is something we would willingly, joyfully do, if the message were believed (the Greek word for repentance, *metanoia*, literally means a "change of mind"). It's not the change of lifestyle that is feared, for that comes naturally. It's whether or not the message is true. If it's true, it's worth the lifestyle change. But why change if it's not true? Why bother at all?

4. *Someone might object that since I think historical claims are open to a great amount of doubt I likewise cannot have any assurance that my historical claims about the Christian faith are any better.*

I just don't see any problem in claiming there is room for doubting many if not most historical claims, especially miraculous claims in the ancient superstitious past. I'm not arguing we shouldn't try to understand what took place in the past, anyway. We should do the best we can. I think I can draw plenty of reasonable conclusions about the past. But if I'm wrong about them, it only serves to prove my point. For it shows that people can be rational and yet be wrong about the past, just like historians cannot all be right even though they rationally disagree with each other on many issues.

The bottom line is that there is a huge difference between trying to establish that some event took place in the past precisely as claimed and trying to show that such a claim is false. Most always there are alternative scenarios, many of them reasonable, leaving room for plenty of doubt. It's the nature of historical studies that although the evidence can lead us to reasonable conclusions about the past, there is always the possibility that the evidence leading to different conclusions did not survive or was destroyed, especially the farther we go back in time. So what I'm doing in this book is disputing the claims of Christians who are trying to establish that the events in the Bible took place precisely as reported. Their conclusions are not probable at all. There are several other alternative conclusions, any one of which is more probable than what they conclude.

5. *If the historical past is a poor medium for God to reveal himself to human beings, how else could God reveal himself? Isn't that all he can do?*

Christians claim God has already verified his revelation in Jesus through miracles in the historical past, and as such it needs no further verification. But as I've argued, history is a poor medium to verify this before the advent of cameras, printing presses, and investigative reporters, especially when it comes to miracles in the superstitious past. I still have not been given sufficient reasons and sufficient evidence to believe.

Sufficient reasons could be provided by God. I need to be able to understand more of the mysteries of Christianity in order to believe it. If everything about Christianity makes rational sense to an omniscient God, then God could've created human beings with more intelligence so that the problems of Christianity are much more intellectually solvable than they are.

Short of God creating us with more intelligence, God could've explained his ways to us. He could've written the "mother of all philosophical papers" by answering such problems as why there is something rather than nothing at all, why there is so much suffering, along with questions about the atonement, the trinity, divine simplicity, the incarnation, the relationship of free will and foreknowledge, and how it's possible for a spiritual being to interact with a material world. Christians born into their faith inside an already Christian culture may claim God has explained the things necessary, but for most people in the world he didn't explain enough. Because he has not done enough to help us understand these things, he is at least partially to blame for those who do not believe, especially if he knew in advance that people wouldn't believe unless he had done so.

Short of helping us to understand these "mysteries," the only thing left is to give us sufficient evidence to believe and less evidence to disbelieve. God could reveal himself to us in every generation in a myriad of ways: What better way to show us that he exists than what the book of Acts says he did for Saul of Tarsus on the road to Damascus! He could become incarnate in every generation and do miracles for all to see. He could spontaneously appear and heal people, or end a famine, or stop a war, or settle an important question like slavery. He could raise up John F. Kennedy from the dead for all to see. He could restore an amputated limb in full sight of a crowd of people that would include all of the best magicians along with the mythbusters and James Randi, who would all find fault if fault could be found. He could do any and all of the miracles he did in the Bible from time to time, including miraculously feeding five thousand men with their families. The list of things God could do in each generation is endless.

God could also have made this universe and the creatures on earth absolutely unexplainable by science, especially since science is the major obstacle for many to believe. He could've created us in a universe that couldn't be even remotely figured out by science. That is to say, there would be no evidence leading scientists to accept a big bang, nor would there be any evidence for the way galaxies, solar systems, or planets themselves form naturalistically. If God is truly omnipotent, he could've created the universe instantaneously by fiat and placed planets haphazardly around the sun, some revolving counterclockwise and in haphazard orbits. God could have even created the earth as a flat disk allowing for no plausible natural explanation at all. Then when it came to creatures on earth, God could've created them without any connection whatsoever to each other. Each species would be so distinct from each other that no scientist could ever conclude natural selection was the process by which they have arisen. There would be no hierarchy of the species in gradual increments. God could've created fish and mammals, but no reptiles or amphibians. Then evolutionary theory could never have gotten off the ground. There would be no rock formations that showed this evolutionary process because it wouldn't exist in the first place. Human beings would be seen as absolutely special and distinct from the rest of the creatures on earth such that no scientist could ever conclude they evolved from the lower primates. There would be no evidence of unintelligent design, either. God didn't even have to create us with brains, if he created us with minds. The existence of this kind of universe and the creatures in it could never be explained by science apart from the existence of God.

Someone could've made a monument to Abraham that still exists and is scientifically dated to his supposed time period. There would be overwhelming evidence for a universal flood covering "all" mountains. Noah's ark would be found exactly where the Bible says, and it would be exactly as described in the Bible. The location of Lot's wife, who was turned into a pillar of salt, would still be miraculously preserved and known by scientific testing to have traces of human DNA in it. There would be noncontroversial evidence that the Israelites lived as slaves in Egypt for four hundred years, conclusive evidence that they wandered in the wilderness for forty years, and convincing evidence that they conquered the land of Canaan exactly as the Bible depicts. But there is none.

Furthermore, Christians would be overwhelmingly better people by far. And God would answer their prayers in such distinctive ways that even those who don't believe would seek out a Christian to pray for them. Scientific studies done on prayer would meet with overwhelming confirmation. We wouldn't see such religious diversity that has divided the world into distinct geographical locations.

If God has foreknowledge, he could've predicted certain events in history like the rise of the Internet, the exact time of the 2004 Indonesian tsunami, or prophesied the day that TV was invented or the atomic bomb, and he could do it using nonambiguous language that would be seen by all as a prophetic fulfillment. God could've predicted several things that would take place in each generation in each region of the earth, so that each generation and each region of the earth would have confirmation that he exists through prophecy.

There would be clear and specific prophecies about the virgin birth, life, nature, mission, death, resurrection, ascension, and return of Jesus in the Old Testament that could not be denied by even the most hardened skeptic. As it is, there is none as we shall see.

The gospel accounts of the resurrection would all be the same, showing no evidence of growing incrementally over the years by superstitious people. The gospels could've been written at about the same time, months after Jesus arose from the dead. And there would be no implausibilites in these stories about women not telling others, or that the soldiers who supposedly guarded the tomb knew the disciples stole the body of Jesus even though they were asleep. Such evidence like a Turin shroud would be found which could be scientifically shown to be from Jerusalem at

that time containing an image that could not be explained away except that a crucified man had come back to life.

Christians will claim God has given us enough evidence to believe, but the existence of billions of sincere nonbelievers is strong evidence that God has not provided the evidence needed for us to believe.

A FINAL NOTE: THE HISTORY OF THE CHURCH IS STRONG EVIDENCE AGAINST CHRISTIANITY

Take a very brief look at some things in church history with me. Because God chose
a poor medium and a poor era to reveal himself, he did not effectively communicate
his perfect will to believers.

The Crusades/Holy Wars

For centuries the church sanctioned the slaughtering of infidels in the name of their
God beginning in the eleventh century against various peoples. The major goal of
the first crusade was to recapture Jerusalem from the Muslims. The history of the
crusades and the deeds done in the name of Jesus are atrocious.

There have been many other wars waged in the name of Jesus and the church—
too many to list. The Spanish conquistadors conducted a holy war against the inhabitants of the Americas demanding them to either "acknowledge the Church as the
Ruler and Superior of the whole world, and the high priest called Pope" or else, "we
shall powerfully enter into your country, and shall make war against you in all ways
and manners that we can, and shall subject you to the yoke and obedience of the
Church and of their Highnesses; we shall take you and your wives and your children,
and shall make slaves of them, and as such shall sell and dispose of them as their
Highnesses may command; and we shall take away your goods, and shall do you all
the mischief and damage that we can, as to vassals who do not obey, and refuse to
receive their lord."[27] In 2002, President George W. Bush called his antiterrorism war
a "crusade."

The Inquisition

The angelic doctor Thomas Aquinas argued from the Bible that heresy was a "leavening influence" upon the minds of the weak, and as such, heretics should be killed.
Since heretical ideas could inflict the greatest possible harm upon other human
beings, it was the greatest crime of all. Heretical ideas could send people to an eternally conscious torment in hell. So logic demands that the church must get rid of this
leavening influence. It was indeed the greatest crime of all, given this logic. So, the
rallying cry for over two centuries beginning with the twelfth century was "convert
or die!"

The Witch Hunts

Christian people actually believed witches flew through the night, met together with others, and had sex with the devil who left a mark on them. Once accused it was extremely difficult to be declared innocent. Any testimony from others could be discounted because she may have cast a spell on them to say she was innocent. No evidence was needed in most cases, and in most cases no evidence was found. Torture was all that was needed to extract the confessions, and it was especially harsh against accused witches because it was believed their magic could help them withstand greater pain. Once they were forced to confess, they were also tortured to find out who their accomplices were, so others were implicated. Witch hunters were mostly paid for their services by confiscating the property of convicted witches, so they had a vested interest in finding them guilty. Convicted witches were then killed by strangulation or by being burned alive.

"Manifest Destiny"

This was a phrase associated with the territorial expansion of the United States during the 1800s. It expressed the general belief that God had given them the divine mission to spread democracy on the North American continent. It was supposedly both obvious ("manifest") and certain ("destiny"). As such it legitimized western expansion and the rape, pillage, and slaughter of Native Americans.

Slavery in the American Antebellum South

I'll say more about this in chapter 12.

There is no justification for God to have allowed his followers to think they were pleasing him by acting in these terrible ways—none! If God was perfectly good, he would've said, "Thou shalt not engage in religiously motivated wars to spread your faith, nor steal land, nor kill witches and heretics, nor buy, beat, or own slaves" (KJV version!), and said it as often as he needed to do so. Then the church couldn't justify all of this horrible violence.

My question is who's at fault here? I'll even grant that human beings are "wicked" and that God knows this about us. If so, then why wasn't he crystal clear about what he wanted believers to do? God is at fault to some degree for the misery and suffering caused by Christians who failed to understand his directives. Add to this the poor job that the Holy Spirit has done in the life of the church, since he's supposed to guide Christians by "illumination," and you see one of the reasons why I reject Christianity. Not only has God failed to communicate effectively, but the Holy Spirit has failed (and continues to fail) to do his job (see note).[28]

NOTES

1. G. E. Lessing, "On the Proof of the Spirit and of Power," in *Lessing's Theological Writings*, trans. Henry Chadwick (Stanford, CA: Stanford University Press, 1956), pp. 51–55.

2. "G. E. Lessing," *The Encyclopedia of Philosophy*, 8 vols., editor in chief Paul Edwards (New York: Macmillan, 1967).

3. C. Stephen Evans, *Subjectivity and Religious Belief* (Grand Rapids, MI: Eerdmans, 1978), p. 83.

4. D. W. Bebbington, *Patterns of History: A Christian View* (Downers Grove, IL: Inter-Varsity Press, 1979), pp. 5–8.

5. E. Schillebeeckx, *God, the Future of Man* (New York: Sheed and Ward, 1968), p. 24.

6. Albert Nolan, *Jesus before Christianity* (Maryknoll, NY: Orbis Books, 1978), p. 4.

7. Bebbington, *Patterns of History: A Christian View*, p. 12.

8. Harry Elmer Barnes, *A History of Historical Writing* (New York: Dover, 1962), pp. 266–71.

9. Karl Popper, *Conjectures and Refutations: The Growth of Scientific Knowledge* (New York: Routledge), pp. 29–31.

10. Carl Becker, "What Are Historical Facts?" in *The Philosophy of History in Our Time*, ed. H. Meyerhoff (New York: Doubleday, 1959), pp. 120–39.

11. Colin Brown, "History and the Believer," in *History, Criticism and Faith*, ed. Colin Brown (Downer's Grove, IL: InterVarsity Press, 1977), pp. 147–216; C. Stephen Evans, *The Historical Christ and the Jesus of Faith* (Oxford: Oxford University Press, 1996), and his "Methodological Naturalism in Historical Biblical Scholarship," in *Jesus and the Restoration of Israel*, ed. Carey C. Newman (Downers Grove, IL: InterVarsity Press, 1999), pp. 180–205. See also Francis J. Beckwith, "History and Miracles," in *In Defense of Miracles: A Comprehensive Case for God's Action in History*, eds. Douglas Geivett and Gary Habermas (Downers Grove, IL: InterVarsity Press, 1997), pp. 86–98. To read a good review of Beckwith's chapter see Richard Carrier's "A Review of *In Defense of Miracles*," to be found at http://www.infidels.org. There are others, of course, but Van Austin Harvey's classic *The Historian and the Believer* (London: SCM, 1967) stands in stark contrast to these other books by arguing that we should use methodological naturalism when approaching the Bible.

12. William Lane Craig, *Apologetics: An Introduction* (Chicago: Moody Press, 1984), pp. 126–50; Norman Geisler, *Christian Apologetics* (Grand Rapids, MI: Baker House, 1976). Geisler's discussion follows a summary of William Lane Craig's master's thesis.

13. Craig, *Apologetics: An Introduction,* pp. 145–49.

14. Bebbington, *Patterns of History: A Christian View*, p. 8.

15. Craig, *Apologetics: An Introduction,* p. 147.

16. Robert M. Price, *The Incredible Shrinking Son of Man* (Amherst, NY: Prometheus Books, 2002), p. 20.

17. I. Howard Marshall, *I Believe in the Historical Jesus* (Grand Rapids, MI: Eerdmans, 1977), p. 59.

18. Ibid., p. 54.

19. Rudolph Bultmann, *The History of the Synoptic Tradition*, 2nd ed. (New York: Harper & Row, 1968), pp. 218–44.

20. This essay can be found at www.infidels.org/library.

21. Ronald A. Wells, *History through the Eyes of Faith* (New York: HarperSanFrancisco, 1989), pp. 8–11.

22. Bebbington, *Patterns of History: A Christian View*.

23. Norman Geisler, *Encyclopedia of Christian Apologetics* (Grand Rapids, MI: Baker Books, 1999), p. 298.

24. Marshall, *I Believe in the Historical Jesus*, pp. 98–101.

25. For two accounts of the earliest days of the church, see John Dominic Crossan's *The Birth of Christianity: Discovering What Happened in the Years Immediately After the Execution of Jesus* (New York: Harper & Row, 1998), and L. Michael White, *From Jesus to Christianity* (New York: Harper & Row, 2004).

26. J. P. Moreland and William Lane Craig, *Philosophical Foundations for a Christian Worldview* (Downers Grove, IL: InterVarsity Press, 2003), p. 158.

27. From the *Requerimiento*, 1510 CE, written by jurist Palacios Rubios, of the Council of Castile.

28. Some scholars are taking another look at all of the crimes of the historical church. See, for instance, Rodney Stark's book *For the Glory of God: How Monotheism Led to Reformations, Science, Witch-Hunts, and the End of Slavery* (Princeton, NJ: Princeton University Press, 2004), and Henry Kamen's book *The Spanish Inquisition: A Historical Revision* (New Haven, CT: Yale University Press, 1997). Stark claims slavery was abolished precisely because of Christianity, and that there were only sixty thousand witches killed during the witch hunts, rather than a hundred thousand. Almost unbelievably Stark rationalizes the witch killings out "to a total number of about two victims per 10,000 population" (p. 203). Why would he put such a fine point on it? Would it equally represent the facts to say a person dove head first into a river without getting hurt that had a statistically overall average depth of two feet? There were communities that suffered a huge loss during the witch hunts even if other communities did not suffer as much. I guess it can be said that neither Stark nor his mother were tried as witches, right? And it says nothing about the terror the Church had on others who were deathly afraid of the Church. Kamen estimates that only two thousand people were killed during the Spanish Inquisition. But the Christian faith isn't really helped by these conclusions at all, even if true. For if God had told his people not to kill heretics or witches and if he had not approved of slavery there would be nothing to reform since such practices would not have been sanctioned by the church in the first place! And even if Kamen is correct that only two thousand lives were snuffed out during the Inquisition in one country, that is still two thousand too many when all God had to do was to condemn such a practice from the beginning. That is why Dinesh D'Souza is extremely heartless when speaking of the twenty-five people killed in the Salem witch trials by callously quipping: "Few Casualties, Big Brouhaha," in *What's So Great about Christianity* (Washington, DC: Regnery, 2007), p. 207.

9

DO MIRACLES TAKE PLACE?

L et's begin for comparison purposes by understanding an important distinction Bart D. Ehrman makes between events the ancients would consider "spectacular," in that they don't happen very often, and what modern scientifically literate people would call a "miracle," which goes contrary/against the laws of nature themselves. Sure, ancient biblical people knew that axe heads don't float, donkeys don't talk, and people cannot walk on water. But "spectacular deeds happened all the time—it was spectacular when the sun came up or the lightening struck or the crops put forth their fruit. . . . For these people there was no 'closed system' of cause and effect, a natural world that was set over against a supernatural realm. Thus, when spectacular deeds, which people today might call 'miracles,' occurred, the only questions for most ancient persons were (a) who was able to perform these deeds, and (b) what was the source of their power?"[1]

SCIENTIFIC PROBLEMS WITH MIRACLES IN THE BIBLE

Some miracles are based on an outmoded cosmological viewpoint in which heaven is above the firmament that holds back water and in which the stars are said to reside: the flat earth is supported by fountains of water beneath it, and hell is the abode of the dead that is in the belly of the earth. Here we have problems with descriptions of the flood, the placement of created stars, the sun stopping in its place for Joshua, and also backing up for Hezekiah. There are also problems with a star that led Magi to the city of Bethlehem, the ascension of Jesus into heaven, and the promised return of Jesus from heaven.

Some miracles are additionally implausible due to the natural sciences: having an ax-head float; walking on water; creating bread and fish to feed five thousand people, changing water into wine; immediately calming the wind and the waves, and cursing of a fig tree that withers on the spot.

Some miracles are implausible due to the biological sciences: the blind, deaf, and lame being instantaneously healed on the spot; a virgin birth; and the dead being raised back to life.

Other miracles seem just strange to modern people today: exorcisms of demonic beings that caused sicknesses; people speaking unlearned foreign languages; both Balaam's donkey and a serpent spoke; Daniel was thrown into a hungry lion's den, yet not eaten; Daniel's friends are thrown into a fire pit, yet not harmed; or being healed by shadows, handkerchiefs, or the stirred waters of the Pool of Siloam.

James D. G. Dunn tells us the problem of myth in the New Testament is that it "presents events critical to Christian faith in language and concepts which are often outmoded and meaningless to 20th century man. (1) Many of the NT metaphors and analogies are archaic and distasteful to modern sensibilities (e.g., blood sacrifice); (2) In the first century world the activity of divine beings is often evoked as the explanation for what we now recognize as natural and mental processes (e.g., epilepsy as demon possession); (3) Out of date conceptualizations determine certain traditionally important expressions of NT faith about Christ—in particular, the problem that 'ascension' and *parousia* [Christ's return] 'in clouds' 'from heaven' were not merely meant as metaphors or analogies but were intended as literal descriptions which derive from and depend on a first century cosmology which is impossible to us."[2]

E. P. Sanders offers five rational explanations for Jesus' reputed miracles: (1) "More or less all the healings are explicable as psychosomatic cures or victories of mind over matter"; (2) "It may be thought that some miracles were only coincidences"; (3) "It has been suggested that some miracles were only apparent"; (4) "Group psychology has often been used to explain the feeding miracles"; and (5) Some miracle stories may be historicizing legends."[3] In any case, Paul Kurtz writes: "Whether Jesus actually cured the people as related in the Gospels is uncertain. We do not have expert medical testimony diagnosing their illness. The conditions of the afflicted are never precisely described. Nor do we have any clear-cut evidence that they were cured and that these cures were permanent."[4]

Deism (Latin *deus* god) provides the initial context for discussing the possibility of miracles. It began with Herbert Cherbury in England during the seventeenth century and went through several different stages in several different countries. It is basically seen as a natural religion where knowledge is acquired solely by the use of reason, as opposed to the Bible or the church. Its adherents held only beliefs that could be supported by reason. The final stage is largely of French origin where God is seen merely as the creator of the universe. God created it and set it in motion, but he does nothing to intervene in its affairs. The analogy for deists was the technological marvel of their time—the pocket watch. What would we think, deists would ask, if the watchmaker had to constantly intervene to fix or repair the watch? Their conclusion was that an inferior watchmaker would have made the watch. Likewise, when it comes to God creating the universe, for him to intervene with miracles means he didn't do a good job of creating it in the first place. It would be an admission that God's original creation was flawed. After Darwin's publication of *Origin of the Species* in 1859, which accounted for the ascent of human beings on earth through natural selection, deism quickly moved in the direction of atheism. David Hume was arguably a deist and his argument against miracles is considered to be the standard against which all discussions about miracles take place.[5]

DAVID HUME'S ARGUMENT AGAINST MIRACLES

Hume's argument is an "even if . . . but in fact" type of an argument. He argues that miracles could never be identified in principle, *even if* they took place, *but in fact* there can't be enough evidence to believe they took place. Hume never said miracles couldn't occur; he only argued that it is not rational to believe that a miracle took place unless it would be more "miraculous" that it didn't. The wise man proportions his belief based upon what is most likely to be the case.[6]

Hume Defines Miracles as Violations of Natural Laws

We couldn't argue that a miracle is just a surprising event that was timed right, or a psychosomatic healing, because then what right do we have to assert that it is a miracle at all? We couldn't argue that a miracle is an event that occurs outside the knowledge and control of natural law as available to the miracle worker *at that time*. Then the problem resurfaces, maybe people believed for less than adequate reasons? Hume's definition of miracles as "violations of natural laws" might seem too strident of a definition, however. What does it mean to violate natural law? While miracles must have a cause that lies outside natural law itself, they wouldn't violate the principle of cause and effect—miracles would just have a supernatural cause. Still, Dr. Eric Mascall insisted that a miracle signifies "a striking interposition of divine power by which the operations of the ordinary course of nature are overruled, suspended, or modified."[7] William Lane Craig merely says it's an event that "neither has physical nor human causes."[8] I can define it no better than that, although I know of many good attempts to define a miracle.

Hume argues that the probability of a miracle happening (i.e., violation of natural law) will always be lower than the probability that a miracle has not occurred (i.e., that natural law was not violated). Why? Because "there must be a uniform experience against every miraculous event, otherwise the event would not merit that appellation." Hence, the wise person should not believe a miracle occurred unless it is more "miraculous" not to believe it occurred than to believe that it did. And in the modern world we have a strong presumption in favor of natural law, based on science as opposed to the miraculous, as Antony Flew explains: "a strong notion of the truly miraculous can only be generated if there is first an equally strong conception of a natural order. Where there is as yet no strong conception of a natural order, there is little room for the idea of a genuinely miraculous event as distinct from the phenomenon of a prodigy, of a wonder, or of a divine sign. But once such a conception of a natural order has taken firm root, there is a great reluctance to allow that miracles have in fact occurred, or even to admit as legitimate a concept of the miraculous. . . . Exceptions are logically dependent upon rules. Only in so far as it can be shown that there is an order does it begin to be possible to show that the order is occasionally overridden. The difficulty (perhaps an insoluble one) is to maintain simultaneously both the strong rules and the genuine exceptions to them."[9] Critical biblical scholar David F. Strauss agreed and wrote: "We may summarily reject all miracles, prophecies, narratives of angels and demons, and the like, as simply impossible and irreconcilable with the known and universal laws which govern the course of events."[10]

Hume Offers Four "But in Fact" Arguments

I find the following four arguments of Hume persuasive:

First, miraculous claims are mainly made by uneducated superstitious people who lack common sense, integrity, or a good reputation. Second, there are many instances of forged miracles, which prove the strong propensity of mankind to believe a wondrous and extraordinary story, and then exaggerate it when they retell it. Third, miracle claims originate among tribes who are uncivilized, ignorant and barbarous. Hume asks, why is it that "such prodigious events never happen in our days?" Finally, competing religions support their beliefs by claims of miracles; thus these claims and their religious systems cancel each other out. That is, any miracles that count for one religion cancel out the miracles of the other, and vise versa.

The late Christian apologist Ronald Nash said the strongest of these four arguments is the fourth one.[11] Richard Swinburne criticized Hume on this by arguing that competing religious claims only cancel each other out if the proclaimed miracles of each religion did in fact occur and if these purported miracles are used to establish the truth of each of these separate religions (since there is nothing prohibiting God from doing a miracle out of kindness to anyone of any faith).[12] But listen to what Hume actually said: "This argument . . . is not in reality different from the reasoning of a judge, who supposes that the credit of two witnesses, maintaining a crime against anyone, is destroyed by the testimony of two others, who affirm him to have been two hundred leagues distant, at the same instant when the crime is said to have been committed." For Hume this is an epistemological problem, and a credibility problem. Against Swinburne the question in Hume's mind is how he can even know whether or not both miracles occurred, since the credibility of both is suspect. And as far as two purported miracles being used to establish the truth of two separate religions go, how about the claim that Muhammad was miraculously inspired to write the Koran (where it states Jesus did not rise from the dead), and compare that with the Christian claim that Jesus did rise from the grave? Hence, the Muslim faith does indeed "cancel out" the credibility and epistemological significance of Christianity, and vice versa.

Hume concludes: "Therefore we may establish it as a maxim that no human testimony can have such force as to prove a miracle, and make it a just foundation for any such system of religion." Should a miracle be ascribed to a system of religion, we are obliged "to compare the instances of the violation of truth in the testimony of men, with those of the violation of the laws of nature by miracles, in order to judge which of them is most likely and probable. As the violations of truth are more common in the testimony concerning religious miracles than in that concerning any other matter of fact; this must diminish very much the former testimony, and make us form a general resolution, never to lend any attention to it, with whatever specious pretence it may be covered."

Can You Refute Hume?

I remember sitting down and talking with Bill Craig at a banquet during an apologetical series of lectures he was giving. While we were talking, he said to me, "Hume has been refuted years ago." To which I replied, "I didn't know Hume could be refuted because he merely said that the wise man proportions his belief based upon what is most likely to be the case." To which Bill admitted, on second thought, that I was right: "You're right, Hume cannot be refuted." He argued that we could believe in miracles in spite of Hume, and I agreed at the time. But Hume makes a great deal of sense. I have about a dozen books that take issue with Hume's argument, showing that it's still possible in spite of Hume to believe in miracles. But again, Hume never said miracles cannot occur, only that there is no reason he knows of to believe in any of them.

Christian philosopher Stephen T. Davis thinks Hume "overstates his case." Still he wrote: "Hume is not the sort of philosopher one can dismiss with a casual wave of the hand. Much of his argument, I believe, is beyond reproach. . . . He is surely correct that rational people will require very strong evidence indeed before they will believe that a miracle has occurred."[13]

There are a great many weird things that people believe took place in history. During the witch hunts people in early modern Europe really believed witches flew through the sky and met with the devil at night for orgies. How do you decide what happened? Whether you know it or not, when it comes to the apparent unexplainable event, you apply Hume's standards, *especially* when it comes to the miraculous claims of religions you don't accept. Likewise, adherents of those religions, apply Hume's standards to the miracles you accept.

Michael Shermer calls skepticism a virtue: "Skepticism is a virtue and science is a valuable tool that makes skepticism virtuous. Science and skepticism are the best methods of determining how strong your convictions are, regardless of the outcome of the inquiry. If you challenge your belief tenets and end up as a nonbeliever, then apparently your faith was not all that sound to begin with and you have improved your thinking in the process. If you question your religion but in the end retain your belief, you have lost nothing and gained a deeper understanding of the God question. It is okay to be skeptical."[14]

TWO MAJOR OBJECTIONS TO HUME'S ARGUMENT

One major objection with Hume's main argument against miracles is that he begs the question of whether miracles have in fact taken place. By defining a miracle as a violation of natural law, it automatically follows for Hume that a miracle is less probable, as it must be for it to be classified as a miracle. Based upon this understanding, Hume claims that a wise man should not believe in miracles because by definition they are less probable. He didn't argue that they were impossible.[15] C. S. Lewis, however, wrote in defense of miracles by saying: "If there is absolute 'uniform experience' against miracles, if in other words they have never happened, why then they never have? Unfortunately we know the experience against them to be uniform only if we know that all reports of them are false. And we know all the reports to be false only if we already know that miracles have never happened."[16] According to William Lane Craig: "To say that uniform experience is against miracles is to implicitly assume already that miracles have never occurred. The only way Hume can place uniform experience for the regularity of nature on one side of the scale is by assuming that the testimony for miracles on the other side of the scale is false. And that, quite simply, is begging the question."[17] Or to put it another way, just because a wise man shouldn't believe in a miracle begs the question of whether or not a miracle occurred.

Robert J. Fogelin dismisses this objection and claims it is a gross misreading of Hume. He says, "Hume nowhere argues, either explicitly or implicitly, that we know that all reports of miracles are false because we know that all reports of miracles are false. . . . Hume begins with a claim about testimony. On the one side we have wide and unproblematic testimony to the effect that when people step into the water they do not remain on its surface. On the other side we have isolated reports of people walking across the surface of the water. Given the testimony of the first kind, how are we to evaluate the testimony of the second sort? The testimony of the first sort does not show that the testimony of the second sort is false; it does, however, create a strong presumption—unless countered, a decisively strong presumption—in favor of its falsehood." Fogelin concludes with these words: "That is Hume's argument, and there is nothing circular or question begging about it."[18]

Hume may have overstated his case somewhat when he indicates that a wise person "shouldn't believe" a miracle occurred because of our confidence in the regular order of the laws of nature. But there's nothing wrong with Hume when he argues that the preponderance of historical, physical, testimonial, and circumstantial evidence should outweigh our confidence in the laws of nature. He could still admit the possibility of a miracle but yet deny that there is enough evidence to lead him to believe one has occurred. Yet, he did say that. He said that it is not rational to believe that a miracle took place unless it would be more "miraculous" that it didn't.

Hume is surely right that we should be skeptical of any claim of a miracle. I believe the issue of question begging can be turned back on both C. S. Lewis and Craig, who defend the truth of the Christian faith. Since they both believe in Christianity, they won't believe any miracles that attest to the major truth claims of other religions. Which one of them, for instance, will take seriously the claim that God spoke "miraculously" to Muhammad so that the Koran is his word? Conversely, since they believe in Christianity, they do not approach the biblical miracles with the same kind of scrutiny or skepticism they use to judge miracles outside of their faith. They have a very strong presumption in favor of Christian miracles, just like Hume—a deist—had a very strong presumption that miracles shouldn't be believed. In practice, Craig and Lewis beg the question when it comes to the miraculous claims of religions they reject.

Walter Kaufmann expressed it this way: "No miracle in the New Testament, Old Testament, or Koran is attested half as well as lots of alleged miracles at Lourdes and other Catholic shrines; and yet these 'Catholic miracles' do not persuade Jews, Protestants, or Muslims. Similarly, Catholics are not swayed by miracles ascribed to some Hassidic rabbis. And members of all three religions are agreed in discounting the miracles performed before our eyes by magicians, witch doctors, mediums, and Yogis."[19]

A second objection has to do with the possibility that Hume commits the logical fallacy of hasty generalization. This fallacy occurs when someone draws a conclusion, or makes a generalization, based upon a small sample of experiences or tests. John King-Farlow and William Niels Christensen ask us to imagine a container hidden from sight so we don't know how large it is. From this container we draw out nothing but red marbles, every time. Based on our limited sampling, we conclude that the container has nothing but red marbles in it. But since we don't know how large the container is, it may actually contain more blue marbles than red ones because it's extremely huge. In the same way, events that seem miraculous to us might prove in the end to be more probable after all. Judging things as Hume does might prove to be too hasty of a conclusion before all experience is in.[20] This could be true, if there is a God. Just because we don't experience miracles today doesn't mean that throughout the history of mankind God may have done a plethora of them, and will do so again when the time is right in the future.

King-Farlow and Christensen are asking us to believe against the overwhelming present-day experience of nearly all modern people that things might turn out differently than we now experience. Is this impossible? No, not at all. But we must still ask whether this is probable given our present-day confirmations of natural law. The only basis for asking us to consider whether events that seem to be miraculous to us might prove in the end to be more probable after all is the existence of God. As C. Stephen Evans writes: "The defender of miracles may claim that whether miracles occur depends largely on whether God exists, what kind of God he is, and what purposes he has."[21] Evans is surely right here: it depends on whether the Christian God exists.

So here's the catch-22. For someone to believe the evidence for the foundational Christian miracle claims, as I'll call them, then as Evans admits, she must first believe in the Christian God. She cannot bring herself to believe those miracles if she begins by first believing in Allah, as we've seen, because then she will apply Hume's standards to those miracle claims. But in order to believe in the Christian

God, as opposed to Allah, she must first have some pretty strong historical, physical, testimonial, and circumstantial evidence to believe in the foundational Christian miracle claims. Think about this. We either start with the Christian God, or the evidence must be very strong. From where comes this starting point? Contrary to my former professor James D. Strauss, we cannot start with the belief in a Christian God "from above" because people born into different religions have a different starting point (or none at all), as we've seen. So we're left with just the evidence. But the available evidence "from below" alone cannot convince someone to believe!

There are Christian evidentialists, like Gary R. Habermas, who think otherwise and argue that the evidence for one particular Christian miracle, the bodily resurrection of Christ, can be strong enough to convince a rational skeptic to believe in Christ and the Christian worldview. However, Stephen T. Davis argued convincingly against Habermas in a debate on the resurrection of Jesus.[22] According to Davis: "The non-believer's position is probably convincing to the non-believer not primarily because of the evidence or arguments in its favor but because it is entailed by the worldview he or she accepts. Similarly, the believer's position is probably convincing to the believer not primarily because of the evidence or arguments in its favor but because it dovetails with the worldview he or she accepts." "There is no such thing as bare uninterrupted evidence or experience, and so the way one evaluates the evidence one sees depends to a great extent on one's worldview, i.e., on whether or not one thinks miracles are possible or probable."[23] "All people interpret their experience within a certain philosophical framework. For many people, their philosophical assumptions exclude God's existence and the possibility of miracles. The odd thing is that a decision a person makes whether to believe in the resurrection is usually made on some basis other than the evidence pro and con. Those who believe in Christ believe in the resurrection; those who accept naturalism do not."[24]

Norman Geisler stated this problem in much stronger terms: "The mere fact of the resurrection cannot be used to establish the truth that there is a God. For the resurrection cannot even be a miracle unless there already is a God. . . . The real problem for the Christian apologist is to find some way apart from the mere facts themselves to establish the justifiability of interpreting the facts in a theistic way. . . . No fact, event, or series thereof within an overall framework which derives all of its meaning from the framework can be determinative of the framework which bestows that meaning on it. For no fact or set of facts can of and by themselves, apart from any meaning or interpretation given to them, establish which of the alternative viewpoints should be taken on the fact(s)."[25]

J. L. MACKIE'S ARGUMENT AGAINST MIRACLES

The late J. L. Mackie, in his book *The Miracle of Theism*,[26] argues against the belief in miracles, along with Hume. Let me quote from him: "The defender of a miracle . . . must in effect concede to Hume that the antecedent improbability of this event is as high as it could be, hence that, apart from the testimony, we have the strongest possible grounds for believing that the alleged event did not occur. This event must, by the miracle advocate's own admission, be contrary to a genuine, not merely supposed, law of nature, and therefore maximally improbable. It is this maximal improbability that the weight of the testimony would have to overcome. . . . Where there is some plausible testimony about the occurrence of what would appear to be a miracle, those who accept this as a miracle have the double burden of showing both that the event took place and that it violated the laws of nature. But it will be very hard to sustain this double burden. For whatever tends to show that it would have been a violation of a natural law tends for that very reason to make it most unlikely that is actually happened."

Mackie then distinguishes between two different contexts in which an alleged miracle might be considered a real one. First, there is the context where two parties "have accepted some general theistic doctrines and the point at issue is whether a miracle has occurred which would enhance the authority of a specific sect or teacher. In this context supernatural intervention, though *prima facie* ("on the surface") unlikely on any particular occasion, is, generally speaking, on the cards: it is not altogether outside the range of reasonable expectation for these parties." The second context is a very different matter when "the context is that of fundamental debate about the truth of theism itself. Here one party to the debate is initially at least agnostic, and does not yet concede that there is a supernatural power at all. From this point of view the intrinsic improbability of a genuine miracle . . . is very great, and that one or other of the alternative explanations . . . will always be much more likely—that is, either that the alleged event is not miraculous, or that it did not occur, or that the testimony is faulty in some way." Mackie concludes by saying: "This entails that it is pretty well impossible that reported miracles should provide a worthwhile argument for theism addressed to those who are initially inclined to atheism or even to agnosticism."[27]

Why is it that someone like Hume has had such a great influence over us, and yet William Lane Craig could say at one point that "Hume has been refuted"? Why is it that I can accept much of J. L. Mackie's argument against miracles, while William Lane Craig can say in the *Truth Journal* that "Mackie's critique of miracles is "*particularly shockingly superficial*" (emphasis mine)?[28] Mackie's arguments are not superficial.

Craig said this when commenting on Alvin Plantinga's critique of Mackie's book *The Miracle of Theism*. So I reread Plantinga's essay "Is Theism Really a Miracle?" in *Faith and Philosophy*.[29] And as I was doing so, I thought to myself that this was superficial too. Really! It's obvious that Plantinga critiques Mackie from a theistic perspective. He even says so. Plantinga refers repeatedly to the phrases "to me," "my evidence," "my experience," or "our evidence." Take, for example, this sentence: "as a matter of fact it could be that what is in fact a violation of a law of nature (a miracle) not only wasn't particularly improbable with respect to *our evidence* [emphasis mine], but was in fact more probable than not with respect to it." What kind of evidence is he speaking to that is specifically his? He's debating Mackie from within a viewpoint Mackie doesn't accept. That is, he totally ignores

Mackie's distinction between the two contexts in which an alleged miracle might be considered a real one. Mackie's debate is inside the second context where it's a "fundamental debate about the truth of theism itself." Plantinga asks the following question: "Why should we think it is particularly improbable that a law of nature be interfered with? . . . I have no reason to suppose that the world is not regularly interfered with. Why couldn't interferences with nature be the rule rather than the exception?" But to people who disagree with Plantinga, that's not a very bright question at all. How often has anyone ever seen a real miracle? Science has progressed on the assumption that miracles don't occur in the laboratory. Plantinga debates with modern science here. Now to those of us who question the believability of miracles, that just seems superficial to us. But in Plantinga's defense, in the next chapter we'll see what he was probably getting at, and it doesn't fare much better.

HUME'S ABJECT FAILURE

Agnostic philosopher John Earman wrote an important work on miracles called *Hume's Abject Failure: The Argument against Miracles*.[30] Since I'm writing on the level of a college student here, I won't be delving into the Bayesian mathematical formula that John Earman uses to argue his case.[31] The basic failure Earman refers to can be described, in William Lane Craig and J. P. Moreland's words, that Hume "incorrectly assumes that miracles are intrinsically highly improbable." With regard to the resurrection of Jesus, Craig and Moreland compare two separate hypotheses: "God raised Jesus from the dead"; and "Jesus rose naturally from the dead." Of course, the second hypothesis is "fantastically, even unimaginably, improbable," they argue, "given what we know about cell necrosis." However, according to them, the first hypothesis can be "highly probable relative to our background information,"[32] by which is meant the sum total of everything they believe. My contention is that the proper hypothesis is neither of the ones they mention. The first one already assumes the Christian God exists, for if the hypothesis instead was that "Allah raised Jesus from the dead," we already know the answer—of course not. And we already know the answer to the second hypothesis—No! The proper hypothesis is simply this: "Jesus rose from the dead," which is reflective of my later chapter on the subject. I deny that he did. From my perspective, only after we arrive at an affirmative answer to this hypothesis can we go on to argue who or what caused him to rise from the dead.

Let me put it this way: When we talk about the probability of some event or hypothesis A, that probability is always relative to a body of background information B. So we cannot merely speak of the probability of A without taking into consideration that background information, B, all of it. And so Earman is absolutely correct about this.[33] Background factors must be considered in evaluating the probability of any miraculous claim, which might subsequently raise the low initial intrinsic probability of that claim to the point where such a claim becomes probable. We assess a miraculous claim based upon other things we know. As I've already argued, whether someone believes in God or not, for instance, is indeed a relevant factor whether she believes in miracles. And I think J. L. Mackie recognized this when he distinguished between the two different contexts from which a people evaluate the truth claims of a miracle. My claim in this book is that the Bayesian background factors are not such that they raise the intrinsic improbability of miracles above what they are initially. If the Bible debunks itself, and the Bible tells us about the miracles of the resurrection of Jesus, then the skeptic has good background factors for not trusting what the Bible says about the resurrection miracle.

MIRACLES AND INVISIBLE CHAIRS

How exactly is it that a spiritual God (John 4:24) can perform miracles in a material universe, anyway? Can he pick up a material box? Humans are material beings, so we have no trouble picking up a box, because our bodily matter makes contact with the matter inherent in the box, and up it goes. How does something that is spirit make contact with something that is matter, unless there is some point of contact between them that they both share?

Take, for example, the idea of ghosts that can walk through walls, and so on. How does a being like that actually move matter, unless there is some point of contact between such a ghost and what he moves on earth? Likewise, how can God speak audibly and be heard by sound waves to our ears, unless he can move sound waves—that is, unless there is once again a point of contact between a spirit being and the material waves in the air?

Imagine an existing chair located in the same room you are in now. It is invisible to your eyes because it's in another dimension, or a parallel universe. It really exists there, but you cannot see it or touch it because it's not a material chair in your universe. Now sit on it. Try to kick it around. Pick it up and throw it as far as you can. Go ahead, experiment all you like. Then report back your findings. Conversely, can that chair act in your world? Let's say it grows a brain, for a minute. And it wants to pick you up and kick you around a while. Can it? How? You couldn't, so how can it?

God, being "spiritual," is like that invisible chair. There can be no physical interaction with an invisible chair, and there can be no action in the world of physical objects by invisible entities, whether they are chairs, ghosts, or God—unless Christians can specify for me what that point of contact might actually be.

Can you precisely describe for me how spirit and matter are the same so they can interact, and yet how they are also different? Analogies are weak, like ghosts and invisible chairs, I suppose. But the question remains, "How can the two interact?" How? Logically they cannot interact, unless they both share a quality or something that they both have. Are spirit and matter two poles of the same reality? Then welcome to *panentheism*, or *process theology*. Are they one and the same? Then welcome to *pantheism* (all is "spirit"), or metaphysical *naturalism* (all is matter). Idealism proclaims there is no material universe. You could go that way, I suppose, like George Berkeley. But then exactly where do we exist? Maybe we're only "dreams" that God is having? Why do we need a heart or a set of lungs? When surgery is performed on our bodies, why do we get better if we don't have bodies?

If a spiritual God can act in this universe, then Christians need to show how it is possible for two different types of, for lack of a better word, "substances" can interact. Energy is, after all, matter. Gases like air are all matter too. And if spirit and matter are not different substances, then what are they? How are they different? How are they the same?[34]

WHAT IF A MIRACLE COULD BE SHOWN TO HAVE OCCURRED?

Even if Christians can show that biblical miracles can take place, there is an additional problem. They must also show that they did take place. But if believers can show how they happened, then doesn't it take all of the force out of the miracle? I have seen a two-tape video series called *Mysteries of the Ancient World* (Sun-Pko Productions, 1993), which is narrated by Dennis Weaver and purports to show how several of the miracles in the Bible may have happened. Take, for example, the segment about Shadrach, Meshach, and Abednego being saved out of the fiery furnace (Daniel 3). The tape tries to show how it all happened naturalistically by quoting from various scholars. Yes, that's right! The tape wants us to see how that the furnace had compartments and the fire was underneath these men in a separate compartment, allowing for pockets of cooler air where they were thrown. But by "proving" this happened, exactly as they claim it did, it takes all of the miraculous out of the event. At that point we no longer need a God to explain what happened.

Robert M. Price noted this when he wrote: "If you can offer scientific proof for the Star of Bethlehem, as popular apologists do every Christmas season, claiming it corresponds to some ancient supernova or planetary alignment, you have thereby evacuated the phenomenon of all its miraculous character. Whatever you prove this way can never transcend the framework of the criteria you try to employ."[35]

So, on the one hand, if Christians cannot explain how a miraculous event took place, outsiders can easily deny it happened at all. On the other hand, if Christians can explain how it might have occurred naturally, then outsiders can easily say it's no longer a miracle. All I can say here is that this is the unavoidable nature of the case when it comes to reported miracles in the prescientific superstitious historical past. *Outsiders* need sufficient evidence of miracles in today's world to accept the Christian faith. Without this evidence, the Christian apologist will always have a near impossible time defending her faith, and as such, I think she should simply abandon this attempt. Without present-day evidence or present-day miracles, Christianity probably cannot be adequately defended at all, and I have seen nothing remotely akin to the purported miracles told to us in the Bible, even as a former Pentecostal in my early years.

On the subject of miracles, I'm with Robert G. Ingersoll, who said: "When I say I want a miracle, I mean by that I want a good one. . . . I want to see a man with one leg, and then I want to see the other leg grow out."[36]

NOTES

1. Bart D. Ehrman, *Jesus: Apocalyptic Prophet of the New Millennium* (Oxford: Oxford University Press, 1999), p. 194. Bernard W. Anderson says it this way: "The Biblical view of miracles is something different from our conception of miracle as a disruption of natural law. As a matter of fact, the Biblical writers had no conception of 'nature' as a realm for which God has ordained laws. Rather, God himself sustains his creation, and his will is expressed in natural events, whether it be the coming of the spring rains or the birth of a child. . . . God is constantly active. His will is discernible in every event." In *Understanding the Old Testament* (Englewood Cliffs, NJ: Prentice-Hall, 1957), p. 43.

2. James D. G. Dunn, "Demythologizing—The Problem of Myth in the New Testament," in *New Testament Interpretation*, ed. I. Howard Marshall (Grand Rapids, MI: Eerdmans, 1977), p. 300.

3. E. P. Sanders, *The Historical Figure of Jesus* (New York: Penguin Books, 1993), p. 158.

4. Paul Kurtz, *The Transcendental Temptation* (Amherst, NY: Prometheus Books, 1991), p. 136.

5. Douglas Geivett and Gary Habermas, eds., *In Defense of Miracles: A Comprehensive Case for God's Action in History* (Downer's Grove, IL: InterVarsity Press, 1997), deals almost exclusively with Hume's arguments.

6. David Hume, *An Enquiry Concerning Human Understanding*, 3rd ed., rev. by P. H. Nidditch (Oxford: Clarendon Press, 1975), sec. X.

7. "Miracles," in *Chamber's Encyclopedia*, as quoted by Anthony Flew in "Miracles," *The Encyclopedia of Philosophy*, editor in chief Paul Edwards (New York: Macmillian, 1967), vol. 5, p. 346. Richard Swinburne did an extensive study of this in *The Concept of Miracle* (Oxford: Oxford University Press, 1970).

8. William Lane Craig, *Apologetics: An Introduction* (Chicago: Moody Press, 1984), p. 114.

9. Flew, "Miracles," p. 347.

10. In David F. Strauss, *The Life of Jesus Critically Examined* (London: Thoemmes Continuum, 2006).

11. Ronald H. Nash, *Faith and Reason: Searching for a Rational Faith* (Grand Rapids, MI: Zondervan, 1988), p. 238.

12. Swinburne, *The Concept of Miracle*, pp. 60–61.

13. Stephen T. Davis, "Is It Possible to Know That Jesus Was Raised from the Dead?" *Faith and Philosophy* (April 1984).

14. Michael Shermer, *How We Believe: The Search for God in an Age of Science* (New York: W. H. Freeman, 2000), p. 23.

15. According to Robert J. Fogelin, to say Hume defined miracles and the laws of nature in a such way that makes them a priori impossible is "a gross misreading of the text." *A Defense of Hume on Miracles* (Princeton, NJ: Princeton University Press, 2003), pp. 32–33.

16. C. S. Lewis, *Miracles: A Preliminary Study* (New York: Macmillan, 1947), p. 105.

17. Craig, *Apologetics: An Introduction*, p. 121.

18. Fogelin, *A Defense of Hume on Miracles*, pp. 19–20.

19. Walter Kaufmann, *Critique of Religion and Philosophy* (Princeton, NJ: Princeton University Press, 1958), p. 128.

20. John King-Farlow and William Niels Christensen, *Faith and the Life of Reason* (Dordrecht, Holland: D. Reidel, 1972), p. 50.

21. C. Stephen Evans, *Philosophy of Religion* (Downers Grove, IL: InterVarsity Press, 1985), p. 113.

22. See *Faith and Philosophy*, April 1984 and July 1985.

23. *Faith and Philosophy* (April 1984): 154–55.

24. *Faith and Philosophy* (July 1985): 306.

25. Norman Geisler, *Christian Apologetics* (Grand Rapids, MI: Baker House, 1976), pp. 94–98.

26. J. L. Mackie, *The Miracle of Theism* (Oxford: Clarendon Press, 1982).

27. Ibid., pp. 18–29.

28. William Lane Craig, "New Arguments for the Existence of God," *Truth: A Journal of Modern Thought* (1991).

29. Alvin Plantinga, "Is Theism Really a Miracle?" *Faith and Philosophy* (April 1986).

30. John Earman, *Hume's Abject Failure: The Argument against Miracles* (Oxford: Oxford University Press, 2000). For a response and a defense of Hume, see Fogelin, *A Defense of Hume on Miracles*. Fogelin also responds to David Johnson's arguments found in his book *Hume, Holism, and Miracles* (Ithaca, NY: Cornell University Press, 1999).

31. For an introduction, see *Bayes's Theorem*, ed. Richard Swinburne (Oxford: Oxford University Press, 2005). Thomas Bayes's theorem essentially says that the probability (P) we attach to a hypothesis (h), given the available evidence (e)—let's call it P(h/e)—depends on the relationship between three quantities: (A) the probability of observing that evidence, if the hypothesis is in fact true; (B) the a priori probability of the hypothesis, based on prior knowledge we have of the world; and (C) the probability of observing the evidence given our prior knowledge of the world. Bayes showed that P(h/e) = (A x B)/C.

32. William Lane Craig and J. P. Moreland, *Philosophical Foundations for a Christian Worldview* (Downers Grove, IL: InterVarsity Press, 2003), p. 571.

33. That being said, Earman is incorrect to claim Hume didn't understand this. See Fogelin, *A Defense of Hume on Miracles*, pp. 40–53.

34. J. P. Moreland defends "substance dualism," in his book *Scaling the Secular City* (Grand Rapids, MI: Baker Book House, 1987), pp. 77–104, but he doesn't answer this question. Sam Harris has asked the important question here: "If we have minds then why did God create us with brains at all?" Paul Copan basically argues that such interactions aren't logically impossible, and then switches the discussion to the problem of consciousness for atheists, in *"How Do You Know You're Not Wrong"* (Grand Rapids, MI: Baker Book House, 2005), pp. 115–22. But even if Copan is correct that such things are not logically impossible, and I don't agree, it doesn't say much about whether they are probable, since we're talking here about probabilities. For great discussions on this whole issue, see Gilbert Ryle's classic book *The Concept of Mind* (New York: Barnes & Noble Books, 1949); Arthur Peacocke's, *Theology for a Scientific Age* (Minneapolis, MN: Fortress Press, 1993), pp. 135–89; Daniel Dennet's *Consciousness Explained* (Boston: Little, Brown, 1991); Francis Crick's, *The Astonishing Hypothesis: The Scientific Search for the Soul* (New York: Charles Scribner's Sons, 1994); and especially Jaegwon Kim's, *Philosophy of Mind* (Cambridge, MA: Westview Press, 1996).

35. Robert M. Price and Jeffery Jay Lowder, eds., *The Empty Tomb: Jesus beyond the Grave* (Amherst, NY: Prometheus Books, 2005), pp. 13–14.

36. Robert G. Ingersoll, *Sixty-five Press Interviews with Robert G. Ingersoll* (Cranford, NJ: American Atheist Press, 1983), p. 23.

THE SELF-AUTHENTICATING WITNESS
OF THE HOLY SPIRIT

I n light of the catch-22 mentioned in the previous chapter (p. 205), William Lane Craig argues that Christians should start with faith in the Christian God. Why? "We know Christianity to be true by the self-authenticating witness of God's Holy Spirit." What does he mean by that? "I mean that the witness, or testimony, of the Holy Spirit is its own proof; it is unmistakable; it does not need other proofs to back it up; it is self-evident and attests to its own truth." Hitchhiking on the philosophical work of Alvin Plantinga's defense of a properly basic belief in God, and citing the Bible (Gal. 3:26; 4:6; Rom. 8:15–16; 1 John 2:20, 26–27; 3:24; 5:7–10), Craig writes: "I would agree that belief in the *God of the Bible* is a properly basic belief, and emphasize that it is the ministry of the Holy Spirit that supplies the circumstance for its proper basically. And because this belief is from God, it is not merely rational, but definitely true" (emphasis mine).[1]

Craig claims that there is a distinction between *knowing* Christianity is true and *showing* Christianity is true. He believes that he knows Christianity is true by the inner witness of the Holy Spirit, period. Such a witness for him is self-authenticating and needs no intellectual arguments on its behalf. When it comes to showing Christianity is true, his arguments can only show probabilities and plausibilites. By offering them up on the table as an apologist, he hopes the Holy Spirit will use his arguments to speak to those who haven't made a commitment to Jesus. But if his arguments don't convince someone, he still has done the best he could do.

At the end of his debate with Gerd Lüdemann on the historicity of the resurrection, Craig provides us with an example of what he means: "So if you ask me why I believe Christ is risen from the dead, I would not only point to the historical evidence, but I would reply in the words of the old hymn, 'You ask me how I know he lives? He lives within my heart!' Now somebody might say I'm deluded. But that's where the historical evidence comes in. In the absence of any good, compelling historical reason to deny the fact of the resurrection of Jesus, it seems to me that it's perfectly rational to believe in Christ on the basis of his living in my life."[2]

When arguing that he knows Christianity is true based on the self-authenticating witness of the Holy Spirit, Craig stands in the steps of some great Christian thinkers like Augustine, Anselm, and even Barth and Bultmann. According to Wolfhart Pannenberg, "the basic presupposition underlying German Protestant theology as expressed by Barth and Bultmann is that the basis of theology is the self-authenticating Word of God which demands obedience."[3] Unlike some of these theologians, though, the basis for Craig's faith is in the inner witness of the Holy Spirit alone, who may use the Bible, evidence, or nothing at all to create faith in the believer.

Does Craig mean to say that he cannot be wrong? Yes! He knows Christianity is true. With this understanding, he has insulated himself from any and all objections to the contrary. He knows he's right because he knows he's right, and that's the end of the matter. Since he knows he's right, Christianity is true.

Mark Smith (of www.jcnot4me.com) set up the following scenario for Craig: "Dr. Craig, for the sake of argument let's pretend that a time machine gets built. You and I hop in it, and travel back to the day before Easter, 33 AD. We park it outside the tomb of Jesus. We wait. Easter morning rolls around, and nothing happens. We continue to wait. After several weeks of waiting, still nothing happens. There is no resurrection—Jesus is quietly rotting away in the tomb."

Smith asked Craig, given this scenario, if he would then give up Christianity, having seen with his own two eyes that Jesus did not rise from the dead. Smith wrote: "His answer was shocking, and quite unexpected. He told me, face to face, that he would STILL believe in Jesus, he would STILL believe in the resurrection, and he would STILL remain a Christian. When asked, in light of his being a personal eyewitness to the fact that there WAS no resurrection, he replied that due to the witness of the 'holy spirit' within him, he would assume a trick of some sort had been played on him while watching Jesus' tomb. This self-induced blindness astounded me." If anyone doubts what Craig said in response, Mark challenges him or her to ask him the same question.

At my prompting, Dr. Zachary Moore did just that. He asked Craig this same question after an invited talk at the First Baptist Church of Colleyville, while Craig was visiting the Dallas/Forth Worth area to record a series of Reasonable *Faith* podcasts in August 2007. Craig clarified his response: "If the question is whether I would be a Christian if Jesus didn't arise from the dead, then the answer to that is obviously 'no.' But if the question is what would count as evidence, then it would always be open for me to say this isn't the right tomb [where Jesus was buried]." Moore then asked him if he could think of any evidence that would counter his faith. Craig answered by saying, "if I were presented with the real tomb of Jesus and his corpse was still there, then I wouldn't have an inner witness of the Holy Spirit." He said the inner witness of the Spirit "trumps all other evidence," so "for other evidence to overpower it, I would not have had it [in the first place]." He said, "it's really an awkward sort of question."

Of course it's an awkward question, and here's why: Craig cannot give up the notion that he has an inner witness of the Holy Sprit no matter what evidence he is presented with. He must continue to claim that if he was presented with incontrovertible evidence to the contrary, then he never would've had the self-authenticating witness of the Spirit in the first place, since this witness "trumps" all evidence to the contrary, and that indeed is awkward, if not epistemologically incoherent. I see no reason why the evidence cannot trump his belief in the witness of the Spirit. So the question remains: if he was presented with incontrovertible evidence that Christianity is a delusion, then even though he also claims to have an inner witness of the Spirit, would he have to reject that inner witness as a delusion as well? Any fair-minded person would have to give up the notion of this witness in the face of incontrovertible evidence. Why didn't he say it? There is no way the witness of the Holy Spirit can be more reliable than his own two eyes if he went back in time and saw for himself, but that's what he said.

It's this view that allows Craig to write: "A believer who is too uninformed or ill-equipped to refute anti-Christian arguments is rational in believing on the grounds of the witness of the Spirit in his heart even in the face of such unrefuted objections. Even such a person confronted with what are for him unanswerable objections to Christian theism is, because of the work of the Holy Spirit, within his epistemic rights—nay, under epistemic obligation—to believe in God."[4]

Even though Muslims and Mormons also claim to have the witness of God in their hearts, Craig denies that other conflicting faiths have this exact same self-authenticating witness of the Holy Spirit, or that their claims are even relevant to the witness he has in his heart. With William Alston, he suggests that their claims are partially true because the people holding to different faith commitments may have had "a veridical experience of God as the Ground of Being on whom we creatures are dependent, or as the Moral Absolute from whom values derive, or even as the loving Father of mankind."[5]

This is a very large claim for him to make when we consider the number of people who believe otherwise, who do so based on the "accidents of birth." Where is the self-authenticating witness of the Christian Holy Spirit among the non-Christian people of the world, more than four billion of them? These believers in other religions could respond in a similar fashion and argue that what Craig experiences is not relevant to their experiences, and that his claims are partially true because the people holding to different faith commitments may have had "a veridical experience of God as the Ground of Being on whom we creatures are dependent, or as the Moral Absolute from whom values derive, or even as the loving Father of mankind." This sounds like an impasse to me.

According to Michael Martin: "To accept Craig's thesis one must believe an outrageous and outlandish hypothesis: namely, that billions of people now and in the past were not telling the truth when they claimed that they never had such an experience."[6] Therefore, the evidence of billions of sincere nonbelievers is evidence that there is no inner Holy Spirit witness of the truth of Christianity. Dr. Craig is trying to explain away the evidence, in my opinion. J. L. Schellenberg reminds us what Craig is doing here: "Of course one might insist in the face of all of this that one's own experience was veridical and all the others unveridical and misleading, but this only brings to mind the child who, presented with evidence contrary to his apparent perception, stubbornly repeats that he 'heard what he heard' or 'saw what he saw,' completely unwilling to admit that he could be mistaken, not recognizing that he is responding with the very evidence that has been challenged."[7]

In a debate with Dr. Corey Washington, Craig offers up an analogy (first used by Plantinga): "Suppose you are accused of a crime that you know you didn't commit, and all the evidence stands against you. Are you obliged to believe that you're guilty because the evidence stands against you? Not at all; you know better. You know you're innocent, even if others think that you may be guilty. Similarly, for the person who has an immediate experience of God, who knows God as a personal, living reality in his life, such a person can know that God exists, even if he's not a philosopher and doesn't understand all of these arguments, and so forth. God can be immediately known and experienced, Christ can be immediately known and experienced in your life today, and that is true even if you've never had the chance to examine the evidence."[8]

But what if you woke up one morning to police officers who arrested you for murder? The case against you is that there were two witnesses who saw you at the scene of the crime, you had no alibi, you had a motive for the murder, your blood and hair were found under the victim's fingernails with corresponding scratches on your back, and the victim's blood was found on your shoes next to your bed. But you "know" you didn't kill anyone. At that point you must consider the evidence against you, and it's overwhelming. Your "knowing" is delusional, no matter what the reason for your delusion. The difference between my suggested "murder" scenario and Craig's scenario for believing in God is that there is hard objective evidence for the "murder," whereas there is no hard objective evidence for Craig's claim. But precisely because there isn't hard evidence for us to debunk Craig's claim, he can go on his merry delusional way all he wants to.

What about third-person outsiders who consider Craig's argument? To the outsider this is circular reasoning. But what an outsider thinks, he says, has no relevance to what he believes. And yet as soon as he argues on behalf of the self-authenticating witness of the Holy Spirit, he has invited outsiders to take a look at this claim. Paul Feinberg sees a problem with this approach: "Persons are in a privileged position with regard to their own experiences. The problem arises with this approach in apologetics because the task is not simply to defend a believer's epistemological rights to believe, but to convince those who are not believers that the Christian understanding of God and reality is true. That requires the third person perspective."[9]

It seems as though it would be akin to a person claiming to have personal experiences of an intelligent alien being from another part of this universe through a wormhole, although actually touching and seeing such a being would be empirical evidence—something Craig does not have. This person knows there is such an alien from personal experiences, and yet she cannot convince anyone else that she had these experiences, nor can she replicate such experiences for anyone else. If I had such experiences, I would probably believe in the existence of that alien too, although I would initially be skeptical about it until proven otherwise. Once I believed this alien existed, however, I should still entertain that I could be mistaken. That's the intellectually honest thing to do. I could still be proved wrong if it's shown that wormholes cannot exist or that some description of the alien or something she said is simply implausible. These are the very questions I'm asking of Craig.

If this kind of evidence were to be shown to me, I would be forced to rethink my experiences of this alien being. And at that point I would have to choose between continuing to believe in spite of the skeptical questions because of a faith that places personal experiences above my inability to answer my critics; or in rejecting my own personal experiences in lieu of the skeptical questions. At that point no one can answer for another person which to choose. But this is what I'll question when it comes to Craig's claims.

Consider the propositional content to this inner self-authenticating witness. Does his inner witness of the Holy Spirit lead Craig to believe that all of the traditional Christian doctrines are true, as he understands them? Does this entail he has the correct understanding of things like God's foreknowledge, predestination, eschatology, and Calvinism? Are his specific views on the deity of Christ, baptism, the atonement, the bodily resurrection of Jesus from the grave, and his second coming all the correct ones? What is the particular content of this self-authentication from the Spirit? There must be some content to the inner witness of the Spirit that gives him assurance he's right. Where does he learn this content? At what point does it stop and he's left on his own to work things out from reading the Bible? That's what I want to know. I believe Craig will have no real satisfying answer to these questions.

I don't think a coherent understanding of this purported inner witness can be adequately described since Christians who claim to have experienced this should've gained some knowledge as a result of it. That is, they should have gained some propositional beliefs about the divine being they experienced, along with some specific beliefs this divine being wants them to have. But since Christians who claim to have had this same experience have theological disagreements, they should be able to explain why there are so many differing doctrinal beliefs among these very Christians. Christians must also distinguish their purportedly unique experience from the experience of people in all other non-Christian religions, or no religion at all. Either there is no content to this experience, in which case I seriously doubt it is a personal experience of some divine being at all, or this witness is so muddled and weak as a religious experience that atheists can deny they have even had one at all.

Craig would surely argue that the Bible teaches this inner witness and that it only assures a person she is a child of God. It probably does not extend to what doctrines are correct. Romans 8:16, for instance, merely says, "The Spirit himself testifies with our spirit that we are God's children." But such a notion echoes the poet whom Paul quoted, who said, "we are his offspring" (Acts 17:28). Surely Paul's point had some content to it besides this, since even polytheistic pagans believed the same thing. Craig is arguing for an inner witness of the third person of the trinity for something more than that. And when Craig further spells this out, he must provide the content to what it means to be a "child" of the kind of "God" he believes in, how one becomes a child of this God, where one can learn additional information about this God, and what he must think of the authority of that source of information.

Plantinga calls the content "the great things of the gospel" and includes the idea that "God exists," "God has forgiven and accepted me," and that "God is the author of the Bible." But before this content can be understood, we have to fill in the details. Without filling in the details there is little to understand about these propositions. For instance, to say "God exists" does not say anything else about this God. What does a believer mean by the word "God"? Without a detailed understanding of what a believer means by the word "God," such a witness might even be consistent with panentheism. And to say "God is the author of the Bible" doesn't say how God authored it, or whether a believer should be conservative or liberal, either, and conservatives do not think liberals are going to heaven.

Even though Craig cannot actually describe the exact propositional content to this inner witness he still must think it witnesses to an undefined evangelical understanding of the Bible. But I'm arguing against the coherence of this whole understanding in this book.

Whether Craig is correct or not depends entirely on whether evangelical Christianity is true, plus some. For instance, how can Craig tell the difference between the witness of the Holy Spirit in his heart and an emotional feeling? We all have had strong feelings about a great many things that turned out to be false. There are Christians who have had strong feelings that God wanted them to do certain things that were wrong. There are Christians who have a strong feeling that God will do something for them in the near future, which may never transpire. There are Christians who feel (or sense) the Holy Spirit in a contemporary (low) church service rather than in an older traditional (high) church type service in an old cathedral, and vice versa. Why does he trust his feelings when feelings are so often wrong? People of other persuasions demur. We must constantly test our feelings in case we err, and it is possible that the cumulative tests we use may someday reveal that our feelings were in error, like I did.

According to J. L. Schellenberg, there is another way to defeat the "first-person experiential justification" of religious beliefs. He argues that the there are a number of natural explanations that better explain religious experiences. They are better explained as "wish fulfillment" which effectively defeats Craig's claim, since we know that it "can produce religious experiences." And since that's the case, "we know that people could be having religious experiences whether anything supernatural is there or not." Furthermore, since "wish fulfillment frequently does lead to unveridical experiences," there is doubt "as to whether the supernatural was perceived in the experiences in question."[10]

Besides all of this, what about Craig's doubts? Children who are taught to believe in Christ at an early age have a "childlike faith"—children pray and act like they have no doubts at all. But as they get older, the experiences of life, the questions they ponder, and their own unanswered prayers cause them to have less and less confidence in that so-called witness. Craig would have to admit that he doesn't have that "childlike faith" anymore. So his adult doubts are a check on the experience he claims to have had of the Holy Spirit.

Can Craig truly say that he doesn't have doubts from time to time? Os Guinness has argued convincingly that while "an element of faith is indispensable to all human knowledge, . . . all of us will doubt at some point, whatever it is we believe." All knowledge comes with some doubt "because we are absolutely certain of nothing. . . . Since our knowledge is finite, none of us can exclude the possibility of our being wrong."[11] So how sure can Craig be about this inner witness of God? Is he as sure of it as he knows he exists? Is he as sure of it as the existence of the chair at his desk, or the truth of a simple mathematical formula? Any philosopher knows, along with Renè Descartes, that all sense data can be doubted because they do not allow us to experience the real world in and of itself. What then is the basis Craig has for saying that he's surer of this inner witness than sense data itself, when that data can be doubted?

Finally, how did Craig come to believe that there is a Holy Spirit and an inner witness in the first place? Through experience? Hardly. Did this inner witness tell him that his views on the self-authenticating testimony of the Holy Spirit are true? The four Christian respondents in *Five Views on Apologetics* take issue with Craig's emphasis and on some of his particulars, too. Norman L. Geisler agrees that my criticisms of Craig's position here are "valid."[12] Are these other Christians not listening to the Holy Spirit? The fact is that Craig learned this at a later age in life by reading the Bible and trying to come up with a Christian apologetic. This is when he first believed in the inner witness and how it functioned for his apologetic. He came up with this in order to justify why he believed, and that's it.

While it might take a great deal to change our minds about our faith, one should never say that she "knows" Christianity to be true, because just like me, she might later come to believe she was wrong. I've tested my experience of the purported witness that I had, and found I was mistaken.

NOTES

1. William Lane Craig, *Apologetics: An Introduction* (Chicago: Moody Press, 1984), pp. 18–22.

2. William Lane Craig and Gerd Lüdemann, *Jesus' Resurrection: Fact or Figment?* (Downers Grove, IL: InterVarsity Press, 2000), p. 65.

3. Wolfhart Pannenberg, *Revelation as History* (New York: MacMillan, 1968), p. 9.

4. In *Five Views on Apologetics*, ed. Steven B. Cowan (Grand Rapids, MI: Zondervan, 2000), p. 35.

5. Ibid., p. 36.

6. "Craig's Holy Spirit Epistemology," found at www.infidels.com.

7. J. L. Schellenberg, *The Wisdom to Doubt: A Justification of Religious Skepticism* (Ithaca, NY: Cornell University Press, 2007), pp. 165–66.

8. Found at: http://www.leaderu.com/offices/billcraig.

9. In Cowan, *Five Views on Apologetics*, p. 72.

10. Schellenberg, *The Wisdom to Doubt*, pp. 184–85.

11. Os Guinness, *In Two Minds: The Dilemma of Doubt and How to Resolve It* (Downers Grove, IL: InterVarsity Press, 1976), pp. 41–43.

12. Norman L. Geisler, "From Apologist to Atheist: A Critical Review," *Christian Apologetics Journal* 6, no. 1 (Spring 2007): 94.

11

THE PROBLEM OF
UNANSWERED PRAYER

I'm not a stranger to unanswered petitionary prayer. When I was a young Christian, I prayed daily for several years that Elton John would become a Christian and record Christian songs. I finally gave up. I also prayed for years that I would be a full-time Bible college professor. Now I am as skeptical of prayer as the late Carl Sagan, who wrote, "We can pray over the cholera victim, or we can give her 500 milligrams of tetracycline every 12 hours . . . the scientific treatments are hundreds or thousands of times more effective than the alternatives (like prayer). Even when the alternatives seem to work, we don't actually know that they played any role."[1] Voltaire said: "Prayer and arsenic will kill a cow." Former slave Frederick Douglass said, "I prayed for twenty years but received no answer until I prayed with my legs."

The problem of unanswered prayer is particularly vexing when many biblical promises of answered prayer seem unqualified (Matt. 7:7; John 14:13; 15:16; and 16:23). The problem is that our experience teaches us otherwise. We all know of someone who has died even though believers had prayed. This is true even of those we deem spiritual giants.

Several biblical examples of unanswered prayer are discernible. They include Jesus' request to avoid the cross (Matt. 27:39; Luke 22:42); Jesus' prayer for Christian unity (John 17:20–22); Paul's request to remove a "thorn in the flesh" (2 Cor. 12:7); and Paul's request that he would be delivered from unbelievers in Jerusalem (Rom. 15:31; compare Acts 21). While it may be true that both Jesus and Paul sought "Thy will not mine," their expressed desires went unanswered as intended.

INADEQUATE SOLUTIONS

Three solutions are inadequate for this problem. First, some Christians simply deny that prayer ever goes unanswered if prayed in faith. This is a radical view and has given rise to the "name it claim it" theology. But this view leads to intense guilt if prayers go unanswered and forces some to paradoxically claim that God healed them even when the symptoms remain! Second, others believe God always answers prayer, but that sometimes his answer is "no." But think about it; how is it possible that a negative answer is not considered an unanswered prayer? Someone who says an answered prayer is one in which God could sometimes say "no" is merely saying God has responded in some way. But in order for us to say that prayer was answered, we really want to know whether the request was granted or not. A denied request is one that goes unanswered, and a request granted is one that is answered. If someone wants to maintain that all prayers are answered, then we merely need to ask that person whether God says "yes" to all prayers, and God clearly doesn't do this. That's the whole reason why unanswered prayer is a problem in the first place, and it *is* a problem. Third, still others rationalize things away so that they can still say God answered their prayer even though God didn't do as they requested. One church prayed for a cancer patient who died. The minister subsequently claimed God had answered their prayer because he said they were praying for her release from the hospital. Since she died, she was in fact released from the hospital and went to be with God. But that was not what they meant when they prayed. While it may be true to say God gives us what is best, that doesn't mean he gives us exactly what we asked him.

SOME OTHER SOLUTIONS

Several other solutions are offered to help explain the problem of unanswered prayer. Believers demand that we see the promises of answered prayer as qualified ones. It's these qualifications that lead David Mills to argue that "believers create the illusion of answered prayer by systematically employing the fallacy known as 'Selective Observation,' a perceptual error also referred to as 'counting the hits and ignoring the misses.'"[2] If a prayer seems to get answered, God gets the credit. But if it goes unanswered, then there was a reason for why God didn't answer it. My question here is whether the biblical promise of answered prayer "dies the death of a thousand qualifications," so to speak. Depending on how one categorizes them, I've discovered several qualifications to answered prayer. I've been helped to a great degree by William Lane Craig's book *Hard Questions, Real Answers*, although, as you can tell, I will draw different conclusions.[3]

Sin in Our Lives

We are told God is under no obligation to answer the specific prayers of one tangled in sin (Ps. 66:18; Isa. 59:1–2; James 5:16; 1 John 3:21–22). This includes all of the outward and inward sins in the Bible, plus not treating family members right (1 Pet. 3:7) and not growing as a Christian (John 15:15–16; Gal. 5:22–23). But a problem surfaces here. Since Christians are washed in the blood of Jesus, God supposedly sees no sin in them. How can God see their sins if they are already washed clean? But if somehow God can see their sins, and if that means seeing inside their so-called filthy hearts, then none of them is clean enough to expect anything from God when they pray.

Wrong Motives in Our Prayer

We are told God is under no obligation to answer selfish prayers (James 4:3). Conversely, God is under no obligation to answer prayers that fail to give glory to God (John 14:13; 2 Cor. 12:9–10). We may not even know what would bring God the most glory (John 9:3). But there are some very strong arguments that indicate there is nothing a human can do or say that is completely free of selfish motives. *Psychological egoism*, for instance, is the theory that everything we do, even if in some small degree, benefits us the most. Even if we don't take that extreme stance, and I don't, most all of what we do is done from motives that benefit ourselves first. Most all of our prayers contain some selfish motives. Even the preacher who prays that his church mature and grow can also want a bigger paycheck, more power, some recognized fame, and fewer problem people as they mature in their Christian faith. So which prayers qualify to be answered when many, if not most of them, are prayed from selfish motives?

Lack of Faith in Prayer

We are told God is under no obligation to answer the prayers of someone who doesn't believe he will (Mark 11:24; James 1:6–8; 5:15). This faith must show itself to be persistent and earnest in prayer (Matt. 7:7; Luke 11:5–8; 18:1–8). Jesus does talk as if all you need is faith and God will intervene for you. He makes it sound easy. All you should have to do is say to that mountain to move over there, and it shall be done. But it doesn't move. So you blame yourself. Something must be wrong with your faith, is the believer's conclusion. Then that failure is a memory and you don't step out so far on the limb next time. And when you fail in faith again, then you hesitate to step out on that limb again. This happens until you find yourself clinging to the tree trunk for fear of stepping out on faith much at all. So you feel guilty about this all over again. Then you hear a good sermon and try again, and when your faith fails, you are back to the tree trunk again. So you feel guilty again. It's simply impossible for adults to have childlike faith because we are no longer children. We've had too many experiences that temper our faith—too many tragedies, too many unanswered prayers, too many setbacks. And all of these things have taught us that believing doesn't always work. So we simply don't believe like we think we should. So we feel guilty, and we struggle some more. And we feel guilty some more for struggling, and so on.

This goes on until all that believers can do is offer up nonfalsifiable prayers that can't be tested to see whether or not God actually did anything as a result of prayer ("God, be with them." "Help them."); and offer up self-fulfilling prayers that are fulfilled because they are the ones praying ("Give me strength." "Give me wisdom to know what to do." "Please encourage me." "Help me stay on the narrow road that leads to you."). I blame the Christian faith for causing this guilt and for these lame, modern, nonfalsifiable, and self-fullfilling prayers. My view doesn't produce guilt because I no longer have such expectations.

It Must Be According to God's Will

We are told God is under no obligation to answer the prayer that is ignorant of God's will (1 John 5:14–15; Matt. 27:39–41; Luke 22:42; John 14:13–14; 15:16; 16:23). Likewise, God is under no obligation to answer a prayer that brings any injustice on others (Luke 18:7–8).

Why would the Christian God answer the prayers of a slave owner who asked that none of his slaves would run away, or the prayers of the KKK for white supremacy, or the prayers of those who want a man standing accused of a crime to be found guilty, if in fact he is innocent? Unjust prayers have no assurance God will answer them. But there are so many ethical and social issues in our world today. How can Christians really claim on every issue that they really know the mind of God enough to pray for what should be done? Most of history is the history of human errors.

It is said that Christians may be praying for an end to AIDS, poverty, teenage pregnancy, and so on, but God doesn't do much to change the situation because as a nation we have to repent first. I cannot see how it's not God's will that more people be saved, yet the Christian faith is losing ground in America today. Jeff, my cousin, told me once that he doesn't think God wants everyone to be saved. Of course, he's a good Calvinist and thinks God wills or decrees everything that happens. But the problem of evil resurfaces here. It takes more faith than I will ever have to say that it was God's will for Hitler to start World War II, or for terrorists to fly planes into the World Trade Center's Twin Towers in New York, or for children to die prematurely, or for people to starve to death. Calvinists believe God decrees those things to happen, and non-Calvinists simply believe that Christians are the ones blamed for not praying enough.

It Must Be within God's Power to Grant the Request

Sometimes believers are praying for contradictory things. Consider two fellows both praying for the romantic affections of one girl, two athletes on opposite teams both praying to win a certain ball game, two people praying for the same job, or the farmer who prays for rain while the vacationer is praying for sunshine, and so on. Then, too, what about mothers who were praying for the lives of their sons on opposite sides of a battle during the Civil War or World War II? Or what of a convicted criminal who prays for a judge to be lenient in his sentencing versus the victim who prays the criminal receives the maximum penalty allowed by law? God cannot answer all prayers because to do so would be to do what is logically impossible. This qualification alone may cause hundreds of thousands of prayers to go unanswered.

Biblical History Teaches Us That When Praying for Certain Things God Is Under No Obligation to Answer Our Requests in Our Lifetime

Believers are told to have patience because of God's timetable. Think of the prayers offered during the purported Israelite Egyptian slavery (Exod. 2:23–25) or the Babylonian captivity (Lamentations 1–5). There were Jews who prayed for the coming of the Messiah, and many Christians down through the centuries have prayed for the promised return of Jesus. There are surely other requests that just don't fit into God's timetable, we are reminded, because we just don't know God's plan for earth. But in the meantime, I wonder why God doesn't help and/or rescue people when they hurt so badly.

Certain Other Requests Must Eventually Be Denied No Matter How Often Christians Pray for Them

Death, sickness, pain, hard work, and strained relationships are part of the curse placed upon humankind because of the supposed fall into sin (Gen. 3:8–19). Prayer can lessen the effects of the Fall, but it cannot eliminate them. We will eventually die. We cannot avoid getting sick from time to time. There will be strained relationships, and work will nearly always be hard. So even if Christians prayed every day to be healthy, they'd still get sick from time to time, and even if they prayed every day not to die, we know that someday they will die despite their prayers.

There Is the Additional Problem of Human Free Will (for Non-Calvinists)

There seems to be the admittance throughout the Bible that human beings have been given free will and that some choose to reject God ("whosoever will, may come"). Given this fact, one must wonder how much change we can expect by praying for an unrepentant person. I recall a conversation Pastor Norm Fuller had with me, as I was becoming a skeptical person:

> Pastor: John, my prayer for you is that you come to your senses before you go off the deep end.

John: Well, if that's your prayer and if prayer works, then I won't go off the deep
    end, will I?
Pastor: But it will depend upon whether or not you have a receptive heart.
John: Well, if it depends upon my heart, then why bother to pray for me?

Had my pastor responded further by saying he will begin praying that I have a receptive heart, I could've responded as I did at first. I could've replied, "Well, if that's your prayer and if prayer works, then I will be given a receptive heart, won't I?" Sometimes I'm just cantankerous.

If Christians want to maintain that God doesn't curtail our free human actions, then how do prayers for people with free will get answered at all? When we pray for safety as we leave our house, how does that prayer have even a remote chance of being answered if there is a predator out there who is going to meet up with us? If God does not stop this predator's free choices, or anyone else's for that matter, how can any prayer that involves free human choices have a remote chance to be answered?

Of course, a Calvinist must admit that God has decreed that I should be a doubter and that I should write this book that will lead others into becoming doubters like me—even though the Bible tells us God desires all people everywhere to be saved! (See 2 Pet. 3:9.)

THREE MORE THOUGHTS

First, even though there are several qualifications for prayer Christians are still chided for not being persistent in prayer. In Hebrews 4:16 they are encouraged to come confidently before God's throne of grace. Even when they are unsure what to pray for, they are assured that God can read the thoughts of their hearts (Rom. 8:26–27). But with all of the qualifications, this is extremely hard for them to do. Second, when it comes to petitionary prayer, why should anyone even ask God to do things? Shouldn't God do the right thing even if we never prayed, regardless of the fact that he wants us to be involved through prayer? Third, prayer is not just asking God for things. There is also praise, thanksgiving, and intercession (1 Tim. 2:1). Believers can always ask for strength to endure, power to obey, love to share, insight to know God's will, and peace in the midst of turmoil. They can pray for a renewed sense of God's forgiveness, for a grateful heart, for joy unspeakable, and so on. I think these are the things that Christians should focus on, and for an atheist like me, it's not much different than positive thinking.

THREE SCIENTIFIC TESTS OF PETITIONARY/INTERCESSORY PRAYER

There are Christians who say we should not test God, but in Malachi 3:10 God says to test him with tithes to see if he won't shower his blessings down on those who give their tithe. The only biblical caution is that a believer must test God with faith, not doubt. So there is nothing inherently wrong with testing the results of prayer either. Let's look at the results of one scientific test and then propose two additional ones.

First, the *American Heart Journal* (151, no. 4 [2006]: 934–42) did a scientific test of prayer on patients who had heart bypass surgery. They were separated into three groups. Group 1 received prayers and didn't know it. Group 2 received no prayers and didn't know it (the control group). Group 3 received prayers and did know it. Groups 1 and 3 were prayed for by different congregations throughout America. The results were very clear. There was no difference between the patients who were prayed for and those who were not prayed for. Moreover, the patients who knew they were being prayed for suffered significantly more complications than those who did not know they were being prayed for.

Second, another scientific test of prayer could be done with amputees. If God answers prayers and heals people, then why are there no reports that he made amputated limbs grow back? This would be observable and it could be easily documented and tested. There is a Web site that makes this challenge: http://whydoesgodhate amputees.com/: "For this experiment, we need to find a deserving person who has had both of his legs amputated. Now create a prayer circle. The job of this prayer circle is simple: pray to God to restore the amputated legs of this deserving person. Pray that God spontaneously and miraculously restores the legs overnight. If possible, get millions of people all over the planet to join the prayer circle and pray their most fervent prayers. Get millions of people praying in unison for a single miracle for this one deserving amputee. Then stand back and watch."

Third, we can test whether prayer works by praying to change a tragic event in the past. If God exists and he foreknows what we will pray for, then prayer can change the past, just as prayers supposedly change the future. What I mean is that prayer would be changing what God foreknows, since he supposedly has foreknowledge of the future. Christian philosopher George Mavrodes argues the past is in fact altered whenever he does something in the present, for in doing so he prevents God from ever having foreknown he did something different.[4] If he's correct, then by praying after a tragic event has already occurred, believers can determine what God foreknows from all eternity. And based upon his foreknowledge, God can prevent the tragic past from happening before it happens. The problem is that since God supposedly foreknows what believers will pray for, he also foreknows they won't be praying for a particular past event to be changed. But if they do pray, God would have this foreknowledge. So here's another test for prayer. Pick an event in the past and have Christians all over the world pray that God changes it. It could be a prayer to stop the Holocaust or the terrorist attacks on the Twin Towers on 9/11, or it could be something as simple as to stop teenagers from getting in a car accident who were killed the night before.

Christians will respond by arguing God has already taken into consideration all prayers in what he allowed to take place in the past. However, most Christian theologians claim God cannot foreknow an event if it doesn't happen. How can he? If an event doesn't happen, there is nothing to foreknow, according to them. So God can only foreknow the prayers that will actually be prayed, and if that's the case, Christians may only need to start praying to help people in the past, just exactly like they pray for their present and future needs!

A scientific test for this was suggested to me by Dr. Joshua Sharp. "Pray for the curing of a genetic disease that is not diagnosed until later in life. For example, Huntington's disease is caused by mutation of a single gene and is dominant (you only need one copy). Except for the juvenile variant, Huntington's is usually not diagnosed until after age twenty. So what you can do is pray in the year 2008 that people born in the year 2000 would not have inherited the Huntington's gene. Pray very hard, then track Huntington's diagnoses. You should see Huntington's diagnoses drop significantly at some point in the future, after which they would go back to normal."

Christians might finally respond that if God does indeed change the past, we would never know he did, since if he does, we would have no memory of even praying for an event in the past to be changed because the event that led to the prayers would never have taken place. That's fine if they wish to hang on to this as a remote possibility. In the meantime just try it, Christian. Pick an event in the past and pray to change it, then another, then another, then another, and so on. My prediction is that all prayers to change the past will fail and that they will also be remembered by those who prayed them precisely because nothing in the past will ever change . . . ever. What's *your* prediction?[5]

NOTES

1. Carl Sagan, *The Demon Haunted World* (New York: Random House, 1996), pp. 9–10.

2. David Mills, *The Atheist Universe: The Thinking Person's Answer to Christian Fundamentalism* (Berkeley, CA: Ulysses Press, 2006), pp. 158–69.

3. In the chapter, "Unanswered Prayer," in *Hard Question, Real Answers* (Wheaton, IL: Crossway Books, 2003), pp. 43–60.

4. George I. Mavrodes, "Is the Past Unpreventable," *Faith and Philosophy* 1, no. 2 (April 1984): 131–46.

5. For some failed scientific experiments on prayer see Victor J. Stenger's *Has Science Found God? The Latest Results in the Search for Purpose in the Universe* (Amherst, NY: Prometheus Books, 2003), and his *God: The Failed Hypothesis* (Amherst, NY: Prometheus Books, 2007), pp. 94–102.

12

THE PROBLEM OF EVIL

Part 1: My Specific Case

et me begin with what Elie Wiesel wrote about the night he arrived at the Birkenau Nazi concentration camp: "Never shall I forget that night, the first night in camp, that turned my life into one long night seven times sealed. Never shall I forget that smoke. Never shall I forget the small faces of the children whose bodies I saw transformed into smoke under a silent sky. Never shall I forget those flames that consumed my faith forever. Never shall I forget the nocturnal silence that deprived me for all eternity of the desire to live. Never shall I forget those moments that murdered my God and my soul and turned my dreams to ashes. Never shall I forget those things, even were I condemned to live as long as God Himself. Never."[1]

The problem of evil is known as "the rock of atheism."[2] Michael Martin considers this problem so significant that out of 476 pages of writing and defending atheism, there are 118 pages in his book on this one issue alone, which is a quarter of his book![3]

Dr. James F. Sennett has said: "By far the most important objection to the faith is the so-called problem of evil— the alleged incompatibility between the existence or extent of evil in the world and the existence of God. I tell my philosophy of religion students that, if they are Christians and the problem of evil does not keep them up at night, then they don't understand it."[4]

I'll be arguing here against the theistic conception of God, who is believed to be all-powerful, or omnipotent, perfectly good, or omnibenelovent and all-knowing, or omniscient. The problem of evil (or suffering) is an internal one to these three theistic beliefs, which is expressed in both deductive and evidential arguments concerning both moral and natural evils.

There is moral evil—suffering as the result of the choices of moral agents. Examples: the Holocaust, terrorist bombings, rape, molestation, slavery, torture, beatings, kidnappings. In 1838 America forced the Cherokees to relocate to the Western states. The march west, known to them as the "Trail of Tears," resulted in the deaths of an estimated four thousand Cherokees. There are witchdoctors in Africa who tell men who have AIDS to have sex with a baby in order to be cured, and as a result, many female babies are being taken from their mother's arms and gang-raped even as I write this. Nearly forty thousand people, mostly children, die every day around the world due to hunger. Then there was Joseph Mengele, who tortured concentration camp prisoners; atomic bombs that devastated Hiroshima and Nagasaki; Soviet gulags; 9/11 Twin Tower terrorist attacks; Cambodian children stepping on land mines; and Columbine shootings. The list of atrocities done by people to each other could literally fill up a library full of books.

There is natural evil: suffering due to nature's tragedies (whether animal or human). **Natural disasters** like floods, tsunamis, droughts, fires, famines, volcanic eruptions, earthquakes, tornados, monsoons, and shipwrecks occur throughout the world. There are heat waves, blizzards, and hurricanes. **Poisonous species** exist like the black widow and the brown recluse spider. There are fifty-eight **poisonous plants**, some lethal. There are **chronic diseases like** cancer (lung, breast, prostrate, throat, brain, etc.), emphysema, leukemia, cardiac problems (many varieties), diabetes, lupus, arthritis, diabetes. There are **birth defects**, including anencephaly, midgets, people born with two heads, deformed limbs, blindness, deafness, dumbness, mental deficiencies including dementia, paranoid schizophrenia, and so on.

Some Major Epidemics Have Decimated Peoples in the Past

162	Possibly measles and smallpox in Eurasian world
542	Bubonic plague in the Middle Eastern world
1331	Bubonic plague in China, Asia, and Europe
1494	Global epidemic of syphilis that started in Italy
1520	Smallpox in the Americas
1556	Influenza in Europe and the Americas
1648	Yellow fever in South America
1817	Cholera spread all over the world
1918	Influenza killed twenty million
Future?	Asian Bird Flu Virus, H5N1 (it could kill 180–360 million people!)

There is also a nonmoral category of evil due to unintentional accidents that are the result of human neglect and inaction. A very significant portion of human suffering is created by people who didn't know the consequences of their actions and did not believe they were doing wrong. The founding of New Orleans, in a bowl below sea level by French explorer Rene-Robert Cavelier is one of them, as evidenced when the 2005 Hurricane Katrina ripped through that city. No one can make the case that he did this on purpose. He had benign reasons.

THE PROBLEM OF EVIL STATED

Here is the argument as stated by David Hume (Philo): "Is he (God) willing to prevent evil, but not able? Then he is impotent. Is he able, but not willing? Then he is malevolent. Is he both able and willing? Whence then is evil?"[5] But I want to be more precise. If God is perfectly good, all knowing, and all powerful, then the issue of why there is so much suffering in the world requires an explanation. The reason is that a perfectly good God would be opposed to it, an all-powerful God would be capable of eliminating it, and an all-knowing God would know what to do about it. So the extent of intense suffering in the world means for the theist that either God is not powerful enough to eliminate it, or God does not care enough to eliminate it, or God is just not smart enough to know what to do about it. The stubborn fact of intense suffering in the world means that something is wrong with God's ability, or his goodness, or his knowledge. I consider this as close to an empirical refutation of Christianity as is possible.

Christians believe God set the Israelites free from slavery, but he did nothing for the many people who were born and died as slaves in the American South. These theists believe God parted the Red Sea, but he did nothing about the 2004 Indonesian tsunami that killed a quarter of a million people. Christians believe God provided manna from heaven, but he does nothing for the more than forty thousand people who starve every single day in the world. Those who don't die suffer extensively from hunger pains and malnutrition all of their short lives. Christians believe God made an axe head to float, but he allowed the *Titanic* to sink. Christians believe God added fifteen years to King Hezekiah's life, but he does nothing for children who live short lives and die of leukemia. Christians believe God restored sanity to Nebuchadnezzar, but he does nothing for the many people suffering from schizophrenia and dementia today. Christians believe Jesus healed people, but God does nothing to stop pandemics, which have destroyed whole populations of people. There are many handicapped people and babies born with birth defects who God does not heal. As God idly sits by, well over 100 million people were slaughtered in the last century due to genocides and wars. The *New York Times* (January 27, 2008) estimates that nearly 10 billion cows, chickens, pigs, and other animals are slaughtered every year for American consumption alone, while animals viciously prey on each other.

Let me tell you two specific cases of suffering. The first comes from a man named Robert, who for four and a half years heard cruel voices in his head. The cruelest voice said that Satan was going to force him to murder his daughter. You may say that these voices were all lies and should have been treated as such. If you say that, then you don't understand the horror of schizophrenia. Schizophrenics wholeheartedly believe these voices. He was so convinced Satan was going to force him to murder his daughter that he fought the urge to commit suicide on a daily basis so he wouldn't be the instrument of his daughter's death. Nothing that he tried helped him either, and he tried it all: exorcisms, repentance from every known sin, medications, and counseling. His wife eventually divorced him in fear he may have been a threat to his daughter, leaving him to live alone in a psychotic state. He's recovered a great deal. But why didn't God care?

Then there's former American slave Frederick Douglass, who described how his Christian master whipped his aunt right before his young eyes. "He took her into the kitchen, and stripped her from neck to waist. He made her get upon the stool, and he tied her hands to a hook in the joist. After rolling up his sleeves, he commenced to lay on the heavy cowskin, and soon the warm, red blood came dripping to the floor. . . . No words, no tears, no prayers, from his gory victim, seemed to move his iron heart from its bloody purpose. The louder she screamed, the harder he whipped; and where the blood ran fastest, there he whipped longest. He would whip her to make her scream, and whip her to make her hush; and not until overcome by fatigue, would he cease to swing the blood clotted cowskin."[6]

Why didn't the Christian God ever explicitly and clearly condemn slavery? Paul Copan defends the notion that biblical slavery was different than American slavery in the antebellum South and shouldn't have been used to justify it.[7] Even if this is true, the Bible was still used by Christians to justify the brutal slavery in the American South. Distinguished Princeton professor Charles Hodge defended American slavery in a forty-page essay written in 1860, just prior to the Civil War. Just read the debates over this issue in Willard M. Swartley, *Slavery, Sabbath, War and Women*.[8] Then you'll see just how unclear this issue really was to them. The Catholic Church didn't condemn slavery until the year 1888, after the Civil War and after every other Christian nation had abolished it.[9] So again, why didn't God tell his people, "Thou shalt not own, buy, sell, or trade slaves," and say it as often as he needed to? Why was God not clear about this in the Bible? Just think how Copan's own arguments would resonate with him if he were born into the brutal slavery of the South! What would he think then as his blood was spilled at the hands of a Bible-quoting master? Sam Harris claims, "Nothing in Christian theology remedies the appalling deficiencies of the Bible on what is perhaps the greatest—and the easiest—moral question our society has ever had to face."[10]

SOME THEISTIC SOLUTIONS

G. W. Leibniz (1646–1716) taught that this is the best of all possible worlds. His reasoning went like this: A perfect God has the power to create any possible world. Being perfect, God would create the best possible world. No creaturely reality can be totally perfect, but must contain some evil. So God created a world possessing the optimum balance of good and evil—this is the best of all possible worlds! But it's clearly not the best possible world I could envision, because with just one fewer murder or drought this would be a better world. This is the view attacked by Voltaire in his novel *Candide*. Atheist William Rowe has argued that if there is a best world for God to create, he would have no other choice than to create it. For, as Leibniz tells us, "to do less good than one could is to be lacking in wisdom or in goodness."[11] Even if the existence of God is not disproved by the fact that this is not the best possible world, Nicholas Everitt argues, "the fact that this is not a perfect world does."[12] When we look at this present world with all of its suffering, it's implausible to believe God created it, since it should be the best that an infinitely powerful, infinitely good being could do in creating a world.

Norman Geisler has instead claimed that this world is the best possible way to get to the best possible world.[13] But again, such a claim is suspect, given the amount of evil in our world. And it's clearly not the best possible way to get to the best possible world either, because with just one fewer murder or drought this would be a better world leading up to the best possible world.

There is also theological determinism, where God decrees everything that happens for his glory (or hyper-Calvinism). According to Clark Pinnock, "One need not wonder why people become atheists when faced with such a theology. A God like that has a great deal for which to answer."[14]

THERE ARE THREE GLOBAL THEISTIC THEODICIES

Augustinian. The traditional Christian answer is that natural and moral evil entered the world as the result of an angelic and then a human fall into sin—freely chosen. God gives us free will in a neutral world and will allow us to reap the full individual, societal, and global consequences of our own free choices. "All evil is either sin or the consequences of sin." God sent Christ to overcome that which brought evil into the world—sin. God will eventually be victorious over evil in the end. Sin that is justly punished is thereby canceled out and no longer mars the universe.[15] This is basically the viewpoint I'll take aim at the most.

John Hick's Irenaean "Soul Making" Theodicy. Two stages of creation are involved: first humans were brought into existence as intelligent animals, and then, through free choices, human beings are gradually being transformed into God's children. Perfection lies in the future of our existence through successive reincarnations. Hick introduces the concept of reincarnation because he's trying to come up with a theology that harmonizes the various religious viewpoints. This theodicy requires an "epistemic distance" from God that allows us to exercise free choices without the direct presence of God to restrain us. It also requires that we reject a historical fall from innocence and accept a universal salvation of all people.[16]

Process Theology of David Griffin. He argues that God has not finished creating the universe—it is still in process. The world is God's body. The natural evil we see in the world is simply a part of the ongoing creative act of God through the evolutionary process—he's not finished yet. In this view, God only has the power to persuade moral agents like us to do well. God cannot intervene to help us, only persuade us. He cares; it's just that he cannot directly intervene because he cannot completely control his creatures. God does not need to be justified for permitting evil, since it is not within his power to prevent it.[17] According to William Hasker, with process theology "the problem of evil, as an objection to belief in the existence of God, virtually disappears," although it has other problems.[18]

The Problem of Evil—Part 1: My Specific Case 233

There are many books and many more journal articles discussing the various issues around the problem of evil. Almost every philosophy anthology textbook and every philosophy of religion book will deal with this issue in varying degrees.[19] It's usually separated into a logical problem and an evidential problem.

THE LOGICAL (DEDUCTIVE) PROBLEM OF EVIL

This is an argument whereby it is claimed that there is a logical (or deductive) inconsistency with the existence of evil and God's omnipotence, omnibenevolence, and/or omniscience. J. L. Mackie's argument was that God is either not good, not omnipotent, or evil doesn't exist. He argues: a good being always eliminates evil as far as it can; and there are no limits to what an omnipotent being can do. Therefore such a God cannot exist—it is a logically impossibility. He asks: "Why couldn't God have made people such that they always freely choose the good?" And, "Why should God refrain from controlling evil wills?"[20] Plantinga's free will defense seeks to answer this problem.[21] He argues that it is logically possible that there is a state of affairs in which humans are free and always do what is right. But he argues God cannot bring about any possible world he wishes that contains free agents with significant choice-making capabilities. Plantinga introduces the concept of *transworld depravity*: it is logically possible that every free agent makes a wrong choice and that everyone suffers from it. This is crucial for the free will defense to work. But as I will argue later, the whole notion of free will has many problems. Plantinga also suggests that it is logically possible that fallen angels cause all of the natural evil in our world. But according to Richard Swinburne, such an explanation for natural evil is an "ad hoc hypothesis," and as such, according to J. L. Mackie, "tends to disconfirm the hypothesis that there is a god."[22]

Most Christians claim the logical problem has been solved. But there are still versions of the logical problem of evil that have not been sufficiently answered. There are those written by Quentin Smith, Hugh LaFollette, and Richard La Croix.[23] Then there is Richard Gale's argument, and Graham Oppy, who argues at length for the thesis that Plantinga's treatment of the logical problem of evil is inconsistent in several respects.[24] A. M. Weisberger also offers a good critique of Plantinga's free will defense in her book *Suffering Belief*.[25] Just because Plantinga answered Mackie's formulation, and just because Mackie admitted this, doesn't mean that all formulations have been answered or that others agree with Mackie's admission.

Even if there is no logical disproof of the existence of God because of intense suffering in this world, that doesn't say much at all. The reason is that there are very few, if any, logical disproofs of anything. Consider this deductive argument from Richard R. La Croix: "If God is the greatest possible good then if God had not created there would be nothing but the greatest possible good. And since God didn't need to create at all, then the fact that he did create produced less than the greatest possible good. . . . Perhaps God could not, for some perfectly plausible reason, create a world without evil, but then it would seem that he ought not to have created at all. . . . Prior to creation God knew that if he created there would be evil, so being wholly good he ought not to have created."[26] After analyzing La Croix's argument, A. M. Weisberger argued that "contrary to popular theistic opinion, the logical form of the argument is still alive and beating."[27]

Why did God create something in the first place? Theists will typically defend the goodness of God by arguing he could not have created a world without some suffering and evil. But what reason is there for creating anything at all? Theists typically respond by saying creation was an expression of God's love. But wasn't God already complete in love? If love must be expressed, then God needed to create, and that means he lacked something. Besides, a perfectly good God should not have created anything at all, if by creating something, anything, it also brought about so much intense suffering.

THE EVIDENTIAL (OR INDUCTIVE) PROBLEM OF EVIL

According to Richard Swinburne, "the crux of the problem of evil. . . . Not the fact of evil or the kinds of evil which are a threat to theism; it is the quantity of evil— both the number of people (and animals) who suffer and the amount which they suffer."[28] Here the skeptical challenge is that theism is not logically inconsistent, but rather it is implausible. That is, given the quantity of evil in our world, it is improbable that a good, all-powerful God exists. Additionally, given the fact that there is pointless or meaningless evil in our world, and there are compelling reasons to think there is, then it's unlikely that a good, all-powerful God exists.

William L. Rowe, is the leading proponent of this evidential argument. He argues (1) There exist instances of intense suffering which an omnipotent, omniscient being could have prevented without thereby losing some greater good or permitting some evil equally bad or worse. (2) An omnipotent, omniscient, wholly good being would prevent the occurrence of any intense suffering it could, unless it could not do so without thereby losing some greater good or permitting some evil equally bad or worse. Therefore: (3) there does not exist an omnipotent, omniscient, wholly good being. According to Rowe, we cannot know with certainty that instances of (1) take place. But it is one thing to prove that (1) is true and quite another thing to have rational grounds for believing (1) to be true. In light of our past experience and knowledge, it is very probable that such events have occurred, thus making (1) reasonable to believe. (1) Taken together with (2), can rationally lead us to the conclusion (3).

Rowe offers two specific instances of evil that support his argument, one involving *moral evil*, and the other involving *natural evil*. The moral evil case came from a *Detroit Free Press* story on January 3, 1986, in which a little girl from Flint Michigan was severely beaten, raped, and then strangled on New Year's Day. He argues that "no good state of affairs we know of is such that an omnipotent, omniscient being's obtaining it would morally justify that being's permitting it."[29] The natural evil case he described was of a fawn that was badly burned and slowly died from a forest fire, without any human observer. Rowe argued that an omnipotent, omniscient being could've "prevented the fawn's apparently pointless suffering." A wholly good omnipotent being could have stopped the lightning from starting the fire, diverted it, kept the tree from starting on fire, or kept the fawn from being burned, or if burned, could have spared it the intense suffering for days by quickly ending its life. But since God didn't do any of these things, such a God doesn't exist, for he would not allow this fawn to suffer if it doesn't serve some outweighing attainable good, and not even a theist can come up with a good reason why such a fawn suffered.[30]

Rowe brings up the problem of gratuitous (or pointless) evil with these two cases. Along these lines theistic scholar Terence Penelhum writes: "Although one cannot require God to do anything, in calling him good one is necessarily expressing the conviction that his behavior will satisfy a certain set of moral standards. In calling God good a theist is committed to saying that God's reasons for permitting evils must be reasons that are acceptable to the believer's own set of moral standards." And since this is the case, "any evils that a Christian will admit to being in the world, he must also say that these evils were allowed by God because their presence is at least compatible with the Christian's own moral principles, and that these evils help with the furtherance of bringing about good in the world. A Christian theist, when faced with what he admits to be an evil, must therefore hold that God allows it because the existence of it brings about good in the world. To admit the existence of an evil which demonstrably cannot have this function would be to admit a proposition inconsistent with Christian theism. For such an evil would be pointless. It is logically inconsistent for a theist to admit the existence of a pointless evil."[31] Gratuitous human suffering, which serves no point, is logically inconsistent with Christian theism, he claims. Why? Simply because it's pointless. It didn't need to happen for some greater good, and hence is inconsistent with a kind and omnipotent God. I'll return to Rowe's argument later in the next chapter, when it comes to theistic responses to the issues he raises (pp. 257–58).

MY SPECIFIC CASE

With all of the above as a background I'll argue my specific case. As I do so, keep in mind a few things. Keep in mind what Dr. Corey Washington said in a debate with Dr. William Lane Craig: "We've got to hold theists to what they say. . . . If they say God is omnibenelovent, God is omnibenelovent, if they say God is omnipotent, God is omnipotent. We can't let theists to sort of play with these words. They mean what they mean. And if God is omnibenelovent, God will not have any more harm in this world than is necessary for accomplishing greater goods."[32]

Keep in mind also what Weisberger wrote: "any proposed solution to the problem of evil which does not account for all kinds of evil in the world, both moral and natural, is deficient in some way, since evil is then not shown to be necessary. And if some evil is not necessary, God's goodness and/or power is called into question" (see note).[33]

Finally, keep in mind that I'm looking at this world and asking whether or not God exists, while a theist already believes God exists and is trying to explain why there is intense suffering in this world given that prior belief. Even if the God hypothesis may be able to explain why this world is the way it is, which I seriously doubt, that's a far cry from this world being the one we would expect to find if there was a good God, and these two different perspectives make all the difference in the world. David Hume first made this distinction in these words: "What if I show you a house or palace where there was not one apartment convenient or agreeable, where the windows, doors, fires, passages, stairs, and the whole economy of the building were the source of noise, confusion, fatigue, darkness, and the extremes of heat and cold? . . . The architect would in vain display his subtilty, and prove to you that, if this door or that window were altered, greater ills would ensue. What he says may be strictly true. But still you would assert in general that, if the architect had had skill and good intentions, he might have formed such a plan of the whole, and might have adjusted the parts in such a manner as would have remedied all or most of these inconveniences. His ignorance, or even your own ignorance of such a plan, will never convince you of the impossibility of it. If you find any inconveniences and deformities in the building, you will always without entering into detail, condemn the architect."[34]

What Hume is getting at can best be described along the same lines as John Rawls's *veil of ignorance*. Let's say we are placed behind a theological Rawlsian veil of ignorance. Behind that veil we are to consider what world we should expect to find if God created that world before experiencing that world. Behind that veil we must think about the kinds of things we could expect to find, based upon a full description of the God that is supposed to exist. What would we expect to find prior to experiencing a world? As I proceed, I'll share what I think.

So let me begin. I'll assume for the sake of argument that God exists. Then why didn't God just create a heavenly world with heavenly bodies in the first place? Theists typically believe that a heaven awaits faithful believers when they die, where there will be no "death, or mourning or crying or pain" (Rev. 21:4), where believers will have incorruptible bodies (1 Cor. 15:30 ff.), in a perfect existence. So why didn't God just create such a perfect existence in the first place? If there's free will in heaven without sin, then God could've created such a world. To say God initially did create such a world but that there was an angelic rebellion in it merely places the problem of evil back in time. How is it possible to be in the direct presence of a being that has absolute goodness and unlimited power and still desire to rebel against him? Even if this is possible, why didn't God prevent such a rebellion? Pierre Bayle argued: "One might as well compare the Godhead with a father who had let the legs of his children be broken in order to display before an entire city the skill which he has is setting bones; One might as well compare the Godhead with a monarch who would allow strife and seditions to spring up throughout his kingdom in order to acquire the glory of having put an end to them."[35]

I could end my argument here. But let's say God decided to create a fleshly world with free creatures in it anyway, even though there is no good reason to do so. If so, God should've had three main moral concerns.

Moral Concern One

That we don't abuse the freedom God gave us. The giver of a gift is blameworthy if he gives gifts to those whom he knows will terribly abuse those gifts. Any mother who gives a razor blade to a two-year-old is culpable if that child hurts himself or others with it. Good mothers give their children more and more freedom to do what they want so long as they are responsible with their freedom. And if children abuse this freedom, their mothers will discipline them by taking away their opportunities to make these choices. It's that simple. Paul Draper wrote, "we would expect God would behave like a good parent, giving humans great responsibility only when we are worthy of it."[36] Besides, why should we as human beings have to learn the consequences of our actions by such Draconian kinds of sufferings when we err? When my children misbehaved or didn't understand the consequences of their actions, I didn't send a proverbial hurricane their way. In fact, as a parent I sought to protect them as much as I could from the extreme consequences of their actions. A little pain was a good thing, so they could learn from their mistakes. But no caring father would let them suffer the full brunt of their mistakes—no father.

Furthermore, if my mother sat by and did nothing while my brother beat me to death, and if she had the means to stop him and didn't, then she is morally responsible for letting me die. She could even be considered an accomplice.

God could keep us from abusing our freedom, too. He could've created us with a stronger propensity to dislike doing wrong just like we have an aversion to drinking motor oil. We could still drink it if we wanted to, but it's nauseating.

God could easily keep a person from molesting a child or raping someone if at the very thought of it, the person began to suffer from severe nausea. We have the ability to do this with alcoholics, so it should be no problem for God to do this with the most heinous of crimes.

God could also implant thoughts into a person's head to prevent him from doing evil; much like in Robert's case above, except these thoughts would be good ones, from God himself.

God has many other means at his disposal here, if we concede for the moment the existence of this present world: One childhood fatal disease or a heart attack could have killed Hitler and prevented World War II. Timothy McVeigh could have had a flat tire or engine failure while driving to Oklahoma City with that truck bomb to blow up the Murrah federal building and the people in it. Several of the militants who were going to fly planes into the Twin Towers on 9/11 could've been robbed and beaten by New York thugs (there's utilitarianism at its best)!

A poisonous snakebite could've sent Saddam Hussein to an early grave, averting the Iraq war before it happened. The poison that Saddam Hussein threw on the Kurds and the Zyklon-B pellets dropped down into the Auschwitz gas chambers could have simply "malfunctioned" by being miraculously neutralized (just like Jesus supposedly turned water into wine). Sure, it would puzzle them, but there are a great many things that take place in our world that are not explainable. Even if they concluded God performed a miracle here, what's the harm? Doesn't God want us to believe in him?[37]

Moral Concern Two

That the environment God places us in will not cause us excessive suffering. If the Christian God wants us to believe in him, then he should've made it a priority to prevent religious diversity by clearly revealing himself in this world such that only people who refuse to believe would do so. In this way he'd prevent all religious wars, Crusades, inquisitions and witch burnings. There'd be no religiously motivated suicide bombers, no Muslim terrorists, and no kamikaze pilots.

God should prevent all natural disasters too, like the 2004 Indonesian tsunami that killed a quarter of a million people. If God had prevented it, none of us would ever know he kept it from happening, precisely because it didn't happen. Any person who is supposed to be good would be morally obligated to prevent it, especially if all it took was a "snap" of his fingers to do so.

God should not have created predation in the natural world, either. The amount of creaturely suffering here is atrocious as creatures prey on one another to feed themselves. There is no good reason for this and every reason against it. Something must die so that something else can eat. The spider will wrap its victim up in a claustrophobic ropelike web and inject a fluid that will liquefy its insides so he can suck them out. The mud wasp will grab spiders and stuff them into a mud tunnel while still alive, and then place its young larva inside so they can have something to eat when they hatch. The cat will play with its victims until they have no strength left, and then will eat them while still alive. The boa constrictor will squeeze the breath out of its victim, crushing some of its bones before swallowing it. Killer whales run in packs and will isolate a calf and jump on it until it drowns in saltwater, whereupon the bloody feeding frenzy begins. The crocodile will grab a deer by the antlers and go into a death spiral, breaking its neck and/or drowning it before the feeding frenzy begins. Nature is indeed "red in tooth and claw."

Listen to Gary Paulsen's depiction of wolves who had captured a doe: "Wolves do not kill 'clean.' (If there can be such a thing.) It is a slow, ripping, terrible death for the prey. Two wolves held the doe by the nose, held her head down to the ice, and the other wolves took turns tearing at her rear end, pulling and jerking and tearing, until they were inside of her, pulling out parts of her and all this time she was still on her feet, still alive. . . . She was still on her feet though they had the guts out of her now, pulled back on the ice, eating and pulling, and I wanted it to end, wanted it to be over for her."[38]

Creatures do experience pain in proportion to the development of their central nervous systems, contrary to what René Descartes claimed. Look at any mammal who is being physically assaulted and see for yourself. Take for instance the mouse, while being attacked by a cat. See him grimace, listen to his squeaks, look at his increased breathing rates, and if you can monitor them, check out his increased heart and brain waves. Even when you spray a spider, a cricket, or an ant with Raid you see the convulsions and the futile attempts to run away from the source of the pain. To say these creatures do not feel pain is to say we cannot know anyone beside ourselves who feels any pain. I can imagine a movie scene of *Planet of the*

Apes where the apes are prodding someone with red-hot pokers all the while claiming he doesn't feel any pain, even though he screams like there is pain. If it looks like pain, it is pain.

In lieu of this, all creatures should be vegetarians or vegans. And in order to be sure there is enough vegetation for us all, God could've reduced our mating cycles and/or made edible vegetation like apple trees, corn stalks, blueberry bushes, wheat, and tomato plants to grow as plenteous as wild weeds do today.[39] Paul Copan has an excellent argument using the Bible to show that there was animal death before Adam and Eve's sin (see Psalms 104; Job 38:39–40; 39:28–29; 41:1, 10, 14), and that God did in fact originally create us as meat eaters (see Gen. 1:28; 4:2–4; 7:2, despite Gen. 9:3).[40] Even if Christians believe we were originally created as vegetarians, why should animals suffer because of the sins in Noah's day (Gen. 9:3)? What did animals do wrong?

God didn't even have to create us such that we needed to eat anything at all. If God created the laws of nature then he could've done this. Even if not, since theists believe God can do miracles, he could providentially sustain us all with miraculously created nutrients inside our biological systems throughout our lives, and we wouldn't know anything could've been different.

The truth is, as Paul Draper has argued, "the theory of evolution of species by means of natural selection explains numerous facts much better than the alternative hypothesis, that each species of plant and animal was independently created by God."[41] Specifically Draper argues, "Both pain and pleasure contributes to two central biological goals of individual organisms, namely, survival and reproduction."[42] But since God doesn't need the biological usefulness of pain and pleasure in attaining these twin goals, and since God additionally needs good moral reasons for allowing for pain, theism is antecedently more implausible than, say, atheism. This is particularly persuasive when we consider how long sentient animals had to suffer through this evolutionary process before the arrival of humans.

In fact, there is no good reason for God to have created animals at all, especially since theists do not consider them part of any eternal scheme, nor are there any moral lessons that animals need to learn from their sufferings. As a result, William Rowe's argument about a fawn that is burned in a forest fire and left to die a slow death without any human observer is gratuitous evil, plain and simple. It serves no greater good.

Animals are grown for human consumption under horrible conditions in intensive factory farms, abused in experimental labs or by abusive owners, and they are left to die slow deaths after being hit by cars or in being trapped. The extent of animal suffering cries out against the existence of a good God.

Moral Concern Three

That our bodies will provide a reasonable measure of well-being for us. All that seems to be required here is that we have rational powers to think and to choose, the ability to express our thoughts, and bodies that will allow us to exercise our choices. So we could've been created much differently—easily.

God could've created all human beings with one color of skin. There has been too much race-based killing and slavery, and too many wars because we are not one race with one language.

God could've made all creatures sexually self-reproducing. Asexual reproduction would eliminate gender harassment and discrimination, since there wouldn't be any gender differences between us. Even if there are social benefits that result from two-parent sexual reproduction, societal ties could still be instilled within us by God. And even though God has supposedly chosen a two-parent reproduction for us, God could've at least repeatedly said "women are not inferior to men" and "women are not to be blamed alone for any sin in the Garden of Eden."

God could've created us with much stronger immune systems such that there would be no pandemics which decimate whole populations of people. At the very least, he could've given us the knowledge to cure these diseases the day after he created us.

God could've created us with self-regenerating bodies. When we receive a cut, it heals itself over time, as does a sprained ankle or even a broken bone. But why can't an injured spinal cord be made to heal itself or an amputated leg grow back in a few weeks? If that's all we experienced in this world, we wouldn't know any different.

We find a lot of things in nature that God could've done for us. God could've created us with a much higher threshold of pain. He could've given us wings on our backs so we could fly to safety if we fell off a cliff, and gills to keep us from drowning.

Only if the theist expects very little from such a being can she defend what God has done. Either God isn't smart enough to figure out how to create a good world, or he doesn't have the power to do it, or he just doesn't care. You pick. These are the logical options given this world.

NOTES

1. Elie Wiesel, *Night*, trans. Marion Wiesel (New York: Hill and Wang, 2006), p. 34.

2. I realize there isn't just one problem of evil depending on one's theology. Still I'm dealing with the evangelical non-Calvinstic problem of evil here in this chapter for the most part. On these distinctions, see John S. Feinberg, *The Many Faces of Evil: Theological Systems and the Problems of Evil* (Wheaton, IL: Crossway Books, 2004).

3. Michael Martin, *Atheism: A Philosophical Justification* (Philadelphia: Temple University Press, 1990).

4. James F. Sennett, *This Much I Know: A Postmodern Apologetic*, unpublished.

5. David Hume, *Dialogues Concerning Natural Religion* (London: Thomas Nelson, 1947), part X.

6. Frederick Douglass, *Narrative of the Life of Frederick Douglass: An American Slave* (1845; reprint, Oxford: Oxford University Press, 1999).

7. In Paul Copan, *"That's Just Your Interpretation"* (Grand Rapids, MI: Baker Book House), pp. 171–78.

8. Willard M. Swartley, *Slavery, Sabbath, War & Women* (Scottsdale, PA: Herald Press, 1983), pp. 31–66. See also Paul Finkelman, ed., *Defending Slavery: Proslavery Thought in the Old South, A Brief History with Documents* (Boston: Bedford/St. Martin's, 2003).

9. John T. Noonan Jr., *A Church That Can and Cannot Change: The Development of Catholic Moral Teaching* (Notre Dame, IN: University of Notre Dame Press, 2005).

10. Sam Harris, *Letter to a Christian Nation* (New York: Knopf, 2006), p. 18.

11. William L. Rowe, *Can God Be Free?* (Oxford: Oxford University Press, 2006). Rowe answers Robert M. Adams's argument in "Must God Create the Best?" *Philosophical Review* 81 (1972): 317–32.

12. Nicholas Everitt, *The Non-existence of God* (London: Routledge, 2004), p. 244.

13. Norman Geisler, *Philosophy of Religion* (Grand Rapids, MI: Zondervan, 1978).

14. Clark Pinnock, in *Predestination and Free Will*, ed. David and Randall Basinger (Downers Grove, IL: InterVarsity Press, 1986), p. 58.

15. See the summary of this view by John Hick in *Philosophy of Religion*, 4th ed. (Englewood Cliffs, NJ: Prentice-Hall, 1990), pp. 41–44.

16. John Hick in *Encountering Evil*, ed. Stephen Davis (Atlanta: John Knox Press, 1981), p. 43.

17. According to David Griffin in Davis, *Encountering Evil*.

18. William Hasker, in *The Openness of God*, ed. Pinnock et al. (Downers Grove, IL: InterVarsity Press, 1994), p. 139. With process theology you no longer have the traditional Christian Omni-God, either.

19. Here are just a few additional books to consider: David Hume, *Dialogues Concerning Natural Religion*, parts X–XI; Daniel Howard-Snyder, ed., *The Evidential Argument from Evil* (Bloomington: Indiana University Press, 1996); William L. Rowe, ed., *God and the Problem of Evil* (London: Blackwell, 2001); A. M. Weisberger, *Suffering Belief: Evil and the Anglo-American Defense of Theism* (New York: Peter Lang, 1999); the essays in *The Improbability of God*, ed. Michael Martin and Ricki Monnier (Amherst, NY: Prometheus Books, 2006), pp. 231–336; and a forthcoming book titled *The Evidential Problem of Evil*, by Paul Draper. From a specifically Christian viewpoint see C. S. Lewis, *The Problem of Pain* (New York: Macmillan, 1962); Henri Blocher, *Evil and the Cross* (Downers Grove, IL: InterVarsity Press, 1990); John W. Wenham, *The Goodness of God* (Downers Grove, IL: InterVarsity Press, 1974); N. T. Wright, *Evil and the Justice of God* (Downers Grove, IL: InterVarsity Press, 2006); Michael Peterson, *God and Evil: An Introduction to the Issues* (Boulder, CO: Westview, 1998); Daniel Howard-Snyder's chapter, "God, Evil, and Suffering," in *Reason for the Hope Within*, ed. Michael J. Murray (Grand Rapids, MI: Eerdmans, 1998); Richard Swinburne, *Providence and the Problem of Evil* (Oxford: Oxford University Press, 1998); and Brian Davies, *Reality of God and the Problem of Evil* (London: Continuum International, 2006). This debate is ongoing. Peter van Inwagen's newest argument, in his book *The Problem of Evil* (Oxford: Oxford University Press, 2006), is answered by J. L. Schellenberg in his *The Wisdom to Doubt: A Justification of Religious Skepticism* (Ithaca, NY: Cornell University Press, 2007), pp. 243–96, in which he offers a new argument against the theistic God from evil. Internet Infidels has a debate between Paul Draper and Alvin Plantinga on evil and evolution at http://www.infidels.org/library/modern/paul_draper/intro2.html.

20. J. L. Mackie, "Evil and Omnipotence" *Mind* 64, no. 254 (April 1955).

21. Alvin Plantinga, *God, Freedom, and Evil* (Grand Rapids, MI: Eerdmans, 1974).

22. Richard Swinburne, *The Existence of God* (Oxford: Oxford University Press, 1979), p. 202; J. L. Mackie, *The Miracle of Theism* (Oxford: Oxford University Press, 1982), p. 162.

23. Quentin Smith, "A Sound Logical Argument from Evil"; Hugh LaFollette, "Plantinga on the Free Will Defense"; and Richard La Croix, "Unjustified Evil and God's Choice" can all be found in *The Impossibility of God*, ed. Michael Martin and Ricki Monnier (Amherst, NY: Prometheus Books, 2003).

24. Richard Gale, *On the Nature and Existence of God* (Cambridge: Cambridge University Press, 1991), pp. 98–178; Graham Oppy, *Arguing about Gods* (Cambridge: Cambridge University Press, 2006), pp. 262–68.

25. A. M. Weisberger, *Suffering Belief: Evil and the Anglo-American Defense of Theism* (New York: Peter Lang, 1999), pp. 163–84.

26. Richard R. La Croix, in Martin and Monnier, *The Impossibility of God*, pp. 19–24.

27. Weisberger, *Suffering Belief*, p. 39.

28. Swinburne, *The Existence of God*, p. 219.

29. William Rowe, "Evil and Theodicy," *Philosophical Topics* 16, no. 2 (1988): 119–32.

30. William Rowe, "The Problem of Evil and Some Varieties of Atheism," *American Philosophical Quarterly* 16, no. 4 (October 1979).

31. Terence Penelhum, "Divine Goodness and the Problem of Evil," in *Readings in the Philosophy of Religion*, ed. Baruch Brody (Englewood Cliffs, NJ: Prentice-Hall, 1974), pp. 214–26.

32. Corey Washington said this in a debate with Dr. William Lane Craig.

33. Weisberger, *Suffering Belief*, p. 102. Christian theists like Victor Reppert argue that since nonbelievers cannot completely explain all of the complexity in the universe, we shouldn't fault him for not being able to completely explain why God allows so much suffering and purportedly commanded the genocide of the Amalekites in the Bible. (See Victor Reppert's blog at: http://dangerousidea.blogspot.com/.) He makes an interesting point. However, I don't think there is any parity here. The main reason is that scientists are indeed making great strides in explaining the complexity of this universe, along with the evolution of life, whereas, if my argument here is correct, Christian theists cannot even begin to adequately explain why God allows so much suffering in this world. Apart from that, I'm not the one who must also justify the miracles in the Bible, or theories about the incarnation and the Trinity. Nor am I asked to justify the atonement, or the five stages of gospel canonization via uninspired people, leading to the claim the New Testament is inspired, from which he gains his Christian beliefs in the first place. Christian theists like Reppert must do this *before* getting to the problem of suffering and why God purportedly commanded the genocide of the Amalekites.

34. Hume, *Dialogues Concerning Natural Religion*, part X.

35. Pierre Bayle, *Historical and Critical Dictionary* (1679), s.v. "Paulicians."

36. Paul Draper, in *The Evidential Argument from Evil*, p. 24.

37. David Hume first suggested such things as these in his book *Dialogues Concerning Natural Religion*, part XI.

38. Gary Paulsen, *Woodsong* (New York: Simon & Schuster, 1990).

39. See Quentin Smith, "An Atheological Argument from Evil Natural Laws," in Martin and Monnier, *The Improbability of God*, pp. 235–49.

40. Copan, *"That's Just Your Interpretation,"* pp. 150–52.

41. Paul Draper, in *The Evidential Argument from Evil*, p. 25.

42. Ibid., p. 15.

13

THE PROBLEM OF EVIL

Part 2: Objections Answered

In this part I'll deal with the various theistic responses to the problem of evil. Christian theists will not concede God's omniscience, or God's omnipotence, or God's omnibenevolence, since they are entailed from many biblical statements and from Anselmian philosophical considerations.

Some theists like C. S. Lewis, in *Mere Christianity*, will argue from the start that there can be no evil without absolute goodness (God) to measure it against. "How do you know a line is crooked without having some knowledge of what a straight line is?" In other words, I need some sort of objective moral in order to say that something is "evil." But the word *evil* here is used both as a term describing the fact that there is suffering and at the same time as a moral term to describe whether or not such suffering makes the belief in a good God improbable, and that's an equivocation in the word's usage. The fact that there is suffering is undeniable. Whether it's considered an *evil* that makes the belief in a good God improbable is the subject for debate. I'm talking about pain—the kind that turns our stomachs. Why is there so much of it when there is a good omnipotent God? I'm arguing that the amount of intense suffering in this world makes the belief in a good God improbable from a theistic perspective, and I may be a relativist, a pantheist, or a witchdoctor and still ask about the internal consistency of what a theist believes.

The dilemma for the theist is to reconcile senseless suffering in the world with her own beliefs (not mine) that all suffering is for a greater good. It's an internal problem for the theist, so it doesn't matter what the beliefs are for the person making this argument. The person making this argument is merely using the logical tool for assessing arguments called the *reductio ad absurdum*, which attempts to reduce to absurdity the claims of a person. The technique is to force a claimant to choose between accepting the consequences of what she believes, no matter how absurd it seems, or rejecting one or more premises in her argument. The person making this argument does not believe the claimant and is trying to show why those beliefs are misguided and false to some degree, depending on the force of the counterargument. It's that simple. If skeptics cannot use this argument on this issue, then we should disallow all *reductio ad absurdum* type arguments.

Christian theists object that in the natural world nothing can count as evil for the atheist, since everything that happens is part of nature. So they claim atheists like me have no objective basis for arguing there is any evil in the natural world that can count against the existence of the Christian God. But this is fallacious reasoning. What counts as evil in my atheist worldview is a separate problem from the Christian problem of evil. They are distinctly separate issues. Christians cannot seek to answer their internal problem by claiming atheists also have a problem with evil. Yet that's exactly what they do here, which is an informal fallacy known as a *red herring*, or skirting the issue. Christians must deal with their internal problem. Atheists must do likewise. I will not skirt my specific problem by claiming Christians have one. I adjure them to do the same.

The fact that many professional philosophers agree with this can be seen in reading through the book *The Evidential Argument from Evil*, edited by Daniel Howard-Snyder.[1] Not one scholarly Christian theist attempted to make this argument in that book; not Swinburne, not Plantinga, not Alston, not Wykstra, not Van Inwagen, and not Howard-Snyder. I suggest it's because they know it is not dealing with the problem at all. They recognize it as a bogus argument, and obviously so.

That this is a theistic problem can be settled once and for all by merely reminding the Christian that she would still have to deal with this problem even if I never raised it at all. That is, even if I did not argue that the existence of evil presents a serious problem for the Christian view of God, the Christian would still have to satisfactorily answer the problem for herself. So to turn around and argue that as an atheist I need to have an objective moral standard to make this argument is nonsense. It's an internal problem that would still demand an answer if no atheist ever argued for it. The problem of evil is one of the reasons why process theologians have conceded that God is not omnipotent. It didn't take atheists to persuade them to abandon God's omnipotence at all. The problem speaks for itself. There is nothing wrong with a Christian who wishes to evaluate the internal consistency of her own belief system. To say otherwise is to affirm pure fideism.

Other than that, the theist has two responses to my argument. The first response is what I call the "God Can't Do It" Defense, and the second response is what I call the Ignorance Defense. On the one hand, God can't remove the suffering in this world because of such things as the independent and neutral laws of nature, or because of "greater goods" like human free will, or because suffering is part of God's plan for "soul-making," which requires "epistemic distance." Or on the other hand, God is so omniscient that we simply cannot understand God's reasons for allowing suffering in this world. I'll take them each in turn.

THE "GOD CAN'T DO IT" DEFENSE

There are several Christian responses to the argument from evil. Let me deal with them each in turn.

"Good cannot exist without evil, and/or pleasure cannot exist without pain." This is obviously false, since the theist believes in the goodness of a heavenly existence without pain. Even in this world where disease causes suffering, I can still experience the pleasure of good health without knowing disease. Besides, if suffering is needed to experience pleasure, then isn't pleasure needed to experience suffering? But this too is obviously false, since someone can suffer a horrible short life and then die without any pleasure.[2] And how does this apply to the sufferings of animals? Weisberger argues: "This type of explanation only serves to account for natural evil among beings who can appreciate its absence in some cognitive fashion."[3] Furthermore, if it's true that we need some suffering to help us experience pleasure, then why do we need so much suffering? That's the whole point. Why all of the senseless suffering?

"Evil is necessary as a means to good." Even if this is so, God could've created a world with far fewer evils, which is my point. Besides, how does this solve the problem of animal suffering? What good do they get out of their suffering? Nonetheless, such a solution assumes a good God initially created the world with the proper balance of suffering. If so, the question becomes whether or not we should try to alleviate suffering. On the one hand, a theist is the first one to say we should alleviate suffering wherever we can, even though God is not obligated to do the same. But if we do, then aren't we also reducing the total good created by God, since suffering is good for us? Maybe we should rue the day that someone found a vaccine for tuberculosis, or polio? Maybe our real duty would be to increase human suffering, since it molds character? On the other hand, if suffering can be alleviated by modern medicine without making it worse off for us as a whole, then those very evils we eliminated were not necessary for our good in the first place. Can the theist have it both ways?[4]

"It's not God's fault that we bring a great deal of suffering on ourselves." After Hurricane Katrina hit New Orleans, someone suggested that people shouldn't have lived there in the first place. But where on earth can we escape from all of the potential evils out there? We may instead move into a tornado zone, or one prone to earthquakes, floods, fires, or the like. While we try to escape from one evil, we run smack dab into another. By escaping a hurricane, we get bit by a black widow spider, or fall prey to a parasite, or a poisonous plant, a poisonous creature, a ravenous wolf, a fire, and so on. And even if there might be one safe place on earth, then such a place would quickly become overcrowded, which would result in other kinds of suffering because of the overcrowding.

We have also created some diseases and viruses because of the use of chemicals to produce crops or because of some scientific experiments. But we don't always know in advance that we are creating these diseases. We are only attempting to make life more comfortable and to save more lives. The diseases are inadvertently created. Our reasons are benign. So it would still be God's fault if we attempt to use the faculties he supposedly gave us in the environment that we have been given. When humans have created such things on purpose, as in chemical warfare, that's a question for why God doesn't control our choices.

"Evil is the punishment for wrongdoing." The supposed fall of man in the Garden of Eden is supposed to account for the sheer amount of our natural suffering in our world. This cannot be since some of it must have been in the garden itself, as Paul Copan has argued. Besides, the whole story is mythical in nature, much like one of Jesus' parables.[5] Even if the Genesis story describes a real event, the punishment is far worse than the crime. The crime was not rebellion, but curiosity, selfishness, and ignorance—the very things God created in them. The whole idea that this world is the result of Adam and Eve's sin is sickening. In Richard Gale's words: "The whole idea of a deity who is so vain that if his children do not choose to love and obey him he will bring down all sorts of horrible evils on them and their innocent descendents is horrendous."[6]

Furthermore, how could Adam and Eve know that God was telling the truth? The serpent questioned this, didn't he? So there wasn't enough evidence for Adam and Eve to know for sure that what the serpent said was not true. Why not? Since God is supposedly omniscient, then he should've known how much evidence they needed. So if they sinned, he knew in advance that he didn't give them enough evidence to believe and heed the warning. If God didn't give them enough evidence to know he was telling the truth, then God shares the blame for their sins. Why? Because if they knew for sure what would happen, they wouldn't have sinned.

People in biblical times defended God against the problem of evil by blaming themselves and their own sins for the natural disasters that God sent them. They believed God controlled all natural happenings (Exod. 12:23, 29, 30; 32:35; Num. 11:33; 16:46–50; 25:18; 2 Sam. 24:15–16). Why don't very many Christians today use this same response to exonerate God from natural disasters? In ancient times, disasters were usually explained in only one way: God was upset with people because of their sins. And that's the explanation we find most often in the Bible, although there are a few notable exceptions (Job; Luke 13; John 9). But even here we see a God who could do anything with the world of nature that he wanted to do without regard for the ordered world and laws of nature.[7]

In Job, for instance, we see the biblical answer for the problem of evil in the first two chapters. The answer was that God is testing us with disasters and he allows Satan to do us harm so that he might be glorified from our actions. That is a sick answer to the problem of evil, and here's why: Medical ethics will not allow us to experiment on human beings with life-threatening procedures, nor with procedures that might cause other serious complications. And they certainly don't allow us to experiment on anyone involuntarily. The other people in the story—like Job's family—don't even matter to God at all. But this is what we find God doing to Job and his family, presumably because he can. What we really want to know is if Job's God cares for him and his family, and he doesn't.

In Job it's further maintained that since God gives life, he can take it away (Job 1:21). In his debate with Keith Parsons, William Lane Craig claimed God was justified in ordering the genocide of the Amalekites because he is the author and giver of life, and as such, he can take life as he chooses. But this is internally problematic and contrary to Christian morality itself. If I give someone a gift, I cannot just take it back. Doing so is both immoral and illegal. I cannot give someone blood to save her life and then demand it back from her. Nor can I give someone money for a life-saving medical procedure and then later demand the money back, or take her life later because I previously saved it. Why can't I? Because once a gift is given it is no longer mine to take back. If Christians respond that God's gifts always have strings attached, like our obedience, then God never truly gives us anything. What kind of gift is it if I save a person's life and then threaten to kill her if she doesn't do as I say? For Christians to retort that God can do whatever he wants to because he's God, still doesn't morally justify his actions.

In Luke 13:1–5 we find Jesus commenting on why a couple of disasters took place. Were these people worse sinners than those who escaped the particular disasters? Jesus' answer is an emphatic, "No!" His point says nothing at all against the culturally accepted view that our sins cause disasters. He only says that these people were no more guilty than those who didn't suffer these disasters. So apparently everyone deserves the disasters that occur; it's just that some do not experience what their sins deserve.

In John 9 Jesus' disciples asked him who sinned that a particular man was born blind. His answer was that neither he nor his parents sinned. But this was a special case, for the reason he was born blind was so "that the work of God might be displayed in him," and then it says Jesus healed him. So his "purpose" in being born blind was for him to later be healed by Jesus.

Many Christians would agree with Rabbi Daniel Lapin, who tried to explain God's goodness in light of the Indonesian tsunami that killed a quarter of a million people. In the process of arguing his case, he said: "God runs this world with as little supernatural interference as possible." Now how does he know that? Such a belief was not shared by most all ancient people before the rise of the repeatable results of modern science. So why don't many theists argue the way biblical writers would argue? Let me suggest that it's because they are modern people after all. And let me also suggest that early Christians would have condemned modern Christians who simply say, "bad things just happen." For them, even the very die cast from a man's hand is controlled by God (Prov. 16:33).

Surely, the punishment for sin by God cannot account for everyone who ever died from a tornado, a hurricane, a fire, a flood, an epidemic, or a famine. Many innocent people have died. The distribution of disease and pain is not related to the virtue of those punished. The so-called punishments simply do not fit the "crimes." Just look at our own "selfish" system of punishments, and compare that with the God's punishments in the Bible. Our punishments are kinder and gentler. They're civil. The punishments of God in the Bible are barbaric. We simply put criminals in jail. We don't break both arms of an infant because her father lied at the office. According to Weisberger: "It is far from clear how infants who die of diseases or are born terribly deformed with paralyzing ailments such as spina bifida, or with other defects such as blindness, deafness or retardation, can be believed to have sinned so that they are deserving of punishment."[8] Furthermore, this solution does nothing to answer the question of why animals suffer. What did they do wrong?

"Evil is necessary for building character, or 'soul-making,' which is a higher good." Again this does not explain the sufferings of animals, and it's difficult to see how this explains senseless evils. Theistic scholars such as Kelly James Clark,[9] Eleonore Stump,[10] and others argue, in William P. Alston's words, that "a perfectly good God would not wholly sacrifice the welfare of one of his intelligent creatures simply in order to achieve a good for others, or for himself. This would be incompatible with his concern for the welfare of each of his creatures."[11] Therefore, the theist has the difficult task of showing how the very people who suffered and died in the Nazi concentration camps were better off for having suffered, since the hindsight lessons we've learned from the Holocaust cannot be used to justify the sufferings of the people involved. It's implausible that their sufferings did more to teach them the virtues of character and cooperation than would banding together to win an athletic contest or helping someone to build a house. Sometimes the pain and suffering of this world is so great that it is unbearable for people who are broken by this world and commit suicide. How does that build character?

"The purpose of intense suffering is to cause us to turn to God." If so, God has done a poor job of this. The pain and the question of human suffering account for more defections from theism than probably any other cause. What else can explain why the problem of evil is the most serious one for Christians? God would be found to be building heaven for the millions on the screams of billions of people who will supposedly wind up in hell.

William Lane Craig and J. P. Moreland have argued that the chief purpose in life is not happiness, but "the knowledge of God," "which can bring eternal happiness" to his creatures. Then by using the statistics in Patrick Johnstone's *Operation World*,[12] they attempt to show that "it may well be the case that natural and moral evils are part of the means God uses to draw people into his kingdom." They report that following disasters in various countries around the world, the number of Christians have increased. They also make the argument that the number of committed Christians in the world has grown significantly across the centuries when compared to the percentage of people in the world, and is growing faster today than ever. Craig and Moreland write, "It is not at all improbable that this astonishing growth in God's kingdom is due in part to the presence of natural and moral evils in the world."[13]

In an online article titled "Human Suffering and the Acceptance of God" (1997), Michael Martin argues against this idea. He questions their statistical facts, of course, but then continues to argue that: "1) If God's aim was to have the maximal number of people believe in God, as Craig has argued, he has not been successful. Billions of people have not come to believe in the theistic God. 2) There are many better ways God could have done to increase belief in him. For example: God could have spoken from the Heavens in all known languages so no human could doubt his existence and his message. God could have implanted belief of God and his message in everyone's mind. In recent times God could have communicated with millions of people by interrupting prime time TV programs and giving his message. 3) Why is there not more suffering since it produces believers, especially in America, since unbelief is on the rise? 4) There is also the ethical issue. Why would an all good, all powerful God choose to bring about acceptance in this way since God could bring about belief in him in many ways that do not cause suffering? Not only does suffering as a means to achieve acceptance conflict with God's moral character, it also seems to conflict with his rationality. Whether or not suffering is a cause of acceptance is one thing. The crucial question is whether it is a good reason for acceptance."[14] This whole argument reminds me of Jeff Lowder's comment: "It's like saying in order to get my wife to love me I have to beat the crap out of her."[15]

"Evil is due to free will." I've already suggested ways God could restrict our freedom to commit senseless evils, and this solution likewise does nothing to solve animal suffering. If God gave us more freedom than we can be responsible for, then he's mainly responsible for the horrible deeds we do. J. L. Mackie asks, "Why would a wholly good and omnipotent god give to human beings—and also, perhaps, to angels—the freedom which they have misused?"[16] Pierre Bayle exposes this difficulty: "It is in the essence of a benefactor to refrain from giving any gift which he knows would be the ruin of the recipient. . . . Free agency is not a good gift after all, for it has caused the ruin of the human race in Adam's sin, the eternal damnation for the greater part of his descendants, and created a world of a dreadful deluge of moral and physical evils."[17]

Like I said, giving us free will is like giving a razor blade to a two-year-old child. Razor blades can be used for good purposes by people who know how to use them, like scraping off a sticker from a window or in shaving. That's because adults know how to use them properly. We could give an adult a razor blade. We cannot give a two-year-old one, for if we did, we would be blamed if that child hurts himself. Just like a younger child should not be given a license to drive or left unattended at the mall, so also if God gives us responsibilities before we can handle them, then he is to be blamed for giving them to us.

Theistic scholar William P. Alston argues that "for all we know, God does sometimes intervene to prevent human agents from doing wicked things they would otherwise have done."[18] My response: First, this is unfalsifiable. Second, it's implausible God has done this at all, since there are obvious cases of senseless suffering in this world he could alleviate. Third, this is known as the fallacy of the beard. To ask us to draw a line here is like asking us to pluck out whiskers until we can say which whisker, when plucked, no longer makes it a beard. Hence, we might not be able to specify how much God should intervene, but we know that with all of the intense suffering caused by free will choices that God doesn't intervene enough, even if he might do so sometimes. Likewise, according to Bruce Russell, "We can know that some penalty (say, a fine of $1) is not an effective deterrent to armed robbery even if there is no sharp cut-off point between penalties that are effective deterrents and those that are not."[19] Fourth, such an objection doesn't say anything about this particular world and the suffering in it. This is the world we are looking at, and there simply isn't any evidence that God has intervened. The question that needs to be asked is whether or not we would expect a good God to avert the Holocaust, and the answer is that morality requires it. Finally, if there was no intense suffering or there was an adequate explanation for suffering, my whole argument would fail.

According to William P. Alston, if God were to act to intervene in every case of incipient wrongdoing, "Human agents would no longer have a real choice between good and evil."[20] However, eliminating intense cases of suffering would still allow humans with significant real choices. Besides, there's a difference between having a real choice and being able to actualize our choices. For all we know, God could turn bullets into butter and baseball bats into rolls of tissue paper whenever they are used to cause harm, for God can surely judge us by our intentions to do wrong alone.

EXCURSUS: THE NATURE AND VALUE OF FREE WILL

This brings up the whole question of the nature and value of free will, so let me address it here, beginning with a statement from A. M. Weisberger: "The free will defender must assume that free will is of such superior value that any evils which result from its use are justified." Since this is so, "the free will defender is compelled to say why free will is of such supreme value. Instead, the free will defender merely assumes that such an assessment of free will as especially valuable is unanimous and offers little, if anything, in way of reasons for this assessment." (On the nature of free will, see note.)[21]

A. M. Weisberger asks us, "Which is more desirable, a world in which there is no free will but where humans always do what is right and in which there is no suffering, or a world such as the present? It seems many of us would opt for the former world, even if that meant we had only the appearance of free will and not the real thing, since all our choices would be predetermined to choose good-producing actions over evil-producing ones."[22] If instead, God did not create us with free will, then Calvinistic theology must justify why our particular world brings God more glory than a different world where he decrees from eternity that his creatures all perfectly obey him. If humans do not have free will, then there can be no rational justification for the suffering that we experience in this world. Such a God as that is only worthy of our disgust, since our world could so easily have been different if he merely pulled our strings to do good and not evil and made us feel as if we were freely choosing what we do.

Furthermore, we must ask ourselves how much freedom human beings actually have in this world. It does absolutely no good at all to have free will and not also have the ability to exercise it. We humans are arbitrarily constrained in what we can choose to do. Most women do not have the upper body strength needed to stop a would-be attacker, while some people don't have the rational capacity needed to spot a con artist. Gender, race, age, brain matter, where we're born, and how we're raised all limit the free choices available to each of us. Both our genes and our environment restrict what choices are available for us to make.

I dare say that if God exists and created a different "soul" inside my mother's womb at the precise moment I was conceived, and if that organism experienced everything I did and learned the exact same lessons throughout life in the same order that I did at the same intensity, then the resulting person would be me, even given free will. And if you won't go that far, the limits of our choices are still set by our genetic material and our environment. We don't have as much free will as we think. All of us have a very limited range of free choices anyway, if we have any at all. So theists should have no objection to God intervening when someone chooses to do horrible deeds, especially since theists also believe God can restrict our choices just like he purportedly hardened Pharaoh's heart against Moses. If we already have limited choices anyway, then there should be no objection to God further limiting our choices when we seek to cause intense suffering in this world. I've already suggested some reasonable ways God had at his disposal to limit our free will given this world.

If having real free will is a good thing, then why is it we ourselves in human societies don't hold it to be so valuable? According to Weisberger: "We do not normally hold freedom to be intrinsically valuable, as evidenced in the willingness we show to limit our freedom to achieve goods, and especially when such freedom gives rise to suffering. . . . The prevention of heinous crimes, even if such prevention limits another's exercise of free will, improves the world."[23] Theists are the first ones to say unrestricted freedom isn't a good thing.

There is also the problem of free will in heaven and in hell. What about free will in heaven? Paul Copan offers three possibilities with regard to free will in heaven:[24] First, that through our truly libertarian free actions on earth we gain access to heaven where we no longer have this freedom to sin. James F. Sennett has argued for this view (see note).[25] But if heaven is a place where we no longer have the freedom to sin, then God could've bypassed our earthly existence altogether. If there is no free will in heaven, then why not just create us all in heaven, as I've argued? What does it matter what we did or didn't do on earth? Second, that God foreknows that no one who enters heaven will freely choose to sin. But if God has that kind of foreknowledge, then again, what is the purpose of creating this particular world? It appears to be a cruel game of hide and seek, where God hides and we must find him, and only the few who find him will be rewarded while the many who don't are punished when they die. If God has foreknowledge, then why didn't he just foreknow who would find him even before creating them, and simply place them in heaven in the first place? That way, there'd be no one punished for not finding him. If heaven is a reward, then "it seems absurd for a wholly good God to force humanity into a position of ignorance regarding correct moral choice and then hold people accountable for such a choice."[26] Furthermore, if this world is to teach us the virtues of courage, patience, and generosity in the face of suffering, then most all of those virtues are irrelevant in a heavenly bliss where there is no suffering or pain. Third, that those who enter heaven will be in "the unmediated presence of God" such that "not sinning will be a 'no brainer'—even though it remains a possibility." But if this is the case, then as I've already argued, why do Christians think the devil rebelled against God, since he was supposedly in the direct unmediated presence of God?

Then there is the problem of free will in hell. Theists like Copan typically claim that people in hell continue in their rebellion against God and so the "doors of hell are locked from the inside." Why is there this difference? Why are the saints in heaven rewarded for their tortures here on earth by the removal of their free will to make moral choices, while the damned are punished by the retention of it? If those who are damned have their free will taken away, then they too could be brought up to heaven. So if free will is such a good thing, then why isn't it such a good thing in the eschatological end? Why not continue to grant it for the saints in heaven and take it away from the damned?

David Wood, of www.answeringinfidels.com, whom I've debated on the problem of suffering, claims that before Satan sinned in heaven, there was free will and that God held him at some sort of "epistemic distance" so that Satan was ignorant about God's absolute love and power. At the consummation of the ages, however, God will allow the saints in his direct unmediated presence, and as a result there will be no moral choices, even if there is free will. By being in God's direct presence there would be no reason to sin against him, since the saints would see his love and power for what it truly is. They wouldn't desire to rebel against God, and even if they did, they would know doing so would be futile. But Wood's proposed solution lacks biblical evidence and goes against the notion of a good, reasonable God. Even if true, it merely places the problem of evil back a step, into heaven itself.

What Wood proposes is that God wanted creatures in heaven who truly loved him and obeyed him, and that this is the best way for God to have done this. But just consider the motivations for God wanting this state of affairs. What is the value of this to God? Why does he want anything? A want is not exactly like a need, but to want something, anything, implies a lack of something. What did God lack? He lacked people who freely choose to love him, Wood will claim. Why was this important? What is there about people who freely love him that is different than people who simply love him? And why does he want anyone to love him in the first place? Why does he care? Does he need to be stroked, appreciated, needed?

Why is it more valuable to a good God that he create free moral creatures at all when the results have been horrific for millions upon millions and probably billions of people down through the centuries? Why? The Christian answer is that God wants creatures who freely choose to love and obey him and that this justifies why he purportedly created us with free will. That is, what God wanted is more important than that people will suffer. At first blush this sounds exactly like God is more concerned with his wants than with our wants. He wants people to freely love and obey him no matter what the consequences are for most of the people who are born into this world. But if this is true, then how can God's love be called *agape*, or self-giving love? God's wants are placed above our wants, and we do not like to experience such intense suffering in this world or the next one.

For many theists there will be "many" compared to the "few" who suffer in hell, however conceived. When we take into consideration the sheer massive weight of suffering in this life and the next life for the "many," it seems entirely rational to conclude that the value of having free moral agents cannot outweigh the pain and suffering caused by these free moral agents to others and to themselves.

THE "GOD CAN'T DO IT" DEFENSE CONTINUED

"Evil is due to the need for 'Epistemic Distance.'" Theists claim that God needs to keep a correct "epistemic distance" from us so he can know for sure we truly love him and that he isn't forcing himself on us with the power and love of his direct presence.[27] This is one of the reasons offered for the perceived "hiddenness of God."[28] He hides himself in the bushes, so to speak, to see if we really want to love and obey him. But think about this. If I did that with my wife, what would be the result? If I didn't let her see the real me, if I hid my real love and strength from her and watched to see if she really loved me, then it would be a false test of her love. I would be wondering whether she loved a caricature of me and not me. Even if it's agreed that God should not over-power us so that we feel forced to obey him, why does he also hide his goodness from us? Let's say I didn't show my wife my true compassionate nature. Should I expect that she will love me the same as if I did show her my true self? No! Why should God think that it's any different when it comes to loving him? We see plenty of suffering in this world and we ask whether or not God is good and deserving to be worshipped. If we conclude he isn't a good God and reject him because of this "epistemic distance," then he should know we have not rejected who he really is. We have merely rejected what he revealed himself to be in his creation. If that's the case, he shouldn't be upset at us when we do reject his love. Why? Because he doesn't show us his true love. There is little by way of our experience that leads us to think he loves us, or that he exists. And if so, then why should he be surprised at our reactions?

Weisberger writes, "The real problem with epistemic distance is in showing how humans can ever do right or discover the will of God intelligently in the apparent absence of God. . . . It is impossible for anyone to intentionally do what is required when it is not known, for how can we be expected to fulfill God's commandments if there is true epistemic distance?"[29]

Christians respond that, since God is omniscient, he knows the proper distance needed to test our love and that he's clearly revealed himself enough for us to love and obey him in the appropriate degree proportionate to this distance. When Christians respond like this, they are reverting to a prior held faith statement that is outside the bounds of the questions I am asking. I'm looking at what I see and I'm questioning the goodness of God and this so-called needed epistemic distance. I'm wondering why this world was created, if it was. I'm questioning whether this God even exists based upon what I see. Christians respond that God knows what he's doing without an argument that makes his actions seem reasonable to me. I question his motivations. I doubt his plans. I reject his purportedly good results. My questions must be answered before I can accept that he knows the proper distance and that he can judge us fairly. In creating this supposed "epistemic distance" between him and us to gain our love, God has also created so much human and animal carnage that I cannot accept his supposed good wisdom in doing so.

"Evil is a necessary by-product of causal natural laws." The theist objects that by making these suggested changes to this world it might go against the laws of nature and/or upset our fine-tuned ecosystem. Theistic philosopher Peter Van

Inwagen claims that for all we know "only in a universe very much like ours could intelligent life, or even sentient life, develop by the nonmiraculous operation of the laws of nature. And the natural evolution of higher sentient life in a universe like ours essentially involves suffering."[30] However, the theist faces a dilemma here: if God created the laws of nature in the first place, then he could've created a different set of laws, and if he didn't create these laws, then where did they come from? Why then did God choose to create this universe rather than a different one, or not create at all?

Besides, since this present ecosystem is causing so much intense suffering, the question for the theist is why this ecosystem is more important to God than one without so much suffering that constantly needs divine miraculous maintenance. People should matter more to God than a fined-tuned ecosystem. If changing the environment in any of these ways requires some adjustment that does not accord with any known laws of nature, what's the problem? The ordering of the world by general laws "seems nowise necessary" to God, as David Hume argued. The theist typically believes God created the universe out of nothing, and if he can do that, he can do anything in his world. Christian scholar Richard Swinburne agrees: "What theism claims about God is that . . . he can make planets move in quite different ways, and chemical substances explode or not explode under quite different conditions from those which now govern their behavior. God is not limited by the laws of nature; he makes them and he can change or suspend them—if he chooses."[31] In a 2003 debate with Eddie Tabash on the existence of God, Swinburne said that instead of gravity, God could've make "bodies repel each other," or that he could "raise this stadium into the air."

God could even perform one or more perpetual miracles here. As far as the theist knows, the whole world operates by perpetual miracles anyway. Are "all things possible with God," or not? Why is it that God can't cause us to levitate whenever we think about levitating, much like how Superman flies through the air by thinking of flying without any known mechanism for propulsion? Why can't God do this miracle? He could miraculously do anything in the physical world regardless of whether or not he could create a different set of natural laws.

A theist might object that it doesn't make sense to say God could ensure that such things happened habitually by means of perpetual miracles. If they happened perpetually, we wouldn't call them miracles, a theist might say. We would just understand them as the laws of nature. So by asking God to do perpetual miracles is like asking, "Could God have had the world operate according to different laws of physics from the ones that actually obtain?" Yet that's exactly what I'm asking. Can God do perpetual miracles or not? Yes or no? I don't care what we might call them if God decides to do them. At that point all we would be dealing with is nomenclature.

Peter Van Inwagen further asks us to consider whether or not the actual sufferings of beasts are a "graver defect" in our world than massive irregularity would be: "massive irregular worlds are not only massively irregular but massively deceptive (i.e., a world created 5 minutes ago, or a world where beasts feel no pain)." He claims, "it is plausible to suppose that deception, and a fortiori, massive deception, is inconsistent with the nature of a perfect being."[32] And he considers these two states of affairs "morally equivalent" such that "a creator could not be faulted on moral grounds for choosing either over the other." However, any philosophically trained person already knows this universe is massively deceptive. We naively think we see and hear reality just as it is, but that is patently false. What we see and hear is filtered by our particular five senses. If we could see and hear the whole electromagnetic and sonic spectra, we would basically see and hear "white noise." Physicists also know that the ground we walk on is actually moving on the microscopic level like swarming bees, even though we're deceived into thinking it doesn't move at all. Given this present massively deceptive universe, if God exists, it's simply not incompatible with the nature of a perfect being. Therefore, to say that a "massively irregular world" might be "morally equivalent" to the massive sufferings of animals is nonsense.

William P. Alston argued that a "conceptual possibility is by no means sufficient for metaphysical possibility. . . . It is much more difficult to determine what is metaphysically possible or necessary than to determine what is conceptually possible or necessary," in our world.[33] However, in response: (1) If this is the case, then as I've already argued, why create anything at all? (2) I see no metaphysical impossibility for many of the suggestions I've made, even within our particular set of natural laws—like creating all humans one color of skin, with better immune systems and as vegetarians, since we already find instances of these things in the natural world. (3) Even if this is the case, the question still remains to be answered, why did God create these particular natural laws in the first place? (4) Finally, why doesn't God do perpetual miracles to avert senseless suffering?

I maintain that the burden of proof is upon the Christian to argue why certain things were metaphysically impossible for God to do. Anything less than this would mean such a God could have done these things. I am suggesting there are things that the Christian God could have done to reduce the amount of human suffering in the world without creating chaos in the world, without inhibiting our character development, that would help draw (rather than repel) humans to him. If he could have done that but didn't, then there is pointless suffering that serves no purpose. It must be metaphysically impossible for God to eliminate this suffering, otherwise God is to be blamed for this gratuitous (or pointless) evil.

THE PROBLEM OF GOODNESS AND THE HYPOTHESIS OF INDIFFERENCE

There is another tactic I can employ when dealing with theistic answers to the problem of evil, and it can be found once again, in David Hume, who offered us four choices about the moral nature of "the first causes of the universe." Either they are perfectly good, they are perfectly evil, they are "opposite and have both goodness and malice," or they have "neither goodness nor malice." (Paul Draper calls the last hypothesis the *Hypothesis of Indifference*, or HI.) Hume (speaking through Philo) argues for HI in these words: "Mixed phenomena can never prove the two former unmixed principles. And the uniformity and steadiness of general laws seem to oppose the third. The fourth, therefore, seems by far more probable."[34]

When it comes to the opposite claims that "the first causes of the universe" are either perfectly good or perfectly evil, it seems implausible to accept either of these extremes given the fact that we see both goodness and suffering in our world. This is what Hume calls "mixed phenomena," in that we see both goodness and malice in our world. Those who argue that these causes are "perfectly good" have to explain why there is so much evil in this world, known as the problem of evil. Those who argue that these causes are "perfectly evil" have to explain why there is so much goodness in this world, known as the problem of goodness.

So let's consider the problem of goodness, rather than the problem of evil, for Hume's first two choices, placed in the context of a Supreme Being. Why is there goodness, we might ask, in a world created by a malicious being? The answers provided would be the same ones that theists who believe in a perfectly good God use to explain the problem of evil, such as: (1) Goodness is the result of truly free actions. (2) Goodness is necessary for evil to exist. (3) Rather than this world being a place for "soul making," it is designed for "soul breaking." (4) Any good in the world will produce greater evils. (5) We may not know why this malicious Supreme Being allows goodness, but he knows what he's doing. Since the same arguments produce two opposite and contradictory conclusions, both conclusions are implausible—they cancel each other out. As Steven M. Cahn argues, "if this is neither the worst of all possible worlds nor the best of all possible worlds, then it could not have been created by either an all-powerful, all-evil demon or an all-powerful, all-good deity."[35]

THE IGNORANCE DEFENSE

The Christian theist will finally punt to mystery, with what I call the "ignorance defense," when she says, "we just don't know why bad things happen, but we can trust God knows what he's doing." Theists claim everything will work out from the perspective of eternity. They claim that the sufferings of this present life are not worthy to be compared with the joys of eternity (Rom. 8:18, 28). But this presupposes what needs to be shown. We are on this side of heaven and hell, and from here we want to know if there really is a heaven and a hell. From here we just don't know. According to David Hume: "Look around this universe. What an immense profusion of beings. How hostile and destructive to each other! How insufficient all of them for their own happiness! How contemptible or odious to the spectator! The whole presents nothing but the idea of a blind nature, impregnated by a great vivifying principle, and pouring forth from her lap, without discernment or parental care, her maimed and abortive children!"[36]

Furthermore, when it comes to the afterlife, what about the damned? No matter what conception of eternity without God the Christian proposes, the fact that most all human beings will suffer this fate is incompatible with the theistic conception of a good God. Such a punishment simply does not fit the crime, just like the punishments from the supposed fall in the *Garden of Eden* don't fit the crime. (See chapter 22.)

Besides, even for those who enter heaven, Madden and Hare argue this is very much like "a torturer telling his victim on the rack that he need not be concerned, for by and by he will be sent to a luxurious spa. To be sure, the victim is delighted to hear that he has such a future ahead of him, but he still cannot understand why he need be tortured before he goes. The torture remains gratuitous for anything the spa argument shows to the contrary."[37] In the absence of good reasons for the torture itself, the final eternal state, even if it's pleasant for all of us, only compensates us for the evils experienced in this life. But compensation for suffering cannot justify the suffering endured; otherwise, anyone could be justified in torturing another person so long as the victim is later compensated.

Theists like Alvin Plantinga and others claim we just don't know how the future will make up for present evils, but that God does, since he's omniscient. Alvin Plantinga wrote: "Say that an evil is inscrutable if it is such that we can't think of any reason God could have for permitting it. Clearly, the crucial problem for this probabilistic argument from evil is just that nothing much follows from the fact that some evils are inscrutable; if theism is true we would expect that there would be inscrutable evil. Indeed, a little reflection shows there is no reason to think we could so much as grasp God's plans here, even if he proposed to divulge them to us. But then the fact that there is inscrutable evil does not make it improbable that God exists."[38]

Theists are indeed correct that we can't understand the reason why God allows the intense suffering we experience in this world. But are they correct to say that if theism is true, we should expect that there would be these particular inscrutable evils? I've already argued that God could've easily done differently.

In response to William Rowe's inductive argument, mentioned in my previous chapter (pp. 234–35), Stephen Wykstra offers the *CORNEA* defense: the Condition of Reasonable Epistemic Access.[39] He writes, "We can argue from 'we see no X' to 'there is no X' only when X has no 'reasonable seeability'—that is, is the sort of thing which, if it exists, we can reasonably expect to see in the situation. . . . In other words, *CORNEA* claims that Rowe's *noseeum* (no-SEE-em) situation justifies his . . . claim only if it is reasonable for Rowe to believe that a God-justifying good for the fawn's suffering would likely be 'seeable.'" And Wykstra argues that since God is omniscient, it's not likely Rowe could see a God-justifying good here.

My response: (1) Even if this CORNEA defense works, it must additionally be shown that the theistic God exists, who knows the reason why there are such evils. (2) If it works, it merely argues that it's possible there's a reason for pointless suffering. But we're talking about probabilities here. In Dr. Weisberger's words, there are "many improbable possibilities."[40] It's possible there are Martians who live beneath the surface of Mars. It's possible that I am dreaming right now. But what we're talking about is probability not possibility. (3) Furthermore, if it works, the same defense could justify continuing to believe in God even though most of the available evidence was against God's existence, since it could be argued that an inscrutable God cannot be shown to exist by means of our limited understanding. Again, this is possible, but how likely is it if most of the evidence is against it? (4) The truth is that it seems very likely that we should see God's reasons for allowing suffering since theists also claim God wants us to believe in him. This is Theodore Drange's argument.[41] (5) Finally, the theistic response here cuts both ways. We're told God is so omniscient that we can't understand his good purposes, and this is true; we can't begin to grasp why there is so much evil in the present world if a good God exists. *But if God is as omniscient as claimed, then he should know how to create a better world, especially since we do have a good idea how God could've created differently.*

Theistic scholars like Michael Bergmann, Stephen Wykstra, and Daniel Howard-Snyder admit they have no expectations of finding a fully adequate solution to the problem of evil. Such a view actually concedes the whole argument from evil. Their defense is that we simply cannot understand God's ways. But this cuts both ways. If we cannot understand God's ways, then there is no reason to think God's ways are good, either. And since that's true, their whole position is also unfalsifiable, because the only way we can test whether or not God is good is by looking at the evidence in the world. If the theist claims God revealed that he is good without any way to evaluate this purported revelation, then how do we know God revealed this about himself? Therefore, the evidence of inscrutable evil speaks loudly against any purported historically conditioned claim of revelation from God, especially if it came from an ancient superstitious people, as I've argued previously.

Theists say God has a higher morality than we do such that God is not bound by the same ethical obligations as we are, because he has "higher purposes." Whatever this higher morality and higher purposes are, we don't have a clue. There are surely specific examples of ethical obligations that should apply to God as well as to us. For instance, it is ethically wrong for anyone, including God, to sadistically kill, maim, or torture innocent people, period. To someone who claims God can do this to any human being because we are all guilty and deserve this kind of treatment, I simply say, as I have already said, that the punishments do not fit the crimes. What they're describing here isn't a higher morality, but a different morality. It's such a different morality that if we treated people like God does in this world through nature, we would be locked up in prison.

John Stuart Mill (1806–1873) observed this: "In sober truth, nearly all the things which men are hanged or imprisoned for doing to one another are nature's everyday performances. Nature impales men, breaks them as if on the wheel, casts them to be devoured by wild beasts, burns them to death, crushes them with stones, starves them with hunger, freezes them with the cold, and has hundreds of other hideous deaths in reserve. She mows down those on whose existence hangs the well-being of a whole people, with as little compunction as those whose death is a relief to themselves."[42]

So, either God is not bound by the ethical standards he sets down for Christians or God's ethical code is absolutely mysterious to us. At this point, the whole notion of God's goodness means nothing to us at all, as John Beversluis has argued (as summarized by Victor Reppert): "If the word 'good' must mean approximately the same thing when we apply it to God as what it means when we apply it to human beings, then the fact of suffering provides a clear empirical refutation of the existence of a being who is both omnipotent and perfectly good. If on the other hand, we are prepared to give up the idea that 'good' in reference to God means anything like what it means when we refer to humans as good, then the problem of evil can be sidestepped, but any hope of a rational defense of the Christian God goes by the boards."[43]

The bottom line is that the evidence of intense suffering in the world is an empirical refutation of the theistic conception of God. There is a group of people who claim the Holocaust is a hoax, apparently including the president of Iran. But the evidence is against this. Likewise, theists believe that a perfectly good all-powerful God exists despite the overwhelming empirical evidence from evil. The evidence is against these two beliefs, period. I think it just goes to show that people can find intellectual reasons to believe what they want to believe and that they can accept and defend what they were taught to believe based on the "accidents of birth," as I've argued earlier.

Is it ever rational to believe against the evidence? I don't think so. Even though there's a possibility that the Holocaust might be a hoax and that the theistic God exists, what we believe should not be in opposition to the evidence. Now it is quite possible to rationally believe something when there is no evidence one way or another, like, for example, that I am not dreaming right now. But it's not reasonable to have a belief when the evidence is against it, and that's the direction the evidence overwhelmingly points. All theistic attempts to fully justify the evil in this world can be likened to a physicist trying to create cold fusion. The naysayers have the weight of evidence behind them.

If God does exist, then at best we would be little more than involuntary animals in a grotesque scientific experiment that God finds pleasure from observing how we act under certain controlled conditions. This might please him, but as animals in that experiment we want to know if God cares about us, even if we aren't equals. And from our perspective, a perfectly good God should really care about us for us to call him "good."

If the Christian still wants to maintain that there is a good purpose for all human suffering, then let her also consider what Ivan Karamazov, Fyodor Dostoyevsky's character, said: "Tell me yourself—I challenge you: let's assume that you were called upon to build the edifice of destiny so that men would finally be happy and would find peace and tranquility. If you knew that, in order to attain this, you would have to torture just one single creature, let's say a little girl who beat her chest so desperately in the outhouse, and that on her unavenged tears you could build that edifice, would you agree to do it? Tell me and don't lie!"[44]

In light of all that has been said, listen to Voltaire: "The silly fanatic repeats to me . . . that it is not for us to judge what is reasonable and just in the great Being, that His reason is not like our reason, that His justice is not like our justice. What!? How do you want me to judge justice and reason otherwise than by the notions I have of them? Do you want me to walk otherwise than with my feet, and to speak otherwise than with my mouth?"[45]

John Stuart Mill forcefully concludes as I do: "In everyday life I know what to call right or wrong, because I can plainly see its rightness or wrongness. Now if a god requires that what I ordinarily call wrong in human behavior I must call right because he does it; or that what I ordinarily call wrong I must call right because he so calls it, even though I do not see the point of it; and if by refusing to do so, he can sentence me to hell, to hell I will gladly go."[46]

NOTES

1. Daniel Howard-Snyder, *The Evidential Argument from Evil* (Bloomington: Indiana University Press, 1996).

2. This is a point that H. L. McCloskey makes in "God and Evil," in *Readings in the Philosophy of Religion*, ed. Baruch A. Brody (Englewood Cliffs, NJ: Prentice-Hall, 1974), pp. 168–86.

3. A. M. Weisberger, *Suffering Belief: Evil and the Anglo-American Defense of Theism* (New York: Peter Lang, 1999), p. 107.

4. This is also a point that McCloskey also makes in "God and Evil."

5. Former Christian Conrad Hyers makes this argument in *The Meaning of Creation: Genesis and Modern Science* (Atlanta: John Knox Press, 1994), pp. 93–137. This can also be seen easily enough in Tim Callahan's book *Secret Origins of the Bible* (Altadena, CA: Millenium Press, 2002), pp. 30–55.

6. Richard Gale in Howard-Snyder, *The Evidential Argument from Evil*, p. 215.

7. See Bart D. Ehrman's book *God's Problem: How the Bible Fails to Answer Our Most Important Question—Why We Suffer* (New York: HarperOne, 2008) where he deals with the biblical passages about suffering, and the notion of free will isn't a part of the biblical solution.

8. Weisberger, *Suffering Belief*, p. 114.

9. http://www.calvin.edu/academic/philosophy/writings/ibig.htm.

10. Eleonore Stump, "Providence and the Problem of Evil," in *Christian Philosophy*, ed. Thomas P. Flint (Notre Dame, IN: University of Notre Dame Press, 1990), pp. 51–91.

11. William P. Alston in Howard-Snyder, *The Evidential Argument from Evil*, p. 111.

12. Patrick Johnstone, *Operation World* (Grand Rapids, MI: Zondervan, 1993), pp. 164, 207–208, 214.

13. William Lane Craig and J. P. Moreland, *Philosophical Foundations for a Christian Worldview* (Downers Grove, IL: InterVarsity Press, 2003), pp. 536–46.

14. Found at www.infidels.org.

15. Lowder/Fernandez debate on Theism vs. Naturalism.

16. J. L. Mackie, *The Miracle of Theism* (Oxford: Oxford University Press, 1982), p. 155.

17. In "Paulicians" in his *Historical and Critical Dictionary* (1697).

18. William P. Alston in Howard-Snyder, *The Evidential Argument from Evil*, p. 113.

19. Bruce Russell in Howard-Snyder, *The Evidential Argument from Evil*, p. 205.

20. Alston in Howard-Snyder, *The Evidential Argument from Evil*, p. 113.

21. Weisberger, *Suffering Belief*, p. 164. There are two philosophical views of the nature of free will. One view is *incompatibilistic* (or libertarian) free will (adopted by Arminians), which is the ability to freely choose to do an action, even though that same person under the same circumstances could've chosen to do differently. The other view is called *compatibilistic* free will (adopted by Calvinists), which is the ability to make choices, even though a person could not have chosen to do otherwise. So long as a person chooses to do an action, then it doesn't matter if she was compelled to make that choice by forces outside of her control. It was still freely chosen. In the nomenclature philosophers simply say this means there is "no free will," since it is a denial of the libertarian view of free will, which is the language I utilize here.

22. Ibid.

23. Ibid., pp. 167 and 171.

24. Paul Copan, *"That's Just Your Interpretation"* (Grand Rapids, MI: Baker Book House, 2001), pp. 106–108.

25. In "Is there Freedom in Heaven?" *Faith and Philosophy* 16, no. 1 (1999): 69–82. Sennett basically argues that through free will on earth (simple libertarian freedom) believers develop their characters, but that in heaven believers will no longer have this same type of freedom. In heaven believers will have compatibilistic freedom of action based upon their character choices on earth. They won't have simple libertarian freedom of action, and as such it will be logically impossible for their choices to be evil choices. Since Christians do not die by first achieving perfect moral characters, Sennett is forced to admit that "there is room for some kind of doctrine of sanctification, whereby God supplies upon our deaths whatever is lacking in our character formations to bring us to the state of compatibilist free perfection" (p. 77). But as we find argued in Graham Oppy's book, "this can't be right. If we can act freely by acting on an aspect of character that has been given to us by a perfect being, then we simply do not have a reply to the problem of heaven: the perfect being can after all just give us characters that determine that we will always do the good. Sennett claims that 'it is the pattern we establish throughout a life of intentional character building that is critical—not our actually attaining the desired character itself in our lifetimes. By establishing such a pattern we are, in effect, giving God permission to fill in the gap' (pp. 77–78). But the perfect being doesn't need permission from us to 'fill in the gaps,' i.e., to endow us with different character traits from those that we actually possess. On the assumption that it is possible for a perfect being to endow us with different character traits from those that we actually possess without impairing our ability to make free choices, it can hardly make any difference to the perfect being what kind of character it begins to work upon." *Arguing about Gods* (Cambridge: Cambridge University Press, 2006), pp. 324–26.

26. Weisberger, *Suffering Belief*, p. 136.

27. John Hick argues for this in *Evil and the God of Love*, 2nd ed. (New York: Harper & Row, 1977).

28. John L. Schellenberg argues that divine hiddenness leads us to think God doesn't exist in his book *Divine Hiddenness and Human Reason* (Ithaca, NY: Cornell University Press, 1993). In evaluating his case, Robert McKim acknowledges Schellenberg is correct when he says that "if God exists, God could do much more than God has done." But beyond that McKim objects to Schellenberg on the same kinds of grounds that theists do in general to the problem of evil. For instance, McKim talks several times about "unknown goods" that might explain divine hiddenness. This is the ignorance defense all over again. See McKim's book *Religious Ambiguity and Religious Diversity* (Oxford: Oxford University Press, 2001), pp. 97–104. In Schellenberg's recent book, *The Wisdom to Doubt: A Justification of Religious Skepticism* (Ithaca, NY: Cornell University Press, 2007), pp. 195–242, he responds to criticisms and strengthens his whole argument.

29. Weisberger, *Suffering Belief*, p. 135.

30. Peter Van Inwagen in Howard-Snyder, *The Evidential Argument from Evil*, p. 160.

31. Richard Swinburne, *Is There a God?* (Oxford: Oxford University Press, 1997), as quoted in Richard Dawkins, *The God Delusion* (New York: Houghton Mifflin, 2006), p 58.

32. Van Inwagen in Howard-Snyder, *The Evidential Argument from Evil*, p. 161.

33. Alston, in *The Evidential Argument From Evil*, p. 117.

34. David Hume, *Dialogues Concerning Natural Religion* (London: Thomas Nelson, 1947), part XI.

35. This is a point made by Steven M. Cahn in "Cacodaemony," in *Contemporary Philosophy of Religion*, ed. Steven M. Cahn and David Shatz (New York: Oxford University Press, 1982), pp. 20–24.

36. Hume, *Dialogues Concerning Natural Religion*, part XI.

37. Edward H. Madden and Peter H. Hare, *Evil and the Concept of God* (Springfield, IL: Charles C. Thomas, 1968), p. 65.

38. Alvin Plantinga in Howard-Snyder, *The Evidential Argument from Evil*, pp. 74–76.

39. Stephen Wykstra in Howard-Snyder, *The Evidential Argument from Evil*, pp. 126–50.

40. A. M. Weisberger, "The Argument from Evil," in *Cambridge Companion to Atheism* (Cambridge: Cambridge University Press, 2006).

41. Theodore Drange, *Nonbelief and Evil: Two Arguments for the Nonexistence of God* (Amherst, NY: Prometheus Books, 1998). See also the essays in *The Improbability of God*, part four: "Nonbelief Arguments against the Existence of God" (Amherst, NY: Prometheus Books, 2006), pp. 337–426.

42. John Stuart Mill, *Nature and the Utility of Religion*, 1871.

43. John Beversluis, *C. S. Lewis and the Search for Rational Religion* (Grand Rapids, MI: Eerdmans, 1985; revised and updated by Prometheus Books, 2007).

44. Fyodor Dostoyevsky, *The Brothers Karamazov* (1880).

45. Voltaire, in his *Philosophical Dictionary*, as quoted to me by Edward T. Babinski.

46. John Stuart Mill, reproduced in an appendix in Richard Taylor, ed., *Theism* (New York: Liberal Arts Press, 1957), pp. 89–96.

THE BIBLICAL EVIDENCE EXAMINED

14

SCIENCE AND THE
GENESIS CREATION ACCOUNTS

N ow that I've defended my controls beliefs, it's time to examine the biblical evidence itself.

Let me start with some preliminary concessions: First, if an omnipotent God existed and could create a universe then he could probably do so instantaneously, by fiat. We merely want to know whether he did. He supposedly has the power to do a great many things but chooses not to use his power that often, especially when it comes to the intense suffering we see in this world. Second, some Christian thinkers claim there is nothing about the concept of creation itself that leads us to conclude God must create by fiat. Arthur Peacock argues that God could use chance as his radar beam searching for the possibilities.[1] Desirable results are then locked in place like a ratchet wrench. God loads the dice, so to speak, so the results are his. While I'll concede this is a Christian possibility, I see no reason to invoke God to explain anything, as I've previously argued. Third, Christians could still hold to the authority of the Bible even if Genesis doesn't speak to the issues of modern science. He or she could maintain that the Bible is authoritative on every issue it speaks about. While I'll concede this too is a possibility, Christians have continually backed off what they claim the Bible speaks authoritatively about because of the onslaught of science. Fourth, according to Phillip Johnson: "Evolution contradicts creation only when it is explicitly or tacitly defined as fully naturalistic evolution—meaning evolution that is not directed by any purposeful intelligence. Similarly, creation contradicts evolution only when it means sudden creation, rather than creation by progressive development."[2] This too I'll grant Christians, although our firmly held scientific model affirms that the universe and life on earth operates uniformly by the same consistent pattern of laws. Any creation theory that denies this is to be rejected, and in that sense creation science is not science.

ONE SCIENTIFIC FACT SEEMS TO BE AGREEABLE TO MOST ALL SCIENTIFICALLY MINDED CHRISTIANS AND ATHEISTS:THE BIG BANG THEORY

There are four scientific models of the origin of the universe: the big bang model, where this universe exploded into existence; the pulsating (oscillating) model, where the universe endlessly explodes and then implodes over and over again; the steady-state model, in which the universe creates new stars as older stars burn out—so that the universe continually recreates itself in a steady state of equilibrium; and also the black hole model of Lee Smolin. Except for the steady state-model, which only has a very small number of supporters, all of them accept the fact that our present universe originated from an initial big bang, even if they quibble about the particulars. According to Ian Barbour, "today big bang theories have clearly won the day."[3] Of the pulsating model, Stanley Jaki says, "There simply is no evidence for this."[4] In fact, the American Astronomical Society met in the summer of 1997 and heard some major scientists claim they now "know" there isn't enough matter in the universe for gravitational attraction to bring the universe back in on itself. So Lee Smolin's model presented in his book *The Life of the Cosmos* is gaining many supporters where he argues that our universe originated from within a *black hole* inside another universe, and that prior universes give rise to baby universes as *black holes* explode into them from a big bang.[5]

Confirmations of the Big Bang

There is overwhelming evidence our universe originated from a big bang. Hubble's law is that the redshifting of light coming from distant galaxies is proportional to their distance. It shows the universe is expanding because light, like sound, changes as it moves away from you from blue to red (much like the sound of a car horn as the sound passes you), and all of the galaxies in our universe are redshifted except Andromeda, which is blueshifted and best explained as locked in gravitational pull with our own Milky Way galaxy. Furthermore, background microwave radiation temperature has been detected and is constant throughout the universe indicating the residual energy from a big explosion. Then too the curvature of space resulting from Einstein's equations along with Ölbers' Paradox shows the universe is finite. German astronomer Wilhelm Ölbers argued that if the universe is infinite containing an infinite number of stars, the night sky should be all lit up with starlight. Finally, there are elements in the universe that cannot be made in stars, like deuterium, helium 3, and lithium 7. The only plausible theory is that the universe began in a big bang.[6]

According to James F. Sennett, "It is not an overstatement to say that denying big bang cosmology requires denying the most fundamental propositions of contemporary physics. In other words, one cannot deny big bang cosmology without denying the reliability of virtually everything that's gone on in physics for the last 100 years. The theory is a rather straightforward deduction from relativity theory and quantum physics aided by uncontroversial astronomical observations. The rational cost of denying big bang cosmology is extremely high. The rational cost of accepting it is relatively small—exchanging one interpretation of the biblical creation stories (which is suspect for other reasons as well) for another."[7]

What Does Astronomy Tell Us about the Age of the Universe?

Astronomy is based on the fact that the universe operates by one set of laws. It allowed for the origin of modern astronomy in the first place. Using a spectroscope, astronomers can determine the actual brightness and know the chemical elements, size, and temperature of a star from its "fingerprint." We can even know its projected life cycle. We can also tell how far away it is and how fast it is moving. The distance is measured in light-years, which is also a measurement of time. The nearest galaxy, Andromeda, is 2.5 million light-years away, which means the universe must be at least that old if that galaxy truly exists! The universe as a whole is judged to be thirteen to fifteen billion years old. But if Genesis 1–2 is taken literally and the earth is only six to ten thousand years old, then only light from stars within that time frame could actually come from existing stars. Nearly all the starlight we see in the sky would not be coming from any existing stars, for it would take thirteen to fifteen billion years for some of it to actually reach us.

This is known among literal creationists as the problem of starlight. One solution to this problem is the "light speed decay" hypothesis put forth by Barry Setterfield. His hypothesis is that the speed of light has been slowing down since the time of God's creation in Genesis, thereby accounting for why the galaxies of stars seem much farther away from us than they really are. The Setterfield hypothesis can be tested. If he's correct and he dates the Creation week to ten thousand years ago, in order for the universe to look like it is thirteen to fifteen billion years old rather than ten thousand years old, physicists could easily calculate the rate of deceleration needed—easily. Once they do this, they can then compare today's measurements of the speed of light with the measurements of five years ago to see if the speed of light has decelerated by the same rate. For them, it would be a simple evidential test. If there was no noticeable deceleration (as is the case), then the evidence would be against this hypothesis, and it is. But Setterfield argues against the results of such a test by asserting the speed of light has reached a stable rate without any evidence for supposing it was different in the past. Thus his theory is an *ad hoc* one brought into the discussion without any reason other than faith for doing so.

Another solution to the problem of starlight is known as "relativistic cosmology" put forth by D. Russell Humphreys.[8] Humphreys claims that the distant starlight problem could be solved if God used the relativistic concept of time dilation. What he proposes is that time in earth's frame of reference was radically different than the frames of reference of the surrounding cosmos. He claims that on the fourth day, billions of years of physical processes would be taking place in the heavens while time would proceed normally here on earth. But Humphreys's claim goes against the lessons we learned in Galileo's day. The universe operates by one set of laws. Time dilutes at the same rate throughout the whole universe, or there should be evidence to the contrary. Any suggestion otherwise is to claim that the universe once operated by a different set of laws, and that supposition must be rejected outright because it undermines the most fundamental fact of astronomy that was fought and won by Copernicus and Galileo, as we saw in a previous chapter.[9] Furthermore, both of these two solutions to the starlight problem misunderstand the creation accounts in Genesis. They go against a straightforward reading of the biblical cosmological world, as we are about to see.

WHAT EXACTLY DOES THE BIBLE SAY WITH REGARD TO CREATION?

In the first place, there are four models of creation found in the Bible, not just one. In Genesis 1 we find: *Creation by Word.* God speaks, "Let there be . . ." and there is. In Genesis 2 we find: *Creation by Action.* God "planted a garden" which he later walked in (3:8); he brought the beasts to Adam for him to name; he took a rib from Adam and created Eve. Here God is shown to be working. We also find *Creation by Birth* in Genesis 2:4; 5:1; 6:9 where the word "generate" (*toledot*) is used; and *Creation by Theomachy or Divine Conflict* (cf. Isa. 51:9–10; Ps. 74:13–14; 89:10–12; Job 26:7–13). The reason why there are so many models of creation in the Bible is because it doesn't claim to tell us how God created, only that he did. When it comes to creation by divine conflict (the fourth model), whom was God fighting? Tim Callahan reminds us that such a divine battle "only makes sense if it is against something God did not originally make, but that existed before him."[10]

THEORIES TO HARMONIZE SCIENCE WITH GENESIS 1–2

There are several theories Christians use to harmonize science with the Genesis creation accounts. Let's take a look at them in turn.

Local Creation is the theory that Genesis 1 speaks only about a localized creation in a Garden of Eden in Mesopotamia, not the whole earth. But how can this be when God created the sun, and the stars on the fourth day? How can they be localized?

Ideal Time (vs. real time) is the theory that God creates with the appearance of age. That is, God created Adam and Eve with age—sixteen, eighteen, or twenty-one years old? Applied to geology and the starry heavens, this means that they, too, were created with the appearance of age. This was first proposed by Philip Henry Gosse. He claimed that the evidence of fossils and geological strata are simply testimonies to the perfection of which God made the world and universe to appear with age. But the lessons of Galileo show us that the universe operates uniformly by the same consistent pattern of laws. It would be treating geological history as unreal and unreliable, and astronomy as a sham. It would mean that God deceived us when he created the fossils in the earth and the stars in the sky and then left us without any evidence that the Bible is his word when it says otherwise. According to Bernard Ramm: "Such a scheme, clever as it is, is a tacit admission of the correctness of geology."[11]

Creation Revealed in Seven Days—Not Performed in Seven Days is a theory defended by Bernard Ramm. "The days of creation are not literal days nor age days indicating the time of creation, but are literal days indicating the time of revelation. . . . The creation record is part topical and part chronological to convey to man: (i) some sense of the order in creation; (ii) that God made everything, so nothing may be worshipped."[12] Ramm also holds that each of the "days" in Genesis 1 could represent a long time, but he does not insist the days are completely chronological. They are instead "part topical or logical." "If Genesis is completely silent about secondary causes, and if geology is ignorant about first causes, then it is only as we bring the first causes and secondary causes together that we will get the truth for the full understanding of the geological record."[13] However, there is nothing in the text to indicate that the days of creation were days of revelation. Furthermore, if he wants to maintain that there is some chronology in the Genesis account, then the only way to know where it can be found is through the sciences, thereby making Genesis 1 superfluous as a source of knowledge about the world. Besides, there is a better alternative.

The Reconstruction Theory (or the Gap Theory) is the view that between Genesis 1:1 and 1:2 is a huge time gap to account for the geological data. This was first proposed by Thomas Chalmers (1780–1847). According to Henri Blocher, this theory, "invented in order to please the scientists, has had considerable difficulty satisfying them." It presupposes three radical phases where there was an early earth, a destroyed earth and a re-created earth. But there are two insurmountable textual difficulties with it. In the first place, to translate verse 2 as, "And the earth *BECAME* formless" is inadmissible. Compare the same Hebrew word used in Genesis 3:1, which reads, "Now the snake *was*. . . ." Second, it also requires that the verb "made" be given the meaning "remake" (cf. 1:31; 2:2f.; Exod. 20:11). Bernard Ramm says that with this theory, "the entire interpretation of geology and Genesis is made to hinge on secondary meanings of two Hebrew words." And "the Gap theory settles nothing in geology," for "harmony with geology is attained by making scripture irrelevant to geology."[14] According to Blocher, the verdict on the whole theory must be "quite impossible."[15]

The Concordist Interpretation is the theory that each day in Genesis 1 is a very long period of time (cf. Ps. 90:4). The first proponent of this interpretation was Hugh Miller (1869 CE). It was meant to harmonize science and the Bible, but it does no such thing. In the Bible, trees (day 3) precede marine life (day 5), and birds (day 5) precede insects (day 6); scientists think the opposite. But the biggest objection is the fourth day—the creation of the sun, moon, stars after the earth and its vegetation and trees. To say God revealed the sun, moon, and stars on the fourth day is an *ad hoc* theory. You cannot turn the word "made" into "reveal" (1:16). Genesis had a perfect word for "appear" when it needed to use it (1:9). "On this reef the concordist boat is wrecked."[16] According to Genesis, God first created the earth, and only later, on the fourth day, did he create the universe of stars. This conflicts with astronomy, and the battle won in Galileo's day.

The Literal Day Theory is that God created in six literal days. This view receives support from earliest of times and has the majority of scholars throughout church history before the advent of modern science. But Henri Blocher reminds us that "the rejection of all the theories accepted by scientists requires considerable bravado. One must be sure that the text demands the literal interpretation. It must not be adopted out of loyalty to the past."[17] In the first place, if the literal interpretation is correct, the term *day* (*YÔM*) would mean for earth-dwellers the twenty-four-hour time period it takes for the earth to revolve. There are two major problems with this view. In the first place, *day* (*YÔM*) is used in Genesis to indicate periods of unspecified time (2:4; 5:1). In the second place, the sun wasn't even created until the fourth day!

Additionally, there are some huge differences between modern science and Genesis 1 that must be acknowledged:

Modern Science	*Genesis 1*
First the universe of stars existed, then the earth was formed.	First the earth was formed, then the universe of stars was created.
Rain comes from clouds.	Firmament holds back the water.
Stars are extremely far away.	Stars in the firmament.
Sun exists before vegetation.	Vegetation before the sun.
Marine life before vegetation.	Vegetation exists before marine life.
Insects exist before birds.	Birds exist before insects.
Classifies life by biological complexity and structure.	Classifies life by habitat and the environment.

The ancient Hebrews viewed the universe much like their contemporaries. There is some disagreement with the sketchy details we have in the Bible itself. But they had contact with Babylonia (Abraham purportedly came from there), Egypt (as purported slaves), the Canaanites (whom they fought with), and other nations around them. It's not likely they would have described the universe totally different from them, except that God created it all. (See Gen. 1:6; 7:11; Job 37:18; Isa. 40:22; Ps. 19:4–6; 78:23–24; 104:2–4; 2 Kings 7:2; Amos 9:6.)

According to *Harper's Bible Dictionary*, "The ancient Hebrews imagined the world as flat and round, covered by the great solid dome of the firmament which was held up by mountain pillars (Job 26:11; 37:18). The blue color of the sky was attributed to the chaotic waters that the firmament separated from the earth (Gen. 1:7). The earth was thus surrounded by waters above and below (Gen. 1:6,7; cf. Ps. 24:2; 148:4, Deut. 5:8). The firmament was thought to be substantial; it had pillars (Job 26:11) and foundations (2 Sam. 22:8). When the windows of it were opened, rain fell (Gen. 7:11–12; 8:2). The sun, moon, and stars moved across or were fixed in the firmament (Gen. 1:14–19; Ps. 19:4, 6). It was also the abode of the birds (Gen. 1:20; Deut. 4:17). Within the earth lay *Sheol*, the realm of the dead (Num. 16:30–33; Isa. 14:9, 15)."[18]

Based on these facts alone, the literal theory has no basis to stand on. The biblical writers could not have written about how God actually created the universe because the Hebrews didn't even have an adequate understanding of the universe. About this James F. Sennett reminds us that "there are many Bible believing Christians who are convinced that the literal historical approach to the creation stories is neither required by the text nor adequate to do the text justice."[19]

Ignoring these insurmountable problems, young-earth literalists will go on to claim that Noah's flood can account for the geological age appearance of the earth. Until the rise of geological science and biblical criticism, most interpreters of the Bible assumed that the story of Noah's flood was about a worldwide flood. Only Noah and his family survived—along with pairs of the earth's animals—in a huge ark that came to rest in the region of Mt. Ararat (Genesis 6–9). But both Biblical criticism and geology have now totally undercut this claim, as we shall see later.

Henri Blocher argues against the *Literal Day Theory* by pointing out that "the signs favoring a 'young earth' belong to a class of facts which are still not properly understood or explained; they do not carry enough weight to counterbalance the much more numerous signs of a great age for the earth. . . . A young earth could never have borne the vegetable mass necessary to create the deposits of coal. . . . There are 600 meters of stratification in the Yellowstone Park which reveal eighteen forests which were covered over by lava one after another, each successive layer which engulfed its predecessor."[20] A young earth simply cannot account for these layers of forestations and volcanic eruptions.

Davis A. Young takes on the young-earth advocates in a chapter titled, "Was the Earth Created a Few Thousand Years Ago?" He examined evidence from sedimentary rocks, igneous rocks, metamorphic rocks, along with radiometric evidence, and concluded: "Geological evidence accumulated over the past three hundred years overwhelmingly indicates that the planet had experienced a dynamic history measurable in billions of years."[21]

Davis A. Young with Howard Van Till and Clarence Menninga[22] have also investigated the so-called evidence for a young earth. Suffice it to say, neither the legend of the shrinking sun, nor the recent decay of the earth's magnetic field, nor the level of dust on the moon, nor the salt levels in the salty sea, nor the claim of missing rock in the Grand Canyon supports the youth-earth theory at all. The young-earth theory is maintained despite the overwhelming geological and astronomical evidence simply because of a particular theory about the literalness of the Bible. But not even the Bible claims to be literal in its descriptions of the creation or the flood. With such evidence abounding, it's time to abandon the theory in total.[23]

The Days of Proclamation Theory of Alan Hayward and Glenn Morton is a newer view.[24] Morton writes: "Genesis 1 is the pre-planning of the universe. God proclaimed things in Genesis 1, but nothing was yet created. It is the human narrator, who lived many billions of years after the origin of the universe who then gives a statement affirming that the proclamation was accomplished. He says to the effect that 'it was so,' but it doesn't say, 'and it was so INSTANTLY!'" Hayward and Morton hold that God gave creative proclamations on these days, and after the week was over, the creative proclamations were set into motion and some of the proclamations were fulfilled earlier than others and sometimes in different order than others.[25] The creation week of Genesis chapter 1 is separated from the later events in chapter 2 by billions of years, which allows for galactic, planetary, geological, and biological evolution until Adam and Eve are created. Morton has gone further and argued that the flood of Noah was not a global flood covering the entire planet but was a local flood. Morton places the Garden of Eden at the bottom of what is now the Mediterranean Sea. He argues that the Strait of Gibraltar was once a dam that God broke which resulted in Noah's flood and produced the Mediterranean Sea five million years ago. Morton also believes Adam was created from a stillborn baby who died from a female apelike hominoid that God refashioned into Adam.[26]

Besides the geological problems of the lack of evidence for the Garden of Eden under the Mediterranean Sea, along with Noah's flood, this theory has two main biblical problems. In the first place, it clashes with the fourth commandment in Exodus 20:11, which says, "For in six days the LORD made the heavens and the earth, the sea and all that is in them, and rested on the seventh day; therefore the LORD blessed the Sabbath day and made it holy." According to this commandment, God just didn't create the heavens and the earth with proclamations and then allow "all that is in them" to evolve eons and eons of time later. No, the heavens and the earth and everything in them were made in the creative week.

Second, the genealogy of Genesis 11 will not allow for gaps, if interpreted properly. Morton thinks there are gaps in this genealogy that allow him to push the flood back five million years in time. In Genesis 11, the Hebrew word for the father-son relationships from Shem in verse 10 to Abram in verse 27 is *yalad*. Both *yalad* and *ben* were Hebrew words meaning "begat," but *ben* was a lot more liberal, and could easily mean a more figurative, ancestor-descendant type of relationship between two individuals. If there were any gaps as Morton argues for in Genesis 11, why wasn't the Hebrew word *ben* used? Morton argues that there was one instance where *yalad* is used as an ancestor-descendent relationship, in Genesis 10:15–18, where Canaan became the father of the Hittites, Jebusites, Amorites, Girgashites, Hivites, Arkites, and other clans of people. As such, he argues it could also indicate an ancestor-descendent relationship in Genesis 11.[27] The problem here is that the context of Genesis 11 demands that *yalad* be interpreted as strict father-son relationships, because each of the generations has the father living a certain number of years as well as having "other sons and daughters." If it was said that "Canaan fathered other sons and daughters," no one would take this to mean that these other sons and daughters just happen to be many other clans in addition to the clans mentioned in Genesis 10:15–18.[28]

Textual Creationist Model/Theory of John Sailhamer.[29] The essence of Dr. Sailhamer's view is that Genesis 1:1 describes the creation of the universe during a prior indeterminate amount of time, while Genesis 1:2–2:4a is describing the preparation of the land (i.e., the Garden of Eden/Promised Land) over six literal days. Sailhamer claims that ancient Jewish readers would naturally understand that the land of Genesis 1 is referring to the Promised Land (p. 52). But this is an implausible claim indeed, considering that none of the Talmudic writers understood Genesis 1 in this way. Sailhamer's interpretation involves many other far-fetched ideas, such as a belief that the sky was still empty of life on day 2 (p. 122). But this is preposterous if birds had been flying around for millions of years as he previously claimed. Sailhamer believes that when the universe, including the sun, was created "in the beginning" (verse 1), it refers to the advent of sunrise. But if the sun had been continuously rising every day for billions of years prior to that day, then what is so noteworthy about this particular sunrise such that it deserves any mention at all? The biblical text is against this model in so many ways.

The Literary Theory is the view that historical chronology is entirely absent— Genesis doesn't tell us anything about how God created, only that he did. This interpretation was advocated by M. J. Lagrange in 1896 and was adopted by other evangelicals such as N. Ridderbos, B. Ramm, M. G. Kline, and D. Payne.

Just consider two facts: First, at the start of the older second account of creation (2:4), we find that the absence of vegetation is explained by the lack of rain and humans to work the land (2:5). This would be a strange explanation if the first account described literal twenty-four-hour days, for it presupposes the regular activity of nature for plant growth. Besides we already had vegetation (1:11–12)! The author connects these two accounts without clearing up this glaring difficulty indicating that he didn't think the days of creation were literal ones. The second fact is the omission of the words *evening* and *morning* on the seventh day when God rested. The natural conclusion: That day is not literal—it was never finished. It is still continuing. Jesus makes an argument that he has the right to work on the Sabbath because God works on his Sabbath (John 5:16–19). His reasoning is sound only if the Father works during his Sabbath. If so, the Son has the same right.

Comparing the widely recognized fact that Genesis 1 and 2 are two different literary accounts of creation, we can better see the literary interpretation.[30] Compare the following differences:

Genesis 1	*Genesis 2*
God alone creates.	God and man in creative harmony.
Begins with watery chaos in which dry land is made to appear.	Begins with not enough water in which water is introduced.
In six days.	In one day.
Creation by divine fiat.	Creation by action.
Vegetation before sun and stars.	Sun and stars before vegetation.
Man created after plants and animals.	Man created before plants and animals.
Adam and Eve created together.	Eve created after Adam.

According to Claus Westermann: "This separation of the two Creation accounts into two literary sources is one of the most important and most assured results of the literary-critical examination of the Old Testament"[31] Most scholars believe Genesis

2 was composed earlier with Genesis 1 much later, reflecting a more pronounced monotheism. Both were combined in one narrative. Genesis 1 reflects civilizations that inhabited river basins and seas, while Genesis 2 is drawn from the imagery of shepherds in semiarid fringes of the fertile plains.

THE OVERALL STRUCTURE OF GENESIS 1

To better see the Literary Theory consider the following chart.[32] In verse 2 we see three problems: darkness, watery abyss, and a formless earth. Then on days 1–3 God prepares his creation for the kinds of things that will populate it in days 4–6, thus solving the three initial problems:

Problem (v. 2)	Preparation (days 1–3)	Population (days 4–6)
darkness	**1a** creation of light (day) **b** separation from darkness	**4a** creation of sun **b** creation of stars
watery abyss	**2a** creation of firmament **b** separation of waters *above*	**5a** creation of birds **b** creation of fish from waters *below*
formless earth	**3a** separation of earth from sea **b** creation of vegetation	**6a** creation of animals **b** creation of humans

Why Seven Days?

Besides everything I've just mentioned, numbers are not always to be taken in a literal sense in the Bible. Conrad Hyers writes: "In the modern world numbers have become almost completely secularized, but in antiquity they could function as significant vehicles of meaning and power. It was important to associate the right numbers with one's life and activity and to avoid the wrong numbers. . . . The symbolic meaning of the number seven and of seven days harks back to the lunar calendar which in Mesopotamia had quite early been divided into four phases of seven days each, followed by the three day disappearance of the moon, thus equaling thirty days. . . . The symbolism of the number of seven was also reinforced in antiquity by association with the seven visible planetary bodies, which had become important in Mesopotamian astrology. . . . Seven has the numerological meaning of wholeness, plenitude, and completeness. This symbolism is derived, in part, from the combination of the three major zones of the cosmos as seen vertically (heaven, earth, underworld) and the four quarters and directions of the cosmos as seen horizontally. Both the numbers three and four in themselves often function as symbols of totality, but a greater totality results from the combination of vertical and horizontal planes. Thus the number seven (adding three and four) and the number twelve (multiplying them) are recurrent biblical symbols of fullness and perfection: seven golden candlesticks, seven spirits, seven words of praise, seven eunuchs, seven churches, the seventh year, the forty-ninth year, the seventy elders, forgiveness seventy times seven, etc."[33] (With this in mind compare the seventy weeks prophecy in Dan. 9:24.)

According to C. Cassuto, the Genesis account is highly structured using the symbolic numbers three, seven, and ten.[34] For instance, the first verse contains seven Hebrew words, the second verse has fourteen Hebrew words (twice 7), and the first section of Genesis is divided into seven sections. This symbolism is undeniable since in Genesis 1 there are at least nine creative acts squeezed into God's six-day workweek: light; firmament; land; vegetation; sun, moon, and stars; birds; fish; animals; and humans.

The Theology of Genesis 1-2

Conrad Hyers tells us: "The crucial question in the creation account in Genesis 1 was polytheism vs. monotheism. . . . For most peoples in the ancient world, all the various regions of nature were divine. Sun, moon, and stars were *gods*. There were sky gods and earth gods and water gods, gods of light and darkness, rivers and vegetation, animals and fertility. . . . In light of this historical context, it becomes clearer what Genesis 1 is undertaking and accomplishing: a radical sweeping affirmation of monotheism vis-à-vis polytheism, syncretism, and idolatry. . . . On each day of creation another set of idols is smashed."[35] There thus runs through the whole Genesis cosmology "a conscious and deliberate anti-mythical polemic'"[36] The question for us today is whether we should believe this polemic, since it was written by a superstitious people who argued for their superstitious view over against other superstitious views.

The fact is that the creation accounts in Genesis are myths, which were abundant in the ancient world. There are Sumerian, Babylonian, Egyptian, and Levantine creation myths. According to Gordon Wenham, Genesis could not have been put into final literary form before 1250 BCE (because for him the events all had to have occurred first; i.e., Jacob's death in Egypt and the Exodus).[37] Yet the Babylonia epic, along with the Atrahasis epic, the Adapa myth, and the Sumerian flood story, were known in the ancient world and dated about 1600 BCE or earlier. According to Wenham: "We believe therefore that the final editor of Genesis had before him an outline of primeval history, an abbreviated version of our present Gen. 1–11, which he reworked to give the present form of the text. . . . Most likely the Biblical authors were conscious of a number of accounts of creation current in the Near East of their day, and Genesis 1 is a deliberate statement of the Hebrew view of creation over against rival views."[38] Bruce K. Watke agrees by saying, "The biblical writers borrowed their imagery, not their theology."[39] But if this is so, it says nothing about whether the Hebrew view is metaphysically correct—only that this is what the Hebrews believed. And as such, the Hebrew view was just a different myth written to exclude *other* mythical accounts.

Just look at the parallel accounts of creation between the older account in the Babylonian "Creation epic" (*Enuma Elish*) and the Genesis 1 account. It seems readily apparent that they both got their views from out of the mythical stories of their day. These stories were merely shaped by them for their own religious purposes.[40]

Babylonian "Creation Epic"	Genesis 1 Creation Account
1. Divine spirit and cosmic matter are coeternal.	1. Divine spirit creates cosmic matter and is independent of it.
2. Primeval chaos: *Tiamat* enveloped in darkness.	2. The earth a desolate waste, with darkness hovering over the deep (*têhŏm*).
3. Light emanating from the gods.	3. Light created.
4. The creation of the firmament.	4. The creation of the firmament.
5. The creation of dry land.	5. The creation of dry land.
6. The creation of the luminaries.	6. The creation of the luminaries.
7. The creation of the human race.	7. The creation of the human race.
8. The gods rest and celebrate.	8. God rests and sanctifies the seventh day.

The similarities here are very striking, although Paul Copan points out what he considers some differences, like the Babylonian epic's coexistence of divine spirit and cosmic matter, the successive rival deities, and polytheism.[41] But even if Copan is correct, which I doubt, these differences are merely the ones that the mythic Hebrew mind developed over time.

The *Phenomenal* Language of Appearances?

Christians will argue that God described his creation of the world to the biblical writers in "the phenomenal language of their day," given that we still talk about the "sun rising" and so forth. But along with everything else I argue for in this book, it's more likely that the Bible merely reflects ancient views of cosmology based upon a mythic nonhistorical consciousness. Isn't it crystal clear God could've described the universe differently in order to teach human beings about the vastness and age of the universe? Why didn't the author of the first creation account in Genesis start out by saying: "In the beginning God created an immeasurable universe of billions of stars, some of which are billions and billions of miles away, through a process that took billions of years out of which he finally created the sun, moon, and a spherical earth which revolves around the sun. On it he created water, land, the beasts of the sea, and eventually every living thing on it through stages as one species evolved into the next one. Finally he created human beings to rule over everything he created." I just don't see why God didn't reveal this, if he exists, or why ancient people couldn't have had a good grasp of what he said. It certainly would be easily understood, and would not be later undermined by the findings of modern astronomy. If God had created Adam and Eve just like we read in Genesis, then he also created the very words they used to communicate, and if that's so, he could've created their language in such a way that they could've understood any of the terms involved, like *billions*, or *universe*, or *miles*. Stating that the earth was spherical or that it went around the sun would've done wonders for biblical credibility with the dawn of modern science, since it would predate what science would later discover.

Apologists will argue that ancient cosmological beliefs were not important for God to correct since all he wanted to do was let humans know that it was HE who created it. But when we reflect on the Galileo affair and the irreparable harm it did to the Christian faith (rightly or wrongly) once astronomers understood the vastness and age of the universe, one can only shake her head in utter amazement that God didn't foresee that because he didn't reveal this, it would lead many of us to doubt the Bible. I am an atheist because this very problem started me down the road of doubt. Does God really not care about the fact that he didn't tell us the truth about the origins of the universe? By not doing so, God has produced many unbelievers who don't see any true divine revelation in the Bible.

Apologists will object that if God had revealed this to the ancient world, it would've been laughed at by the ancients who knew differently, just like Socrates was laughed at in Aristophanes' play *The Clouds*, for suggesting rain came from the clouds rather than from the sky (firmament) itself. Several things can be said about this objection. In the first place, if God had directly revealed this to Adam and Eve, then all humanity would've accepted what God revealed. It would be the consensus opinion that would require evidence to prove differently. Second, if God actually did the many miracles claimed in the Bible, they would be considered strong evidence to believe what he said about the universe as well. Third, God could also have provided Adam and Eve with the knowledge to confirm what he said by telling them how to make a telescope, for instance. Fourth, if God had revealed the truth about the universe, then human beings, especially believers, would find ways to confirm what he said, just like believers today try to confirm the stories in the Bible. So revealing this would also speed up what we know about the universe. Fifth, if God revealed the truth of the origin of the universe before we discovered it, then such a revelation would be strong evidence that the God of the Bible exists. Last, we must place this lack of divine foresight in the context of other things God could've revealed, but didn't. He could've revealed to us how to discover penicillin; but he didn't. He could've unambiguously condemned slavery; but he didn't. He could've condemned honor killings, witch burnings, and inquisitions; but he didn't. In fact, the Bible does not contain one single statement that could not have been written by a person living in the time period in which he wrote. The best explanation for this is that the God of the Bible doesn't exist.

A Much Better Understanding of Days 1–4 in Genesis 1

Let me offer a much better understanding of the first four days in Genesis 1 than anything proposed by so-called Bible-believing Christians who merely seek to defend their faith. We see several prefatory comments before several different accounts in Genesis 1–11, one of which reads: "This is the account of the heavens and the earth when they were created" (2:4; see also 5:1; 6:9; 10:1; 11:10; 11:27). The prefatory comment introduces (and sometimes briefly summarizes) what the author is about to give a detailed account of following that comment. What follows the prefatory comment is a detailed description of the comment itself. These prefatory comments keep getting smaller and smaller until we simply read, "This is the account of Terah" (11:27).

With this context in mind, Genesis 1:1 is basically a prefatory comment that says, "The following is an account of when God created the heavens and the earth." Then beginning in verse 2, we read the account of when God created the heavens (sky) and the earth. The reason the prefatory comment translation is better is because of the whole context. In addition to this, Dr. Gary Rendsberg argues that according to the syntax of the Hebrew text, "Genesis 1:1 is actually a dependant clause, dependant on Gen 1:2–3. That is, the earth is in a state of preexistent matter and then God creates the world."[42] I've heard scholars debate the correct Hebrew translation back and forth, but even if scholars like Rendsberg are incorrect, then because of the prefatory comment context alone it seems fairly clear that creation *ex nihilo* (out of nothing) is not to be found in Genesis 1. Such an interpretation is not supported by the Hebrew text itself, one way or another. That's why *The New Revised Version* translates Genesis 1:1 like this: "In the beginning when God created the heavens and the earth." An already existing earth in Genesis 1 parallels ancient polytheistic beliefs where the gods merely formed the earth. They did not create the earth out of nothing, either.

Creation "out of nothing" is a viewpoint that was developed in late antiquity (ca. 200–700 CE) rather than in biblical times, anyway. Biblical scholar Hector Avalos tells us (via e-mail) "We don't know the earliest date of the *ex nihilo* doctrine, but, insofar as the whole universe is concerned, it cannot be traced back prior to Hellenistic times in Jewish literature. It is not found in the Hebrew Bible, unless you speak of the light ("let there be light"), but not of the materials in verses 1–2 of Genesis 1. The Hebrew word *BARA'* (for create) used in Genesis 1:1 is used synonymously with words for making things from preexisting materials. Even in the first few centuries of Christianity there were contradictory positions, so the issue was not settled then. In Aquinas's *Summa* part I, question 45, article 1, objection 1, we find Aquinas acknowledging that Augustine did not believe in *creatio ex nihilo* where he says: "It would seem that to create is not to make anything from nothing. For Augustine says (Contra Adv. Leg. et Proph. i): 'To make concerns what did not exist at all; but to create is to make something by bringing forth something from what was already.'"[43]

According to Genesis 1:2, then, what exists before the heavens or the earth is the water, chaotic water. We shouldn't assume that if an ancient writer talks about earth, he means the planet Earth, or that it already exists. To the ancients of this time period, the sea and sky were distinct from the earth. The land was thought to come out of the sea. The author was surely aware of new islands appearing in the midst of the sea. We explain them today as due to plate tectonics. So the "earth" of verse 2 is described in its initial state as a formless void because it had not yet risen from out of the chaotic waters, and as such it did *not* truly exist as land at all.[44] An analogy would be clay in the potter's hands. A pot does not exist until it is formed by the potter.

According to Genesis 1, on day 1 God causes daylight. Because daylight occurs even when the sun is not seen, the author thought the sun merely makes the day brighter. On day 2 God created the heavens by taking the primordial water and dividing it into the blue sea below and the blue sky above, and placing a firmament (or metal dome) to prevent the sky water from falling down.

On day 3 God creates the earth out of the sea below. The land rises in the midst of the sea and constitutes the beginning of the earth. 2 Peter 3:5 confirms this when we read that "scoffers" in the last days "deliberately forget that long ago by God's word the heavens existed and the earth was formed out of water and by water." Then on day 4 God creates the sun, moon, and stars and hung them in the firmament dome that was supported by the mountains at the edges of the earth.

I can stop here. I think I've proven my point. The Genesis creation accounts are mythical stories, period.

NOTES

1. See Arthur Peacock, *Theology for a Scientific Age* (Minneapolis, MN: Fortress Press, 1993), pp. 115–21, 156.

2. Phillip Johnson, *Darwin on Trial* (Washington, DC: Regnery, 1991), p. 4.

3. Ian Barbour, *Religion in an Age of Science* (New York: Harper & Row, 1990), p. 129.

4. In Stanley L. Jaki, *Science and Creation: From Eternal Cycles to an Oscillating Universe* (Edinburgh: Scottish Academic Press, 1974).

5. Lee Smolin, *The Life of the Cosmos* (Oxford: Oxford University Press, 1999).

6. See Richard Morris, *Cosmic Questions* (New York: Wiley, 1993).

7. James F. Sennett, *This Much I Know: A Postmodern Apologetic* (unpublished).

8. Barry Setterfield, *The Velocity of Light and the Age of the Universe* (Adelaide: Creation Science, 1983). I thank Matthew J. Green for describing the arguments in this book and the next one that follows. D. Russell Humphreys, *Starlight and Time: Solving the Puzzle of Distant Starlight in a Young Universe* (Green Forrest, AR: Master Books, 1994).

9. On this whole subject see Howard Van Till, *The Fourth Day* (Grand Rapids, MI: Eerdmans, 1986), pp. 95–277.

10. Tim Callahan, *The Secret Origins of the Bible* (Altadena, CA: Millenium Press, 2002), p. 39.

11. Bernard Ramm, *The Christian View of Science and Scripture* (Grand Rapids, MI: Eerdmans, 1954), p. 134.

12. Ibid., pp. 151–53.

13. Ibid., p. 154.

14. Ibid., pp. 139, 142.

15. Henri Blocher, *In the Beginning: The Opening Chapters of Genesis*, trans. David G. Preston (Downers Grove, IL: InterVarsity Press, 1984), p. 42.

16. Ibid., p. 45.

17. Blocher, *In the Beginning*, p. 48.

18. See "Genesis Knows Nothing of Scientific Creationism: Interpreting and Misinterpreting the Biblical Texts," by Conrad Hyers, and "Biblical Views of Creation," by Frederick E. Greenspahn, both found at the National Center for Science Education Web site, http://www.ncseweb.org/resources/articles. See also Edward T. Babinski, "Evolving Interpretations of the Bible's 'Cosmological Teachings,'" at his Web site, http://www.edwardtbabinski.us, along with the *Anchor Bible Dictionary* entry on "Cosmogony, Cosmology."

19. Sennett, *This Much I Know: A Postmodern Apologetic*.

20. Blocher, *In the Beginning*, pp. 218–19.

21. In Ronald Youngblood, ed., *The Genesis Debate* (Grand Rapids, MI: Baker Book House, 1990), pp. 56–85.

22. In their book *Science Held Hostage: What's Wrong with Creation Science and Evolutionism?* (Downers Grove, IL: InterVarsity Press, 1988).

23. See also the debate in *Three Views on Creation and Evolution*, ed. J. P. Moreland and John Mark Reynolds (Grand Rapids, MI: Zondervan, 1999).

24. Alan Hayward, *Creation and Evolution: Rethinking the Evidence from Science and the Bible* (Minneapolis, MN: Bethany House, 1995); Glenn Morton, *Foundation, Fall, and Flood*, 3rd ed. (Woodlands, TX: DMD, 1999).

25. Morton, *Foundation, Fall, and Flood*, pp. 12–14.

26. Ibid., pp. 169–70.

27. Ibid., p. 18.

28. I want to thank Matthew J. Green for alerting me to this theory.

29. See his book *Genesis Unbound: A Provocative New Look at the Creation Account* (Portland, OR: Multnomah Press, 1996).

30. See Youngblood, *The Genesis Debate*.

31. Claus Westermann, *Creation* (Minneapolis, MN: Fortress Press, 1974), p. 6.

32. See Conrad Hyers, *The Meaning of Creation* (Atlanta: John Knox Press, 1984), p. 69.

33. Ibid., pp. 76–79. The phases of the moon began on the 28th day.

34. Israel Adams, trans., *A Commentary on the Book of Genesis*, vol. 1 (Jerusalem: Magnes Press, 1992).

35. Hyers, *The Meaning of Creation*, pp. 44–45.

36. Alexander Heidel, *The Babylonian Genesis: The Story of Creation*, 2nd ed. (Chicago: University of Chicago Press, 1963), p. 91.

37. Gordon Wenham, *Genesis 1–15* (Dallas: Word Incorporated 1987), p. xliv.

38. Ibid., pp. xli, 9.

39. "Creation Myths," in the *Baker Encyclopedia of the Bible*, general editor Walter A. Elwell (Grand Rapids, MI: Baker Books, 1988).

40. The following comparison is found in Heidel, *The Babylonian Genesis*, p. 129.

41. Paul Copan, *"That's Just Your Interpretation"* (Grand Rapids, MI: Baker Book House, 2001), pp. 149–50.

42. Gary Rendsberg, *Redaction of Genesis* (Winona Lake, IN: Eisenbrauns, 1986).

43. For more information on this, Dr. Avalos recommends Gerhard May, *Creatio Ex Nihilo: The Doctrine of "Creation out of Nothing" in Early Christian Thought* (Edinburgh: T&T Clark, 1994); Jonathan A. Goldstein, "The Origins of the Doctrine of Creation *Ex Nihilo*," *Journal of Jewish Studies* 35 (1984): 128–35; David Winston, "The Doctrine of *Ex Nihilo* Revisited," *Journal of Jewish Studies* 37 (1986): 88–91; and the counterreply by Goldstein in *Journal of Jewish Studies* 38 (1987): 187–94.

44. I thank both John Powell and Ed Babinski for this understanding.

15

SCIENCE AND GENESIS 1–11

Professing Christian philosopher John Hick admits that the picture of a fall from grace by angelic beings and then by humanity in Adam and Eve cannot, strictly speaking, be disproved. The reason is obvious, he wrote, "because those who believe the Bible also believe God can do these things." But he goes on to say, it "is fatally lacking in plausibility. For most educated inhabitants of the modern world regard the biblical story of Adam and Eve, and their temptation by the devil, as myth rather than as history."[1]

SCIENTIFIC PROBLEMS WITH GENESIS 1–11

Let's review some of the scientific problems with Genesis 1–11.

1. The order of creation depicted in chapter 1 is totally out of sync with what cosmology teaches—in Genesis the earth existed first, then the universe of stars; there was plant life before the sun; a fully formed man existed before there was a female, and so on
2. Evolutionary theory describes death as something natural to plants, animals, and human beings—not the result of a particular act of punishment by God for human sin.
3. Mythical elements like serpents that talk, trees that have magical powers to confer eternal life, and human beings who supposedly live to be quite old (Adam lived 930 years).
4. The idea that brothers married sisters and produced children is very disturbing.
5. The origin of different races among humanity is not sufficiently explained in Genesis (the curse of Ham has been proven wrong for this).

6. A universal flood that covered every mountain would upset the earth's orbit and not dissipate in the time allotted.

7. That every species of animal life could be gathered in Noah's ark completely lacks plausibility, especially since new species are found every year in remote parts of the world (dinosaurs?).

8. The origin of languages at the Tower of Babel is counter to how linguists view language development (Chinese? African languages? Australian Outback?).

9. That human beings could cohabit with angels to produce children is completely mythical and to be rejected.

10. Astronomy, geology, and anthropology show that the universe, the earth, and humanity are much older than the genealogies allow.

OPTIONS WITH REGARD TO ADAM AND EVE IN THE GARDEN OF EDEN

Here are several Christian quotes with regard to the various options about the historicity of Adam and Eve. As you will see, most all of them admit there are mythic elements in the story, which provides a good reason to reject it as history, since this comes from Christian scholarship itself!

Literal/historical. The stories are actual historical events despite what science teaches us. Francis Schaeffer, in reference to the serpent in Genesis 3, wrote, "The Bible is a book for fallen man. Whenever it touches upon anything, it does so with true truth, but not exhaustive truth. That is, where it speaks of the cosmos, science, what it says is true. Likewise, where it touches history, it speaks with what I call true truth, propositional, objective truth."[2]

Quasi-Literal/historical. These stories are merely based on actual historical events. John Stott writes: "I have long held and taught that [Genesis 2–3] contain figurative or symbolic elements, so that we should not dogmatize about the snake and the trees. But I cannot agree that the Adam and Eve story is myth, whose truth is purely symbolical. Adam's body may well have evolved from hominids. But alongside this continuity with the animal creation, he enjoyed a radical discontinuity, owing this to his having been created in God's image.[3]

Henri Blocher argues that "the presence of symbolic elements in the text in no way contradicts the historicity of its central meaning. . . . The real problem is not to know if we have a historical account of the fall, but the account of a historical fall."[4]

Gordon Wenham states, "To affirm that Gen. 2–3 is a 'factual report' is not to say it is history, at least history in the normal meaning of the term. Some have suggested 'pre-history,' and 'mytho-historical'."[5] Wenham thinks "the story offers a proto-historical account of man's origins and his sin."[6]

Derek Kidner states: "nothing requires that the creature into which God breathed human life should not have been a species prepared in every way for humanity, with already a long history of practical intelligence, artistic sensibility and the capacity for awe and reflection. On this view, Adam, the first true man, will have had as contemporaries many creatures of comparable intelligence, widely distributed over the world. Yet it is at least conceivable that after the special creation of Eve, which established the first human pair as God's vice-regents and clinched the fact that there is no natural bridge from animal to man, God may now have conferred his image on Adam's collaterals, to bring them into the same realm of being. Adam's 'federal' headship of humanity extended outwards to his contemporaries as well as onwards to his offspring, and his disobedience disinherited both alike."[7]

Clark Pinnock wrote that "it is not necessary to understand the story of the fall of Adam as a historical, eyewitness account, which it could not have been."[8] "The literary genre . . . is figurative rather than strictly literal . . . the hints are very strong that it is symbolic: Adam (which means 'Mankind') marries Eve (which means 'Life'), and their son Cain (which means 'Forgerer') becomes a wanderer in the land of Nod (which means 'Wandering')!"[9] He still maintains: "It makes sense to think of the Fall as being historical. There must have been a moment when the decision was first taken and a new direction was first chosen. . . . Such a turning point would have had to be posited had the Bible not reported it."[10]

Donald Gowan claims that the stories of Genesis 1-11 can only be misunderstood if they are "thought to be a historical account of what happened to two people who lived long ago in a world utterly different from ours." Instead, they "lie somewhere between a purely imaginative story and straightforward accounts of historical events." So he rejects labeling them as "saga," "legend," and "tale" but chooses to call them "archetypal stories" in that their experiences are to be seen as "archetypal, repeated in each of us."[11]

Nonhistorical/mythical stories. They are divinely inspired parabolic stories. They are not historical stories at all, but they teach us spiritual truths about the universe in which we live and our place in it. The stories are told by human beings (men) who tried to explain why the world and society operates the way it does.

H. Wade Seaford argues that "the ecological and cultural data contained in Genesis 1-4 [e.g., iron metallurgy and domesticated food], if compared to established archeological knowledge, places the events somewhere between ten thousand and two thousand years ago," that is, "at the dawn of the Neolithic Age." But "there is overwhelming, staggering evidence that humans inhabited the world millennia before the Neolithic/Iron Age setting of the creation story." So he asks: "Can we understand the Genesis account as an allegory, written by persons who used the ecological setting with which they were acquainted to tell the story of human alienation from God and of God's redemptive purpose? If we wish to claim Adam and Eve as symbolic progenitors of the entire human race, we must consider them as representing an event occurring thousands or millions of years before the setting in which the text of Genesis places them. Unfortunately . . . the paleontological record thoroughly establishes that one population is always preceded by another, making the idea of a single pair of humans procreating an entire species unthinkable."[12]

Conrad Hyers states that "Genesis 2-3 is mythical." Myths account for "why snakes have no legs like other reptiles, why they 'eat dust,' why there is special 'enmity' between snakes and humans, why humans and not animals are embarrassed by their nakedness and wear clothes, why there is pain in childbirth. Other, more substantial features of existence are also accounted for in like manner: the relationship between male and female, between animals and humans, and between humans and God, as well as the sources of toil, suffering, and death."[13]

Alan Richardson wrote, "The time element in the myths of the Creation and Fall (as in all biblical myths) must be discounted; it is not that ONCE . . . God created man perfect and then fell from grace. God is . . . eternally making man . . . so the 'Fall' is an ingredient of every moment of human life; man is at every moment 'falling,' putting himself in the centre, rebelling against the will of God. Adam is Everyman."[14]

John C. L. Gibson boldly states that "there never was a place as the Garden of Eden, nor was there ever a historical person called Adam who lived in it and conversed with snakes and with God in Hebrew. . . . Animals only speak in fables." The garden is a garden of the mind, a garden of 'men's' dreams, the kind of place they would like this world to be, the kind of place indeed they know this world ought to be. And Adam is each one of us, he is Everyman. . . . Each and every day Paradise beckons us, but each and every day we eat the forbidden fruit and are banished from it."[15]

Emil Brunner claims Adam and Eve were not actual persons but that there is no loss in abandoning the historicity of the record. For the story is about you and me and everyone in the world. If anything, the story represents a "fall upward"—as an ascent to consciousness and individual responsibility and maturity.[16]

Let's look at two additional case studies from Genesis 1–11 to show why even some Christian scholars think the Bible starts off describing the origin of the Hebrew people with myths.

CASE IN POINT ONE: THE STORY OF CAIN (GEN. 4:1–25)

According to Genesis 4 God's judgment upon Cain for killing his brother Abel was to be a wanderer. Cain is deathly afraid of this and says: "whoever finds me will kill me." So God places a mark on him so that "no one who found him would kill him" (v.14). Now who is Cain afraid of here? Supposedly the only people on earth were his mom and dad, and a few sisters. Then it says, "Cain lay with his wife" (v.17). Where did he get a wife? Nothing was said about that, but presumably the author isn't interested in such matters. Why? It's because the author of chapters 3–11 was stressing the sinfulness of human beings. God created the world good, but look how his highest creation behaves—he behaves very, very badly. Human beings are very sinful beginning with Adam and Eve's disobedience, to Cain killing his brother, to the flood where God destroyed everyone but Noah and his family, to the Tower of Babel. Human beings are very sinful and ungrateful for what God has done. To try to make sense of where Cain got his wife is to miss the point of these chapters. These chapters have the feel of a story with a point, not a statement about marrying sisters. Then Genesis says when Cain's wife gave birth to his firstborn, Enoch, Cain was in the process of "building a city" (v.17). If we try to make sense of this, we simply cannot do it. Cain is banished from his parents and marked so that no one who finds him will kill him. He gets a wife and starts to build a city, and while doing so, Enoch is born. None of this makes much sense given the whole setting. A city? Instead, maybe it should have read, "Cain was building a house." But a whole city? Do fugitives build cities?

It doesn't make sense to think there was a massive amount of incest going on, producing babies. Even then the text would still be incorrect, for Cain should've said: "any of my brothers or sisters who finds me will kill me." And since this whole problem is obvious, the author/editor surely would've cleared it up if he considered it to be something that needed to be cleared up at all.

Donald Gown claims this whole scenario "seems to presuppose a different background from that provided by chapters 2–3, one in which Cain and Abel live in an already well-populated world. Furthermore, the genealogy at the end (vv. 18–22), leading to the founding of guilds of cattle raisers, musicians, and metallurgists, seems strangely irrelevant when we realize that all the descendants of these people will be wiped out by the flood (chapter 6). Originally, then, the story of Cain and Abel was probably told as a self-contained narrative, without having any relationship to the stories of the garden or the flood."[17]

This should surprise no one. Even the gospels do not present the same chronology of events in the life of Jesus or stress the same things about him. The events in the life of Jesus were arranged by each of the four authors to stress certain distinct things in the life of Jesus, and very few, if any, New Testament authorities think otherwise. See almost any conservative scholarly introduction to the gospels for this.[18]

But with the story of Cain, if so many things are inserted without the need to correct the setting, like his wife, the people he fears, and the city he is building, then when the editor/author earlier said "Eve would become the mother of all the living" (Gen. 3:20), we can see it for what it really is. It is just a folk story with a point, like one of Jesus' parables. According to John Gibson: "Genesis is essentially folk literature. The vast bulk of it consists of stories which still carry about them the marks of having been composed to entertain and to instruct ordinary folks. . . . In effect we are treating this and other opening chapters of Genesis as imaginative stories, approaching them as we would a modern short story or, to use a Biblical parallel, one of our Lord's parables."[19]

This view undercuts what both Jesus and Paul purportedly thought about Adam and Eve, and Cain and Able too. Either they were both wrong to think of them as real historical people, or they thought these were imaginative folk tales.

CASE IN POINT TWO: THE FLOOD STORY OF GENESIS 6-9

The first thing to notice in the flood story is that there is a great deal of repetition. We are told that Noah is commanded by God to make an ark, load it with food and animals, and then board it. Afterward it says Noah "did everything just as God had commanded him" (6:14–22). But after doing all of this once, God repeats similar instructions to Noah, and once again the text says Noah "did all that the Lord had commanded him" (7:1–5). Did Noah make two arks and board them twice? But we're not done yet. Genesis goes on to say Noah and his family boarded the ark again (7:7–9), and again (7:13–16). There are also discrepancies in these chapters. In 6:14–22 God is referred to as "Elohim" and only one pair of each species of animal was put in the ark, whereas in 7:1–5 the word for God is "Yahweh" and Noah is told to put in the ark seven pairs of clean animals and one pair of unclean animals. There are also discrepancies with how long the flood lasted: 40 days (7:17), 150 days (7:24), or one year (compare 7:11 with 8:13)?

Biblical scholars now see the way the flood is presented here as reflecting two ancient sources that were combined into one account. This was done by "following a very conservative principle of keeping virtually everything from both sources, even though that produced considerable repetition," and, I might add, discrepancies.[20] The closest stories we find to the flood story in the Bible are from Mesopotamia: the Epic of Gilgamesh and Atrahasis. According to Gordon J. Wenham, the Epic of Gilgamesh was written about 1600 BCE and it "may be based on the flood story told in Atrahasis." These stories have several striking similarities, including a flood hero, an ark, a universal worldwide flood because of man's disobedience, and even a dove.[21] Donald Gowan concludes, "These texts are evidence for the transmission of a very popular story from century to century and from people to people; among the recipients of this tradition were the Greeks and the Hebrews."[22]

Since this is the case, the flood story in Genesis was taken and reshaped to fit the purposes of the final editor of Genesis 1–11. And if we consider prior sources to be the more authentic sources (and historical scholars consider this to be so in every other case), then the true account of the flood (if there is one and it reflects something that historically happened) is to be found in Atrahasis along with the Epic of Gilgamesh. Genesis 6–9 is very late and therefore unreliable, historical analysis would reveal. Atrahasis and the Epic of Gilgamesh would be our primary sources for information about a great universal flood that covered the whole world. And in them neither a person named Noah nor a God named "Yaweh" are to be found!

How much of the flood story can truly be regarded as historical if it is based upon ancient superstitious polytheistic folk tales that were handed down throughout the centuries?—tales which have been told by almost every ancient culture, except most of Africa and in central and eastern Asia?[23] Textual analysis cannot really lead us to think all of these tales speak of the same event. Rather, these tales are based upon local devastating floods, which most ancient cultures believed were sent by the gods to punish people for their disobedience. We now know why local floods take place, and it isn't because of our sins, but because of atmospheric and oceanic conditions.

PROBLEMS CONNECTED TO THE FLOOD STORY

Bernard Ramm's critical analysis of a universal flood (while dated a half century ago) is still a good one containing a good summation of the evidence, from which I draw on here. Ramm admits: "There is no known geological data to support those who defend a universal flood."[24] Donald Gowan sums up the evidence with these words: "Not only have all archeological excavations failed to uncover any such evidence (for a universal flood), the record of the earth's history discovered by geology virtually rules out the possibility that anything of that sort has ever happened."[25] There is a recent discovery by Robert Ballard that the Black Sea shoreline increased by 60,000 square miles around 7,500 years ago. But he admits this could have been the result of an earthquake, a massive storm, or perhaps the sheer weight of the ocean waters, none of which demands a worldwide flood.[26] Ramm argues: "The problems in connection with a universal flood are enormous." First, "It would have required eight times more water than we now have." Second, the mixing of saltwater and freshwater along with the pressure of the waters would have been devastating to marine life. Freshwater fish would die in saltwater and saltwater fish would die in freshwater. The pressure of the water six miles high (to cover the Himalayas) would crush to death the vast bulk of marine life that lives within the first fifty fathoms in the water. Third, getting rid of such a vast amount of water would be impossible— think of it! Fourth, "The astronomical disturbances caused by the increase of the mass of the earth would have been significant." Fifth, there are improbabilities with regard to the animals involved. How did Noah get them all into the ark? Bringing them from all four corners of the globe would take considerable time. How did they get along in the ark? Some are carnivorous and would be prone to eating the other animals, while others would have vegetarian diets. Where did the food come from to feed all of these animals from around the world? How could a few people care for them all in the ark? Some animals need a moist climate, and others a dry one; some need it very cold, while others need it warm. Finally, after the flood, how did these animals all migrate back to their original lands, like the kangaroo from Australia? All of this leads me to state categorically that there was no universal flood, and since that's the case, creation scientists cannot use it to explain away the mountains of geological evidence leading scientists to believe the earth is billions of years old. Even the *Anchor Bible Dictionary* ("Noah's Flood") admits: "Scholars are agreed that archaeological evidence for a universal flood in the historical past is wanting," and this admission comes from Christian scholarship on the issue!

NOTES

1. See John Hick, "An Irenaean Theodicy," in *Encountering Evil*, ed. Stephen T. Davis (Atlanta: John Knox, 1981), pp. 40–41.

2. Francis A. Schaeffer, *Genesis in Space and Time* (Downers Grove, IL: InterVarsity Press, 1972), p. 78.

3. David L. Edwards and John Stott, *Evangelical Essentials* (Downers Grove, IL: InterVarsity Press, 1988), p. 96.

4. Henri Blocher, *In the Beginning: The Opening Chapters of Genesis*, trans. David G. Preston (Downers Grove, IL: InterVarsity Press, 1984), pp. 155–57.

5. Gordon Wenham, *Genesis 1–15* (Dallas: Word Incorporated 1987), p. 54.

6. Ibid., p. 91.

7. Schaeffer, *Genesis in Space and Time*, p. 29.

8. Clark Pinnock, *The Scripture Principle* (New York: Harper & Row, 1984), p. 67.

9. Ibid., p. 116.

10. Clark Pinnock and Robert C. Brow, *Unbounded Love* (Downers Grove, IL: Inter-Varsity Press, 1994), p. 62.

11. Donald Gowan, *From Eden to Babel: Genesis 1–11* (Grand Rapids, MI: Eerdmans, 1988), pp. 35–36.

12. Ronald Youngblood, ed., *The Genesis Debate* (Grand Rapids, MI: Baker Book House, 1990), pp. 154–62.

13. Conrad Hyers, *The Meaning of Creation: Genesis and Modern Science* (Atlanta: John Knox Press, 1984), pp. 125–26.

14. Alan Richardson, *A Theological Word Book of the Bible* (London: SCM, 1957), p. 14.

15. John Gibson, *Genesis Vol. 1* (Philadelphia: Westminster Press, 1981), pp. 100–101, 121–25.

16. Emil Brunner, *Man in Revolt* (Louisville, KY: Westminster Press, 1947), pp. 85–88.

17. Gowan, *From Eden to Babel: Genesis 1–11*, pp. 62–63.

18. For a good introduction to the New Testament see L. Michael White, *From Jesus to Christianity* (New York: HarperSanFrancisco, 2004).

19. Gibson, *Genesis Vol. 1*, pp. 2, 11.

20. See, for instance, Gowan, *From Eden to Babel: Genesis 1–11*, p. 89.

21. See "Ancient Parallels to the Flood Story," in Wenham, *Genesis 1–15*, pp. 159–66.

22. Gowan, *From Eden to Babel: Genesis 1–11*, p. 91.

23. To read ninety-seven pages of summaries of these tales, see Sir James G. Frazer's book *Folklore in the Old Testament: Studies in Comparative Religion Legend and Law* (Whitefish, MT: Kessinger Publishing, 2003).

24. Bernard Ramm's, *The Christian View of Science and Scripture* (Grand Rapids, MI: Eerdmans, 1954), pp. 163–69.

25. Gowan, *From Eden to Babel: Genesis 1–11*, p. 89.

26. See "Mysteries of the Bible," *U.S. News & World Report*, November 2004.

16

PROPHECY AND BIBLICAL AUTHORITY

Predictive prophecy is used as a support to biblical authority. In this chapter we'll look at both of these two issues. Let's start with predictive prophecy. In order to predict the future, God must have foreknowledge. Can he predict the future, especially of free-willed human beings? What is the basis of God's foreknowledge? There are philosophical as well as biblical considerations.[1]

PHILOSOPHICAL CONSIDERATIONS

What would be the basis of God knowing the future? That is, how is it logically possible for God to know with absolute certainty that a specific kind of event performed by a free-willed human being would take place? As a Molinist, William Lane Craig believes God not only knows what people will actually do in the future but that God also knows what the future would've been like as the result of every free choice of every person if said persons had done differently.[2] God knows the outcome of every possible choice from the beginning of time. This seems wildly implausible, since every single alternative choice would lead to a different outcome, which, in turn, means that God would have to know the outcome of all alternative choices in that new future as well, and so on, and so on, ad infinitum. One problem for the Molinist is that if God knows the possible outcomes of every potential choice, how can he distinguish between those outcomes that occur from those that don't? Regardless whether one is a Molinist or not, one still needs to know the basis for God's having foreknowledge. There are four possible bases for this.

1. Theological Determinism

God sovereignly decrees/determines what happens (i.e., Calvinism). If God decrees everything that happens, then he can know the future of every human action since he decrees each one of them. But there are serious problems with such a theology. It means God decrees every evil deed that we do. It also means that God decrees every evil desire that we have to do every evil deed that we do. We cannot do otherwise. We cannot even desire to do otherwise. It also means God decrees everything that we believe. None of us can believe other than that which God decrees. Therefore, God decrees people to hell, since those who end up there could not have believed differently. I only have the harshest kinds of comments for such a theology. That God is an evil monster requiring nothing but disgust and loathing. Such a theology creates atheists and motivates me like no other theology to attempt to demolish the Christian faith.

2. God Is Outside of Time So He Sees Everything as Present

If this were so, God would have no problems predicting the future because it is not actually in the future. He's merely seeing the present from his perspective. Stephen T. Davis argues against this view by claiming that such a timeless being is "probably incoherent." If God created this universe, then there was a time when it didn't yet exist, and then there was a later time when it did exist. So he argues: "it is not clear how a timelessly eternal being can be the creator of this temporal universe." It would also make 2005 BCE and 2005 CE simultaneous in God's eyes. But they are not simultaneous in human historical space and time. Davis argues, "We have on hand no acceptable concept of atemporal causation, i.e., of what it is for a timeless cause to produce a temporal effect."[3]

The notion of a timeless God can be traced to Greek philosophers. Plato argued that God must be an eternally perfect being. And since any change in an eternally perfect being must be a change for the worse, God cannot change. Aristotle argued that all of God's potentialities are completely actualized. Therefore, God cannot change because he cannot have unactualized potentialities. Christian thinkers like Augustine, Boethius, and Aquinas brought these concepts to the Bible. Boethius argued: "God lives in an everlasting present." According to Aquinas, God has no past, present, or future since everything is "simultaneously whole" for him.

Christian philosopher William Hasker argues that Plato's argument, for instance, "is straightforwardly fallacious, because it rests on a false dichotomy. It rests on the assumption that all change is either for the better or for the worse, an assumption that is simply false." We want a watch to reflect the correct time, and so it must change with the time of day. The watch that stays the same all day long, and didn't change, would be imperfect. Likewise, "when God began to create the universe he changed, beginning to do something that previously he had not done." Such a change implies no imperfection in God.[4]

The whole notion that God doesn't change seems to imply that God never has a new thought, or idea, since everything is an eternal NOW, and there is nothing he can learn. This is woodenly static. God would not be a person but a block of ice, a thing. To say he does nothing NEW, thinks nothing NEW, feels nothing NEW, basically means he does nothing, thinks nothing, feels nothing, for it's all been done. What would it mean for a person not to take risks, not to plan (for it's already been planned), or to think (thinking involves weighing temporal alternatives, does it not?). But if God cannot have a new thought then he cannot think—he is analogous to a block of ice.

3. The Inferential View

God figures out from the range of options which choices we will make. He does this because he knows who we are completely and thoroughly as the "ultimate psychoanalyst." He can take us in our present state and know with certainty what we will do next, and next, and next, and so on, and so on. He knows the future because he deduces it from who he knows us to be now. This option actually means, however, that what we do is somehow "programmed" into us. The determinist claims that it's all in the genes and environment, so this viewpoint commits the believer to the same position as the determinist. If God can predict future human actions five hundred years from now, based upon what he knows about people living today, then we are merely environmentally and genetically programmed rats. There is no human freedom.

4. The Innate View

God just has comprehensive knowledge of the future. He just "sees it" because he is omniscient. But this isn't an explanation at all! When I asked Professor William Lane Craig in class how it is that God has foreknowledge, Craig, who would normally have elaborate arguments and defenses for his views, merely said, as if this is all that needed to be said, "It's innate, God just has it." What? How? Eventually this answer led me to reject God's foreknowledge of future human free-willed choices since it is not an answer.

Socrates argued that humans have innate knowledge, and he offered an explanation for why we do. His answer was that the soul is immortal, so all learning is a recollection of that which we already knew prior to being born in this world. Descartes also argued we have innate knowledge, and he too offered an explanation for why we do. His answer was that God gave it to us. According to Descartes, human innate knowledge was limited to principles like "something greater does not come from something lesser," not historical knowledge, anyway. Still, both of them offered a reason for their claims—a mechanism for how this was possible, which were disputed by John Locke. That's what's lacking in Craig's claim. Craig offers us no reason to explain how this kind of divine innate knowledge is possible. He offers us no mechanism for understanding how this is possible, especially when it comes to his very unusual claim that God has innate foreknowledge of future free-willed historical actions of human beings.

Craig and J. P. Moreland mainly assert that unless I can prove otherwise, such a thing is possible. They take the offensive by claiming that "unless the detractor of divine foreknowledge can show some incoherence in the notion of innate knowledge, his objection cannot even get off the ground."[5] This is a fine way of saying that such a view as theirs must be shown to be impossible, which is an impossible standard. I have evaluated and found wanting several of the known bases for God having foreknowledge, and that's all I can do. How, for instance, can anyone living in the year 2008, God or otherwise, innately know what someone will do on January 1, 2031? The bottom line for me is that if there is no known mechanism or reason given for how God could know future truly free actions, then I have reasons to reject that God can foreknow such actions. I don't know of any such mechanisms, so without one, I am justified in thinking one isn't available.

From these philosophical considerations, I just don't see any real basis for believing that God can have absolute and certain foreknowledge of future truly free-willed human actions. Therefore, along with a great many recent Christian philosophers, I do not believe God can predict the future of human history with certainty. And since I also reject theological determinism, then there is no basis for predestination either, whether due to God's supposed foreknowledge of what we will do or in God's decrees.

BIBLICAL CONSIDERATIONS OF PREDICTIVE PROPHECY

God is described as declaring what will happen in the future (Ps. 139:4,16; Isa. 46:10–11; Heb. 4:13). But these verses do not demand that God has absolute certain foreknowledge of what we humans will do. Just as God does not have the power to do an absurdity (Can he create a rock so large that he cannot lift it? Can he ride a horse he isn't riding?), neither can God know our future free-willed choices because they simply cannot be known. The Bible speaks often as if God doesn't know the future (Gen. 22:12; Deut. 13:3; Jer. 3:7, 19–20; 26:3; 32:35; Ezek. 12:3 and Jon. 3:10).

Even from a biblical perspective, predictive prophecy can be explained in one of three ways: (1) God is announcing ahead of time what he plans to do (Exod. 6:6–8; 7:3; Isa. 46:10–11). (2) God offers predictions based upon his exhaustive knowledge of the past and present (Exod. 3:19–21). Knowing people as intimately as God does, he can pretty much predict what they will do in certain limited situations, although, the further into the future human history moves, the more it becomes impossible even for God to predict. (3) Prophecy can also be understood as a warning, and is thus conditional and based upon human responses (Jon. 3:2, 5, 10; Isa. 38:1–6; and Jer. 18:7–10).[6]

How the New Testament Writers Used Predictive Prophecy

One of the major things claimed by the New Testament in support of Jesus' life and mission is that Jesus fulfilled Old Testament prophecy (Luke 24:26–27; Acts

3:17–24). But if not even God can predict the future as it moves farther and farther into the distance, then neither can any prophet who claims to speak for God. As we will see with regard to the virgin birth of Jesus, the claim that he was God Incarnate, and of his resurrection, none of the Old Testament passages in the original Hebrew prophetically applied singularly and specifically to Jesus. Early Christian preachers simply went into the Old Testament looking for verses that would support their view of Jesus. They took these Old Testament verses out of context and applied them to Jesus in order to support their views of his life and mission.[7]

In an important work on this subject Catholic scholar Joseph A. Fitzmyer did an exhaustive study of how the Messiah was understood by the Jews in the Old Testament. Fitzmyer claims that "one cannot foist a later Christian meaning on a passage that was supposed to have a distinctive religious sense in guiding the Jewish people of old."[8] So when examining every potentially prophetic Messianic passage in the Old Testament, except perhaps for a couple of passages in the book of Daniel (a book which was "finally redacted c.a. 165 BC"), Fitzmyer rightly argues that the Christian writers interpreted these passages anachronistically due to hindsight understandings of who they concluded Jesus to be.

Many of the claimed prophecies came from the book of Psalms, believed by Christians to be "Messianic Psalms" (i.e., Psalms 2, 16, 22, 35, 40, 69, 110, and 118). But these Psalms in their original contexts are simply devotional prayers. Among other things in the Psalms we find prayers for help in distress, for forgiveness, and for wisdom, and so on. They declare praise to God, and they express hope that their enemies will be defeated. There is nothing about them, when reading them devotionally, that indicates they are predicting anything at all. Yet the New Testament writers quoted from several of them and claimed they predicted several things in the life, death, and resurrection of the Messiah, Jesus.

Psalms 2, according to Christians, expresses hope for the Messiah, the anointed one. Even if this is the case, any Jew writing about his hope for a future Messiah could have said these same hopeful things. A hope is not a prediction. But, in fact, according to Fitzmyer, "Psalm 2 is not 'messianic' in any sense."[9] "There is not even a hint of a 'messianic' connotation of the term or of a remote future, when a Messiah might appear."[10] Besides, Psalms 2 and 110 were most likely to be read at the coronation of Jewish kings. Psalms 110:1 reads: "The Lord says to my lord: 'Sit at my right hand until I make your enemies a footstool for you feet.'" The New Testament writers make a big deal out of the belief that David wrote this Psalm in which he calls someone else "lord." This supposedly refers to David's future Messianic son, Jesus—his divine nature and mission. But it's fairly obvious that if David wrote this Psalm, he did it upon the coronation of his son Solomon, whom he subsequently called "lord." He did this because of Solomon's new status, which placed him as a ruler even above the aged David himself. The fact is that David probably didn't even write Psalm 110, if we're to believe he was on his deathbed when Solomon was crowned his successor (1 Kings 1–2:12). Given the prevalence of pseudonymity in the Bible, it's more likely that someone else did. Nonetheless, Fitzmyer claims Psalm 110 "could hardly refer to any eschatological ideal in the distant future."[11]

The other Psalms do not predict anything at all. They are prayers to be interpreted within the range of the writers' experiences alone. Any extrapolation of them to Jesus is reading Jesus into the text, and not justified by the text itself. After discussing several of the key "Messianic Psalms," Fitzmyer concludes, "The attempt to interpret these Psalms anachronistically in a 'messianic' sense is misguided."[12] It is more probable that the New Testament writers were influenced in the construction of their stories about Jesus by making his life fit some of these details. That may explain Luke's concoction of a census in order to get Mary to Bethlehem so that Jesus could be born there according to "prophecy" (Mic. 5:2, Matt. 2:6), as we will see later.

When it comes to the "Suffering Servant" of Isaiah 53, in the context of post-exilic 2 Isaiah, the servant was not a redeemer messiah, since even Christians think no one in Jesus' day thought that text referred to such a person, otherwise they would not have crucified him. In the book of Isaiah the suffering servant is identified with the people of Israel themselves (42:18–24; 44:1–2; 49:3). Fitzmyer argues there is no room here to see a Messiah as a ruler of the age of salvation. In fact, "there is no passage in the book of Isaiah that mentions a 'Messiah' in the narrow sense, and all attempts to speak of Isaiah's 'messianic prophecies' are still-born."[13] He claims that the Servant Song of Isaiah 53 "has no messianic connotation" per se.[14] "The idea of a suffering Messiah . . . is found nowhere in the Old Testament or in any Jewish literature prior to or contemporaneous with the New Testament. It is a Christian conception that goes beyond the Jewish messianic tradition."[15] Even according to Christian scholarship, Isaiah's servant is "almost certainly to be identified with Israel."[16] The identification of Isaiah's servant with Jesus was based upon the Christian recasting of Isaiah 52–53 in light of the apocryphal book of *The Wisdom of Solomon* (chaps. 1–6).

For a specific look at how the New Testament writers wrote their stories based upon the Old Testament, notice that Matthew 21:2 has Jesus requesting both a donkey and also a colt to ride into Jerusalem on, based upon a misunderstanding of Zechariah 9:9, which reads: "Rejoice . . . your king comes to you . . . gentle and riding on a donkey, on a colt, the foal of a donkey." Zechariah's prophecy is an example of Hebraic parallelism in which the second line retells the point of the first line. There is only one animal in Zechariah, but Matthew thinks he means there is a donkey and also a colt, so he wrote his story based upon this misunderstanding in order to fit prophecy! The gospels of Mark (11:1) and Luke (19:30) both say it was a "colt." John's gospel (12:14–15) says it was a "donkey," and then he misquoted Zechariah 9:9 as saying: "your king is coming, seated on a donkey's colt."

How Matthew's gospel uses the Old Testament is a case in point for us. Since we'll discuss some examples in later chapters, let's just look at three from Matthew. First, 2:14–15: "Then Joseph got up, took the child and his mother by night, and went to Egypt, and remained there until the death of Herod. This was to fulfill what had been spoken by the Lord through the prophet, 'Out of Egypt I have called my son.'" According to the conservative *Bible Knowledge Commentary: An Exposition of the Scriptures*: "This is a reference to Hosea 11:1, which does not seem to be a prophecy in the sense of a prediction. Hosea was writing of God's calling Israel out of Egypt into the Exodus. Matthew, however, gave new understanding to these words. Matthew viewed this experience as Messiah being identified with the nation."[17] Other scholars go further than this: "The total disassociation of that quotation from its context is completely at odds with our own exegetical preferences."[18] "Matthew naturally understands his quotation from Hosea as prophetic; he did not share the insight, common since Zwingli . . . and Calvin . . . that his interpretation does not correspond to the original meaning."[19]

Second, 2:17–18 sees Jeremiah 31:15 as fulfilled when Herod the king ordered all boys two years old and younger in Bethlehem to be killed. But Jeremiah is mourning for those who will be cast into Babylonian captivity. According to R. Schnackenburg, "it seems far-fetched to quote this text as fulfillment of prophecy."[20]

Third, 2:22–23: "Then after being warned by God in a dream, he left for the regions of Galilee, and came and lived in a city called Nazareth. This was to *fulfill* what was spoken through the prophets: 'He shall be called a Nazarene.'" Again, according to *The Bible Knowledge Commentary*, "The words 'He will be called a Nazarene,' were not directly spoken by any Old Testament prophet, though several prophecies come close to this expression. Isaiah said the Messiah would be 'from [Jesse's] roots' like 'a Branch' (Isa. 11:1). 'Branch' is the Hebrew word *nezer*, which has consonants like those in the word 'Nazarene' and which carry the idea of having an insignificant beginning."[21] So this so-called prophecy does not specifically say that the Messiah would be from the town of Nazareth. That's a clear misreading of the texts.

What is the point of these quotations? What do they add to Matthew's narrative? What do they confirm about Jesus? Contextually, there is simply no way on grammatical-historical lines that Hosea 11:1 could be used as evidence of the nature or mission of Jesus in Matthew 2:15. It just isn't there. Matthew uses the verse so loosely that it would show evidence of nothing at all to us today were we the ones weighing the claims of another Messiah. Matthew's claim that Jesus is a "Nazarene" isn't specifically quoted from any Old Testament source, and even if the Messiah was to be a "branch" from David, that only could mean to the Old Testament reader that he would be from David's blood line, not that he would live in Nazareth. No wonder professor C. F. D. Moule claims that Matthew's use of the Old Testament "to our critical eyes, [is] manifestly forced and artificial and unconvincing."[22] And if this is the case, then with S. V. McCastland we can legitimately ask how Matthew distorts his other sources when writing his gospel: "What we have observed about the liberties Matthew took with passages of Scripture he quoted suggests that he may have done the same thing with his more contemporary sources of the life and sayings of Jesus."[23] Why not then be skeptical of his whole gospel?

Steve Moyise acknowledges that "in our day, copyright laws mean that authors need to quote accurately, attend to the original setting of the utterance and then draw conclusions. In the ancient world, texts were living traditions, regularly updated to apply to new situations. The task of an interpreter then was not to discern what the text meant in the past but what it means today. . . . Scholars have sometimes used words like 'arbitrary' or '*ad hoc*' to describe the use of the Old Testament in the New. And from our point of view, it sometimes appears that way."[24] But this is exactly my point. Our methods for discerning correctness have changed, for the better. If we were to judge them by our standards of hermeneutics, they wouldn't measure up—that is, we would be laughed at by our contemporaries if we employed the same methods in scholarly studies—try it and see!

James D. G. Dunn stated that Matthew's use of the sayings of Jesus is similar to the way he used the Old Testament in that: "the texts used were often significantly different in sense from the original. It was evidently quite an acceptable procedure in Matthew's time to incorporate the interpretation into the saying itself by modifying the form of the saying."[25] Today we think this way of interpreting the Old Testament is wrong. New Testament evangelical scholar Richard N. Longenecker argues that "Christians today are committed to the apostolic faith and doctrine of the New Testament, but not necessarily to the apostolic exegetical practices as detailed for us in the New Testament. . . . [L]et us admit that we cannot possibly reproduce the revelatory stance of *pesher* interpretation, nor the atomistic manipulations of Midrash, nor the circumstantial or *ad hominem* thrusts of a particular polemic of that day—nor should we try."[26] Paul Copan admits this: "We should not seek to imitate the Jewish methods of interpretation (of the New Testament)."[27] Of course we shouldn't! But the question is why Christians accept the results of the New Testament writers when they also must reject their hermeneutical method? I defy someone to come up with one statement in the Old Testament that is specifically fulfilled in the life, death, and resurrection of Jesus that can legitimately be understood as a prophecy and singularly points to Jesus as the Messiah using today's historical-grammatical hermeneutical method. It cannot be done.[28]

Randel Helms argues that the way the New Testament writers used the Old Testament "involved interpretive methods that to modern ears seen bizarre."[29] He goes further to argue that many of the very events in the life of Jesus, including his miracles, his death on the cross, and his resurrection, are fictionalized creations based upon Old Testament stories, to show Jesus was the Messiah who fulfilled prophecy by what he did.

On the nature of Old Testament fulfilled prophecy there are several options available. One might be that the New Testament writers were simply wrong in many of their interpretations. Hence, maybe the Messiah hasn't yet come, or no Messiah exists. A second option is that the way they interpreted Old Testament prophecy is correct and it serves as a model for interpreting all texts since the authors were inspired interpreters with inspired methodology. Once we claim the New Testament writers were correct in their interpretations, then it's extremely difficult not to canonize their interpretive methods, including some Midrash, *pesher*, and so on. A third option is possible based upon the fact that the methods for interpretation have changed over the centuries, some for better, some for worse. God foreknew what methods of interpretation would exist at the time of Jesus, so when God prophesied of Jesus, he knew in advance which hermeneutical principles would force people of that day to the conclusion that Jesus was the Messiah. A particular difficult New Testament interpretation might be incorrect based upon the grammatical-historical method yet still be a confirmation that Jesus was its intended object for New Testament–era people. But I've already argued philosophically against the third option, and the second option is not a live option to me.

The Flawed Reasoning of Jesus and Paul

The way Matthew interpreted the Old Testament is flawed by today's standards, but then we see this same flawed reasoning with Jesus and Paul too. Look, for instance, at how Jesus purportedly argued on behalf of the resurrection: "And as touching the dead, that they rise: have ye not read in the book of Moses, how in the bush God spoke unto him, saying, 'I am the God of Abraham, and the God of Isaac, and the God of Jacob?' He is not the God of the dead, but the God of the living: ye therefore do greatly err" (Mark 12:26–27). How this argument of Jesus' is supposed to lead to the belief that the dead do in fact arise is convoluted to say the least. This Old Testament text, taken in its original context, is merely identifying the God who was speaking to Moses from out of the so-called burning bush. No thinker today would ever conclude that God was proclaiming anything about a resurrection from the dead, even if Jesus and his contemporaries may have thought so.

Look also at how Paul argued on behalf of the general resurrection:

If there is no resurrection of the dead, then not even Christ has been raised.
Christ has been raised.
Therefore, there is a resurrection of the dead. (1 Cor. 15:13)

This is a logically valid argument form, called *Modus Tollens*, even if I don't think it's a sound or convincing argument. Why does it follow merely from the fact that Christ arose that there shall be a resurrection of the dead? There seems to be nothing in the belief that Jesus arose that would lead me to think that there is a general resurrection. It just might be the case that Jesus arose because he's special and that's it.

The answer for Paul is that Christ is the head of those who believe, just like Adam is the head of humanity (vv. 21–22), so what is true of the head will likewise be true of his followers. But this kind of inferential argument makes no sense in today's world, no matter what Christian scholars say people believed in the past. Paul's logic is flawed here. It could equally be argued from this same logic that since Jesus ascended into heaven, so will all believers, since what is true of the head will likewise be true of his followers. But of course, that logic doesn't work because even in Paul's day, some Christians had already died and didn't ascend into heaven as Jesus purportedly did from Mount Olivet.

My position is that these ancient standards are pathetic in comparison to today's standards. Their reasoning was inadequate, their scientific testing was lame, and their understandings were infantile. So to continue believing what they tell us, when we know this about their standards, is utter foolishness.

Now here's the rub. If I misapplied an Old Testament text, or misquoted it to make a point, or if I used *pesher*, *midrash*, typological, or allegorical methods today to understand the Old Testament, or the Bible as a whole, Christians today would be the first ones to jump down my throat based upon the grammatical-historical method. Christians would not believe someone today who claimed some strange ideas about an incarnate God who rose from the dead, if the person presenting the evidence used quotations from an ancient text out of context or their reasoning was flawed. They wouldn't, and neither do I.

The bottom line is that in order for today's Christians to believe Jesus rose from the dead, they must first believe in the hermeneutical method of the New Testament. It cannot be reversed because we want to know whether or not Jesus arose from the dead "according to the Scriptures." Northrop Frye wrote: "How do we know that the Gospel story is true? Because it confirms the prophecies of the Old Testament. But how do we know that the Old Testament prophecies are true? Because they are confirmed by the Gospel story. Evidence, so called, is bounced back and forth between the testaments like a tennis ball; and no other evidence is given us. The two testaments form a double mirror, each reflecting the other but neither the world outside."[30] Therefore, I believe there is no solid Old Testament support for any of their claims about Jesus from the Old Testament. The New Testament writers misused Old Testament sources and subsequently reasoned as Paul did to show that Jesus was truly born of a virgin, that he was the messiah, that he atoned for our sins, and that he arose from the dead. None of their quotes or offered reasons support their claims (by the way, typology is all in the mind of the beholder, like horoscope readings).[31]

But it's precisely their hermeneutical methods and reasoning here that led them to argue the way they do on behalf of Jesus. I simply argue that if their approach is so flawed in how they argue, then we should not trust their claim that Jesus rose from the dead. If one is flawed, then so is the other. Both stem from a faulty and inadequate way of understanding the world and of assessing the evidence for or against any historical claim, much less a miraculous one.

Against this argument, Christians will argue that the New Testament writers knew that Jesus was born of a virgin, raised from the dead, and so on, but that to substantiate it for those who believed the Old Testament as scripture, they sought out passages that could be read typologically as a double fulfillment to verify that these events were foreseen in the Old Testament. But this is the very question I'm asking. How do we know today that the historical events led them to discover these texts, and not vice versa? Based on the reasoning of the New Testament writers, it is much more likely that Old Testament texts led them to tell the stories they did about Jesus, not vice versa. The best way to understand their use of the Old Testament is that they wrote about the life of Jesus from the perspective of their superstitious beliefs about Jesus. That is, they made Jesus' life fit the details of their flawed understanding of the Old Testament, even if it was out of context and even if their reasoning was flawed by today's more rigorous standards.

What Christian apologists will have to show is that early Christians were concerned in the first place about what actually happened. For that's what is needed to prove their point. Christians might as well argue that the early Christians weren't superstitious or that they had a good grasp of science too, but I've already dealt with that earlier in this book.

The Prophetic Paradigm

In the Bible we have a few prophets proclaiming the "word of God," which has become a model for understanding the Bible as a whole, known as the *prophetic paradigm*. Paul J. Achtemeier wrote: "It is precisely because the prophet is the one into whose mouth God placed his own words that the prophet became the model for an understanding of the inspiration of Scripture. This way of understanding the inspiration of Scripture was then applied to the other books of the Bible, and to other literary forms: poems, songs, histories, wisdom sayings and all the rest. Behind the books of the Bible stand the inspired authors, each of whom wrote down what God wanted to be written down."[32]

But the model of the prophet receiving the very words of God is not a good paradigm for understanding the Bible as a whole. In the first place, prophetic speech claiming "thus says the Lord" is not seen much at all in the Old Testament, although it is true that it is common in the prophetic books. We don't see the phrase "thus says the Lord," for instance, after we read in the Bible that "the priests, who were heads of families, numbered 1,760" (1 Chron. 9:13). Nor do we see it after the phrase, "I am the rose of Sharon, a lily of the valleys" (Song of Songs 2:1). According to James Barr, in his excellent discussion on this whole subject, such a prophetic paradigm "is not applied to the total literature of the Old Testament by that literature itself. Large tracts of Old Testament material are not in any normal sense 'prophetic' and these tracts make no pretension to possessing the features of being words directly given by God such as we find in the speeches of the prophets themselves."[33]

When we do look at those passages where the prophets use phrases like "thus says the Lord," what do we find? According to Barr, "for the most part the content concerns the divine judgment and the divine promise upon Israel, Judah and other peoples (see Amos). . . . It is a warning of disaster that will come unless one's ways are mended. What a prophet says, then, is characteristically not an absolute. What the prophet says is conditioned. It may be affected by repentance of the persons affected, or by the pleas and prayers of the righteous on their behalf."[34] Jeremiah 18:5–10 describes this best. It reads: "The word of the Lord came to me: 'If at any time I announce that a nation is to be uprooted and destroyed, and if that nation I warned repents of its evil, then I will relent and not inflict on it the disaster I had planned. And if at another time I announce that a nation is to be built up and planted, and if it does evil in my sight then I will reconsider the good I had intended to do for it.'" This of course, is used to explain away why God failed to keep the "land promise" he made to Joshua that he would conquer the whole land of Palestine in his day, but which never happened.[35] Contrast this understanding with Deuteronomy 18:21–22, where it says the test of a true prophet is that what a prophet said must come true.

Isaiah prophesied that Hezekiah would die, but because he prayed to live, God purportedly gave him an additional fifteen years (38:1–6). Technically speaking, what the prophet Isaiah predicted was not fulfilled. But that didn't bother Isaiah because he wasn't concerned about predicting the future. He was mainly offering warnings and threats for disobedience. Jonah obeyed "the word of the Lord" by prophesying to the people of Nineveh, "forty more days and Nineveh will be over-turned." They repented and God did not destroy them (3:2, 5, 10). But didn't Jonah prophesy that Nineveh would be overturned? We see this throughout the prophets. Barr argues: "Prophecy was not concerned with accuracy, but with communicating the will and judgment of God. The belief that the prophetic paradigm supports ideas of accuracy and inerrancy can be maintained only if the actuality of what the Old Testament prophets were like is ignored."[36]

Where the prophets do predict the future, according to Barr, "the vast majority" of them are fairly short-term ones, and as we've seen, most all of these are condi-tioned upon the responses of the hearers. The prophets did describe a future ideal messianic age in which pain and suffering would be eliminated (Isa. 11:6–9), but "these are not really 'predictions.' They are expressions of aspirations and ideals which, the prophet is confident, God will bring to realization. They do not 'predict' how or when or in what degree these expectations may be realized." Furthermore, "it is not the case that prediction is possible only with supernatural aid or guidance. People do it all the time. A number of the predictions which Old Testament prophets make could have been made by a capable newspaper columnist of the period."[37]

Tim Callahan has examined a hundred or more so-called prophetic passages in the Bible and subjected them to four simple questions: (1) Is the prophecy true, and if so, to what degree, or is it too vague as to be open to many interpretations? (2) If the prophecy is true, was it written before or after the fact? (3) Was the prophecy deliberately fulfilled by someone with knowledge of the prophecy? (4) Was the prophecy a logical guess? Was its fulfillment something that could be predicted based on a logical interpretation of the events of the prophet's own day? After exam-ining these texts, he concludes that not a single biblical prophecy satisfies the demands of these four questions.[38]

If a foretelling God were truly behind the Bible, then in Sam Harris's words, "Why doesn't the Bible say anything about electricity, or about DNA, or about the actual size of the universe?" "You would expect it to contain a passage such as, 'In the latter half of the 20th century, humankind will develop a globally linked system of computers . . . and this system shall be called the Internet.'"[39]

JESUS WAS A FAILED DOOMSDAY PROPHET

Let me focus on the one major failed prophecy in the New Testament from the lips of Jesus himself, who is best understood as a failed apocalyptic doomsday prophet.[40] The *eschaton* never happened as Jesus prophesied in his generation. In Matthew's gospel we read about it when Jesus says: "Immediately after the tribulation of those days the sun will be darkened, and the moon will not give its light, and the stars will fall from heaven, and the powers of the heavens will be shaken; then will appear the sign of the Son of man in heaven, and then all the tribes of the earth will mourn, and they will see the Son of man coming on the clouds of heaven with power and great glory; and he will send out his angels with a loud trumpet call, and they will gather his elect from the four winds, from one end of heaven to the other. From the fig tree learn its lesson: as soon as its branch becomes tender and puts forth its leaves, you know that summer is near. So also, when you see all these things, you know that he is near, at the very gates. Truly, I say to you, this generation will not pass away till all these things take place" (Matt. 24:29–34; Mark 13:24–30). This event and the establishment of God's kingdom describe what is called the *eschaton*, from which we get the word *eschatology*, or the study of end times. It was never fulfilled as prophesied.

Theologians have tried to construe the word *generation* in the above passage to mean "race," as in "this race of people will certainly not pass away until all these things have happened." But that is not the obvious meaning, given the context. Edward Adams states it forthrightly: "It is virtually certain that 'this generation' means the generation living at the time of utterance. The time frame in this verse is thus the lifetime of Jesus' own contemporaries."[41] When we factor in the other sayings attributed to Jesus, it seems obvious the gospel writers have him talking about an imminent *eschaton*: "some of those standing here will not taste death until they see the kingdom coming in power" (Matt. 16:28; Mark 9:1; Luke 9:27); and "I tell you the truth, you will not finish going through the cities of Israel before the Son of Man comes" (Matt. 10:23). Speaking to the Sanhedrin during his trial Jesus reportedly said, "you will see the Son of Man seated at the right hand of power, and coming on the clouds of heaven" (Matt. 26:64; Mark 14:16).

The rest of the New Testament writers interpreted Jesus in this natural way. So, for example, we find Paul saying this: "What I mean, brothers, is that the time is short. From now on those who have wives should live as if they had none; those who mourn, as if they did not; those who are happy, as if they were not; those who buy something, as if it were not theirs to keep; those who use the things of the world, as if not engrossed in them. For this world in its present form is passing away" (1 Cor. 7:29). This also explains Paul's sense of urgency and his racing with all his might to preach the Gospel to every nation, since Jesus reportedly said the Gospel must first be preached to the ends of the earth before the *eschaton* occurs (Matt. 24:14). We find the author of 1 John saying he knows it's the "last hour" since many antichrists have arisen (2:18) because Jesus purportedly predicted false Christ's would arise just before the *eschaton* (in Mark 13:21–23). We have the author of the book of Revelation (13:18), who identifies the beast with Nero through the cipher language of using numbers to double as letters, so that 666 adds up to Nero Caesar, in which case the *eschaton* has a statute of limitations with the people alive during Nero's time.

All of this fits nicely with Jesus' and the early church's radical "interim ethic" where his disciples are to sell all and give to the poor (Luke 12:33), and where Jesus said "Follow me, and leave the dead to bury their own dead" (Matt. 8:22). According to Bart D. Ehrman, Jesus "urged his followers to abandon their homes and forsake families for the sake of the kingdom that was soon to arrive. He didn't encourage people to pursue fulfilling careers, make a good living, and work for a just society for the long haul; for him, there wasn't going to be a long haul."[42] This makes perfect sense. Jesus believed and preached an imminent *eschaton*, given that he accepted John the Baptist's eschatological message of repentance: the kingdom is at hand because "the axe is already laid at the root" (Luke 3:9).

This interpretation also fits nicely with the fact that the eschatological "kingdom of God" talk and the imminent prediction was successively watered down (from Mark to Matthew to Luke), to the point where such talk of an imminent *eschaton* is completely removed in John's gospel, and the language about "the kingdom of God" is replaced with non-eschatological "eternal life" language. (See note.)[43] In the second-century pseudonymous epistle of 2 Peter, which almost didn't make it into the canon of scriptures, scoffers were already questioning why Jesus didn't return. These things were an embarrassment to the church of that day. The answer given was expressed in these words: "But do not forget this one thing, dear friends: With the Lord a day is like a thousand years, and a thousand years are like a day. The Lord is not slow in keeping his promise, as some understand slowness. He is patient with you, not wanting anyone to perish, but everyone to come to repentance. But the day of the Lord will come like a thief" (2 Pet. 3:3–10). But this answer falls on deaf ears. It comes across as an excuse for why the *eschaton* didn't occur in the very generation Jesus said it would.

For these sorts of reasons, the vast majority of New Testament scholars take such language attributed to Jesus to be of an imminent *eschaton*. Some conservative Christian scholars take a Preterist interpretation of eschatology in which the things Jesus predicted would occur imminently in that Jesus was only referring to the destruction of Jerusalem and the temple in 70 CE, and not the end of the world. They believe the prophecies about the *eschaton* were fulfilled either partially or in full in the first century. But I believe Preterism is a frank concession of the fact that Jesus did not return as was expected from the earliest days of Christianity until recently. It is one thing for skeptics to scoff, it's quite another to see Christians reinvent their eschatology to accommodate this glaring problem. Now it is true that the *eschaton* had to do with the destruction of Jerusalem (see the parallel passages in Matt. 24:15–17 and Mark 13:14 compared with Luke 21:20, where it says to watch for when "Jerusalem is surrounded by armies"). But Preterists deny the obvious meaning of what Jesus was saying—not to mention that the rest of the New Testament authors who assumed such talk implied the destruction of the Roman Empire itself. How else can we understand the following words on Jesus' lips: "Nation will rise against nation and kingdom against kingdom, and there will be great earthquakes, and in various places plagues and famines; and there will be terrors and great signs from heaven" (Luke 21:10)? It was not only going to be the end of all of the kingdoms of men on earth but a total cosmic catastrophe in which the stars literally "fall from heaven" following which God inaugurates a literal kingdom with the son of man (Jesus?) reigning from Jerusalem.[44] This never happened in their lifetimes as was predicted. The only reason Christians gerrymander around the plain sense of these New Testament texts, in Michael Martin's words, "is that apologists have reinterpreted Scripture in an implausible way in order to save Christianity from refutation."[45]

IS THE BIBLE REALLY THE AUTHORITATIVE WORD OF GOD?

Evangelicals will typically quote from the Bible to settle any question it speaks directly about, since they believe it's God's word. Some fundamentalists will repeat the phrase, "God said it; I believe it; that settles it." Using proof texts like those found in 2 Peter 1:21, where it's said the prophets of old "spoke the words of God," and 2 Timothy 3:16, which says scripture is "God breathed," they claim the very words in the Bible are from God (see also Matt. 5:18; 24:35; John 10:35; 17:17; Rom. 3:2; 1 Cor. 2:13; 15:3; 1 Thess. 2:13; 4:15; 1 Tim. 5:18; Heb. 1:1; 1 Pet. 1:25; 2 Pet. 3:2).[46]

There are several serious problems with this view. It should be noted from the outset that there are several Christian theories of what it means to say the Bible is inspired. First, there is the "dictation" or "mechanical" theory, in which it's believed God woodenly dictated the very words to the biblical writers like someone might dictate a letter to a secretary. This is now almost universally rejected by Christians, since it's obvious that each of the biblical writers had a distinct style and vocabulary. Second, there is the "verbal-plenary" theory. It is "verbal" in that the very words in the Bible are God's, although (somehow) not dictated by God. The end product is all that's affirmed here, that the Bible is the very word of God, not how God accomplished this. It is "plenary" in that it's believed that the Bible is completely inspired in all of its parts. Some of those who believe in the verbal-plenary theory believe that the Bible is the "inerrant" word of God, containing no errors at all; while others maintain that the Bible may be regarded as their "infallible" rule of faith and practice in all religious and ethical matters, but not in historical and scientific matters. Third, there is the "illumination" theory, where it's believed God "breathed on" or illuminated the biblical writers, who then translated this so-called religious experience into words. Thus, the Bible does not contain the exact words of God; it only contains God's thoughts as expressed through human beings, and as such, only the main thoughts of the Bible are inspired. Fourth, Karl Barth, along with other neo-orthodox Christian thinkers, affirms that the Bible is a "witness" to God's revelation and not God's revelation itself. God uses the Bible in a unique way when read or proclaimed to speak to people, although God could also use a Russian flute concerto to do so. Last, liberal Christians have adopted what can be called the "natural" theory, in that biblical writers were only inspired in the sense that a poet is inspired. According to them, the spark of divine inspiration that is supposedly in us all burned a little brighter in their lives, and as such, inspiration refers to the Christian community of faith.

None of these theories have any evidence for them. Norman L. Geisler, for instance, claims that the resurrection of Jesus proves he is the divine Son of God, and as such, his words are God's words. Therefore, since Jesus purportedly said to his disciples that the Spirit of God will "guide you into all truth" (John 16:13) and that it will "teach you all things and will remind you of everything I have said to you" (John 14:26), Geisler claims Jesus "guaranteed the inspiration of the New Testament."[47] Clark Pinnock agrees and wrote, "Jesus preauthenticated the New Testament canon when he called the apostles to be with him and promised the Holy Spirit to guide them."[48] There are a few problems with this, as I will shortly argue. In another chapter

I'll argue we cannot trust much, if anything, that John's gospel says that Jesus said (see my chapter 18). The truth of the matter is that Jesus is being used in the Gospel of John to authenticate the Gospel of John, since it was obvious that it departed from the style and content of the three synoptic Gospels. Robert M. Price argues that the Gospel of John (16:12–14) "even admits pretty overtly that Johannine teaching comes not from the historical Jesus but from the *Paracletos* (the Holy Spirit Comforter), one sent after Jesus to clarify and update his doctrine. . . . We do not need to think very hard to see this *Paracletos* is none other than the gospel writer himself."[49]

Besides, even most conservative biblical scholars do not think many of these twelve disciples, whom Jesus was directly speaking to, wrote anything. Paul was not there, nor was Mark, nor Luke, nor the author of Hebrews, nor the brothers of Jesus who supposedly wrote James and Jude. Some conservative scholars do not think the disciples Matthew or John wrote the gospels attributed to them, but that they were the product of two schools of thought. This leaves us with little (1 John and 1 Peter?) or nothing that any of the disciples who might have been present when Jesus purportedly spoke the words Geisler refers to wrote.[50] And to claim, as Pinnock does, that Jesus "preauthenticated" the canon itself, goes way beyond what the text actually says. Pinnock is proof texting. James Barr reminds us that "Jesus in his teaching is nowhere portrayed as commanding or even sanctioning the production of a written Gospel, still less a written New Testament. He never even casually told his disciples to write anything down, nor did he even, short of writing, command them to memorize his words exactly for future committal to the medium of writing."[51]

I've discussed several "errors of interpretation," by arguing that the New Testament writers misinterpreted many Old Testament texts, along with some failed prophecies. I've also addressed some of the "scientific errors" when it comes to the Genesis creation accounts. And if my arguments against the historicity of the fall in the garden of Eden, Noah's flood, the Israelite exodus from Egypt, the virgin birth of Jesus, the existence of Joseph of Arimathea, and Jesus' resurrection are correct in this book, I'm addressing "historical errors," some of which are fatal to the Christian faith itself. I also mention "ethical errors" when it comes to the Inquisition, witch burnings, honor killings, and slavery. Bishop John Shelby Spong, in his book *The Sins of Scripture*, adequately reveals the Bible's atrocious record when it comes to the environment, women, homosexuality, children, and anti-Semitism.[52] Besides all of this, when it comes to the Bible itself, the authors disagree with each other on things like racism, their own history, the discrepancies in the wisdom literature, Apocalyptic predictions, views of Jesus, and Paul's debates with James and the Judaizers. According to Randel McCraw Helms, "The Bible is a war zone, and its authors are the combatants."[53] These kinds of arguments are strong evidence against those Christians who affirm the Bible is God's word whether "infallible" or "inerrant."

But "inerrantists" are the most difficult to convince, so let me take aim here at the inerrancy verbal-plenary view of inspiration. I'll address some biblical "inconsistency errors" that provide strong evidence against the claim that the Bible is "inerrant." To do this, I can utilize the arguments of those Christian thinkers who affirm the Bible is "infallible" against those who affirm "inerrancy."

Biblical Inconsistencies

Stephen T. Davis argues against "inerrancy" and affirms instead "infallibility." He claims that "the Bible is or ought to be authoritative for every Christian in all that it says on any subject unless he encounters a passage which after careful study and for good reason he cannot accept."[54] He argues that "the phenomena of Scripture do not support the claim that the Bible is inerrant."[55] Among the problems he argues for is the brutality of the Canaanite genocide (see Josh. 11:1–23). Davis says, "I frankly find it difficult to believe that it was God's will that every Canaanite—man woman, and child—be slaughtered." There's also David's numbering of his people (did God provoke him to do this as in 2 Sam. 24:1–2, or did Satan, as in 1 Chron. 21:1–2?); the mustard seed problem (Jesus said it was the smallest seed in Matt. 13:31–32, but it's not the smallest seed); Matthew 27:9–10 claims to be quoting from Jeremiah (but "the quoted words are found nowhere in Jeremiah"); and the staff problem (did Jesus tell his disciples to take a staff with them, as we see in Mark 6:8, or not, as seen in Matt. 10:9–10?).

Paul J. Achtemeier, a Christian thinker who understands biblical inspiration as a "witness" inside the ongoing progressive nature of the community of faith, wrote: "That there are errors in the 'plain and obvious' sense of Scripture has long been seen by those not committed to their denial."[56] Then he fills several pages with examples of these types of errors.[57] One of the most interesting errors he uses to illustrate his point concerns how many times the cock will crow before Peter has denied Jesus three times. In Mark 14:30, Jesus says the cock will crow *twice* before Peter denies Jesus three times, while in Matthew 26:34; Luke 22:34, and John 13:38, Jesus is reported to have said before the cock crows *once* Peter will deny him three times. And true to what each gospel says would happen is what happened. But they disagree with each other. Such a problem as this forced inerrantist Harold Lindsell, in his book *Battle for the Bible*, to suggest that Peter didn't just deny Jesus three times, but six times, with three of them taking place before the first crowing (following Matthew, Luke, and John) and three of them taking place before the second crowing (as in Mark).[58] Achtemeier, however, doesn't let him get away with this. Of Lindsell's argument he wrote, "He has thus convincingly demonstrated that none of the four (gospels) is inerrant, since none of them know what really happened, i.e., six denials. All claim three."

Bart D. Ehrman, a former Christian who is now an agnostic, highlights the crisis of faith he had in believing the Bible was inspired when doing a research paper trying to answer who the priest was when King David and his hungry men went into the temple to eat. In 1 Samuel 21:1–6 it says Ahimelech was the priest, but in Mark's gospel (2:25–26) we find Jesus saying Abiathar was the priest. Ehrman said he developed a "bit convoluted" argument trying to harmonize this discrepancy. But when his professor suggested that Mark might have "just made a mistake," he realized, in his words, "I had to do some pretty fancy exegetical footwork to get around the problem, and that my solution was in fact a bit of a stretch. I finally concluded, 'Hmmm . . . maybe Mark *did* make a mistake. Once I made that admission, the floodgates opened. For if there could be one little, picayune mistake in Mark 2, maybe there could be mistakes in other places too."[59]

David L. Edwards[60] lists several biblical inconsistencies, as do Joe Holman and Valerie Tarico.[61] Let me mention a few of them that troubled me the most as I was thinking about the inspiration and authority of the Bible. First: In Galatians 3:8 and 3:16, Paul indicates the promise to Abraham was to one child, or "seed," which he says is Christ. In Genesis 12:7, 13:15, and 24:7, however, the original word in Hebrew is a plural word, "seeds." The promise was not, as Paul said, to one particular seed, Jesus, but to Abraham's children. Second: In Galatians 3:17 Paul claimed that the law came 430 years after Abraham received the promises from God, but according to Exodus 12:40–41, long after Abraham and yet before the law was given, the Israelites lived in Egypt 430 years. They both cannot be accurate. Third: In Ephesians 4:8 Paul misquotes Psalms 68:18. Did Christ give gifts to the church (Ephesians) or did he receive gifts from the church (Psalms)? To say Paul captured the intent of the quote due to Christ's coronation, in which the giving and receiving of gifts usually take place, is not the same thing as quoting it accurately. Fourth: When did Jesus cleanse the temple? It's simply not credible that he did it twice. Compare John 2:13–25, where Jesus did this at the beginning of his ministry, with Matthew 21:12, Mark 11:15–17, and Luke 19:45–46, where it's claimed he did it during Passion Week (the week in which he was crucified). There is even disagreement between Matthew, Mark, and Luke on which day during that week Jesus cleansed the temple. Fifth: How many Israelites were killed by a plague? Were twenty-three thousand killed, as reported in 1 Corinthians 10:8, or twenty-four thousand, as seen in Numbers 25:9? Sixth: Who killed the large and mighty Goliath of the Philistines? Did David (1 Samuel 17), Elhanan (2 Sam. 21:19), or did Elhanan kill Goliath's brother (1 Chron. 20:5)? Seventh: Was Jarius's daughter dying or already dead when he approached Jesus to ask him to do a miracle in her life (Matt. 9:18 or Mark 5:23)? Eighth: What did the Centurion do and say concerning his servant who needed healing (Matt. 8:5–13; Luke 7:1–10)? What did Jesus say? What did the people say? Who said what and when? In one account Jesus makes a statement, but in another account it was the people who made it. Ninth: The writer of the book of Hebrews uses a mistranslation to argue a point. The word in Hebrews 10:5 is *body*, but in Psalms 40:6 it is *ears*. Finally, What exactly happened on the day Jesus supposedly resurrected and in what order? I'll deal with this one later. There were others.

Dr. Valerie Tarico reveals just how Christians argue with regard to Bible inconsistencies. She writes, "a whole industry has sprung up to convince believers and non-believers alike that these difficulties are inconsequential." She quotes from Gleason Archer's *Encyclopedia of Bible Difficulties*, where he tells his readers that when looking at the Bible, one must first assume God inspired the authors and preserved them from error or mistake. Then she writes, "Archer says, essentially that the reader must start the process of inquiry by assuming a certain outcome. Don't look for the most likely hypothesis suggested by the evidence, he says, nor the one that is most likely straightforward or reasonable. Start by believing that a certain conclusion is already true. . . . Examine the evidence through the lens of that conclusion. . . . Ask yourself, 'What explanations or interpretations can I come up with that would allow me to maintain my belief that these texts are not contradictory?' If you can find any at all, then you have succeeded in your task. By implication, if you cannot, the problem lies with you, not the text. Archer's approach, in almost any other field of inquiry, would be considered preposterous."[62] I wholeheartedly agree.

THE FIVE STAGES OF THE GOSPEL TRADITION

What many Christians fail to realize is how we got the final product of the four Gospels in the first place (as well as the New Testament itself). The Gospel of Luke acknowledges three stages in the origin of his work: "Many have undertaken to draw up an account of the things that have been fulfilled among us, just as they were handed down to us by those who from the first were eyewitnesses and servants of the word. Therefore, since I myself have carefully investigated everything from the beginning, it seemed good also to me to write an orderly (Lit. 'chronological') account for you, most excellent Theophilus" (from Luke 1:1–4). The first thing to be said here is that even though Luke states his account is chronological, it is anything but that. Nonetheless, he admitted to three stages in the production of his gospel.[63] There are two additional stages for a total of five.

STAGE ONE: Oral Traditions Stemming from Eyewitnesses

Stories about Jesus and what he taught circulated among early Christians. At some point they began to write these stories down and circulated them as independent units, probably as a way to teach and disciple others. *Form Criticism* tries to determine which stories were earlier by evaluating the stories themselves according to their form and style. The working assumption is that the earlier stories would be more accurate because of the tendency of people to lengthen their stories by adding details to them to fit the needs of the progressing Christian community. Scholars use tests like the "criterion of dissimilarity" to determine authenticity, which states that if a story or saying of Jesus reflects primarily the concerns of the progressing primitive church, it probably didn't originate with Jesus.[64]

STAGE TWO: Written Accounts of Jesus

Eventually Christians needed a written account containing these stories in an orderly whole, and according to Luke there were "many" of them. *Source Criticism* seeks to understand what written sources, if any, the evangelists used in compiling their gospels. In the first three gospels there are a number of passages that contain exact verbal agreement, even when describing the events leading up to when Jesus speaks. At the same time there are also many differences in verbal agreement. Likewise, there is a certain sequence of events usually adopted by the writers, but quite a divergence in sequence as well. So the goal is to seek a hypothesis that best accounts for both exact agreement and wide divergences in these gospels. According to most scholars, the oral traditions were gathered together in the form of teaching material for new converts. This teaching was complied into a document dubbed "Q" (short for *Quelle* or "source"). Early tradition says Matthew wrote the first gospel in the Aramaic language. Mark wrote his gospel from the content of Peter's preaching, we're told. Matthew may have later transformed his Aramaic gospel into a Greek gospel using Mark and "Q." Luke used several sources, including "Q," Mark, Matthew, and perhaps a separate source. This is known as the "two-source" hypothesis (Mark and "Q") and is widely accepted today. This is a fine way for God to inspire a book, eh?

STAGE THREE: The Final Composition of the Gospels

The gospel writers have written (or edited) these stories to form a whole Gospel account of Jesus with a different emphasis (or purpose) to meet the needs of the particular Christian community at the time they were written. In so doing, each gospel writer relates different events in the life of Jesus with a differing chronology of the events he chose to include—events that help each writer stress his particular point of view. *Redaction Criticism* seeks to describe these purposes by analyzing the way they use their sources, and by comparing the final product with the time and place and people to whom it was written. Luke, for instance, heavily emphasizes the poor, women, and the downtrodden in the life of Jesus, whereas John's gospel hardly says anything about them. So the question becomes this: Even if we have Jesus' words, what did Jesus actually emphasize in his ministry if it's filtered through the eyes of the gospel writers? Even if they were all inspired, we still cannot determine with a great deal of confidence what Jesus actually stressed.

STAGE FOUR: The Transmission of the Texts of the Gospels

Earlier I said it would've been better for God to reveal himself after the rise of printing presses. Here is the reason why. In reference to the original manuscripts of the New Testament being copied and recopied by hand, Bart Ehrman writes, "Not only do we not have the originals, we don't have the first copies of the originals. We don't even have copies of the copies of the originals, or copies of the copies of the copies of the originals. What we have are copies made many centuries later. And these copies all differ from one another, in many thousands of places. . . . There are more differences among our manuscripts than there are words in the New Testament."[65] Hector Avalos argues that "the findings of textual critics devastate any claim that the Bible has been transmitted faithfully from any original text," and as such, "the whole idea of an original text is an illusion." He even argues that "there is no longer any strong rationale for why textual criticism, as a discipline, should matter to those outside communities of faith, or even to communities of faith themselves. In short, the subdiscipline of textual criticism has helped to put itself and biblical studies out of business. All that is left is for textual critics to come to terms with what they have done to themselves."[66]

Some of these differences are very important for theology.[67] This makes it very difficult for us to know exactly what God had inspired in the New Testament itself, or in some cases what we should even believe. This is especially forceful since the initial copying of these manuscripts took place for several centuries by amateur scribes (scribes who, in a few cases, couldn't even understand what they were copying) before we find any good complete manuscripts of the New Testament.

STAGE FIVE: The Canonization of the New Testament Itself and the Variety of Early Christianities

The process of determining the present collection of twenty-seven books that Christians now call the New Testament took just over three hundred years before the Third Council of Carthage (397 CE) declared them to be scripture. That being said, James Barr reminds us that when it comes to questions of the canon, "it was impossible to provide *scriptural* proof for this central of questions, namely, which precisely were the books which had been divinely inspired. No passage in either Old or New Testament gave a list." There was "no scriptural evidence to decide what were the exact limits of the canon. Books do not necessarily say whether they are divinely inspired or not, and many books that do in some fashion claim divine inspiration were nevertheless not accepted as canonical."[68] Bart Ehrman discusses these other writings and calls them "Lost Scriptures,"[69] coming from "Lost Christianities."[70]

The first known canon was proposed by Marcion (ca. 110–160), who rejected the whole Old Testament and only accepted Luke's gospel and ten letters of Paul, which excluded the Pastoral Epistles. The Muratorian Fragment (ca. 170) generally lists the books now recognized as the New Testament, but the first historian of the church, Eusebius (ca. 325), talks about disputed books such as James, Jude, 2 Peter, 2 John and 3 John, and perhaps the book of Revelation. The Cheltenham manuscript (ca. 360) excludes Hebrews, James, and Jude. The debate about the canon came to the foreground again during the Protestant Reformation, when Martin Luther rejected the book of James, and the Catholic Church decided at the Council of Trent (which was convened three times between 1545 and 1563) to include several additional books into their canon that Protestants think are apocryphal.[71]

Protestant Christian thinkers claim the church did not "establish" what books should be in the canon of scriptures, but rather the church "recognized" them.[72] Such a distinction makes no sense at all, since to recognize them is to establish them, and to establish them is to recognize them. Helmut Koester argues that the whole notion of a canon should be abolished, since there is no significant difference between the early Christian literature, and as such, "whatever sources shed light on the early Christian movement should be treated the same way."[73]

Christian thinkers claim there were some precise objective criteria that the early church used to establish canonicity, like whether it was written by an apostle, widely recognized as authentic, and conformed to what Christians believe, called the "rule of faith."[74] But apart from Paul, whose apostolic credentials were questioned by the people in Corinthians (2 Corinthians), the apostles wrote little or nothing about this

in the New Testament itself. And if being widely recognized as authentic was important, then the issue of canonicity was settled by the majority. Is the majority always
correct? Should we trust the majority to settle this issue? If conformity to the "rule of
faith" was important to canonicity, then what exactly is this "rule of faith" such that
the church can determine which books conform to it? Isn't this arguing in a circle,
since what Christians believed was based upon the texts they thought were authentic?

The truth is, according to James Barr, "we seldom know very well the grounds
on which decisions about canonical questions were reached, and even when some
grounds are mentioned it is often difficult to know whether they were the ones that
were really effective. . . . [I]n so far as such things existed [they] existed in the form
of the different opinions of different groups; and a settlement was eventually reached
not through a 'decision' but through the fact that one group became dominant, its
opinion became more powerful and important, and that other views simply faded
away with the fading of the groups which had maintained them." Barr goes on to say,
"Arguments for and against the canonicity of books may in many cases be . . . arguments for what has been done after it had already been done. A good example is
Irenaeus' famous argument over the necessity that there should be precisely four
Gospels, as there are four regions of the world, four winds, four faces of the
cherubim: if, however, there had been three Gospels, e.g., if Mark had dropped out,
one could (and no doubt would) have argued decisively that there could in the nature
of things only be three gospels, since three is the number of the Holy Trinity, the
number of the basic cosmic elements (heaven, earth, and sea)—who knows?"[75]

This whole five-stage process looks entirely like a human not a divine endeavor,
as Bart Ehrman suggests. It really does! Christians must believe God guided this
whole process from start to finish when it involved so many uninspired people (the
original stories; "Q"; other compositions; the many gospels; scribal copyists; and
church canonical pronouncements). The funny thing about this, to me anyway, is
that while Christians believe God guided this whole process perfectly, which
involved controlling free-willed uninspired people, Christians also deny God controls (or restrains) the free will of evil people intent on doing harm. Why would God
do one thing and not do another?

THE EXAMPLE OF THE LORD'S PRAYER

If looking at the errors in the Bible isn't good enough of a reason to reject the verbal-
plenary view of inspiration, understanding the five stages of the gospel tradition and
the nature of the Bible itself will. Let's now focus on one example, the Lord's Prayer:

From the New International Version (NIV):

From Matthew:
   [9] "Our Father in heaven,
   hallowed be your name,

[10] your kingdom come,
your will be done
on earth as it is in heaven.
[11] Give us today our daily bread.
[12]Forgive us our debts,
as we also have forgiven our debtors.
[13] And lead us not into temptation,
but deliver us from the evil one.[a]"

[a] Or "from evil"; some late manuscripts "one, for yours is the kingdom and the power and the glory forever. Amen."

From Luke:
"Father"[b]
hallowed be your name,
your kingdom come.[c]
[missing verse]
[3] Give us each day our daily bread.
[4] Forgive us our sins,
for we also forgive everyone who sins against us.[d]
And lead us not into temptation."[e]

[b] Some manuscripts "Our Father in heaven"
[c] Some manuscripts "come. May your will be done on earth as it is in heaven."
[d] Greek "everyone who is indebted to us."
[e] Some manuscripts "temptation but deliver us from the evil one."

In this simple example of what believers should pray, we find many of the difficulties with which biblical scholars wrestle. We see manuscript and translation differences. We see word differences. What prayer did Jesus actually teach his disciples to pray? The prayer itself is memorable, and not likely to have been forgotten, as evidenced by most believers today. Yet here we have two versions of it. As I just mentioned, Mark's gospel is accepted by the overwhelming number of scholars to have been written first. But why didn't Mark include this prayer? It seems to be a glaring omission on his part since the prayer itself is so memorable, not unlike the "I am" sayings of Jesus mentioned only in John's later gospel. With such memorable things as these it's hard to explain why only the later gospel writers wrote about them.

Look at the differences themselves. If the gospel writers were supposed to tell us exactly what Jesus said, then they did not do this. If inerrancy requires no errors, then this is indeed an error. Inerrantists qualify what it means to say the Bible is inerrant, and in so doing this doctrine dies the death of a thousand qualifications, so to speak (see note).[76]

Evangelical Christian scholars admit that we do not have the very words of Jesus. (Instead they argue that we have the "voice" of Jesus through the gospel writers.) Jesus spoke in Aramaic, so his words would have been first translated into Greek. Since the verbal agreement among the Gospels is very close in the Greek when they relate the same story, these stories were already in Greek before they reached the gospel writers. So again, what exactly are the words we should use when saying the Lord's Prayer?

Look at the whole verse missing from Luke's later gospel. The rest of the prayer is pretty much the same in the Greek, but why delete this verse? What exactly is there about the phrase "your will be done on earth as it is in heaven" that didn't fit with Luke's gospel to the poor and downtrodden? Could it be that since ancient people believed God's will is done through the rulers and kings of the earth (see Rom. 13:1–2) that it would offend the very people Luke was writing for? Scholars ask these types of questions. And why did Luke replace the word *debts* with *sins*? Could it be that the poor had no debts to forgive? Scholars think Matthew wrote down *debts* because he was a tax collector, if it was actually Matthew who wrote the gospel. But how do we explain this discrepancy? Did Matthew get it wrong? Did he "translate" what Jesus actually said into terms he could understand? Or did Jesus repeat this prayer several times using the word *debts* on some occasions and *sins* on others? How likely is that? When it comes to the words of Jesus, a complete harmonization of what he said and what others said in response to him cannot be done. It's more likely that Luke changed the word *debts* to *sins* for his readers. What else did he change? Since Luke was not one of the apostles, why should we accept this change? Who or what guarantees that Luke's gospel is inspired? He's not an apostle and he never claims his work is inspired.

These sorts of scholarly questions can be duplicated for almost everything told in the Gospels. These are the kinds of questions that scholars wrestle with that lead some to say we can know little about what Jesus himself actually stressed or taught.[77] And if that's even partially the case, how can the Gospels be authoritative for us as the word of God? I'll tell you how; they can't.

NOTES

1. On other biblical considerations, see especially Nicholas Wolterstorff, "God Everlasting," in *God and the Good*, ed. Clifton Orlebeke and Lewis B. Smedes (Grand Rapids, MI: Eerdmans, 1975).

2. William Lane Craig, *The Only Wise God: The Compatibility of Divine Foreknowledge* (Grand Rapids, MI: Baker Book House, 1987).

3. Stephen T. Davis, *Logic and the Nature of God* (Grand Rapids, MI: Eerdmans, 1983), pp. 8–24.

4. William Hasker, in *The Openness of God* (Downers Grove, IL: InterVaristy Press, 1994), pp. 132–33. For balanced discussions of this problem, see Thomas Morris, *Our Idea of God* (Downers Grove, IL: InterVarsity Press, 1991); and the late Ronald Nash, *The Concept of God* (Grand Rapids, MI: Zondervan, 1983).

5. J. P. Moreland and William Lane Craig, *Philosophical Foundations for a Christian Worldview* (Downers Grove, IL: InterVarsity Press, 2003), p. 521.

6. On these points see Richard Rice, "Divine Foreknowledge and Free-Will Theism," in *The Grace of God, The Will of Man* (Grand Rapids, MI: Zondervan, 1989), pp. 135–37.

7. Randel McCraw Helms shows this in *The Bible against Itself: Why the Bible Seems to Contradict Itself* (Altadena, CA: Millennium Press, 2006), pp. 81–99.

8. Joseph A. Fitzmyer, *The One Who Is to Come* (Grand Rapids, MI: Eerdmans, 2007), p. ix.

9. Ibid., p. 20.

10. Ibid.

11. Ibid., pp. 44–45.

12. Ibid., p. 25.

13. Ibid., pp. 42–43.

14. Ibid., p. 141.

15. Ibid., p. 142.

16. *Anchor Bible Dictionary*, s.v. "Lamb."

17. John F. Zuck and Roy B. Walvoord, eds., *The Bible Knowledge Commentary: An Exposition of the Scriptures* (Wheaton, IL: Victor Books, 1985), see Matt. 2:14–15.

18. J. Gnilka, *Das Matthausevangelium I Kommentar zu Kap 1.1–13.58* (Freiburg: Herder, 1986), p. 55.

19. U. Luz, *Das Evangelium nach Matthaus I Mt 1–7*, p. 129.

20. Gnilka, *Das Mathausevangelium 1.1–16.20* (Die Neue Echter Bibel, 1.1; Wurzburg: Echter Verlag, 1985), p. 27.

21. Zuck and Walvoord, *The Bible Knowledge Commentary*, see Matt. 2:22–23.

22. C. F. D. Moule, *The Origin of Christology* (Cambridge: Cambridge University Press, 1977), p. 129.

23. See his essay in G. K. Beale, ed., *The Right Doctrine from the Wrong Text?* (Grand Rapids, MI: Baker Academic, 1994), p. 149.

24. Steve Moyise, *The Old Testament in the New: An Introduction* (London: Continuum, 2001), pp. 4–5.

25. James D. G. Dunn, *The Living Word* (Philadelphia: Fortress Press, 1987), pp. 115–22.

26. Quoted in Beale, *The Right Doctrine from the Wrong Text?* p. 385. G. K Beale disagrees. He claims the proposal that "the New Testament's exegetical approach to the Old Testament is characteristically non-contextual is a substantial overstatement." He is furthermore convinced that "there are no clear examples where they (the NT writers) have developed a meaning from the Old Testament which is inconsistent or contradictory to some aspect of the original Old Testament application" (p. 398). Even granting with Beale that there will be some "enigmatic passages," most scholars disagree, and he has yet to prove his case. Maybe he thinks he does (with D. A. Carson) in his book, *Commentary on the New Testament Use of the Old Testament* (Grand Rapids, MI: Baker Academic, 2007), but I seriously doubt it.

27. Paul Copan, *"That's Just Your Interpretation"* (Grand Rapids, MI: Eerdmans, 2001), p. 194.

28. To see Christians argue about this and what it means for their faith, see Beale, *The Right Doctrine from the Wrong Text?* Phillip Barton Payne, for instance, claims it's a fallacy to equate meaning with the human author's intention, since ultimately "God is the author of Scripture" (p. 70). Hence, "our primary task is to understand God's intention, not fundamentally the human author's. After all, the Bible is God's word" (p. 81). But that assumption is the one I'm testing and finding the lack of evidence for in this book. See what George Bethune English (1787–1828) wrote about Old Testament prophecies in a book titled *The Grounds of Christianity Examined by Comparing The New Testament with the Old*, available for free online at http://www.gutenberg.org/etext/15968.

29. Randel Helms, *Gospel Fictions* (Amherst, NY: Prometheus Books, 1988), p. 131.

30. Northrop Frye, *The Great Code: The Bible and Literature* (New York: Harcourt Brace, 1982), p. 78.

31. After noting that the standard treatment of typology was done by Leonhard Goppelt, in his book *Typos*, where he claims typology is the dominant hermeneutical method of exegesis in the New Testament understanding of the Old, Christian exegete David L. Baker still maintains that "typology is not exegesis." He wrote, "the exegete has to find the meaning of the text and its witness to an event and for this the tool is grammatical-historical exegesis." See his essay in Beale, *The Right Doctrine from the Wrong Text?* pp. 313–30.

32. Paul J. Achtemeier, *The Inspiration of Scripture* (Philadelphia: Westminster Press, 1980), pp. 30–32.

33. James Barr, *Beyond Fundamentalism* (Philadelphia: Westminster Press, 1984), pp. 21–23.

34. Ibid., pp. 23–24.

35. Farrell Till makes this argument at http://www.infidels.org. Just do a search there for the "Land Promise." Matthew Green makes this same argument at http://tektonontrial .blogspot.com/2007/11/failed-land-promise.html.

36. James Barr, *Beyond Fundamentalism*, p. 29.

37. Ibid., p. 102.

38. Tim Callahan, *Bible Prophecy: Failure or Fulfillment?* (Altadena, CA: Millennium Press, 1997).

39. Sam Harris, *Letter to a Christian Nation* (New York: Knopf, 2006), pp. 60–61. From what I've said it will be clear that I do not believe Michael Drosnin's claims in his 1997 book, *The Bible Code* (New York: Touchstone), that there are any hidden meanings or prophecies in the Bible. On this see Jeffery L. Sheler's book *Is the Bible True? How Modern Debates and Discoveries Affirm the Essence of the Scriptures* (New York: HarperSanFrancisco, 1999), pp. 233–52.

40. I've been helped here by Dr. Felipe Leon. That Jesus was an apocalyptic prophet has been the dominant Christian view since the time of Albert Schweitzer and given a robust defense recently by Christian scholar Dale Allison in *Jesus of Nazareth* (Minneapolis: Fortress Press, 1998). For an excellent overall treatment of Jesus as a failed prophet see Bart D. Ehrman, *Jesus: Apocalyptic Prophet of the New Millennium* (Oxford: Oxford University Press, 1999).

41. Edward Adams, *The Stars Will Fall from Heaven* (New York: T & T Clark, 2007), p. 164.

42. Bart D. Ehrman, *Jesus: Apocalyptic Prophet of the New Millennium* (Oxford: Oxford University Press, 1999), p. 244.

43. To see how the biblical writers progressively changed their position regarding the *eschaton*, the restoration of Israel, and the return of Jesus, see Helms, *The Bible against Itself*, pp. 153–65, and Randel McCraw Helms, *Who Wrote the Gospels?* (Altadena, CA: Millennium Press, 1997), pp. 19–39. Jeremiah spoke of seventy years for the restoration of Israel (25:1), which never happened as prophesied, so the book of Daniel claims Jeremiah meant seventy weeks of years (Daniel 9), which meant the prophecy was for his day (in the second century BCE). Since the restoration of Israel and the *eschaton* did not happen in that day, Mark's gospel informs us that Daniel's prophecy was about the destruction of Jerusalem, which was a prelude for the *eschaton* to happen a few years afterward (Mark 13). In the book of Revelation the author makes Daniel's "time, times and half a time" into an indeterminate period that would end "soon" in his day, which as we know did not happen.

44. Edward Adams documents these things sufficiently in his book *The Stars Will Fall*

from Heaven. We see this from additional passages like Heb. 12:25–29, 2 Pet. 3:5–13, and Rev. 6:12–27.

45. Michael Martin, *The Case against Christianity* (Philadelphia: Temple University Press, 1991), p. 119.

46. To see how the passages used to support inerrancy do not actually support it, see James D. G. Dunn's chapter, "The Authority of Scripture According to Scripture," in *The Living Word* (Philadelphia: Fortress Press, 1987).

47. Norman Geisler, *Christian Apologetics* (Grand Rapids, MI: Baker Book House, 1976), p. 368.

48. Clark Pinnock, *The Scripture Principle* (New York: Harper & Row, 1984), p. 47. Pinnock is a prominent evangelical who changed his mind about inerrancy and now affirms the infallibility of scriptures. He previously had defended inerrancy in *Biblical Revelation* (Chicago: Moody Press, 1971).

49. Robert M. Price, *The Incredible Shrinking of the Son of Man* (Amherst, NY: Prometheus Books, 2003), p. 35.

50. To see these issues discussed from a conservative Christian perspective, see Ralph Martin, *New Testament Foundations: A Guide for Christian Students*, vols. 1–2 (Grand Rapids, MI: Eerdmans, 1975–78); Donald Guthrie, *New Testament Introduction* (Downers Grove, IL: InterVarsity Press, 1970); and D. A. Carson, Douglas Moo, and Leon Morris, *An Introduction to the New Testament* (Grand Rapids, MI: Zondervan, 1992). See also L. Michael White, *From Jesus to Christianity* (New York: HarperSanFrancisco, 2004). For a provocative and insightful book discussing the authorship of the four gospels, see Helms, *Who Wrote the Gospels?* For a popular book of these issues, see John Shelby Spong, *Rescuing the Bible from Fundamentalism* (New York: HarperSanFrancisco, 1991).

51. James Barr, *Holy Scripture: Canon, Authority, Criticism* (Philadelphia: Westminster Press, 1983), p. 12.

52. John Shelby Spong, *The Sins of Scripture: Exposing the Bible's Texts of Hate to Reveal the God of Love* (New York: HarperSanFrancisco, 2005).

53. Helms, *The Bible against Itself*, p. i.

54. Ibid., p. 116. Of course, if that's the case, then like me he should reject most of it!

55. Stephen T. Davis, *The Debate about the Bible: Inerrancy versus Infallibility* (Philadelphia: Westminster Press, 1977), pp. 94–113.

56. Paul J. Achtemeier, *The Inspiration of Scripture: Problems and Proposals* (Philadelphia: Westminster Press, 1980), p. 60.

57. Ibid., pp. 60–75.

58. Harold Lindsell, *Battle for the Bible* (Grand Rapids, MI: Zondervan, 1978), pp. 174–76.

59. Bart Ehrman, *Misquoting Jesus* (New York: HarperSanFrancisco, 2005), pp. 8–10.

60. David Edwards and John Stott, *Evangelical Essentials* (Downers Grove, IL: InterVarsity Press, 1988), pp. 79–82.

61. Joe E. Holman, *Project Bible Truth: A Minister Turns Atheist and Tells All* (Morrisville, NC: Lulu Press, 2008). Valerie Tarico, *The Dark Side: How Evangelical Teachings Corrupt Love and Truth* (Seattle: Dea Press, 2006), pp. 52–64.

62. Ibid., pp. 62–63.

63. For the best scholarly description of the first three stages, see Helmut Koester, *Ancient Christian Gospels* (Philadelphia: Trinity Press International, 1990), pp. 1–348.

64. Other criteria include "coherence" (does a saying in question cohere with material already established as authentic) and "multiple attestation" (in how many strata underlying

the four gospels can the saying in question be found). To see this in practice, read Robert W. Funk, *Honest to Jesus* (New York: HarperSanFrancisco, 1996), pp. 121–240.

65. Ehrman, *Misquoting Jesus*, p. 10.

66. Hector Avalos, *The End of Biblical Studies* (Amherst, NY: Prometheus Books, 2007), p 66.

67. To see this, take a look at Bart D. Ehrman's book *The Orthodox Corruption of Scripture: The Effect of Early Christological Controversies on the Text of the New Testament* (Oxford: Oxford University Press, 1993).

68. Barr, *Holy Scripture*, pp. 23, 25.

69. Bart D. Ehrman, *Lost Scriptures: Books That Did Not Make It into the New Testament* (Oxford: Oxford University Press, 2005).

70. Bart Ehrman, *Lost Christianities: The Battles for Scripture and the Faiths We Never Knew* (Oxford: Oxford University Press, 2005).

71. For an accessible account of the development of the canon, go to http://en.wikipedia.org and do a search for "development of the New Testament canon."

72. See Carson, Moo, and Morris, *An Introduction to the New Testament*, p. 498; and Norman L. Geisler (with William E. Nix), *A General Introduction to the Bible* (Chicago: Moody Press, 1968), pp. 136–37.

73. See Koester's *Introduction to the New Testament: History, Culture, and Religion of the Hellenistic Age, Volume 1* (Philadelphia: Fortress, 1982), p. xxi.

74. For which see Geisler and Nix, *A General Introduction to the Bible*, pp. 137–47, along with Carson, Moo, and Morris, *An Introduction to the New Testament*, pp. 494–95.

75. Barr, *Holy Scripture*, pp. 57–59.

76. To see one example of this, read Paul D. Feinberg's chapter, "The Meaning of Inerrancy," in *Inerrancy*, ed. Norman L. Geisler (Grand Rapids, MI: Zondervan, 1980), pp. 267–304. Feinberg argues that inerrancy does not demand strict adherence to the rules of grammar; nor historical or semantic precision; nor does it demand the technical language of modern science; nor verbal exactness in its use of quotations; nor does it demand we have the exact words of Jesus. He even goes so far as to say "inerrancy does not demand the infallibility or inerrancy of the non-inspired sources used by biblical writers" (p. 302). But as we've just seen, that means much of the Bible can be in error.

77. See Funk, *Honest To Jesus*; Robert J. Miller, ed., *The Complete Gospels: Annotated Scholars Version* (New York: HarperCollins, 1994); and Robert Funk and the Jesus Seminar, ed., *The Acts of Jesus: The Search for the Authentic Deeds of Jesus* (New York: Harper-Collins, 1998).

17

WAS JESUS BORN OF
A VIRGIN IN BETHLEHEM?

Some skeptics have gone so far as to deny that Jesus ever was a historical person.[1] Even though I personally don't think Adam, Eve, Noah, Abraham, Moses, Joshua, Joseph of Arimathea, or Judas Iscariot existed, and even though the cases they make seem reasonable, I'm just not that skeptical. Robert M. Price claims that if there is a kinship of the New Testament writers and belief with those of adjacent cultures, "the real issue of debate ought to be whether there was a historical Jesus at the core of all the mythology."[2] Price does have a good point. Still, I believe there was a person named Jesus. I just don't think he was a Messiah/Christ/Son of God. The Gospels and the rise of the church serve as prima facia justification for believing the man Jesus really existed.[3] But there is every reason to question whom early Christians claimed he was, what he actually did, and what he actually said, since the myths surrounding him exponentially grew.[4]

WAS JESUS BORN IN BETHLEHEM?

Let's first look at the prophecy Matthew reports about Jesus being born in Bethlehem (2:5): "When Herod the king had heard these things, he was troubled, and all Jerusalem with him. And when he had gathered all the chief priests and scribes of the people together, he demanded of them where Christ should be born. And they said unto him, 'In Bethlehem of Judea: for thus it is written by the prophet, "And thou Bethlehem, in the land of Judah, art not the least among the princes of Judah: for out of thee shall come a Governor, that shall rule my people Israel."'" The Greek word for *governor* can be translated in English as "ruler" or as "shepherd" depending on the context. To the Greek mind, a ruler is a shepherd and a shepherd is a ruler.

In the first place, "Bethlehem Ephratah" in Micah 5:2 refers not to a town, but to a clan: the clan of Bethlehem, who was the son of Caleb's second wife, Ephrathah (1 Chron. 2:19, 2:50–51, 4:4). Second, the prophecy, as understood by Herod's scribes (if they actually did think this), refers to a military commander, as can be seen from the context of Micah 5:6, which says, "He will be their peace. When the Assyrian invades our land and marches through our fortresses, we will raise against him seven shepherds, even eight leaders of men. They will rule the land of Assyria with the sword, the land of Nimrod with drawn sword. He will deliver us from the Assyrian when he invades our land and marches into our borders." This leader is supposed to defeat the Assyrians, which, of course, Jesus never did. This is basic exegesis. If Jesus is who Micah referred to as having been born in Bethlehem, then Jesus was also supposed to conquer the Assyrians.

Gleason Archer deals with this Bible difficulty in his book *The Encyclopedia of Bible Difficulties*. He claims Matthew did not quote from the Septuagint version (LXX), which was the standard Greek translation of the Hebrew text, but from some other Greek paraphrase. A paraphrase wasn't meant to be literal translation; it was more expressive. It brought out the implications of the prophecy, and Archer claims that this was what Matthew used. He also claims Matthew conflated two different prophecies when quoting Micah 5:2. Archer claims Matthew also was quoting from 2 Samuel 5:2, where "all of Israel" came to King David and said, "In the past, while Saul was king over us, you were the one who led Israel on their military campaigns. And the Lord said to you, 'You will shepherd my people Israel, and you will become their ruler.'" Afterward the people anointed David as their king. Archer claims the phrase "You will shepherd my people Israel, and you will become their ruler" is what Matthew is referring to when speaking about Jesus, not that he would conquer the Assyrians. Archer further states that it was actually "Herod's Bible experts," not Matthew, "who quoted from more than one Old Testament passage." So, "in a sense, therefore, they were the ones responsible for the wording, rather than Matthew himself."[5]

Now it is true that New Testament writers repeatedly "conflate" Old Testament quotations in the New Testament, and Archer offers a couple of examples. We see this in Matthew 27:9–10, which combines elements from Zechariah 11:12–13, Jeremiah 19:2, 11, and Jeremiah 32:6–9. We also see this in Mark 1:2–3, which combines elements from Isaiah 40:3 and Malachi 3:1. But Matthew (2:5) explicitly says the prophecy was from a "prophet," not from the people of Israel in 2 Samuel 5:2. Furthermore, if Matthew takes Micah's prophecy out of context, as I've explained, then it doesn't help anything by claiming he was also referring to 2 Samuel 5:2, since that too is taken out of context. It isn't even a prophecy. It's about David shepherding the people of Israel. If, however, Archer wants to blame the scribes in Herod's court for misapplying Micah 5:2, then why did Archer expend so much ink trying to show what Matthew was attempting, if Matthew wasn't attempting to do anything here but merely record what these scribes said? If Herod's scribes are to be blamed for misunderstanding Micah 5:2, along with 2 Samuel 5:2, then exactly where is there in the Old Testament any prophecy for the birth of Jesus in Bethlehem? There is none!

Now let's turn to the Star of Bethlehem. Craig Chester, then president of the Monterey Institute for Research in Astronomy, offered a detailed and elaborate understanding of the rising star in the Bethlehem sky at Jesus' birth, in "The Star of Bethlehem."[6] He claims it was Jupiter, the planet known to represent kingship to astrologers in the ancient East, which came into conjunction with Regulus, the star of kingship, which is located in the constellation of Leo, also known as the constellation of kings. Mark Kidger discusses several different astronomical possibilities: the star couldn't be Halley's comet, nor unusual meteors, nor Venus, nor the occultation of the moon, nor a supernova. Kidger argued that it was a triple conjunction of Jupiter and Saturn in Pisces.[7] Michael R. Molnar claims that it was a lunar occultation of Jupiter in the constellation of Aries.[8] Catholic physicist Frank J. Tipler argues that it must have been a Type Ic hypernova, located in the Andromeda galaxy, or a Type Ia supernova in a globular cluster of this galaxy.[9]

These theories all assume the star reported in Matthew's gospel (2:1–10) was a natural astronomical event or events, and they may explain some things the Magi saw, but E. P. Sanders asks, "Why take the star of Matthew's story to be a real astral event and ignore what the author says about it?"[10] Here's what Matthew said: "the star, which they (the Magi) had seen in the east, went on before them until it came and stood over the place where the child was. When they saw the star, they rejoiced exceedingly with great joy" (2:9–10). How is it truly possible for the star that Matthew describes leading the Magi from Jerusalem to a specific inn located in Bethlehem less than five miles away be the one that modern Christian astronomers describe? H. R. Reimarus (CE 1768) observed long ago that if it were some sort of comet with a tail, "it is too high to point to a specific house."

Where is there any record of this event outside of Matthew, if it truly was an astronomical event? Gleason Archer bit this bullet when he wrote, "it is highly unlikely that any normal star (or a planetary cluster) was capable of directing its glow so specifically over Bethlehem that the wise men (Magi) could identify the place where the Christ child was then residing."[11] Bernard Ramm agreed by writing: "We believe that it was a special manifestation for the birth of Jesus and that it was seen only by the wise men (Magi)."[12] But if it was a miraculous star, then exactly why didn't everyone in the vicinity see it? Pope Leo I (CE 461) proposed that the star was invisible to the Jews because of their blindness. But then why did it appear to pagan astronomer-astrologers? Given the whole nature of apocalyptic literature in the Bible, in which, according to Joel's prophecy as interpreted by Peter on the Day of Pentecost, the moon is "turned to blood" and "the sun will be turned to darkness" (Acts 2:19–20), and given the whole nature of the cosmogony of the ancients, it's more reasonable to simply reject the idea that there was an actual star that shone down on a specific house in Bethlehem, period. This whole story presupposes a pre-scientific three-tired universe with the stars hung in the firmament. In such a universe early Christians could claim a star was moved over a house by God.

If Luke is taken literally, Jesus was not born in Bethlehem anyway, according to E. P. Sanders.[13] What husband would take a nine-month-pregnant woman on such a trek from Nazareth at that time when only heads of households were obligated to register for a census and when the census would've been stretched out over a period of weeks or even months? But if he did, why did he not take better precautions for the birth? Why not take Mary to her relative Elizabeth's home just a few miles away from Bethlehem for the birth of her baby? According to Luke's own genealogy (3:23–38) David had lived forty-two generations earlier. Why should everyone have had to register for a census in the town of one of his ancestors forty-two generations earlier? There would be millions of ancestors by that time, and the whole empire would have been uprooted. Why forty-two generations and not thirty-five or sixteen? If it was just required of the lineage of King David to register for the census, what was Augustus thinking when he ordered it? He had a king, Herod. "Under no circumstances could the reason for Joseph's journey be, as Luke says, that he was 'of the house and lineage of David,' because that was of no interest to the Romans in this context."[14] The fact is, even if there was a worldwide Roman census that included Galilee at this specific time, there is evidence that census takers taxed people based upon the land they owned, so they traveled to where people lived.

According to Robin Lane Fox, "Luke's story is historically impossible and internally incoherent." But he says, "Luke's errors and contradictions are easily explained. Early Christian tradition did not remember, or perhaps ever know, exactly where and when Jesus had been born. People were much more interested in his death and consequences. . . . After the crucifixion and the belief in the resurrection, people wondered all the more deeply about Jesus' birthplace. Bethlehem, home of King David, was a natural choice for the new messiah."[15] "Luke's real source for the view that Jesus was born in Bethlehem was almost certainly the conviction that Jesus fulfilled a hope that someday a descendant of David would arise to save Israel," because the Messiah was supposed to come from there (Mic. 5:2).[16]

Matthew's account of Jesus' birth fares no better. According to Fox: "Bethlehem was not Jesus' birthplace but was imported from Hebrew prophecies about the future Messiah; the Star had similar origins (Num. 24:17). Matthew's story is a construction from well-known messianic prophecies (Bethlehem; the Star), and the Wise Men (Magi) have been added as another legend. . . . Where the truth had been lost, stories filled the gap, and the desire to know fabricated its own tradition. Luke told a tale of angels and shepherds, bringing some of the humblest people in society to Bethlehem with news of Jesus' future. Instead of shepherds, Matthew brought Wise Men, following a star in the East and bringing gifts. . . . In one version, there are simple shepherds, the other, learned Wise Men: the contrast sets our imaginations free, and perhaps like the Wise Men we too should return by 'another way.'"[17]

Raymond Brown is the author of the massive 752-page book titled *Birth of the Messiah* and "Gospel Infancy Narrative Research from 1976 to 1986."[18] Here are four points about the contents of Matthew and Luke that Brown mentioned in his *Anchor Bible Dictionary* article "Infancy Narratives in the NT Gospels":

(1) Brown discusses the agreements between Matthew and Luke's gospels, but those are obvious and not part of my point.
(2) "Matthew and Luke disagree with each other on several significant points.

In chapter 1, Luke's story of John the Baptist (annunciation to Zechariah by Gabriel, birth, naming, growth) is absent from Matthew. At the time of the annunciation, Mary is detectably pregnant in Matthew, while the annunciation takes place before conception in Luke. In chapter 2 in each gospel, the basic birth and postbirth stories are totally different to the point that the two are not plausibly reconcilable."

Before moving on to the third and fourth points Brown makes, it's worthwhile to spend a little time on one particular problem. Matthew and Luke actually tell contradictory stories. Luke has Joseph and Mary living in Nazareth from where they traveled to Bethlehem for the Roman census (Luke 1:26; 2:4). After Jesus was born, Joseph took his family from Bethlehem to Jerusalem for up to forty days (Luke 2:22), and from there straight back to Nazareth (Luke 2:39). But Matthew has Joseph's family already living in Bethlehem, and after the birth of Jesus, staying there for up to two years (Matt. 2:16). After the Magi leave, Joseph is warned in a dream to flee to Egypt and stay there until Herod died (Matt. 2:15). After Herod died, Joseph was told in a dream to return to the land of Israel, and he headed for his home in Bethlehem of Judea. But since he was afraid to go there, he settled in Nazareth (Matt. 2:21–23), for the first time! S.V. McCasland simply tells us "Matthew's conclusion contradicts the testimony of Luke."[19] This Bible difficulty is not even dealt with by Gleason Archer in his monumental *Encyclopedia of Bible Difficulties.*[20]

The attempt to harmonize these gospel accounts by resorting to some very sophisticated intellectual gymnastics requires that a person create an entirely new account of its own not to be found in any of the Gospels—a gospel of one's own. But in fact it cannot be done without the addition of several ad hoc hypotheses. So such an attempt "dies the death of a thousand qualifications," so to speak.

Back to Raymond Brown.

(3) "None of the significant information found in the infancy narrative of either gospel is attested clearly elsewhere in the NT." The following claims are found only in the infancy narratives: (a) "The virginal conception of Jesus"; (b) "Jesus' birth at Bethlehem"; and (c) "Herodian knowledge of Jesus' birth and the claim that he was a king." Later Herod's son seems not to know anything of Jesus (Matt. 14:1–2). (d) "Wide knowledge of Jesus' birth, since all Jerusalem was startled (Matt. 2:3), and the children of Bethlehem were killed in search of him." Later we read that no one seems to know of the miraculous origins of Jesus (Matt. 13:54–55). (e) "John the Baptist was a relative of Jesus and recognized him before birth (Luke 1:41, 44)." But later on John seems to have "no previous knowledge of Jesus and to be puzzled by him (Luke 7:19; John 1:33)."

(4) "None of the events that might have been 'public' find attestation in contemporary history." (a) "There is no convincing astronomical evidence identifiable with a star that rose in the East, moved westward, and came to rest over Bethlehem," as we've just shown. (b) "Even though the Jewish histo-

rian Josephus amply documents the brutality in the final years of Herod the Great, neither he nor any other record mentions a massacre of children at Bethlehem." (c) "A census of the whole world (Roman provinces?) under Caesar Augustus never happened, although there were three Augustan censuses of Roman citizens. It is not unlikely that Luke 2:1 should be taken as a free description of Augustus' empire-cataloguing tendencies." (d) "Luke's implication that Quirinius was governor of Syria and conducted a 'first census' (2:2) before Herod's death (1:5) has no confirmation." (e) "Although this item differs somewhat from the immediately preceding one, Luke's idea that the two parents were purified ('their purification according to the Law of Moses': 2:22) is not supported by a study of Jewish law, whence the attempts of early textual copyists and of modern scholars to substitute 'her' for 'their' or to interpret the 'their' to refer to other than the parents."

Here's what Raymond Brown concludes: "A review of the implication of nos. 1–4 explains why the historicity of the infancy narratives has been questioned by so many scholars, even by those who do not *a priori* rule out the miraculous. Despite efforts stemming from preconceptions of biblical inerrancy or of Marian piety, it is exceedingly doubtful that both accounts can be considered historical."[21]

WAS JESUS BORN BY A MIRACULOUS VIRGIN BIRTH?

Uta Ranke-Heinemann tells us, "If we wish to continue seeing Luke's accounts of angelic messages and so forth, as historical events, we'd have to take a large leap of faith: We'd have to assume that while on verifiable matters of historical fact Luke tells all sorts of fairy tales (just mentioned above) but on supernatural matters— which by definition can never be checked—he simply reports the facts. By his arbitrary treatment of history, Luke has shown himself to be an unhistorical reporter—a teller of fairy tales."[22]

When Mary first hears from the angel Gabriel that she is to give birth, she objects by saying, "How shall this be, since I know not man?" (Luke 1:34). According to Ranke-Heinemann, "psychologically this sentence can never be spoken, because it states that Mary has relations neither with her husband nor with any other man. She does not say the only thing that she could have said: 'since I have had no sexual relations with *my husband*.' Instead she says, 'with man,' meaning with any man. This proves that Mary's objection to the angel is a literary invention."[23] The way it's phrased is to justify her virginity to the reader rather than to historically retell what might have actually been said.

According to David L. Edwards: "Paul's surviving letters do not refer to the virgin birth. Mark's gospel also does not mention this miracle. John's gospel is also silent about a miraculous conception, except that all Christians are 'born' not through sex but 'of God' (1:13). . . . Herod's massacre of 'all the boys in Bethlehem . . .' is not mentioned in the indignantly careful list of Herod's atrocities given by the Jewish historian, Josephus. But it is suspiciously like the story of Pharaoh's massacre of Hebrew boys in Exodus 1:22. In Luke's narrative the characters, sayings and experiences of John the Baptist's parents (1:5–25; 57–80) are suspiciously like those of Abraham and Sarah in the book of Genesis, and Mary's song (1:46–55) resembles the song of Hannah (1 Sam. 2:1–10)."

It is furthermore interesting that the church developed the legend that Mary was a perpetual virgin even though we are told in the Gospel of Mark that Jesus had brothers and sisters (6:3). It seems clear, according to Edwards, that "births avoiding human sex were thought of as being purer and more wonderful than the mystery of the sexual creation of a new human being."[24]

The fact is, as Dr. Theodore Drange reminds us, "the idea of a virgin birth was a common notion among some other ancient groups, including the Greeks and Romans. Many famous people and mythical heroes were said, by one group or another, to have been born of a virgin. Among them were Julius Caesar, Augustus, Aristomenes, Alexander the Great, Plato, Cyrus, the elder Scipio, some of the Egyptian Pharaohs, the Buddha, Hermes, Mithra, Attis-Adonis, Hercules, Cybele, Demeter, Leo, and Vulcan."[25]

There were also savior-gods, like Krishna, Osiris, Dionysus, and Tammuz, who were born of virgins. They also did miracles. Justin Martyr was a second-century Christian apologist who tried to convince the pagans of his day of the truth of Christianity. In his *First Apology* Justin Martyr wrote, "And when we say also that the Word, who is the first-birth of God, was produced without sexual union, and that he, Jesus Christ, our teacher, was crucified and died, and rose again, and ascended into heaven, *we propound nothing different from what you believe regarding those whom you esteem sons of Jupiter.* For you know how many sons your esteemed writers ascribed to Jupiter: Mercury . . . Aesculapius . . . Bacchus . . . Hercules; and the sons of Leda, and Dioscuri; and Perseus, son of Danae; and Bellerophon. And what kind of deeds are recorded of each of these reputed sons of Jupiter, it is needless to tell to those who already know. . . . [I]f we even affirm that he (Jesus) was born of a virgin, accept this in common with what you accept of Perseus. And in that we say that he (Jesus) made whole the lame, the paralytic, and those born blind, we seem to say what is very similar to the deeds said to have been done by Aesculapius."[26]

The Virgin Birth Prophecy Mistake

In Matthew 1:20–23 the author claims that Isaiah 7:14 refers to Jesus' virgin birth: "Immanuel with us." The context for the prophecy in Isaiah tells us that before any "young woman" (not virgin) shall conceive and bear a son who grows to maturity, that Syria, the northern kingdom of Israel, along with the southern Israelite kingdom of Ahaz, would all lie devastated. The prophecy in the original Hebrew of Isaiah says nothing whatsoever about a virginal conception. And it says nothing about a messiah, either. God will indeed be with Ahaz, not in salvation, but in judgment. The prophecy was actually fulfilled in Isaiah 8:3 with the birth of Isaiah's son Maher-shalal-hash-baz (meaning, "Hasten the booty, the spoil is running away").

Gleason Archer claims instead that Isaiah's second son, mentioned in 9:1–7, refers to the redeemer son of God, Jesus, and that the first son, mentioned in 7:14 (i.e., Maher-Shalal-hash-baz), was a "type" of Jesus, who is the anti-type son, "God with us."[27] Implicit in what Archer argues for is that what is true for the type, Maher-shalal-hash-baz, is also true of the anti-type, Jesus. Isaiah 9:6–7 reads: "For to us a child is born, to us a son is given, and the government will be on his shoulders. And he will be called Wonderful Counselor, Mighty God, Everlasting Father, Prince of Peace. Of the increase of his government and peace there will be no end. He will reign on David's throne and over his kingdom, establishing and upholding it with justice and righteousness from that time on and forever."

What can we say about this? In the first place, there is nothing in these two texts that connects these two sons. Sometimes in Isaiah we see different back-to-back topics without any connection to what went on previously, presumably because the prophet(s) simply wrote down a series of disconnected visions. Second, such a type/anti-type view of these two sons is superstitious to the core. I've already argued we find this in the Bible and that we should reject this kind of thinking. Third, even if there was this type/anti-type analogy with a future Messiah, how does Archer know which details in the type, Maher-shalal-hash-baz, are to be found in the anti-type, Jesus, and which ones don't apply? Fourth, I have reasons to think God cannot predict future free-willed contingent human actions anyway. (For which, see my chapter 16.) Fifth, there is nothing in the description of this second son that would ever be considered to be a God who took up human flesh, from the Jewish perspective. In the context of Isaiah, it only offers a hope for a king after the period of the Exile (8:21–22). Later, Cyrus came to be viewed in these terms (Isaiah 44–45). Kings were, after all, called "gods" in the Ancient Near East (see my discussion in chapter 18). The names of that king are just that, names (or titles) that describe him. Joseph A. Fitzmyer tells us the names "given to the child are to be understood as symbolic throne-names, rhetorically summing up the names that he will win for himself in the people's estimation, when he sits upon the throne."[28] Native Americans have names like "walking bear" and "tall tree," but that has nothing to do with whether a child is a bear or a tree, so there is no reason to think these names refer to a child being God, either. There are plenty of men named "Immanuel," like Immanuel Kant, too. But Kant wasn't an incarnate God just because he was given that name. In the sixth place, even if Isaiah is expressing a hope in this prophetic child-redeemer who will reign on David's throne named "Immanuel," that says nothing much about whether his hope was fulfilled in Jesus, nor does it demand we think he was inspired to prophecy this. Any Jew writing in that time period might have expressed the same hope in the midst of the struggles they were facing. But an expressed hope for a future savior is not to be considered a prediction, unless along with that expressed hope are specific details whereby we can check to see if it was fulfilled in a specific person. Last, Joseph A. Fitzmyer forcefully reminds us that "the greatest objection to the messianic interpretation of this passage is this: 'How can Emmanuel, the Messianic child of the distant and impenetrable future, be a true sign for the eighth-century king, Ahaz?'"[29]

In the original Hebrew of Isaiah 7:14, we find the word *'almah*, which means any young woman, not necessarily meaning virgin in the strict sense. Gleason Archer himself begrudgingly admitted this when he wrote of that word, "It is therefore not as precise a word for virgin as the Hebrew *betulah*, which is defined in Genesis 24:16 as a young woman who has never had sexual relations."

The Greek translation of the Hebrew word *'almah*, in the Septuagint (LXX), is *parthenos*. According to James Barr, "What happened was a shift in the semantic identification of the word. When the Septuagint translators rendered it *parthenos*, they did not mean 'virgin'; they meant the Greek word in the general sense of 'girl'—this usage is found in a majority of cases in the Greek Genesis, as well as in Maccabees." But the Greek word *parthenos* went through a semantic shift over the years until it was understood by the time of Matthew's gospel to mean "virgin." This is not unlike how the words *nice* and *gay* have changed in meaning over the years. According to Barr, "For the Christians, however, it was a different matter. Given the conviction of the mysterious origin and birth of Jesus, the word *parthenos* leapt out of the page at them: surely it must be used in the stricter, narrower, and more technical, and also more common and characteristic, sense of 'virgin.' They thus understood the Isaiah passage in this sense and used it so."[30] Therefore, "the traditional Christian interpretation, which points to the Messiah Jesus, is not tenable as an exegesis of Isaiah 7:14."[31]

John Dominic Crossan wrote: "Clearly, somebody went seeking in the O.T. for a text that could be interpreted as prophesying a virginal conception, even if such was never its original meaning. Somebody had already decided on the transcendental importance of the adult Jesus and sought to retroject that significance onto the conception and birth itself. I understand the virginal conception of Jesus to be a confessional statement about Jesus' status and not a biological statement about Mary's body. It is later faith in Jesus as an adult retrojected mythically onto Jesus as an infant."[32]

GENETICS AND THE VIRGIN BIRTH

The ancient and medieval church believed that Jesus' humanity was a new creation, and therefore sinless. The ancients commonly believed that the woman contributes nothing to the physical being of the baby to be born. Ancient people thought the child was only related to the father. The mother was nothing but a receptacle for the male sperm, which grew to become a child, which we now know to be a false understanding of genetics. Since this is so, it makes a mockery of the attempt to harmonize the genealogies of Jesus given in Luke (3:23–37) and Matthew (1:1–17). They cannot be legitimately harmonized anyway, but the best attempt is to argue that Luke traces Jesus' royal lineage back through Mary, while Matthew traces his lineage back through Joseph. Even if this is the case, there are additional serious problems. If Jesus' royal lineage is to be traced back through Mary, as it's claimed Luke does, then Mary was just the receptacle of God's seed, contributing nothing. And if that's so, how can Jesus legitimately be of the Davidic lineage? However, if Jesus' royal lineage is to be traced back through Joseph, as it's claimed Matthew does, and if Joseph was not the father, then we have the same problem. In either case, how can Jesus legitimately be of the Davidic lineage? On this problem, according to Paul Kurtz, "the Gospels are impaled on an irreconcilable contradiction."[33]

Today, with the advent of genetics, most Christian thinkers try to defend the virgin birth on the grounds that the humanity of Jesus was derived from Mary and his sinlessness and deity were derived from God. Today's Christian thinkers do this because they know something about genetics and now know Mary must have contributed the female egg that made Jesus into a man. But even if this is a better explanation, it doesn't adequately explain how Jesus is a human being, since a potential human being is conceived when a human male sperm penetrates a human female egg. Until that happens, we do not have the complete chromosomal structure required to have a human being in the first place. If modern Christian thinkers want to use genetics to explain the virgin birth, then the question still left unanswered is how Jesus can be a human being.

One last thing before we move on. If someone holds to a pre-incarnate existence for Jesus, then there has been one human in the entire course of history who actually got to choose—before birth—whether he would be predominantly right-handed, left-handed, or ambidextrous.[34] In fact, it was absolutely necessary for Jesus to pick out his specific DNA, prior to being born. He could not let the chips fall where they may, because Joseph purportedly was not providing any.

What DNA did Jesus choose? It would seem that many people have a genetic predisposition toward certain sins. If Jesus was to be tempted in "all ways," did he include those predispositions in his DNA? Did he include a propensity toward alcoholism, so that he could be tempted in the same way that a human with a similar propensity is? Since there is evidence to suggest there is a genetic inclination to homosexuality, did Jesus include that as well? Or toward gambling? Or a higher libido? As we look about us, we see that many humans struggle with various problems at different levels. Did Jesus include all that in the mix as well, so as to be intimately familiar with how a person could be tempted in those regards?

At the time the Gospels were written, concepts such as DNA or genetic manipulation would be inconceivable. Now we've gained knowledge in these fields that render even more problems to the stories of a God creating a human form for himself. How does a God pick how much IQ to give himself if he is to interact with humans? How much pain threshold does he give himself? If he is to be tempted by hunger, how much metabolic rate does he give his body? But given this edge that God had over human beings who must deal with the DNA that they had no choice in, how much less remarkable is it for a God to appear in human form, if he has picked the best DNA from the crop?

All of which leads us to our next topic, the Incarnation.

NOTES

1. See G. A. Wells, *Did Jesus Exist?* (Amherst, NY: Prometheus Books, 1986); and his *The Historical Evidence for Jesus* (Amherst, NY: Prometheus Books, 1988); as well as Earl Doherty, *The Jesus Puzzle: Did Christianity Begin with a Mythical Christ? Challenging the Existence of an Historical Jesus* (Ottawa, ON: Age of Reason Publications, 2005); and S. Acharya, *The Christ Conspiracy: The Greatest Story Ever Sold* (Kempton, IL: Adventures Unlimited Press, 1999).

2. Robert M. Price and Jeffrey Jay Lowder, eds., *The Empty Tomb: Jesus beyond the Grave* (Amherst, NY: Prometheus Books, 2005), p. 150. See also Robert M. Price's *Deconstructing Jesus* (Amherst, NY: Prometheus Books, 2000.

3. See Jeffery Jay Lowder, "Independent Confirmation and the Historicity of Jesus" (1997) at http://www.infidels.org. Of the existence of Jesus, Paul Kurtz writes, "[I]t seems to me that some such man lived, most likely in Palestine in the first half of the first century, that he was crucified or hanged, and that a sect of Christians developed proclaiming his divinity. We know very few authentic facts, however, about Jesus beyond this bare outline." *The Transcendental Temptation* (Amherst, NY: Prometheus Books, 1991), p. 114. To read a comprehensive book on the sources for the historical Jesus, see Gerd Theissen and Annette Merz, *The Historical Jesus: A Comprehensive Guide*, trans. John Bowden (Minneapolis, MN: Fortress Press, 1998).

4. The scholars in the Jesus Seminar produced several books that argue we know very little about what Jesus said and did. See Robert W. Funk and Roy W. Hoover, *The Five Gospels: The Search for the Authentic Words of Jesus* (Sonoma, CA: Polebridge Press, 1993); Robert J. Miller, ed., *The Complete Gospels* (Sonoma, CA: Polebridge Press, 1994); and Robert W. Funk and the Jesus Seminar, eds., *The Acts of Jesus: The Search for the Authentic Jesus* (New York: HarperCollins, 1998). For a good description of their method leading to these results, see Robert Funk, *Honest to Jesus: Jesus for a New Millennium* (New York: HarperSanFransisco, 1996).

5. Gleason Archer, *Encyclopedia of Bible Difficulties* (Grand Rapids, MI: Zondervan, 1982), pp. 318–20.

6. Craig Chester, "The Star of Bethlehem," *Imprimis* (December 1993).

7. Mark Kidger, *The Star of Bethlehem* (Princeton, NJ: Princeton University Press, 1999).

8. Michael Molnar, *The Star of Bethlehem: The Legacy of the Magi* (New Brunswick, NJ: Rutgers University Press, 1999).

9. Frank J. Tipler, *The Physics of Christianity* (New York: Doubleday, 2007), pp. 140–53.

10. E. P. Sanders, *The Historical Figure of Jesus* (New York: Penguin Press, 1993), p. 55.

11. Archer, *Encyclopedia of Bible Difficulties*, p. 318.

12. Bernard Ramm, *The Christian View of Science and Scripture* (Grand Rapids, MI: Eerdmans, 1954), p. 14.

13. Sanders, *The Historical Figure of Jesus*, pp. 84–91.

14. Uta Ranke-Heinemann, *Putting Away Childish Things* (New York: HarperCollins, 1992), p. 10.

15. Robin Lane Fox, *The Unauthorized Version: Truth and Fiction in the Bible* (New York: Knopf, 1992), pp. 31–32.

16. Sanders, *The Historical Figure of Jesus*, p. 87.

17. Fox, *The Unauthorized Version*, pp. 35–36.

18. Raymond E. Brown, *Birth of the Messiah* (New York: Anchor Bible, 1999); and "Gospel Infancy Narrative Research from 1976 to 1986," *Catholic Biblical Quarterly* 48 (1986): 469–83, 661–80.

19. Quoted from his essay in G. K. Beale, ed., *The Right Doctrine from the Wrong Text?* (Grand Rapids, MI: Baker Academic, 1994), p. 147.

20. Archer, *Encyclopedia of Bible Difficulties.*

21. For a very detailed examination of the "Date of the Nativity in Luke," see Richard Carrier's essay at http://www.infidels.org by that title.

22. Ranke-Heinemann, *Putting Away Childish Things*, p. 14. For a book-length treatment of the issues here, see John Shelby Spong, *Born of a Woman: A Bishop Rethinks the Birth of Jesus* (New York: HarperSanFransisco, 1992). Just before debunking the virgin birth of Jesus, Spong wrote that to readers of his book, "It will be incomprehensible to them how one who calls himself a Christian . . . could entertain the possibilities this book suggests" (p. xv). I am one of those readers. It is indeed incomprehensible to me.

23. Ranke-Heinemann, *Putting Away Childish Things*, pp. 16–17.

24. David Edwards and John Stott, *Evangelical Essentials: A Liberal–Evangelical Dialogue* (Downers Grove, IL: InterVarsity Press, 1988), pp. 190–94.

25. See Theodore Drange, "The Argument from the Bible," at http://www.infidels.org/library/modern.

26. Chapters 21–22, found at http://www.earlychristianwritings.com. Emphasis mine.

27. Archer, *Encyclopedia of Bible Difficulties.*

28. Joseph A. Fitzmyer, *The One Who Is to Come* (Grand Rapids, MI: Eerdmans, 2007), p. 37.

29. Ibid., p. 36.

30. James Barr, *Beyond Fundamentalism* (Philadelphia: Westminster Press, 1984), p. 144.

31. U. Luz, *Das Evangelium nach Matthaus I Mt 1–7* (EKKNT, 1.1; Zurich and Neukirchen-Vluyn: Neukirchener Verlag, 1985), p. 107. A friend translated this for me.

32. John Dominic Crossan, *Jesus: A Revolutionary Biography* (New York: HarperCollins, 1989), pp. 16–23.

33. Paul Kurtz, *The Transcendental Temptation* (Amherst, NY: Prometheus Books, 1991), p. 120.

34. I thank fellow blogger DagoodS for this point.

18

WAS JESUS GOD INCARNATE?

I can do little better here than to share the arguments of John Hick and to argue for them.[1] His argument has three major points. We'll briefly review and illustrate his main points in order.

His first point is that the traditional view that Jesus was literally God in the flesh was not something Jesus himself believed or taught, but was written into the Gospels after the Easter event. For Palestinian Jews living in the first century, a close encounter with Jesus could be considered a conversion experience of some sort. The conviction in his eyes as he preached that the kingdom is at hand, the authority of his words and deeds, the way he expressed love, the "miraculous" healings and his apocalyptic conviction of living in the last days of the present age could lead super-stitious people to think God is indeed in this person.

How this conversion experience led up to John's claim in his gospel that Jesus was "the only begotten Son of God" (1:18) is a large and complex topic. In Mark's gospel, the first one written, a man comes to Jesus saying, "Good teacher what must I do to inherit eternal life," and Jesus says to the man, "Why do you call me good? No one is good but God alone" (10:17–18). According to James Barr, "This only makes sense if Jesus is **not** claiming to be God," because "it fits with the fact that Jesus fully accepted Jewish monotheism."[2] But by the time Matthew's gospel was written, the church had developed a higher, more glorified view of Jesus, so this same conversation is amended to read, "'Teacher, what good **deed** must I do to have eternal life?' And he (Jesus) said to him, 'Why do you ask me about what is good? There is only one who is good'" (19:16). Gone is the description of Jesus as a "good teacher," so that Jesus' rhetorical question can be deleted and his statement revised. Jesus now merely asks him, "Why do you call me good?" Noticeably absent is where Jesus said, "No one is good but God **alone**." By contrast, John's gospel, dated conservatively around 100 CE, thirty (to forty-five?) years after Mark's, reveals a very exalted view of Christ.

This process of the deification of Jesus took at least seventy years among ancient superstitious people. Paula Fredricksen summarizes the different cultural milieu in which this deification of Jesus took place, in contrast to the original locus of the events: "from oral to written; from Aramaic to Greek; from the end of time to the middle of time; from Jewish to Gentile; from Galilee and Judea to the Empire."[3]

Marcus Borg shows us the progression of thought from Mark's gospel to Matthew's later gospel. Borg points out that in Mark, the earliest gospel, "a messianic self-claim is not part of Jesus' own message." Only once did Jesus deal with this issue in his public ministry, at Caesarea Philippi. When Jesus asked his disciples "Who do you say that I am?" Peter gives the answer, "You are the Messiah!" (Mark 8:27–30). According to Borg, Mark's story "concludes on an enigmatic note: Jesus neither accepted nor rejected Peter's affirmation but instead sternly told him to say nothing about it." But when Matthew used Mark and constructed his own account, two things were added. "To Peter's exclamation, 'You are the messiah,' Matthew adds a second Christological affirmation: 'The Son of the Living God.'" And, rather than ending it as Mark's gospel did, "Matthew adds a response from Jesus strongly commending Peter and explicitly affirming Jesus' own special status" (16:16–17).

Borg also points out the difference between Mark and Matthew when it comes to the story of Jesus walking on the water. Mark's story concludes with "the disciples being confused about what they had experienced." ("They were utterly astounded" NRSV, 6:45–52.) But "as Matthew copies this story from Mark, he deletes the disciples' lack of understanding and replaces it with a Christological affirmation: 'Truly you are the Son of God.'" Matthew also adds, "and those in the boat worshipped him" (14:32). Beyond Matthew's gospel, John's gospel provides "further evidence that early Christian communities projected post-Easter understandings of Jesus back into the ministry itself."[4]

One huge piece of evidence that leads most scholars to believe John's gospel was written very late is his usage of the phrase "the Jews." It occurs about seventy times, in contrast to five occurrences in the other gospels. In John's gospel it is a stereotype for Jesus' opponents. Compare 7:13: "for fear of the Jews no one spoke openly of him (Jesus)." (See also John 2:18–20; 5:15, 18; 7:1; 9:18, 22; 10:31; 12:9; 18:28; 19:38; 20:19.) But these people were all Jews! How do Jews fear the Jews? The gospel writer himself was a Jew, if it was John! A Christian apologist might object that the phrase "the Jews" merely meant those people who lived in the province of Judea, but several of these occurrences could not be just about people in Judea (John 2:3; 4:22; 5:1; 6:4, 41; 18:20, 33; 19:3, 21, 19, 40). Such a usage reveals the complete breakup between official Judaism and Christianity, which occurred after the destruction of Jerusalem in 70 CE by the Roman army. It is a very odd use of the phrase, leading most scholars to believe John the Apostle didn't even write this gospel, because he himself was a Jew. At the minimum it reveals that the author was not so much interested in historical facts but in elaborating on history, and even creating history.

Christian scholar James D. G. Dunn tells us the specific problem. It's "whether we can use John's Gospel as direct testimony to Jesus' own teaching. . . . This problem was not invented by modern scholarship; it was rather discovered by modern scholarship."[5] John's gospel is "obviously different" from the other three earlier gospels in terms of style and content. With regard to style, in the three synoptic Gospels Jesus speaks in proverbs (Matthew 5–7), and in parables (Luke 15), whereas in John's gospel Jesus often speaks in long involved discourses (14–17). With regard to content, in the three synoptic Gospels Jesus speaks often of the "kingdom of God" and hardly anything about himself, whereas in John's gospel he speaks often about himself ("I am the light of the world . . . the bread of life . . . the way the life and the truth."), but he hardly says anything about the kingdom of God.

At best, scholars see these differences as indicative of the fact that John's gospel is a theological elaboration of history, while still others see them as indicating it is wholly theological in nature with not much historical value at all when it comes to what Jesus taught. Case in point is the question of the high view of Christ revealed in John's gospel. Even Dunn acknowledges that the number of times Jesus speaks of God as his "Father" or "the Father" in John's gospel (173 times—Dunn's count), when compared to the number of times we see this in all three earlier synoptic gospels (a sum total of 43 times), leads him to say that John's Jesus is "the truth of Jesus in retrospect rather than as expressed by Jesus at the time. . . . [I]t is expanded teaching of Jesus."[6] Yet it is precisely because of John's Jesus that we get a very high Christology. John's Jesus is quoted as saying: "I and the Father are one" (10:30), and "He who has seen me has seen the Father" (14:9). But, based on what we've just seen, he never said those things. This is John's Jesus speaking, not the historical Jesus.

Furthermore, Dunn asks a very important question with regard to the "I am" claims of Jesus: "If they were part of the original words of Jesus himself, how could it be that ONLY John has picked them up, and NONE of the others [emphasis his]? Call it scholarly skepticism if you will, but I must confess that I find it almost incredible that such sayings should have been neglected HAD they been known as a feature of Jesus' teaching."[7] John Shelby Spong, an American bishop, goes farther by claiming: "I do not believe I can make a case for a single word attributed to Jesus in the Fourth Gospel to be a literal word actually spoken by the historic Jesus."[8]

Wolfhart Pannenberg argues that the belief that Jesus claimed anything like this "has been demonstrated with growing certainty by critical study of the Gospels to be the work of the post-Easter community. Today it must be taken as all but certain that the pre-Easter Jesus neither designated himself as Messiah (or Son of God) nor accepted such a confession to him from others."[9]

According to John Hick: "Among mainline NT scholars, both conservative and liberal, Catholic and Protestant, there is today a general consensus that these are not pronouncements of the historical Jesus but words put into his mouth some sixty or seventy years later by a Christian writer expressing the theology that had developed in his part of the expanding church. To create speeches in this way for famous or revered figures of the past, embodying the writer's sense of the real significance of the past figure, was standard practice in the ancient world; and the discourses attributed to Jesus in the Fourth Gospel are seen today by most contemporary scholarship as examples of this."[10] Hick provides additional support for his view from several scholars on this issue: C. F. D. Moule, "a pillar of orthodoxy," wrote: "Any case for a high Christology that depended on the authenticity of the alleged claims of Jesus about himself, especially in the 4th Gospel, would be precarious."[11] Another pillar of orthodoxy, Michael Ramsay, said, "Jesus did not claim deity for himself." Besides, "the title 'son of God' need not of itself be of high significance, for in Jewish circles it might mean no more than the Messiah . . . and in popular Hellenism there were many sons of God, meaning holy inspired men."[12] Dunn wrote, "There was no real evidence in the earliest Jesus tradition of what could fairly be called a consciousness of divinity."[13] And according to Brian Hebblethwaite: "It is no longer possible to defend the divinity of Jesus by referring to the claims of Jesus."[14]

It's these kinds of considerations that render C. S. Lewis's "tri-lemma" ineffective as a Christian apologetic. Lewis argued that either Jesus was a liar, a lunatic, or the Lord. In his words, "either this man was, and is, the Son of God: or else a madman or something worse."[15] The fact is however, that Jesus never claimed to be God in the flesh in the first place.

The second point in Hick's argument is that we can trace how Jesus was deified by his followers leading ultimately to the Nicean/Chalcedonian view of Christ as a way of expressing the Lordship of Jesus over the gods and goddesses of the Roman Empire. According to Hick: "In general it seems that the early Christians, seeking to understand and communicate the significance of their Lord, grasped at concepts and titles within their culture and that the usage of these developed under the pressures of preaching and controversy."[16]

Jewish tradition in Jesus' time had three major images of the redeemer who would bring in the coming new and glorious age. One was the "Messiah" (Hebrew for "king"), who was to reign in a new kingdom in which Jerusalem would be the center of the world, and where God's will would be done on earth. There was nothing about this Messiah/king that was considered to be anything other than a reigning human Jewish king, a mere hope of the Jews and nothing more, as we've seen (in my chapter 16).

The second image was that of the "Son of man" prophesized in Daniel 7:13–14. Hick reminds us that "with a view to the later Christian doctrine of the incarnation, that neither the Messiah nor the Son of man was, in Jewish thinking, divine . . . it was emphatically not equivalent to being God incarnate."[17] Besides this, there are strong indications that Jesus did not think of himself as the *Son of Man* anyway. Just look closely at what Jesus said in Mark 8:38 as one example of a "Son of Man" saying: "For whoever is ashamed of me and of my words in this adulterous and sinful generation, of him will the Son of man also be ashamed, when he comes in the glory of his Father with the holy angels." Bart D. Ehrman argues that when we look at what Jesus actually said about the Son of Man, "there is no indication that he is talking about himself. In fact, if you didn't know in advance the Christian idea that Jesus was the Son of Man, there'd be no way you would infer it from this saying. On the contrary, just taking the saying on its own terms, Jesus appears to be referring to someone else. To paraphrase the saying: 'whoever doesn't pay attention to what I'm saying will be in big trouble when the Son of Man arrives.'"[18]

A third image was "Son of God," which was common in the ancient world as well as in biblical literature. Oscar Cullman argues: "The origin of the 'son of God' concept lies in ancient oriental religions, in which above all kings were thought to be begotten of gods."[19] In the Bible we find kings and even the people of Israel themselves are known as God's sons, but they aren't supernatural beings at all (Ps. 2:7; 2 Sam. 7:14; Hos. 11:1). And when it comes to divine supernatural beings, if Christians actually looked at what is said in the Old Testament, they'd find God has many divine sons, not just one. There are many divine beings in the Bible who have the exact title "sons of God." (Job 1:6; 38:7), which were later understood to be angels. Furthermore James Dunn says: "Some of the legendary heroes of Greek myth were called sons of God," like Dionysus and Heracles, who were sons of Zeus. "Famous philosophers also, like Pythagoras and Plato, were sometimes spoken of as having been begotten by a god (Apollo). . . . The language of divine sonship and divinity was in widespread and varied use in the ancient world and would have been familiar to the contemporaries of Jesus, Paul and John in a wide range of application."[20]

How this divine language was used in the time of the Apostle Paul is interesting. Geza Vermes argues that the title "Son of God" was understood "metaphorically" in Jewish circles at the time, such that "if the medium in which Christian theology developed had been Hebrew and not Greek, it would not have produced an incarnation doctrine as this is traditionally understood."[21] John Hick tells us that it's "not in the least surprising that Jesus, as a spirit-filled prophet, a charismatic healer, perhaps as Messiah, believed to be of the royal line of David, should have been thought of and should have thought of himself as, in this familiar metaphorical sense, a son of God. What happened, as the gospel went out beyond the Hebraic milieu into the Greek-dominated intellectual world of the Roman Empire, was that the metaphorical son of God was transformed into the metaphysical God the Son."[22] Pannenberg argues: "Only in Gentile Christianity was the divine Sonship understood physically as participation in the divine essence."[23] The progression of this train of thought led up to the very strong affirmation of Nicene/Chalcedonian Christology of the fourth and fifth centuries. Hick again: "It could well be that its deification of Jesus helped the early Christian community to survive its period of intermittent persecutions and that subsequently, if the church was to be the spiritual, moral, and cultural director of the Roman Empire, and thus of Western civilization, it needed the prestige of a founder who was none other than God, in the person of the eternal Son."[24]

But the Apostle Paul seems to be the exception to this Jewish thinking. Paul grew up in Tarsus and had been educated under the great Jewish teacher Gamaliel (Acts 21:39; 22:3), but it's crystal clear when reading Acts that he must have had a good Hellenistic education too. It's in Paul's writings that we first see Jesus' spoken of as God's son (see Rom. 1:3–4; 8:3; 1 Cor. 15:23–28; Phil. 2:5–11; Gal. 4:4; Col. 1:15–20). About this Hick asks, "what did this language mean to the writer and his readers in the first century?" Paul's language suggests "the subordination of the son to the father. And in Paul's writings God and God's Son cannot be said to be co-equal, as Persons of the Holy Trinity were later declared to be. The notion of Jesus as God's Son is indeed pre-trinitarian. Paul's carefully stated theological view, in the

Epistle to the Romans, seems . . . to be that Jesus was a man who was raised by God in his resurrection to a special and uniquely important status."[25]

We also may rightly wonder about the gospel that Paul was preaching, for he claims the gospel he preached was given to him by revelation. After three years he had spent only fifteen days with Peter and James (Gal. 1:11–22). Paul claims he was taught the gospel by a revelation. Did this objectively happen? And if it was only a vision, how can we be sure of the truth of everything he preached? Fifteen days with Peter may not be enough to sort out all of his theological views. They clearly had debates about some things (Gal. 2:11–21; Acts 15), which has led some scholars to see a major divide in the churches between those associated with Paul and those associated with Peter.

What we do know is that Paul tried to reach people in the Roman Empire who thought it possible that the gods could take up human form. In Acts, when the crowd in Lystra saw how Paul had healed a man, "they shouted in the Lycaonian language, 'The gods have come down to us in human form!' Barnabas they called Zeus, and Paul they called Hermes, because he was the chief speaker" (Acts 14:11–12). In addition, in Acts 28:6, Paul is called a "god" on the island of Malta. Paul was probably using the language that only they could appreciate when he preached to them about Jesus, since they might only be interested in the gospel of Jesus if he were a god, or a son of God. And didn't Paul say "I have become all things to all people, that I might by all means save some" (1 Cor. 9:22). He was an evangelist who sought to communicate to his hearers in ways that they would understand, and he simply wanted them to know of the greatness of Jesus over that of their gods and goddesses.

Robert W. Funk summarizes the four stages of Christology in the New Testament: Stage one: *Exaltation Christology*. This is an evaluation of Jesus that "assigns him the role of a son of Adam at his death and resurrection. . . . In this view, Jesus became, or was elevated to, a son of God by virtue of his resurrection" (Rom. 1:3–4; Acts 2:36). Stage two: *Adoptionistic Christology.* "The first stage of Christology did not require the creation of a gospel because the words and deeds of Jesus were not essential to his function; the real role of Jesus was to return as the messiah in the very near future. When he did not return immediately as expected, his followers began to review what they remembered of him and decided that his life, after all, had exhibited some unusual traits. Now they started to fashion another version of his story in which he was designated son of God, not at his resurrection but at his baptism" (Mark 1:10–11). Stage three: "The next step came with the gospels of Matthew and Luke, and these gospels 'moved the messianic status of Jesus back to his birth.' If there was someone who had a noteworthy life, he must have had a noteworthy birth. If a hero is human, as in the case of John the Baptist, the miracle is that of a barren woman. . . . If the hero is considered superhuman, as in the case of Hercules and Alexander, the male parent is a god." Stage four: "The gospel of John's prologue (1:1–18) makes Jesus pre-existent from the beginning."[26]

Hick's third point is that the belief that Jesus was fully man and fully God has never been shown to be consistently defined, explained, or defended. The Council of Chalcedon (451 CE) finally defined the orthodox doctrine of the incarnation. The problem is that the council "merely asserted that Jesus was 'truly God and truly man' without attempting to say how such a paradox is possible. . . . Merely to assert that two different natures coexisted in Jesus 'without confusion, without change, without division, without separation' is to utter a form of words which as yet has no specific meaning."[27] Many attempts before and after Chalcedon were made, but none of them were accepted by the Church, from Docetism, Adoptionism, Apolli-narianism, Nestorianism, Arianism, and Monophysitism.

Here then are four conceptual problems with an incarnate God, that is, how can one person be truly and fully God and at the same time truly and fully a man: (1) God is necessarily an uncreated being. Humans are essentially created beings. Therefore Jesus is both created and uncreated. (2) God is necessarily omniscient—he knows everything. Human beings are not omniscient beings. Therefore, Jesus is both an omniscient and also not an omniscient being. (3) God is a morally perfect being, and as such could not be tempted to do wrong. Human beings, however, can be tempted to do wrong and are imperfect. Therefore, Jesus could not be tempted, nor do any wrong, yet we're told that he was tempted to do wrong. (4) God is omnipresent, everywhere, but Jesus as a human being was not.

THOMAS MORRIS'S THEORY OF TWO MINDS

One modern attempt to defend the notion that Jesus was God incarnate has been made by Thomas Morris, in which he defends the proposition that "Jesus of Nazareth was one and the same person as God the Son, the second person of the Trinity."[28]

Initially, such a view raises certain questions. Christians like Morris have three successive beings to reconcile with each other: There was a second person of the Trinity, known as the Logos, who existed before time; then there was Jesus, who is God-in-the-flesh—a unique and new being in history; and finally, there is the resur-rected and glorified Jesus who now is purportedly "sitting at the right hand of God."

Now keep in mind that the God-man Jesus was a fully human being, so any res-urrected God-man must have a body in keeping with his humanity; otherwise, the human part of the God-man ceased to exist, died, or his body was simply discarded. But it can't be that God would destroy a sinless man—the man Jesus. There are a few Christian attempts to deal with this problem, none of which I find plausible.

One possibility is that Jesus was not a new creature at all, but instead he was/is the exact embodiment of the second person of the Trinity, the "Logos of God." That is to say, Jesus was/is the essential nature of the second person of the Trinity, and he was always embodied as he existed on earth from eternity. But this solution is rejected by J. P. Moreland and William Lane Craig, in that it would deny that "the Logos (the second person of the Trinity) preexisted as a member of the Trinity in incorporeal form."[29]

Still another possibility is that after the resurrection and ascension events of Jesus there are now two beings rather than one. In heaven there is the human Jesus, and then there is the second person of the Trinity. There are now two beings who exist and arose out of one being, one person, here on earth. That is, the second person of the Trinity discarded his human form to live for the rest of eternity unhindered, letting the human part of him exist as a separate person in heaven with him. But this solution is not considered by Christians to be orthodox, because the Chalcedon creed speaks of there being a "union" of the God-man such that the result is "but one and the same Son and Only-begotten God the Word, Lord Jesus Christ." How can such a metaphysical union be separated into two beings? The traditional orthodox doctrine is that Jesus is one person!

When I asked about this problem of the glorified Jesus, my former professor Dr. Ron Feenstra had no trouble accepting the conclusion that the second person of the Trinity took on a human form and now must keep it for all of eternity.[30] But this whole belief is extremely troublesome and implausible. If the human nature of Jesus is forever linked to the second person of the Trinity, then the full Trinity now includes a man, that is, the human side of Jesus. In heaven, the second person of the Trinity must now forever live encapsulated within a human body (a glorious body, nonetheless, but a body). We now have an embodied God, forever! This whole thing seems contrived and is the result of believing, along with ancient superstitious people, that human beings could be gods (see Acts 14:11; 28:6).

But this God-man union is exactly what Morris is trying to defend. To do this he proposes a two-minds theory: "In the case of God Incarnate, we must recognize something like two distinct ranges of consciousness. There is first what we can call the eternal mind of God the Son with its distinctively divine consciousness. . . . And in addition there is a distinctively earthly consciousness that came into existence and grew and developed as the boy Jesus grew and developed."[31] In this way the second person of the Trinity could know what was going on in both the conscious and the unconscious mind of Jesus although Jesus could be totally unaware that he is even there.

Morris has some major difficulties when he tries to work out this theory involving two minds, even though he uses the results of modern psychology. If there are two separate minds, each with its own separate consciousness, then a major question is this: Was the earthly Jesus conscious of the second person of the Trinity, or not? If he wasn't conscious of the divine mind, then Jesus would act and think like a human being in every respect. However, there would be no guarantee that his behavior is a model for us, nor would there be any guarantee that he spoke the very words of God to us. The only possible guarantee that he did so would be to claim the divine mind directed the human mind of Jesus to act and say the things he purportedly did. But at that point it's not really possible to say that this accurately describes a human being "like us in every respect." For if God directed our human minds in the same way, then we too would be sinless and we too would speak the very words of God. In this sense the human side of Jesus would be merely a puppet of God.

If the human side of the God-man was conscious of the divine mind, then why didn't he exhibit the attributes of deity, like omniscience (Matt. 24:36, Luke 8:45–46) and omnipotence (Matt. 14:3–13; 26:53)? The reason Stephen T. Davis suggests is that Jesus couldn't do this and still be fully human: "At any point in his earthly ministry, I suspect, Jesus could have called on his omniscience (or omnipotence, for that matter), but had he done so, it would have been tantamount to his no longer being truly human."[32]

So on the one hand, if the human side of the God-man was not conscious of the divine mind, then how can his actions be guaranteed to be Godlike? But on the other hand, if he was conscious of the divine mind, or if the divine mind infallibly directed the human side of the God-man, then we no longer have a true human being who was "just like us in every respect."

This whole problem can be seen most forcefully when trying to understand what took place if and when the human and divine minds of Jesus ever came into conflict, as in the case of temptation. Which mind made the final decision in what to say or in how to act? How can one person have two minds but one will? Does the "divine will" override the "human will"? Jesus himself said that human beings could sin in their thoughts alone (Matt. 5:22, 28). Was Jesus able to fully act as a human being, or was his will to sin always restrained? Morris suggests that Jesus had free will but that if he ever acted to sin the second person of the Trinity would have stopped him from doing so. But if Jesus' will was restrained in this way, then how can it be said Jesus was truly like us? He would have a divine consciousness that we don't have, and as such he didn't have the same choices and freedoms we have as human beings. Being restrained from sinning is not praiseworthy at all, because being praiseworthy demands that we acted on our own accord and we thought and did good things, not bad things. But apparently Jesus couldn't totally act freely, so there's nothing praiseworthy about what he thought and did as a human being. And if that's so, how does his purportedly sinless life do anything to atone for our sins?

We're told that Jesus was tempted (Matt. 4:1; Heb. 4:15). To be tempted would entail having thoughts about sinning. One cannot be tempted to do something if there is no desire to do it. If someone tries to tempt me to rob a bank, it cannot be done, because I do not have that desire, and never will. This is no temptation for me at all. Theologians have been trying to make sense of this whole idea of the distinction between temptation and the sinful thoughts that Jesus condemns, I think, unsuccessfully. But since Jesus was tempted to sin, there seems to be some small imperfections in him, since to be tempted means to have desires that do not accord with the nature of God, especially when we take seriously the whole idea that there are no imperfections in the Godhead at all. According to John Hick: "Even unfulfilled beginnings of evil must themselves count as imperfections; for in order for the divine mind to overrule them there must have been something there that required to be overruled." Jesus exhibited what we'd now call a racist attitude toward a woman (Mark 7:27); Jesus didn't respect his parents like the law would demand (Mark 3:31–5; Luke 14:26); and he used violence in the temple when he cast out the money changers (Matt. 21:12).[33]

Paul Copan understands the seriousness of this problem, but to solve it he introduces an ad hoc theory. Without any biblical support, he claims Jesus was voluntarily ignorant of the fact that "he was necessarily good," and as such he really was tempted to sin but couldn't, because of his divine nature.[34] Just how Jesus could be divine and still lack the recognition that as a divine being he was necessarily good

Copan doesn't explain. Instead Copan offers an analogy. He answers by saying this is the same problem with how Jesus could know he was divine and yet not know the time of his purported second coming (Matt. 24:36). But, this doesn't solve either problem. One bad analogy doesn't solve another one. He still hasn't answered how Jesus could be divine and yet not have divine foreknowledge.

What we have left is a man, Jesus, who was chosen for a specific role by God such that God never allowed him to do anything wrong. If this is the case, then God could do that with any human being, and as such, any human being could be considered God incarnate. So the question that Morris leaves unexplained is whether Jesus was free to sin. This, according to Hick, is the specific problem "that proved fatal for Morris' theory."[35]

MORELAND AND CRAIG'S PROPOSED MIND BEHIND THE MIND CHRISTOLOGY

J. P. Moreland and William Lane Craig's proposal fares no better.[36] They affirm with the Chalcedon creed that in Jesus is one person with one single will "who exemplifies two distinct and complete natures, one human and one divine." They argue that "the Logos (or the 2nd person of the trinity) contained perfect human personhood archetypically in his own nature. The result was that in assuming a hominoid body the Logos brought to Christ's animal nature just those properties that would serve to make it a complete human nature." As such, the nature of Jesus "was made complete by the union of the flesh with the Logos, the archetype of humanity." Claiming that man was made in the image of God in the first place (Gen. 1:27), Moreland and Craig argue: "The Logos already possessed in his preincarnate state all the properties necessary for a human self. In assuming a hominoid body, he brought to it all that was necessary for a complete human being." Therefore, "Christ is both fully God and fully man, that is to say, he is all that God is and all that man ought to be."

Left unexplained by Moreland and Craig is an exegesis of what it means to say human beings are made in the image of God, which I examined in an earlier chapter (pp. 128–30). Leaving that issue aside, what could Moreland and Craig mean by the concept of a "complete human being" when it comes to Jesus? I take it that other human beings are not "complete." If they're referring to the fact that human beings are sinners, then shouldn't Adam and Eve before the fall be considered by them to be incarnations of the Logos? Hardly. So it must mean something else, even though they argue Christ is "all that man ought to be." The word "ought" here implies an obligation to be like Christ, but that makes no sense to me in this context, since they're not just talking about someone who is sinless, but trying to describe a metaphysical union of the divine and human. If they are talking about a metaphysical union, then we cannot be complete human beings unless we too are incarnations of the Logos, and that cannot be, for then it should also be possible for us to become members of the Trinity who've existed eternally!

So what exactly is a complete human being and how is it possible for us to be complete human beings? What exactly is an incomplete human being? Moreland and Craig never spell these things out for us. Is it that we have power but Jesus had infinite power; that we have knowledge but Jesus had infinite knowledge; that we are "present" but Jesus was omnipresent? Jesus didn't exhibit these infinite characteristics, and he surely wasn't omnipresent. If it's impossible for us to be complete human beings with omniscience, omnipotence, and omnipresence, then there is a real metaphysical difference that still needs to be reconciled within the nature of Jesus. From what they've argued, the only complete human being was/is Jesus, and he is metaphysically different than all other human beings. And if Jesus was indeed metaphysically different from us, how can he be like us "in every respect" and still atone for our sins (Heb. 2:17)?

Leaving these insurmountable problems unresolved, Moreland and Craig argue that "the divine aspects of Jesus' personality were largely subliminal during his state of humiliation." They borrow from William James's notion of the "subliminal self" and apply it to Jesus, according to which "the subliminal facets of a person's personality do not possess a distinct faculty of the will, even though those subconscious aspects of one's own personality may, indeed, powerfully influence what one wills in ways that one does not suspect." Based on this view, they argue that "the 'subliminal self' is the primary locus of the superhuman elements in the consciousness of the incarnate Logos." As such, "the Logos allowed only those facets of his person to be part of Christ's waking consciousness which were compatible with typical human experience, while the bulk of his knowledge and other cognitive perfections, like an iceberg beneath the water's surface, lay submerged in his subconscious."

I just don't see this as an improvement over Morris's "two-minds" theory. The locus of the divine mind now resides in the subconscious human mind of Jesus, and as such, it's still impossible to see how this solves anything left unresolved from Morris's view. I merely have to rephrase some of my objections. Instead of a "two-minds" theory, what we now have is a "mind behind the mind" theory. Instead of having the problem of two conscious minds in Jesus, now we have the problem of two subconscious minds in Jesus. But it's the same problem moved back a step. We still have serious problems understanding the relationship of the divine subconscious mind to the human subconscious mind of Jesus. We still have to ask how much control the divine side of his subconscious mind had over the human side of his subconscious mind.

What took place when the human subconscious mind of Jesus and his divine subconscious mind came into conflict, as in the case of temptation? Which one had the overriding influence in what to say, or in how to act? To say there was never any conflict is an act of faith without any basis in human psychology, since as human beings we are often led by fleshly desires. Moreland and Craig suggest that the conscious mind of Jesus was controlled by the divine subconscious mind. They wrote: "The will of the Logos had in virtue of the Incarnation become the will of the man Jesus." But that could only be the case if the human subconscious mind of Jesus was always overridden whenever he wanted to do something contrary to the Logos that controlled his subconscious mind. So even if Moreland and Craig do not argue for two conscious wills in the incarnate Jesus with two separate minds, they have a divine mind behind the human mind and a divine will behind the human will of Jesus. On their view Jesus was not "like us" in every respect." He couldn't be.

To be a human being in the first place, is to have *both* a conscious and a subconscious part to the human mind. To make human decisions is to fully utilize both parts of our minds. If the human subconscious mind was taken over by the divine subconscious mind, as they suggest, then how is it also to be described as a fully human subconscious mind? Again, as I've argued, it does no good to merely say Jesus was a complete human being without also telling us what this means. It's just obvious to me that without spelling out these differences what we have in Moreland and Craig's "mind behind the mind" proposal are the same problems as Morris's "two-minds" theory, which are subject to the same objections.

DIVINE KENOSIS THEORIES

According to Clark Pinnock, "Kenotic Theory is, I think, the most important fresh contribution to Christology since the early centuries."[37] This idea comes from Philippians 2:5–11 and claims that the second person of the Trinity laid aside his nonessential attributes in order to be a man, like omniscience. It was first proposed by Lutheran theologian Gottfried Thomasius. Thomasius proposed that the metaphysical attributes of the second person of the Trinity were temporarily laid aside in the incarnation while the moral attributes were retained, so that Jesus' attributes were divine goodness, love, and justice, but not omnipotence and omniscience. The questions to be answered are whether there is any room in this Jesus left for God, and whether or not Jesus can still be God incarnate without the attributes of God, as defined by the Chalcedon Council?[38]

When it comes to describing Jesus as God incarnate, Kenotic theologians mainly offer analogies that don't explain anything, and then they "punt to mystery." I had a master's class with William Lane Craig called the "Concept of God." In this class, we read and discussed Stephen T. Davis's book *Logic and the Nature of God* very thoroughly.[39] It was a good book for discussion since there was so much room for it. I remember the analogy that Dr. Craig proposed to help us understand Kenotic theology. He drew a square, and then he drew a circle next to it that connected with the square at one corner. He said the square would represent the attributes of a man, and a circle would represent the attributes of God. The point at which they touch each other is the person of Jesus Christ.[40] But what does this analogy show? Not much as far as I can tell at this point, because the question is still begged as to how many properties God can lose and still be God, and how many properties a man can gain and still be a man.

Take, for instance, Davis, who claims, "If Jesus was God; and if Jesus was non-omnipotent; then being omnipotent is not essential to God."[41] And the same is said for his other divine attributes. But after emptying the divine nature of so much, Davis is just left with the properties of "being divine," "being self-identical," and "existing." John Hick argues that "existing and being self-identical must indeed be properties of anything that exists, including God." So the only other property is divine existence. But without some characteristics or properties of what it means to have divine existence, we are left with nothing specific. Hick says: "Thus in making space for divine incarnation, Davis has had to reject much of the traditional Christian understanding of God."[42] Davis senses the problems of his view and says: "Of course we cannot use kenosis (or any other theory) to remove the mystery of the classical doctrine." Davis continues, "As Brian Hebblethwaite said, 'incarnation is a baffling act of a being whose essence we will never fully understand; it is highly unlikely, therefore, that we will ever completely grasp the incarnation.'"[43]

P. T. Forsyth is quoted as saying, "We cannot form any scientific conception of the precise process by which a complete and eternal being could enter on a process of becoming, how Godhood could accept growth, how a divine consciousness could reduce its own consciousness by volition."[44]

E. P. Sanders sums it up: "It lies beyond my meager abilities as an interpreter of dogmatic theology to explain how it is possible for one person to be 100 per cent human and 100 per cent divine, without either interfering with the other."[45]

It would seem much more likely to me, given these serious intellectual problems in understanding the incarnation, that it should simply be rejected. It is based upon historical claims, and as we've seen, history is subject to all kinds of differing interpretations. But if we try to make sense of these historical claims and simply cannot do it, then it's high time we reject those claims.

NOTES

1. John Hick's books are (ed.) *The Myth of God Incarnate* (London: SCM Press, 1977); and *The Metaphor of God Incarnate* (Louisville: Westminster, 1993), and in a chapter for *Encountering Jesus: A Debate on Christology*, ed. Stephen T. Davis (Atlanta: John Knox Press, 1981). See also *Incarnation and Myth: The Debate Continued*, ed. Michael Goulder (London: SCM Press, 1979).

2. James Barr, *Beyond Fundamentalism* (Philadelphia: Westminster Press, 1984), p. 58.

3. Paula Fredricksen, *From Jesus to Christ* (New Haven, CT: Yale University Press, 1988), p. 8.

4. In Marcus Borg and N. T. Wright, *The Meaning of Jesus: Two Visions* (New York: HarperSanFrancisco, 1999), pp. 56–57.

5. James D. G. Dunn, *The Evidence for Jesus* (Louisville, KY: Westminster Press, 1985), p. 31.

6. Ibid., p. 45.

7. Ibid., p. 36.

8. Jon Shelby Spong, *Rescuing the Bible from Fundamentalism* (New York: HarperSanFrancisco, 1991), p. 191.

9. Wolfhart Pannenberg, *Jesus—God and Man* (Louisville, KY: Westminster Press, 1968).

10. Hick in *More Than One Way? Four Views on Salvation*, ed. Dennis L. Okholm and Timothy R. Phillips (Grand Rapids, MI: Zondervan, 1995), p. 53.

11. C. F. D. Moule, *The Origins of Christology* (Cambridge: Cambridge University Press, 1977), p. 136.

12. Michael Ramsey, *Jesus and the Living Past* (Oxford: Oxford University Press, 1980), pp. 39, 43.

13. James D. G. Dunn, *Christology in the Making* (Louisville, KY: Westminster/John Knox Press, 1980), p. 60.

14. Brian Hebblethwaite, *The Incarnation* (Cambridge: Cambridge University Press, 1987), p. 74.

15. C. S. Lewis, *Mere Christianity* (New York: Macmillian, 1952), p. 41. For an excellent critique of C. S. Lewis's argument, see John Beversluis, *C. S. Lewis and the Search for Rational Religion*, rev. and updated ed. (Amherst, NY: Prometheus Books, 2007), pp. 111–41.

16. Hick, *Encountering Jesus*, p. 14. Three books that deal with this progression of thought in the early centuries are John Dominic Crossan, *The Birth of Christianity* (New York; HarperCollins, 1998); L. Michael White, *From Jesus to Christianity* (New York: HarperSan-Franscico, 2004); and Fredricksen, *From Jesus to Christ.*

17. Hick, *Encountering Jesus*, pp. 7–9.

18. Bart D. Ehrman, *Jesus: Apocalyptic Prophet of the New Millennium* (Oxford: Oxford University Press, 1999), p. 135.

19. Oscar Cullman, *The Christology of the New Testament* (London: SCM Press, 1971), pp. 271–73.

20. Dunn, *Christology in the Making*, p. 17. For more on these titles see the *Anchor Bible Dictionary.*

21. Geza Vermes, "Jesus the Jew," in *Jesus' Jewishness: Exploring the Place of Jesus in Early Judaism*, ed. James H. Charlesworth (New York: Crossroad, 1991), p. 113; see also Geza Vermes, *Jesus and the World of Judaism* (London: SCM Press, 1983).

22. Hick, *Encountering Jesus*, p. 14.

23. Pannenberg, *Jesus—God and Man*, p. 117.

24. Hick, *Encountering Jesus*, pp. 15–16.

25. Hick, *The Metaphor of God Incarnate*, p. 43.

26. Robert W. Funk, *Honest to Jesus* (New York: HarperSanFrancisco, 1996), pp. 279–96.

27. Hick, *The Metaphor of God Incarnate*, p. 48.

28. Thomas V. Morris, *The Logic of God Incarnate* (Ithaca, NY: Cornell University Press, 1986), p. 13.

29. J. P. Moreland and William Lane Craig, *Philosophical Foundations for a Christian Worldview* (Downers Grove, IL: InterVarsity Press, 2003), p. 606.

30. He edited, along with Cornelius Plantinga Jr., *Trinity, Incarnation, and Atonement* (South Bend, IN: University of Notre Dame Press, 1989).

31. Morris, *The Logic of God Incarnate*, p. 102.

32. Stephen T. Davis, *Logic and the Nature of God* (Grand Rapids, MI: Eerdmans, 1983), p. 126.

33. Hick, *The Metaphor of God Incarnate*, p. 77.

34. Paul Copan, *"That's Just Your Interpretation"* (Grand Rapids, MI: Baker Book House, 2001), pp. 138–43.

35. Hick, *The Metaphor of God Incarnate*, pp. 58, 60; See also Michael Martin's critique of Morris's theory in *The Case against Christianity* (Philadelphia: Temple University Press, 1991), pp. 125–61.

36. Moreland and Craig, *Philosophical Foundations for a Christian Worldview*, pp. 606–12.

37. Clark Pinnock and Delwin Brown, *Theological Crossfire: An Evangelical/Liberal Dialogue* (Grand Rapids, MI: Zondervan, 1990), p. 146.

38. For a recent examination of Kenotic Christology, see C. Stephen Evans, ed., *Exploring Kenotic Christianity: The Self-Emptying of God* (Oxford: Oxford University Press, 2006). I haven't seen this book yet, but I'm sure it fails from the same pitfalls.

39. Davis, *Logic and the Nature of God.*

40. At the time I thought Craig was supportive of Kenotic theology, but it's clear he rejects Kenotic theology from reading J. P. Moreland and his book *Philosophical Foundations for a Christian Worldview*, pp. 606–13, where they argue that to accept Kenotic theology whereby "Christ divested himself of any attribute essential to divinity, then he thereby ceased to be God" (p. 606).

41. Davis, *Logic and the Nature of God*, p. 72 (as quoted by Hick).

42. Hick, *Metaphor of God Incarnate*, p. 73.

43. Brian Hebblethwaite, *Encountering Jesus: A Debate on Christology* (Atlanta: John Knox Press, 1988), p. 53.

44. P. T. Forsyth, *The Person and Place of Jesus Christ* (London: Hodder & Stoughton, 1911), p. 293.

45. E. P. Sanders, *The Historical Figure of Jesus* (New York: Penguin Books, 1993), p. 134.

19

"THE PASSION OF THE CHRIST"

Why Did Jesus Suffer?

The major atonement theory among evangelical Christians is the Reformer's *penal substitutionary theory*, which dominates in the conservative churches.

This theory hasn't always been the one Christians adopted from the biblical texts. The earliest attempt to conceptualize what Jesus did for the world on the cross was first advanced by Irenaeus and developed by Origen. Based upon Mark 10:45, it is called the *ransom theory*. According to this theory, human beings fell under the jurisdiction of Satan when we fell into sin, and Jesus' death paid the ransom for our release. John Hick comments: "Ransom had a poignant meaning in the ancient world, when a considerable proportion of the population lived in the state of slavery. . . . Being ransomed, and thus made free, was accordingly a vivid and powerful metaphor whose force most of us can only partially recapture today."[1] Such a version of the atonement stood for roughly nine hundred years as the generally accepted one.

St. Anselm set forth another theory in a different social climate for the people of his day in the eleventh century. Of the ransom theory, he asked why anyone should believe that the devil has any valid legal rights over the infinite Creator God to demand a ransom in the first place? Anselm then proceeded to argue for a *satisfaction atonement theory*. According to Anselm, our sins are an insult to God and detract from his honor. Therefore God's honor must be restored and the insult must be undone. But only through the death of the God-Man can God's honor be restored and satisfaction be made, since the satisfaction must be in proportion to the amount of sin, and the amount of sin is infinite.

According to John Hick, Anselm's theory "made sense within the culture of medieval Europe," in that it reflected "a strongly hierarchical and tightly knit society." The whole idea of satisfaction "had long operated in both church and society. . . . The idea of disobedience, whether to God or to one's feudal lord, was a slight upon his honour and dignity, and required for its cancellation an appropriate penance of gift in satisfaction. . . . When one did something to undermine the dignity and authority of one's earthly overlord, one had either to be punished or to give sufficient satisfaction to appease the lord's injured dignity." Leon Morris writes: "In the end Anselm makes God too much like a king whose dignity has been affronted. He overlooked the fact that a sovereign may be clement and forgiving without doing harm to his kingdom."[2] Michael Martin adds that "the very idea of God's pride being so wounded and demanding such satisfaction that the voluntary sacrifice of his innocent son is required, assumes a view of God's moral nature that many modern readers would reject."[3] Anslem's theory makes little sense to democratic loving people in today's world. It presupposes a feudal society that we have rejected a long time ago.

In the sixteenth century, the Reformers introduced the penal substitutionary theory, which still holds sway in most conservative Christian circles. The Reformers used Paul's understanding of justification as their biblical backdrop. They claimed God's sense of justice demanded a payment for the sins of humanity and that Jesus paid that infinite debt with his substitution in our place for our sins on the cross. Upon the acceptance of the payment Jesus made for our debt, we are now forgiven for our sins.

According to John Hick, the society that the Reformers lived in had changed since Anselm's day. In the medieval world the law was the expression of a king. To disobey the king brought dishonor to the king, for which satisfaction by punishment was needed in order to restore the honor due to the king. "But the concept of an objective justice, set over ruled and ruler alike, had been developing in Europe since the Renaissance. Law was now thought to have it's own eternal validity, requiring a punishment for wrongdoing which could not be set aside even by the ruler. It was this new principle that the Reformers applied and extended in their doctrine that Christ took our place in bearing the inexorable penalty for human sin—a powerful imagery that has long gripped the Christian imagination."[4]

A GENERAL CRITIQUE OF THESE THEORIES

What I say here will apply in various ways to these three theories. If Jesus suffered in my place so that I can go to heaven rather than hell, then apart from Jesus' suffering, I should be punished for my sins by being sent to hell when I die. But what has any one of us ever done to deserve the kind of punishment Jesus suffered, much less to deserve hell itself? All through my entire life I have never met, nor even heard of, one person who deserved such a punishment. Never.

In our modern society we punish people in a humane way. We don't flog them or crucify them or put them on the rack, or in stocks, nor do we brand them or tar and feather them for public disgrace. These are things only the most bloodthirsty people would do to their enemies. We put them in jail to keep them from hurting more people, and we do so to deter others from a life of crime. Then there is the motive of simple retaliation—retribution. Many people are arguing that such a motive is unethical and unbecoming of a humane society, especially when it comes to capital punishment. Now my point here is to ask which motive is it that God has that makes him a just God when he punishes us, if in fact we deserve it? And how do his methods of punishment compare with our more humane ones? Most all of us wouldn't want our worst enemies to suffer as Jesus did. Even those of us who believe in capital punishment would still want it done humanely.

To say that my sins are an infinite wrong because they are committed against an infinite God, and thus demand an infinite punishment, seems mistaken for several reasons.

In the first place, does justice really demand this much punishment? Can it really be true that justice demands I suffer for all eternity in hell for one little white lie? Who creates the demands of justice, anyway? What judge would think this is a fair punishment? What picture of God lies behind this view of justice— a caring father or an aloof vengeful medieval potentate? Jesus describes God as the former, a caring father. We see this in the Lord's Prayer (Matt. 6:9–15) and the Parable of the Prodigal Son (Luke 15:11–32), where no one pays any penalty for their sins—they merely have to ask for forgiveness. Asking forgiveness was all a Pharisee had to do to (Luke 18:13–14). Jesus himself said, "I desire mercy, and not sacrifice" (Matt. 9:13).

Second, if God became incarnate to relate to us, then why can't he also see what sin is from our perspective, as a finite offense from partly good and partly bad human beings? We intend no infinite wrong against God when we sin. God should know this, especially since it's claimed he related to us by being one of us. To claim otherwise makes God's justice misguided and inappropriate. To say that the punishment depends on the status of the one being offended would mean that someone who offends the President's son should be punished more severely than any other offender, and this makes a mockery out of the notion of a fair justice for all.

Third, did Jesus really suffer an infinite punishment for our sins? If Jesus was merely being punished for all of the wrongdoing of every person who ever lived on earth based on human standards of punishment and not infinite standards, we'd still have to ask whether he was punished enough. After all, if every person who ever lived deserved to be slapped in the face just one time, then the equivalent of sixty billion slaps would surely amount to more punishment than Jesus physically endured.[5] But if it's true to say that each and every one of us deserved an infinite punishment for our sins, then how much less is it true to say Jesus suffered infinitely for each one of us? More to the point, if we were given a choice to suffer as Jesus did or else be cast in hell for eternity (which would be our infinite punishment), we would all choose to suffer as Jesus did. Jesus didn't suffer forever, nor did he stay dead.

But it is said that Jesus endured more than just physical pain. He also endured the pain of being separated from God. How can we make sense of this claim? If it's merely a metaphor for the mental pain of not sensing God's help when we need it, then we have all felt that pain throughout our lives. Otherwise, it must somehow mean Jesus ceased to be God while on the cross. However, Christians cannot believe that. Because if Jesus in fact ceased to be God, then since Christians believe a triune God exists, that means God also ceased to exist when Jesus ceased to be God.

In the fourth place, in order for someone to be forgiven, why must there be punishment at all? We know of victims who have forgiven their assailants even though they have never been punished, and we know of other victims who won't forgive their assailants even after they have been punished. To forgive someone doesn't mean that you must first punish the offender at all. Forgiveness doesn't really depend upon the remorse of the offender, either, although it does help quite a bit. At this point it's not up to the offender at all, but the victim, who must find a way to forgive. To forgive means bearing the suffering of what that person has done to you without retaliation. If I stole something from you, then forgiveness means bearing the loss without recompense. If I slandered you, forgiving means bearing the humiliation without retaliating. If the cross of Christ means someone got punished for my sins, then that's not offering forgiveness—that's punishing someone for what I did wrong.

If the cross was needed to pay the punishment for my sins, then how can God really be a forgiving God? Forgiveness doesn't require punishment. To put it bluntly, if I can't forgive you for striking me on the chin until I return the blow back to you, or to someone else, then that's not forgiveness—that's retaliation, or sweet revenge! Revenge is never an ethical motive for action, even if we are led to take revenge on others sometimes. John Hick again: "A forgiveness that has to be bought by the bearing of a just punishment . . . is not forgiveness, but merely acknowledgment that the debt has been paid in full."[6]

Fifth, even if punishment is needed, which I seriously question, then how does punishing Jesus help God forgive us? This Christian theory says God himself bore our punishment on the cross in Jesus. This means the divine way to forgive us when we sin against him is to turn around and punish his Son? If you see me along the roadway and beat me to a pulp, the divine way to forgive you is to turn around and beat myself up all over again, or my son? This is because "someone's got to pay," and a loving divine guy like myself just shouldn't beat you up in retaliation? It doesn't make any rational sense at all. There's no reason for additional punishment, especially to an innocent person like Jesus.

Furthermore, if we die outside of faith in Jesus, what kinds of reasons would God have for punishing us when we die? Maybe God punishes us when we die to deter others from doing wrong? But then why is it we don't see any evidence of this punishment while we're still alive? Maybe God punishes us in order to teach us to do better, like a father who corrects a child? How can this be, since hell would be final and horrible? Maybe God punishes us because he is angry with us? That doesn't seem to fit either. If God foreknows everything we do, or rather, if he knows every background experience and genetic makeup that goes into every decision we make, then we can never surprise him by what we do. I have found that the more I understand someone's background, the easier it is for me to love and have sympathy for that person. By the same reasoning, do you think God can ever get angry with us enough to punish us with hell? How can he? What judge would do this? What father would do this? He understands everything about us. But what other motives are there for God to punish us when we die? If there are none, then our only punishment is what we do to ourselves here and now. When we do wrong, we hurt ourselves. God doesn't need to punish us. By "sinning" we punish ourselves.

If, however, being sent to hell is not about punishment for our sins, but rather about God not tolerating sin in his presence, then exactly where does sin reside in us? Can it be located somewhere in our bodies and seen by an x-ray machine, or does it somehow make an actual black mark on our soul? The truth is that sin isn't an existing thing at all, nor is sin something we have. We cannot hold a cupful of sin in our hands. Sin is an action we do. Once we do it, sin becomes a memory of a hurtful deed done. We don't carry sin on us; we do sinful things. So there is no sin to bring with us into God's presence.

In a sermon delivered by Tom Smith, pastor of the Presbyterian Chapel of the Lakes, in Angola, Indiana, he said, "For some strange reason God believed the cross was necessary for our salvation." See him struggle with this? There must be a reason why Jesus died on the cross. But what is it? According to John Hick: "The idea that guilt can be removed from a wrongdoer by someone else being punished instead is morally grotesque."[7] Bishop John Shelby Spong wrote: "I, for example, do not believe in a God who willed Jesus to suffer for my sins. I do not believe in a God whose inner need for justice is satisfied when his son is nailed to a cross. I regard the substitutionary version of the atonement as a barbaric attack on both the truth of God and the meaning of human life."[8]

RICHARD SWINBURNE'S RELATIONSHIP THEORY

Richard Swinburne has recently produced a somewhat different atonement theory based upon a modern understanding of relationships between people.[9] According to him, there is a fourfold way to restore a relationship when we damage it. We must repent, apologize, offer reparations, and do penance. This, he claims, is also what we must do when we damage our relationship with God, and the same general conditions for reconciliation apply. Swinburne argues we cannot offer adequate reparations and do adequate penance for our sins, since that would require living a "perfect human life."[10] That perfect human life was provided by Jesus, who subsequently voluntarily endured a death, which he intended as a sacrifice that we can now offer to God as our required reparations and penance.[11]

Some of the same criticisms mentioned earlier still apply to this theory, because now the words "reparation" and "penance" are used rather than "punishment." Why, for instance, do my sins require this much penance or reparations in the torture and death of Jesus on the cross? Swinburne still must circumvent the whole idea of the gruesome nature of the reparations Jesus offered for us, since we live in a more humane modern society in the way we deal with offenders.

John Hick argues correctly that Swinburne cannot take this fourfold way to restore human relationships and carry it over "unchanged into our relationship with God." This is Swinburne's "fundamental error." Hick writes: "The idea that something further, corresponding to this repentance-plus-penance towards our human neighbour, is required by God for Godself, seems to me groundless. It rests upon a category mistake in which God is treated as another individual within the same moral community as ourselves. For a moral relationship with another person presupposes the possibility of actions that can benefit or injure that other person; but we cannot benefit or injure our creator over and above our actions in benefiting and injuring our fellow creatures."[12]

Even if "a benefit solely to God were possible and required," Hick argues, that "a perfect human life would constitute it is, surely, illogical." For a perfect human life is already owed to God by all of us, according to Swinburne, and "therefore could not constitute a reparation-plus-penance for not having lived a perfect life in the past." How can one single perfect human being make up for the sinful lives of every person when God purportedly demands that every person live a perfect life in the first place? A perfect life in Jesus doesn't give to God anything above what he already demands from every person.

Swinburne's answer to this problem is morally repugnant, for he says, "God could have chosen one supererogatory act of an ordinary man as adequate for the sins of the world. Or he could have chosen to accept some angel's act for this purpose."[13] If this is so, then Jesus suffered an agonizing death when other ways to accomplish the same results were available. In the end, Swinburne's view leads us to think the cross of Jesus was not required. But if the cross wasn't required, and other less morally grotesque ways of restoring sinful people to God were available, then it makes God's character morally repulsive.

Even though I have not considered all of the atonement theories here, none of the ones we've considered actually makes sense of the supposed atonement offered to God on our behalf, in Jesus. And given nearly two millennia of theological discussions, I'd venture to say there will never be a cogent, well-argued theory that can ever pass muster in the future either. I think the whole idea of Jesus dying for my sins to restore me to God is built upon the beliefs of a superstitious ancient world, where gods and goddesses were pleased with sacrifices, whether they were human or animal ones. This ancient world is long gone now, and it's time to give up believing in an incarnate God who offered a sacrifice for us on the cross to atone for our sins.[14]

NOTES

1. John Hick, *The Metaphor of God Incarnate* (Louisville, KY: Westminster Press, 1993), p. 114.

2. Walter A. Elwell, ed., *Evangelical Dictionary of Theology* (Grand Rapids, MI: Baker Book House, 1984), s.v. "Atonement," p. 101.

3. Michael Martin, *The Case against Christianity* (Philadelphia: Temple University Press, 1991), p. 256.

4. Hick, *The Metaphor of God Incarnate*, pp. 118–19.

5. This is the estimate Frank J. Tipler gives for the number of people (*Homo sapiens*) who have lived on the earth. *The Physics of Christianity* (New York: Doubleday, 2007), p. 172.

6. Hick, *The Metaphor of God Incarnate*, p. 127.

7. Ibid., p. 119.

8. John Shelby Spong, *Rescuing the Bible from Fundamentalism* (New York: Harper-SanFranscisco, 1991), p. 69.

9. Richard Swinburne, *Responsibility and Atonement* (Oxford: Clarendon Press, 1989).

10. Ibid., p. 157.

11. Ibid., p. 154.

12. Hick, *The Metaphor of God Incarnate*, p. 123.

13. Swinburne, *Responsibility and Atonement*, p. 160.

14. For a critique of other atonement theories, see Martin, *The Case against Christianity*, pp. 252–63.

20

DID JESUS BODILY RISE
FROM THE DEAD?

L et's say you meet a sincere, well-dressed friendly man who seems to enjoy life very much, who's very intelligent, very caring, and very religious. After being convinced of his sincerity, he proceeds to tell you the following story.

"I am a missionary/disciple from Iran. For the past few years I have been a follower of the life and teachings of a man named Achmed, who was born of a virgin, preached a message of love and forgiveness to Muslims, and did many miracles. But Achmed was tortured and then killed by the authorities for sedition." This missionary had been a former persecutor of Achmed's followers and claims to have had a vision/revelation/encounter that Achmed was truly a resurrected Son of God. Before leaving Iran he himself was subject to persecution too. But he swears that Achmed arose from the dead and now has ascended into heaven to be with his Father-God and Jesus Christ, as an incarnation of the third person of the Trinity. He tells you that "the third person of the Trinity, Achmed, died for the sins of those who have never personally heard the gospel of Jesus."

"God decided to take world evangelism in his own hands because the message of the gospel was not getting out like it should, and too many people were being damned to hell. The only people who now will ever receive punishment in hell will be those who personally heard the gospel and obstinately rejected it." This missionary friend came to America because there are many such people to evangelize who have heard the gospel but rejected it. Those who have never heard will now be saved, so he doesn't need to reach them. He would use double-fulfillment type prophetic statements in the Bible to show that Achmed fulfilled the same passages that Jesus did, and he would use a lot of allegory, "pesher," typology, and "midrash" type interpretations, like the New Testament writers did to show that Achmed was the Son of God, too. And although the Bible says Jesus was a final revelation to man, "it was meant to the people in his day, not to people in our day," he says, just like Mormons believe Jesus also came to America. And Achmed did some miracles to back up his claims, this friend says. The evidence for Achmed's resurrection would be the same as that for Jesus' resurrection, except that you couldn't personally check any of the facts out for yourself.

Now there are no pictures of Achmed, nor any video, either. Just this man's word. And you cannot check out his story, either, since you cannot go there, because Iranian authorities won't allow it.

You would be in the same position as most all of the Roman world who listened to Paul, because, like you, they could not check out such a story, either. But they believed it. Would you? What would it take for you to believe it? How open would you be to considering it? Pretty skeptical, eh? Why? Because you are a modern person, as opposed to an ancient superstitious person. You might even share some of the same worldview assumptions of this missionary friend, and yet you would still be skeptical.

Today we can check some of the story of the resurrected Jesus out, but not all of it, because we are separated in history by two thousand years. I am skeptical of the Christian claim, just as you would be skeptical of the story Achmed's disciple told you. Neither story fits with the other things you believe, so you begin by being skeptical, both you and I—each from our different perspectives.

The truth is we should approach such stories with a large measure of skepticism. I'll say it this way: *in order for me to believe that a miracle happened in the past (or present), then the evidence should be such that it "requires" a supernatural intervention.* Anything less than that would render my critical thinking faculties null and void.

If there is doubt in some small measure, then I can reasonably reject such an event as miraculous. So this burden of proof is on the Christian, just like the burden of proof is on this hypothetical missionary friend from Iran. I don't think requiring Christians to have the burden of proof is unreasonable at all here. After all, a miracle would be such a rare event; it would have to have some overwhelming evidence on its behalf for reasonable people to believe it. So if the case I present here is faulty by a 20 percent to 80 percent ratio in the minds of the readers, then I still win, because it will take a higher percentage than that to win this debate. The evidence for such a miracle must be simply overwhelming.[1]

I'm not looking for certainty, either. But if there is just a 50–50 chance, or even 70–30 chance, that Jesus rose from the dead when I have many other problems with miraculous claims and the inherent problems with Christianity, should this be enough to convince reasonable people? NO! It must be an overwhelming case, not unlike our skepticism regarding Achmed. If, for instance, Christians thought there was a 70–30 chance that Jesus was going to return this week, would that be enough for them to sell everything and give to the poor in hopes of converting them, and then to wait on a mountain top for him? No? 80–20? It would have to be an overwhelming case, wouldn't it?

WHAT IF YOU WENT BACK IN TIME?

Let's say that you lived in the time of Jesus and you heard him preach, but you went away unconvinced that he was the Messiah for various reasons, including the fact that you believed the Messiah was someone who would throw off Roman rule. Then you learn he was crucified. Later you talk to someone who claims he had risen from the dead, and that several people had seen him too. Would you believe? What if someone showed you an empty tomb and said he was buried here and now he's gone? What if you heard reports that these same people were performing miracles in the name of a risen Jesus to show that he gave them this power from on high (Acts 3, 5:12)? As a modern person, as opposed to an ancient superstitious person, would this be enough to convince you, even if we hypothetically grant for a moment that this was the evidence back then? You know of many reports of miracles by Oral Roberts and assertions by psychics. Do you believe them? There are religious leaders like Joseph Smith, who claimed the angel Moroni visited him, and Sun Myung Moon, whose followers believe he is the Messiah. Do you believe them? The curious fact is that while the book of Acts says many people believed, most people in Jesus' day did not. With rare exceptions, there is no record that Pilate nor his soldiers, Caiaphas nor the Sanhedrin, King Herod nor his court, nor the mob that yelled, "Crucify him" were converted to Christianity because of the weight of evidence for his resurrection. Even King Herod and some others were easily convinced that someone could come back from the dead: "At that time Herod the ruler heard reports about Jesus; and he said to his servants, 'This is John the Baptist; he has been raised from the dead'" (Matt. 14:1, Mark 6:14–16). This, of course, is superstitious thinking. What would you think if someone claimed Babe Ruth was risen in Hank Aaron and/or in Barry Bonds because they both beat his home run record? It also tells us that the belief in a resurrection from the dead of a single person was accepted at the time. However, there's no record Herod believed that Jesus himself resurrected, and the Gospels would surely point that out, if he did. If the evidence of this miracle didn't convince most people in Jesus' day, even ancient people who were very superstitious, how is the evidence supposed to convince us two millennia later?

We do know that according to the New Testament there were other purported miracle/magic/sorcery workers in Jesus and Paul's day (Mark 9:38–39; Acts 8:9; 19:13–14; 19:19). It just wasn't as difficult to believe in miracles for them back then as it is for us today. According to Richard Carrier, "It is crucial to understand how different the situation was in the first century, in comparison with what we take for granted today. Skeptics and informed or critical minds were a small minority in the ancient world. Superstition and credulity ruled the day. Though the gullible, the credulous, and those ready to believe or exaggerate anything are still abundant, they were far more common in antiquity and taken far more seriously. We are talking about an age of fable and wonder, where magic, miracles, ghosts, and gods were everywhere and almost never doubted." Besides all of this, Carrier asks, "how would a myth be exploded in antiquity? They had no newspapers, telephones, photographs, or access to public documents to consult to check a story. There were no reporters, coroners, forensic scientists, or even detectives. If someone was not a witness, all people had was a man's word, and they would most likely base their judgment not on anything we would call evidence, but on the display of sincerity by the storyteller, by his ability to persuade, and impress them with a show, by the potential rewards his story had to offer, and by his 'sounding right' to them. . . . In times like these, legends had it easy."[2]

THE BIBLICAL RECORD

In order to overcome our modern-day inclination not to believe in miracles, the evidence for the resurrection of Jesus must be extremely strong. Michael Martin lays down five factors that would affect the reliability and strength of the evidence, which I want to highlight here. "First, if various accounts of an event are consistent, this would tend to increase their evidential weight whereas inconsistencies would tend to lower it. . . . Second, eyewitness accounts are generally more reliable than accounts that are second or third hand. . . . Third, if the eye-witnesses to some event are known to be reliable and trustworthy, this should increase their evidential worth. . . . Fourth, independent testimony that is in agreement should tend to increase our confidence of its reliability; failure of independent confirmation should lower our confidence. . . . Finally, if an author's purpose in writing a document leads us to believe that the document was not a reliable historical account, then this would lower the evidential weight of the document."[3] This is fair enough of a challenge.

1. Do We Have Eyewitness Accounts?

We don't have any eyewitnesses to the actual resurrection itself. According to Willi Marxsen, "There were no eyewitnesses to this event. We do not know anyone in the earliest church who claimed, 'I was there when the dead Jesus came to life.'"[4] What we actually have are New Testament writings that were composed anywhere from 50 CE to 100 CE maybe later, which were doctored up by the church from time to time pseudonymously for a couple of centuries, as we've seen. None of these authors were there when Jesus was first seen for them to know precisely what took place, and only the Gospel of John claims that John ran to the empty tomb (with Peter). The only eyewitness account claim we have of a post-resurrection appearance of Jesus is from Paul.

According to Keith Parsons, "What we have are, at best, second-, third-, or fourth-hand reports of those experiences as recounted in the Gospels. There is no reason to think that the Gospel records are particularly reliable. On the contrary, how much confidence can we have in documents (1) written by persons unknown, (2) composed forty or more years after the events they purport to describe, (3) based on oral traditions, (4) containing many undeniably fictional elements, (5) each with a clear theological bias and apologetical agenda, (6) contradicting many known facts, (7) inconsistent with each other, (8) with very little corroboration from non-Christian sources, (9) testifying to occurrences which, in any other context, would be regarded as unlikely in the extreme."[5]

Christian scholar Richard Bauckham disagrees. He argues that "in the period up to the writing of the Gospels, gospel traditions were connected with named and known eyewitnesses, people who had heard the teaching of Jesus from his lips and committed it to memory, people who had witnessed the events of his ministry, death, and resurrection and themselves had formulated the stories about these events that they told."[6] Such a contention belies some of the facts for several reasons, so no wonder it takes him 508 pages to establish what he thinks happened in the historical past based upon supposition after supposition.

Bauckham himself admits that historical studies are fraught with some serious problems when mentioning the various current views of Jesus coming from scholars like John Dominic Crossan, Marcus Borg, N. T. Wright, Dale Allison, Gerd Theissen, J. P. Meier, E. P. Sanders, S. McKnight, M. Bockmuehl, B. Chilton, R. W. Funk, J. D. G. Dunn, E. Schüssler Fiorenza, and G. Vermes. He wrote: "Historical work, by its very nature, is always putting two and two together and making five—or twelve or seventeen."[7] So what confidence can we truly have of his own attempts to establish what happened in the historical past?

Nonetheless, if Bauckham had the same control beliefs I do, which I have previously argued for, he'd see things differently, as I do. And while I think he presents a good case for the historicity of the person of Jesus, and for thinking more of Jesus' sayings are authentic, I fail to see much of interest that follows, especially since we cannot have any regard for the so-called fulfilled prophecies in Jesus' life, or know what Jesus actually taught his disciples to pray in the so-called Lord's Prayer (see my chapter 16). Bauckham's case depends heavily on a particular interpretation of what fourth-century church historian Eusebius quoted Papias as saying in the second century. Other scholars disagree with Bauckman on this. Besides, there were two centuries for pseudonymous comments to be added to what Papias actually wrote before Eusebius saw his text. That's some real solid historical evidence, right? Bauckham's case also rests to some degree on the use of names in the Gospels for people who would've still been alive to confirm or deny the stories told about Jesus. But I think a good case can be made that neither Judas Iscariot nor Joseph of Arimathea existed, as I'll argue later in this chapter about Joseph. Bauckham also rests his case on the claim in the Gospel of John that the writer was an eyewitness of the things he wrote about (John 21:24). But this is preposterous given the anti-Jewish nature of that gospel itself, since if the writer was a disciple of Jesus, he must have been a Jew (see my chapter 18). Bauckham doesn't deal adequately with the discrepancies in the early testimonies to the resurrection of Jesus, nor with the arguments that these testimonies were actually visions, which I'll address in this chapter. And so when it comes to this testimonial evidence, what exactly were these people testifying about? I'll argue against the notion there is a hell and a devil later on, so what then becomes of their testimonies to Jesus' purported sayings about hell and of his exorcisms? Benny Hinn and Oral Roberts surely have testimonial evidence from people that they too can perform miracles by God, and I've already addressed the believability of miracles in the ancient superstitious past. So let's move on.

All of the Gospel writers including Paul spoke of postresurrection appearances of Jesus, except for Mark. But this is very significant. In Mark's gospel "there was the stunning absence of the risen Lord. Mark's gospel recorded no sightings nor visions of the risen Christ. Once the stone had sealed the tomb, in Mark's story, Jesus was never again seen by human eyes. The women who were visiting the tomb were told that Jesus had been raised, but that risen presence was simply not available to them."[8] This is significant because most all scholars consider Mark's gospel to be written first, and that Matthew and Luke used his gospel when writing their accounts. So even on a conservative account, Mark stopped writing at verse 8. At that point the women who went to the tomb didn't see the risen Jesus, and when they left they told no one about what they had seen, because they were afraid.

Those who heard the stories of Jesus' resurrection didn't initially believe them (Luke 24:11), including "Doubting" Thomas (John 20:24–29). Because there were doubters, Christians will claim these people were not gullible—they demanded evidence before they would believe. In the case of the disciple Thomas, when he saw the risen Jesus, he "said to him, 'My Lord and my God!'" But we've already seen that John's gospel takes quite a few liberties with what actually was said and done (see my chapter 18). Such a high exclamation coming through the lips of Thomas never happened. So we have reason to wonder if the event itself ever took place. John describes a risen Jesus who appeared to Thomas, even "though the doors were locked," indicating that Jesus either walked through the doors or just appeared out of thin air. And then Jesus proceeds by asking Thomas to put his finger in his hands and his hand in Jesus' side. How can both of these descriptions of Jesus be of a flesh and blood person? The way Jesus appeared to Thomas leads us to think that this was nothing but a ghost or a vision. How then could Thomas touch the flesh of Jesus, which still had open fatal wounds? Did the post-resurrected Jesus still have blood running in his veins? We now know that blood is necessary for the body to function and that breathing gives the blood its oxygen, which is pumped though the body by the heart. Did he have a functioning heart and a set of lungs? Did the post-resurrected Jesus breathe? To speak, as it's claimed Jesus did, demands a functioning set of lungs. John specifically said that he breathed (John 20:22). But didn't Jesus lose all of his blood on the cross, and didn't the post-resurrected body of Jesus still have open fatal wounds, according to John? These fatal wounds would cause him to lose any remaining blood out of his body. All of this leads me to suspect, at best, it was a vision.

The stories also tell of a post-resurrected Jesus who is usually not immediately recognized by his disciples (John 20:14; Luke 24:16). It's also worth noting that even among those who saw the risen Jesus, "some doubted" (Matt. 28:17). How is that really possible? What is it that made them doubt? The fact that Matthew tells us of this may indicate his honesty in telling the story, or it may be his way of dealing with those doubters out there who told a different story.

2. Are the Various Gospel Accounts Consistent?

When comparing the four gospel accounts there are incompatibilities with how many women came to the tomb (1, 2, or 3 plus "others"), when they came ("while it was still dark" or "just after sunrise"), why they came ("to look at the tomb" or "to anoint the body with spices"), who they saw (one angel, two angels, a man dressed in white, or Jesus himself), what was said, who said what, who else came (Peter, or both Peter and John), who saw the resurrected Jesus first (Peter or Mary Magdalene), and what they did as they left the tomb ("they said nothing to anyone" or "they ran to tell his disciples"). Matthew seems to imply that the stone was rolled away in the presence of the women who came to the tomb, while Mark, Luke, and John say the women arrived to discover the stone had already been rolled away. Matthew and Mark have Jesus on his way to Galilee by the time the women arrive at the tomb, while Luke and John have Jesus in Jerusalem on the night of the first Easter Sunday. Luke's gospel says the disciples "stayed continually in the temple" because Jesus had told them to wait in Jerusalem until they had been "clothed with power from on high." But John's gospel has the disciples returning to their fishing trade in Galilee, where Matthew has Jesus appearing and commissioning the eleven in Galilee. John's gospel mentions an appearance of Jesus and says: "this was now the third time Jesus appeared to his disciples" (21:14), but Paul's list and order of appearances (1 Cor. 15:5–8) doesn't square with John's order of appearances. Paul doesn't mention any appearances to women.

There are three major discrepancies. First, the synoptic Gospels disagree with John, by having women visit the tomb, encounter angels, and successfully relay the angelic message, while John has the women encounter no angels on their first visit and no message is relayed. Second, Matthew describes the angelic descent, earthquake, and removal of the stone after the women arrive, in contrast to the other gospels, which have the stone already rolled away before the women arrive. Third, Luke mentions that Jesus appeared on the first Easter Sunday to eleven men (24:13, 36), which would imply Doubting Thomas was present (minus Judas), while John denies that Thomas was there (20:19–24). These are three explicit contradictions in the resurrection narratives.

There is more. The belief in the resurrection of Jesus also demands the belief in the ascension into heaven of Jesus' resurrected body. When it comes to Jesus' ascension, the New Testament writers assumed an ancient three-tiered universe in which he ascended into heaven above, as I've described before, a view that has been shattered by modern science. Since these twin beliefs stand or fall together, modern cosmology makes them both exceedingly implausible. (see note)[9] We also find that the stories told about the ascension in the New Testament have their own discrepancies as well. In Luke 24:51, Jesus' ascension takes place from Bethany on the same day of his resurrection, whereas in Acts chapter 1, Jesus ascended from the Mount of Olives forty days after his resurrection.

Gleason Archer has made a good but failed attempt at harmonizing the accounts, as did Simon Greenleaf.[10] Most scholars disagree with them. David Edwards writes: "It has proved impossible to construct a fully harmonized version of the resurrection stories, despite many attempts to do so . . . the stories as given constitute not a jigsaw puzzle but an insoluble mystery."[11] According to Michael Martin, the Gospels are either inconsistent or they "can only be made consistent with the aid of implausible interpretations."[12] Willi Marxsen argues: "The conclusion is inescapable: a synchronizing harmony of the different accounts of the resurrection proves to be impossible."[13] John Shelby Spong adds: "When we embrace all of their versions in our minds at one time, we discover that all we have in the Bible about Easter is an inconsistent, contradictory, mutually exclusive witness."[14]

Looking at these discrepancies, one can come away with two different understandings of them. On the one hand, Christian scholars have argued that the lack of consistency in the resurrection stories themselves show that there was no collusion among the authors to create and fabricate an identical story. On the other hand, other scholars see the lack of consistency in the stories as evidence that the stories had a long oral stage of telling and retelling which lends itself toward exaggerating the claims of what actually happened. Which of these is more plausible given my control beliefs? According to Michael Martin, "the great differences among postresurrection appearance stories and the difficulty of reconciling them certainly suggests that oral transmission has generated inaccuracies."[15]

3. Are the Eyewitnesses Trustworthy?

Michael Martin says that we really don't know if they are trustworthy. He writes: "Without independent reason to believe their reliability one must be suspicious. Further, we do not know who reported these stories or how many times they were told and retold before they were finally written down. They were presumably passed down by word of mouth and not recorded until several decades after the event."[16]

Jan Vansina is widely recognized as one of the leading authorities on the subject of the oral transmission of history. Even if we assume that there are genuine eyewitnesses to the resurrection, which there are not, there is still the question of the reliability of that testimony. Here's what he says about eyewitness testimony: "In the best of circumstances, even the best of witnesses never give a movie-like account of what happened, as all accounts of accidents show. Eyewitness accounts are always a personal experience as well and involve not only perception, but also emotions. Witnesses often are also not idle standers-by, but participants in the events. Furthermore, an understanding of what happened cannot occur through mere data of perception. Perceptions must be organized in a coherent whole and the logic of the situation supplies missing pieces of observation. The classical cases of car accidents or purse snatchings document this to satiety. A witness reporting a car accident typically first heard a smash, then saw it, then deduced how it happened—how both cars were traveling before the accident after which he or she built up a coherent account of the incident. Usually he did not see the two cars before the accident drew attention to them. Most witnesses cannot resolve themselves to build up a story starting with a noise and the result of the accident first. If a witness was traveling in one of the stricken cars, much of what took place happened at a speed greater than his own reaction time allowed him to perceive. Such persons often only remember one or two images of the accident. Yet when called upon to tell what happened, they must become coherent and build up a tale in which the logic of the situation makes up most of the account."

Vansina continues: "Eyewitness accounts are only partly reliable. Certainly it is true that complex or unexpected events are perhaps rarer than simple, expected events. Yet even here the account remains imperfect. The expectation of the event itself distorts its observation. People tend to report what they expect to see or hear more than what they actually see or hear. To sum up: mediation of perception by memory and emotional state shapes an account. Memory typically selects certain features from the successive perceptions and interprets them according to expectation, previous knowledge, or the logic of 'what must have happened,' and fills the gaps in perception." [17]

The truth is that there are certain elements in the stories themselves that are hard to believe. Why would Nicodemus carry about one hundred pounds of a mixture of myrrh and aloes to place on Jesus' body when he was buried (John 19:39)? Such an amount would smother the body. And if John's gospel is correct that Jesus was given a proper Jewish burial (19:40), then it is inexplicable why the women came on Sunday morning to finish the job (Mark 16:1), since they had supposedly watched this burial in the first place (Mark 16:47). W. G. Kümmel writes: "In view of the Palestinian climate, it is not conceivable that the women intend to anoint a corpse on the third day after death. Nor is it comprehensible that the women go to the tomb with the intention of anointing the body although they do not know who will roll away the heavy boulder in front of the tomb. Besides, among the Jews it was not the custom to use spices in caring for the dead. In view of these improbabilities, it is hardly possible to regard this account as historically reliable."[18] Furthermore, why would the disciples return to their fishing trade after seeing and believing in the risen Jesus (John 21)?

There is also the improbability of the story that the chief priests and elders were reported to have started about the missing body of Jesus. They most likely wouldn't have even heard that Jesus was to rise from the dead, much less believe that Jesus would do so enough to want to post a guard at a tomb in the first place (Matt. 27:62–66). Not even the believing disciples themselves expected it, even though it is claimed Jesus predicted it—which calls into doubt whether Jesus actually predicted his resurrection. But even if the chief priests and elders did want to post a guard at the tomb, Matthew's report of their conversation isn't credible (Matt. 28:11–15). We are told that the guards at the tomb saw the angel of the Lord roll back the stone and sit on it. The angel's appearance was like lightning and his clothes as white as snow (Matt. 28:2–4). They were so afraid that "they shook and became like dead men." They saw all this, plus the empty tomb, yet somehow they were paid off to spread a stupid denigrating lie about themselves? Not likely.

In the first place, Matthew tells us that the guard wasn't placed there until the day after Jesus was crucified (27:62–65). This is one reason that leads Richard Carrier to argue for the plausibility that Jesus' body might have been stolen, because it could've been stolen before the guard was posted. He also suggests that if Matthew didn't have a problem showing these guards took bribes, then it's not unbelievable to think these guards might have been bribed to allow the theft.[19]

These soldiers wouldn't have reported to the chief priest and elders, but to Pilate whose soldiers they were (Matt. 28:64). And what was the lie? They are to say "we were asleep" while the disciples stole the body. Now it's one thing to lie, but another thing for soldiers to spread the word that they were derelict in their duty in order to help people they didn't care for, especially in light of their vivid experience and with the possibility of being severely punished or killed for it. But again, these soldiers would report to Pilate, not the chief priests and elders. Would they lie to Pilate when brought in by him? Plus, in the face of the soldier's testimony, why would the chief priests tell them to lie in the first place? These soldiers would have presented a very powerful witness on behalf of the resurrection.

The truth is that it's a useless and stupid lie. If they were asleep, how did they know what happened? Anyone who heard them tell the lie would know they didn't actually know what happened, but rather inferred the disciples stole the body. This inference wouldn't be enough to stop the belief that Jesus rose from the dead. The lie would additionally be unbelievable because rolling a stone back and taking the body of Jesus would surely have woke the soldiers. So why is it easy for Christians to believe the chief priest, elders, and soldiers all acted contrary to the intelligent people they surely were and not question the historical trustworthiness of the Gospel accounts themselves?

William Lane Craig maintains that "the real value of Matthew's story is the incidental—and for that reason all the more reliable—information, that the Jewish polemic never denied that the tomb was empty, but instead tried to explain it away. Thus, the early opponents of the Christians themselves bear witness to the fact of the empty tomb."[20] But why is it that if the Jewish polemic didn't deny any of these facts, then it must be true? Where are there any independent Jewish sources that attest to this claim of his? Nonetheless, his scenario demands that the Christian claims of an empty tomb were made very early in the life of the church. According to conservative scholar Ralph Martin, Matthew's gospel was written "in the ninth or final decades of the first century."[21] If Matthew is late in origin, then when he writes the story of the guards at the empty tomb of Jesus, he's probably responding to the Jewish opponents of his own day who are reacting to the late church's proclamation that there was an empty tomb. It was not to "the early opponents" that Matthew was responding, as Dr. Craig asserts.

Matthew's gospel is merely responding, as it does throughout the book, to the struggles of the church of his day. Along with the later claims of an empty tomb came the counterclaims by the later Jewish opponents that the disciples stole the body and perpetrated a fraud. And if this is so, Stephen T. Davis admits that if the empty tomb story itself was invented by Mark and "written outside Palestine during or after the Jewish war," then verification of this claim would have been difficult."[22]

Furthermore, the prophecies used to support the resurrection on the third day, which Paul referred to as "according to the Scriptures" (1 Cor. 15:3–4), don't say anything of the kind. Some cross-reference Bibles list Hosea 6:2 in reference to this passage. But what Hosea 6:2 actually says is this: "After two days he will revive us; on the third day he will restore us, that we may live in his presence." Hosea 6:2 originally was meant as an exhortation to Israel to hope in a forgiving God after being punished by him. Another supposed prophetic passage is Psalms 16:9–10, which is quoted by Peter in Acts 2:26–27, saying, "you will not abandon me to the grave, nor will you let your Holy One see corruption." The original meaning of this passage was King David's prayer for recovery from sickness. According to David Edwards: "The relevance of these passages to a resurrection believed to have occurred about thirty-six hours after a death depends on a method of interpreting Scripture which is ancient rather than modern."[23]

What doesn't count as evidence for the truth of the resurrection, according to Michael Martin, are eyewitnesses to Jesus' post-resurrection appearances who were transformed people willing to die for their beliefs. Many people who weren't eyewitnesses of Jesus were willing to die for their beliefs too, especially since they also believed they would go to hell if they didn't. Christian heretics have also been willing to die for their beliefs. "Let us not forget that Muslims, Mormons, followers of James Jones, kamikaze pilots, and many others have been willing to die for what they believed. The fact that people are willing to die for their beliefs can show . . . strength of character, extreme devotion, and even fanaticism. But it is hard to see that it indicates that what is believed is true or even that the evidential bases of the beliefs should be taken seriously." Furthermore, "if we count Paul's conversion as being evidence for the truth of the resurrection, should we not count Muhammad's conversion to Islam from polytheism as being evidence for the truth of the claim that Jesus was not resurrected (Muslims reject Jesus' resurrection)? The evidential value of Paul's conversion and Muhammad's conversion for the truth of the resurrection tend to cancel each other out."[24]

4. Is There Any Independent Testimony in Agreement with the Gospel Record?

This is a question that one must ask of any historical event, miraculous or otherwise. However, the problem is a somewhat circular one. If the testimony is by a Christian believer, then it's not an independent one, but if it is an independent testimony, then it will not reveal the belief that Jesus was resurrected from the dead. Nonetheless, we have no confirmation by either Jewish or pagan sources to show that Jesus rose from the dead. There is a pseudonymous quote inside Josephus to that effect (Antiquities 18:3, 3), but even conservative Christian scholars agree that it was a later interposition placed there by Christian scribes (see pp. 174–75). The only other independent testimony is from the Shroud of Turin, which is a strip of cloth believers say covered the body of Jesus as he arose from the dead that produced a stunning image of a man who fits the description of someone who had been crucified. It was first noticed around the year 1355 CE. The problem is that recent radiocarbon dating of the shroud revealed it was 99.9 percent certain the shroud originated from the period 1000 to 1500, and 95 percent certain that the cloth dated from between 1260 and 1390.[25]

Where is the independent confirmation that the whole land was covered by darkness for three hours (Mark 15:33), or that the temple curtain miraculously tore in two (Mark 15:38), or that there was an earthquake (Matt. 27:51), or that "the tombs also were opened, and many bodies of the saints who had fallen asleep were raised. After his resurrection they came out of the tombs and entered the holy city and appeared to many" (Matt. 27:52). Surely at least one of these events would have been recorded by Josephus or some other writer at that time. This is not arguing from silence here, because I believe the silences are telling. Where is there any record of these things having occurred except in the Gospels? I'll tell you where—nowhere!

Some apologists make a big deal about Paul's claim to the Corinthians that five hundred people saw the risen Jesus at the same time (1 Cor. 15:6). However, in a debate with William Lane Craig, Robert M. Price said that if there were really five hundred brethren who saw the risen Jesus, he finds it "incredibile" such a story "never makes it into any of the gospels." He said, "it's impossible that no one would've thought it worth mentioning."[26] Nonetheless, consider the impact such a statement would have for the Corinthians. Keith Parsons asks, "How many of the Corinthian Christians, probably mostly persons of rather modest circumstances, would have had the means or the disposition to travel from Greece to Palestine to track down the witnesses?"[27] It would still just be Paul's word on it. Did he know them all . . . by name?

5. Do the Gospel Writers Intend to Be Historically Accurate?

There were three groups of people in relationship to Jesus. There were neutral observers, there were his opponents, and finally there were people who had been changed by Jesus, Christians. According to Willi Marxsen, "We do not have any narratives told by neutral observers or by Jesus' opponents. This means that everything that has come down to us is presented from a certain point of view, and that it has been so from the very beginning. Put in a modern way, they wanted to win people for Jesus."[28] The Gospel writers all had theological and evangelistic aims. From this we don't know for sure if their stories are like preacher's stories today that illustrate truths even though the stories themselves may or may not have happened. Because of this, Michael Martin claims, "we should be suspicious of their reliability."[29]

But what if they never intended to tell the literal historical truth in the first place? The New Testament writers have been mistaken to write the literal truth ever since the Gospel left Jewish soil when non-Jewish western European people began to read their writings. What they wrote contained a lot of *Midrash*. What is *Midrash*? According to *The Jewish Encyclopedia*, Midrash is "the attempt to penetrate into the spirit of the text, to examine the text from all sides, to derive interpretations not immediately obvious, to illuminate the future by appealing to the past."[30] It is the ability to tell stories that are illustrative of the truths they believe. We have just seen the way they used the Old Testament prophecies to illustrate Jesus' resurrection. We have also seen it with regard to the virgin birth of Jesus in Bethlehem. Bishop John Shelby Spong claims that, "the question to ask of this *Midrash* tradition is not, 'Did it really happen?' That is a Western question tied to a Western mind-set. . . . The proper question is 'What was there about Jesus of Nazareth that required the meaning of his life to be interpreted through the stories of Abraham and Isaac, Moses and Passover, Exodus and wilderness, Sinai and Promised Land, Hannah and Samuel, David and Solomon, Elijah and Elisha, the Servant figure, the Son of Man, Pentecost and Tabernacles, and a thousand other choices that served to incorporate the life of Jesus into the meaning of God known in the history of the Jewish people?'" As Christianity was denied its Jewish roots and ignored its Jewish home, "it resulted in extravagant literal claims for the historicity of what were in fact Midrashic retellings of ancient themes in new moments of history."[31]

WHAT IS MEANT BY "RESURRECTION"?

The only thing all the New Testament writers agree on is that God raised Jesus from the dead. Should this unanimous agreement alone be enough of a reason to believe Jesus was resurrected from the dead? It is a reason, no doubt. But there is the problem of knowing exactly what early Christians thought of the resurrected body of Jesus. It was a body that could be touched (Luke 24:39, John 20:27), could eat fish (Luke 24:42–43), but sometimes it was unrecognizable even to his disciples (Luke 24:16; John 20:14). It could pass through walls (John 20:19, 26), or appear out of thin air (Luke 24:36) and then disappear at will (Luke 24:31, 51). There is also the minor problem of where Jesus got his clothes (rather than angelic robes) that made him look normal to the disciples. What kind of body was this?

The only description we have of resurrected bodies is written by Paul in 1 Corinthians 15. It is also the earliest written account we have of the resurrection, dated around 55 CE. Paul argues that the resurrected body will be a "spiritual body" (v. 44). "There are heavenly bodies and there are earthly bodies" (v. 40). "Flesh and blood cannot inherit the kingdom of God, nor does the perishable inherit the imperishable" (v. 50). Our new bodies will be as different as a wheat plant differs from its seed (vv. 36–37). And while there is some continuity between the seed and the plant, David Edwards reminds us "in the ancient world it was believed that a seed dies in the ground (cf. John 12:24). The continuity pictured by Paul is continuity through death, which is why Paul dwells on the contrast."[32] Elsewhere Paul wrote that "if the earthly tent we live in is destroyed, we have a building from God, an eternal house in heaven, not built by human hands (2 Cor. 5:1–8). In Philippians (3:20–21) Paul tells us that someday Christ will "transform our lowly bodies so that they will be like his glorious body."

What little Jesus himself said about the resurrection leads us to think both he and Paul shared the same view. Jesus said there is no marriage in heaven because believers "will be like the angels in heaven" from which they "will shine like stars" (Mark 12:24–27; Matt. 13:43).

Paul lists six appearances of the risen Jesus to various people in chronological order and then says, "last of all, he appeared to me" (v. 8). The only record we have of Jesus' appearance to Paul is on the Damascus Road recounted three times in Acts (9, 22, 26). He seems to be saying the appearance of Jesus to him was the same as his appearance to the others. But there is no clue what exactly Paul saw. He saw a bright light and heard a voice identifying himself as Jesus. But Paul had never seen Jesus before. Did he claim to see a physical body? We don't know. What scholars lead us to believe is that the word for "appeared" (*ophthē*) used here by Paul is an important clue in understanding what Paul saw. According to Willi Marxsen, "what is being spoken of is a vision."[33] Paul even says as much (see Acts 9:17; 26:19). If Paul's experience of Jesus was a vision, then Paul can be understood to say that the people he listed in 1 Corinthians 15 had "a vision" of Jesus too, not that they were witnesses of the physical resurrection of Jesus from the dead. This same word, *ophthē*, is also used in the Greek Septuagint translation of the Hebrew Old Testament (LXX) to describe appearances of God and angels (Gen. 12:7; Exod. 3:2; 6:2–3). It is also used in the Gospels of Zechariah's vision of the angel Gabriel (Luke 1:22), of Abraham's vision of God (Acts 7:2), and in the Epistles several times to describe Jesus' appearances (1 Cor. 9:1).[34]

When we realize all of this, we can see why Bishop John Shelby Spong summarizes the results of modern scholarship with these words: "There is no sense at all in Paul of a physical resurrection of Jesus back into the life of this world. God did not, for this apostle, raise Jesus from the grave to life on this earth. Rather, for Paul, God raised Jesus from death into God's presence; from the grave to God's right hand. . . . The essential thing to note about Paul's understanding of the appearances to him is that it was identical with every other appearance on his list. That is, it was not a physical, historical encounter but a revelatory manifestation of the living Christ from heaven."[35] At the very least, David Edwards admits, "the long dispute of the scholars shows that it is uncertain whether or not Paul believed in the physical resurrection of Jesus."[36] But if it isn't a physical body, then hear what former atheist Antony Flew said: "To the unsanctioned eye . . . seeing spiritual bodies is indiscernible from having visions to which no mind-independent realities correspond."[37]

If what I've just written accurately describes Paul's understanding of the resurrection, then how can we reconcile this with the Gospel claims that the disciples touched Jesus' body, watched him eat, and walked with him? (Although, the Gospels themselves also make us wonder what kind of physical body Jesus had.) We could either say that Paul believed in a bodily resurrection as the Gospels report, which doesn't seem to fit Paul's statements at all, or we could say the Gospel writers embellished their stories using the aforementioned writing style of *Midrash*, or symbolism, or typology, or all three. I believe the evidence points to this second option. That being said, I simply reject the idea that I should believe based upon *Midrash*, symbolism, and typological descriptions of such an "event." I want to know what happened, and there are discrepancies among the biblical writers themselves. These are the two options. This is not unlike the problem biblical scholars have in comparing the tongues experience in Acts 2 with Paul's description of the tongues experiences in the church at Corinth in 1 Corinthians 14. Do we interpret them to be describing the same tongues experience? If so, do we interpret Acts 2 in light of 1 Corinthians 14, or do we interpret 1 Corinthians 14 in light of Acts 2? With my control beliefs I've made my choice.

Richard Carrier argues that Paul's understanding of Jesus' resurrection didn't require a resurrected body, but that independent from Paul and later in time, the author of Mark invented the story of the empty tomb. Mark did this, as other biblical authors did, making the empty tomb a metaphor symbolizing either the corpse of Jesus or the ascension of Jesus. "On my theory," he writes, "the empty tomb story originated as a symbol, not a historical fact. It then became the subject of legendary embellishment over the ensuing generations, eventually becoming an essential element in the doctrine of a particular sect of Christians, who spurned Paul's original teachings, and insisted on a resurrection of the flesh instead."[38]

THE EMPTY TOMB

This brings us to the empty tomb. There is more to the evidence for the bodily resurrection of Jesus, as Stephen T. Davis tells us: "spiritual resurrection theories do not require an empty tomb."[39] What about the empty tomb? Several major mainline Christian scholars, both Catholic and Protestant, argue against the empty tomb, including C. H. Dodd, Rudolf Bultmann, Raymond Brown, Reginald Fuller, Hans Küng, Karl Rahner, D. H. Nineham, along with many others.

Listen to Uta Ranke-Heinemann: "The empty tomb on Easter Sunday morning is a legend. This is shown by the simple fact that the apostle Paul, the most crucial preacher of Christ's resurrection, says nothing about it. Thus it also means nothing to him, that is, an empty tomb has no significance for the truth of the resurrection, which he so emphatically proclaims. Since he gathers together and cites all the evidence for Jesus' resurrection that has been handed down to him, he certainly would have found the empty tomb worth mentioning. That he doesn't proves that it never existed and hence the accounts of it must not have arisen until later. . . . The belief in the resurrection is older than the belief in the empty tomb; rather, the legend of the empty tomb grew out of the faith of Easter."[40]

It's argued that the belief in the empty tomb was just presupposed by Paul (1 Cor. 15:3–5; cf. Acts 13:29–31), as well as Peter on the Day of Pentecost (2:29–33; 3:15). It's true that Peter's Pentecost sermon in Jerusalem, the city where Jesus' tomb was supposedly located, is a shortened summary written by Luke. But why didn't Peter say, "See for yourselves, the tomb where he lay is empty?" While it can still be argued that Peter presupposed the empty tomb because it may have already been known to those people, it has much less plausibility with regard to Paul. Just compare their emphasis on the empty tomb, when preaching to convince people Jesus was resurrected, which is nothing, with evangelistic writings today that all emphasize it as the number one piece of evidence needing to be explained, and you'll know what is meant. If it's so important to a Christian apologetic, why didn't the apostles emphasize it?

According to Gerd Lüdemann, the logic of what Paul wrote in 1 Corinthians 15:3–5 is as follows: "'See, he (Jesus) was buried; hence he was dead. See, he appeared to Cephas; hence he was raised.' It's not possible (or at least it's difficult) to read the empty tomb into this text—all the more so, since Paul is dealing here with opponents (or friends) in Corinth who denied the resurrection. If he had known about the empty tomb, he would certainly have referred to it in order to have additional arguments for the resurrection. . . . Paul obviously did not know anything about the empty tomb."[41]

Richard Carrier argues that Matthew and Luke embellished on Mark's metaphor of the empty tomb. Mark tells a simple story, but by the time we get to Matthew, several things are added: Joseph of Arimathea is now "a disciple of Jesus" (27:57), who buried Jesus' body "in his own new tomb" (27:60). The boy in Mark has now become an angel (28:2–3, 5), and added was "a massive earthquake" (28:2), along with "a guard at the tomb" (28:4). Also added are the women who meet Jesus (28:9). Carrier says. "There can be no doubt that we are looking at extensive legendary embellishment upon what began as a much more mundane story."[42] We see further embellishment in Luke and John. The same trends can be seen in the appearance narratives, from none in Mark, to "clasping Jesus' feet" in Matthew (28:9), to handling and eating with Jesus, and a description of Jesus' body in Luke (24:37–43), to the Doubting Thomas story where Jesus "proves" his bodily presence (John 20:24–29). According to Peter Kirby, "Since all accounts of the empty tomb are dependent on Mark, the story hangs by a slender thread."[43]

The Pseudepigrapha shows us that any telling and retelling of a story gets expanded as time goes by. We can actually trace such things in the case of a virgin birth story to the Immaculate Conception story, to the story that Mary was a perpetual virgin, even though the New Testament says Jesus had siblings (Mark 3:31–35). And since there was an oral tradition before such things were put into the Gospels, then we have reason to believe the same kind of expanded storytelling took place before all of the Gospels were compiled, and then was further expanded upon until the New Testament itself was canonized.

Mark's gospel ends with these words from "a young man" at the empty tomb: "'But go, tell his disciples and Peter that he is going ahead of you to Galilee; there you will see him, just as he told you.' So they went out and fled from the tomb, for terror and amazement had seized them; and they said nothing to anyone, for they were afraid" (Mark 16:7–8). (The longer ending is now universally rejected as a pseudepigraphal later addition and not part of Mark's original gospel.)[44]

The original ending of Mark is inconclusive. No one had seen Jesus, and the women said nothing about what they had seen. No wonder later Christians wanted to write out the further details and add more verses to Mark's gospel. But why Mark ends it this way is a subject for debate. It could be to explain why the story of the empty tomb did not exist before Mark's gospel. The reason was because the women "said nothing to anyone." So in his gospel Mark is purportedly telling "their story" for the first time. According to Peter Kirby: "If the story had been known far and wide, from the beginning of Christianity, ending with the women conveying their message, I would suggest that the author of Mark would not have received it in the form he tells it. For that reason, the story is probably of recent origin in the Gospel of Mark."[45]

Richard Carrier argues: "Mark's 'empty tomb' account cannot be regarded as historical with any more confidence than his claim that at Christ's death the whole land was covered by darkness for three hours or that the Temple curtain miraculously tore in two. Neither claim is corroborated in other texts, which could not have failed to record them, and so neither claim is credible. . . . But like the empty tomb, these two 'wonders' have obvious symbolic and metaphorical meaning, so it is not even necessary to suppose Mark imagined himself as writing history when he added them. As easily as he could add them, he could add the empty tomb, and for all the same reasons. And as later Christians began to believe Mark was reporting those events as history, they could just as easily come to believe the empty tomb was history, too."[46]

On the Christian side, Stephen T. Davis and William Lane Craig, along with many others, have presented strong arguments for an empty tomb. One piece of evidence Craig offers is the Gospel indication that Joseph of Arimathea gave Jesus' body an honorable burial, and if that's the case, then the early disciples knew where the tomb was located to verify that it was empty.[47] Let me just deal with two major problems with this view: the lack of tomb veneration among the early disciples and the probability that Joseph of Arimathea was a literary fiction.

Let's deal with the first problem first. If Jesus was given an honorable burial by Joseph as told in the Gospels, then why was there no record of tomb veneration by the early church? Jesus' empty tomb was not venerated by early Christians until the fourth century, according to Eusebius (*Via Constantini* 3.25–32). James D. G. Dunn argues: "There is no evidence whatsoever for Christians regarding the place where Jesus had been buried as having any special significance" with pilgrimages and veneration. Dunn claims this was "because the tomb was empty." However, even Dunn admits "that it was quite customary at the time of Jesus for devotees to meet at the tomb of the dead prophets for worship (Matt. 23:29). And it continues today in the veneration accorded the tombs of Abraham in Hebron and of David's tomb in Jerusalem."[48] Just the very fact that Christians since the fourth century have "venerated" what they thought was the empty tomb of Jesus is evidence for this. I myself visited both sites claimed to be Jesus' empty tomb while in Jerusalem.

One very plausible suggestion for why the tomb of Jesus wasn't venerated for the first few centuries was made by Byron McCane. He argued that Jesus was given a dishonorable burial, based upon Jewish customs of that day, along with the hints in the Gospel texts themselves. He concludes that the body of Jesus was placed in the Jewish graveyard of the condemned, in disgrace. According to him: "The shame of Jesus' burial is not only consistent with the best evidence, but can also help to account for an historical fact which has long been puzzling to historians of early Christianity: why did the primitive church not venerate the tomb of Jesus?"[49]

JOSEPH OF ARIMATHEA WAS PROBABLY A LITERARY CREATION

Concerning the second problem of Joseph of Arimathea, I believe with John Dominic Crossan and Keith Parsons that the accounts of Joseph of Arimathea giving Jesus an honorable burial are probably a literary fiction. This shouldn't surprise the reader since there are good reasons to also be suspicious of the existence of Judas Iscariot, who conspired with the Sanhedrin to betray Jesus with a kiss the night before his crucifixion. [50]

With regard to Joseph being a literary creation, there are several lines of evidence that point in this direction. In the first place we have no idea where the location of the town of Arimathea is, whereas we do know the location of other biblical cites like Bethlehem, Jerusalem, Capernaum, and Damascus. According to Roy W. Hoover, "the location of Arimathea has not (yet) been identified with any assurance; the various 'possible' locations are nothing more than pious guesses or conjectures undocumented by any textual or archaeological evidence."[51] Hoover means we don't have any other textual reference to the town in any ancient text apart from those influenced by the biblical narrative, and there is no archaeology confirming the location of this town. No wonder that Luke's gospel, written to the Greeks from someplace in the Roman Empire after the gospels of Mark and Matthew, had to explain why they had never heard of this town before, so it says Arimathea was a "Jewish town," one with which they probably weren't so familiar (Luke 23:51).

In the second place, there are some implausible aspects about just what this Joseph did and when. In none of the Gospels do we find him mentioned at the scene of the crucifixion. Yet we're told he asked to take Jesus' body down to bury it. Three gospels tell us Jesus died specifically at 3 PM (Mark 15:34–37; Matt. 27:46–50; Luke 23:44–46). When did he learn that Jesus had died if he wasn't at the scene? Purportedly someone went to him and told him. So it wasn't until "evening approached" that Joseph went to Pilate to ask for the body of Jesus. To confirm that Jesus had died, Pilate dispatched a centurion to see for sure, and upon returning he told Pilate Jesus was dead, so he granted Joseph his request. This had to have taken some additional time. Does anyone expect that gaining access to Pilate was a quick and easy thing, or that it didn't take time to walk back and forth like they were to have done? Then, upon having his request granted, Joseph had to go home and get a shroud; find Nicodemus, who bought one hundred pounds of myrrh and aloes (John 19:38); take Jesus' body down; bury it; and roll a stone across the entrance—all before sundown. There wasn't enough time!

The noncanonical Gospel of Peter first saw this problem when it says Joseph asked to have Jesus' body at the same time Pilate sent him to be crucified. At least then Joseph would be able to make all the preparations. If the Gospel of Peter's scenario is correct, the canonical Gospels are probably wrong, but if the canonical Gospels are correct, then there either wasn't enough time for the burial, or the Gospels placed Jesus' death incorrectly at 3 PM for theological reasons, or Joseph buried Jesus on the Sabbath Day after sundown (contrary to Jewish law), or Joseph of Arimathea is a literary fiction of sorts.

In the third place, we never hear of Joseph again. This is significant, I think, as explained by Roy W. Hoover: "He is not among the witnesses to the empty tomb in the Gospel stories and is never subsequently said to have become a believer and a member of the early church. His cameo appearance only serves the immediate narrative interest of the Gospel authors—to 'establish' the location of Jesus' tomb, the emptiness of which he was no longer around to verify."[52]

There are other good reasons to think Joseph is a literary fiction. Look at the texts themselves. In Acts 13:28–29, we're told Jesus was buried by his enemies who had him crucified: "Even though they found no cause for a sentence of death, they asked Pilate to have him killed. When they had carried out everything that was written about him, they took him down from the tree and laid him in a tomb." This doesn't seem to describe Joseph of Arimathea, whom Matthew and John both claim was one of Jesus' disciples (Matt. 27:57; John 19:38). Also problematic is that earlier in Mark's gospel we read where all the members of the Sanhedrin high court voted to condemn Jesus to death: "Then the high priest tore his clothes and said. . . . 'What is your decision?' All of them condemned him as deserving death" (Mark 14:62). How could Joseph condemn Jesus if he was his disciple? The Gospel of Matthew solves this problem by saying Joseph was "a rich man," not a member of the Sanhedrin, while John's gospel solves it by claiming Joseph was a "secret" disciple, "because of his fear of the Jews." Left unresolved is how a Jewish member of high standing in the Sanhedrin itself would fear the "Jews," since he was one.

The Gospel of Mark's own attempt to resolve what was said earlier in his own gospel is with deliberate ambiguity. According to John Dominic Crossan: "Joseph is described not as a member of the *synedrion*-council but as a member of the *boulē*-council, as if there were two councils in charge of Jerusalem, a civil council and a religious council, with Joseph a member of the former body (*bouleutēs*) but not in the later one at all (*synedrion*). There was, of course, no such distinction in historical life; there was only one council by whatever name."[53] Thus Mark's gospel is deliberately ambiguous with regard to whether or not Joseph was a member of the council he had previously told us condemned Jesus.

Mark's gospel is also deliberately ambiguous as to whether or not Joseph was a believing disciple of Jesus. In Mark we read that Joseph "was looking for the kingdom of God" (15:43). Crossan asks, "Is 'looking for' it the same as accepting it, entering it, believing in it? That oblique expression 'looking for' makes it impossible to be sure whether Joseph was among the followers of Jesus."[54]

When it comes to the two other thieves who died next to Jesus, we have a tradition in John (19:31) in which "the Jews" asked Pilate that the bodies of Jesus and the two thieves would be removed, indicating that all three crucified victims were removed that same day, even though John indicates later that Jesus was given a separate burial by Joseph (19:38–42). Here we have the problem of the two thieves. If Joseph's duty was to bury condemned criminals, or if he was just a pious humanitarian, he would've buried them all. But this presents some serious problems, for if he buried them all together in a single tomb or in a communal grave for criminals, then how could anyone prove Jesus' corpse was the one missing when the other two bodies would've decomposed by the time of the first proclamation that Jesus was raised from the dead? So Matthew's gospel rephrases Mark by saying Jesus was buried "in his own new tomb," and instead of just a "stone" being placed in the entrance, it has now become a "great stone" (27:60). Luke adds it was a tomb "where no one had ever been laid" (23:53).

Crossan argues that all of this leads him to think Joseph's honorable burial is creative fiction based upon "prophecy historicized," by which he means the New Testament writers created their accounts based to some extent on the attempt to show that prophecy was fulfilled by the events they told.[55] We've already seen this in Luke's concoction of a census to get Mary to give birth to Jesus in Bethlehem, as but one example of many. Crossan wrote, "First, if Joseph was in the council, he was against Jesus; if he was for Jesus, he was not in the council. Second, if Joseph buried Jesus from piety or duty, he would have done the same for the two other crucified criminals; yet if he did that, there could be no empty-tomb sequence."[56] In the end he argues that Mark "did his best with an impossible problem: those in power were against Jesus; those for him had no power. How could you invent a person with power (at least access to Pilate) but for Jesus? He created Joseph as both a Sanhedrist and almost-a-disciple of Jesus."[57]

Two objections come to the forefront at this point. William Lane Craig charges that "the figure of Joseph is startling dissimilar to the prevailing attitude in the church toward the Sanhedrin. Therefore, Joseph is unlikely to have been a fictional creation of the early church."[58] Yet, if Crossan's argument is correct, in order to provide some evidence that there was an empty tomb, Mark probably invented the perfect figure in Joseph of Arimathea for the task. Such a literary invention would also satisfy the antagonism of the early church toward the Sanhedrin for condemning Jesus.

The second objection is why Mark would provide a name (Joseph) and a place of residence (Arimathea) for the person who buried Jesus? He didn't need to do that, did he? So it's likely such a person existed, and if he did, it's likely he did something like what Mark said he did. Crossan answers this objection in these words: "The general early Christian tradition was to name those significant characters left nameless in the passion accounts."[59] The Gospel of Peter gives the name "Petronius" to the centurion who was in charge of the soldiers who were supposed to guard the tomb. Pilate's wife, the centurion at the cross, and the two thieves crucified with Jesus were all given subsequent names. There are examples of this in the Gospels themselves. The sword wielder and the person whose ear was cut off in the Garden of Gethsemane in Mark's gospel are later named in John 18:10 as "Simon Peter" and "Malchus." Crossan asks, "If you create the events, why not create names as well?"

Then there's the parable of the rich man and Lazarus in which Luke gives one of its characters a name, "Lazarus." Names in the Bible meant something, and this is the case with Lazarus too, which means "God has helped." The rich man is later called "Dives" in the Latin Vulgate version of the Bible, meaning "wealthy." Even conservative scholars regard the story as one of Jesus' parables, and it is treated as such by Simon J. Kistemaker and by William Hendricksen, without so much as giving the reader a reason why it's considered a parable.[60] It's considered a parable because it has the same format as one of Jesus' parables and because Jesus begins many of his parables in Luke with the same phrase, "a certain man," or something similar (13:6; 14:16; 15:11; 16:1; 16:19; 18:2; 19:12). In the parable of the shrewd manager that precedes this one, Luke starts out with the same exact phrase, "There was a rich man . . ."

There is also the intriguing notion presented by Richard Carrier that "Arimathea" can be translated as "Best Disciple Town."[61] Taken together with Mark's penchant for literary motifs, and the lack of a distinct town, it causes me to believe Mark was doing yet another play on words. The twelve disciples had abandoned Jesus, and now an unknown person, who was from "Best Disciple Town," was the one who stayed with Jesus to the end. *The Last Disciple of Christ* would have been the title of his biography.[62] In fact, if the Creation and Exodus accounts in the Old Testament are mythic parabolic stories, then the Bible contains several literary figures with places of residence who never existed, like Adam and Eve, Cain and Abel, Enoch, Noah, Moses, and Joshua.

In a well-argued chapter, Jeffery Jay Lowder has defended the idea that Jesus' body was hastily buried before the Sabbath Day by Joseph of Arimathea but that it was relocated on the Sabbath Day to the public graveyard of the condemned, which would make the identification of Jesus' decomposed body unidentifiable by the time Christians first proclaimed the resurrection of Jesus.[63] The problem with Lowder's scenario is that it seems improbable that in obedience to Jewish law, the body of Jesus was buried before the Sabbath, and yet in defiance of Jewish law, those who buried it worked on the Sabbath by removing the body of Jesus from the initial tomb and burying it elsewhere.

Even if Joseph of Arimathea was not a literary creation, then at best he was the official whose duty it was to bury condemned criminals, who were buried in the public graveyard of the condemned, which Jewish law proscribed. And if that's so, all three crucified men would have been buried together, and Jesus' body would have decomposed beyond the point of identification by the time of the first Christian proclamation that Jesus was raised from the dead seven weeks later (Acts 1:3; 2:1).

Stephen T. Davis suggests the remote possibility that Jesus was "buried in an unmarked or even a mass grave by a Roman functionary and two underlings who three days later, without having told anyone how they had disposed of the body, were transferred back to Rome," although he clearly doesn't believe that scenario.[64] David Edwards suggests the possibility that "the corpse of Jesus was thrown into the same grave as the corpses of other crucified criminals and was beyond recovery and recognition by the time that the story of the resurrection reached the ears of the authorities—a time which may have been months or years after the death." Although, Edwards doesn't believe this scenario, either.[65]

My point is that there are several reasonable natural theories about the so-called empty tomb that don't fit with the supernatural explanation that God bodily raised Jesus from out of it. If any of these reconstructions has a degree of improbability, these reconstructions are still more probable than that Jesus was bodily raised from the dead by God, given my control beliefs.

According to Davis, the question in the minds of the people in Jerusalem was not "Was the tomb empty?" but rather "Why was the tomb empty?"[66] Even if this is the question, and I doubt it, then along with Luis M. Bermejo we can still affirm the empty tomb but deny Jesus' bodily resurrection.[67] And even if Jesus did rise bodily from the dead, that doesn't prove that he's God or that the Christian interpretation of his life and death are correct. Jewish theologian Pinchas Lapide accepts that Jesus arose, but still denies Christianity in favor of Judaism.[68]

Upon finished arguing for an empty tomb, Davis concluded: "The empty tomb, by itself, does not prove the resurrection. It is a necessary but not sufficient condition for the bodily resurrection of Jesus. . . . Perhaps the tomb was empty because of quite natural circumstances that are now unknown."[69] Later in his book Davis admits that an unbeliever, atheist, or naturalist can rationally respond to the evidence for the empty tomb and the resurrection by saying, "The rationalistic explanations do seem weak, and I don't claim to know what in fact happened, but one thing I do know is that it wasn't a resurrection." These people, he claims, are not guilty of ruling out the evidence before examining it "only if the evidence for the resurrection of Jesus is very strong indeed—so strong, in fact, as to outweigh the commitment virtually all rational people have made to the notion that dead people do not get up and walk around again. It seems to me perfectly possible for the naturalist to examine the relevant evidence objectively and carefully and still decide that no miracle occurred."[70]

In debating the resurrection of Jesus, former-atheist-turned-deist Antony Flew does just that: "Confronted with testimonial evidence for the occurrence of a miracle, the secular historian must recognize that however unlikely it may seem that all the witnesses were in error, the occurrence of a genuine miracle is, by definition, naturally impossible."[71] There are several biblical scholars who have examined the biblical evidence and concluded Jesus did not physically rise from the dead. This is just what biblical critic John Dominic Crossan has concluded: "I do not think that anyone, anywhere, at any time brings dead people back to life."[72] Robert Funk and the scholars in the Jesus Seminar reached a fairly firm consensus: "Belief in Jesus' resurrection did not depend on what happened to his corpse."[73] Thomas Sheenan writes, "Jesus, regardless of where his corpse ended up, is dead and remains dead."[74] Marcus Borg claims that "the discovery of Jesus' skeletal remains would not be a problem. I see the empty tomb and whatever happened to the corpse of Jesus to be ultimately irrelevant to the truth of Easter."[75] Cutting through all of this theological rhetoric, former Christian scholar, member of the Jesus Seminar, and atheist Robert M. Price simply concludes *Jesus Is Dead*.[76]

WHAT REALLY HAPPENED?

Episcopal Bishop John Shelby Spong, of New Jersey, offers a speculative reconstruction of what might have initially happened soon after Jesus' death. While several such scenarios have been suggested, I'll use his.[77]

Simon Peter felt depressed after the crucifixion of Jesus. He had placed years of his life in Jesus' hands and heard him and seen his beautiful life, and now his hopes were all gone. He went back to Galilee to fish again, and the events of the last few years replayed themselves over and over in his mind. Then it all became clear to him in a vision he had in which he realized that Jesus' whole life and death was a parable of divine love for mankind, and at that moment he felt resurrected—"he saw Jesus alive." "It was as if scales fell from his eyes." This vision was indeed real, but not objectively so. So "Peter rallied his mates with his vision, and together they decided that now they should go up to Jerusalem for the feast of Tabernacles, and in this setting they must share this vision with others so they also might see." This vision came "as much as six months after the death of Jesus." Peter then "opened the eyes of his fellow Galilean disciples so that they, too, could see Jesus risen." In Jerusalem and "inside the liturgy of the celebration of Tabernacles, the story of Easter unfolded." In a subsequent chapter Spong grounds his speculation in the way the disciples used the Midrashic understanding of the feast of Tabernacles; Psalms 16, 22, and 118; passages from Zechariah; Moses and the Passover; and so forth, to point to Jesus.[78]

Now it's not uncommon for someone to feel dejected when some hope is dashed and then to see something new in order to continue what he had started. The Seventh Day Adventists, for instance, began interpreting much of the Bible differently once they experienced a failed prediction of Jesus' return. What were they to think now? The answer came in a vision. Jesus entered a "heavenly sanctuary." Likewise, the Jehovah's Witnesses experienced a failed prediction of Jesus' return, and again, the answer came in a vision. Jesus did in fact return after all—he just returned "spiritually."[79] Plus, given the nature of the hallucinations surrounding the Salem witchcraft trials, Michael Martin reminds us, "Surely, it is not beyond the realm of psychological possibility, that in first-century Palestine, among the unsophisticated people who believed in the divinity of Jesus, one disciple's hallucination of Jesus could have triggered corresponding hallucinations in the others." (see note)[80]

Bruce Malina and Richard Rohrbaugh discuss the nature of visions in their excellent book, *Social Science Commentary on the Synoptic Gospels*.[81] Their commentary shows us that in the ancient social world of the New Testament, visions involved altered states of consciousness, which were regarded as normal and occurred frequently— before, during, and after the time of Jesus. Such visions were common among holy men, and it was common for group visions to happen where two or more people would share in the same vision. Malina and Rohrbaugh consider the postmortem appearances of Jesus to be "visions." Michael Goulder succinctly and brilliantly defended this as the basis for the belief in the resurrection of Jesus, as does Gerd Lüdemann.[82] This provides, I believe, the social-scientific basis for claiming that Christianity originated with a series of visions.

After this possible initial "vision" of Peter, several scenarios of viewing the progress from vision to resurrected body are possible, and they all involve the belief that Jesus did not physically rise from the grave. The appearances of Jesus were merely visions or hallucinations, or "revelatory encounters."[83] Then with the belief that Jesus was alive, the original stories were embellished. Paul thought of Jesus' resurrected body as a spiritual one, but beginning with Mark's invention of an empty tomb, the storytellers started to emphasize the physical nature of Jesus' body. According to Robert Funk, "As time passed and the tradition grew, the reported appearances become more palpable, more corporeal."[84] With the later church conflict over Paul's view and the Gospels' different view, the followers of Paul lost out, and from then on Christians believed in the bodily resurrection of Jesus. Robert Funk argues that there were other rivalries in the early church that helped formulate the final resurrection doctrine. For instance, "the concern over appearances as the gospel took shape has to do primarily with apostolic right and succession, or, as we would say, with empire building and office politics." Furthermore, "The move to replace a disembodied, supernatural figure with a more tangible, material bodily resurrection was actually triggered by a conflict with Gnostic views."[85]

CONCLUSION

At every juncture of this study of the resurrection, there is some doubt about the bodily resurrection of Jesus. In Paul Kurtz's words, "one thing seems clear, that the evidence in the four Gospels for Jesus' alleged historical resurrection is flimsy. . . . What is clear is this: the evidence presented is neither remarkable nor convincing. This momentous event in history is thus not proven. It is not even likely or probable. It remains, in the last analysis, only an article of faith."[86] It would seem as though if our eternal destiny were at stake based upon the evidence of the bodily resurrection of Jesus, then God should have made the evidence much stronger for those of us who hear about it centuries later. While it does convince some, it didn't convince most people in Jesus' day, and it doesn't convince most people in our day. It's not an airtight case by any stretch of the imagination. The sum total of my entire modern life experience is that truly dead bodies stay dead. Dead bodies don't get up and walk around again. Until I experience people bodily rising up from the dead—and why wouldn't God do that once in a while just to show that it's a possibility?—I will continue judging the past by the present.

The bottom line is that an outsider to the Christian faith would not believe God raised Jesus from the dead with the paucity of historical evidence there is for it. Since the defender in miracles has the double burden of proof I mentioned earlier, the outsider could conclude, quite reasonably, that Jesus did not rise up from the dead. The historian would not have a reason for thinking Jesus rose from the dead, qua historian. Given the immense problems I have with believing in the incarnation, the supposed atonement by Jesus on the cross, and his ascension into heaven, I see no reason why I should also accept the claim that God raised Jesus from the dead. As I've argued, there are way too many superstitious beliefs in the Bible. The resurrection of Jesus is another one of them.

Jesus died on the cross. He did not bodily arise from the grave. His body has rotted away.

THE FINAL NAIL IN THE COFFIN: PHILOSOPHICAL CONCERNS

The Apostle Paul informs us that just as Jesus arose from the dead so shall we (1 Cor. 15:23, 48–49). But when it comes to the general notion of a bodily resurrection, there are some insurmountable philosophical problems with it. Suffice it for me to mention a few of them: First, the bodies of many people have been eaten by cannibals, by animals like lions, bears, and sharks, and by parasites like maggots. This means many bodies have shared atoms. If eaten by maggots, are those atoms still human atoms, or are they now maggot atoms? Other bodies have decomposed into nothing but dust in the ground, and/or have provided the fertilizer for weeds to grow from them. Are those atoms still human atoms, or are they now weed atoms? Some bodies have been lost or buried at sea, burned at the stake, or cremated with their ashes spread to the four winds. These human bodies no longer exist. How can there be a bodily resurrection for them if their bodies no longer exist?

Second, the bodies we have today are not the bodies we had in months or in years past, for as J. D. Bernal wrote: "It is probable that none of us have more than a few atoms with which we started life, and that even as adults we probably change most of the material of our bodies in a matter of a few months."[87] So which body gets resurrected: the one someone had when she was ten years old, forty years old, or the one she died with while suffering from Alzheimer's disease? This raises questions about what age a person will look like if resurrected, what bodily characteristics she will have, what her mental capacity will be, and what level of responsibility said person will have, since we cannot expect a ten-year-old to have the same level of responsibility of a forty-year-old, nor that of an Alzheimer's affected person.

Third, genetics have shown that our bodies have a great deal to do with who we are as people. Linda Badham notes: "Our personal experience and emotions are intimately linked to our body chemistry. Indeed, the limits to what we are able to think at all are set by our genetic endowment; so that one man's physiochemical equipment enables him to be a brilliant mathematician, while another's lack condemns him to lifelong imbecility. . . . The 'subject of my conscious experiences' would seem to be very much at the mercy of my physiochemical constitution."[88] Since this is the case, who I am is directly related to my body. I cannot do without my body and still be the same person. So if I'm given a perfect body in the resurrection, I will not be the same person. Besides, does it even make sense to say resurrected people will all receive perfect bodies? What does a perfect body look like? What would be considered an imperfection in a resurrected body such that none of them will have any? Aren't differences to be considered imperfections when it comes to perfect bodies? Will some bodies have lesser stamina or strength? Will others not be as beautiful? Will some of them not allow for as much intelligence, or verbal skills? Are these things not imperfections? But if these resurrected bodies don't have any imperfections, doesn't that entail there will be no differences, and if that's so, will everyone be exactly the same? We are distinguished from one another precisely because we have these bodily differences. Lacking these differences, how can resurrected people be distinguished from one another, or recognized for who they were on earth, or even recognize themselves? For Christians to say resurrected people will be rewarded differently with these differences, or imperfections, because of sins of omission here on earth (i.e., the lack of obedience) simply means not all sins were forgiven by God after all!

One attempted Christian solution to this philosophical problem is that God will create a replica of our bodies with our personal memories programmed into it, proposed by John Hick, among others.[89] But if so, several problems emerge. If the *Mona Lisa* painting was burned in a fire, would a re-created replica be the same painting? No! Would a replica of our earthly bodies be something we even want, since some of us are physically or mentally challenged? And given our physical imperfections, how could a replica of our present body be transformed into a glorified perfect spiritual body and yet still be a replica of our body? Furthermore, with Linda Badham we must ask: "What would we say . . . if the replica were created *before* my death?" Would that replica really be me? The replica body "would only be something very similar to the one who died, a replica, and not a continuation of the dead person."[90] And if it's possible for God to create one replica of me, then he could also create multiple replicas of me, and if that's so, how can it be said each replica is truly me? There can only be one me.

Christians have attempted other solutions for these kinds of problems. Trenton Merritt, for instance, distinguishes between numerical identity and qualitative identity when it comes to bodily existence through time. To be numerically identical is to be the same person regardless of the qualitative changes. He argues that he can be numerically identical to the one-year-old child he used to be and to the person he will be millions of years from now in heaven with God, even though he has changed through the years and will undergo many unimaginable qualitative changes when glorified in heaven. "Great qualitative change . . . is consistent with numerical identity," he argues. Based on this distinction, Merritt argues we can be numerically identical with ourselves in the resurrection but also qualitatively different from what we are now.[91] That being said, Merritt himself admits "we cannot survive just any sort of qualitative change."[92] Just how much change we can survive he doesn't say, but it seems crystal clear that if my whole body upon death becomes the same with the bodies of a thousand maggots who eat it, that is not just a qualitative change. It's a numerical one. It would no longer be my body.

The whole reason why Merritt accepts his view is because he believes the Bible teaches our resurrected bodies will be numerically the same. End of story for him. He has a "divine revelation" from God which teaches "that a body which has ceased to exist will come back into existence on the Day of Resurrection. And since what will happen must be possible, scripture implies that it is possible for a thing that has ceased to exist to come back into existence. So we know that this *is* possible." (see note)[93] But I think that throughout this book of mine I've established time after time that there is no reason to trust what the Bible says just because it says it. And if my argument is correct, then Merritt's whole philosophical case unravels since he admits: "There are no conclusive philosophical arguments one way or another on this issue. So if all we have are the tools of philosophy, perhaps we ought to say we have no idea whether a thing can utterly cease to exist and then come back into existence."[94]

In the final analysis Merritt retreats to the "it's still possible" and/or "it's not impossible" defense I've mentioned earlier, reflected in what I just quoted from him above ("it is possible"). Remember, if a belief cannot be shown to be impossible (which is an unreasonable standard), then the believer can continue to believe. Merrick writes: "Suppose that we have no satisfactory account of what makes for the identity of the earthly body with the resurrected one. All that follows is that none of us has any clear idea how resurrection will work. . . . What would be a genuine threat to the doctrine of resurrection would be some sort of proof or argument that temporal gaps in the career of a body are *impossible* [my emphasis]. But the fact that we cannot see how resurrection is supposed to go, that we cannot explain what God does to bring an annihilated body back into existence, does not imply that God's doing this is *impossible* [again, my emphasis]; it implies only that we are ignorant."[95] As I said earlier, this is a frank admission once again that the evidence and the arguments are not on the believer's side.

A FINAL NOTE

The weekend before my book went to press I received the third edition of William Lane Craig's book *Reasonable Faith: Christian Truth and Apologetics*. In it Craig said of Dale C. Allison's book *Resurrecting Jesus* that it contains the "best presentation of skeptical arguments against inferring Jesus' resurrection."[96] I had Allison's book in my library but I hadn't read it until now.

As a liberal Christian professor, Allison presents a book that is challenging to both sides of this debate. He argues against a few of the things I've argued for in this chapter, which, even if he's correct, changes nothing, for he too is skeptical about the bodily resurrection of Jesus.[97] Echoing what I had argued for earlier (in my chapter 8), Allison wrote: "History keeps its secrets better than many historians care to admit. Most of the past—surely far more than 99 percent, if we could quantify it—is irretrievably lost; it cannot be recovered. This should instill modesty in us." Allison continues: "The accounts of the resurrection, like the past in general, come to us as phantoms. Most of the reality is gone. It is the fragmentary and imperfect nature of the evidence as well as the limitations of our historical-critical tools that move us to confess, if we are conscientious, how hard it is to recover the past. That something happened does not entail our ability to show that it happened, and that something did not happen does not entail our ability to show that it did not happen. . . . Pure historical reasoning is not going to show us that God raised Jesus from the dead."[98]

Echoing what I have been arguing for in this book with regard to control beliefs, Allison wrote: "We inevitably evaluate matters by means of our presuppositions. . . . Probability is in the eye of the beholder. It depends upon one's worldview, into which the resurrection fits, or alternatively, does not fit. . . . Arguments about Jesus' literal resurrection cannot establish one's *Weltanschauung* (i.e., worldview)." So the resurrection of Jesus, he argues, "belongs to the Christian web of belief, within which alone it has its sensible place. Outside that web it must be rejected or radically reinterpreted. . . . One who disbelieves in all so-called miracles can, with good conscience, remain disbelieving in the literal resurrection of Jesus after an examination of the evidence."[99]

Since I have argued at length for my control beliefs in the first part of this book,

I indeed have the needed confidence to deny Jesus resurrected, especially given the paucity of historical evidence on its behalf.

NOTES

1. On this point see Michael Martin, "The Resurrection as Initially Improbable," in *The Empty Tomb: Jesus beyond the Grave*, ed. Robert M. Price and Jeffery Jay Lowder (Amherst, NY: Prometheus Books, 2005), pp. 43–54.

2. "The Spiritual Body of Christ," in Price and Lowder, *The Empty Tomb*, pp. 171–72.

3. In Michael Martin, *The Case against Christianity* (Philadelphia: Temple University Press, 1991), p. 77. Richard Swinburne argues, in his book *The Resurrection of God Incarnate* (Oxford: Oxford University Press, 2003), that it's 97 percent probable that if God exists, then Jesus arose from the dead. I hardly think his supposed "new" approach proves anything. He still must show that God exists, that Jesus needed to atone for my sins, and that the concept of incarnation is plausible, which I have already examined and found wanting. It seems wildly implausible that any Bayesian analysis of the resurrection of Jesus can show it to be 97 percent probable.

4. Willi Marxsen, *Jesus and Easter: Did God Raise the Historical Jesus from the Dead?* trans. Victor Paul Furnish (Nashville: Abingdon Press, 1990), p. 41.

5. Price and Lowder, *The Empty Tomb*, p. 439. In footnote 19 Parsons documents each one of these claims.

6. Richard Bauckham, *Jesus and the Eyewitnesses: The Gospels as Eyewitness Testimony* (Grand Rapids, MI: Eerdmans, 2006), p. 93.

7. Ibid, pp. 3–4.

8. John Shelby Spong, *Resurrection: Myth or Reality?* (New York: HarperSanFrancisco, 1994), pp. 60–61.

9. Ray Hoover argues that the resurrection and ascension depend upon two basic concepts: God is the creator and sovereign ruler of this world; and the cosmos has a three-level structure with heaven above and hell beneath the earth. He argues that when these two concepts lose their credibility, "the ideas and beliefs that are dependent on them lose their credibility as well. And that, in fact, is what happened with the coming of modern scientific knowledge about the physical and natural world." See, *Jesus' Resurrection: Fact or Figment? A Debate between William Lane Craig and Gerd Lüdemann*, ed. Paul Copan and Ronald K. Tacelli (Downers Grove, IL: InterVarsity Press, 2000), pp. 138–39.

10. In Gleason Archer, *Encyclopedia of Bible Difficulties* (Grand Rapids, MI: Zondervan, 1982), pp. 347–56; Simon Greenleaf, *The Testimony of the Evangelists Examined by the Rules of Evidence Administered in Courts of Justice* (1847).

11. David Edwards and John R. W. Stott, *Evangelical Essentials* (Downers Grove, IL: InterVarsity Press, 1988), p. 205.

12. Martin, *The Case against Christianity*, p. 81.

13. Willi Marxsen, *The Resurrection of Jesus of Nazareth*, trans. Margaret Kohl (Philadelphia: Fortress Press, 1970), p. 74.

14. Spong, *Resurrection: Myth or Reality?* p. 105.

15. Martin, *The Case against Christianity*, p. 83.

16. Ibid., p. 83.

17. Jan Vansina, *Oral Tradition as History* (Madison: University of Wisconsin Press, 1985), pp. 4–5. See also John Dominic Crossan, *The Birth of Christianity: Discovering What*

Happened in the Years Immediately after the Execution of Jesus (New York: Harper & Row, 1998), pp. 59–67.

18. W. G. Kümmel, *The Theology of the New Testament according to Its Major Witnesses: Jesus-Paul-John* (Nashville: Abingdon Press, 1973), p. 100.

19. Richard C. Carrier, "The Plausibility of Theft," in Price and Lowder, *The Empty Tomb*, p. 358.

20. William Lane Craig, "The Guard at the Tomb," *New Testament Studies* 30 (1984): 273–81.

21. Ralph Martin, *New Testament Foundations*, vol. 1 (Grand Rapids, MI: Eerdmans, 1975), p. 243. See also G. D. Kirkpatrick, *The Origins of the Gospel according to Matthew*, 1946; B. H. Streeter, *The Four Gospels*, 1924; and F. V. Wilson, *The Gospel according to St. Matthew*, 1960.

22. Stephen T. Davis, *Risen Indeed* (Grand Rapids, MI: Eerdmans, 1993), p. 74.

23. Edwards and Stott, *Evangelical Essentials*, p. 202.

24. Martin, *The Case against Christianity*, pp. 77, 91–92.

25. On the Shroud of Turin, see Joe Nickell's book *Relics of the Christ* (Lexington: University Press of Kentucky, 2007), pp. 111–79.

26. This debate took place on the campus of Ohio State University in 1999. An MP3 of it can be found at http://www.bringyou.to/CraigPriceDebate.mp3.

27. Keith Parsons, in Price and Lowder, *The Empty Tomb*, p. 438.

28. Willie Marxsen, *Jesus and Easter: Did God Raise the Historical Jesus from the Dead?* trans. Victor Paul (Nashville: Abingdon Press, 1990), pp. 23–25.

29. Martin, *The Case against Christianity*, p. 78.

30. *The Jewish Encyclopedia* (New York: Funk & Wagnall, 1925).

31. Spong, *Resurrection: Myth or Reality?* pp. 11–17.

32. Edwards and Stott, *Evangelical Essentials*, p. 207.

33. Marxsen, *Jesus and Easter*, p. 69.

34. On this whole point see the excellent argument by Richard Carrier, "The Spiritual Body of Christ," in Price and Lowder, *The Empty Tomb*, pp. 105–232.

35. Spong, *Resurrection: Myth or Reality?* pp. 50, 53.

36. Edwards and Stott, *Evangelical Essentials*, p. 202.

37. Antony Flew (with Gary R. Habermas), *Did Jesus Rise from the Dead?* (New York: Harper & Row, 1987), p. 12.

38. Richard Carrier, "The Spiritual Body of Christ," in Price and Lowder, *The Empty Tomb*, pp. 158–59.

39. Davis, *Risen Indeed*, p. 60.

40. Uta Ranke-Heinemann, *Putting Away Childish Things* (New York: HarperCollins, 1992), p. 131.

41. Gerd Lüdemann in Copan and Tacelli, *Jesus' Resurrection: Fact or Figment?* p. 44.

42. Carrier, "The Spiritual Body of Christ," p. 165.

43. Peter Kirby, "The Case against the Empty Tomb," in Price and Lowder, *The Empty Tomb*, p. 237.

44. See Bruce Metzger, *A Textual Commentary on the Greek New Testament* (London: United Bible Societies, 1971), pp. 122–26.

45. Kirby, "The Case against the Tomb," p. 240. Richard Carrier looks at Plutarch's biography of Romulus, the founder of Rome, and claims that it is "so obviously a parallel to Mark's ending of his gospel that nearly anyone would have noticed—and gotten the point. It certainly looks like the Christian passion narrative is a deliberate tranvaluation of the Roman

Empire's ceremony of their founding savior's incarnation, death, and resurrection." *The Empty Tomb*, pp. 180–81.

46. Richard C. Carrier, in Price and Lowder, *The Empty Tomb*, pp. 176–77.

47. As succinctly argued, for instance, in Dr. Craig's closing response of the book edited by Copan and Tacelli, *Jesus' Resurrection: Fact or Figment?* pp. 160–204.

48 James D. G. Dunn, *The Evidence for Jesus* (Philadelphia: Westminster Press, 1985), pp. 67–68.

49. Byron McCane, *Roll Back the Stone: Death and Burial in the World of Jesus* (Harrisburg, PA: Trinity Press International, 2003), pp. 89–108. I thank Matthew J. Green for alerting me to McCane's arguments.

50. For the evidence for this see John Shelby Spong, *The Sins of Scripture* (New York: HarperSanFrancisco, 2005), pp. 199–204.

51. Roy Hoover in Copan and Tacelli, *Jesus' Resurrection: Fact or Figment?* p. 130.

52. Ibid.

53. Crossan, *The Birth of Christianity: Discovering What Happened in the Years Immediately after the Execution of Jesus*, p. 554.

54. Ibid.

55. John Dominic Crossan, *Who Killed Jesus?* (New York: HarperSanFrancisco, 1995), pp. 1–13. For those unfamiliar with how the New Testament writers constructed stories based upon Old Testament passages, see Randel Helms, *Gospel Fictions* (Amherst, NY: Prometheus Books, 1988), p. 131.

56. Crossan, *The Birth of Christianity: Discovering What Happened in the Years Immediately After the Execution of Jesus*, p. 555.

57. Crossan, *Who Killed Jesus?* p. 173.

58. As quoted in Copan and Tacelli, *Jesus' Resurrection: Fact or Figment?* p. 166.

59. Crossan, *Who Killed Jesus?* p. 177.

60. As seen in Kistemaker's book *The Parables of Jesus* (Grand Rapids, MI: Baker Book House, 1980), and Hendriksen's book *New Testament Commentary: An Exposition of the Gospel according to Luke* (Grand Rapids, MI: Baker Book House, 1978).

61. Price and Lowder, *The Empty Tomb*, p. 238.

62. I thank fellow blogger DagoodS for this description.

63. In Price and Lowder, *The Empty Tomb*, pp. 261–306.

64. Davis, *Risen Indeed*, p. 80.

65. Edwards and Stott, *Evangelical Essentials*, pp. 200–201.

66. Davis, *Risen Indeed*, p. 72.

67. Luis M. Bermejo, *Light beyond Death: The Risen Christ and the Transfiguration of Man* (Chicago: Loyola Press, 1985).

68. Pinchas Lapide, *The Resurrection of Jesus: A Jewish Perspective* (Minneapolis, MN: Augsburg Fortress, 1983).

69. Davis, *Risen Indeed*, p. 84.

70. Ibid., pp. 170–71.

71. Flew, *Did Jesus Rise from the Dead?* p. 6.

72. John Dominic Crossan, *Jesus: A Revolutionary Biography* (New York: HarperSanFrancisco, 1994), p. 95.

73. Robert W. Funk, *Honest to Jesus: Jesus for a New Millennium* (New York: HarperSanFrancisco, 1996), p. 259.

74. Thomas Sheenan, *The First Coming: How the Kingdom of God Became Christianity*, repr. ed. (New York: Vintage, 1988), pp. 172–73.

75. Marcus Borg (with N. T. Wright), *The Meaning of Jesus: Two Visions* (New York: HarperSanFrancisco, 1999), pp. 130–31.

76. Robert M. Price, *Jesus Is Dead* (Cranford, NJ: American Atheist Press, 2007).

77. For other similar conjectures see the following books: John Hick, *The Metaphor of God Incarnate* (Louisville, KY: Westminster, 1993), pp. 23–26; Marcus Borg and Wright, *The Meaning of Jesus: Two Visions*, pp. 130–35; Gerd Lüdemann, *What Really Happened to Jesus?* (Philadelphia: Westminster, 1995); and the authors in *The Empty Tomb* book, just to mention a few. Some have criticized my use of Bishop John Shelby Spong here, since some people don't consider him a scholar, but if William Lane Craig can debate him on the resurrection of Jesus (Easter Sunday 2005, at Bethel College, and aired on CBN), then he's worthy to quote from. He does a good job of summarizing the results of scholarship.

78. Spong, *Resurrection: Myth or Reality?* pp. 233–60.

79. On this see Walter Martin, *The Kingdom of the Cults* (Minneapolis, MN: Bethany House, 1985).

80. Martin, *The Case against Christianity*, p. 95. Dale C. Allison agrees with Martin here, for once one disciple had told others about seeing Jesus "then the idea would have been planted in the mind of others, so how can we exclude the thought of psychological contagion?" Allison also writes: "The plurality of witnesses does not settle anything. Hypnotists can persuade a group of good subjects that they all see the same phantasmal object, and religious enthusiasm can work the same trick. Furthermore, more than one person has sincerely reported having a vision of the departed Elvis Presley. And if counting heads were all that mattered, there would be no question that short, large-headed, bug-eyed aliens have kidnapped thousands of sleeping Americans: the stories are legion." *Resurrecting Jesus* (New York: T. & T. Clark, 2005), p. 297.

81. Bruce Malina and Richard L. Rohrbaugh, *Social Science Commentary on the Synoptic Gospels*, 2nd ed. (Minneapolis, MN: Augsburg Fortress, 2003), pp. 327–29.

82. Michael Goulder, "The Explanatory Power of Conversion-Visions," in Copan and Tacelli, *Jesus' Resurrection: Fact or Figment?* pp. 86–103; Gerd Lüdemann, *The Resurrection of Jesus: History, Experience, Theology* (Minneapolis, MN: Fortress Press, 1994), pp. 173–79.

83. Reginald H. Fuller, *Formation of the Resurrection Narratives* (New York: Macmillan, 1971), p. 49.

84. Funk, *Honest to Jesus*, p. 260.

85. Ibid., pp. 269, 272.

86. Paul Kurtz, *The Transcendental Temptation* (Amherst, NY: Prometheus Books, 1991), pp. 157–58.

87. J. D. Bernal, *Science and History*, vol. 3 (Harmondsworth, UK: Penguin, 1969), p. 92.

88. Linda Badham, "Problems with Accounts of Life after Death," in *Philosophy of Religion: Selected Readings*, ed. Michael Peterson et al. (Oxford: Oxford University Press, 1996), pp. 446–47.

89. John Hick, *Philosophy of Religion*, 4th ed. (Englewood Cliffs, NJ: Prentice Hall, 1990), pp. 120–25; and his *Death and Eternal Life* (New York: Macmillan, 1987).

90. Badham, "Problems with Accounts of Life after Death," pp. 445–46.

91. Trenton Merritt, "The Resurrection of the Body and Life Everlasting," in *Reason for the Hope Within*, ed. Michael J. Murray (Grand Rapids, MI: Eerdmans, 1999), p. 267.

92. Ibid., p. 265.

93. Ibid., p. 270. Dale C. Allison correctly reverses Merritt's whole approach: "My own

considered opinion is that staking our postmodern identity to a literal resurrection because the Bible tells us so is akin to insisting on finding science in Genesis or seeing blueprints for the future in Revelation. . . . Apart from scriptural fundamentalism, I see no reason why we should, on the other side of the grave, need to come back for our rotting or disassembled corpses." *Resurrecting Jesus* (New York: T. & T. Clark, 2005), p. 225.

94. Merritt, "The Resurrection of the Body and Life Everlasting," p. 270.

95. Ibid., p. 276.

96. William Lane Craig, *Reasonable Faith: Christian Truth and Apologetics* (Wheaton, IL: Crossway Books, 2008), p. 401. Craig was referring to Allison's long chapter "Resurrecting Jesus," in *Resurrecting Jesus*, pp. 199–375.

97. He argued that Mary Magdalene probably had the first visionary encounter with Jesus, not Peter; that skeptics like me make an empty claim when we point out neither Peter nor Paul mentioned the empty tomb of Jesus; that Joseph of Arimathea probably existed; that the Apostle Paul probably believed in a bodily resurrection, and that there was a very slight probably Jesus' tomb was empty (although Allison remains "in permanent irresolution" about this). If someone believes Joseph of Arimathea existed, then an empty tomb becomes a bit more probable.

98. Allison, *Resurrecting Jesus*, pp. 337–42.

99. Ibid., pp. 340–42.

21

THE DEVIL MADE ME DO IT!

"*Satan*" is the Hebrew word for "adversary." "*Devil*" is the Greek word for "accuser." The conception of this being, no matter what he's called, comes from the mythical human imaginations of the ancient superstitious past.

In the Old Testament, Satan is seen as a servant of God. Walter Wink tells us, "The original faith of Israel actually had no place for Satan. God alone was Lord, and thus whatever happened, for good or ill, was ascribed to God. 'I kill and I make alive,' says the Lord, 'I wound and I heal' (Deut. 32:39; Isa. 45:6–7; 1 Sam. 2:6–7). It was not inconsistent, on the one hand, to believe that God might call Moses to deliver Israel from Egypt, and on the other hand, for God to want to murder him on the way (Exod. 4:24–26). When Pharaoh resisted Moses it was not ascribed to his free will, but to God's hardening of his heart (Exod. 4:21; 7:3; 9:12; 10:1, 20, 27; 11:10; 14:4, 8, 17; Josh. 11:20, etc). Likewise, it is God who sent an evil spirit on Saul (1 Sam. 16:14–16, 23), and it was God who sent a lying spirit to enter the mouths of the four hundred prophets of Ahab (1 Kings 22:22; see 2 Sam. 17:14)."[1]

Walter Wink continues: "One possible translation of 'Yaweh,' God's name, is 'He causes to happen what happens.' If, then, God has caused everything that happens, God must also cause evil. But God was also the God of justice (Gen. 18:25). So how could God be just and still be the one to cause evil? This was the terrible price Israel had been forced to pay for its belief that God was the primary cause of all that happens. Gradually God became differentiated into a 'light' and a 'dark' side, both integral to the Godhead. The bright side came to be represented by the angels, the dark side by Satan and his demons."[2]

There are four important instances in the Old Testament where the word "Satan" is mentioned to describe a celestial being or his work. "In Numbers 22:22–32 we see a clear instance where the word *śāṭān* describes a celestial being who is not in any way doing anything wrong (as "an adversary"). This being is described as the 'Angel of Yahweh' and is sent by God to be a *śāṭān* to Balaam. The angel blocks Balaam's path so that his donkey may not pass on by. Then the angel rebukes Balaam."[3] In Job 1–2, Satan cannot be an evil being if he is a fully accepted member of the heavenly court, one of the "sons of God." "Satan's role here is somewhat like an overzealous district attorney, where in his zeal to uncover injustice steps over the edge into entrapment. In all of this Satan manifests no power independent of God, and there is no condemnation of him by God. . . . There is nothing in the context to indicate that the angel is evil."[4] In 2 Samuel 24:1 an angry God incites king David to carry out a wrongful census. But in 1 Chronicles 21:1, which is a post–Babylonian captivity revision of Samuel and Kings, it is now revised to read that "Satan" (used here for the first time as a proper name) is blamed as the one who incited David to carry out the census. Of course, if God indeed used Satan to accomplish his purposes here, then why not just do it himself? Such a relationship seems contrived. In Zechariah 3:1–5, Satan is seen in the role of prosecuting attorney who brings a valid accusation against Joshua, which God rejects because of his mercy. While we don't like prosecutors, they aren't evil just because they are doing their job. It does, however, say a great deal about us as people if we greatly fear and greatly dislike the prosecutor. If we think the prosecutor is evil, then it's most likely because we are the evil ones.

WHAT ABOUT THE SERPENT IN THE GARDEN OF EDEN (GEN. 3:1-15)?

If Satan was the serpent who tempted Adam and Eve to rebel against God, then why is he later found in God's heavenly court doing his will in the Bible passages mentioned above? That makes no sense if God cannot tolerate sin in his presence. According to Bernard Anderson: "There is no basis here for identifying the serpent with Satan."[5] John Gibson offers, "It was one of the animals named by the man [and created by God] in the previous chapter. . . . It is clear that one of the reasons the snake has been selected for the role it plays is that like the fox it is universally credited with cunning, and it was slimy and treacherous to boot. [The author] doesn't want a Satan or a Devil brought into the picture, in case that would be thought to detract from man's responsibility for his own sin. . . . Paradise is lost to humankind through its own fault. . . . No one else was to blame. . . . The serpent is temptation personified. . . . This is of course fantasy . . . animals only speak in fables, but fables contain much wisdom."[6] According to Donald Gown: "The curse on the snake (Gen. 3:14–15) clearly shows that the author is thinking of a real snake"—it is condemned to crawl on its belly from henceforth. The author "clearly rejected the belief in evil deities or spirits, which his polytheistic neighbors would have offered as an easy explanation, for his God is the Creator of all that is, and he made it all to be good. So he chooses one of God's creatures to become the source of temptation, and the snake is the best candidate. It had an ambiguous reputation in the ancient East. . . . The instinctive human hatred for snakes made him a logical choice for the one who initiated the human grasp for independence. . . . Eventually, when the concept of a personal tempter, the source of evil, had developed, interpreters found it easy to identify the serpent with the devil. . . . But this happened long after the O.T. period (see Wisdom of Solomon 2:24; Rev. 12:9; 20:2)."[7] Gordon J. Wenham writes: "Within the world of the O.T. animal symbolism, a snake is an obvious candidate for an anti-God symbol, notwithstanding its creation by God . . . [anyone] familiar with the symbolic values of different animals, a creature more likely than a serpent to lead man away from his creator could not be imagined. . . . The serpent symbolizes sin, death, and the power of evil."[8]

The only way Isaiah 14:12–17 and Ezekiel 28 can be seen as referring to Satan is by reading him back into the text.[9]

THE CONCEPT OF SATAN EVOLVED

Over time, the concept of Satan evolved from that of a heavenly public prosecutor to the leader of an angelic host at war with God and man. The original model for the figure of Satan may have been an Oriental spy, who in the absence of a state police served as the eyes and ears of the king. The whole notion of a "devil's advocate" is that of a lawyer "who has the job of being an adversary in the interests of discovering the truth."[10] Logic supports this view too. According to Sidney Harris, "If God is really all-powerful, no devil would have a chance against him. So if a devil really exists, it must be because he's secretly in cahoots with God."

Satan was transformed into the "Evil One" by two trains of thought, according to Walter Wink. First, since in Job we see Satan provoking God to bring on sickness, catastrophes, pillage, and death, it would not take long for the popular imagination to turn Satan into the New Testament "god of this world" (2 Cor. 4:4). Second, was the need to explain the origin of evil. The sheer massiveness of evil in the world pointed to a more malevolent source than puny human beings. The allusion to a fall of angels through intercourse with women (Gen. 6:1–4) provided the seedbed of a whole new set of ideas which led to that of Satan and his fallen angelic host (see 1 Enoch 6–14).

Bart D. Ehrman connects the rise of the concept of Satan as a personal force of evil pitted against God and his angels with the rise of Jewish apocalypticism around 170–150 BCE. This occurred about the time of the Maccabean revolt (ca. 167 BCE) against the attack of Jerusalem by Antiochus Epiphanes IV, his desecration of the temple, and the subsequent persecution of the Jews. Previously, the typical answer to why people suffered was because they had sinned. But that couldn't explain this horror. According to them there must be a supernatural being who is causing this suffering. Taking their cue from the beasts in Daniel 7, Ehrman argues they saw a new solution: "suffering comes to God's people because of evil forces in the world (the beasts), forces that are opposed to God and those who side with him."[11]

From that point on Satan was gradually transformed into the leader of an evil kingdom whose battleground was the earth over human souls. Several different names were used to designate the leader of these hostile evil forces: the devil, Belial (also Beliar), Mastemah, Apollyon (meaning the "Destroyer"), Sammael, Asmodeus, or Beelzebub. Satan, however, came to be the name that was used the most. This is the being reflected in the New Testament and in the Dead Sea Scrolls (ca. 150 BCE to 68 CE), where he is seen ". . . as the leader of the evil forces and attacker of the righteous."[12] In the New Testament we see an evil God-hating satanic kingdom pitted against God's kingdom. However, this being is nothing but a human invention to distance God from evil and to also exonerate human beings from the source of evil.

The bottom line is that if Satan was the brightest creature in all of creation, and he knew of God's immediate presence, absolute goodness, and omnipotent power like no one else, then to rebel against God makes him pure evil, suicidal, and dumber than a box of rocks! How is it really possible that any creature in the direct unmediated presence of God would want to rebel against the absolute goodness and love of an infinitely all-powerful being? Even if a creature wanted to rebel, he would know that such a rebellion would be absolutely futile. But since no one can be that evil or stupid, he doesn't exist at all.

NOTES

1. Walter Wink, *Unmasking the Powers* (Philadelphia: Fortress Press, 1986), pp. 11–44. For two book-length treatments on Satan, see Wink's *Unmasking the Powers*, from whom much of the following was taken, and Elaine Pagels, *The Origin of Satan* (New York: Random House, 1995).

2. Wink, *Unmasking the Powers*, pp. 11–44.

3. *The Anchor Bible Dictionary*, s.v. "Satan."

4. Walter A. Elwell, gen ed., *Baker's Encyclopedia of the Bible*, 2 vols. (Grand Rapids, MI: Baker Book House, 1988), s.v. "Satan," pp. 1907–1908.

5. Bernard Anderson, *Understanding the Old Testament* (Englewood Cliffs, NJ: Prentice-Hall, 1957), p. 169.

6. John Gibson, *Genesis Vol. 1* (Philadelphia: Westminster Press, 1981), pp. 121–25.

7. Donald Gown, *Genesis 1–11: From Eden to Babel* (Grand Rapids, MI: Eerdmans 1988), pp. 51–52.

8. Gordon J. Wenham, *Genesis 1–15* (Dallas: Word Incorporated, 1987), pp. 72–80.

9. Even the conservative NIV Study Bible says of the Isaiah text that "the passage clearly applies to the king of Babylon."

10. Uta Ranke-Heinemann, *Putting Away Childish Things*, trans. Peter Heinegg (New York: HarperSanFrancisco, 1992), p. 59.

11. Bart Ehrman, *God's Problem: How the Bible Fails to Answer Our Most Important Question—Why We Suffer* (New York: HarperCollins, 2008), p. 214.

12. *Baker's Encyclopedia of the Bible*, s.v. "Satan," pp. 1907–1908.

There are at least four positions to take when understanding the doctrine of hell. The first three can be found among conservative Christians. The last one is how liberals and atheists view it. I'll describe them and argue against the first three, each in turn. I'll argue that the whole notion of hell is mythical, based upon ancient superstitious beliefs, and that the whole notion of punishment after the grave is uncharacteristic of a loving God.

1. THE BIBLICAL LANGUAGE OF HEAVEN AND HELL IS METAPHORICAL NOT LITERAL

This first view of hell is the dominant view among evangelicals. Just like depictions of heaven are figurative describing a place of pleasure and rest, so also depictions of hell describe a place of misery where the wicked are banished from the presence of God forever.

Heaven is described as first-century people would picture perfect bliss. Before the use of gunpowder, thick walls surrounded ancient cities for protection, with sturdy gates. In Revelation (chapter 21) heaven is described as the most safe and beautiful city ever, even though there can be no use for walls in heaven. Every conceivable precious stone was used in the heavenly city, except the diamond—because it was too difficult to cut and polish back then. Platinum was unknown until the sixteenth century, so it's not in the heavenly city either. Since pearls were known in antiquity and were extremely important adornments, the heavenly city gates were made from one single pearl. When people worked from dawn to dusk simply to feed themselves, a heavenly rest (Hebrews 3–4) beginning with a sumptuous feast (Rev.

19:6–9) was the perfect picture of heaven to laborers in Jesus' day. To people who lived in one-room dark houses, heaven could best be described as filled with light and space (John 14:2; Rev. 21:10–27). When only kings could wear a few trinkets of gold, heaven could best be described as having "streets of gold" (Rev. 22:1–3). We're told God was communicating truth to people "in ways they can understand at their particular time in history."[1]

By contrast, hell, or in the Greek, *Gehenna*, is a valley outside Jerusalem where rubbish was burned. I actually visited this place called hell, and rubbish is still burned there today. So when the Jews wanted to talk about punishment in the afterlife what better image could they use but *Gehenna*? It was a garbage heap. In a garbage heap fire and worms (maggots) consume the trash. To literally say that sinners who die go to hell would quite frankly mean they end up in this valley. But how can that be? Hell is described as a place where there are fire, worms, and darkness (Matt. 8:12; 22:13; 25:30; etc). But fire gives light, not darkness. Furthermore, do the damned get eaten by maggots, or are they burned? The wicked are to weep and gnash their teeth while some are beaten with many blows (Matt. 13:42; 24:51; 25:30; Mark 9:48; Luke 12:47). The wicked person's teeth could be knocked out if beaten with many blows. How then can they gnash their teeth if they don't have any? What is meant by "the worm never dies?" Do worms live forever in hell? Physical fire and worms can only cause pain to earthly physical bodies. The picture of heaven and hell here is not literal, but metaphorical and figurative, so it's argued. For Christians who believe this, like C. S. Lewis, hell is described as "the absence of God" in the afterlife, although it is still very painful. The serious problem to be dealt with here is that if God's gift to the saved is described as "life," or "eternal life" (John 3:16; 17:3; 20:31; 1 John 5:11–20; Jude 21; Rev. 2:7), then the absence of God is death. This conclusion has led many Christians to adopt the next position on hell, Annihilationism.

PAUL COPAN'S DEFENSE OF THE METAPHORICAL VIEW

As an evangelical, my friend Paul Copan takes the conservative position (1) above, that the biblical language of heaven and hell is figurative, not literal.[2] What do these images depict according to Copan? Hell is "the ultimate, everlasting separation from the source of life and hope: God." Therefore, "the pain of hell should not be seen in terms of something physical but rather as pain within a person's spirit. . . . Hell at its root is the agony and utter hopelessness of separation from God." However, here I must wonder if Copan has done any deep thinking about what it might mean to be separated from the source of life. There are many evangelicals who conclude that this means the damned cease to exist—position (2) next. And while it appears Copan is trying to soften the horrors of hell, if correct, such a view of hell is still a horrible fate for a loving God to inflict upon human beings. The punishment does not fit the crime, period. No thinking person should believe this is what our so-called sins deserve.

Copan further argues that "hell is the logical outcome of living life away from God." Those who find themselves in hell have committed "not simply a string of finite sins," but "the infinite sin," for unbelievers have resisted "the influence of God's Spirit" and "refused to honor God as God" by "not lovingly responding to God's kind initiative." Instead, I find it almost absurd that the Christian God blames us for living our lives as if he didn't exist, because there simply isn't enough reason to believe in him over any of the other gods, or no god at all, especially when we usually adopt the religion we were born into. I furthermore find it absurd that God is so upset that we don't acknowledge him in this life that he will punish us forever for it, as if it hurts him that much for us not to acknowledge him. If he is omniscient, then he knows why we do what we do and why we believe what we do, and I fail to see how such a God cannot empathize with how we live our lives. We all do the best we can do, given our environment and brain matter.

Copan continues to argue that "to force someone into heaven who would hate the presence of God . . . would be horrible," and he agrees with D. A. Carson, who said "heaven would surely be hell for those who don't enjoy and desire the blessing of God's presence."[3] According to Copan, "Hell is getting what one wants (and deserves)—no God." Copan also quotes with approval C. S. Lewis that "the doors of hell are locked on the inside."[4] Copan claims even though the damned are in anguish, "they still choose to remain in it," rather than to prefer "a God-centered existence in heaven." And so "resistance to God continues in hell."

To soften the force of this view believers will argue there will be gradations of punishment in hell for the unsaved just as there will be gradations to their reward in heaven, with some in the "nosebleed" section (based on passages like Luke 12:47–48). But why? Either Jesus washed away all of their sins or he didn't. If he did, then why are there different rewards in heaven? Any lack of obedience from a believer on earth is to be considered a sin of "omission," and yet all sins were supposedly forgiven . . . all of them. But if those sins are not forgiven then based on their own logic there will be some believers in heaven who may not enjoy it there and prefer hell, or at least have periods where they would rather be there. Why not?

I understand Copan is trying to do his best with the Bible, based upon philosophical or theological grounds. But to claim that the damned prefer the anguish of hell over the bliss of heaven through repentance is simply absurd. Anyone in such anguish would repent of their "sins" if she could experience the purported joys of heaven. Every single person in hell would willingly desire to change if she could escape the torments of hell for the joys of heaven. Every single one of them!

Christians might claim such repentance wouldn't be true repentance. However, *repentance* (Greek: *metanoia*) is "a change of mind." People would automatically change their minds if they could know the truth about God with this kind of certainty. Once someone believes something different, she automatically changes her lifestyle in keeping with that new belief. This is undeniably true and noncontroversial. Socrates went so far as to argue that once someone knows what is good, she will then automatically do good deeds.

The parable of the rich man and Lazarus (Luke 16:19–31), for instance, shows that the rich man in hell (*Hades*) was now a believer. The rich man now knew the truth about God and hell. The difference between the rich man and believers still alive is the fact that his fate was sealed, along with the "demons who believe." The difference is that there are no promises from God to him about a change of lifestyle leading to heaven. His final destiny is sealed, and that makes all the difference in the world.

Copan's claim is that the rich man doesn't want to "repent" or change his lifestyle. What possible lifestyle did he have in hell that was preferable to a heavenly existence? Just picture yourself in the rich man's shoes. If you were in hell, you would easily be willing to change your lifestyle for a lifestyle in heaven, especially if you now believed the Bible was true. The rich man did not ask to be admitted into heaven, not because he didn't want to go there, but rather because in this parable Jesus reflects the commonly held belief that this was impossible, since his fate was sealed. So the rich man requests the only two other things he could: (1) for personal relief from his pain, and (2) on behalf of his family so they might escape the horrors he now experiences.

This parable doesn't show that the doors of hell are locked from the inside to me at all. It's exactly the opposite! The doors of hell cannot be locked from the inside if it's painful to be there. For Christians like Copan to claim the inhabitants of hell prefer the pain of hell to the pain of being in heaven simply makes no sense at all. What sane person who was led to believe by virtue of her experience in hell would not prefer to repent and be in heaven?

2. CONDITIONAL IMMORTALITY (OR ANNIHILATIONISM)

This second view of hell was an important conclusion I came to on my intellectual journey, for my skeptical questions would've been hamstrung by a fear of everlasting punishment in hell if I got it wrong. The loss of the fear of an eternal conscious punishment allowed me to pursue my doubts.

According to this view, we should not confuse the reality of hell with its images. The images of hell are of "everlasting punishment" (Matt. 25:46); "eternal destruction" (Matt. 10:28); and banishment into the "darkness" (Matt. 22:13; 25:30). How we interpret these images depends on other Bible verses. In the Old Testament the wicked will cease to exist (Psalm 37, Mal. 4:1–2). Jesus in the New Testament shows us that the purpose of fire in punishment is to destroy or burn up the wicked (Matt. 3:10–12; 13:30, 42, 49–50). According to Evangelical John R.W. Stott: "The main function of fire is not to cause pain, but to secure destruction."[5] Paul likewise emphasized destruction (2 Thess. 1: 9; 1 Cor. 3:17; Phil. 1:28; 3:19). Peter likewise stressed the sinners' fate as that of destruction (2 Pet. 2:1, 3, 6; 3:6–7). Even in John's book of Revelation, the lake of fire will consume the wicked (Rev. 20:14–15). According to G. B. Caird, "John believed that, if at the end there should be any who remained impervious to the grace and love of God, they should be thrown, with Death and Hades, into the lake of fire which is the second death, i.e., extinction and total oblivion."[6]

Clark Pinnock argues that "the Bible uses language of death and destruction, of ruin and perishing, when it speaks of the fate of the impenitent wicked. It uses the imagery of fire that consumes whatever is thrown into it." But "linking together images of fire and destruction suggests annihilation. One receives the impression that 'eternal punishment' refers to a divine judgment whose results cannot be reversed rather than to the experience of endless torment (i.e., eternal punishing)."[7]

Biblically speaking, human beings are not immortal. God alone has immortality (1 Tim. 6:16); well-doers seek immortality (Rom. 2:7); immortality is brought to light through the gospel (2 Tim. 1:10); and those in Christ will put on immortality (1 Cor. 15:54), so that they now partake of the divine nature (2 Pet. 1:4).

In an interesting book called *The Problem of Hell*, Jonathan L. Kvanvig utilizes biblical, moral, and philosophical arguments on behalf of the view that based upon God's character "in which his love is the primary motivational characteristic," God will not abandon any person until that person has made a settled, final decision to reject God, under favorable circumstances. Once a person has finally and competently chosen to reject God, then out of respect for that person's autonomy, God allows him or her to be annihilated, as a sort of rational suicide when all other alternatives are too painful and/or hopeless. Kvanvig claims that "the fundamental flaw of the traditional conception of hell and the standard alternatives is easy to appreciate. All such views rely intrinsically on a retributive punishment model of hell."[8] These theories cannot pass the moral test. While Kvanvig admits his view of hell involves punishment, the punishment "is not motivated by retribution and for the cause of retribution." God's "primary motivation in sending people to hell is not to punish them. His primary motivation is always love, and in loving the depraved he is forced to act in such a way that persons in hell are punished."[9]

In its place Kvanvig suggests a nonretributive view: "The choice of heaven or hell is not a choice of residence, as if one were picking between two new countries in which one might wish to reside. The choice of heaven or hell is rather a choice between ultimate union with God and ultimate independence from God. Choosing to aim against ultimate union with him is choosing ultimate independence from him, which is to choose nonexistence."[10]

I think I've already sufficiently debunked his views earlier when asking why God needs to have our love in the first place, along with asking how God could expect us to choose him when he hides himself from us. Exactly how can God fully expect human beings to make a rational, settled, and final choice if we don't know exactly what we are choosing between? To assert that we do belies the sociological data that forms the basis of the Outsider Test for Faith.

Kvanvig does admit that his "strictly philosophical investigation of the doctrine of hell does not imply many of the aspects of biblical teaching about hell."[11] Whether this is actually what we find in the Bible is a much disputed conclusion among evangelicals. It certainly was not the dominant view of the church for millennia, and it still leaves unresolved why we human beings need to be punished in the first place when we all do the very best we can given our brain matter and social environment.

3. THE TRADITIONAL VIEW OF HELL

The first two views of hell in the Bible are more "reasonable" views than the traditional view of hell, in that they are trying to come to grips with the horrible consequences the traditional view places upon a loving God. But that doesn't mean these views are biblically correct. John Walvoord presents an excellent case for the traditional view of an everlasting conscious torment in a literal place of fire, if we believe the Bible.[12]

After surveying the Bible on the topic, Walvoord states that "the ultimate convincing argument for eternal punishment is found in Revelation 20:10–15." There we read: "And the devil, who deceived them, was thrown into the lake of burning sulfur, where the beast and the false prophet had been thrown. They will be tormented day and night for ever and ever." Notice that the lake of fire does not depict their destruction, for they will be tormented day and night for ever and ever. Later (v.15) when it says that people who are condemned by God were thrown into the lake of fire, it can only mean they would suffer likewise, forever. This suffering, which they first experience temporarily in Hades, becomes a permanent place of conscious suffering forever in the lake of fire. And according to Walvoord, it is a place of fire. Walvoord argues that "the frequent mention of fire in connection with eternal punishment supports the conclusion that this is what the Scriptures mean." Here he cites passages like Matthew 5:22; 18:8–9; 25:41, Mark 9:43, 48; Luke 16:24; James 3:6; and Jude 7. His best case is the story of the rich man and Lazarus (Luke 16:19–31). We are told that the rich man was "in agony in this fire," and that's about as clear as we get.

Walvoord argues that objections to this view "have to be on philosophic or theological grounds rather than on exegetical ones." In my opinion, the whole reason the traditional view is attacked today is because Christian theologians are cherry-picking the Bible based upon our modern, more humane notions in light of the global awareness that billions of sincere people do not accept Jesus as their savior. The whole reason this is called the "traditional view" of hell is because it is the one that received the overwhelming support throughout the history of the church until the advent of modernity and the recognition through global religious diversity that people sincerely do not believe in Jesus. This view was codified and explicated in gruesome detail by Dante in his *Divine Comedy*, complete with artwork depicting the tortures of hell. The truth is that most traditionalists don't actually take what the Bible says literally in our modern era. But creationists Henry M. Morris and Martin E. Clark do. They wrote, "So far as we can tell from Scripture, the present hell, Hades, is somewhere in the heart of earth itself. . . . The Biblical descriptions are quite matter-of-fact. The writers certainly themselves believed hell to be real and geographically 'beneath' the earth's surface."[13]

That being said, C. S. Lewis reminds us that the traditional doctrine of hell "is one of the chief grounds on which Christianity is attacked as barbarous and the goodness of God impugned."[14]

Jonathan Edwards described it this way: "The God that holds you over the pit of hell, much in the same way as one holds a spider, or some loathsome insect, over the fire, abhors you, and is dreadfully provoked; his wrath towards you burns like fire. . . . You hang by a slender thread, with flames of divine wrath flashing about it and ready every moment to singe it, and burn it asunder. . . . Consider this, you that yet remain in an unregenerate state. That God will execute the fierceness of his anger, implies, that he will inflict wrath without any pity . . . you shall be tormented in the presence of the holy angels, and in the presence of the Lamb. . . . There will be no end to this exquisite horrible misery. . . . So that your punishment will indeed be infinite."[15]

So here's a question Hans Küng asks: "What would we think of a human being who satisfied his thirst for revenge so implacably and insatiably?"[16] "If this were true" (i.e., the traditional view), Nels Ferre claims it would make Hitler "a third-degree saint, and the concentration camps . . . a picnic ground."[17]

Clark Pinnock argues that "the idea that a fully conscious creature would undergo physical and mental torture through endless time is plainly sadistic and therefore incompatible with a God who loves humanity. . . . In terms of justice, the traditional view of hell is simply unacceptable. It is a punishment in excess of anything that sinners deserve. . . . Besides, no purpose is served by the unending torture of the wicked except vengeance."[18]

Pinnock asks, "Is it not plain that sins committed in time and space cannot deserve limitless divine retribution? Hell is the ultimate big stick to threaten people with . . . this monstrous belief will cause many people to turn away from Christianity. . . . What human crimes could possibly deserve everlasting conscious torture?"[19] Pinnock adds, "Surely the idea of everlasting conscious torment raises the problem of evil to impossible heights."[20] And "Any doctrine of hell needs to pass the moral test. . . . The traditional belief . . . is unbiblical, is fostered by a Hellenistic view of human nature, is detrimental to the character of God, is defended on essentially pragmatic grounds, and is being rejected by a growing number of biblically faithful, contemporary scholars."[21]

John McTaggart has argued convincingly against the traditional view of hell. Since there is no empirical evidence for it, the only way we would know it exists is if God reveals this to us. However, the concept of hell is just too vile and repulsive for us to believe, so this calls into question anything of importance that such a God might reveal to us. Since a God who would consign people to hell cannot be trusted, we would have no good reason to trust that he is telling us the truth about anything important. So on the one hand there is no reason or evidence to believe in hell, and on the other hand there would be no reason to trust what God would say if he revealed it to us.[22]

Marilyn Adams argues that damnation in hell is so inconceivable of a horror that human beings cannot fully understand the consequences of choosing for or against God. She claims people do not have a free will with respect to this matter "with fully open eyes," and as such, argues they should not be held fully responsible for such a choice. In her view, for God to give humans this choice is like an adult giving a child a loaded handgun. Hell, as the final consequence for sin, is so disproportionate to the sinful acts themselves that a person's eternal destiny cannot hinge on whether or not she behaves correctly. If God does this, then he places unreasonable expectations on human beings, who cannot fathom the consequences of their choices.[23]

Uta Ranke-Heinemann claims that "as the Church's threat against all sinners and all its enemies, hell serves the holy purpose of cradle to grave intimidation."[24]

4. HELL IS A NONEXISTENT MYTHICAL PLACE

The notion of a punishment after we die is sick and barbaric. The concept of hell developed among superstitious and barbaric peoples, and tells us nothing about life after death. The concept of life after death mostly developed in the Apocryphal literature during the intertestamental time between the Old and New Testaments (based on passages like Job 19:26, Isa. 26:19, and Dan 12:1–3). Just like we've seen with the concept of Satan, it wasn't accepted until the second century BCE, in the days of the Maccabean crisis when the return to life of the dead came about.[25]

The whole concept of hell developed during the Hellenistic period and then was adopted by the New Testament writers. There was the idea of a fiery judgment (1 Enoch 10:13; 48:8–10; 100:7–9; 2 Bar. 85:13), in a fiery lake or abyss (1 Enoch 18:9–16; 90:24–27; 103:7–8; 2 Enoch 40:12; 2 Bar. 59:5–12; 1QH 3). Here's what we read in 1 Enoch 48:8–9: "For in the day of their anxiety and trouble their souls shall not be saved; and they shall be in subjection to those whom I have chosen. I will cast them like hay into the fire, and like lead into the water. Thus shall they burn in the presence of the righteous, and sink in the presence of the holy; nor shall a tenth part of them be found."

The Valley of Hinnom (*gehenna*), often referred to simply as "the accursed valley" or "abyss," came to signify the place of eschatological judgment of the wicked Jews by fire (1 Enoch 26–27; 54:1–6; 56:1–4; 90:24–27). Thus we read in the *Anchor Bible Dictionary*, under "*Gehenna*": "The judgment of the wicked occurred either as a casting of their soul in Gehenna immediately upon death or as a casting of the reunited body and soul into Gehenna after the resurrection and last judgment (2 Esd. 7:26–38; 4 Ezra 7:26–38; Ascension of Isaiah 4:14–18; cf. Sib. Or. 4.179–91). This understanding divorced Gehenna from its geographical location, but retained its fiery nature. Gehenna had become hell itself." Would Christians want to claim that these apocryphal texts are inspired too? Hardly. These texts are reflective of an ancient barbaric superstitious people, period.

NOTES

1. As defended by William Crocket, who also edited *Four Views of Hell* (Grand Rapids, MI: Zondervan, 1992), pp. 43–76. See also Michael J. Murray, "Heaven and Hell," in *Reason for the Hope Within* (Grand Rapids, MI: Eerdmans, 1999).

2. From Paul Copan, *"That's Just Your Interpretation"* (Grand Rapids, MI: Baker Books, 2001), pp. 101–109.

3. D. A. Carson, *How Long, O Lord?* (Grand Rapids, MI: Baker Book House, 1990), p. 103.

4. C. S. Lewis, *The Problem of Pain* (New York: Macmillan Paperbacks, 1962), p. 127.

5. John R. W. Stott with David Edwards, *Evangelical Essentials* (Downers Grove, IL: InterVarsity Press), p. 316.

6. G. B. Caird, *A Commentary on the Revelation of St. John the Divine* (Peabody, MA: Hendrickson, 1987), p. 186.

7. Clark Pinnock in Crocket, *Four Views of Hell*, p. 144.

8. Jonathan L. Kvanvig, in *The Problem of Hell* (Oxford: Oxford University Press, 2001), p. 136. Kvanvig argues against "second chance" theories and "universalism" too (pp. 25–66).

9. Ibid., p. 155.

10. Ibid., p. 148.

11. Ibid., p. 158.

12. John Walvoord in Crocket, *Four Views of Hell*, pp. 11–28. For a detailed examination of the traditional view of hell, see Jonathan L. Kvanvig's, *The Problem of Hell*, pp. 25–66.

13. Henry M. Morris and Martin E. Clark, *The Bible Has the Answer: Revised and Expanded* (El Cajon, CA: Creation Life Publishers, 1987), p. 312.

14. Lewis, *The Problem of Pain*, pp. 118–28.

15. Jonathan Edwards, sermon, "Sinners in the Hands of an Angry God."

16. Hans Küng, *Eternal Life* (New York: Doubleday, 1984), p. 136.

17. Nels Ferre, *Christian Understanding of God* (New York: Harper and Brothers, 1951), p. 540.

18. Clark H. Pinnock and Robert Brown, *Unbounded Love* (Downers Grove, IL: InterVarsity Press, 1994), pp. 88, 93.

19. Pinnock in Crockett, *Four Views of Hell*, pp. 39, 140.

20. Ibid., p. 150.

21. Ibid., p. 165.

22. John McTaggart, *Some Dogmas of Religion* (London, 1906), section 177.

23. Marilyn McCord Adams, "The Problem of Hell: A Problem of Evil for Christians," in *Reasoned Faith: Essays in Philosophical Theology in Honor of Norman Kretzmann*, ed. Eleonore Stump (Ithaca, NY: Cornell University Press, 1993), pp. 308–11.

24. Uta Ranke-Heinemann, *Putting Away Childish Things*, trans. Peter Heinegg (New York: HarperSanFrancisco, 1992), pp. 228–47.

25. *The Anchor Bible Dictionary*, s.v. "Resurrection."

Part 3

WHAT I BELIEVE TODAY

23

WHY I BECAME AN ATHEIST

I know what I reject. I reject Christianity. But after the demolition is done, what could I now believe about how we got here on earth and why? In a letter I wrote to Dr. Strauss (written in 1996), I said I could be described as a deist, a theological existentialist, and perhaps a panentheist (as in process theology). It wasn't long afterward I described myself as an agnostic.

This initial agnosticism of mine was unsettling to me. It simply wasn't an answer. To say "I don't know," means just that, I don't know. I don't think I'll gain any new information with further research that will help me figure it out. I know about everything I will know to make a decision. According to William James, we must choose. This is the problem he spoke of when it came to *forced options*, and it is a forced one for me. There's no such thing as living like an agnostic. So why couldn't I decide? Why? As I pondered this question, the answer just hit me like a proverbial ton of bricks. Let me explain.

FAITH AND REASON REVISITED

The relationship of faith to reason is sort of a catch-22 for me. If we initially try to figure it out with reason, we cannot figure it out. Take, for instance, the existence of God. It's undeniable that something now exists, without even trying to come to a common understanding of the nature of that which exists, be it spirit, matter, or a combination of both. That means there are basically two choices for us, or we can just say that it's all completely absurd to the core. Either something has always and forever existed or something popped into existence out of absolutely nothing. Either horn you grab onto presents us with deep problems. On the one hand, it's extremely difficult to understand what it means for something, let's say God, or the universe for that matter, to have always existed without a beginning. Can anyone say they truly comprehend that? On the other hand, it's extremely difficult to understand how something (either the universe as we know it, or even God for that matter) popped into existence out of absolutely nothing. Can anyone say they truly comprehend that? In fact, almost every scientific attempt I've read to describe how our universe began to exist always begins with something—from the "swerving atom" of ancient Greek philosopher Democritus, to Paul Davies's "cosmic repulsion in a quantum vacuum," to what Edward Tryon and Stephen Hawking both describe as a "quantum wave fluctuation"[1] These things are not nothing.

Mark William Worthing claims, "For a true creation out of nothing there can be no scientific explanation. Any theory explaining how something has come from nothing must assume some preexisting laws or energy or quantum activity in order to have a credible theory. It could be claimed, naturally, that there was nothing and then suddenly there was, without apparent physical cause or ground, something. But this would be more a statement of philosophical or theological belief than a genuine scientific theory."[2]

Our choice is between an infinite regress of events or an uncaused cause. Our choice is between the cosmos having no explanation for its existence or the universe having a final explanation that needs no further explanation. Concerning the origin of our universe, Sam Harris writes, "The truth is that no one knows how or why the universe came into being. It is not clear that we can even speak coherently about the creation of the universe, given that such an event can be conceived only with reference to time, and here we are talking about the birth of space-time itself. Any intellectually honest person will admit that he does not know why the universe exists."[3]

The best attempt to understand how something exists is what I had mentioned in my chapter 5, as argued by Victor J. Stenger. His argument is that "nothing" is unstable, and as such there is a 60 percent chance that something should exist given the laws of nature. I have to admit this is an extremely interesting argument, one that I don't have the knowledge or expertise to properly evaluate at this time. If true, it would settle the whole debate about why there is something rather than nothing. Still it's difficult to grasp what it means to say that the laws of nature just simply exist.

With regard to the origin of this reality we experience, it appears that reason cannot help us. The catch-22 here—damned if I do, damned if I don't—is that if I start with reason, I may get nowhere, but if I start with faith, the question becomes this: what if I start out by believing the wrong set of things?

THE RELIGIOUSLY AMBIGUOUS NATURE OF THE UNIVERSE

John Hick is arguably the most important philosopher of religion in the past century, and this is one of the reasons I quote from him so much. He has called for religious Copernican revolution when it comes to world religions.[4] We've already discussed the Copernican revolution, in which our whole understanding of how we viewed the universe changed from the geocentric view (where earth was viewed as the center) to the heliocentric view (where the sun was viewed as the center). Immanuel Kant called for a philosophical Copernican Revolution when it came to our notion of how we experience reality. For him, in short, categories in our mind structure reality, instead of reality shaping our mind (i.e., there is no mind-independent reality).

According to Hick: "The universe is religiously ambiguous in that it is possible to interpret it, intellectually and experientially, both religiously and naturalistically. The theistic and anti-theistic arguments are all inconclusive, for the special evidences to which they appeal are also capable for being understood in terms of the contrary worldview. Further, the opposing sets of evidences cannot be given objectively quantifiable values." That is, "our environment is capable of being construed —in sense perception as well as ethically and religiously—in a range of ways." Thus, "all conscious experiencing is experiencing—as."[5]

The internationally revered authority on world religions Huston Smith stated it this way: "the world is ambiguous. It does not come tagged 'This is my Father's world' or 'Life is a tale told by an idiot.' It comes to us as a giant Rorschach inkblot. Psychologists use such blots to fish in the subterranean waters of their patients' minds. The blots approach the patient as invitations: Come. What do you see here? What do you make of these contours? The sweep of philosophy supports this inkblot theory of the world conclusively. People have never agreed on the world's meaning, and (it seems safe to say) never will."[6]

Even though Hick believes that the universe is religiously ambiguous, he still chooses the tradition of liberal Christianity to interpret all of the religions—the one he inherited. But if he is correct about the ambiguous nature of it all, then it would also be rational for someone to believe in atheism, and he admits this.

Anglican philosopher Terence Penelhum agrees with Hick. He wrote: "An ambiguous world is one in which there are always reasonable grounds for hesitation, and is therefore one in which such hesitation is probably not blameworthy. The world could not be ambiguous if there were no people in it who could reasonably interpret it in more than one way." But we all know that there are such people.[7]

"We appear to be confronted not with a simple theist-naturalist ambiguity, either side of which can justify itself at least in negative terms; we are confronted, rather, by a world that exhibits multiple religious and ideological ambiguity. . . . It is possible to be conscientiously unable to decide between two or more worldviews and life-options. . . . Those who insist that unbelief must be willful, and not merely that it may be, have the onus of showing that the world is not ambiguous. Only then can we be sure that unbelief is due to the willful refusal to grant what the accuser thinks is true."

Penelhum concludes: "I think there is one unqualified obligation for all rational beings, whether they have a faith or not: to remove it—to seek the disambiguation of their world. To find some truth that eliminates some alternative reading of the world, or a truth that establishes some essential part of a hitherto merely possible reading of the world. But we can't all wait, can we, for the philosophers to determine what it is rational to do before we make life-forming decisions? Of course not; but this is the problem. There are many beliefs we have to go on holding whether philosophers can sustain them for us or not. But an ambiguous world is a world in which it is rational to go on holding this or that or the other worldview, but also rational to hold many others, and in which the informed thinker knows this." Therefore, the first thing we must do "is what committed but intellectually responsible adherents of a faith should do," and that is "to try their best to find a disambiguating argument in favor of the position they are living by."[8]

I believed that I must try to disambiguate this religiously ambiguous universe, too. In doing this, I previously chose to believe in deism and the philosopher's God who created this universe. This God is not the particular God of Abraham who demands worship and obedience, so much as a God who solves the question of how we got here. While I granted the religiously ambiguous nature of this universe, I struggled to believe in God. It was probably a Kierkegaardian leap of faith for me, which also made me an existentialist, a deistic existentialist. But this wasn't satisfying, for according to Marcus Borg: "There is little difference between a distant and absent God and no God at all."[9]

MY FORMER POSITION WAS UNTENABLE

Since this universe is religiously ambiguous, then there are several religious or nonreligious options available to rational people when they seek to disambiguate this ambiguous universe. But if this is so, why did I existentially choose deism, and not atheism, or panentheism, or pantheism? Why not even return to some form of Christianity, since Christians too can claim, at least to themselves, to be rational in holding to it? Why not choose as John Hick, Huston Smith, or Terence Penelhum does?

This was a tough question for me. I wasn't even sure if reason applied to ultimacies, so how could I judge anyone else's worldview by the standards of reason? All I could do was to say that most Christians welcome reason to examine their beliefs, so I examined them rationally. They think their faith wins in the marketplace of ideas and that it's supported by reason. So in this book I have done what they asked me to do. I've examined and evaluated Christianity with the standards of reason and modern science and concluded the Christian faith is not a reasonable faith.

Then the question hit me. Why is this universe religiously ambiguous, capable of being interpreted in various rational and sometimes even mutually exclusive ways? Why does it all appear absurd when we approach it all with reason? Why must I resort to giving up on reason and punting to the view that I just don't know or that it cannot be rationally figured out? Why?

THEN THE ANSWER HIT ME

When we seek for a cause of it all, we run into apparent absurdities, precisely because blind chancistic events cannot be figured out. Chance events can produce order. We know this. Even if the odds are extremely unlikely for this universe to exist, once there is some order in the universe and someone to look upon the order that's there, it cries out for an explanation. Pascal would be right here to say all over again, "I look on all sides and see nothing but obscurity; nature offers me nothing but matter for doubt." We may even have to say, like I had previously said, that it cannot be figured out with reason, and initially it can't. *But when we reflect on why we can't figure it all out, the best reason I can offer is that random chance events can't be figured out by hindsight, because there is nothing but chance to account for them.* So in the end, I do have a reason for what I believe. Nature is ultimate. According to the late Carl Sagan, "the cosmos is all there is, was, or ever will be." According to Bertrand Russell, the universe is simply "a brute fact." I am an atheist. There is no God. And there is at least one reason for me not to believe in God, and that is because this universe is absurd when we try to figure it out. Any attempt I know of to figure it out fails, except the conclusion that it arose because of chance. According to Jacques Monod, "our number came up in a Monte Carlo game."[10]

Christians and I reject all other religions. I simply reject their Christian religion with the same confidence they have when rejecting these other religions. The rejection of a religious viewpoint is the easy part. We all do it. And we're all confident when doing so. The hard part after the rejection is to *affirm* a religious viewpoint. That's where a person must argue that she has the correct one. And from what I see, these Christians are just as confident that they are right as that the others are wrong, unlike me. I think the default position is (soft or weak) agnosticism, which simply says, "I don't know." That's right; I don't know what to believe after rejecting all religious viewpoints. I could even concede that there is a God, a deist god, a philosopher's god. But as I said, such a distant god is practically no different than none at all. That's why I've chosen to be an atheist, since it makes no difference to me even if a god does exist. But I could be wrong, and I admit it.

Many Christians seem absolutely confident that they are correct in what they *affirm*, and that's a huge difference between us. Given the proliferation of religious viewpoints separated by geographical location around the globe, the fact that believers have a strong tendency to rationally support what they were taught to believe (before they had the knowledge or capability to properly evaluate it), along with the lack of compelling evidence to convince people who are "outsiders" to the Christian faith, mine is the reasonable viewpoint to *affirm*; that's all.[11]

My wife, Gwen, is an atheist, as I have said. While she's not an intellectual, her argument is quite simple. She asks a very simple question: "If God exists, then why doesn't he show me?" It can be developed into a sophisticated argument, however, and it does have some force to it. Surely if God exists, he knows what it would take for us to believe. So why doesn't he do what it takes? From the theistic perspective, this is the so-called problem of divine hiddenness, which is an extension of the problem of evil. This problem is best explained by the fact that God doesn't even exist.[12]

Michael Scriven claims that "if we take arguments for the existence of something to include all the evidence which supports the existence claim to any significant degree, i.e., makes it at all probable, then the absence of such evidence means there is no likelihood of the existence of the entity. And this, of course, is a complete justification for the claim that the entity does not exist, provided that the entity is not one which might leave no traces (a God who is impotent or who does not care for us) and provided we have comprehensively examined the area where evidence would appear if there was any."[13] What I have examined leads me to the conclusion that a divine being does not exist, so I am rational and justified in being an atheist.

In another sense, by declaring myself an atheist it can be seen as a protest against a religiously ambiguous world. I don't think there is a supreme being of any kind, but even if I can't be sure that such a being does not exist, I still proclaim myself an atheist. Theologian John K. Roth has argued for a "Protest Theodicy" in which he thinks protesting the amount of suffering in this world is the only appropriate response when it comes to a God who fails to act compassionately toward us. He thinks our moral responsibility is to shame God into doing what is right.[14] So like Roth, I too am shaming God, if he exists. I am an atheist to protest the fact that even if he exists he has not revealed himself clearly to his creatures, or shown us divine compassion. Even if there is a God after all, I will shame him for not providing sufficient evidence and reasons to believe.

However, atheism is a very unsettling conclusion to me, in one sense. It means I have no hope in a resurrection, that I no longer have the hope that there is someone outside the space-time matrix who can help me in times of need or give me any guidance. In a real sense I actually prefer such a delusionary belief would turn out to be true (so long as I could cherry-pick out from it the evil inherent within it). This unsettling fact is probably the main reason why people refuse to consider atheism as a live option and prefer instead what Paul Kurtz calls, the *Transcendental Temptation*.[15] But it's finally a conclusion. I now can believe something, and as I've said, it's better over here. It's very relieving to reach a conclusion. It just seems plausible to me because everything I have examined so far has failed to provide a satisfying answer, except atheism. So ends my attempt to disambiguate this religiously ambiguous universe. Others may seek to do so in other ways.

No matter what position you take on the nature of existence, you must start with something seemingly absurd. It's like the Englishman who traveled to India and inquired about the Indian legend that the world rests on the backs of four giant elephants. He asked an Indian man what the elephants rested on, and the Indian man told him a huge turtle. Of course, our traveler then asked the next, rather obvious question: What does this turtle rest on? The Indian man replied, "Oh, sahib, after that it is just turtle all the way down." (To read the Christian alternative see note.)[16]

NOTES

1. Edward Tryon in *Nature* (December 1973) and Stephen Hawking in *Physical Review* (December 1983).

2. Mark William Worthing, *God, Creation, and Contemporary Physics* (Minneapolis, MN: Fortress, 1996), p. 105.

3. Sam Harris, *Letter to a Christian Nation* (New York: Knopf, 2006), pp. 73–74.

4. John Hick, *An Interpretation of Religion: Human Responses to the Transcendent* (New Haven, CT: Yale University Press, 1989).

5. Ibid., p. 12.

6. Huston Smith, *Why Religion Matters* (New York: HarperSanFrancisco, 2001), pp. 205–206.

7. http://www.ucalgary.ca/UofC/faculties/HUM/RELS.

8. We see him struggling with his faith in "A Belated Return," in *Philosophers Who Believe*, ed. Kelly James Clark (Downers Grove, IL: InterVarsity Press, 1993), pp. 223–36.

9. Marcus Borg, *The God We Never Knew* (New York: HarperSanFrancisco, 1997), p. 23.

10. Jacques Monod, *Chance and Necessity* (New York: Knopf, 1971).

11. This conclusion is one J. L. Schellenberg argues for at length in his book *The Wisdom to Doubt: A Justification of Religious Skepticism* (Ithaca, NY: Cornell University Press, 2007).

12. J. L. Schellenberg, "Divine Hiddenness Justifies Atheism," in *The Improbability of God*, ed. Michael Martin and Ricki Monnier (Amherst, NY: Prometheus Books, 2006), pp. 413–26.

13. Michael Scriven, *Primary Philosophy* (New York: McGraw-Hill, 1966), p. 102. See also J. L. Schellenberg's updated arguments in his book *The Wisdom to Doubt*, pp. 195–242.

14. See John Roth's essay in *Encountering Evil: Live Options in Theodicy*, ed. Stephen T. Davis (Atlanta: John Knox Press, 1981), pp. 7–37.

15. Paul Kurtz, *The Transcendental Temptation* (Amherst, NY: Prometheus Books, 1991).

16. James Sire uses a similar story as told from a scientific approach. To the question what holds the world up, the answer is that gravity does. To the question of why gravity holds the world up, the answer given is that gravity is the expression of the uniformity of causes operating in the universe. To the question of why the universe works this way, the answer is "that's just the way it is . . . it's uniform all the way down." See his book *Discipleship of the Mind* (Downers Grove, IL: InterVarsity Press, 1990), pp. 36–38.

24

WHAT IS LIFE WITHOUT GOD?

F rancis Schaeffer has initiated a Christian "cultural apologetic" based upon the human predicament. This apologetic, according to William Lane Craig, "simply explores the disastrous consequences for human existence, society, and culture if Christianity should be false."[1]

After noting what Pascal, Dostoyevsky, Kierkegaard, and Schaeffer said about the human predicament without God, Craig offers his own assessment. According to Craig, if there is no God or immortality, "then man and the universe are doomed. . . . It means that life itself is absurd." It means that the life we have "has no ultimate meaning . . . no ultimate value . . . and no ultimate purpose." The biblical book of Ecclesiastes typifies this view. "All is vanity" without God ("under the sun"), in an ultimate sense. I now feel the force of that book like never before. It describes the plight of human existence.

Dr. Craig is careful to point out that arguing for this "cultural apologetic" doesn't prove that the Christian point of view is correct, only that "if God does not exist, then life is [ultimately] futile." I certainly agree that it doesn't prove the Christian faith, but since he considers this argument to have considerable force, let's see what could be said in response.

We can have three options in our lives:

1. A reasoned hope in life after death (belief in a true religion, if one exists);
2. A reasoned despair or pessimism about death (e.g., agnosticism or atheism);
3. A false and/or delusional hope in life (e.g., false religions or existentialism).

The despair or pessimism I refer to in the second option is due to the idea that life has no "ultimate meaning" beyond this life. That is, our lives have no significant ultimate purpose beyond this life, much like an animal or an insect. When we die, and our children die, and their children die, there will barely be a remembrance of us. When the ever-swelling sun swallows up this whole earth and human life is extinguished, there will be no remembrance of the human species as a whole, unless we can find a way to populate other planets in our solar system, but they too will be swallowed up by the sun, until the sun burns out. But to travel to another inhabitable planet from our solar system seems absolutely remote. Even if we could, this universe itself will expand until it reaches absolute zero degrees, in which humans cannot survive. So there is no ultimate significance to human beings, and that's what I mean about a reasoned despair. Albert Camus simply asks us, "why not commit suicide?" After all, if there is no ultimate purpose, then at least you can determine the time of your death.

I personally just don't think the first option is a live option. I've chosen the second since the third option is no hope to me at all. According to Michael Martin, "If pessimism is justified by the evidence, then we must be pessimistic. If we are optimistic when pessimism is justified, we are irrational."[2] Yet this simply does not mean I shouldn't go on living my life as a good person who seeks to be good to other people at all. It doesn't mean that a society that adopts such a position does not have a reason to contribute to the common good either, as I will argue here.

Let me offer six responses to this cultural apologetic. In the first place, Schaeffer and Craig point out the moral troubles in Western societies and decry the days when Christianity was a stronger force in Western societies. They argue that as Christianity was being rejected, our society began to go to hell in a handbasket. Now it is a fact that we have indeed raised many narcissists in our modern Western societies, which probably means the West is in moral decline. Many great societies of the past went into moral bankruptcy too. It may just be the natural bent of we human beings. The increase in crime could be partially due to population growth and overcrowded cities.

It may be that because of the worldwide media we are just more aware of these problems. The media may even contribute to this problem in other ways, too. Neil Postman has argued that a visual media culture like ours has adversely affected much of what we do. Postman argues that the media (qua media) has denigrated us into an entertainment culture, which, in turn, has adversely affected journalism, religion, politics, and the teaching profession. We no longer think as rationally as in a print type culture. We seek to be entertained. Thus we are *Amusing Ourselves to Death*.[3]

Besides, we can see plenty of moral progress. We abhor slavery. Women, gay men, lesbians, and African Americans have gained many needed rights in the West, along with freethinkers. We are more health conscious with the foods we eat, and there is a movement against smoking. We no longer have lynchings in the West. When we do execute a murderer, we've come up with more humane ways to do it, and many people are against the death penalty altogether. Richard Dawkins talks about the "steadily shifting standard of what is morally acceptable." Hitler, who is widely regarded as a monster, "would not have stood out in the time of Caligula or of Genghis Khan. . . . Hitler seems especially evil only by the more benign standards of our time." Even Donald Rumsfeld, who "sounds so callous and odious today, would have sounded like a bleeding-heart liberal if he had said the same things during the Second World War."[4]

Just remember this, prior to our day and age, Christianity was the "myth" that held us together. And since the Enlightenment, scholars have been dismantling it piece by piece. With it in decline, pluralism reigns for many people, along with many bankrupt ethical people. There is probably no longer a uniting myth to Western societies. And while Schaeffer and Craig may be right to point out our moral malaise, the real problem isn't necessarily the loss of Christian truth and values in our society. The real problem is that there is no longer something that unites or binds us together. That may be more of our problem in America today, not the fact that we're rejecting Christianity. I think human dignity, freedom, and democratic capitalism should unite us as a society, and it does. I also believe we should export these values around the globe; not only because it's good for humanity, but it's also in our own self-interest as an American society at war with Islamic terrorists who seek our demise.

In the second place, let me say that anyone who tries to show that no society can be a good society without Christianity needs a history lesson. She needs to study some of the great societies of the past, like Greece during the golden ages, or the Roman Empire, or several of the dynasties in ancient China, or the Islamic empire under Muhammad, or the historic Japanese culture. None of these societies were influenced by Christianity, but they were great societies by all standards of history. And yes, there was corruption in every one of these societies, just like we see in any ancient or modern society. But even biblical Judaism and Christian America have had corruption in their societies too.

If Christians want to maintain that a Christian society is a better society, then just let them volunteer to go back in time to medieval Christianity and see if they like it. Probably all Christians today would be branded as heretics and persecuted or burned to death. And if today's Christians will say that medieval Christianity doesn't represent true Christianity, then which Christian society truly represents Christianity? Even in the first few years of the early church there was corruption. There was sin in the camp (Acts 5); grumbling about food (Acts 6); and a major dispute that threatened to split the church (Acts 10–11, 15; Galatians 2). Then there were the constant disputes among these Christians over a very wide assortment of issues (1 and 2 Corinthians).

Christian inclusivist scholar Charles Kimball argues that certain tendencies within religions cause evil. "Religious structures and doctrines can be used almost like weapons."[5] Religion becomes evil, according to Kimball, whenever religion: has absolute truth claims; demands blind obedience; tries to establish the ideal society; utilizes the end justifies any means when defending their group identity; or sees itself in a holy war. He says, "A strong case can be made that the history of Christianity contains considerably more violence and destruction than that of most other major religions."[6]

Christians like Dinesh D'Souza claim that the crimes of Christianity's past were not that big of a deal when compared to the mass killings under recent atheist regimes in the past century, especially Mao, Stalin, Hitler, and Pol Pot.[7] However, if the atrocities committed by professing Christians of the past do not represent true® Christianity, and if many Muslims today can say that the militant Muslim terrorists do not represent true® Islam, then atheists can do likewise and argue the crimes done in the name of atheism do not represent true® atheism, and I do.

D'Souza needs to understand that there is a big difference in the means people had to commit these crimes. In our modern era we have guns and tanks and bombs. People with guns kill more people than people without them. So I wonder how many more people would've been killed in the past by Christians if they had this arsenal at their disposal? Surely many, many more. D'Souza excuses some of the wars done in the name of religion as based on ethnic rivalries and/or over territory. But surely it can be said likewise that Hitler's war was based on territorial expansion and ethnic tension.

D'Souza also fails to realize the role of a dictator in a totalitarian government. Most all of the Russian tsars, for instance, were hated because they were cruel. Ivan the Terrible was one such example unrelated to his religious preferences. Saddam Hussein was cruel too. Most dictators ruled with an iron fist because of fear they would be assassinated. Those of us who have never been a dictator will not understand this. So they terrorize their people into fearing them. This is just what most dictators do, and it's a defense mechanism unrelated to their religion, or none at all.

The goal of world domination under a totalitarian regime by cultic societies was the dominating factor in the atrocities committed during the past century in world history, not atheism. Case in point is the fact that Hitler, Mao, and Stalin, weren't the only ones killing masses of people at that time in history. Japan was a religious society that worshiped the emperor as "a god." The Japanese committed many atrocities against other people, especially the Chinese. Mussolini was a Catholic whose thugs were largely practicing Roman Catholics.

The fact is that religious views, or nonreligious views, are used by people to justify whatever they want to do. It's not clear Hitler was an atheist, but he was certainly the type of maniac who would use anything he could to advance his egomaniacal power over people. Besides, Hitler had the support of Germany, which was a Christian nation at the heart of the Protestant Reformation. These German Christians had a built-in hatred for the Jews due to centuries of Christian propaganda that they were "Christ killers," most notably from Martin Luther himself, which made it easy for them to plunder, rape, and kill up to six million of them (see note).[8] The bottom line is that civilized people today are less likely to commit such crimes because we have all learned our lessons from history, both Christians and atheists. Why? Because that's how human beings learn our morality, through trial and error and the lessons of history.

I just don't see where a Christian society is a better one. And even if Christianity was the main motivator in starting most all early American universities, most all of our hospitals and many food kitchens, and the like, these things still would have been started anyway, if for no reason other than necessity. Every society has these kinds of things in it, not just those dominated by Christianity. It just so happened that Christianity has been the dominant religion in America for a couple of centuries; that's all. Besides, these things were probably not started by Christian churches out of pure altruism, or a desire for a better society, but as a way for church groups to convert people. After all, who are most vulnerable to the Christian message? They are the sick (hospitals), the poor (food kitchens), and young people leaving home for the first time to enter universities (which in our earlier days were started to train preachers).

In the third place, rather than religions producing societies, societies produced religions because of the search for meaning. We have a great intellectual need to make sense of something that cannot be made sense of, to find purpose when there isn't any to be found, and to find meaning in a meaningless world. This need to make sense of the universe will tend to push us to believe in God, for then we have meaning and security in knowing who we are, why we're here, and where we're going. Paul Kurtz effectively argued that this "transcendental temptation" is why it seems religious beliefs dominate the landscape even in the midst of modernity, and that it "is no doubt the deepest source of the religious impulse, the transcendental yearning for something more."[9]

In my opinion, this human need may be the reason why people believe in God in the first place, not because of the arguments pro and con. As humans we simply cannot bear to believe we have no ultimate purpose in life and that our existence is absurd. We think we're more important than that.

Harvard professor and evolutionary psychologist Steven Pinker has argued that the mysteries of our existence first provoked the belief in God or gods in the first place. He asked, "who benefits" from the pervasive religious belief in our world? There are the "consumers of religion," who are confronted with the mysteries of death, dreams, and questions about existence. Then there are the "producers of religious beliefs," who seek to come up with answers to these questions. As these producers come up with satisfying answers to these mysteries, the consumers grant them power, some measure of fame, and money. In this way everyone benefits, but the producers benefit much more. In this way religion is propagated all over the globe.[10]

And what better answers are there than that we are significant and that life does have meaning? These are the answers we desperately want to hear, so it's no surprise to me that there are more religious believers in the world. The producers of religion offer solutions that are very fulfilling indeed, especially the story about a God who cared about us so much that he came down in Jesus and died in our place! The question is how many people would follow a "producer" if his answer was that life is ultimately in vain?

When these originating producers of religion gained a foothold of power in a society and that society economically and militarily flourished, it validated those religious answers. According to Edward O. Wilson, "All great civilizations were spread by conquest, and among the chief beneficiaries were the religions validating them."[11] In my opinion, Christianity is a legendary development from a person named Jesus that lucked its way into political power.

In the fourth place, we need to consider the dangers of someone who claims to have ultimate values in life. Edward T. Babinski has documented Christianity's "grotesque past" where he discusses some of the atrocities committed by Christian people who claimed to have had ultimate values. Christians don't have a good track record when it comes to slavery, wars, inquisitions, witch hunts, scientific progress, and so on.[12] The Crusaders had an ultimate reason for slaughtering Muslims in Jerusalem, didn't they? The German church was behind Hitler, claiming ultimate purposes too. There are abortion clinic bombers who claim to have ultimate values. Right now there are American Christian Dispensationalists who support the Jews no matter what they do, because they have "ultimate" knowledge that the Jews are linked with biblical prophecy. These Christians have actually helped perpetuate the conflict we now have with the Muslims of the world.

Consider also the harm that has been done by Christians with regard to inhibiting scientific progress through some inaccurate notions about the nature of human beings, by forbidding stem cell research, prohibiting someone by law from following a desire for a same-sex relationship, impeding the progress of feminism, advocating some forms of censorship, intolerance, bigotry, and discrimination to those who are agnostics and atheists.

Militant Muslims have their own ultimate purposes and values, don't they? They are extremely dangerous people because they will die for their ultimate cause and go to heaven to be with seventy-two virgins (what those virgins did wrong to be in heaven at their service I just don't know). As John Debbyshire comments, "You can point to people who were improved by faith, but you can also see people made worse by it. Anyone want to argue that, say, Mohammed Atta was made a better person by his faith? Can Christianity make you a worse person? I'm sure it can. If you're a person with, for example, a self-righteous conviction of your own moral superiority, well, getting religion is just going to inflame that conviction."[13]

According to Bertrand Russell, "one of the most interesting and harmful delusions to which men and nations can be subjected is that of imagining themselves special instruments of the Divine Will. . . . Cromwell was persuaded that he was the Divinely appointed instrument of justice for suppressing Catholics and malignants. Andrew Jackson was the agent of *Manifest Destiny* in freeing North America from the incubus of Sabbath-breaking Spaniards." Of course, such a political program "assumes a knowledge of the Divine purposes to which no rational man can lay claim, and that in the execution of them it justifies a ruthless cruelty which would be condemned if our program had a merely mundane origin. It is good to know that God is on our side, but a little confusing when you find the enemy equally convinced of the opposite. . . . Belief in a divine mission is one of the many factors of certainty that have afflicted the human race. . . . Most of the greatest evils that man has afflicted upon man have come through people feeling quite certain about something which, in fact, was false."[14]

The bottom line is, in Steven Weinberg's words, "with or without religion, good people can behave well and bad people can do evil; but for good people to do evil— that takes religion."[15] Pascal is reported to have said, "Men never do evil so completely and cheerfully as when they do it from religious conviction." In light of Christianity's past, it would be better if Christians didn't consider the values that they have to be ultimate ones. Better is a healthy measure of skepticism about such claims.

In the fifth place, while there may be no ultimate reasons for being a good person, as Craig argues, there are plenty of nonultimate reasons for being good.[16] There is no meaning for human existence beyond the life we humans share on earth. Any meaning is to be found here and now without the help of God, and there is plenty of meaning and purpose to be found.

Here then, are some nonultimate reasons for being good. Human beings do not like pain, unless they are testing their own physical endurance level for an upcoming sports contest, in which case the pain is worth the reward. There is mental pain, social pain, physical pain, financial pain, and so on. The avoidance of pain for humans is a huge motivator. This means the opposite is the seeking of holistic pleasure. Holistic pleasure, then, is its own reward, as Plato and Aristotle argued.

The values of tolerance, family, and friendship in a political democracy under democratic capitalism provide a society with the best chance to avoid pain for most people in it. According to democratic capitalism, for instance, we receive money from people we serve, so we serve people to get what we want. Anyone who doesn't serve others in this way will not be financially rewarded. If we want fame and power, the same thing applies. We must have something that people want, and so by serving people, we get what we want. As social human beings we need approval from others, which is a motivator for doing good deeds and for contributing to society.

Like most people, my wife and I are good to others. We like the approval of people, and we like knowing we helped out in humanitarian ways. It gives us pleasure to please others, so we do. It makes us feel good about ourselves. That's not why we do it, but it's what we receive for doing it. And we need no ultimate values for this, either. It's just a better life when we have friends who we can count on in times of need because we were good to them in their times of need. When someone is shunned or ostracized as a human being, it's very painful, so it's in our best interests to be good people.

These reasons may not be ultimately enough, but I believe they are values everyone can share. Many Muslims want what we have in the Western world too. It was said by Bernard Lewis, who is an authority on Islam, that when American planes were flying over Iran to drop bombs on Iraq, people held up signs that read, "Drop bombs here!" People all over the world want what the Western world has in a free society based upon democratic capitalism. When they have a chance, they "vote with their feet."

You don't need an "ultimate" anything to live life in this world. There just aren't any ultimacies. But there are nonultimate reasons. And while I don't think what I do in life will matter for all of eternity, it matters very much, both to the ones I love and to me. This life is all there is: a short blip of existence in the cosmos. So it makes what I do here of utmost importance. I should therefore be motivated to give all I have today, for this is all I have.

Michael Shermer asks the Christian, "What would you do if there were no God? Would you commit robbery, rape, and murder, or would you continue being a good and moral person? Either way the question is a debate stopper. If the answer is that you would soon turn to robbery, rape, or murder, then this is a moral indictment of your character, indicating you are not to be trusted because if, for any reason, you were to turn away from your belief in God, your true immoral nature would emerge. . . . If the answer is that you would continue being good and moral, then apparently you can be good without God. QED."[17]

Here's what atheist Bertrand Russell said: "United with his fellow men by the strongest of all ties, the tie of a common doom, the free man finds that a new vision is with him always, shedding over every daily task the light of love. The life of man is a long march through the night, surrounded by invisible foes, tortured by weariness and pain, toward a goal that few can hope to reach, and where none may tarry. One by one, as they march, our comrades vanish from our sight, seized by the silent orders of omnipotent death. Very brief is the time in which we can help them, in which their happiness or misery is decided. Be it ours to shed sunshine on their path, to lighten their sorrows by the balm of sympathy, to give them the pure joy of never-tiring affection, to strengthen failing courage, to instill faith in hours of despair . . . let us remember that they are fellow sufferers in the same darkness, actors in the same tragedy with ourselves. And so when their day is over . . . be it ours to feel that, where they suffered, where they failed, no deed of ours was the cause."[18] This is my goal.

But what about someone who is self-seeking in all of his ways, and harms people who get in his way? Well, we ostracize these people, and we lock up many of them in our jails and prisons. They are not deemed by any society to contribute to the well-being of that society. So the avoidance of any kind of pleasure that leads to the pain of prison is better than unmitigated pleasure. And since we cannot turn our character on and off like a faucet without changing who we are by degrees, we'd be better off being good people in any society we live in.

On the fringes of society we will have some sociopaths, thieves, and sexual predators who seek to do others wrong for their selfish pleasure. This is unavoidable in a free society containing human beings with all of our psychological problems and undisciplined desires. But that isn't what any society considers the norm, and what they do certainly isn't rational, either. We put people in jail for seriously harming others. We do the same things to Christians on the fringes of our society who think they have an ultimate goal in life and who seek to do others wrong, like the KKK or Catholic priests who are molesters. They too do harm. The monthly circular *Free Thought Today*, published by Dan Barker's "Freedom From Religion" organization, documents many crimes done by Christians, from embezzlement to rape to molestation. You'll have that on both sides of the fence, whether religious or not.

In the sixth place, if I am correct that there isn't a reasoned hope, then no one has any ultimate meaning in this life, precisely because this life is the only one we have to live. Those Christians who think they have a reasoned hope are living their life based upon a delusion. They have a false and irrational hope, but just don't know it. They are simply deluded into thinking their lives have some grand ultimate purpose. So who's better off? Someone who lives a life of delusion, doing things because she thinks it will matter for eternity, along with the daily guilt for not having lived up to those standards, or someone who lives with her feet planted squarely on the ground?

Consider the medieval monks, for instance. They lived ascetic lives on the bare bones of existence, spending their lives reading a biblical text that was false, rather than living the fullest life possible. Consider modern-day Catholic priests, who live life without knowing the warmth of an intimate embrace in the arms of a woman and the joys of being a father and a grandfather. Consider the fundamentalist Baptist minister who never may know what it's like to get drunk. Consider the many nights Christians spend evangelizing others, when those same nights might be better spent with their families or friends. Consider the time many Christians spend reading the Bible, when they could enjoy the great novels of their day. Consider the joy one might have in alleviating the person who is suffering for the pure joy of it, rather than doing it for some false heavenly reward. Consider the money that was spent in building great cathedrals and temples to this false sense of ultimate reality that could be better spent on the needs of people, or with what is leftover, a cruise in the Bahamas.

Contrary to the whole Christian cultural apologetic, *all is vanity when you live a life of delusion!* The Christian life is ultimately in vain, because it is built on a false hope.[19]

NOTES

1. William Lane Craig, *Reasonable Faith: Christianity and Apologetics* (Wheaton, IL: Crossway Books, 1994), formerly, *Apologetics: An Introduction* (Chicago: Moody Press, 1984), pp. 31–53. See also J. P. Moreland, *Scaling the Secular City: A Defense of Christianity* (Grand Rapids, MI: Baker Book House, 1987), chap. 4.

2. Michael Martin, *Atheism: A Philosophical Justification* (Philadelphia: Temple University Press, 1990), p. 15.

3. This is the title to his book *Amusing Ourselves to Death: Public Discourse in the Age of Show Business* (New York: Penguin Books, 1985).

4. Richard Dawkins, *The God Delusion* (New York: Houghton Mifflin, 2006), pp. 268–69.

5. Charles Kimball, *When Religion Becomes Evil* (New York: HarperSanFrancisco, 2002), p. 32.

6. Ibid., p. 27.

7. Dinesh D'Souza, *What's So Great about Christianity* (Washington, DC: Regnery, 2007), pp. 213–21.

8. On my blog, Dr. Hector Avalos summarized this case, in "Avalos Contra Weikart":

Luther's seven-point plan is similar to that of Nazi policy. In order to understand this point, let's quickly summarize Luther's seven-point plan, which is found in "Martin Luther, On the Jews and Their Lies" (translated by Martin H. Bertram, in *Luther's Works: The Christian in Society IV*, ed. Franklin Sherman [55 volumes; Philadelphia: Fortress Press, 1971], pp. 268–72:

"First, to set fire to their synagogues or schools and to bury and cover with dirt whatever will not burn, so that no man will ever again see a stone or cinder of them.

This is to be done in honor of our Lord and Christendom, so that God might see that we are Christians, and do not condone or knowingly tolerate such public lying, cursing, blaspheming of his son and of his Christians. . . .

Second, I advise that their houses also be razed and destroyed. . . .

Third, I advise that all their prayer books and Talmudic writings, in which such idolatry, lies, cursing, and blasphemy are taught, be taken from them.

Fourth, I advise that their rabbis be forbidden to teach henceforth on pain of loss of life and limb. . . .

Fifth, I advise that safe-conduct on the highways by abolished completely for the Jews.

Sixth, I advise that usury be prohibited to them, and that all cash and treasures of silver and gold be taken from them for safekeeping. . . .

Seventh, I recommend putting a flail, an ax, a hoe, a distaff, or a spindle into the hands of young strong Jews and Jewesses and letting them earn their bread in the sweat of their brow, as was imposed on the children of Adam (Gen. 3:19)."

Avalos tells us: "Every single point in Luther's plan was implemented by Nazi policy."

9. Paul Kurtz, *The Transcendental Temptation* (Amherst, NY: Prometheus Books, 1991), p. 21.

10. Steven Pinker, "The Evolutionary Psychology of Religion," *Free Thought Today* (January/February 2005); see also Daniel C. Dennett, *Breaking the Spell: Religion as a Natural Phenomenon* (New York: Viking 2006); Michael Shermer, *How We Believe: The Search for God in an Age of Science* (New York: W. H. Freeman, 2000); and Dawkins, *The God Delusion*, pp. 161–207.

11. Edward O. Wilson, *Consilience: The Unity of Knowledge* (New York: Knopf, 1998), p. 44.

12. Edward T. Babinski, *Leaving the Fold* (Amherst, NY: Prometheus Books, 2003), pp. 35–60 and also online in an essay called "The Civil War, Slavery, and the Bible," http://www.edwardtbabinski.us. On witch hunts see Carl Sagan's book *The Demon Haunted World* (New York: Random House, 1986), pp. 118–23, 406–13. See also Brian P. Levack, *The Witch-Hunt in Early Modern Europe*, 3rd ed. (London: Pearson Education, 2006).

13. John Debbyshire, "God & Me," *National Review Online*.

14. Bertrand Russell, "Ideas That Have Harmed Mankind," in *Unpopular Essays* (New York: Simon & Schuster, 1950), pp. 146–65.

15. Quoted by him in *Science and Religion: Are they Compatible?* ed. Paul Kurtz (Amherst, NY: Prometheus Books, 2003), p. 40. On the dangers of religious faith in a modern world containing weapons of mass destruction, see Sam Harris, *The End of Faith: Religion, Terror and the Future of Reason* (New York: Norton, 2005). See also Dawkins, *The God Delusion*, pp. 279–308.

16. On my blog I argue that "rational self-interest" can account for morality, and that the Christian actually operates by the same moral standard. Go to www.debunkingchristianity .blogspot.com and do a search for "An Atheistic Ethic."

17. Michael Shermer, *The Science of Good and Evil* (New York: Henry Holt, 2005), pp. 154–55.

18. Bertrand Russell, "A Free Man's Worship," in *Why I Am Not a Christian* (New York: Touchstone, 1957), pp. 104–16.

19. For further discussions on the values and meaning of life without God, see Louise M. Antony, *Philosophers without Gods: Meditations on Atheism and the Secular Life* (Oxford:

Oxford University Press, 2007); Albert Camus, *The Myth of Sisyphus and Other Essays* (New York: Knopf, 1955); Daniel C. Dennett, *Darwin's Dangerous Idea: Evolution and the Meanings of Life* (New York: Simon & Schuster; 1996); J. L. Mackie, *Ethics: Inventing Right and Wrong* (New York: Penguin Books, 1977); Kai Nielsen, *Ethics without God* (London: Pemberton Books, 1973); Kurt Baier and Kai Nielsen, *The Meaning of Life*, ed. E. D. Klemke (New York: Oxford University Press, 1981); Richard Robinson, *An Atheist's Values* (London: Clarendon Press, 1964); Kai Nielsen, *Naturalism and Religion* (Amherst, NY: Prometheus Books, 2001); Richard Carrier, *Sense and Goodness without God* (Bloomington, IN: Authorhouse, 2005); Michael Martin, *Atheism, Morality, and Meaning* (Amherst, NY: Prometheus Books, 2002); Erik J. Wielenberg, *Value and Virtue in a Godless Universe* (Cambridge: Cambridge University Press, 2005), and Dawkins, *The God Delusion*, pp. 209–33.

BIBLIOGRAPHY OF SELECTED WORKS

Abraham, William J. *An Introduction to the Philosophy of Religion*. Englewood Cliffs, NJ: Prentice-Hall, 1985.

Achtemeier, Paul J., ed. *Harper Bible Dictionary*. 1st ed. San Francisco: Harper & Row, 1985.

———. *The Inspiration of Scripture*. Philadelphia: Westminster Press, 1980.

Adams, Edward. *Stars Will Fall from Heaven: Cosmic Catastrophe in the New Testament and Its World*. Edinburgh: T. & T. Clark, 2007.

Adams, Robert Merrihew. "Kierkegaard's Arguments against Objective Reasoning in Religion," *Monist* 60, no. 2 (1977).

Allen, Diogenes. *Christian Belief in a Postmodern World*. Louisville, KY: Westminster Press, 1989.

Allison, Dale C. *Jesus of Nazareth: Millenarian Prophet*. Minneapolis, MN: Fortress, 1998.

———. *Resurrecting Jesus*. New York: T. & T. Clark, 2005.

Anderson, Bernard W. *Understanding the Old Testament*. Englewood Cliffs, NJ: Prentice-Hall, 1957.

Antony, Louise M., ed. *Philosophers without Goals: Meditations on Atheism and the Secular Life*. Oxford: Oxford University Press, 2007.

Archer, Gleason. *The Encyclopedia of Bible Difficulties*. Grand Rapids, MI: Zondervan, 1982.

Avalos, Hector. *The End of Biblical Studies*. Amherst, NY: Prometheus Books, 2007.

———. *Fighting Words: The Origins of Religious Violence*. Amherst, NY: Prometheus Books, 2005.

Babinski, Edward T. *Leaving the Fold*. Amherst, NY: Prometheus Books, 2003.

Badham, Paul, and Linda Badham. *Death and Immortality in the Religions of the World*. New York: Paragon Press, 1987.

Baier, Kurt, and Kai Nielsen. *The Meaning of Life*. Edited by E. D. Klemke. New York: Oxford University Press, 1981.

Barbour, Ian. *Religion in an Age of Science*. New York: Harper & Row, 1990.

———. *When Science Meets Religion: Enemies, Strangers, or Partners?* New York: HarperCollins, 2000.

Barker, Dan. *Losing Faith in Faith: From Preacher to Atheist.* Madison, WI: Freedom From Religion Foundation, 1992.

Barr, James, *Beyond Fundamentalism.* Philadelphia: Westminster Press, 1984.

———. *Holy Scripture: Canon, Authority, Criticism.* Philadelphia: Westminster Press, 1983.

Barrow, John D., and Frank J. Tipler. *The Anthropic Cosmological Principle.* Oxford: Oxford University Press, 1988.

Barth, Karl. *The Word of God and the Word of Man.* New York: Harper & Row, 1928.

Bartsch, Hans Werner, ed. *Kerygma and Myth: A Theological Debate.* New York: Harper & Row, 1961.

Bebbington, D. W. *Patterns of History: A Christian View.* Downers Grove, IL: InterVarsity Press, 1979.

Behe, Michael. *Darwin's Black Box: The Biochemical Challenge to Evolution.* New York: Simon & Schuster, 1996.

Betty, L. Stafford, with Bruce Cordell. "The Anthropic Teleological Argument." *International Quarterly* 27, no. 4 (December 1987).

Beversluis, John. *C. S. Lewis and the Search for Rational Religion.* 2nd ed. Amherst, NY: Prometheus Books, 2007.

Biagioli, Mario. *Galileo, Courtier: The Practice of Science in the Culture of Absolutism.* Chicago: University of Chicago Press, 1993.

Blocher, Henri. *In the Beginning: The Opening Chapters of Genesis.* Translated by David G. Preston. Downers Grove, IL: InterVarsity Press, 1984.

Boa, Kenneth D., and Robert M. Bowman Jr. *Faith Has Its Reasons: An Integrative Approach to Defending Christianity.* Colorado Springs, CO: Paternoster, 2006.

Borg, Marcus. *The God We Never Knew.* New York: HarperSanFransisco, 1997.

———. *Meeting Jesus again for the First Time.* New York: HarperSanFrancisco, 1994.

Borg, Marcus, and N. T. Wright. *The Meaning of Jesus: Two Visions.* New York: HarperSanFrancisco, 1999.

Brodsky, Garry, et al., eds. *Contemporary Readings in Social and Political Ethics.* Amherst, NY: Prometheus Books, 1984.

Brody, Baruch, ed. *Readings in the Philosophy of Religion.* Englewood Cliffs, NJ: Prentice-Hall, 1974.

Brogaard, Betty. *Dare to Think for Yourself: A Journey from Faith to Reason.* Frederick, MD: Publish America, 2004.

Brown, Colin, ed. *New International Dictionary of New Testament Theology.* 4 vols. Grand Rapids, MI: Zondervan, 1986.

———. *Philosophy and the Christian Faith.* Downers Grove, IL: InterVarsity Press, 1968.

Brown, Raymond E. *Birth of the Messiah.* Updated ed. Anchor Bible Reference Library. New York: Doubleday, 1999.

Bruce, F. F. *New Testament History.* New York: Doubleday, 1969.

Bultmann, Rudolph. *The History of the Synoptic Tradition.* 2nd ed. New York: Harper & Row, 1968.

Cahn, Steven M., and David Shatz, eds. *Contemporary Philosophy of Religion.* Oxford: Oxford University Press, 1982.

Callahan, Tim. *Secret Origins of the Bible.* Altadena, CA: Millennium Press, 2002.

Carrier, Richard. *Sense and Goodness without God.* Bloomington, IN: Authorhouse, 2005.

Charlesworth, James. *The Old Testament Pseudepigrapha and the New Testament.* Cambridge: Cambridge University Press, 1985.

———. *The Pseudepigrapha and Modern Research with a Supplement.* Chico, CA: Scholars Press, 1981.

Cialdini, Robert B. *Influence: The Psychology of Persuasion*. New York: William Morrow, 1993.

Clark, Kelly James. *Philosophers Who Believe*. Downers Grove, IL: InterVarsity Press, 1993.

Clifford, W. K. "The Ethics of Belief." In *Lectures and Essays*. New York: Macmillan, 1897.

Copan, Paul. *"How Do You Know You're Not Wrong."* Grand Rapids, MI: Baker Book House, 2005.

———. *"That's Just Your Interpretation."* Grand Rapids, MI: Baker Book House, 2001.

Copan, Paul, and Ronald K. Tacelli, eds. *Jesus' Resurrection: Fact or Figment? A Debate between William Lane Craig and Gerd Lüdemann*. Downers Grove, IL: InterVarsity Press, 2000.

Cowan, Steven B., ed. *Five Views on Apologetics*. Grand Rapids, MI: Zondervan, 2000.

Craig, William Lane. *Apologetics: An Introduction*. Chicago: Moody Press, 1984.

———. *The Cosmological Argument from Plato to Leibniz*. New York: Macmillan, 1980.

———. "The Guard at the Tomb." *New Testament Studies* 30 (1984): 273–81.

———. *Hard Questions, Real Answers*. Wheaton, IL: Crossway Books, 2003.

———. *The Kalam Cosmological Argument*. London: Macmillan, 1979.

———. "'Lest Anyone Should Fall': A Middle Knowledge Perspective on Perseverance and Apostolic Warnings." *International Journal for Philosophy of Religion* 29 (1991): 65–74.

———. "Must the Beginning of the Universe Have a Personal Cause? A Rejoinder." *Faith and Philosophy* 19, no. 2 (April 2002): 233–44.

———. *The Only Wise God: The Compatibility of Divine Foreknowledge*. Grand Rapids, MI: Baker Book House, 1987.

———. *Reasonable Faith: Christian Truth and Apologetics*. Wheaton, IL: Crossway Books, 1994; 3rd ed., 2008.

Craig, William Lane, and Paul Copan. *Creation Out of Nothing: A Biblical, Philosophical, and Scientific Exploration*. Grand Rapids, MI: Baker Academic Books, 2004.

Craig, William Lane, and Gerd Lüdemann. *Jesus' Resurrection: Fact or Figment?* Downers Grove, IL: InterVarsity Press, 2000.

Craig, William Lane, and Quentin Smith. *Theism, Atheism, and Big Bang Cosmology*. Oxford: Oxford University Press, 1993.

Crick, Francis. *The Astonishing Hypothesis: The Scientific Search for the Soul*. New York: Charles Scribner's Sons, 1994.

Crocket, William, ed. *Four Views of Hell*. Grand Rapids, MI: Zondervan, 1992.

Crossan, John Dominic. *The Birth of Christianity: Discovering What Happened in the Years Immediately after the Execution of Jesus*. New York: Harper & Row, 1998.

———. *The Historical Jesus: The Life of a Mediterranean Jewish Peasant*. New York: HarperSanFrancisco, 1991.

———. *Jesus: A Revolutionary Biography*. New York: HarperCollins, 1989.

———. *Who Killed Jesus?* New York: HarperSanFrancisco, 1995.

Davies, Brian. *An Introduction to the Philosophy of Religion*. Oxford: Oxford University Press, 1993.

———. *Reality of God and the Problem of Evil*. London: Continuum International, 2006.

Davies, Paul. *God and the New Physics*. New York: Pelican Books, 1984.

———. *Superforce: The Search for a Grand Unified Theory of Nature*. New York: Touchstone, 2002.

Davis, Stephen T., ed. *Encountering Evil*. Atlanta: John Knox Press, 1981.

———, ed. *Encountering Jesus: A Debate on Christology*. Atlanta: John Knox Press, 1988.

———. "Is It Possible to Know That Jesus Was Raised from the Dead." *Faith and Philosophy* (April 1984).

———. *Logic and the Nature of God*. Grand Rapids, MI: Eerdmans, 1983.

————. *Risen Indeed: Making Sense of the Resurrection.* Grand Rapids, MI: Eerdmans, 1993.

Dawkins, Richard. *The Blind Watchmaker: Why the Evidence of Evolution Reveals a Universe without Design.* New York: Norton, 1996.

————. *Climbing Mount Improbable.* New York: Norton, 1997.

————. *The God Delusion.* Boston: Houghton Mifflin, 2006.

Delaney, C. F., ed. *Rationality and Religious Belief.* Notre Dame, IN: University of Notre Dame Press, 1979.

Dembski, William A. *The Design Revolution: Answering the Toughest Questions about Intelligent Design.* Downers Grove, IL: InterVarsity Press, 2004.

Dembski, William A., and Michael Ruse, eds. *Debating Design: From Darwin to DNA.* Cambridge: Cambridge University Press, 2004.

Dennett, Daniel C. *Breaking the Spell: Religion as a Natural Phenomenon.* New York: Viking, 2006.

————. *Consciousness Explained.* Boston: Little, Brown, 1991.

————. *Darwin's Dangerous Idea: Evolution and the Meanings of Life.* New York: Simon & Schuster, 1996.

Dever, William G. *Did God Have a Wife? Archaeology and Folk Religion in Ancient Israel.* Grand Rapids, MI: Eerdmans, 2005.

————. *Recent Archaeological Discoveries and Biblical Research.* Seattle: University of Washington Press, 1990.

————. *Who Were the Early Israelites and Where Did They Come From?* Grand Rapids, MI: Eerdmans, 2003.

Douglass, Frederick. *Narrative of the Life of Frederick Douglass: An American Slave.* Oxford: Oxford University Press, 1999.

Drange, Theodore. *Nonbelief and Evil: Two Arguments for the Nonexistence of God.* Amherst, NY: Prometheus Books, 1998.

Draper, Paul. "A Critique of the Kalam Cosmological Argument." In *Philosophy of Religion: An Anthology.* 4th ed. Edited by Louis P. Pojman. Belmont, CA: Wadsworth, 2002.

D'Souza, Dinesh. *What's So Great about Christianity?* Washington, DC: Regnery, 2007.

Dulles, Avery Cardinal. *A History of Apologetics.* San Francisco: Ignatious Press, 2005.

Dunn, James D. G. *Evidence for Jesus.* Louisville, KY: Westminster Press, 1985.

————. *The Living Word.* Philadelphia: Fortress Press, 1987.

————. *Unity and Diversity in the New Testament: An Inquiry into the Character of Earliest Christianity.* 3rd ed. London: SCM, 2006.

Earman, John. *Hume's Abject Failure: The Argument against Miracles.* Oxford: Oxford University Press, 2000.

Edwards, David L., and John Stott. *Evangelical Essentials: A Liberal–Evangelical Dialogue.* Downers Grove, IL: InterVarsity Press, 1988.

Edwards, Paul, editor in chief. *The Encyclopedia of Philosophy.* 8 vols. New York: Macmillan, 1967.

Ehrman, Bart D. *God's Problem: How the Bible Fails to Answer Our Most Important Question —Why We Suffer.* New York: HarperOne, 2008.

————. *Jesus: Apocalyptic Prophet of the New Millennium.* Oxford: Oxford University Press, 2001.

————. *Lost Christianities: The Battles for Scripture and the Faiths We Never Knew.* Oxford: Oxford University Press, 2005.

————. *Lost Scriptures: Books That Did Not Make It into the New Testament.* Oxford: Oxford University Press, 2005.

————. *Misquoting Jesus: The Story behind Who Changed the Bible and Why*. New York: HarperCollins, 2005.

————. *The Orthodox Corruption of Scripture*. Oxford: Oxford University Press, 1993.

Evans, C. Stephen. *Philosophy of Religion*. Downers Grove, IL: InterVarsity Press, 1985.

————. *Subjectivity and Religious Belief*. Grand Rapids, MI: Eerdmans, 1978.

Everitt, Nicholas. *The Non-existence of God*. New York: Routledge, 2004.

Feenstra, Ronald, and Cornelius Plantinga Jr. *Trinity, Incarnation, and Atonement*. South Bend, IN: University of Notre Dame Press, 1989.

Feinberg, Joel., ed. *Reason and Responsibility*. 9th ed. Belmont CA: Wadsworth, 1996.

Finkelstein, Israel, and Neil Asher Silberman. *The Bible Unearthed: Archaeology's New Vision of Ancient Israel and the Origin of Its Sacred Texts*. New York: Free Press, 2001.

————. *David and Solomon: In Search of the Bible's Sacred Kings and the Roots of the Western Tradition*. New York: Free Press, 2006.

Fitzmyer, Joseph A. *The One Who Is to Come*. Grand Rapids, MI: Eerdmans, 2007.

Flew, Anthony. *God, Freedom, and Immortality: A Critical Analysis*. Amherst, NY: Prometheus Books, 1984.

————. *The Logic of Mortality*. London: Blackwell, 1987.

————. *The Presumption of Atheism*. Amherst, NY: Prometheus Books, 1976.

Flew, Anthony, and Gary R. Habermas. *Did Jesus Rise from the Dead?* New York: Harper & Row, 1987.

Fogelin, Robert J. *A Defense of Hume on Miracles*. Princeton, NJ: Princeton University Press, 2003.

Forrest, Barbara. "Methodological Naturalism and Philosophical Naturalism: Clarifying the Connection." *Philo* 3, no. 2 (Fall–Winter 2000).

Fox, Robin Lane. *The Unauthorized Version: Truth and Fiction in the Bible*. New York: Knopf, 1992.

Frazer, James G. *Folklore in the Old Testament: Studies in Comparative Religion Legend and Law*. Whitefish, MT: Kessinger Publishing, 2003.

Fredricksen, Paula. *From Jesus to Christ*. New Haven, CT: Yale University Press, 1988.

Freedman, David Noel, editor in chief. *Anchor Bible Dictionary*. New York: Doubleday, 1992.

Friedman, Richard Elliot. *The Bible with Sources Revealed*. New York: HarperOne, 2005.

————. *Who Wrote the Bible?* New York: Harper & Row, 1997.

Funk, Robert W. *Honest to Jesus: Jesus for a New Millennium*. New York: HarperSanFrancisco, 1996.

Funk, Robert W., and Roy W. Hoover. *The Five Gospels: The Search for the Authentic Words of Jesus*. Sonoma, CA: Polebridge Press, 1993.

Furlong, Andrew. *Tried for Heresy: A 21st Century Journey of Faith*. Winchester, UK: O Books, 2003.

Gale, Richard. *On the Nature and Existence of God*. Cambridge: Cambridge University Press, 1991.

Geisler, Norman. *Baker's Encyclopedia of Christian Apologetics*. Grand Rapids, MI: Baker Books, 1999.

————. *Christian Apologetics*. Grand Rapids, MI: Baker Books, 1976.

————. *Philosophy of Religion*. Grand Rapids, MI: Zondervan, 1978.

Geisler, Norman, and William D. Watkins. *Worlds Apart: A Handbook on Worldviews*. 2nd ed. Grand Rapids, MI: Baker Books, 1989.

Geivett, Douglas, and Gary Habermas, eds. *In Defense of Miracles: A Comprehensive Case for God's Action in History*. Downers Grove, IL: InterVarsity Press, 1997.

Gibson, John. *Genesis Vol. 1*. Philadelphia: Westminster Press, 1981.

Gowan, Donald. *From Eden to Babel: Genesis 1–11*. Grand Rapids, MI: Eerdmans, 1988.

Grant, Michael. *Myths of the Greeks and Romans*. Boston: Dutton, 1989.

Guinness, Os. *In Two Minds: The Dilemma of Doubt and How to Resolve It*. Downers Grove, IL: InterVarsity Press, 1976.

Harris, Sam. *The End of Faith: Religion, Terror, and the Future of Reason*. New York: Norton, 2004.

———. *Letter to a Christian Nation*. New York: Knopf, 2006.

Helm, Paul. *John Calvin's Ideas*. Oxford: Oxford University Press, 2006.

Helms, Randel McCraw. *The Bible against Itself: Why the Bible Seems to Contradict Itself*. Altadena, CA: Millennium Press, 2006.

———. *Gospel Fictions*. Amherst, NY: Prometheus Books, 1988.

———. *Who Wrote the Gospels?* Altadena, CA: Millennium Press, 1997.

Hick, John. *Death and Eternal Life*. Louisville, KY: Westminster/John Knox Press, 1994.

———. *Evil and the God of Love*. 2nd ed. New York: Harper & Row, 1977.

———. *An Interpretation of Religion*. New Haven, CT: Yale University Press, 1989.

———, ed. *The Metaphor of God Incarnate*. Louisville, KY: Westminster, 1993.

———. *The Myth of God Incarnate*. London: SCM, 1977.

———. *Philosophy of Religion*. 4th ed. Englewood Cliffs, NJ: Prentice-Hall, 1990.

Hitchens, Christopher. *God Is Not Great: Why Religion Poisons Everything*. New York: Twelve, 2007.

Hoffman, Joshua, and Gary S. Rosenkrantz. *The Divine Attributes*. London: Blackwell, 2002.

Holman, Joe E. *Project Bible Truth: A Minister Turns Atheist and Tells All*. Morrisville, NC: Lulu Press, 2008.

Holmes, Arthur F. *All Truth Is God's Truth*. Grand Rapids, MI: Eerdmans, 1977.

———. *Ethics: Approaching Moral Decisions*. Downers Grove, IL: InterVarsity Press, 1984.

Howard-Snyder, Daniel, ed. *The Evidential Argument from Evil*. Bloomington: Indiana University Press, 1996.

Hoyle, Fred, and N. C. Wickramasinghe. *Evolution from Space: A Theory of Cosmic Creationism*. New York: Simon & Schuster, 1981.

Hume, David. *Dialogues Concerning Natural Religion*. London: Thomas Nelson, 1947.

———. *An Enquiry Concerning Human Understanding*. 3rd ed. Revised by P. H. Nidditch. Oxford: Clarendon Press, 1975.

Hyers, Conrad. *The Meaning of Creation: Genesis and Modern Science*. Atlanta: John Knox Press, 1984.

James, William. *Essays in Pragmatism*. New York: Hafner Press, 1948.

Johnson, Phillip. *Darwin on Trial*. Washington, DC: Regnery, 1991.

Kaufmann, Walter. *Critique of Religion and Philosophy*. Princeton, NJ: Princeton University Press, 1958.

Kennedy, Ludovic. *All in the Mind: A Farewell to God*. London: Hodder & Stoughton, 1999.

Kenny, Anthony. *Faith and Reason*. New York: Columbia University Press, 1983.

———. *The Five Ways*. London: Routledge & Kegan Paul, 1969.

———. *The God of the Philosophers*. Oxford: Oxford University Press, 1987.

Kim, Jaegwon. *Philosophy of Mind*. Cambridge, MA: Westview Press, 1996.

Kimball, Charles. *When Religion Becomes Evil*. New York: HarperSanFrancisco, 2002.

King-Farlow, John, and William Niels Christensen. *Faith and the Life of Reason*. Dordrecht, Holland: D. Reidel, 1972.

Kirsch, Jonathon. *God against the Gods: The History of the War between Monotheism and Polytheism*. New York: Viking Compass, 2004.

———. *A History of the End of the World: How the Most Controversial Book in the Bible Changed the Course of Western Civilization*. New York: HarperCollins, 2006.

Kitcher, Philip. *Living with Darwin: Evolution, Design, and the Future of Faith*. Oxford: Oxford University Press, 2006.

Knopp, Richard A., and John D. Castelein, eds. *Taking Every Thought Captive: Essays in Honor of James D. Strauss*. Joplin, MO: College Press, 1997.

Kuhn, Thomas S. *The Structure of Scientific Revolutions*. 2nd ed. Chicago: University of Chicago Press, 1970.

Kurtz, Paul, ed. *Science and Religion: Are they Compatible?* Amherst, NY: Prometheus Books, 2003.

———. *The Transcendental Temptation*. Amherst, NY: Prometheus Books, 1991.

Kvanvig, Jonathan L. *The Problem of Hell*. Oxford: Oxford University Press, 2001.

Lapide, Pinchas. *The Resurrection of Jesus: A Jewish Perspective*. Minneapolis, MN: Augsburg Fortress, 1983.

Layman, C. Stephen. *The Shape of the Good: Christian Reflections on the Foundations of Ethics*. Notre Dame, IN: University of Notre Dame Press, 1991.

Leick, Gwendolyn. *A Dictionary of Near Eastern Mythology*. London: Routledge, 1991.

Lessing, G. W. *Lessing's Theological Writings*, translated by Henry Chadwick. Stanford, CA.: Stanford University Press, 1956.

Levack, Brian P. *The Witch-Hunt in Early Modern Europe*. 3rd ed. London: Pearson Education Limited, 2006.

Lewis, C. S. *The Grand Miracle*. New York: Ballantine Book, 1970.

———. *Miracles: A Preliminary Study*. New York: Macmillian, 1947.

———. *The Problem of Pain*. New York: Macmillian Paperbacks, 1962.

Lewis, Gordon R. *Testing Christianity's Truth Claims*. Lanham, MD: University Press of America, 1990.

Lüdemann, Gerd. *The Resurrection of Jesus: History, Experience, Theology*. Minneapolis, MN: Fortress Press, 1994.

———. *What Really Happened to Jesus?* Philadelphia: Westminster Press, 1995.

Mackie, J. L. *Ethics: Inventing Right and Wrong*. New York: Penguin Books, 1977.

———. *The Miracle of Theism*. Oxford: Clarendon Press, 1982.

Madden, Edward H., and Peter H. Hare. *Evil and the Concept of God*. Springfield, IL: Charles C. Thomas, 1968.

Malina, Bruce. *The New Testament World: Insights from Cultural Anthropology*. Louisville, KY: Westminster John Knox Press, 2001.

Malina, Bruce, and Richard L. Rohrbaugh. *Social Science Commentary on the Synoptic Gospels*. 2nd ed. Minneapolis, MN: Augsburg: Fortress, 2003.

Marshall, I. Howard. *I Believe in the Historical Jesus*. Grand Rapids, MI: Eerdmans, 1977.

Martin, Michael. *Atheism: A Philosophical Justification*. Philadelphia: Temple University Press, 1990.

———. *Atheism, Morality, and Meaning*. Amherst, NY: Prometheus Books, 2002.

———, ed. *Cambridge Companion to Atheism*. Cambridge: Cambridge University Press, 2006.

———. *The Case against Christianity*. Philadelphia: Temple University Press, 1991.

———. "Justifying Methodological Naturalism." http://www.infidels.org/library.

Martin, Michael, and Ricki Monnier, eds. *The Impossibility of God*. Amherst, NY: Prometheus Books, 2003; repr. 2006.

Marxsen, Willi. *Jesus and Easter: Did God Raise the Historical Jesus from the Dead?* Translated by Victor Paul Furnish. Nashville: Abingdon Press, 1990.

———. *The Resurrection of Jesus of Nazereth.* Translated by Margaret Kohl. Philadelphia: Fortress Press, 1970.

Mayers, Ronald B. *Balanced Apologetics.* Grand Rapids, MI: Kregel Academic & Professional, 1996.

McCane, Bryon. *Roll Back the Stone: Death and Burial in the World of Jesus.* Harrisburg, PA: Trinity Press International, 2003.

McDowell, Josh. *Evidence That Demands a Verdict.* Los Angeles: Campus Crusade for Christ, 1972.

———. *He Walked among Us: Evidence for the Historical Jesus.* San Bernadino, CA: Here's Life Publishers, 1988.

McKim, Robert. *Religious Ambiguity and Religious Diversity.* Oxford: Oxford University Press, 2001.

Metzger, Bruce. *The Canon of the New Testament: Its Origin, Development, and Significance.* Oxford: Oxford University Press, 1997.

———. *A Textual Commentary on the Greek New Testament.* 2nd ed. London: United Bible Societies, 2005.

Miller, Ed L. *Questions That Matter: An Invitation to Philosophy.* 4th ed. New York: McGraw-Hill, 1984.

Miller, Robert J., ed. *The Complete Gospels.* Sonoma, CA: Polebridge Press, 1994.

Mills, David, *Atheist Universe.* Berkeley, CA: Ulysses Press, 2006.

Mitchell, Basil. *The Justification of Religious Belief.* Oxford: Oxford University Press, 1981.

Monod, Jacques. *Chance and Necessity.* New York: Knopf, 1971.

Moreland, J. P. *Christianity and the Nature of Science.* Grand Rapids, MI: Baker Book House, 1989.

———. *Scaling the Secular City: A Defense of Christianity.* Grand Rapids, MI: Baker Book House, 1987.

Moreland, J. P., and William Lane Craig. *Philosophical Foundations for a Christian Worldview.* Downers Grove, IL: InterVarsity Press, 2003.

Moreland, J. P., and Kai Nielsen. *Does God Exist: The Great Debate.* Nashville, TN: Thomas Nelson, 1990.

Moreland, J. P., and John Reynolds, eds. *Three Views on Creation and Evolution.* Grand Rapids, MI: Zondervan, 1999.

Morris, Thomas V. *Francis Schaeffer's Apologetics: A Critique.* Chicago: Moody Press, 1976.

———, ed. *God and the Philosophers.* Oxford: Oxford University Press, 1994.

———. *The Logic of God Incarnate.* Ithaca, NY: Cornell University Press, 1986.

———. *Our Idea of God.* Downers Grove, IL: InterVarsity Press, 1991.

Morriston, Wes. "Causes and Beginnings in the Kalam Argument: Reply to Craig." *Faith and Philosophy* 19, no. 2 (April 2002): 233–44.

———. "Must the Beginning of the Universe Have a Personal Cause? A Critical Examination of the Kalam Cosmological Argument." *Faith and Philosophy* 17, no. 2 (2000): 149–69.

———. "Must the Past Have a Beginning?" *Philo* 2, no. 1 (1999): 5–19.

Murray, Michael J., ed. *Reason for the Hope Within.* Grand Rapids, MI: Eerdmans, 1999.

Nash, Ronald H. *The Concept of God.* Grand Rapids, MI: Zondervan, 1983.

———. *Faith and Reason: Searching for a Rational Faith.* Grand Rapids, MI: Zondervan, 1988.

Nickell, Joe. *Relics of the Christ.* Lexington: University Press of Kentucky, 2007.

Nielsen, Kai. *Ethics without God.* London: Pemberton Books, 1973.

———. *Naturalism and Religion*. Amherst, NY: Prometheus Books, 2001.

Nolan, Albert. *Jesus before Christianity*. Maryknoll, NY: Orbis Books, 1978.

Nowacki, Mark R. *The Kalam Cosmological Argument for God*. Amherst, NY: Prometheus Books, 2007.

Okholm, Dennis L., and Timothy R. Phillips, eds. *More Than One Way? Four Views on Salvation*. Grand Rapids, MI: Zondervan, 1995.

Olshansky, S. Jay, Bruce Carnes, and Robert N. Butler. "If Humans Were Built to Last." *Scientific American*, March 2001.

Oppenheim, A. L. *The Interpretation of Dreams in the Ancient Near East*. Philadelphia: American Philosophical Society, 1956.

Oppy, Graham. *Arguing about Gods*. Cambridge: Cambridge University Press, 2006.

———. *Ontological Arguments and Belief in God*. Cambridge: Cambridge University Press, 1995.

Orr, James, general editor. *The International Standard Bible Encyclopedia*. 5 vols. Grand Rapids, MI: Eerdmans, 1956.

Outka, Gene, and John P. Reeder, eds. *Religion and Morality: A Collection of Essays*. Garden City, NY: Anchor Books, 1973.

Pagels, Elaine. *The Origin of Satan*. New York: Random House, 1995.

Parsons, Keith. *God and the Burden of Proof*. Amherst, NY: Prometheus Books, 1990.

Peacocke, Arthur. *Theology for a Scientific Age*. Minneapolis, MN: Fortress Press, 1993.

Penelhum, Terence. *Survival and Disembodied Existence*. New York: Humanities Press, 1970.

Pennock, Robert T. *Tower of Babel: The Evidence against the New Creationism*. Cambridge, MA: MIT Press, 2000.

Perakh, Mark. *Unintelligent Design*. Amherst, NY: Prometheus Books, 2003.

Peterson, Michael. *God and Evil: An Introduction to the Issues*. Boulder, CO: Westview Press, 1998.

Peterson, Michael, William Hasker, Bruce Reichenbach, and David Basinger. *Reason and Religious Belief*. Oxford: Oxford University Press, 1991.

Petty, Richard E., and John T. Cacioppo. *Attitudes and Persuasion: Classic and Contemporary Approaches*. Dubuque, IA: William C. Brown, 1981.

Pinnock, Clark. *The Scripture Principle*. New York: Harper & Row, 1984.

Pinnock, Clark, and Robert C. Brow. *Unbounded Love*. Downers Grove, IL: InterVarsity Press, 1994.

Pinnock, Clark, and Delwin Brown. *Theological Crossfire: An Evangelical/Liberal Dialogue*. Grand Rapids, MI: Zondervan, 1990.

Pinnock, Clark, Richard Rice, John Sanders, William Hasker, and David Basinger. *The Openness of God*. Downers Grove, IL: InterVarsity Press, 1994.

Plantinga, Alvin. *Does God Have a Nature?* Milwaukee, WI: Marquette University Press, 1980.

———. *God, Freedom, and Evil*. Grand Rapids, MI: Eerdmans, 1974.

———. "Methodological Naturalism?" Parts 1 and 2. *Perspectives on Science and Christian Faith* 49 (1997). Available at http://www.arn.org.

———. *Warrant and Proper Function*. Oxford: Oxford University Press, 1993.

———. *Warranted Christian Belief*. Oxford: Oxford University Press, 2000.

———. *Warrant in Contemporary Epistemology*. Lanham, MD: Rowman & Littlefield, 1996.

———. *Warrant the Current Debate*. Oxford: Oxford University Press, 1992.

Plantinga, Alvin, and Nicholas Wolterstorff, eds. *Faith and Rationality: Reason and Belief in God*. Notre Dame, IN: University of Notre Dame Press, 1983.

Pojman, Louis P. *Ethics: Discovering Right and Wrong.* 5th ed. Belmont, CA.: Wadsworth, 2006.

———. "Faith without Belief." *Faith and Philosophy* 3 (1986): 157–76.

Popper, Karl. *Conjectures and Refutations.* London and New York: Routledge Classics, 2002.

Porteus, Skipp. *Jesus Doesn't Live Here Anymore: From Fundamentalist to Freedom Writer.* Amherst, NY: Prometheus Books, 1991.

Postman, Neil. *Amusing Ourselves to Death: Public Discourse in the Age of Show Business.* New York: Penguin Books, 1985.

Price, Robert M. *Deconstructing Jesus.* Amherst, NY: Prometheus Books, 2000.

———. *The Incredible Shrinking Son of Man.* Amherst, NY: Prometheus Books, 2003.

———. *Jesus Is Dead.* Cranford, NJ: American Atheist Press, 2007.

———. *Paperback Apocalypse: How the Christian Right Was Left Behind.* Amherst, NY: Prometheus Books, 2007.

Price, Robert M., and Jeffery Jay Lowder, eds. *The Empty Tomb: Jesus beyond the Grave.* Amherst, NY: Prometheus Books, 2005.

Quinn, Phillip. *Divine Commands and Moral Requirements.* Oxford: Oxford University Press, 1978.

Rachels, James. *The Elements of Moral Philosophy.* 2nd ed. New York: McGraw-Hill, 1993.

Ranke-Heinemann, Uta. *Putting Away Childish Things.* New York: HarperCollins, 1992.

Ramm, Bernard. *The Christian View of Science and Scripture.* Grand Rapids, MI: Eerdmans, 1954.

———. *Varieties of Christian Apologetics.* Grand Rapids, MI: Baker Book House, 1961.

Robinson, John A. T. *Honest to God.* Philadelphia: Westminster Press, 1963.

Robinson, Richard. *An Atheist's Values.* Oxford: Clarendon Press, 1964.

Rowe, William L. *Can God Be Free?* Oxford: Oxford University Press, 2006.

———, ed. *God and the Problem of Evil.* London: Blackwell, 2001.

Rowe, William L., and William J. Wainwright, eds. *The Philosophy of Religion: Selected Readings.* 3rd ed. Orlando, FL: Harcourt Brace, 1998.

Rundle, Bede. *Why Is There Something Rather Than Nothing?* Oxford: Clarendon Press, 2004.

Russell, Bertrand. *Unpopular Essays.* New York: Simon & Schuster, 1950.

———. *Why I Am Not a Christian.* New York: Simon & Schuster, 1957.

Sagan, Carl. *The Demon Haunted World.* New York: Random House, 1996.

Sanders, E. P. *The Historical Figure of Jesus.* New York: Penguin Books, 1993.

Schaeffer, Francis. *He Is There and He Is Not Silent.* Wheaton, IL: Tyndale House, 1972.

Schellenberg, John L. *Divine Hiddenness and Human Reason.* Ithaca, NY: Cornell University Press, 1993.

———. *The Wisdom to Doubt: A Justification of Religious Skepticism.* Ithaca, NY: Cornell University Press, 2007.

Sennett, James F. *This Much I Know: A Postmodern Apologetic.* Unpublished book.

Sennett, James F., and Douglas Groothuis, eds. *In Defense of Natural Theology: A Post Humean Assessment.* Downers Grove, IL: InterVarsity Press, 2005.

Shanks, Hershel. *Ancient Israel.* Englewood Cliffs, NJ: Prentice-Hall, 1999.

Sheler, Jeffery L. *Is The Bible True? How Modern Debates and Discoveries Affirm the Essence of the Scriptures.* New York: HarperSanFrancisco, 1999.

Shermer, Michael. *How We Believe: The Search for God in an Age of Science.* New York: Freeman, 2000.

———. *The Science of Good and Evil.* New York: Henry Holt, 2004.

———. *Why Darwin Matters: The Case against Intelligent Design.* New York: Times Books, 2006.

———. *Why People Believe Weird Things*. 2nd ed. New York: Henry Holt, 2002.

Sire, James. *The Universe Next Door*. Downers Grove, IL: InterVarsity Press, 2004.

Smith, Huston. *Why Religion Matters*. New York: HarperSanFranscisco, 2001.

Smolin, Lee. *The Life of the Cosmos*. Oxford: Oxford University Press, 1999.

Spong, John Shelby. *Born of a Woman: A Bishop Rethinks the Birth of Jesus*. New York: HarperSanFrancisco, 1992.

———. *Rescuing the Bible from Fundamentalism*. New York: HarperSanFrancisco, 1991.

———. *Resurrection: Myth or Reality?* New York: HarperSanFrancisco, 1994.

———. *The Sins of Scripture*. New York: HarperSanFranscisco, 2005.

Sproul, R. C., John H. Gerstner, and Arthur W. Lindsley. *Classical Apologetics*. Grand Rapids, MI: Zondervan, 1984.

Stahlecker, Scott R. *How to Escape Religion Guilt Free*. Lincoln, NE: iUniverse, 2004.

Steele, David Ramsey. *Atheism Explained: From Folly to Philosophy*. Peru, IL: Open Court, 2008.

Stenger, Victor J. *The Comprehensible Cosmos: Where Do the Laws of Physics Come From?* Amherst, NY: Prometheus Books, 2006.

———. *God: The Failed Hypothesis. How Science Shows That God Does Not Exist*. Amherst, NY: Prometheus Books, 2007.

———. *Has Science Found God? The Latest Results in the Search for Purpose in the Universe*. Amherst, NY: Prometheus Books, 2003.

Stump, Eleonore, ed. *Reasoned Faith: Essays in Philosophical Theology in Honor of Norman Kretzmann*. Ithaca, NY: Cornell University Press, 1993.

Swartley, Willard M. *Slavery, Sabbath, War and Women: Case Issues in Biblical Interpretation*. Scottsdale, PA: Herald Press, 1983.

Sweeney, Julia. *Letting Go of God*. http://www.juliasweeney.com.

Swinburne, Richard, ed. *Bayes's Theorem*. Oxford: Oxford University Press, 2005.

———. *The Concept of Miracle*. Oxford: Oxford University Press, 1970.

———. "Could There Be More Than One God? *Faith and Philosophy* 5, no. 3 (July 1988): 225–41.

———. *The Existence of God*. Oxford: Oxford University Press, 1979.

———. *Is There a God?* Oxford: Oxford University Press, 1997.

———. *Providence and the Problem of Evil*. Oxford: Oxford University Press, 1998.

———. *Responsibility and Atonement*. Oxford: Clarendon Press, 1989.

———. *The Resurrection of God Incarnate*. Oxford: Oxford University Press, 2003.

Tarico, Valerie. *The Dark Side: How Evangelical Teachings Corrupt Love and Truth*. Seattle: Dea Press, 2006.

Tarnas, Richard. *The Passion of the Western Mind*. New York: Ballantine Books, 1991.

Taylor, Richard. *Metaphysics*. 4th ed. Englewood Cliffs, NJ: Prentice-Hall, 1992.

———, ed. *Theism*. New York: Liberal Arts Press, 1957.

Tempelton, Charles. *Farewell to God: My Reasons for Rejecting the Christian Faith*. Toronto, ON: McClelland & Stewart, 1999.

Theissen, Gerd, and Annette Merz. *The Historical Jesus: A Comprehensive Guide*. Translated by John Bowden. Minneapolis, MN: Fortress Press, 1998.

Toulmin, Stephen, and Harry Wolf, eds. *What I Do Not Believe, and Other Essays*. Dordrecht, Netherlands: D. Reidel, 1971.

Tucker, Ruth. *Walking Away from Faith: Unraveling the Mystery of Belief and Unbelief*. Downers Grove, IL: InterVarsity Press, 2002.

Van Fraassen, Bas. *Laws and Symmetry*. Oxford: Oxford University Press, 1989.

Van Inwagen, Peter. *The Problem of Evil*. Oxford: Oxford University Press, 2006.

Vansina, Jan. *Oral Tradition as History*. Madison: University of Wisconsin Press, 1985.

Van Till, Howard J. *The Fourth Day*. Grand Rapids, MI: Eerdmans, 1986.

Vermes, Geza. *Jesus and the World of Judaism*. London: SCM, 1983.

Vitz, Paul. *Faith of the Fatherless: The Psychology of Atheism*. Dallas: Spence, 2000.

Vogel Carey, Toni. "The Ontological Argument and the Sin of Hubris." *Philosophy Now*, December 2005.

Wall, James, ed. *How My Mind Has Changed*. Grand Rapids, MI: Eerdmans, 1991.

Walsh, Brian J., and Richard J. Middleton. *The Transforming Vision*. Downers Grove, IL: InterVarsity Press, 1984.

Weinberg, Steven. *The First Three Minutes: A Modern View of the Origin of the Universe*. 2nd ed. New York: Basic Books, 1993.

Weisberger, A. M. *Suffering Belief: Evil and the Anglo-American Defense of Theism*. New York: Peter Lang, 1999.

Wells, Ronald A. *History through the Eyes of Faith*. New York: HarperSanFrancisco, 1989.

Wenham, Gordon. *Genesis 1–15*. Dallas, TX: Word Incorporated, 1987.

Wenham, John W. *The Goodness of God*. Downers Grove, IL: InterVarsity Press, 1974.

Westermann, Claus. *Creation*. Minneapolis, MN: Fortress Press, 1974.

White, L. Michael. *From Jesus to Christianity*. New York: Harper & Row, 2004.

Wielenberg, Erik J. *Value and Virtue in a Godless Universe*. Cambridge: Cambridge University Press, 2005

Wiesel, Elie. *Night*. Translated by Marion Wiesel. New York: Hill and Wang, 2006.

Winell, Marlene. *Leaving the Fold*. Berkeley, CA: Apocryphile Press, 2006.

Wink, Walter. *Unmasking the Powers*. Philadelphia: Fortress Press, 1986.

Wogman, J. Philip. *Christian Ethics: A Historical Introduction*. Louisville, KY: Westminster Press, 1993.

Wolterstorff, Nicholas. *Reason within the Bounds of Religion*. Grand Rapids, MI: Eerdmans, 1984.

Worthing, Mark William. *God, Creation, and Contemporary Physics*. Minneapolis, MN: Fortress Press, 1996.

Young, Matt, and Taner Edis. *Why Intelligent Design Fails: A Scientific Critique of the New Creationism*. New Brunswick, NJ: Rutgers University Press, 2004.

Youngblood, Ronald, ed. *The Genesis Debate*. Grand Rapids, MI: Baker Book House, 1990.